# Studies in the Economics of Central America

Victor Bulmer-Thomas

*Reader in the Economics of Latin America*
*Queen Mary College*
*University of London*

St. Martin's Press New York

First published in the United States of America in 1988

Printed in Hong Kong

ISBN 0–312–02395–2

Library of Congress Cataloging-in-Publication Data
Bulmer-Thomas, V.
Studies in the economics of Central America
Bibliography: p.
Includes index.
1. Central America—Economic conditions. I. Title.
HC141.B783 1988 330.9728'053 88–15822
ISBN 0–312–02395–2

STUDIES IN THE ECONOMICS OF CENTRAL AMERICA

For Oscar Arias Sánchez, President of Costa Rica,
whose efforts have shown that the pen can indeed be
mightier than the sword

# Contents

# List of Tables

# List of Illustrations

# Preface

This book brings together a number of my essays on the economics of Central America written over the last five years. Some of the essays have already been published, but they appeared in edited works with more general themes and are therefore not easily accessible to students of Central America. I am grateful to Cambridge University Press for permission to reproduce Chapter 2 (published in the *Journal of Latin American Studies*, 1983, Vol. 15, Part 2) and Chapter 8 (published in E. Duran (ed.), *Latin America and the World Recession*, 1985). Chapter 3 was published in R. Thorp (ed.), *Latin America in the 1930s*, Macmillan, 1984; Chapter 7 was published in R. Thorp and L. Whitehead (eds), *Latin American Debt and the Adjustment Crisis*, Macmillan, 1987; and Chapter 4 in A. El-Agraa (ed.), *International Economic Integration*, Macmillan, 1988.

VICTOR BULMER-THOMAS

# 1 Introduction

The transformation of the economies of Central America before 1979 rested on three pillars. The first was rapid growth and diversification of agricultural exports to the rest of the world. The second, based on the first, was stable exchange rates and very low rates of inflation. The third, based on the first and second, was exports of manufactured goods within the Central American Common Market (CACM). Since the Central American crisis began in 1979, all three pillars have crumbled and the task of economic reconstruction has become one of the most pressing facing the region. The work of reconstruction is complicated, however, by the knowledge that the three traditional pillars were in some respects deficient; they could not prevent a descent into civil war in three countries of the region (El Salvador, Guatemala and Nicaragua) nor interstate conflict between two (El Salvador and Honduras in 1969). Thus, reconstruction will have to address the failings of the old order, while adding new elements of dynamism to permit the countries of the region to regain and surpass the pre-1979 levels of income per head.

This book of essays, written between 1983 and 1987, addresses these issues. The first part, entitled long-run studies, looks at the transformation of the economy in the period from 1920 and tries to identify both the strengths and weaknesses of an export-led model based on agricultural exports to the rest of the world. The second part, entitled Central American co-operation, is primarily concerned with the CACM; the first essay (Chapter 4) is an overview of the CACM from its successful origins in the 1960s to its current demise, while the next essay (Chapter 5) proposes a reform of the CACM which would allow intra-regional trade to expand alongside non-traditional exports to the rest of the world. The final essay in this section (Chapter 6) examines co-operation between Central America and Western Europe in the light of the latter's renewed interest in the region. The third section, entitled Central America in crisis, explores the current economic malaise. Chapter 7 is a detailed study of the role of internal and external factors in the economic decline; Chapter 8 compares the depression of the 1980s with the slump in the 1930s; Chapter 9 represents the author's written evidence to the Kissinger Commission (appointed by President Reagan in 1983 to find bipartisan solutions to the regional crisis), while Chapter 10 is a case study of Costa Rica's efforts to escape from the current economic crisis through the promotion of non-traditional exports to the rest of the world.

There is general agreement that economic factors played an important part in the regional crisis which struck Central America in 1979 and which has plagued it ever since. Publications from all sides of the political spectrum, inside and outside the region, reflect the consensus that in some way the economic model pursued by the five republics before 1979 contributed to the unfolding of the regional crisis.

The consensus, however, is very superficial. When it comes to determining why the model was defective, there is a great deal of confusion (reflected, for example, in many parts of the Kissinger Report) and division. This is understandable. We have all been conditioned to accept the notion that a fast rate of growth of real Gross Domestic Product (GDP) is a 'good thing', easing social tensions and paving the way for political stability. Yet the five republics enjoyed rapid growth in the three decades before 1979, while Nicaragua – from the end of the 1940s to the beginning of the 1970s – achieved the highest rate of growth throughout all Latin America (including Brazil). Similarly, the two countries in the region which have escaped civil war and a breakdown of the social order – Costa Rica and Honduras – stand at opposite ends of the economic spectrum: the richest and the poorest in the region respectively.

The role of economics in explaining the regional crisis is therefore complex. Before 1979, all five republics followed roughly the same model, yet the social and political consequences were very different. By conventional criteria, e.g. real income per head, the model would have to be judged a success, but the conviction remains – however poorly articulated – that the model was deeply flawed. Meanwhile, policy-makers – from San José to Washington – are left with the task of developing new economic strategies for the region, while remaining ignorant of why the previous policies failed.

The key to understanding the part played by economics in the regional crisis lies in analysis of the model itself. The latter has several layers, reflecting the evolution of the regional economy since its integration into the world economy in the second half of the nineteenth century. That integration took place on the basis of exports of coffee and bananas – two products that remain central to the functioning of the regional economy. The two exports have frequently registered spectacular rates of growth, making the region a major supplier of both products to the world market, but have produced in their wake a series of problems; in the case of coffee, private estates were frequently established through alienation of communal lands, while labour was often obtained through coercion: in the case of bananas, control has rested in foreign hands and the industry has enjoyed a privileged tax position which has distorted fiscal systems in the region in a number of undesirable ways.

Since the Second World War, regional exports have been diversified through the promotion of cotton, sugar and cattle. These new products complete the first pillar on which transformation of the economy before 1979 was based; growth rates have been dramatic and the new exports have served as an engine of growth, but they have brought in their wake a series of consequences which many regard as unacceptable. These include excessive deforestation, the marginalisation of the peasantry and an unhealthy tension between agriculture for export (EXA) and agriculture for domestic use (DUA).[1]

Although the diversification and growth of agricultural exports produced a series of adverse social consequences, it was extremely successful at earning foreign exchange. Between 1945 and 1979, the dollar value of exports from the region rose from $105.7 million to $4668.2 million with coffee, bananas, cotton, sugar and beef accounting for 65 per cent of all exports and 80 per cent of extra-regional exports by the end of the period. The increase in dollar earnings was by no means swamped by increases in dollar import prices; the purchasing power of exports over the same period rose twenty-fold in Costa Rica with impressive, if less spectacular, increases elsewhere.[2]

This boom in foreign exchange and the purchasing power of exports distinguished Central America from the rest of Latin America, where inward-looking development was marked by foreign exchange bottlenecks and exchange-rate instability. By contrast, Central America enjoyed virtually unchanged nominal exchange rates to the dollar after the Second World War and this brought in its wake a remarkable period of price stability which was only undermined in the 1970s as a result of the first oil crisis and an acceleration in imported inflation.

Stable exchange rates and negligible levels of inflation provided a solid basis for the growth of intra-regional trade in the 1960s. With each country's exchange rate pegged to the dollar, the cross-border exchange rates were also fixed. The region was in effect on a dollar standard with CACM enjoying a form of monetary union. Full currency convertibility and an absence of capital controls persuaded many capitalists in the agricultural sector to try their hand at industrial production, while the widening of the market persuaded numerous multinational companies to invest in the CACM.

Intra-regional trade produced imbalances between pairs of countries with deficit nations expected to settle their accounts in dollars. The risk to currency convertibility from these deficits was avoided by the spectacular performance of extra-regional agricultural exports which provided dollars in sufficient quantities to meet any intra-regional payments imbalances. Thus, the CACM – the third pillar in the region's economic transformation – rested firmly on the first two pillars.

The CACM provided a convenient vehicle for the promotion of industry in the region through the creation of a free trade area protected from outside competition by a common external tariff. Thus, the CACM was a halfway house between industrial import substitution in one country (e.g. Peru) and industrial export promotion (e.g. Hong Kong). It was, in effect, a case of regional import substitution and it produced spectacular rates of growth of manufactured exports in Central America until the war between El Salvador and Honduras in 1969 and the withdrawal from CACM of Honduras in 1970. The CACM, now in deep crisis, was formerly held up as the most successful example of regional integration among developing countries, but also attracted criticism for the unbalanced way it distributed benefits to member countries, for its penetration by multinational companies, for its poor employment record and for its failure to break the dominance of traditional exports and the agro-export model.

The export-led model of growth may have transformed the regional economy, but it produced losers as well as winners. The winners were fairly easy to identify. They were the agro-exporters, where medium- and large-scale farms were generally dominant, and the urban-based industrialists with foreign capital present in both sectors. In addition, the growth of foreign exchange earnings underpinned a notable expansion of domestic commerce, the rise in incomes per head was accompanied by a shift of demand towards services (both business and personal) and the increase in government revenue linked to economic expansion permitted a sharp rise in public services and the size of the state bureaucracy.

The main losers were the small-scale farmers and traditional peasantry. The expansion of EXA exacerbated the pressure on the peasantry from other sources (notably population growth) and reduced many farmers to the status of landless labourers with only seasonal work to sustain them. Given world prices for agricultural exports coupled with fixed exchange rates made nominal labour costs a major determinant of profitability in the export sector. This produced a rigid wage discipline in the rural sector so that the benefits of export-led growth were very unequally distributed.

The seasonal nature of many jobs in export agriculture coupled with demographic pressure produced an explosion in rural–urban migration, which has left the urban population almost as large as the population in rural areas.[3] The industrial urban sector, protected from foreign competition by high tariffs, has never exhibited the same degree of wage discipline as export agriculture, but its capital-intensive nature prevented it from absorbing labour in sufficient quantities to cope with the rising supply. In the absence of comprehensive social security programmes, the informal urban sector was left to take up the slack with competitive wage rates well below those ruling in either the public sector or modern manufacturing enterprises.

The dislocations associated with the export-led model gave rise to two possible responses. The first was to reject the model altogether, arguing for a more inward-looking policy based on an extension of import-substitution and regional industrialisation; this policy, embraced by many intellectuals inside and (later) outside the region, was emphatically rejected by policy-makers in Central America. The second response was to offer a programme of reforms, designed to compensate the losers for the unequal distribution of benefits associated with the export-led model.

All five republics implemented reform programmes, but their scope and impact varied enormously between the countries. In an effort to offset the impact of EXA growth on landlessness, the marginalisation of the peasantry and the threat to domestic food production, land reform legislation was adopted in all countries except El Salvador.[4] Only in Honduras, however, during part of the 1970s could it be said that land reform had made a significant impact towards ameliorating the condition of the losers from export-led growth. Costa Rica, on the other hand, did implement a credit policy through its nationalised banking system which favoured small-scale farmers and supported a healthy expansion of domestic food crops in the 1970s.

The strains imposed by demographic pressure and rapid urbanisation demanded buoyant fiscal revenues to pay for an expansion of services in education, health and social security. The antiquated fiscal system, heavily dependent on indirect taxes in general and external trade taxes in particular, came under pressure in the 1960s from the formation of CACM and the decline in tariff revenues. Only Costa Rica and Honduras were able to overhaul their fiscal systems significantly, paving the way for major increases in social expenditure in the 1970s.[5] Elsewhere, the fiscal system remained regressive and its buoyancy low so that government revenue failed to match the growth in the economy and social expenditure continued to receive a very low priority.

The final area for reform was labour legislation. The rigid wage discipline favoured by agro-exporters could be countered to some extent through minimum wage legislation or the spread of rural labour organisations. In El Salvador, Guatemala and Nicaragua, however, the state remained so closely identified with the interests of agro-exporters that rural labour failed to achieve the minimal strength required to extract benefits from rising world prices or increases in labour productivity, while trade unions in all three countries – even in urban areas – continued to be regarded with deep suspicion. The Honduran government, on the other hand, gradually adopted a more tolerant attitude towards organised labour, while the democratic system in Costa Rica ensured that labour's demands were given recognition by the political parties.

The threat to social and political stability from the workings of the export-led model, which had accumulated slowly in the 1950s and 1960s, accelerated in the 1970s when rising inflation threatened the fragile social equilibrium. Only in Costa Rica and Honduras was labour able to reverse the initial sharp falls in real wages provoked by imported inflation associated with the overheating of the world economy and the first oil crisis. Elsewhere, the discontented labour movement made common cause with the frustrated political aspirations of the middle classes to provoke a descent into civil war and the beginning of the regional crisis.

The sequence of events which led to the fall of Somoza in Nicaragua, the resignation of General Romero in El Salvador and the unleashing of indiscriminate terror in Guatemala could be traced in part to the economic history of the previous decades, although ironically the short-term economic indicators against which the crisis unfolded in 1979 were generally favourable. The net barter terms of trade were still benefiting from the boom in the price of coffee after 1975, trade within the CACM was still growing and only El Salvador and Nicaragua were subject to economic decline as a result of civil unrest. By 1981, however, it was clear that the region was in the grip of a major economic crisis and in 1982 the real Gross Domestic Product fell in every republic for the first time for fifty years. Since then, real income per head has declined dramatically and even on optimistic assumptions El Salvador and Nicaragua will not regain the 1970s peak until well into the twenty-first century.

The first indication of the economic crisis was the decline in the net barter terms of trade at the start of the 1980s. This was bad enough, but in addition to falling prices for the main agro-exports quantity restrictions also began to be increased. Beef quotas for several republics exporting to the United States were cut, the reimposition of coffee quotas under the International Coffee Agreement pushed supplies into non-traditional markets with huge price discounts and the US sugar quota was slashed in response to falling demand and rising US domestic supplies.[6] The multinational fruit companies responsible for marketing bananas exerted constant pressure for a cut in export taxes and United Brands (formerly the United Fruit Co.) finally withdrew from Costa Rica. Cotton suffered not only from the collapse of world prices (caused in part by the stimulus to US production from artificial domestic prices), but also from the ecological damage caused by several decades of indiscriminate insecticide use and the spread of disease.

The double squeeze from falling prices and quantity restrictions drove down foreign exchange earnings from agro-exports and the first pillar on which the region's economic transformation had been based began to crumble. At the same time, balance-of-payments pressures were exacerbated by capital flight from the region in response to political uncertainty, interest rate differentials and exchange rate fears. The last reason proved to be a self-fulfilling prophecy as each republic except Honduras dropped its commitment to exchange rate stability in the wake of the balance-of-payments crisis. Devaluation, however, brought with it a sharp increase in inflationary pressures and the region's reputation for price stability disappeared rapidly. Thus, the second pillar of the regional economy collapsed in the first half of the 1980s.[7]

With the first two pillars swept away, it was only a matter of time before intra-regional trade within the CACM suffered. The position was made even worse, however, as a result of the serious imbalances in intra-regional trade in 1980 when both Nicaragua and El Salvador boosted CACM imports without a corresponding rise in their exports. The corresponding deficits led to the accumulation of debts within CACM which could not be serviced and intra-regional trade fell by two-thirds between 1980 and 1986. In the final year recorded exports and imports, which in theory should be equal, differed by 10 per cent as traders resorted to countertrade and contraband as a way out of the payments impasse.[8]

By the mid-1980s the old order in Central America, on which economic growth had been based, had disappeared. New obstacles to growth, however, had now emerged. The first was the rise in external debt. Although, as elsewhere in Latin America, the origins of this debt could be traced to the 1970s (particularly in Nicaragua), most of it was contracted in the 1980s in a forlorn attempt to underpin the balance of payments and prevent economic collapse. Two of the republics (Costa Rica and Nicaragua) are now among the most heavily indebted in the world on a *per caput* basis, but the other three republics have seen their reputation for fiscal prudence vanish in a mountain of external obligations. The debt problem, coupled with its other economic problems, pushed Nicaragua into passive default after 1983, while Costa Rica, Guatemala and Honduras have found themselves locked into almost permanent negotiation with the International Monetary Fund, the World Bank and other representatives of the creditor nations. Only El Salvador, whose debt has been contracted on exceptionally soft terms (mainly from the US administration) has escaped the worst effects of the debt crisis.

The second problem has been the tension between Central American states as a result of political upheaval and the consolidation of the Sandinista regime in Nicaragua. Efforts to revive the CACM have been impeded not only by the deterioration in the external environment, but also by the mutual suspicion between the Sandinistas on the one hand and the governments in El Salvador and Costa Rica on the other.[9] At the same time, the US administration has refused to fund any regional initiatives from which Nicaragua might benefit; since the institutions of CACM had been from their origin heavily dependent on US support, this made it very difficult for the CACM to function normally. The political tension in the region, both between and within states, also contributed to the massive capital flight in the first years of the 1980s. By the time effective exchange controls were put in place, an estimated $2 billion had been drained from the region with little prospect of a reversal of capital flight for many years to come.

The refugee problem is a further obstacle to economic recovery. The terror used against the Indian majority in the highlands of Guatemala, the continuing civil war in El Salvador and the US-backed efforts to overthrow the Sandinistas in Nicaragua have produced massive migrations of refugees, many of whom have settled in other countries of the region. This has added to the burden of host governments (e.g. Costa

Rica) at the same time as it has taken out of production a substantial proportion of the labour force in the war-torn countries. Resettling the refugees will not be a simple matter, since inevitably the competition for land has encouraged those that remained to take over abandoned farms.

Finally, natural disasters – a constant threat on the isthmus – have further complicated the task of economic reconstruction. Droughts in Nicaragua and Costa Rica have taken their toll of agricultural production in several recent years, while the earthquake in El Salvador in October 1986 was yet another blow to the fragile civilian regime of President Duarte. Even malaria, efficiently contained until recently, has reasserted itself as a major cause of illness, while dengue fever has grown in importance on the Atlantic coast.

The depth of the economic crisis in Central America has brought with it some compensations. The geopolitical implications of the Sandinista revolution have persuaded the US administration to adopt trade and aid measures intended not only to punish Nicaragua, but also reward US allies in the region. The bilateral aid flows from the United States to Nicaragua's neighbours (see Table 6.5) have reached levels which make Central America comparable with Israel and Egypt in the amount of US aid received on a *per caput* basis. Nicaragua's sugar quota in the US market was reallocated to the rest of Central America after 1983 and the trade embargo against Nicaragua in 1985 provided a further opportunity for the rest of Central America to increase its exports to the United States at the expense of the Sandinista regime. The Reagan administration has used its influence in the IMF, the World Bank and the Interamerican Development Bank to increase the flow of resources from multilateral agencies to the region (excluding Nicaragua) and has applied discrete pressure on occasions to soften the conditions attached to increased multilateral lending.[10]

The most innovative feature of US economic policy towards the region has been the Caribbean Basin Initiative (CBI). Launched at the beginning of 1984, it offers duty-free access to the US market for an initial twelve-year period for a wide range of non-traditional exports. Nicaragua was denied participation in the scheme, but the rest of Central America was invited to join. The politically-motivated nature of the CBI drew heavy criticism from a number of sources, but its economic features were also attacked. The CBI, which is expected to be renewed for a further twelve years, excludes many traditional products as well as a number of 'sensitive' exports (e.g. textiles) and therefore the proportion of exports in 1984 that could qualify was very small. Many of these criticisms were justified, although the case study of Costa Rica (see Chapter 10) shows that under certain circumstances the scheme can be beneficial.

The rest of the world also responded to the Central American economic crisis. The two regional powers, Mexico and Venezuela, provided oil on soft terms from 1980 under the San José accord. Like the CBI, the San José accord (renewed every year) applies to many Caribbean states as well as Central America. Unlike the CBI, Nicaragua was included in the scheme until the accumulation of unpaid oil debts compelled Venezuela to withdraw supplies in 1983.[11] Mexico, anxious to maintain an influence on the Sandinistas in the light of their deteriorating relations with the United States, maintained supplies until 1985 despite non-payment. Since then, however, most of Nicaragua's oil has come from the Soviet bloc, although it continues to be refined by a US multinational company.

The Soviet bloc's economic support for the region mainly benefited Nicaragua, although a trade agreement was also signed with Honduras in 1987. Yet Nicaragua's huge balance-of-trade deficit, which exceeded the total value of exports in every year after 1983, was also funded by Western Europe on both a bilateral and multilateral basis. Bilateral support came in the form of aid from friendly countries (e.g. Scandinavia) as well as funds from non-governmental agencies (e.g. Oxfam). It also came in the form of commercial credits with Spain in particular playing a leading role. Multilateral support came from the European Economic Community (EEC), whose multilateral aid programme for the region was upgraded following the signing of a Co-operation Agreement between Central America (including Panama) and the EEC in 1985. Western European economic measures have been applied on a non-discriminatory basis to the whole region, but the highest share of aid has flowed to Nicaragua in an effort to avoid the Sandinista regime becoming even more dependent on the Soviet bloc.

The response by the international community to the Central American economic crisis, although motivated by very different political considerations, has undoubtedly alleviated the situation. For example, while most of the Latin American republics have been forced since 1982 to run large trade surpluses in response to the debt crisis and transfer as much as 5 per cent of their GDP to the rest of the world in debt service payments, all of the Central American republics have been able to run trade and balance-of-payments deficits while receiving a net inflow of funds from official sources on concessional terms.

The international response must be put in context, however, since

Central America is suffering its worst economic crisis since the early 1930s and on some criteria its worst economic crisis ever. Thus, while there are some problems which the new trade and aid measures can solve, there are others which require alternative solutions and even some problems which may be made worse by the international response.

The problems which the international response can solve are mainly concerned with the balance of payments. Increased capital flows from abroad, soft terms for oil imports and access to markets for non-traditional exports ease the foreign exchange constraint and make available a higher level of imports than would otherwise be possible. In turn, this permits a modest recovery in real GDP and some growth in employment. Increased capital flows also help to stabilise the exchange rate and reduce inflationary pressures. Finally, the higher level of imports made possible by capital flows provides tariff revenue and eases the fiscal problem.

Parts of this virtuous circle have been observed in Central America. The dollar value of imports has risen since 1982 in Costa Rica, El Salvador and Honduras and all three countries have experienced a modest recovery in real GDP, although only in Costa Rica has this exceeded population growth. Exchange-rate stability has been preserved in Honduras, while the rate of devaluation has declined sharply in Costa Rica; El Salvador and Guatemala are both trying to defend new dollar parities for their domestic currencies and inflation rates have been falling in Costa Rica, Guatemala and Honduras. Nicaragua is the exception which proves the rule; the capital flows from abroad may be high, but they have not increased enough to permit a rise in the dollar value of imports since 1982. Real GDP has declined, the budget deficit has widened to accommodate the demands of a war economy, the exchange rate has collapsed and the inflation rate (fuelled by an explosion in the money supply) has accelerated to the point where the social base of the revolution has been put at risk.

The international response also helped to make some impact on implementing the structural reforms, which had been so seriously neglected in the period before 1979. Some progress has been made in the area of land reform with the Salvadorean programme in particular heavily underwritten by US aid; the more radical Nicaraguan land reform owed nothing, of course, to US funding, but the high level of balance-of-payments support from other countries enabled the Sandinistas to discount the impact on traditional exports that the distribution of land to landless peasants after 1984 was likely to have.

In the field of fiscal modernisation, reform has been achieved both through the carrot of extra foreign resources as well as the stick of IMF and World Bank conditionality in Costa Rica and Honduras, while Guatemala under President Cerezo appeared at the end of 1987 to have made some progress towards extracting government revenue from the undertaxed rich.

There can, however, be no room for complacency. The economic crisis since 1979 has made the need for structural reforms even more pressing; land reform in Guatemala, the country with the greatest inequality of land tenure in Latin America, is still not on the agenda and fiscal modernisation in El Salvador has hardly begun. Even Costa Rica has found it very difficult to reform its tax system in a way that combines equity with efficiency, while fiscal reform in Nicaragua has been distorted by hyperinflation and a budget deficit equal in some years to a quarter of GDP. Land reform in Honduras has been stalled in favour of a US-funded titling programme which has done little to relieve the pressure on land and throughout the region the reforms needed to promote a vigorous, independent labour movement have been avoided in favour of either repression or cooption.

Recognition of the positive achievements associated with the international response cannot disguise the fact that it has not addressed a number of Central America's most pressing economic problems. Export earnings remain dominated by traditional agro-exports (coffee, bananas, cotton, sugar and beef) with all five products continuing to face exceptionally difficult world market conditions. The EEC reduced its tariff on coffee exports from Central America; there was a recovery in coffee prices in 1986, but it proved short-lived and the reimposition of coffee export quotas in 1987 under the International Coffee Agreement (ICA) restored the *status quo ante*. High domestic prices for US sugar prices coupled with a decline in consumption squeezed US sugar imports and forced cuts in the US sugar quota from which not even Washington's regional allies were exempt. Export quotas for beef suffered further cuts and the World Bank began to re-evaluate its support for cattle-raising projects in the light of protests from environmental lobbies. The volume of traditional exports has therefore been stagnant and the sector has been unable to make an effective contribution to employment or balance-of-payments problems.

The international response has also failed to make much impact on the region's debt problems. The largesse by official creditors has not been matched by private creditors, who remain unwilling to commit additional resources to the region and who have imposed tough terms in debt renegotiations. Even the Paris Club has failed to adjust its terms for debt owed to official creditors to take into account the special problems of the region. Thus, several countries in the region have had to use a large part of the additional funds from official sources to provide debt service payments to private creditors.

The international response has also failed to make any impact on the decline in the CACM. Only creditors in Western Europe have given the recovery of CACM any serious attention, but their efforts so far must be deemed a failure. The Co-operation Agreement between the EEC and Central America puts a premium on projects which promote regional integration, but the EEC in practice has continued to offer multilateral aid mainly to individual countries. The most serious efforts to revive the CACM have come, quite appropriately, from Central Americans themselves and led in 1986 to a scheme for replacing the dollar with a domestic resource in settling intra-regional trade imbalances. This resource, Derecho de Importación Centroamericana (DICA), is issued by the Central Bank of each country to importers to pay for exports from CACM countries and exporters can trade it for domestic currency or CACM imports. Yet the DICA scheme could not clear off the backlog of unpaid debts between pairs of CACM countries and this remains the fundamental obstacle to the recovery of intra-regional trade.

There are also problems inherited from the past which may have been exacerbated by the recent international response. There is widespread agreement among scholars of the regional economy that the export-led model had two major deficiencies. First, it took export specialisation to a point where macroeconomic performance was dangerously vulnerable to fluctuations in world market conditions for a handful of products. Secondly, the market and institutional mechanisms through which growth in export earnings could be translated into economic development were generally inadequate, although some countries had gone further than others in introducing the necessary reforms.

The main thrust of the response by the Western international community has been to increase the emphasis on exports in general and non-traditional exports to the rest of the world in particular. Thus, the Central American countries subject to Western influence (all except Nicaragua) are being driven towards even greater dependence on exports, while at the same time the mechanisms for translating export growth into development remain largely unreformed.

An optimist might argue that the new emphasis, by focusing on non-traditional exports to the rest of the world, will avoid the pitfalls of the previous export-led model and establish a satisfactory framework for 'trickledown' effects to operate so that all social classes can benefit from the dynamism of the export sector. This is unlikely to be so. The new exports in many cases demand the same wage discipline and social control if the owners of capital are to be ensured a high rate of profit. Investment in non-traditional exports is often footloose and foreign capital in particular will be attracted to countries with low labour costs, real wage discipline and weak labour organisations. Where, as in Costa Rica, relatively high labour costs are compensated by an educated labour force, public investment in social infrastructure and political stability, the investment climate may still be favourable; it will take the rest of Central America many years, however, to match Costa Rica in these departments. Thus, the ability of the rest of the region to capture investment in non-traditional exports appears to require the maintenance of anti-labour policies; furthermore, the urban industrial labour force – relatively protected from the impact of international competition by high tariffs – will now be expected to maintain rigid wage discipline in order to guarantee the profitability of non-traditional manufactured exports.

International pressure is not pushing Nicaragua in the direction of export intensification. On the contrary, the importance of exports for the Nicaraguan economy has fallen sharply in recent years, as the export sector has declined in absolute terms and the informal urban sector has mushroomed. This decline in export dependence does not, however, bring any comfort. The growth of the non-export economy has been based mainly on the needs of a war economy on the one hand and on the other a retreat into the black market in response to hyperinflation. The only bright spot has been the growth in food production for the local market as a consequence of the emphasis in the land reform programme on the small peasantry and landless labourers. Furthermore, the decline in the export sector (both traditional exports to the rest of the world and manufactured exports to CACM) has been so severe that it has swamped any increases in the non-export economy and left real GDP below the level in 1983 and far below the level before the revolution.

The limitations of the massive international response in the first half of the 1980s emphasise the need for peace in the region. Without peace, it is very difficult to revive regional integration or implement the needed domestic reforms. Peace is also a precondition for the reversal of capital flight and an improvement in the investment climate, while an end to civil war and regional tension would permit governments to shift resources away from security towards economic and social development. The peace plan for the region, first proposed by President Arias of Costa Rica and adopted by all Central American presidents in August 1987, gives a glimmer of hope that peace will prevail and that we may indeed see peace in our time.

## Notes

1. I have estimated the division of agricultural net output between EXA and DUA for the whole period 1920–84. See Bulmer-Thomas (1987), Tables A.5 and A. 6, pp. 316–9.
2. The index (1970 = 100) for the purchasing power of exports in 1945 was as follows (with 1979 levels in parentheses):

| | |
|---|---|
| Costa Rica | 7.5 (152.4) |
| El Salvador | 17.9 (194.1) |
| Guatemala | 19.3 (127.9) |
| Honduras | 31.4 (174.8) |
| Nicaragua | 12.7 (159.7) |

   See Bulmer-Thomas (1987), Table A.15, pp. 336–7.
3. By 1987, Costa Rica and Nicaragua had a higher share of their populations in urban than rural areas.
4. El Salvador introduced land reform legislation in 1975, but dropped its implementation following protests from the private sector.
5. The weakness of tax effort in Central America is borne out by the fact that Honduras, the poorest country, had the highest ratio of government revenue to GDP by 1979. See Bulmer-Thomas (1987), Table 10.5, p. 213.
6. In the case of Nicaragua, the US sugar quota was reduced to zero in 1983 as part of the Reagan administration's campaign against the Sandinista regime.
7. Guatemala maintained the fiction of an unchanged official exchange rate by allowing the Central Bank to service foreign debt at the old parity.
8. See SIECA (1987), Table 1.
9. There has been deep suspicion between Honduras and Nicaragua as well, but Honduras is not a member of the CACM.
10. For example, US pressure persuaded the IMF to change the target for the budget deficit as part of the conditions for a standby credit to Costa Rica.
11. Venezuela was also concerned over the direction of the Nicaraguan revolution under the Sandinistas.

# Part I

# Long-run Studies

# 2 Economic Development over the Long Run – Central America since 1920

## INTRODUCTION

The development of Central America in recent decades presents a paradox. As measured by the growth of real Gross Domestic Product (GDP) per head, the region's performance compares favourably with the rest of Latin America and other less developed countries (LDCs). At the same time, political convulsions have become more acute, and in no part of the isthmus – not even in Costa Rica – is political stability assured.

There are several possible responses to this paradox. One is a virulently anti-Marxist response, denying the relevance of any form of historical materialism, in which the evolution of the political system is divorced entirely from its economic substructure. Another is to downgrade the economic achievements of Central America, arguing that conventional measures of performance are a poor indicator of economic health.

Neither response will be adopted in this chapter. I do not wish to deny either the achievements of the Central American economies or the connection between the political and economic systems. By taking the long view, however, one may observe how the model of economic development adopted has involved resource shifts which make untenable the old political systems; these shifts, which in the short run can be dismissed as 'marginal', only acquire significance in the long run since their influence takes many years to be felt.

A study of Central American development over the long run is hampered by the absence of official statistics. Official national accounts for each country go back, in most cases, only to 1950. As part of my work for a study of Central America in the inter-war years, I have prepared the national accounts back to 1920 (see Bulmer-Thomas, 1987), which together with the official statistics gives a time-series for each country of 65 years (1920–84). While in no sense perfect, a time-series of this length for five republics makes it possible to distinguish between permanent and temporary changes in the economy and to observe the operation of any long-term cyclical forces.[1]

This chapter does not attempt a complete overview of the Central American economies since 1920; given the limitations of space, that would be neither possible nor appropriate. Instead, I shall focus primarily on the agricultural sector, which to this day remains dominant in terms of employment, foreign exchange earnings and (at least at world prices) output.

This continuing dominance of agriculture is at first sight surprising in view of the deliberate attempt to foster industrialisation through a Customs Union in the late 1950s and 1960s. These attempts, inspired by the UN Economic Commission for Latin America and carried through by regional technocrats, led to a wave of optimism that Central America was in transition towards a new model of development in which economic, social and political modernisation would occur simultaneously (see Torres Rivas, 1973).

Such optimism can now be seen to be premature. Throughout most of the isthmus, agrarian interests (the traditional oligarchy) exercise preponderant influence over political affairs and have successfully neutralised the efforts of the region's technocrats to breathe new life into the Central American Common Market (CACM).

The formation of CACM was not the first occasion on which the oligarchy survived a challenge to its political hegemony. An earlier crisis had occurred during the depression of the 1930s; on that occasion, however, the oligarchy survived by increasing the power of the state, over which it continued to exercise great influence either directly or indirectly.

This increased state power ensured that the challenge presented by the CACM was potential only. The traditional interests of the oligarchy (export agriculture) were safeguarded and the extra resources needed by industrialisation and urbanisation has to come from elsewhere; furthermore, industry's need for an expanding internal market based on income redistribution was averted through carrying out import-substitution at the regional level. The effort, therefore, to steer Central America towards industrial modernity without generating a political or social crisis must be deemed a failure.[2]

The oligarchy never abandoned the export-led model of growth which had proved so successful in the half century up to the Great Depression. Indeed, during the heyday of the CACM one may observe two models of development co-existing uneasily at the same time. The collapse of the CACM, however, led to further intensification of the traditional export-led model.

It is the implications of this intensification which form the principal focus of this chapter; as we shall see, the price which must be paid for the continuing dominance of the oligarchy based on its agricultural export interests is a breakdown of social and economic relations in the rural economy. This breakdown is presenting a third challenge to the oligarchy, which may yet prove to be decisive.

## ECONOMIC PERFORMANCE OVER THE LONG RUN

At the economy-wide or aggregate level, the measure of performance most commonly used in country descriptions is provided by the growth of real GDP. These growth rates for each country are reported in Table 2.1 for various periods; the entry for Central America is an unweighted arithmetic average of the growth rates recorded for the five republics.

Several features of Table 2.1 are worthy of comment; one may note, first, that the economic depression of the last few years has been intensely severe, surpassing in extent for several countries the drop in real output recorded after the 1929 depression. With the exception of these two periods, real GDP fell only in three cases: Nicaragua from 1974 to 1979 (which was mainly due to a massive 25 per cent reduction in real GDP during the 1979 civil war year) and Costa Rica and Guatemala during the Second World War.

Secondly, if we ignore the periods of falling real output (1929–34 and 1979–84), the real GDP growth rate for the region comes close to 5 per cent per annum – a respectable performance by international standards. This rate tends only to be surpassed when exceptional conditions prevail (e.g. the period 1944–9, when the productive forces artificially restrained during the Second World War were released, and the period 1949–54 when the commodity boom triggered off by the Korean War prevailed).

The figures in Table 2.1 suggest the following periodisation:

(*a*) 1920–9. A decade in which the traditional model of export-led growth is consolidated after the dislocations of the First World War. During this period, export specialisation reaches its peak, with coffee and bananas accounting for more than 70 per cent of export earnings in all republics and more than 90 per cent in Costa Rica, El Salvador and

*Table* 2.1 Rate of growth of Gross Domestic Product at 1970 prices. (Rates expressed as geometric annual averages.) 1920–84

| | *Costa Rica* | *El Salvador* | *Guatemala* | *Honduras* | *Nicaragua* | *Central America** |
|---|---|---|---|---|---|---|
| 1920–4 | 2.2 | 3.1 | 3.3 | 2.6 | 1.8 | 2.6 |
| 1924–9 | 1.7 | 3.7 | 4.0 | 6.9 | 3.9 | 4.0 |
| 1929–34 | 0.8 | − 0.4 | 0.1 | − 3.0 | − 2.2 | − 0.9 |
| 1934–39 | 6.0 | 2.9 | 12.4 | 0.6 | 0.9 | 4.6 |
| 1939–44 | − 0.7 | 3.5 | − 4.8 | 1.8 | 5.4 | 1.0 |
| 1944–9 | 8.8 | 7.7 | 6.3 | 5.7 | 4.3 | 6.6 |
| 1949–54 | 7.6 | 3.8 | 3.4 | 3.3 | 8.8 | 5.4 |
| 1954–9 | 6.1 | 4.7 | 5.1 | 3.8 | 3.4 | 4.6 |
| 1959–64 | 6.4 | 6.4 | 5.0 | 4.7 | 8.3 | 6.2 |
| 1964–9 | 7.2 | 5.1 | 5.6 | 5.2 | 5.2 | 5.7 |
| 1969–74 | 6.8 | 4.6 | 5.9 | 3.2 | 4.8 | 5.1 |
| 1974–9 | 5.5 | 3.7 | 5.5 | 5.2 | − 1.5 | 3.7 |
| 1979–84 | − 0.5 | − 4.3 | − 0.3 | 0.8 | 0.3 | − 0.8 |
| 1920–9 | 1.9 | 3.4 | 3.7 | 5.0 | 3.0 | 3.4 |
| 1929–39 | 3.4 | 1.3 | 6.1 | − 1.2 | − 0.6 | 1.8 |
| 1939–49 | 3.9 | 5.6 | 0.7 | 3.8 | 4.8 | 3.8 |
| 1949–59 | 6.8 | 4.3 | 4.3 | 3.6 | 6.1 | 5.0 |
| 1959–69 | 6.8 | 5.7 | 5.3 | 4.9 | 6.8 | 5.9 |
| 1969–79 | 6.1 | 4.1 | 5.7 | 4.2 | 1.6 | 4.3 |
| 1920–49 | 3.1 | 3.4 | 3.5 | 2.4 | 2.3 | 2.9 |
| 1949–79 | 6.6 | 4.7 | 5.1 | 4.2 | 4.8 | 5.1 |

*Figures for Central America are unweighted arithmetic averages of country rates.

*Source*: Derived from Table A.1 in V. Bulmer-Thomas, *The Political Economy of Central America since 1920* (Cambridge: Cambridge University Press, 1987).

Guatemala. In the second half of the decade problems of excess supply in world coffee markets start to be felt, causing a reduction in the rate of growth of GDP for Costa Rica.[3] In Nicaragua and Honduras, however, the rate of growth accelerates, as virgin banana lands are opened for production.

(*b*) 1929–34. A quinquennium in which most of the output-reducing impact of the depression is experienced. In one case (Costa Rica) the fall in output begins before 1929 and in several republics (Costa Rica, El Salvador, Guatemala) the turning-point is reached before 1934. In all cases, the fall in output is much more modest than the fall in prices.

(*c*) 1934–9. A period of strong recovery in the 'coffee republics' (i.e. those whose principal export was coffee), while the performance of the 'banana republics' (Nicaragua,[4] Honduras) was much less impressive. Recovery was based primarily on import substitution in agriculture (ISA) and only secondarily on import substitution in industry (ISI) and/or increases in the export quantum. The hypothesis suggested by this dichotomy (see Chapter 3) is that ISA was easier to achieve in the coffee than banana republics, since in the former the land and labour required for an increase in home output were more readily available.

(*d*) 1939–44. A quinquennium in which economic performance is determined primarily by the impact of the Second World War. On the export front, the requisitioning of the banana fleets by the US navy posed severe problems, but new markets also appeared for war-related products (e.g. quinine), or products whose supply to the US market was interrupted by the Japanese occupation of parts of Asia (e.g. rubber, abacá). The poor growth record of Costa Rica in this period (GDP actually fell) was due to the collapse of banana exports after 1941 caused by transportation problems. Similar problems occurred in Honduras and Nicaragua, but these were more than offset by strong ISA and gold export performances respectively.[5]

(*e*) 1944–9. The exploitation of idle resources in the post-war years caused a boom of almost unparalleled proportions in all republics. The major beneficiary in each case was the export sector, which successfully recaptured markets lost in the war. During this period, exports also became more diversified; timber, cacao and abacá acquired significance in Costa Rica,[6] while sesame and cotton increased in importance in Nicaragua. Cotton also started to make an important contribution to export earnings in El Salvador.

(*f*) 1949–54. Despite high commodity prices caused by the Korean war, the export quantum did not expand rapidly in this period and the rate of growth decelerated in all republics except Nicaragua.[7] The indirect impact of high commodity prices proved beneficial, however, through its impact on government revenue and expenditure and the relaxation of the foreign exchange constraint. In El Salvador, ISI proved to be important for the first time.

(*g*) 1954–9. Despite the fall in their price, the quantum of traditional exports rose sharply in this period and contributed substantially to the rise of real GDP. Export diversification also continued with cotton and sugar increasing in importance throughout the isthmus, while coffee exports expanded rapidly in Honduras.

(*h*) 1959–69. A decade of rapid growth dominated by the formation of the Central American Common Market (CACM). In all republics, the industrial share of GDP rose, although the rise was least marked in Costa Rica and in Honduras the share fell between 1964 and 1969. The diversion of resources from agriculture, however, was in relative terms only and the agricultural sector continued to grow in all republics, with beef added to the list of major agricultural exports.

(*i*) 1969–74. Although GDP continued to grow rapidly in all the republics, the difficulties facing CACM in the wake of the war between El Salvador and Honduras in 1969[8] began to manifest themselves in the performance of the industrial sector. The deceleration in the latter's rate of growth, however, was compensated for by the rise in world commodity prices after 1971, which favourably influenced the volume of agricultural exports in all republics.

(*j*) 1974–9. Despite the continued weakness of CACM and the world economy, real GDP continued to rise rapidly in all republics except Nicaragua.[9] The main stimuli were provided by the extraordinary rise in commodity prices (mainly coffee and sugar) and by the sharp rise in foreign capital inflows.

(*k*) 1979–84. A period in which the economic crisis, which had been threatening for many years, was finally realised. The weaknesses of CACM were brought into the open with the closing of frontiers, the intra-regional payments crisis, the collapse of exchange rate stability and the adoption of unilateral action by partner countries. The fall in commodity prices proved more rapid than anticipated and the drying up of new capital inflows focused attention on the foreign exchange constraint as the major obstacle to future growth.

The growth of real GDP is not intended as a measure of economic welfare. It can be adjusted, however, in a number of ways to approximate the change in welfare; one such adjustment allows for changes in population, another for the difference between the growth of product and home expenditure with or without terms of trade effects. The first adjustment will be presented here, while the second will be left to the next section.

Unlike the case of many other LDCs, rapid population growth in Central America is not exclusively a post-1950 phenomenon.[10] While it is true that the annual rate of growth of population has accelerated in the last three decades, it stood around 2 per cent even in the 1920s. Since 1950 the rate of growth of population has regularly exceeded 3 per cent p.a. in all republics except Costa Rica, where the demographic transition began in the late 1960s.[11]

As elsewhere, the cause of the acceleration in the rate of growth of population has been primarily the fall in the death rate. The Crude Death Rate (CDR), which in the 1920s was roughly 20, is now much closer to 10 – a drop which in the absence of any change in the Crude Birth Rate (CBR) is sufficient to add 1 per cent to the rate of growth of population.[12] Several countries, however, noticeably Nicaragua and El Salvador, have also experienced sharp rises in the CBR, giving a further stimulus to population growth.[13]

The results obtained from adjusting GDP growth for population changes are given in Table 2.2, the most striking feature of which is the ability of the recent crisis to wipe out the gains of decades; Nicaragua and El Salvador, for example, recorded in 1984 much the same GDP per head as in 1956. The stagnation of GDP per head in Honduras over the whole period is also a marked feature of the table; not only has

*Table* 2.2 GDP per head (in 1970 dollars) for selected years, 1920–84
(Figures in parentheses refer to home expenditure per head)

| *Year* | *Costa Rica* | *El Salvador* | *Guatemala* | *Honduras* | *Nicaragua* |
|---|---|---|---|---|---|
| 1920 | 278 (227) | 164 (142) | 235 (214) | 217 (207) | 173 (179) |
| 1929 | 285 (264) | 186 (162) | 247 (247) | 264 (192) | 213 (212) |
| 1939 | 321 (312) | 185 (157) | 354 (341) | 193 (178) | 167 (163) |
| 1949 | 370 (345) | 283 (254) | 300 (303) | 226 (203) | 211 (205) |
| 1959 | 463 (483) | 325 (316) | 335 (352) | 236 (237) | 287 (284) |
| 1969 | 635 (669) | 404 (387) | 413 (410) | 277 (289) | 423 (434) |
| 1979 | 894 (977) | 452 (512) | 514 (509) | 307 (327) | 355 (348) |
| 1984 | 790 (752) | 310 (330) | 445 (409) | 274 (276) | 293 (309) |

Three-year averages. (1920 and 1984 two-year averages).

*Source*: Derived from Tables A.1, A.2, A.12 and A.13 in V. Bulmer-Thomas, *The Political Economy of Central America since 1920* (Cambridge: Cambridge University Press, 1987).

Honduras (since 1951) acquired the dubious status of being the poorest Central American country, it has also not yet recorded the income per head of Costa Rica in 1950.[14]

With the exception of Honduras, income per head more than doubled between 1920 and the beginning of the recent crisis (1978–80). This increase, however, has been very unevenly distributed, with most of it occurring in the second half of the period; from 1944 to 1979, GDP per head grew at more than 2 per cent p.a. in Costa Rica, El Salvador and Guatemala, while from 1938 to 1978 GDP per head in Nicaragua grew at more than 3 per cent p.a.

It would be tempting to look only at the figures for 1984 in Table 2.2 and argue from this that the present crisis results from economic backwardness. This is a temptation which should be resisted; the sharp fall in GDP per head in recent years is as much a consequence of the present crisis as its cause and for much of the period (particularly since the Second World War) the growth in GDP per head has been high by international standards. Furthermore, the poor performer (Honduras) is the exception which proves the rule, since Honduras is not in the midst of a social revolution, while the fastest growing country (Nicaragua) was the first in recent years to experience one.

## HOME EXPENDITURE AND TERMS OF TRADE EFFECTS

In the previous section, economic performance has been measured using Gross Domestic Product (GDP). GDP, however, measures output (net) and includes exports while excluding imports as can be seen very clearly when written as:

$$y = e + x - m \tag{2.1}$$

where $y$ represents real GDP, $e$ represents real home expenditure, $x$ represents real exports and $m$ real imports.

Real home expenditure ($e$) includes consumption and investment (both private and public); it therefore represents a better guide to the standard of living than real GDP. In the absence of direct measurements, it can be approximated from equation (2.1) as

$$e = y - x + m \tag{2.2}$$

where this time it will be noted that $e$ varies negatively with $x$ and positively with *m*. Thus real imports – by adding to the resources available for consumption and investment – increase real home expenditure while exports subtract from it.

The data on real home expenditure per head are given in parentheses in Table 2.2.[15] A pattern emerges for most republics of a post-war period in which real home expenditure per person has either exceeded or come close to real GDP per person, while falling short of the latter in the pre-war period.

Starting from a given year, if the external terms of trade improve, then a given volume of exports will permit a higher volume of imports, i.e. real imports and real home expenditure will rise. The opposite will be true if the external terms of trade deteriorate. One possible interpretation, therefore, of Table 2.2 is that movements in the external terms of trade for Central America since 1920 account for the change in the ratio between home final expenditure and real GDP.

The net barter terms of trade for the Central American republics are presented in Fig. 2.1.[16] While the terms of trade before 1950 except for Honduras are generally adverse (i.e. less than 100), the post-1950 picture is much more mixed with periods of sharp improvement at the beginning and in the late 1970s, but a tendency towards 'secular decline' in the intervening years. Honduras, however, is again the exception, since banana prices did not profit from the commodity boom in the Korean war so that the post-1950 period is marked by more stable terms of trade.[17]

Movements in the external terms of trade, therefore, explain much of the gap between real home expenditure and real GDP per person in Table 2.2, but not all of it. Real imports, however, can grow faster than real exports for reasons other than favourable movements in the barter terms of trade; even with constant prices, a growing deficit on commodity trade is possible if capital inflows are rising, and this certainly did occur in Central America during the 1960s and much of the 1970s.

We can establish the following key periods in the evolution of Central America's external terms of trade; an initial period of decline as a result of the 1921 depression is followed by a sharp improvement which passes its peak in the late 1920s. This is followed by a lengthy period of deterioration which is only reversed in the later stages of the Second World War. There follows a spectacular improvement which reaches its peak at the end of the Korean war, leading into nearly two decades of deterioration; the improvement in the early 1970s is almost as dramatic as that thirty years before, but the turning point (1977) is reached more quickly.

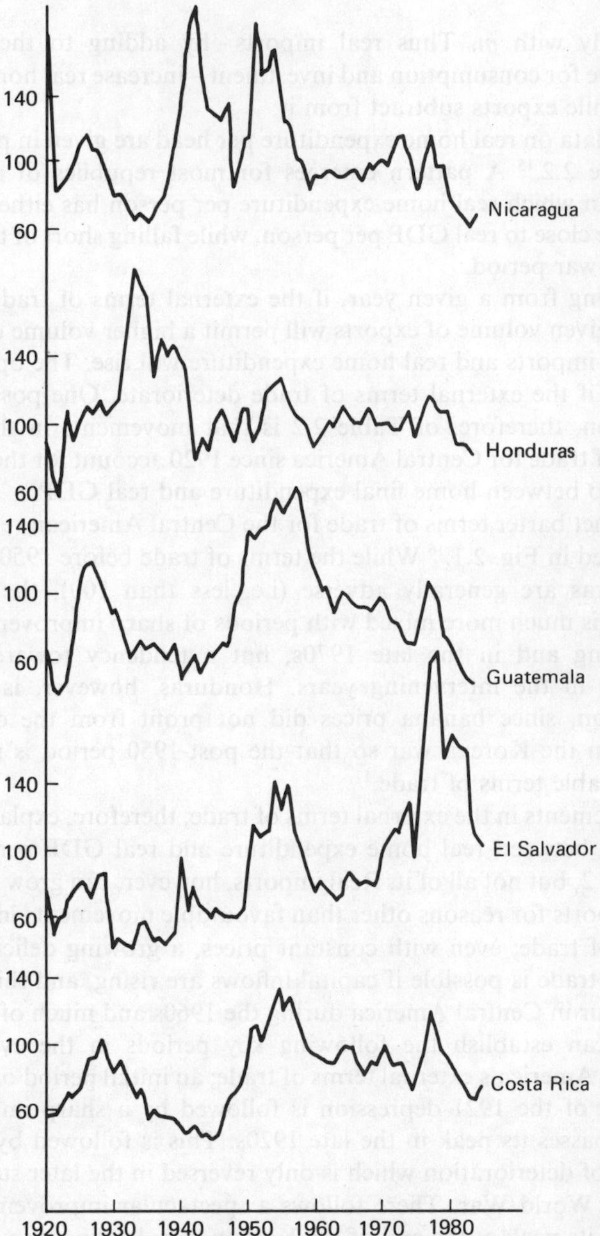


*Figure* 2.1 Net barter terms of trade, 1920–84 (1970 = 100)

*Source*: Table A.14 in V. Bulmer-Thomas, *The Political Economy of Central America since 1920* (Cambridge: Cambridge University Press, 1987).

What conclusions can be drawn from the evidence on GDP and home expenditure per head in Table 2.2? In general, the results confirm the picture presented in Table 2.1 of steady (but not spectacular) economic growth, with the exceptions provided by the long-run stagnation of Honduras and the collapse of the last few years. There is little support here for the notion of Central America as an area locked into traditional methods of production and isolated from advances in the world economy.

On the contrary, the evidence on growth presented in Tables 2.1 and 2.2 suggests an economy which over the last sixty years has been subjected to a considerable degree of transformation. As we shall see, the roots of the present crisis lie to a large extent in the tensions and dislocations generated during the course of that transformation; it is change, not stagnation, which lies at the heart of Central America's problems.

The data presented so far, however, are all highly aggregated and do not permit us to establish the exact nature of the economic transformation which has occurred in Central America. We must, therefore, turn from aggregate to sectoral performance, beginning with the all-important agricultural sector.

## CHANGES IN AGRICULTURE'S RELATIVE SHARE

Both cross-section and time-series studies (Chenery and Syrquin, 1975) of LDCs suggest that the agricultural sector's share of GDP will decline as income per head rises. The decline is explained in a number of ways (Johnstone and Kilby, 1975), of which one of the most persuasive is Engel's law; according to the latter, the proportion of income spent on foodstuffs declines as income rises, which suggests that the output of the agricultural sector will rise less rapidly than GDP itself.

The relative decline in agriculture is assumed to be accompanied by rapid urbanisation, which attracts rural out-migration and a net capital inflow from the rural economy. The migration of rural labour permits in turn a rise in the productivity of agricultural labour, raising rural real incomes and expanding the market for industrial goods. This accentuates the tendencies towards further urbanisation and a virtuous circle is established, leading towards the transformation of a primarily agrarian economy into an industrial one.

The time period dealt with in this paper is long enough to assess the validity of this model for Central America, since GDP per head since

1920 (see table 2.2) has risen substantially in all cases except Honduras. We may begin, therefore, by looking at the change in agriculture's share of GDP over time (see Table 2.3).

When the beginning and end of the period are compared, a sharp decline in the relative importance of agriculture can be observed. However, the rate of decline is by no means constant over time, and there are sub-periods of considerable length when the share either does not decline or in some cases actually rises.[18] Furthermore, the decline is very sharp (when end periods are compared) in the case of Honduras, for whom the rise in GDP per head was the smallest, while the decline is least dramatic in the case of Guatemala, which experienced a substantial rise in income per head.

The model outlined above refers, in any case, to a relationship between agriculture's share of GDP and income per head, and time may be only a poor proxy for the latter. A more precise test is therefore provided by regression analysis using the equation:

$$\log (Va/P)_t = \alpha + \beta \log (y/P)_t + \gamma \log P_t \qquad (2.3)$$

where *Va* represents net output (value added) in agriculture, *P* stands for population and *y*, as before, represents real GDP.[18]

The use of logarithms in equation (2.3) means that the parameters (β, γ) can be interpreted as elasticities (growth and size elasticities respectively). *A priori* reasoning suggests that the growth elasticity (β) will be

*Table* 2.3 Agriculture's share of GDP (%). Three-year averages

| *Year* | *Costa Rica* | *El Salvador* | *Guatemala* | *Honduras* | *Nicaragua* |
|---|---|---|---|---|---|
| 1920* | 46.9 | 45.6 | 41.8 | 49.8 | 56.5 |
| 1929 | 42.1 | 45.9 | 36.2 | 56.0 | 66.0 |
| 1939 | 35.1 | 47.6 | 44.9 | 49.9 | 53.1 |
| 1949 | 39.0 | 43.2 | 37.7 | 45.8 | 35.3 |
| 1959 | 30.3 | 37.1 | 33.1 | 36.3 | 30.7 |
| 1969 | 25.8 | 29.9 | 30.3 | 35.6 | 28.4 |
| 1979 | 19.6 | 28.9 | 28.2 | 24.9 | 29.6 |
| 1984* | 21.5 | 30.3 | 28.4 | 26.8 | 27.8 |

*Two-year averages.

*Source*: Derived from Tables A.1 and A.4 in V. Bulmer-Thomas, *The Political Economy of Central America since 1920* (Cambridge: Cambridge University Press, 1987).

positive but less than unity; this implies that a rise in real income per head (*cet. par.*) will raise value added per head in agriculture, but not in the same proportion; thus the share of agriculture in GDP will fall. By contrast the size elasticity (γ) is expected to be negative; the increase in population, *cet. par.*, expands market size and permits above proportionate growth in non-agricultural activities, so that agriculture's share of GDP again falls.

The results of equation (2.3) are given in Table 2.4 and provide a severe challenge to the model outlined at the beginning of this section.[19] While the size elasticity comes out as negative in all cases (as expected),

*Table* 2.4 Agricultural response patterns in Central America

| | *Regression coefficients in equation (2.3a) with respect to:*† | | | | |
|---|---|---|---|---|---|
| | *Intercept* α* | log (*y*/*P*) (β) | log *P* (γ) | $\bar{R}^2$ | *Durbin–Watson statistic* |
| Costa Rica | 1.74 (5.91) | 1.2 (14.8) | − 0.48 (8.9) | 0.98 | 1.77 |
| El Salvador | 2.74 (7.05) | 1.09 (12.09) | − 0.53 (6.99) | 0.94 | 2.2 |
| Guatemala | 0.39 (1.22) | 1.13 (16.99) | − 2.28 (5.87) | 0.97 | 2.19 |
| Honduras | 1.17 (2.13) | 1.24 (12.37) | − 0.41 (8.27) | 0.97 | 2.15 |
| Nicaragua | 1.82 (2.84) | 0.82 (9.99) | − 2.27 (2.72) | 0.92 | 2.09 |

*Note*: Figures in brackets are *t*-statistics.

†Estimation of equation (2.3) by Ordinary Least Squares revealed a high degree of serial correlation. The equation was therefore re-estimated using a maximum likelihood iterative technique (see Beach, 1978)

$$\left(\log\frac{Va}{P}\right)_t - \rho\left(\log\frac{Va}{P}\right)_{t-1} = \alpha^* + \beta\log\left(\frac{y}{P}\right)_t - \log\left(\frac{y}{P}\right)_{t-1} + \gamma[\log P_t - \log P_{t-1}] \tag{2.3a}$$

where $\alpha^* = \alpha(1-\rho)$. The results in Table 2.4 refer to the parameter estimates in equation (3a), from which it can be seen that the Durbin–Watson statistic is in each case within the acceptance region for no autoregression.

the growth elasticity is less than one for one country only (Nicaragua). In all other republics, the β-coefficient exceeds unity, which implies that an increase in real income (population unchanged) will raise, not lower, agriculture's share of GDP. Thus the observed long-run decline of agriculture's share only comes about because the share-increasing tendency of the growth elasticity is subdued by the share-reducing tendency of the size elasticity.

A further challenge to the received wisdom on agriculture's declining share and rural out-migration is provided by the figures on urbanisation. By 1950, for example, the proportion of the population classified as rural (see Torres Rivas, 1973, Table 16) was over 70 per cent in all republics and over 80 per cent in Honduras. These figures are so high that it is difficult to see how the decline in agriculture's share between 1920 and 1950 (see Table 2.3) could have been accomplished by much rural–urban migration. Indeed, in the case of El Salvador (see Durham, 1979, p. 55) there was only a six-percentage-point drop in the proportion of the population classified as rural between 1892 and 1950.

The validity of Engel's law is not in question among economists; indeed, it is one of the few empirically established laws of economics which have stood the test of time. The problem, therefore, is to explain the performance of the agricultural sector in Central America in a manner which does not contradict Engel's law.

Engel's law, however, refers to the demand for foodstuffs; even if we ignore the fact that much agricultural output does not consist of foodstuffs, it is possible for supply to outstrip home demand if there are favourable export opportunities. We need, therefore, to distinguish between two branches of agriculture: one producing goods for the home market, the other producing goods for the world market. I shall call the first branch Domestic Use Agriculture (DUA) and the second Export Agriculture (EXA).

Many products are sold in both home and world markets; none the less, in the case of Central America, world markets are dominant in the case of coffee and bananas and, to a lesser extent, cotton and sugar. I have therefore defined EXA in terms of these four commodities, so that DUA refers to all other agricultural products.[20]

Engel's law can be said to apply to DUA. It does not, however, apply to EXA unless the country producing the export crop is a dominant supplier to the world market; this is not the case in Central America, with the possible exception of bananas. A shift of resources into EXA can, therefore, move agriculture's share in a perverse direction in terms of the conventional model.

The division of agriculture into two branches has further implications of great social importance. EXA tends to be large-scale, land-extensive, using hired labour and sometimes highly mechanised; DUA, by contrast, tends to be small-scale land- and labour-intensive using family labour. According to the CIDA study of the 1960s (reported in Dorner and Quiros, 1983, Table 3), while 80 per cent of the output of sub-family farms was destined for the home market, only 25 per cent was similarly allocated in the case of the largest size category of farms. A movement from one branch of agriculture to the other therefore carries implications for land use, land–man ratios and rural out-migration which turn out to be of great importance.[21]

## THE TWO BRANCHES OF AGRICULTURE

The share of EXA in agriculture's net output is shown in Table 2.5 (there is no need to show DUA's share as this is a residual and can, therefore, be derived from Table 2.5 very easily).

The first feature to note is the extraordinary importance of EXA. In the late 1920s, for example, when the export-led model reached its peak, EXA accounted for more than 60 per cent of agriculture's net output in Honduras and Costa Rica and nearly 50 per cent in a further two republics (El Salvador and Guatemala).

The ability of several republics (El Salvador, Honduras, Nicaragua) to increase EXA's share in the 1920s helps to explain why in Table 2.3 agriculture's share of GDP for these same countries actually rises during this decade. A rapidly expanding EXA permits agriculture to

*Table* 2.5 Export agriculture's share of agricultural net output (%), 1920–84

| *Year* | *Costa Rica* | *El Salvador* | *Guatemala* | *Honduras* | *Nicaragua* |
|---|---|---|---|---|---|
| 1920 | 59.9 | 44.3 | 54.1 | 45.5 | 17.8 |
| 1929 | 62.6 | 46.4 | 47.6 | 69.0 | 23.6 |
| 1939 | 40.9 | 46.4 | 26.4 | 44.6 | 27.8 |
| 1949 | 50.8 | 46.2 | 27.4 | 42.6 | 14.1 |
| 1959 | 37.3 | 50.9 | 34.4 | 34.1 | 41.5 |
| 1969 | 44.7 | 50.8 | 32.2 | 42.6 | 55.4 |
| 1979 | 43.2 | 50.6 | 33.6 | 49.2 | 58.7 |
| 1984 | 47.8 | 46.6 | 30.1 | 48.0 | 55.7 |

*Source*: Derived from Tables A.4 and A.5 in V. Bulmer-Thomas, *The Political Economy of Central America since 1920* (Cambridge: Cambridge University Press, 1987).

grow at a rate faster than that implied by the growth of home demand.

A high (and increasing) EXA share also implies specialisation in EXA and a neglect of DUA, as resources are reallocated from the latter to the former. This implies an increase in imports of foodstuffs, which Central America certainly experienced in the late 1920s when such imports represented 20 per cent by value of the total import bill.

The presence of food imports, however, means that growth of DUA is no longer determined (at least in the short run) by the growth of home demand. In the 1930s, for example, several republics enjoyed rapid increases in DUA (see Chapter 3), which were achieved in part through import substitution. This accounts for the rise in the share of agriculture in GDP in Guatemala and, to a lesser extent, in El Salvador during the 1930s. The fall in EXA's share in the 1930s, therefore, is due not so much to the collapse of export markets (the quantum of exports – but not the value – held up well) as to the rise in importance of DUA.

The second feature to note about Table 2.5 is the substantial rise in EXA's share after the Second World War. Indeed, in several republics export specialisation has come close to, if not surpassed, the levels achieved in the 1920s. Significantly, the formation of CACM seems to have made little, if any, impact on this process of specialisation, which suggests that the incipient industrial sector did not compete seriously with EXA for scarce resources.[22]

Several republics for part of the post-war period have experienced a constant or even rising share of agriculture in GDP despite rising income per head. Nearly all these observations can be explained by a sharp increase in EXA's share in the same period; thus, favourable world market conditions permit EXA to grow faster than DUA and a rising EXA share permits agriculture to grow faster than GDP.

The decline in EXA's share in the two decades up to 1950 means that DUA's share was rising. DUA, however, is by hypothesis the labour-intensive sector, so that the 'push' factors influencing rural out-migration are likely to be less severe in periods when DUA's share is increasing. This, it is argued, helps to account for the low levels of urbanisation in 1950.

By contrast, when EXA's share is rising, the push factors influencing rural out-migration increase substantially; EXA competes with DUA for land and labour (not capital), which in turn either increases landlessness among the peasantry, or reduces the median size of family farms; in both cases the supply of labour for hire (wage labour) increases, since even those with farms must now seek off-farm work to supplement their farm earnings. Wage labour in EXA, however, is highly seasonal so that annual incomes are usually low and often insecure. The gap between labour supply and demand in EXA then exerts downward pressure on real wages, which ensures that a large share of the value of the product consists of economic rent (see Reynolds, 1978b). These rents are not eroded through competition, because Central America is a price-taker in international markets, and their size discourages an outflow of capital resources, until comparable rents can be earned elsewhere.[23]

## EXPORT AGRICULTURE AND THE PRESSURE ON LAND

The hypothesis that a rapid expansion of EXA contributes sharply to the push factors influencing rural out-migration assumes that most of the increase in EXA's production occurs through increases in area cultivated rather than through increases in yields. If the increase is achieved through changes in yields, then the demand for hired labour rises sharply (labour is being substituted for land), but the supply of labour is not affected. Far from encouraging rural out-migration, an increase in yield would increase real wages and discourage any outflow.

Before presenting the data on yield/area increases in EXA, the special case of banana production must be mentioned. It has always been the case that bananas are cultivated on only a fraction of the area owned by banana companies (national or multi-national). This is because of the ever-present threat of disease, although it is also designed to forestall competition and reduce alternative occupations for the local labour force.

Within the cultivated fraction (see Ellis, 1983, Table C.3) yields have risen substantially; in the period 1947–76, yields increased by some 200 per cent in Costa Rica and Guatemala and by nearly 100 per cent in Honduras. At the same time, the cultivated area remains only a small part of the total available for banana production so that it does not serve as a useful guide to changes in man–land ratios.

Figures for the remaining export crops are presented in Table 2.6. While the increases in yields have not been negligible, they have in general been dwarfed by the increases in area. This is particularly noticeable in the case of cotton where, for example, area sown in Guatemala increased by 2307 per cent between 1950 and 1980, but the difference between the increase in area and yield is also very marked in the case of cane sugar.

Coffee provides a qualification to the hypothesis that increases in

*Table* 2.6 Increases in area and yield for export agriculture (%)

| *Period* | *Costa Rica* | *El Salvador* | *Guatemala* | *Honduras* | *Nicaragua* |
|---|---|---|---|---|---|
| Cotton | | | | | |
| Area (1950–80) | — | 289 | 2307 | — | 829* |
| Yield (1950–80) | — | 94 | 349 | — | 95* |
| Cane sugar | | | | | |
| Area (1950–80) | 130 | 154 | 392 | 279 | 131 |
| Yield (1950–80) | 36 | 25 | 83 | 35 | 81 |
| Coffee | | | | | |
| Area (1935–80) | 73 | 72 | 136 | 340† | 103‡ |
| Yield (1935–80) | 261 | 65 | 54 | 41† | 51‡ |

*The terminal year is 1978 (three-year average) rather than 1980, because the civil war played havoc with the cotton crop in that year.
†There are no data on area and yield in Honduras for 1935, so the period 1945 (three-year average) to 1980 has been used instead.
‡Figures for 1935 are based on a single observation rather than a three-year average.
—Neither Costa Rica nor Honduras can be considered a serious exporter of cotton, so they have been omitted from the table.

*Sources*: The figures have been obtained from the *F.A.O. Production Yearbook*, with annual data estimated as three-year averages. Pre-war data are taken from the Institute of Agriculture's *International Yearbook of Agricultural Statistics*.

EXA have been achieved primarily through increases in area cultivated; Costa Rica, for example, experienced a much sharper rise in yields than area between 1935 and 1980, while the increase was roughly similar over the same period in El Salvador. This is not particularly surprising, as much coffee is still grown in small units where the more intensive use of family labour and/or material inputs is a legitimate alternative to increases in area. It remains true, however, that in the other three republics area increases were much more important than changes in yield.

The expansion of EXA has not been the only source of competition for the land devoted to DUA by the peasantry. The spectacular rise of the livestock industry (the most land-extensive of all branches of agriculture) and its transformation into an export activity in the 1960s has exacerbated the problem of land pressure considerably. In Nicaragua, for example, the area recorded as under permanent pasture at the end of the Second World War was 280,000 hectares and this had risen to 3,420,000 hectares by 1980. Comparable increases have been recorded in the other republics.

In order to determine land pressure quantitatively, it is necessary to deduct from the total land area the area devoted to (i) EXA, (ii) permanent pasture, (iii) forest and woodland, (iv) uncultivated land; this gives the Net Arable Land (NAL) available for production of crops for the home market (including subsistence). Division of NAL by the economically active population (PEA) in agriculture then gives a rough measure of the land–man ratio and, by implication, a measure of land pressure.[24]

The results of this experiment are presented in Table 2.7 for the years for which data could be obtained. They present a very striking picture, in which the pre-1950 relative decline of EXA is accompanied by an improvement in the land–man ratio, while the post-1950 relative increase in EXA is accompanied by a sharp deterioration in the land–man ratio. A comparison between countries reveals the desperate position of El Salvador, since the estimate of NAL available per member of the agricultural PEA has fallen well below that of the other republics.

The data presented in Table 2.7 suggest a serious deterioration over the last three decades in the land–man ratio. This, in turn, implies a reduction in real incomes among tenant farmers and owner-occupiers not involved in EXA, which prompts a search for additional sources of income. This encourages two types of migration: rural–rural migration (in search of wage labour within the rural economy) and rural–urban migration. Within the context of the model of economic development

*Table* 2.7 Land–man ratios in Central America (in hectares): arable land and permanent crop area (net of EXA) divided by agricultural labour force

| *Year* | *Costa Rica* | *El Salvador* | *Guatemala* | *Honduras* | *Nicaragua* |
|---|---|---|---|---|---|
| 1980 | 1.150 | 0.558 | 1.092 | * | * |
| 1975 | 1.328 | 0.553 | 1.102 | 1.133 | 1.908 |
| 1970 | 1.299 | 0.663 | 1.111 | 1.222 | 2.092 |
| 1965 | 1.620 | 0.706 | 1.159 | 1.280 | 2.133 |
| 1960 | N.A. | 0.928 | 1.341 | 1.906 | 2.296 |
| 1955 | 1.084 | N.A. | N.A. | 2.183 | N.A. |
| 1950 | 0.893 | 0.961 | 1.701 | 2.076 | 3.327 |
| 1945 | 0.563 | 0.824 | N.A. | 1.352 | 1.845 |
| 1940 | 0.569 | N.A. | 1.576 | N.A. | N.A. |
| 1935 | N.A. | N.A. | N.A. | N.A. | N.A. |
| 1930 | 0.539‡ | 0.587 | 0.989 | N.A. | N.A. |
| 1925 | 0.634 | N.A. | N.A. | N.A. | N.A. |

*Figures on arable land and permanent crops for 1980 were revised drastically by the FAO, making them inconsistent with earlier years.
‡ = 1929.

*Sources*: Same as for Table 2.6. Estimates of the agricultural labour force were not always consistent, however, and where necessary earlier figures were revised to make them consistent with later estimates.

adopted by Central America, both types of migration have tended to be socially and politically destabilising. The urban demand for labour has not kept pace with the increase in supply, while the rural demand for hired labour (particularly in EXA) has not provided work of a permanent nature and has frequently required the separation of the head of the household from the rest of the family.

The picture presented in Table 2.7 is complemented by the more familiar data on concentration of ownership from the agricultural census. By 1979, for example, farms in Guatemala with less than one *manzana* accounted for 41.1 per cent of all farms compared with 21.3 per cent in 1950 (see Inforpress, 1982). In El Salvador, farms with less than one hectare accounted for 2.55 per cent of the total land area (see Montgomery, 1982, p. 29) compared with 4 per cent in 1971, while the proportion of properties in this category was 37.2 per cent. In Costa Rica, between 1963 and 1973, the smallest farm size increased in number by 80 per cent compared with an increase in all farms of 29 per cent (see Seligson, 1980, p. 147).

Agricultural census data, however, have too often been interpreted as if the increased concentration of land ownership was simply due to rapid population growth. While the latter exacerbates the situation, the relative expansion of EXA (and land for livestock) is also an important contributory factor. While population growth is to a considerable extent beyond the control of the authorities – at least in the short run – the same is not true of the allocation of resources within the agricultural sector. Table 2.7 therefore, points to the need for explicit recognition of the role of government policy in a way which census data do not.

## CONCLUSIONS

With rare exceptions, the source of dynamism in the Central American economy since 1920 has been provided by EXA.[25] The most important exceptions are the periods of import substitution in agriculture (1930s) and import substitution in industry (1960s); specialisation in EXA has made possible rapid growth in real GDP and, to a lesser extent, income per head (except in Honduras). The expansion of EXA, however, has disrupted economic and social relations in agriculture to the point where the political model underpinning EXA is called into question.[26] Political and social stability in Central America, therefore, threatens to break down *because* of the success of export-led growth rather than *despite* it.

This interpretation of Central America's economic development is inconsistent with the Prebisch–Singer thesis of a secular decline in the net barter terms of trade of primary producers. As Fig. 2.1 shows, there has been no long-term tendency for terms of trade to deteriorate, although there is perhaps a disturbing asymmetry between rapid (but brief) improvements in the terms of trade and slow (but lengthy) declines.

It is quite possible that Central America's external trade exhibits unequal exchange in Emmanuel's sense (see Emmanuel, 1972). However, the strength of the theory of unequal exchange lies in its ability to predict a deterioration in the net barter terms of trade of the periphery irrespective of the initial pattern of specialisation (see Evans, 1981). Since such a deterioration has not come about, it is not of great interest to establish whether trade between Central America and the rest of the world involves unequal exchange in a static sense.

Nor is it true that Central America's growth has been growth without development. Although social indicators (e.g. literacy, life expectancy) stand at low levels today, they are still much higher than they were sixty years ago and compare reasonably well with other countries with similar levels of income per head. The test of development should not be the performance of advanced countries, but the past record of a country and the present record of comparable countries. If one does not use such a yardstick, the charge of growth without development becomes tautologically true.

The success of the CACM in the 1960s (see Chapter 4) led to the illusion that the dominance of the export-led model of growth had ceased. The CACM experiment, however, was incorporated within the very same political model which had spawned export-led growth with only minor modifications. With the benefit of hindsight, we can now see that CACM never really threatened the export-led model and when (in the 1970s) hard choices had to be made, it was the industrial sector which suffered.

The export-led model is justified in terms of the Ricardian theory of comparative advantage: by specialising in those activities (EXA) in which she has a comparative advantage, Central America can increase the level of consumption permitted by its human and physical resources.

There are several problems with the theory, however, two of which are relevant in the context of Central America. First, the theory does not account for the neglect of DUA; if anything, Central America has a comparative advantage in all natural resource-intensive products (EXA and DUA) and a comparative disadvantage in manufactured goods. If export-led growth had taken place on the basis of those crops currently produced under DUA, the implications for factor use, employment, income distribution and so on would have been very different.

Secondly, the theory does not say how the gains from trade will be distributed. Substantial gains from trade can coincide with an increase in inequality in the size distribution of income – something which has quite clearly occurred in Central America.[27] In related theories (e.g. the Hecksher–Ohlin theorem), there is a presumption of factor price equalisation between different countries; this equalisation, however, is stated as a tendency only and is conditional upon a number of restrictive assumptions.

At the present time, the export-led model is deep in crisis. This is not just a matter of falling commodity prices, which have occurred at various stages in the last sixty years; it is much more to do with the breakdown of social relations within the agricultural sector as a result of the specific way in which the export model has operated.

If the political system surrounding the export-led model now collapses, it may prompt a search for an alternative and herald a retreat into autarchy. It is not export-led growth, however, which is at fault, so much as the policies which have promoted it and which have encouraged excessive increases in area together with low returns to labour.

Significantly, the revolutionary government in Nicaragua has not turned its back on EXA, much of which remains in private hands; the distribution of the gains from trade, however, is different in Nicaragua from, say, Guatemala, and employment in EXA is becoming much more permanent in character (see Barraclough, 1982).

Nevertheless, even revolutionary governments would be well advised to avoid the extremes of export specialisation which Central America has experienced. Sharp changes in the barter terms of trade impose severe strains on very open economies, making macroeconomic stability very difficult to achieve. It is one thing to propose the reform of international commodity markets; it is altogether another to act as if they were already reformed.

## Notes

1. The complete time-series is given in the Appendix to Bulmer-Thomas (1987) along with the methodology used in its preparation.
2. These points are discussed more fully in Chapters 8, 9 and 10 of Bulmer-Thomas (1987).
3. Disease on the banana plantations after 1925 was also responsible for the sharp fall in the rate of growth of GDP in Costa Rica.
4. In general, coffee has been a more important source of export earnings than bananas in Nicaragua, but this was not true for most of the 1930s. It should be clear that the use of the phrase 'banana republics' is not intended in the pejorative sense used by O. Henry.
5. On the importance of gold to the Nicaraguan economy in this period, see Cantarero (1949).
6. The export of cacao from Costa Rica began in the late 1930s, when the United Fruit Company turned over idle banana lands for alternative uses (see Seligson, 1980).
7. The exceptionally high growth of GDP in Nicaragua was due to a boom in social infrastructure developments linked to the rapid expansion of cotton exports.
8. It is now generally accepted that the CACM's present difficulties would have arisen without the 1969 war. See, in particular, Delgado (1978).

9. Even in Nicaragua, GDP increased rapidly up to 1978 when it fell by 8 per cent, falling by a further 25 per cent in 1979.
10. Estimates of population are given in the Appendix to Bulmer-Thomas (1987), Table A.2.
11. The present Costa Rican annual growth rate of population, however, still exceeds 2 per cent – similar to the rate recorded in the pre-war period.
12. The CBR is measured as the number of live births per thousand of the population; the CDR measures the number of deaths per thousand of the population. The difference between the two measures the net increase in population on the assumption of no international migration.
13. In Nicaragua, however, this stimulus has been moderated by the fact that the CDR was already low in the 1930s, varying between 11 and 14 (see Cantarero, 1949, p. 38).
14. An explanation of Honduras's poor performance would require an article to itself. Much of the explanation, however, has to do with Honduras's heavy dependence on banana exports; production, prices and markets of these exports have, for much of the period, been controlled by multinational fruit companies concerned with the maximisation of global, not national, profits. Banana exports have also generated less government revenue than other exports in Central America.
15. Data on real GDP, population, real exports and real imports are provided in the Appendix to Bulmer-Thomas (1987).
16. The net barter terms of trade are given in Bulmer-Thomas (1987), Table A.14.
17. The relevant banana price is f.o.b. It does not follow that banana retail or auction prices did not rise.
18. In a classic study, Chenery (1968) used agriculture's share as the dependent variable rather than agricultural value added per head; in this case, *a priori* reasoning suggests that the '$\beta$' coefficient will be negative; I have experimented with this equation and the results confirm those given in Table 2.4. Many studies on sectoral performance also use the square of real income per head as well as real income per head in order to capture any non-linearities in the relationship between agriculture's share and real income. The omission of this additional variable, however, is much less serious in a time-series study, where the range of observed real incomes is much smaller than in cross-section work.
19. The results in Table 2.4 are taken from the earlier version of this chapter (see *Journal of Latin American Studies*, November, 1983).
20. There is a case for including beef production in EXA. Before 1960, however, beef was mainly sold in the domestic market so that the narrower definition of EXA is preferable.
21. This description of the two branches of agriculture should not be taken too literally; coffee (part of EXA) is often produced in small-scale, labour-intensive units, while rice (part of DUA) is sometimes the opposite. Despite these qualifications, the contrast remains valid – as can be seen for El Salvador in figure 2.17 and for Honduras in figure 4.9 of Durham (1979).

22. The absence of competition for scarce resources between the industrial sector and EXA is one of the themes of the paper by Reynolds (1978a). This lack of competition is surprising, given the initial impact of ISI on the internal terms of trade, until one considers the political economy of Central America in this crucial period. The export agricultural interests were able to influence fiscal, credit and exchange rate policy in a way which neutralised the initial adverse movement in the internal terms of trade. In El Salvador, for example, the proportion of private credit allocated to EXA actually increased between 1961 and 1975 (see Baloyra, 1982, p. 187).
23. The difficulty of attracting resources away from EXA, when economic rents are high, helps to account for the high nominal and effective rates of protection offered to industry during the CACM experiment. Indeed, one may generalise from this and argue that the path to industrial development is likely to be very different in a region rich in natural resources (such as Central America) when compared with the path followed in less favourably endowed regions (such as East Asia), precisely because the attraction of agricultural investment is much smaller in the latter.
24. It could be argued that if Net Arable Land (NAL) is the numerator, then the denominator should be the agricultural labour force net of those employed in EXA. There is a strong argument against this, however, in addition to the more mundane consideration of data availability. Employment in EXA is typically neither permanent nor secure; in Guatemala, for example, the *Instituto Guatemalteco de Seguridad Social* reported that agricultural employment had fallen from 412 400 in 1981 to 168 000 in 1982 (see *Central America Report*, 18 March 1983, p. 82); since nearly all this 'employment' is in EXA, its precarious nature in the wake of a deterioration in world market conditions is made abundantly clear.
25. This remains true despite the increase in importance of industry achieved through CACM. In a recent study of the latter, it was stated (Reynolds, 1978a, p. 288 no. 2): 'A striking feature of econometric models of income determination in the region is the evidence of the continuing dominating effect of terms of trade and other export-related fluctuations on the level of domestic income and product. This is so, despite almost two decades of integration policy designed to diversify these economies to reduce their vulnerability to foreign trade cycles.'
26. Many works have looked at the relationship between EXA and the political system. See, for example, Monteforte Toledo (1972).
27. See, for example, table 23 in Reynolds (1978a).

# 3 Central America in the Inter-war Period

## INTRODUCTION

This chapter[1] will concentrate on economic developments in Central America in the two decades spanning the Great Depression.[2] This period (1920–40) has been seriously neglected in Central American scholarship, so that the region's performance has not been taken adequately into account in works purporting to offer an overview of the Latin American experience (e.g. Furtado, 1970).

In place of studies based on primary sources, a 'received wisdom' has been built up derived from *a priori* reasoning. Thus, it has been argued, since industrialisation did not begin seriously in Central America until the 1960s, the impact of the Depression must have been particularly severe. This in turn has justified the most sweeping generalisations regarding economic performance.[3]

The main reason for the neglect of this period in Central American economic studies has been the lack of appropriate statistics. Before writing this chapter, therefore, it was necessary to construct estimates of national income for each republic from available primary sources. These estimates are in real terms and have been built up sector by sector, so that the performance of the main branches of the economy can be assessed.

After allowing for all the well-known problems associated with national income estimates, the results show a very different picture from the prevailing one; despite the severity of the impact of the Depression, which was felt above all in the form of falling commodity prices, regional Gross Domestic Product (GDP) recovered fairly quickly in real terms and the second half of the 1930s was marked by steady growth in several republics. How this was possible, despite the weakeness of industry, will be discussed below, but first the main features of the Central American economy in the 1920s must be outlined.

## CENTRAL AMERICA IN THE 1920S

The liberal reforms which swept Central America in the 1870s created the framework for the economic structure which exists in large part to this day. Communal ownership of land was abolished, banks were started, railroads laid down and ports improved; an export economy, based first on coffee and later on bananas as well, was established to the interests of which the State was completely subservient.

The First World War interrupted the consolidation of the liberal reforms, but did not lead to any change in direction. The ruling class waited patiently for an end to the war, which had disrupted its European markets (particularly for coffee), and then proceeded to re-establish even more firmly the dominance of the two traditional exports – bananas and coffee. This was helped in the early 1920s by a series of currency reforms which led to the adoption of fixed exchange rates under the gold standard (see Young, 1925). These rates were rigidly adhered to and even today one of the republics (Honduras) preserves the parities established during this period.

The model of export-led growth based on traditional exports[4] reached its highest expression in the 1920s. By 1926, for example, earnings from coffee and bananas accounted for over 90 per cent of exports by value in Costa Rica, Guatemala and El Salvador, while in Honduras and Nicaragua (where exports of precious metals continued to be important), traditional exports represented over 70 per cent of export earnings.

The growth of exports in real terms was achieved through increases in acreage rather than yields. This brought with it a number of implications of great importance; first, the increase in area devoted to coffee began to encroach on land used for domestic crops (particularly in El Salvador); second, the increased use of labour by the export sector also reduced the workforce available for supplying the home market, so that for both these reasons imports of foodstuffs rose;[5] third, the expansion of the volume of banana exports through increases in acreage depended crucially on direct foreign investment, so that the influence of the multinational fruit companies rose sharply in the 1920s.

The region's financial system was largely built around the export sector in the 1920s. Exports paid for imports and taxes on external trade accounted for the bulk of public revenues;[6] the budget of each republic was usually balanced and total public debt (both internal and external) was very modest;[7] movements in the money supply were therefore determined above all by surpluses and deficits in the balance of payments and the credit extended to the export sector was usually supplied from abroad. The commercial banking system played only a minor role in stimulating productive economic activity other than coffee.

The export-led model was therefore very simple. Increases (decreases) in sales of traditional exports brought rises (falls) in factor incomes in the export sector, with profits being the most volatile element in income; with a high marginal propensity to import out of profits, imports responded quickly to changes in exports and external equilibrium became almost automatic. Public revenues also rose (fell) with increases (decreases) in external trade and public expenditure moved in line with revenue; thus, both private and public consumption moved pro-cyclically and adverse developments in the export sector set in motion a train of events, which restored external equilibrium at a lower level of output, incomes and employment.

The failure to operate any sort of countercyclical demand management policy can be explained in several ways; first, governments were very weak and controlled directly only a small part of total expenditure; second, the ideology of *laissez-faire* was embraced whole heartedly by the political leadership and, third, the belief that adverse developments in the export sector would only be temporary was widespread. Thus, the response to the 1920/1 world recession, which savagely reduced the value of export earnings from Central America, was one of non-intervention and, indeed, export prices and earnings did recover very quickly.

The consolidation of the traditional model of export-led growth in the 1920s was achieved in an atmosphere of comparative political stability, with the exception of Nicaragua, which continued to be occupied by US marines (see Black, 1981); in Guatemala, the liberals José Maria Orellana (1921–6) and Lázaro Chacón (1926–30) gave the republic a chance to recover from the suffocating dictatorship of Estrada Cabrera, while in El Salvador the Meléndez family governed in the interest of the coffee aristocracy until 1927. In Honduras, after the civil war of 1923, a unique decade of political stability was achieved under alternating presidents and in Costa Rica two conservatives (Ricardo Jiménez and Cleto González) succeeded each other in power from 1924 to 1936; thus Costa Rica became the only country not to institute a long dictatorship in the wake of the Depression.

Some efforts at export diversification were made in the 1920s,[8] but in general the leadership in each country felt content to consolidate the achievements of the past half-century based on traditional exports (coffee and bananas). Throughout the isthmus, the political élite concurred in the belief that the market was too small to justify industrialisation[9] and that demand for the region's traditional exports could be expected to grow without limit; the main problems were seen as smoothing the obstacles to expansion on the supply side. In Guatemala, for example, the leadership remained preoccupied with the problem of ensuring an adequate labour supply,[10] while in Honduras the emphasis was on improving transportation and encouraging foreign investment. In El Salvador, however, the main constraint on export expansion was becoming a shortage of suitable land.[11]

Only a few voices were raised against the dominance of the traditional model in the 1920s, but with the benefit of hindsight its diminishing utility becomes apparent. On the supply side the expansion of coffee was increasing dependence on imported foodstuffs and reducing the region's ability to secure an automatic adjustment to external equilibrium (since food imports cannot be cut so easily). In the case of bananas, expansion involved mortgaging vast tracts of land in perpetuity to banana companies,[12] while the accompanying social infrastructure served the needs of the banana sector only.[13]

The main criticism, however, of the traditional model concerns the distortions it introduced into the allocation of resources. The region's investment effort was geared almost exclusively to the needs of the traditional export sector so that alternative activities were squeezed out. Non-traditional agriculture suffered from a shortage of land where infrastructure was available and an absence of infrastructure where land was available; manufacturing developments, where permitted by market size, were choked off by a shortage of credit and the region's mineral potential went largely unexploited.

## THE ONSET OF THE DEPRESSION

For most of the 1920s the value of exports and imports rose steadily in Central America (see Figure 3.1). This was due principally to the persistent and sharp rise in coffee prices from 1921 to 1925[14] and the less marked tendency for upward revision of the administered export price for bananas.[15] The advent of the Depression, however, was signalled by a collapse of export values.

The turning-point in the cycle (see Figure 3.1) did not coincide with the year (1929), often thought of as marking the arrival of the Depression in developed countries. On the contrary the value of

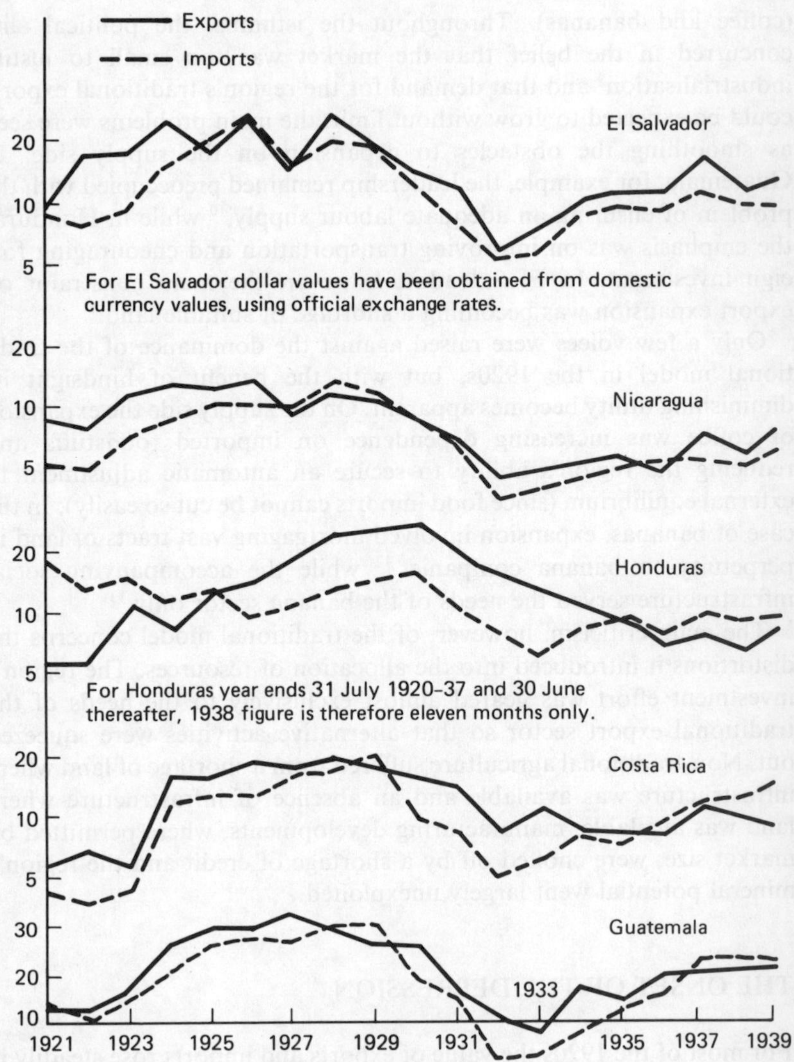


*Figure* 3.1 Central America: imports and exports 1921–39 (million dollars)

*Note*: Exports valued f.o.b. exclusive of export duties. Imports valued c.i.f. (El Salvador, Costa Rica), f.o.b. (Nicaragua, Honduras) and f.a.s. (Guatemala)

*Sources*: 1920–9 League of Nations, *International Trade Statistics*. 1930–9 UN, *Yearbook of International Trade Statistics*.

exports peaked as early as 1927 in Guatemala and 1926 in Nicaragua. In Costa Rica and El Salvador the down-turn commenced after 1928, while in Honduras it was delayed until after 1930.[16]

The difference in timing can be most easily explained by reference to the prices of traditional exports. Much Central American coffee in the 1920s was being sold in forward markets,[17] which appear to have anticipated the Depression; thus, Guatemalan coffee prices reached their peak in the period 1925–7 and fell steadily thereafter until 1934.

Banana prices, by contrast, held up much better and did not decline until the period 1931–2. There were two reasons for this: first, the export price – being an administered price – reflected auction prices in consumer countries only after a considerable lag; second, retail banana prices did not fall anything like as far or as fast as retail coffee prices in the Depression.

A third factor affecting the timing of the decline in export values was the volume of banana exports;[18] in Costa Rica, for example, production of bananas went into decline as a result of disease as early as 1926 and fell in each of the following ten years; in Honduras, the export of bananas rose sharply in the late 1920s and continued to rise until 1931 when a dramatic decline (also caused by disease) set in.

The initial decline in export values was not considered very serious in Central America. The cyclical nature of export earnings was accepted and reserves built up in good years were used to support imports in bad years; thus in all the republics except Honduras[19] a visible trade deficit was at first tolerated (see Figure 3.1). By 1930, however, the severity of the Depression had become apparent and imports by value fell even more rapidly than the value of exports; thus all Central American countries ran surpluses on visible trade in the worst years of the Depression.

The sharp decline in the value of imports during the Depression (to about one-quarter of peak levels) was not all due to volume changes. Import prices in dollar terms did fall, although the evidence is rather indirect.[20] The barter terms of trade, however, initially rose or fell depending on whether a republic specialised in bananas or coffee (see Figure 3.2).[21] Thus in the case of Honduras (where the bulk of exports was accounted for by bananas) the terms of trade index rose steadily until 1930 and did not fall below the 1928 level until 1933.

Coffee-producers were not so fortunate. The steep fall in coffee prices brought a sharp decline in the barter terms of trade after 1928 which was only reversed in 1934 (see Figure 3.2). El Salvador, for example, whose export earnings came almost entirely from coffee, was the worst

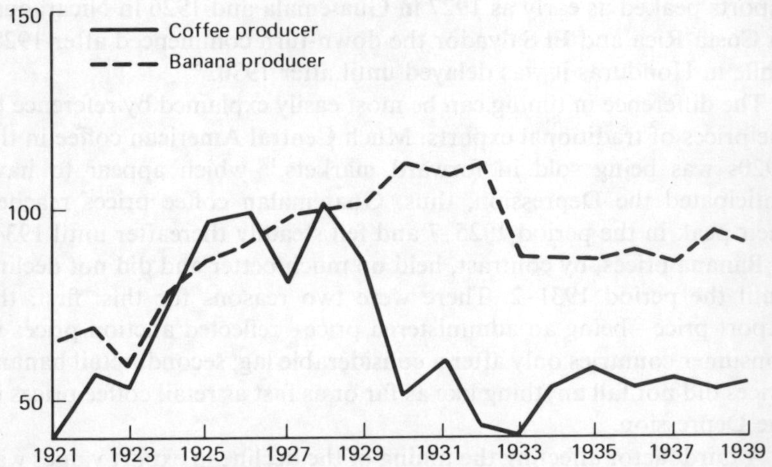


*Figure* 3.2 Net barter terms of trade, 1921–39 (1928 = 100)

*Note*: Import prices have been derived from data on real and money values of imports for Honduras (see Banco Central de Honduras, 1956).

Coffee prices are unit values for El Salvador and banana prices are unit values for Costa Rica.

affected, although the other coffee-producing countries also experienced a deterioration in the barter terms of trade.

The decline in the value of external trade reduced government income from trade taxes, the most important component of public revenue. The latter peaked in the period 1928–9 and fell sharply in the following three years (see Table 3.1). Public expenditure reductions followed with a short lag, although the fall was generally of a smaller amount than in the case of revenue and budget deficits were therefore common in the first half of the 1930s.[22]

## SHORT-RUN RESPONSE TO DEPRESSION

The steep fall in the value of external trade, beginning in the late 1920s, did not at first cause undue problems. The region had experienced such declines before, most notably in 1921, and the long-run repercussions had been minimal; each republic had the resources and the means to run a trade and/or budget deficit for a year or so; the former was made

*Table* 3.1 Central America: summary of budget accounts
(Receipts in millions of units of domestic currency. Expenditure in parentheses)

| *Year* | *Costa Rica* | *Year* | *El Salvador* | *Nicaragua* | *Honduras* | *Guatemala* |
|---|---|---|---|---|---|---|
| 1928 | 33.3 (26.9) | 1928/9 | 27.0 (27.2) | n.a. | 13.7 (13.1) | 15.4 (16.4) |
| 1929 | 35.4 (36.2) | 1929/30 | 24.6 (25.8) | 5.9 (3.8) | 14.3 (15.0) | 13.4 (14.3) |
| 1930 | 27.5 (32.5) | 1930/1 | 20.5 (n.a.) | 5.4 (4.9) | 11.8 (13.9) | 10.7 (13.2) |
| 1931 | 24.8 (27.6) | 1931/2 | 14.4 (17.9) | 4.7 (4.8) | 10.9 (10.1) | 9.2 ( 9.9) |
| 1932 | 23.1 (25.0) | 1932/3 | 17.4 (16.6) | 3.8 (4.2) | 9.0 (12.3) | 8.3 ( 8.3) |
| 1933 | 23.9 (24.2) | 1933/4 | 14.6 (15.6) | 4.2 (4.7) | 10.1 (12.7) | 8.6 ( 8.2) |
| 1934 | 26.4 (25.9) | 1934/5 | 19.4 (16.1) | 5.0 (4.9) | 10.8 (12.5) | 9.6 ( 8.8) |
| 1935 | 27.2 (30.8) | 1935/6 | 17.7 (19.9) | 5.3 (5.5) | 10.0 (14.1) | 10.5 (10.0) |
| 1936 | 34.5 (32.5) | 1936/7 | 19.9 (19.4) | 7.5 (6.9) | 11.7 (11.7) | 11.6 (10.4) |

*Sources*: League of Nations, *Public Finance, 1928–37*.

possible by healthy exchange reserves, while the latter depended on a pliable banking system.

During the period 1930–1 it had become clear that the recession was much deeper and might last longer than previous downturns in the trade cycle. The collapse in the value of external trade, which had fallen to half of its peak levels by 1931, was putting intolerable strain on public revenues and salary bills in the public sector were in many cases simply 'deferred' (see, for example, Grieb, 1979, p. 55).

A political crisis was therefore inevitable and the first casualty was Guatemala. A period of constitutional confusion in the latter half of 1930 (see Grieb, 1979) was resolved when Jorge Ubico was elected president as the sole candidate in 1931. In El Salvador the victor in the presidential elections in 1930, Arturo Araujo, was overthrown and his constitutional successor General Maximiliano Hernández Martínez ruled like Ubico through a policy of *continuismo* until 1944 (see White, 1973).

In Nicaragua and Honduras the transfer of power did not occur until 1933, but the Depression contributed to the discontent against the Moncada regime and the presence of US marines in Nicaragua; the Sandinista revolt ended when the liberal Juan Bautista Sacasa took office in 1933, but this was to prove merely a temporary interlude and Anastasio Somoza succeeded to the presidency after 1936 (see Black, 1981). In Honduras the better export performance may have contributed to the survival of the Mejía Colindres regime until 1933, when Tiburco Carías – the successful conservative candidate in the 1932 elections – took power and ruled through *continuismo* until 1948 (see Stokes, 1950).

In Costa Rica the electoral system survived the crisis and power changed hands peacefully in 1932, 1936 and 1940 (see Bell, 1971). None the less, political developments in the depths of the recession were of some importance; the Communist Party was formed by Manuel Mora Valverde and was powerful enough to lead a successful strike against the United Fruit Company in 1934.

The most serious problem faced by each government in the immediate wake of the Depression was the maintenance of external equilibrium. International reserves could not be expected to finance imports at their previous levels and foreign capital flows (both public and private) virtually dried up.[23] The decline in imports was initially achieved through a non-price rationing of available foreign exchange by commercial banks and was in most cases highly successful (with the value of imports falling more steeply than exports).

The key to the success in reducing imports was provided by their structure; the import bill was dominated by consumer goods, whose purchase could be indefinitely postponed without affecting the profitability of the export sector or the rate of growth of GDP. None the less, that imports fell *more* steeply suggests that foreign exchange was required for repatriated profits and/or capital outflows;[24] little evidence is available for this, although the need for foreign exchange to meet fixed interest charges on the public external debt was rising in proportionate and, in some cases, absolute terms.[25]

With the collapse of the gold standard in 1931, the Administration in each republic faced a new crisis – the management of the exchange rate. The initial response was to peg to the US dollar in the case of Guatemala, Honduras and Nicaragua, although Costa Rica and El Salvador allowed their rates to float. The Costa Rican colón, which throughout the second half of the 1920s, had been quoted at 4 to the US dollar, fell gradually to 6 colones to the dollar by 1936,[26] while in El Salvador a depreciation of 33 per cent between 1932 and 1933 was followed by a mild appreciation until the rate was pegged in 1935 at an official parity which survived for fifty years.

It is fair to say, therefore, that Central America followed a passive exchange-rate policy, since the rates even in Costa Rica and El Salvador did not change very dramatically. They preferred to avoid active use of an instrument which proved very useful in promoting recovery elsewhere in Latin America.[27] Despite this it is difficult to question the wisdom of the policy; exchange-rate depreciation alone was not capable of promoting a programme of import-substituting industrialisation (ISI) and the government of each republic preferred other methods to stimulate the external sector (see next section).[28]

The fall in the value of exports, imports and public revenue increased in proportionate terms the burden of the service on the external debt[29] and forced several republics into default and renegotiation. Costa Rica, Guatemala and El Salvador defaulted in the year 1932/3, while Honduras defaulted on its *domestic* debt only. Nicaragua had to postpone the repayment of certain foreign loans starting in 1932, although interest payments on the external debt were met promptly. By 1937, however, the foreign debt had been successfully renegotiated in each case.

The extreme difficulty of obtaining additional capital from abroad[30] forced several governments to increase their internal public indebtedness to meet the budget deficits during the early years of the Depression. In Costa Rica, Guatemala and El Salvador there was a sharp rise in the public debt (see Table 3.2), although the fiscal rectitude of Nicaragua and Honduras (until 1931) made such an increase unnecessary. In Honduras, however, the floating debt rose sharply, when the government failed to pay civil servants on time and this became increasingly serious between 1931 and 1934.

With such abrupt falls in the value of exports, imports, public revenue and expenditure, combined with the rise in indebtedness, it is easy to see why the impact of the Depression on Central America has been assumed to have been very severe. When the monetary veil is stripped from the figures, however, the position does not look so bad. The volume of agricultural exports in general held up well and the decline in real GDP from its peak in the late 1920s was quite mild for all countries except Nicaragua (see Table 3.3).

As elsewhere in much of Latin America, therefore, the impact of the Depression was felt more through price than quantity changes. Employment, real incomes and real consumption certainly fell,[31] but the declines were less steep and less rapid than those experienced, for example, by Nicaragua in the period 1977–9 and El Salvador in the period 1979–81.[32] Why the impact in real terms was so mild and why Central America was able to grow rapidly in the second half of the 1930s is something to which we must now turn.

*Table* 3.2 Central America: total public debt (internal debt in parentheses) (in millions of units of domestic currency)

| *Year* | *Costa Rica** | *El Salvador** | *Nicaragua†* | *Honduras‡* | *Guatemala** |
|---|---|---|---|---|---|
| 1928 | 83.6 (15.0) | 45.8 ( 4.7) | 23.5 (20.2) | 28.4 (17.2) | 17.6 (2.9) |
| 1929 | 87.8 (17.9) | 42.7 ( 3.7) | 23.2 (20.1) | 29.4 (18.6) | 15.6 (2.1) |
| 1930 | 94.1 (25.8) | 43.6 ( 7.6) | 22.5 (19.7) | 27.0 (16.6) | 20.0 (4.6) |
| 1931 | 101.8 (27.4) | 46.6 (11.8) | 21.9 (19.3) | 25.5 (17.0) | 20.9 (6.4) |
| 1932 | 108.4 (30.9) | 49.0 (12.3) | 21.6 (19.2) | 25.6 (16.2) | 21.3 (7.1) |
| 1933 | 114.5 (30.6) | 46.9 ( 9.8) | 17.9 (15.5) | 28.0 (19.1) | 22.2 (7.6) |
| 1934 | 115.5 (31.8) | 45.3 ( 8.6) | 10.0 ( 7.7) | 28.7 (21.1) | 22.1 (7.6) |
| 1935 | 119.7 (36.7) | 45.7 ( 6.2) | 8.2 ( 5.9) | 27.8 (20.8) | 22.2 (7.2) |
| 1936 | 141.9 (37.7) | 42.1 ( 6.2) | 9.0 ( 6.7) | 28.3 (21.8) | 20.2 (6.0) |

*31 December.
†1928–32, 31 March. 1932–6, 28 February.
‡31 July.

*Sources*: League of Nations, *Public Finance 1928–37*.

*Table* 3.3 Real Gross Domestic Product, 1920–40
1970 prices (thousand dollars). Net factor cost

| *Year* | *Costa Rica* | *El Salvador* | *Guatemala* | *Honduras* | *Nicaragua* |
|---|---|---|---|---|---|
| 1920 | 119 208 | 193 521 | 290 407 | 157 477 | 108 806 |
| 1921 | 116 717 | 193 930 | 318 958 | 159 091 | 112 926 |
| 1922 | 127 144 | 205 450 | 300 983 | 172 966 | 103 435 |
| 1923 | 117 539 | 214 173 | 331 001 | 171 999 | 110 669 |
| 1924 | 134 379 | 229 118 | 357 909 | 160 704 | 117 328 |
| 1925 | 133 939 | 213 315 | 351 099 | 193 943 | 129 517 |
| 1926 | 148 066* | 252 080 | 354 466 | 195 714 | 112 603 |
| 1927 | 134 378 | 221 653 | 377 747 | 214 914 | 113 086 |
| 1928 | 141 375 | 259 947 | 386 277 | 241 714 | 143 306 |
| 1929 | 135 563 | 260 228 | 431 065 | 239 314 | 160 074* |
| 1930 | 142 154 | 266 891* | 449 595* | 254 857 | 129 452 |
| 1931 | 140 360 | 239 118 | 419 222 | 260 400* | 121 005 |
| 1932 | 129 122† | 214 598† | 366 919† | 233 257 | 108 936 |
| 1933 | 153 814 | 243 578 | 370 676 | 218 800 | 137 051 |
| 1934 | 135 596 | 251 592 | 419 296 | 211 943 | 124 464 |
| 1935 | 146 910 | 276 855 | 484 637 | 202 514 | 126 461 |
| 1936 | 156 676 | 270 659 | 665 639 | 206 229 | 100 622† |
| 1937 | 182 660 | 296 365 | 652 826 | 197 143† | 109 096 |
| 1938 | 193 630 | 275 560 | 670 863 | 208 571 | 112 832 |
| 1939 | 199 245 | 295 591 | 754 982 | 214 343 | 140 112 |
| 1940 | 191 138 | 321 027 | 862 410 | 229 086 | 153 216 |

*Pre-Depression peak.
†Post-Depression trough.

*Source*: V. Bulmer-Thomas, *The Political Economy of Central America since 1920* (Cambridge: Cambridge University Press, 1987), Table A.1.

## RECOVERY FROM THE DEPRESSION – EXPORT PROMOTION

Although export volumes held up well in the early years of the Depression they did fall below their previous peak levels and the deterioration of the barter terms of trade (see Figure 3.2) meant that even the maintenance of previous export levels would still reduce the capacity to import. The road to recovery was therefore likely to depend on more than just the promotion of traditional exports.

This, as we shall see, was the case. Policy, however, concentrated heavily on the traditional export sector for a number of reasons; first, it was felt that world commodity prices for traditional exports would improve and the level of activity in the export sector should therefore be maintained; second, influencing the level of exports through variations in policy instruments was a familiar role for Central American Administrations and, third, the political élite throughout the Depression and despite its severity remained wedded to the traditional export-led model.

There was a sharp contrast, however, between the positions of coffee and banana exports. Coffee production and sales, being largely in national hands,[33] could be influenced with the policy instruments available, but banana exports were quite different; first, they were almost entirely controlled[34] by the United Fruit Company and the Standard Fruit and Steamship Company, and these two giants of the fruit trade determined production in individual Central American republics on a global basis; second, banana production was very susceptible to disease for which at that time (see Karnes, 1978) no known antidote existed.[35]

Coffee production could be influenced through variations in export duties, the availability of credit, exchange rate changes and special funds.[36] All these instruments were used by one or other republic in the Depression and the impact of low world prices on profitability was also mitigated by the reduction in labour costs. Perhaps the most important contribution, however, which the State made towards maintenance of coffee production was the protection of growers from foreclosure by exporters and bankers when debts were not paid. This was of particular importance in El Salvador (Wilson, 1970), where General Hernández Martínez intervened on behalf of the growers shortly after taking office.[37]

The result of these endeavours was the maintenance or even increase in the volume of coffee exports during the 1930s over peak levels achieved in the 1920s (see Figure 3.3). At the same time banana production dropped steeply as disease spread through plantations, although activity was maintained close to previous levels in Guatemala. The overall performance of traditional exports therefore depended on the relative importance of coffee and bananas in the total; this helps to account for the poor GDP performance of Honduras in the 1930s (see Table 3.3), since she had virtually no coffee exports and banana exports were seriously affected by disease.

Efforts at export diversification during the 1930s were rather disappointing. Even in the 1920s the dominance of traditional exports was not absolute; in several republics sugar had grown into a minor export crop of some importance and timber was a useful source of foreign

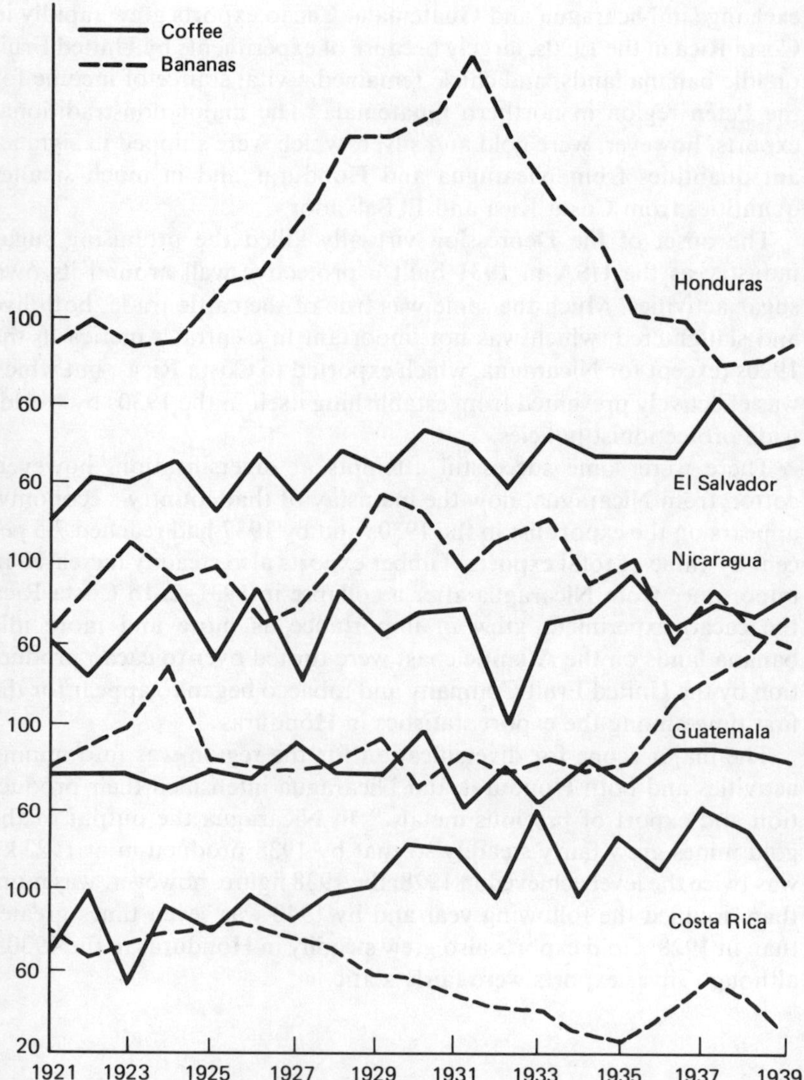


*Figure* 3.3 Central America: exports of coffee and bananas by volume, 1921–39 (1950 = 100 except banana exports from Nicaragua, where 1928 = 100.)

exchange in Nicaragua and Guatemala. Cacao exports grew rapidly in Costa Rica in the 1920s, largely because of experiments by United Fruit on idle banana lands, and chicle remained a vital source of income for the Petén region in northern Guatemala. The major non-traditional exports, however, were gold and silver, which were shipped in significant quantities from Nicaragua and Honduras and in much smaller quantities from Costa Rica and El Salvador.

The onset of the Depression virtually killed the promising sugar industry as the USA in 1931 built a protective wall around its own sugar activities. Much the same was true of the cattle trade, both live and slaughtered, which was not important in Central America in the 1920s (except for Nicaragua, which exported to Costa Rica), but which was effectively prevented from establishing itself in the 1930s by worldwide protectionist policies.

There were some successful attempts at diversification, however; cotton from Nicaragua, now the mainstay of that country's economy, appears on the export list in the 1930s and by 1937 had reached 7.5 per cent by value of total exports. Timber exports also steadily increased in importance from Nicaragua after a collapse in 1931–2. In Costa Rica the cacao experiment grew in importance as more and more idle banana lands on the Atlantic coast were turned over to cacao production by the United Fruit Company and tobacco began to appear for the first time among the export statistics in Honduras.

The major scope for diversification for the region was into mining activities and both Honduras and Nicaragua intensified their production and export of precious metals.[38] In Nicaragua the output of the gold mines grew fairly steadily so that by 1938 production at 1522 kg was twice the level achieved in 1928; the 1938 figure, however, was more than doubled the following year and by 1940 was seven times greater than in 1928. Gold exports also grew steadily in Honduras in the 1930s, although silver exports were fairly static.

## RECOVERY FROM THE DEPRESSION – IMPORT-SUBSTITUTION

The decline in the barter terms of trade combined with a (slight) fall in the volume of traditional exports brought about a deterioration in the income terms of trade for Central America and a reduction in the capacity to import. With the tightness of the international reserve position, and the drying up of capital flows from abroad, the capacity to import proved to be a fairly accurate determinant of real imports and Central America was faced with a choice between forgoing consumption of goods previously imported or producing them herself.

This was a similar choice to that faced elsewhere in Latin America, but there were differences. The level of industrial (and particularly manufacturing) output was extremely low in the 1920s[39] and the spare capacity to increase production without importing additional equipment simply did not exist; on the other hand, half a century's reliance on the traditional export-led model had left the region heavily dependent on imported foodstuffs.

Import-substitution therefore occurred in two quite separate activities in Central America and import-substituting agriculture (ISA) turned out to be more important than import-substituting industrialisation (ISI). The performance of domestic use agriculture and industry in each republic between 1921 and 1938 is summarised in Table 3.4 and a number of patterns can be discerned . First, in the case of domestic use agriculture, there is a marked contrast between the stagnation of the 1920s and the rising trend in the 1930s;[40] second, in the case of industry modest growth was achieved in the 1920s, while the following decade was rather disappointing in some republics.

No serious attempt to promote ISI was made by governments in Central America,[41] but incentives none the less were available. Tariffs on imported goods were increased;[42] although this was conceived as a revenue-raising measure it clearly operated as a protective device as well.[43] Exchange-rate changes (at least in Costa Rica and El Salvador) offered some incentive to ISI activities, and the difficulty of obtaining foreign exchange for imports of consumer goods may have permitted the domestic price of the latter to rise above world prices plus tariffs.[44]

The obstacles to a rapid growth of industry, however, remained considerable; virtually no credit was available from the organised financial market and foreign exchange for essential capital equipment was hard to obtain. On the demand side, although income per head began to rise in the late 1930s, the market remained too small for the production of many goods and efforts at regional integration in this period came to nothing.

The obstacles to the expansion of domestic use agriculture in the 1930s were much less severe; the stagnation of the 1920s in production for the home market (in some cases a decline) reflected the profitability of the traditional export sector, as resources switched into the latter. The replacement of imports of maize, beans, rice, wheat and cattle did

*Table* 3.4 Annual average rates of growth (%) for domestic use agriculture (DUA) and manufacturing (MAN) value added at constant (1970) prices, 1921–38

| *Period** | *Costa Rica* | | *El Salvador* | | *Guatemala* | | *Honduras* | | *Nicaragua* | |
|---|---|---|---|---|---|---|---|---|---|---|
| | *DUA* | *MAN* | *DUA* | *MAN* | *DUA* | *MAN* | *DUA* | *MAN* | *DUA* | *MAN* |
| 1921–8 | 0.9 | 3.2 | 1.5 | 2.8 | 2.1 | 4.6 | 0.6 | 2.3 | 5.2 | − 3.5 |
| 1928–32 | 1.5 | 3.8 | − 1.8 | − 6.4 | 4.6 | − 0.5 | 1.3 | − 2.5 | − 3.4 | − 5.3 |
| 1932–8 | 5.7 | 8.8 | 4.4 | 3.6 | 16.8† | 4.3 | 4.6 | 5.0 | − 2.9 | 6.9 |

*Three-year average.

†This is biased upwards by a distortion in the underlying statistics. See Bulmer-Thomas (1987) Methodological Appendix, p. 306.

*Source*: V. Bulmer-Thomas, *The Political Economy of Central America since 1920* (Cambridge: Cambridge University Press, 1987), Table 4.2, p. 80.

not depend greatly on the availability of foreign exchange and credit was not so necessary as with ISI.

Although capital may not have been a serious problem, ISA clearly required land and labour. The latter was provided by those made redundant or required less intensively by the export sector. In the case of the coffee-producing zones, migrant workers could often return full-time to their own farms or, in the case of the *colonos*, they could rent a bigger plot on the unoccupied part of the estate; in the banana zones, however, the labour force in general had no access to land of its own and the presence of a large, depressed banana zone was a serious impediment to economic recovery.

Other factors were also at work in promoting ISA. In Guatemala, for example, which experienced a particularly sharp rise in domestic-use agriculture in the 1930s, production for the home market was affected in two quite separate ways; first, the labour laws were changed in 1934 and the legalised system of debt peonage was replaced by an anti-vagrancy law. The latter was intended to ensure a regular supply of labour to the export sector, but it also had the effect of increasing the labour-time supplied by a given workforce (see Jones, 1940, p. 164); with the weakness of the traditional export sector, much of the increase in labour-time supplied must have gone into domestic-use agriculture.[45]

The second influence in Guatemala (felt to a lesser extent throughout the region) was the massive road-building programme initiated by Ubico in the 1930s, which brought an almost fivefold increase in the road network in a decade (see Grieb, 1979, p. 137). As the programme relied essentially on forced labour, it gave Ubico a highly unsavoury reputation in liberal circles, particularly when coupled with his whole-hearted admiration for European fascism; the new roads, however, did open up parts of the country which had previously been isolated and gave remote villages the opportunity to market a surplus where none had existed before.

## THE PUBLIC SECTOR

In the early years of the Depression there was no element of final expenditure which operated countercyclically. Real consumption and investment followed traditional exports downwards and this was true also of government expenditure on current and capital account. Public expenditure peaked in real terms (see Table 3.5) between 1929 and 1930 and fell steadily until the mid-1930s.[46]

The pro-cyclical nature of government expenditure is not hard to explain. The ideology of *laissez-faire* during the hey-day of the traditional export-led model had kept government participation in the economy to very modest levels. In 1929, for example, the contribution of general government to GDP[47] was between 3 per cent and 9 per cent, except in Nicaragua where it did not even reach 1 per cent.

A further constraint was provided by the difficulty of financing public-sector deficits. As explained above (see p. x ref), each republic ran a budget deficit in the worst years of the Depression, which was mainly funded through increases in the domestic debt; the non-floating domestic debt was essentially a euphemism for unpaid salary bills. There were, therefore, political obstacles to the expansion of the latter and financial obstacles to the expansion of the former.

Despite these obstacles the domestic debt did rise sharply in several republics (see Table 3.2, p. 54); the Nicaraguan government, for example, contracted loans from the National Bank in 1932, 1933 and 1934 to cover budget deficits, while the Guatemalan government obtained a US $3 million loan in 1931 from the local subsidiary of a foreign bank; the sharp rise in the non-floating debt in Costa Rica (from 1.2 million colones in 1931 to 10.0 million colones in 1934) was due almost entirely to borrowing from the banking system.[48]

These efforts to fund budget deficits did not, however, amount to much, and the contribution of general government to GDP actually

*Table* 3.5 Value added by general government, 1928–38. 1970 prices (thousand dollars). Net factor cost

| *Year* | *Costa Rica* | *El Salvador* | *Guatemala* | *Honduras* | *Nicaragua* |
|---|---|---|---|---|---|
| 1928 | 5 589 | 15 395 | 37 124 | 7 429 | 985 |
| 1929 | 7 333 | 16 312 | 41 560 | 8 286 | 1 095 |
| 1930 | 6 757 | 17 462 | 37 494 | 8 286 | 734 |
| 1931 | 6 022 | 16 580 | 33 351 | 8 743 | 857 |
| 1932 | 5 626 | 13 992 | 26 548 | 6 971 | 822 |
| 1933 | 5 607 | 13 325 | 20 115 | 7 429 | 838 |
| 1934 | 5 914 | 13 633 | 20 189 | 7 714 | 889 |
| 1935 | 6 740 | 14 092 | 22 554 | 7 714 | 851 |
| 1936 | 7 369 | 15 969 | 23 221 | 7 886 | 1 002 |
| 1937 | 7 819 | 16 773 | 23 960 | 8 057 | 1 818 |
| 1938 | 8 860 | 17 806 | 23 886 | 8 743 | 1 919 |

*Source*: V. Bulmer-Thomas, *The Political Economy of Central America since 1920* (Cambridge: Cambridge University Press, 1987), Table A.9.

declined between 1929 and 1934 in Costa Rica, Guatemala and El Salvador, although it remained virtually the same in Nicaragua and Honduras. The position, moreover, was not very different in 1939, and we may conclude that the *direct* impact of government expenditure on economic recovery was minimal.

Despite this it is worth singling out a few examples of government intervention, for there were areas where expenditure actually increased. In El Salvador a special fund for Social Improvement was set up (with incomings earmarked from the duty on coffee exports), to be used for the acquisition of land and houses by the peasantry. In Honduras 'law and order' expenditure rose between 1929 and 1931 and in Costa Rica money expenditure on public works and agriculture nearly trebled in 1929 (although they fell back sharply thereafter).

In no sense can these interventions be described as Keynesian, and government expenditure was essentially pro-cyclical. The *indirect* influence of government intervention, however, was considerable, and examples are provided by the road-building programme in Guatemala, the rescue of producers of traditional exports from foreclosure and the impact of exchange control and/or tariff changes on import-substitution.

## RECOVERY FROM THE DEPRESSION – DEMAND-SIDE CHANGES

The short-run response to falling world commodity prices was sufficient to prevent a downturn in real economic activity, but in most of Central America the bottom of the Depression had been reached by 1932 (see Table 3.3).[49] The drop in the level of activity was surprisingly modest, although the impact on real living-standards is much more severe when population growth and the terms of trade effect are taken into account.

After 1932, however, there follows nearly a decade of steady growth in Guatemala, El Salvador and Costa Rica (in Nicaragua and Honduras recovery does not begin until the period 1936–8). During the five-year period 1934–9 only Honduras and Nicaragua failed to achieve an increase in real product per person and in several republics the rise in living-standards was impressive. By 1935 Costa Rica, Guatemala and El Salvador had all surpassed or reached the pre-Depression peak in GDP.

In previous sections we have considered what factors contributed to the recovery of the economy and how these were made manifest through changes in the output of different sectors. This, however, is the economics of the supply-side and it should be possible to relate a consistent story on the demand-side.

In two cases – export agriculture and mining – the consistency is automatic; demand-side changes in the main refer only to foreign demand. Similarly, the supply- and demand-side of public administration are not independent.

With agriculture for domestic use, however, and industry (other than mining) the two sides are independent and it is important to consider how demand for these sectors could have changed at a rate consistent with the estimated change on the supply-side.

One approach to this question might be to use some variant of the Chenery 'sources of growth' equation (see, for example, Robinson and Kubo, 1979). This enables us to decompose the change in output of any sector into the change due to variations in (a) home demand, (b) foreign demand, (c) import coefficients and (d) technological coefficients. Neither (b) or (d) is of much relevance in the 1930s for the two sectors in question, so we are left with (a) and (c).

We have already argued that import-substitution in agriculture and industry was important in initiating economic recovery. It is doubtful, however, if it could account for the dramatic increases recorded by some republics in these two sectors. It follows that changes in home demand must also have been important.

The change in demand for any sector depends on the change in real income, the income and price elasticity of demand, and income distribution. Ignoring import-substitution this means that a sector can only grow faster or slower than GDP if the elasticities and/or income distribution changes permit it.

In Central America, after 1932, the growth of domestic-use agriculture and manufacturing was faster than GDP in several countries. This can be explained satisfactorily in the case of manufacturing by income elasticities greater than unity together with import-substitution effects; in the case of domestic-use agriculture, however, it is at first somewhat puzzling.

The key to the puzzle is provided not by income elasticities (which are unlikely to have exceeded unity) nor by price elasticities nor by import-substitution (although this certainly played a part). The answer, on the contrary, must be found in income distribution changes.

As we have seen, the arrival of the Depression in Central America was heralded by a sharp fall in world commodity prices. This put a squeeze on the profit share of national income, to which capitalists and landowners responded by trying to drive down money-wage costs. The scanty evidence at our disposal suggests that these efforts were only partially successfully[50] and that the worst years of the Depression were marked by a shift away from profits in the export sector.

In the period of recovery after 1932, world commodity prices continued at low levels while coffee and banana workers, for example, achieved modest increases in money wages.[51] In the urban economy it is not unreasonable to argue that a similar shift in income distribution was taking place, since the profitability of the most important sector (commerce) would have been highly dependent on the level of imports and labour-intensive activities (e.g. construction) were growing significantly.[52] Thus, we may surmise that in the urban economy and export agriculture, labour incomes rose faster than non-labour incomes in the 1930s.

If the shift in the functional distribution of income did occur, it helps to explain how domestic-use agriculture grew faster than real GDP. The marginal propensity to consume foodstuffs must have been higher for labour than non-labour incomes. At the same time a shift towards greater equality in the distribution of income during the 1930s is not inconsistent with what one might expect in primary-producing countries where the non-labour share of national income is heavily dependent on world commodity prices.

## CONCLUSIONS

The most obvious conclusion from this study of Central America is that the Depression was less severe than had previously been thought. The received wisdom on this question can now be seen to have arisen from a confusion of price and quantity changes; while the former fell sharply in the worst years of the Depression, the decline in volumes was much more modest and in this respect the performance of Central America mirrors that of the other Latin American countries.

Real GDP, however, did fall in every case from the peak level achieved in the late 1920s and real consumption per person fell further for two reasons; first, population growth in the period was quite rapid (around 2 per cent per annum) and the terms-of-trade effect was negative. The hardships associated with the Depression were greatest in the banana zones; although banana exports held up well in the first years of the Depression, the eventual collapse from disease led to unemployment among banana workers, who usually had no lands of their own to which they could return.[53]

Many factors contributed to the recovery from the Depression; one of the most important was the willingness of the government to intervene in the coffee sector to maintain or even increase the volume of exports despite low world prices. This intervention did not come easily to governments accustomed to minimising the role of the State in economic affairs, although the rise of *caudillos* in four of the five republics may have helped. Other factors contributing to recovery were import-substitution in domestic use agriculture and industry and income-distribution changes; export diversification, however, played only a minor part.

One important consideration in the timing and speed of the recovery was the composition of traditional exports. Republics with a large, foreign-owned banana enclave were at a severe disadvantage. They could not influence the level of banana exports with the instruments at their disposal, while a reduction in activity led to unemployment of both the land and the labour force[54] rather than to resource reallocation. This hampered efforts at import-substitution in agriculture and export diversification.

Despite the speed of recovery from the Depression, the 1930s is not a decade to which Central America can turn back with pride. It was in many ways a decade of missed opportunities; there was no fundamental break with the traditional export-led model and only a few serious attempts at export diversification were made. Although new export crops were introduced in the 1950s (cotton) and 1960s (sugar, meat), the region remains to this day over-dependent on the export of coffee and bananas and the grip of the fruit companies is still considerable.

There were, nevertheless, some changes made in the 1930s which had favourable long-term implications. First, recognition of the need for some degree of state intervention in the economy is indispensable in a primary-producing region such as Central America and the first real steps in this direction were taken after the onset of the Depression.

Second, the traditional export-led model had led to the sad neglect of financial institutions. Credit for the export sector came from foreign merchants in the case of coffee and the fruit companies in the case of bananas and loans for new productive activities from domestic financial sources were virtually unavailable. This began to change in the 1930s with the emergence of new banks,[55] and the strengthening of old ones and financial institutions started to play a much more active part in determining the allocation of resources.

It is tempting to conclude by looking for parallels between the present economic decline in Central America and the Depression initiated fifty years before. Both downturns have been marked by falling commodity prices (particularly for coffee) and changes in political regimes. In both periods an earlier export boom had led to increased dependence on imported foodstuffs, local production of which could take the edge off the impact of the recession. There, however, the parallels cease; much of the present economic crisis in Central America is the result of internal disturbances – fiscal and monetary (Costa Rica), as well as political (Nicaragua, El Salvador, Guatemala) – and by no means all export commodity price movements have been unfavourable in the last few years. The complexity of the economy has increased considerably and political and social developments since the 1930s mean that no government, however authoritarian, can now afford to ignore internal equilibrium.

## Notes

1. I have been helped considerably in the writing of this chapter by the comments of Carlos Díaz Alejandro and Laurence Whitehead, although the latter in particular may not agree with all its contents. I am also very grateful to Rosemary Thorp for suggesting the idea in the first place.
2. The phrase 'Great Depression' in fact is something of a misnomer, as we shall see, because other periods in Central American history have been equally (if not more) traumatic in terms of their economic consequences. The phrase is maintained here, however, because of its long-established tradition.
3. Anderson (1971) p. 12, for example, claims that national income in El Salvador fell by 50 per cent in the Depression.
4. Throughout this chapter the phrase 'traditional exports' refers to coffee and bananas; in El Salvador, however, there were no banana exports, while in Honduras coffee exports were negligible during the inter-war period. In the other republics both products were of great importance.
5. By 1929 imports of food and drink (excluding live animals) represented nearly 20 per cent of the import bill in each republic.
6. Trade taxes accounted for some 65 per cent of government revenue in the 1920s.
7. Public debt per person in nominal terms varied from US $42 for Costa Rica to US $9 in Guatemala. The external public debt was less than US $15 per person in each republic except Costa Rica.
8. Attempts were made to establish cotton as an export crop in El Salvador, but the experiment failed through disease.
9. By the end of the 1920s the population of Central America was 5.2 million, of which 1.8 million lived in Guatemala and 1.4 million in El

Salvador. Natural and artificial barriers to trade between the republics meant that intra-regional commerce was negligible and within each country much of the rural population was not in a position to purchase industrial goods. The effective market for industrial output was therefore limited to the main urban centres in each republic.

10. The problem of labour supply is a recurring theme in Guatemalan colonial and post-colonial history (see Jones, 1940).
11. The alienation of communal lands in El Salvador continued long after the initiation of liberal reforms in the 1870s and was one factor accounting for the peasant uprising of 1932, brutally suppressed by General Maximiliano Hernández Martínez (see Anderson, 1971).
12. In Costa Rica, for example, the United Fruit Company controlled 274 000 hectares on the Atlantic coast at the start of the Depression, although the area cultivated never rose above 20 000 hectares. By the end of the 1930s the Company had added another 118 000 hectares to its holdings on the Pacific (see Seligson, 1980, ch. 3).
13. The best example is provided by Honduras, where the transport system could be used for little else but the movement of bananas. It did not even connect the capital with the coast.
14. Coffee prices peaked in 1925 in all republics except Costa Rica, where the peak is reached in 1927/8. Costa Rica coffee data in this period, however, are quoted c.i.f. and this might account for the difference.
15. Throughout the inter-war period the export price of bananas reflected nothing more than the fruit companies' needs for local currency expenditure. Thus the companies did not have to surrender foreign exchange from export sales before purchasing imported equipment, repatriating profits, etc. (see May *et al.*, 1952, pp. 231–2). Since local currency costs were dominated by labour expenses, the export price tended to vary in line with the wage rate. For an excellent description of this and other aspects of the banana industry see Kepner and Soothill (1935) and Kepner (1936).
16. This is fiscal year 1930, i.e. 1 August 1929 to 31 July 1930.
17. This was not true of Nicaraguan coffee, which (being of inferior quality) was sold in spot markets. Nicaragua, however, is the exception which proves the rule, because its coffee prices only fell sharply after 1929.
18. The volume of coffee exports, by contrast, held up well in the Depression. See Figure 3.3, p. 57.
19. Honduras had no need to run a deficit in the first years of the Depression because the value of exports did not peak until 1930.
20. The only source for import prices in Central America in the inter-war period is unit values constructed from trade data. In Honduras, however, official estimates of real imports (see Banco Central de Honduras, 1956) have been obtained from *weighted* unit values, using as weights the five classes in the Brussels trade nomenclature and the implicit price deflator obtained by comparing the real and money values of Honduran imports is therefore the best guide to import prices in Central America. For that reason, I have used Honduran import prices in constructing the barter terms of trade indices in Figure 3.2.
21. The terms of trade indices in Figure 3.2 are theoretical. They represent

the case of a republic which obtains all its export revenue from either coffee or bananas. In practice the indices reflect closely the reality in Central America, because Honduras obtained 75 per cent of export earnings from bananas while in 1928 Costa Rica, Guatemala, Nicaragua and El Salvador obtained 62, 82, 58 and 93 per cent of export earnings from coffee respectively.

22. In no sense, however, can these budget deficits be regarded as Keynesian in spirit. Internal equilibrium (full employment) was not a policy objective in this period.
23. The book value of foreign direct investment, for example, which had built up rapidly during the 1920s to reach $288 million by the end of 1929, fell thereafter and was estimated at $197 million in the period 1935–9 (see Rosenthal, 1973, pp. 74–6).
24. Other than the profits of the international fruit companies – see n. 15.
25. In Costa Rica, for example, the service on the public debt (most of which was external) as a proportion of government expenditure rose from 17 per cent in 1928 to 28 per cent in 1932. This also represented a rise in absolute terms.
26. The Costa Rican colón was pegged in 1937 at c5.6 to the US dollar.
27. In the case of Nicaragua and Honduras the adoption of a passive exchange-rate policy was undoubtedly influenced by their semi-colonial status. In Guatemala, however, the same policy may have been adopted in reaction to the chaotic monetary conditions prevailing in the early 1920s before the 1925 currency reform.
28. Central America experienced in the inter-war period some of the structural rigidities of countries which run the risk of price increases and output falls following a devaluation (this is known in the literature as a 'contractionary devaluation' – see Krugman and Taylor, 1978). A contractionary devaluation also involves a worsening of income distribution and this would certainly have occurred in Central America if greater use had been made of exchange-rate depreciation.
29. Exchange-rate depreciation added further to this burden, although the devaluation of the British pound sterling against the US dollar reduced the domestic currency cost of servicing the British-held debt. Sterling obligations formed a part of the public external debt for most of the republics.
30. An example is provided by the Swedish Match loan to Guatemala in 1930, which was only obtained after the republic had agreed to humiliating and onerous terms (see Grieb, 1979, p. 179).
31. Although the fall in real product was not as severe as one might have expected, real consumption per person must have fallen further because of population growth and the adverse terms-of-trade effect. Serious labour unrest, however, was not common in the Depression, the most important exceptions being the peasant revolt in El Salvador in 1932 and the banana strike in Costa Rica in 1934. The civil war in Nicaragua broke out before the onset of the Depression and had much broader origins.
32. GDP fell by 32.2 per cent in Nicaragua from 1977 to 1979 and by 22.8 per cent in El Salvador from 1978–83.

33. Both the production and export of coffee in Guatemala, however, involved a high level of participation by foreigners, although the foreigners concerned (mainly German) did reside in the country (see Fergusson, 1940).
34. The United Fruit Company bought out Sam Zemurray's Cuyamel Company in 1929, leaving only Standard Fruit as a serious rival (see Wilson, 1947). It should be pointed out that, although these two companies totally dominated the export of bananas, they did not exercise the same control over production, part of which remained in the hands of independent growers (see Kepner, 1936).
35. In the inter-war period, the preferred method of dealing with disease was to abandon affected plantations and start new ones. This is the main reason why the companies owned far more land than they cultivated.
36. El Salvador, for example, set up a special fund administered by the Mortgage Bank to aid coffee-growers.
37. This interpretation is disputed by Anderson (1971), who argues that forced sales of coffee estates in the Depression brought about a sharp rise in the concentration of ownership. It seems certain, however, that without the intervention of the state concentration would have risen still further.
38. In both countries the mines were foreign-owned and the rate of production was outside the scope of government influence.
39. The proportion of GDP accounted for by manufacturing in each republic at the end of the 1920s varied from 5 per cent in Honduras and Nicaragua to 13.7 per cent in Guatemala. See Bulmer-Thomas (1987), Table 12.3.
40. There is no rising trend in Nicaragua, where – on the contrary – there is a sharp fall in agricultural production for domestic use from 1933 to 1937. This could have been in reaction to the earlier civil war, although the latter would in any case have made the estimate of production somewhat unreliable.
41. With the possible exception of Costa Rica (see Soley Güell, 1949, vol. II, pp. 329–32).
42. In Nicaragua, for example, the ratio of the value of tariffs collected to the value of imports rose from 34 per cent in 1928 to 50 per cent in 1933. It should also be remembered that some duties were specific, not *ad valorem*, and in a period of declining export prices the *ad valorem* equivalent of such taxes would have been rising.
43. The incentive to producers is measured by the *effective* not *nominal* rate of protection, but even in this period of their history Central American Administrations taxed consumer good imports more heavily than intermediate and capital goods. It is quite possible, therefore, that the effective rate of protection also rose in the 1930s.
44. The most important industrial developments in Central America after 1929 were the establishment of a textile industry in Nicaragua and El Salvador, using in the main locally grown cotton, the establishment of cement production in Nicaragua and the expansion of the shoe industry throughout the isthmus.
45. Agricultural workers cultivating 'with their personal work' three manzanas of corn in a hot zone, four manzanas in a cold zone, or four

manzanas of wheat, potatoes, vegetables or other products in any zone were exempted from the provisions of the anti-vagrancy law. If Wagley's (1941) study of Chimaltenango is representative, a significant minority of the rural population would have had access to farms of this size and the incentive to increase production of domestic crops would have risen accordingly. This incentive was reinforced in 1937, when rural workers cultivating at least $1\frac{5}{16}$ manzanas of land on their own account were required to work for others a minimum of 100 days per year rather than the 150 days applied to landless labourers.

46. Table 3.5 refers to value added by general government, but this corresponds closely to real public expenditure.
47. See Bulmer-Thomas (1987), Table 12.3, p. 273.
48. Despite the rise in the internal public debt in Central America, monetary contraction rather than expansion was the rule. This occurred, because of the downward pressure on the money supply exerted by the fall in international reserves. Throughout the inter-war period, changes in the stock of net foreign assets held by the banking system (money of external origin) is a much better guide to changes in the money supply than changes in net domestic assets (money of internal origin).
49. In Honduras the turning-point was not reached until 1937, while in Nicaragua 1932 represented only a *local* minimum – the global minimum was not reached until 1936.
50. We must again distinguish between those republics for which coffee was the dominant export crop and those for which it was bananas. In the latter the fall in the export price reflected the fall in labour costs in the banana zones (see n. 15), so that, *ceteris paribus*, such republics would not have experienced a shift in income distribution.
51. In Guatemala the rise in money wages in the mid-1930s was considerable, as employers reacted to the change in the labour laws by competing for workers (see Jones, 1940, p. 165). Guatemala is also the country which experienced the sharpest rise in domestic-use agriculture.
52. The shift in the distribution of income within the urban economy runs against what was happening in the larger Latin American republics in the 1930s. In the latter case, however, the shift towards profits is associated with the sharp rise in industrial output – a phenomenon which, as we have seen, did not occur in Central America.
53. It is in fact the thesis of one author (Seligson, 1980) that in Costa Rica at least many workers only took jobs in the banana zones because they had lost access to land in the coffee-producing highlands. It is also well-documented that in Honduras many banana labourers were landless migrants from El Salvador.
54. In Costa Rica banana lands ravaged by disease were eventually leased to former employees by the United Fruit Company for growing cacao. This did not, however, become important until nearly a decade after disease started spreading. In Costa Rica there were also legal impediments to the migration of the banana workers (mainly black) to the rest of the country (see Seligson, 1980, ch. 3).
55. The Banco Central de Reserva, for example, was established in El Salvador in 1934.

# Part II

# Central American Co-operation

# 4 The Central American Common Market

## ORIGINS OF THE CENTRAL AMERICAN COMMON MARKET (CACM)

The Central American Republics of Costa Rica, Nicaragua, El Salvador, Guatemala and Honduras have a tradition of union, both of the political and economic kind. Ruled as one territory by Spain under the *Audiencia de Guatemala* in the colonial epoch, they continued as one nation for the first twenty-one years of independence (1821–42). There followed a century of attempts at political (and sometimes economic) union among sub-groups of the five republics (Karnes, 1961), before the final, successful movement towards economic integration began in the 1950s.

Despite the rhetoric, it is doubtful whether the tradition of union has really been of much benefit in the most recent integration experience. Although the CACM has survived despite the intense ideological differences among its members, this is due more to the perceived sharing of mutual benefits than to traditions of union; furthermore, it is significant that the one country (Honduras), which considered itself to be a net loser from integration, could not be persuaded to remain a member despite appeals to the powerful union myth and in fact left the market in 1970.[1]

The prime mover in the preliminary drive towards integration in the 1950s was the Economic Commission for Latin America (ECLA). Awareness of this fact is important for a true understanding of the CACM, because ECLA thinking was at that time dominated by the model of '*desarrollo hacia dentro*' – import-substituting industrialisation (ISI). The size of the individual republics, in terms of GDP, income per head and population (see Table 4.1), made it clear that industrialisation could only be carried out at the regional level, otherwise high-cost, inefficient plants would be duplicated across the isthmus.

The initial efforts towards economic integration were hampered by the fact that the traditional export-orientated model ('*desarrollo hacia afuera*') was working well in the wake of the commodity boom brought about by the Korean war. This soon changed, however, and by the

*Table* 4.1 Basic data for the Central American Common Market (1970 prices)

| | *1950* | *1960* | *1970* | *1978* | *1983* | *1986* |
|---|---|---|---|---|---|---|
| *Costa Rica* | | | | | | |
| Population (thousands) | 800 | 1250 | 1730 | 2120 | 2370 | 2600 |
| GDP per head ($) | 372 | 474 | 659 | 884 | 775 | 822 |
| Share of industry in GDP (%) | 11.6 | 12.5 | 15.2 | 17.3 | 16.3 | 22.7 |
| Share of agriculture in GDP (%) | 38.5 | 29.7 | 25.0 | 20.2 | 21.5 | 19.1 |
| *El Salvador* | | | | | | |
| Population (thousands) | 1860 | 2450 | 3440 | 4350 | 4720 | 4910 |
| GDP per head ($) | 275 | 329 | 406 | 487 | 312 | 316 |
| Share of industry in GDP (%) | 13.9 | 14.2 | 17.8 | 18.4 | 16.4 | 17.6 |
| Share of agriculture in GDP (%) | 41.0 | 36.0 | 30.6 | 27.7 | 30.3 | 24.0 |
| *Guatemala* | | | | | | |
| Population (thousands) | 2810 | 3830 | 5270 | 6840 | 7930 | 8200 |
| GDP per head ($) | 315 | 336 | 417 | 508 | 450 | 412 |
| Share of industry in GDP (%) | 11.3 | 12.1 | 14.7 | 15.4 | 15.2 | 16.3 |
| Share of agriculture in GDP (%) | 36.6 | 33.4 | 30.1 | 28.8 | 28.2 | 25.6 |
| *Honduras* | | | | | | |
| Population (thousands) | 1430 | 1950 | 2639 | 3439 | 4092 | 4510 |
| GDP per head ($) | 226 | 240 | 280 | 302 | 275 | 274 |
| Share of industry in GDP (%) | 11.4 | 17.2 | 16.2 | 16.4 | 15.9 | 14.9 |
| Share of agriculture in GDP (%) | 44.8 | 32.8 | 34.6 | 24.7 | 26.7 | 24.9 |
| *Nicaragua* | | | | | | |
| Population (thousands) | 1060 | 1410 | 1830 | 2370 | 3017 | 3400 |
| GDP per head ($) | 225 | 282 | 424 | 441 | 303 | 259 |
| Share of industry in GDP (%) | 12.3 | 14.2 | 19.9 | 22.8 | 23.0 | 26.9 |
| Share of agriculture in GDP (%) | 36.6 | 29.5 | 27.0 | 29.9 | 28.8 | 22.9 |

*Source*: V. Bulmer-Thomas, *The Political Economy of Central America since 1920* (Cambridge: Cambridge University Press, 1987), Statistical Appendix. Data for 1986 derived from Consejo Monetario Centroamericano, *Boletín Estadístico*, San José, 1987.

mid-1950s, the world price of Central America's traditional exports (coffee and bananas)[2] had begun a secular decline which continued through most of the 1960s. The result was a surge of interest in the ISI model and there followed in quick succession a series of treaties, culminating in the General Treaty on Economic Integration signed at the end of 1960 by Guatemala, El Salvador, Honduras and Nicaragua with Costa Rica signing two years later. It is this treaty which established the CACM.[3]

Judged by the orthodox tenets of customs union theory (Viner,

1950), the CACM could hardly be other than a failure. In the absence of a significant industrial base before union for all but non-traded manufactured goods,[4] trade creation was expected to be slight; trade diversion, however, was likely to be significant because the dominant source of imports was low-cost goods from third countries. Furthermore, the conditions suggested in the literature (Lipsey, 1960) for a successful union just did not exist in Central America; pre-union intra-regional trade was negligible (2–3 per cent of total trade for most of the 1950s) and none of the five economies could be regarded as competitive with each other, except in the case of primary products which were in any case effectively excluded from the General Treaty.

We have already seen, however, that industrialisation was one of Central America's major objectives in forming the CACM. Consequently, even within the context of the orthodox theory and assuming net trade diversion, the CACM could be judged a success if the social utility attached to the collective consumption of industrial activity should exceed the welfare loss associated with net trade diversion (see Johnson, 1965).

There are, however, additional reasons why Central American policy-makers could afford to ignore the likelihood of net trade diversion (quite apart from the cynical observation that much of the welfare loss would be sustained by the politically powerless consumers!). First, the assumption that trade creation is welfare-improving rests crucially on the assumptions of fixed external terms of trade and full employment. If the domestic resources freed by trade creation cannot find employment or can only do so in the export sector at the expense of a deterioration in the terms of trade, then trade creation may reduce welfare.

Secondly, trade diversion is only welfare reducing if factors of production are valued at their social opportunity costs. If, in the presence of un- or under-employment, resources can be attracted to the high-cost industrial activities without loss of output elsewhere (particularly in the export sector), then trade diversion can bring improvements in welfare. The principal distorted factor prices in Central America are labour and foreign exchange and this has profound implications for measuring the net benefits realised by the CACM, as we shall see below.

Thirdly, even if trade diversion leads to a fall in output in the (traditional) export sector, this need not matter if there is an improvement in the external terms of trade. With Central America an important supplier in several world markets for traditional exports (particularly bananas), this was a real possibility and enabled policy-makers to view the CACM as a means to reduce dependence on the external sector, improve the terms of trade and achieve industrialisation at one and the same time.

The fact that the CACM, therefore, was likely to be net trade diverting did not trouble policy-makers unduly. However, it had one important implication which was not adequately perceived at the time. If a union is, on balance, net trade creating, the balance of payments and the distribution of net benefits between members are not likely to be serious problems; with trade creation, the balance of payments deficit of one member in intra-regional trade should be matched by a surplus in trade with the rest of the world, while net trade creation ensures that consumers throughout the region benefit, if not in equal proportions.

The same is not true of a trade diverting union. Here the distribution of net benefits (assuming these are positive) is all important and can to some extent be identified with surpluses in intra-regional trade, because the principal means by which trade diversion improves welfare is through an increase in domestic production and intra-regional exports (see below). Consequently, there must be adequate means in a trade diverting union to ensure that benefits are more or less equally distributed and this was not the case in the CACM.[5]

The CACM achieved an initial success, which led many observers to herald it as a model of its kind (Wionczek, 1972). The first difficulty the CACM encountered was the loss of government revenue consequent upon the combination of net trade diversion and prohibitively high tariffs on imports from third countries. This resulted in the San José Protocol, ratified in 1967, a desperate and ill-conceived measure which allowed countries to bolster government revenues by imposing a surcharge of 30 per cent on the common external tariff (CET). The next crisis occurred with the '*guerra inutil*' between El Salvador and Honduras in 1969,[6] which led to Honduras' departure from the CACM in the following year. Since then, the CACM has virtually stagnated despite various high-level attempts to revive it.

In what follows, we concentrate on the achievements and failures of the CACM, the controversial role played by multinational companies (MNCs) and the prospects for a revived market. First, however, it is important to examine the instruments by which the CACM was brought into being and their effectiveness for achieving the region's objectives.

## INSTRUMENTS OF INTEGRATION

We have seen in the preceding section how the CACM was formed to meet the objective of rapid industrialisation of the region subject to a mutual sharing of the net benefits expected from its formation. Industrialisation in turn was expected to bring with it rising incomes and a decreased dependence on the rest of the world. The instruments of integration must therefore be examined in this context.

The industrialisation objective was pursued through the freeing of trade within Central America subject to a CET on third countries. The freeing of trade was effectively restricted to industrial products[7] and was carried out quickly and efficiently; as soon as the General Treaty went into effect, 74 per cent of all items listed in the tariff schedule entered intra-regional trade free of all restrictions and this figure had increased to 94 per cent by the end of 1966 (see Hansen, 1967). The remaining items not subject to free trade[8] accounted for only 5 per cent of the value of intra-regional trade by the end of the decade. Where tariffs were reduced over a period of years, this was done automatically and no doubt accounted for the CACM's great success in this area – a lesson not lost on those responsible for the Cartagena Treaty setting up the Andean Pact.

Before union, the Central American republics imposed different tariff rates on imports from the rest of the world; the adoption of a CET required the harmonisation of the tariff structure. The result was (pre-union figures in brackets) the following average nominal tariff rates by type of good: consumer goods 82.5 per cent (64 per cent); raw materials and intermediate goods 34.4 per cent (30 per cent); building materials 32.2 per cent (30 per cent) and capital goods 13 per cent (12 per cent) (see Hansen, 1967, p. 27). In fact, these figures are somewhat misleading, because – as a result of generous incentives (see below) – firms were often able to import their intermediate and capital goods requirements duty free.

The general picture, however, is clear. The CET raised the nominal rate of protection on consumer goods (thereby causing 'trade suppression') and lowered the nominal rate of protection on other goods (thereby causing 'external trade augmentation'). Trade suppression involves a switch from low-cost to high-cost sources of production and is therefore exactly like trade diversion, while external trade augmentation encourages imports from the lowest-cost source and is therefore like trade creation. Because external trade augmentation was so substantial, it was claimed by some economists that the CACM was on balance net trade creating (see Wilford, 1970). Although this is an exaggeration (see Willmore, 1976), external trade augmentation remains important and is one reason why the region's dependence on the rest of the world has not declined.

The combination of free trade within the region, together with almost prohibitive tariffs on consumer goods and low tariffs on other goods, brought about a dramatic decline in government revenue from trade taxes. The latter have traditionally been the major source of tax revenue in Central America (see Wilford, 1978) and the problem was to some extent anticipated. As a result, the republics reached agreement in 1962 on uniform fiscal incentives for industrial development, the aim being to prevent a competitive reduction of the tax rates applied to the newly established industries.

Unfortunately, the agreement was never ratified;[9] the result has been wasteful competition among the countries to provide the most generous incentives to new firms (see Joel, 1971) and a progressive deterioration in the public finances of all the republics. In an effort to restore fiscal health, the San José Protocol was signed (see above) and indirect taxes on sales were introduced or increased on a national basis, but the result was far from satisfactory.

In the preliminary discussions before the formation of the CACM, the weaker industrial members (Honduras and Nicaragua particularly, but Costa Rica also to a smaller extent) expressed their fears that the freeing of intra-regional trade would lead to a concentration of new activity in the stronger industrial countries (Guatemala and El Salvador). Honduras was especially vocal (see Delgado, 1978) about the need for mechanisms which would ensure relatively equal distribution of the benefits from industrialisation; at the same time, it was recognised that Central America was too economically small to support more than one firm in many industrial sectors; with several firms in these sectors, as ECLA repeatedly stressed, the potential cost-savings through economies of scale would be dissipated.

The result was the Régime for Central American Integration Industries, signed in 1958 by all countries. The Régime is one of the more remarkable features of the CACM and has been studied in depth (cf. Cohen Orantes, 1972); the firm[10] receiving status as an integration industry would receive duty free treatment on its inputs while being guaranteed free access to the regional market; at the same time, the same products produced by firms not accorded integration industry status would be subject to trade taxes within the region. The Régime therefore conferred a virtual monopoly position on any firm lucky enough to receive its benefits, although in return it would be subject to price and other controls.

By locating firms equitably among the member countries, it was hoped to achieve balanced industrial development in the region. Unfortunately, only two firms have received benefits under the scheme[11] and the scheme went into abeyance soon after the foundation of the CACM. It has often been claimed (cf. Vaitsos, 1978) that the USA killed the Régime because of its ideological opposition to enforced monopolies. This, in fact, is not so; the Régime was effectively destroyed by the signing of the General Treaty, which established free trade on a *product* basis (thereby leaving little room for protection by *plant*), although it is also true that El Salvador and Guatemala, who stood to gain most by unrestricted free trade, were not unhappy to see the Régime lapse.

Deprived of its principal mechanism for ensuring an equal distribution of benefits, the CACM was left with only a number of minor instruments for achieving this objective. These included the Central American Bank for Economic Integration (CABEI), whose lending policy does in fact favour the less industrialised members (see Cline, 1978, Table 17) and the Regional Secretariat (SIECA), which has laboured hard, if unsuccessfully, to secure a more equitable sharing of benefits.

Many regional organisations, other than SIECA and CABEI, have been set up in an effort to promote economic union in Central America. The most important of these is the Central American Economic Council, which consists of the ministers of economy of the respective countries, but mention should also be made of the Central American Institute for Industrial and Technical Research (ICAITI), whose establishment in 1956 showed an early awareness of the need for the transfer and adaptation to Central American conditions of advanced country technology. There is also a monetary clearing house, the original purpose of which was to enable the bulk of intra-regional trade to be settled in domestic currencies.

A casual visitor to Central America today, returning after an absence of thirty years, would probably be most struck by the improvement in transport and communications. Although these are a precondition for successful integration, it is also legitimate to view them as instruments of integration. The Pan-American Highway, linking many of the major industrial centres, was completed just in time for the inauguration of the CACM and has proved most beneficial in allowing countries to take advantage of the incentives which intra-regional free trade offered.

## SUCCESS AND FAILURE IN THE CACM

The most tangible evidence of the CACM's success has been achieved in the field of intra-regional trade. From the negligible levels recorded in the 1950s, intra-regional trade rose to great importance (see Table 4.2); the CACM's share of total Central American trade rose rapidly from 6 per cent in 1960 to nearly 25 per cent in 1968. From then on the share has tended to fall away, suggesting that 1968 (the last 'normal' year of operation of the CACM before the war between El Salvador and Honduras) was a critical turning-point in the market's fortunes.

The increase in the proportion of intra-regional trade has been achieved primarily at the expense of the USA. In the 1950s, the USA accounted for 60–70 per cent of exports and imports by value; these shares were reduced to 33 per cent and 39 per cent respectively by 1968, since when the shares have stabilised. Some countries, however, notably El Salvador and Guatemala, have *increased* their dependence on the USA in the last decade both as a market for exports and as a source of imports (see Table 4.2).

The CACM, therefore, has in general reduced the geographic concentration of Central American trade and geographic concentration has often been cited as a source of export instability (cf. Soutar, 1977), which in turn has been claimed to be prejudicial to economic growth.[12] Furthermore, since trade within Central America is almost exclusively in manufactured goods, the CACM has reduced the importance of primary products in total exports – a further cause of export instability, as some claim.

Although the relationship between export instability and economic growth is a controversial one, the impact of the CACM on export instability is an empirical question, which can fairly easily be settled. We are therefore fortunate to have a study (Caceres, 1979), which examines the total variance of exports over the 1962–73 period using a portfolio model. The results, however, suggest that on balance the CACM has *increased* export instability[13] and the explanation is not hard to find. The principal determinant of any one member's intra-regional exports is the value of their trading partners' traditional exports. The variance of the latter is positively correlated for most pairs of countries, so that extra- and intra-regional exports tend to move together.

Apart from the pattern of trade, the CACM has brought a further structural change in the form of the increased share of industry in GDP. As Table 4.1 makes clear, this has risen from the 'floor' level of

*Table* 4.2 Central America: external transactions (m. US $)

| | *1950* | *1960* | *1970* | *1977* | *1983†* | *1986†* |
|---|---|---|---|---|---|---|
| *Costa Rica* | | | | | | |
| Exports (fob) | 56.0 | 86.0 | 231.0 | 798.0 | 852.5 | 1074.0 |
| % to CACM | 0.6* | 2.9 | 19.9 | 21.0 | 23.2 | 8.4 |
| % to USA | 65.7* | 52.3 | 42.5 | 31.3 | 47.0 | 41.0 |
| Imports (cif) | 46.0 | 110.0 | 317.0 | 1026.0 | 987.8 | 1160.7 |
| % from CACM | 0.4* | 3.2 | 21.7 | 15.9 | 12.2 | 8.2 |
| % from USA | 60.1* | 46.8 | 34.8 | 35.2 | 40.0 | 37.0 |
| *El Salvador* | | | | | | |
| Exports (fob) | 68.0 | 117.0 | 228.0 | 973.0 | 757.9 | 713.0 |
| % to CACM | 3.3* | 11.0 | 32.3 | 16.3† | 22.6 | 12.8 |
| % to USA | 82.1 | 35.1 | 21.4 | 32.3 | 38.7 | 46.6 |
| Imports (cif) | 48.0 | 122.0 | 214.0 | 942.0 | 891.5 | 934.9 |
| % from CACM | 9.0* | 10.5 | 28.4 | 23.2† | 26.1 | 17.2 |
| % from USA | 59.9* | 42.9 | 29.6 | 29.4 | 32.4 | 42.8 |
| *Guatemala* | | | | | | |
| Exports (fob) | 79.0 | 117.0 | 299.0 | 1160.0 | 1091.7 | 1119.1 |
| % to CACM | 1.7* | 4.3 | 35.5 | 24.4† | 29.4 | 17.9 |
| % to USA | 76.6* | 55.6 | 28.3 | 33.1 | 30.1 | 33.6 |
| Imports (cif) | 71.0 | 138.0 | 284.0 | 1084.0 | 1135.0 | 1050.0 |
| % from CACM | 1.0 | 5.6 | 22.9 | 13.6 | 20.2 | 7.6 |
| % from USA | 64.5 | 46.0 | 35.3 | 39.3 | 31.6 | 35.2 |
| *Honduras* | | | | | | |
| Exports (fob) | 65.0 | 63.0 | 179.0 | 504.0 | 694.0 | 900.9 |
| % to CACM | 6.2* | 12.9 | 10.6 | 8.5 | 8.8 | 2.6 |
| % to USA | 77.8* | 57.4 | 54.6 | 49.2 | 53.7 | 49.0 |
| Imports (cif) | 33.0 | 72.0 | 220.0 | 581.0 | 822.7 | 978.1 |
| % from CACM | 3.7* | 7.4 | 24.9 | 12.3 | 13.0 | 8.7 |
| % from USA | 71.6* | 56.1 | 41.5 | 42.9 | 47.5 | 43.2 |
| *Nicaragua* | | | | | | |
| Exports (fob) | 27.0 | 63.0 | 179.0 | 627.0 | 428.8 | 242.5 |
| % to CACM | 2.0 | 4.5 | 26.3 | 21.2 | 7.8 | 6.5 |
| % to USA | 45.5 | 40.3 | 33.2 | 23.6 | 24.0 | 0 |
| Imports (cif) | 25.0 | 72.0 | 198.0 | 755.0 | 834.0 | 826.5 |
| % from CACM | 2.5 | 3.9 | 25.3 | 21.6 | 14.8 | 5.6 |
| % from USA | 65.1 | 52.7 | 36.5 | 28.8 | 18.2 | 0 |

*Taken from J. B. Nugent, *Economic Integration in Central America* (Baltimore: Johns Hopkins University Press, 1974) Table 1-1. Figures refer to 1953.
†Taken from Consejo Monetario Centroamericano, *Boletín Estadistico*.

*Note*: Honduras is treated as a member of the CACM even after 1970.

*Source*: United Nations, *Yearbook of International Trade Statistics*.

9–14 per cent in 1950 to an average of 18 per cent in 1978 with all countries (even Honduras) benefiting to some extent. We may also note for further reference that the industrial share tended to peak around 1970, suggesting again that the CACM has stagnated or declined since then.

Given that the CACM was conceived as a mechanism for rapid industrialisation, it is safe to assume that much of this increased share was due to regional integration. The same cannot be said of the acceleration of the rate of growth of GDP (see Table 4.3), which also coincided with the foundation of the CACM. Various attempts (cf. McClelland, 1972; SIECA, 1973 and Nugent, 1974) have been made to isolate the contribution of the CACM to the annual growth rate of GDP, ranging from a 'high' of 1.6 per cent to a 'low' of 0.6 per cent per annum. The methodologies employed in these studies, however, leave a lot to be desired (see Lizano and Willmore, 1975).

When net welfare benefits are defined by orthodox customs union theory, it is possible for regional integration to promote an increase in the rate of growth of GDP with negative welfare benefits (net trade diversion). This is an unsatisfactory state of affairs and it seems preferable to postpone discussion of the CACM's impact on growth until we have observed its net welfare impact according to the non-orthodox interpretation outlined earlier.

Part of the interest in industrialisation in the 1950s stemmed from the need for an alternative to agriculture as a source of employment generation. In order to evaluate the impact of the CACM in this respect, it is necessary to know the proportion of the increment in output which can be attributed to integration; from this, on the basis of employment elasticities, the number of jobs created directly in industry can be estimated, as well as the indirect employment effects (if input–output tables are available).

This approach is used in a major study of employment in Central America (see Frank, 1978), where it is estimated that some 3000 new manufacturing jobs were created directly every year by integration from 1958 to 1968 and 2500 new jobs from 1968 to 1972. When indirect employment effects are taken into account,[14] these figures increase to 4200 and 3500 respectively, with between 50 per cent and 66 per cent of the indirect job creation occurring in the urban economy itself.

Whether these increases are significant or not depends, of course, on the impact of integration in providing employment for those entering the labour force over the same period. The study estimated that for every 100 workers entering the labour force, between 10 and 14 found

*Table* 4.3 Real rates of growth of GDP (annual averages); *per caput* rates of growth in brackets (%)

| | *1950–5* | *1955–60* | *1960–65* | *1965–70* | *1970–75* | *1975–78* | *1978–83* |
|---|---|---|---|---|---|---|---|
| Costa Rica | 7.4 (3.5) | 4.8 (1.1) | 3.9 (0.2) | 6.9 (3.8) | 6.4 (3.9) | 6.9 (4.3) | − 0.4 (− 2.7) |
| El Salvador | 4.5 (1.8) | 3.8 (1.2) | 7.7 (4.2) | 4.3 (0.7) | 5.3 (2.3) | 5.7 (2.7) | − 5.7 (− 9.7) |
| Guatemala | 2.3 (− 0.9) | 5.3 (2.2) | 6.2 (3.1) | 5.9 (3.1) | 5.9 (2.9) | 7.0 (4.0) | 0.5 (− 2.2) |
| Honduras | 4.1 (1.0) | 4.4 (1.3) | 4.8 (1.7) | 4.8 (1.7) | 2.9 (− 1.0) | 8.1 (4.3) | 1.7 (− 3.9) |
| Nicaragua | 8.3 (5.5) | 2.3 (− 0.8) | 8.2 (5.2) | 4.0 (1.5) | 5.9 (2.5) | 1.7 (− 1.9) | − 2.7 (− 7.8) |

*Source*: For the period 1950 to 1965, data taken from R. Hansen, *Central America: Regional Integration and Economic Development* (Washington DC: National Planning Association, 1967) Table II. For the period 1965–83, data taken from United Nations, *National Accounts Yearbook*.

jobs which were due to the CACM (i.e. these jobs would not have been available if a customs union had not been formed). This is by no means a negligible impact, although it must be remembered that the study is somewhat partial because it ignores the impact of integration on working conditions in the agricultural sector.[15]

We may now turn to the principal concern of this section – measurement of the social costs and benefits of integration. As stated earlier, the formation of the CACM would be expected to lead to net trade diversion and this is confirmed by a number of studies (see Willmore, 1976). However, with a changing tariff structure *vis-à-vis* the rest of the world pre- and post-union and with distortions in factor markets, net trade diversion is unlikely to give a satisfactory guide to net welfare benefits. This conclusion is strengthened when dynamic considerations are taken into account.

In an illuminating analysis of costs and benefits in the CACM, Cline (1978) has attempted to remedy some of the major deficiencies in the orthodox theory and his results are presented in Table 4.4. Cline continues to treat trade creation and diversion as leading to welfare gains and losses respectively, but notes that these effects will be compounded by those of external trade augmentation and trade suppression; in terms of these four criteria, as Table 4.4 shows, the costs of integration far exceed the benefits and this is true of all member countries. It is particularly interesting to note the importance of trade suppression as a result of setting the CET on consumer goods at a rate far exceeding the pre-union average for the five union members.

The study then goes on to take account of factor price distortions; the increased domestic production in country 'A' made possible *both* by trade creation in country 'B' *and* trade diversion in country 'A' attracts factors of production at rates assumed to be well above their social opportunity costs. In the case of labour, the difference between the market wage and the shadow wage gives rise to a welfare benefit which is based on the net increase in output; this gain is estimated in Table 4.4 using a shadow wage varying from $93 per annum in El Salvador and Honduras to $340 in the case of Costa Rica.[16] This welfare gain proves to be substantial for Guatemala and El Salvador.

The next static gain considered in Table 4.4 relates to the economies of scale effect. With factors valued at their social opportunity cost, a 1 per cent change in all inputs leading to a $(1 + x)$ per cent change in output will generate a welfare gain of $(x/1 + x)$ per cent of the change in output. Estimates of economies of scale in Central American industry must be considered rather crude, but there is some evidence (Williams,

*Table* 4.4 Costs and benefits (static and dynamic) of integration in CACM 1972 in '000 US $

| | *Costa Rica* | *El Salvador* | *Guatemala* | *Honduras* | *Nicaragua* |
|---|---|---|---|---|---|
| (A) *Static costs* (−) *and benefits* (+) | | | | | |
| Trade creation | + 1 933 | + 446 | + 1 802 | + 1 748* | + 3 061 |
| Trade diversion | − 3 475 | − 2 943 | − 3 787 | − 1 970* | − 2 473 |
| External trade augmentation | + 60 | 0 | + 551 | + 416* | + 234 |
| Trade suppression | − 1 870 | − 8 435 | − 4 375 | − 1 671* | − 2 263 |
| Labour opportunity cost | + 1 876 | + 9 269 | + 10 231 | + 1 210* | + 1 912 |
| Economies of scale | + 1 932 | + 1 228 | + 1 977 | + 254* | + 986 |
| Foreign exchange savings | + 16 292 | + 36 324 | + 39 810 | + 5 547* | + 17 463 |
| Industry intermediate effects | − 3 668 | − 2 345 | − 2 934 | − 1 226* | − 2 441 |
| **Sub-total** | **+ 13 080** | **+ 33 544** | **+ 43 275** | **+ 4 308*** | **+ 16 479** |
| (B) *Dynamic net benefits* | + 1 673 | + 1 640 | + 16 583 | + 11 019 | + 23 161 |
| **Total** | **+ 14 753** | **+ 35 184** | **+ 59 858** | **+ 15 327** | **+ 39 640** |
| Ratio, share in gains/ share in population | 0.78 | 0.94 | 1.03 | 0.55 | 1.80 |

*Refers to 1968.

*Source*: Derived from W. R. Cline, 'Benefits and Costs of Economic Integration in Central America', in W. R. Cline and C. Delgado (eds), *Economic Integration in Central America* (Washington DC: Brookings Institution, 1978) Tables 5, 6, 7 and 16.

1978) to suggest that, where constant returns do not prevail, increasing returns are the rule rather than the exception. These estimates are responsible for the scale effects in Table 4.4.

Trade diversion, by locating production within the region of goods which were previously imported from the rest of the world, tends to improve the extra-regional balance of payments. A net trade-diverting customs union, therefore, will save on foreign exchange and the savings can be considered as leading to a welfare benefit if the shadow price of foreign exchange exceeds the market rate. Using a variety of approaches to calculating this shadow price,[17] the study then estimates the welfare benefit and finds (even with a shadow price only 25 per cent above the market rate) a massive gain (see Table 4.4).[18]

The 'dynamic' effects of integration are hard to measure, but are usually considered to be important. There is the impact which integration has on foreign capital flows (i.e. in attracting funds which – in the absence of union – would not have come) as well as the impact which structural transformation might have in raising utility for a risk-averting nation. An attempt is made to measure these effects in the study referred to above, and is included in Table 4.4 under the rubric 'dynamic effects', although it must be admitted that the methods of estimation are somewhat unreliable.

The 'static' gains from integration represent 1.9 per cent of the region's GDP in 1972. Adding in the 'dynamic' gains, this figure rises to about 3 per cent, which is very substantial and helps to account for the relatively robust nature of the CACM, despite the political upheavals which afflict the region. Although one cannot extract the increase in GDP attributable to the CACM precisely from these figures, it is clear that it could have been important. Indeed, if the 'static' gain is spread over the 1960–72 period and added to the 'dynamic' gain, it suggests a 1.2 per cent rise in the annual growth rate above what it would otherwise have been.

According to Table 4.4, all countries have enjoyed net welfare benefits from the CACM, although the distribution is very unequal. Honduras' share of 'static' net benefits is about 4 per cent, far less than her share in population or Regional GDP (see Table 4.1), while El Salvador and Guatemala – as was suspected from the outset – have been the principal beneficiaries.

The position changes somewhat when 'dynamic' benefits are considered; Honduras' share of these benefits is closer to 20 per cent while El Salvador and Costa Rica appear to benefit very little. When both benefits are added together, we can observe how the benefits are shared relative to population shares (see last line in Table 4.4). Honduras still benefits least, but Nicaragua does best (thanks to 'dynamic' benefits, which brought a great flow of investment to Nicaragua and which it is claimed would not have occurred in the absence of integration).

It would be easy to criticise the methodology employed in the construction of Table 4.4 and no doubt other investigators, using slightly different assumptions, could come up with very different results. The most suspect gain, in this context, is likely to be that due to foreign exchange savings, which dominates all other 'static' gains (losses) and prevents the CACM from being net welfare reducing on 'static' criteria.[19]

Despite this, the important point to note is that, in the context of distorted factor prices, the extra output made possible by integration can have welfare improving effects. Although first-best policy is no doubt the removal of the underlying distortions, this may not be possible in practice; in that case, integration among countries is an important second-best policy for welfare improvement and Table 4.4 suggests that the gains could be substantial.

## THE CAUSES OF THE CACM'S FAILURE

The value of intra-regional trade within the CACM has been declining in relative terms since 1970 and in absolute terms since 1980. This decline is a very serious matter and its causes will shortly be investigated. None the less, it must be put into perspective: intra-regional exports still account for nearly 10 per cent of total Central American exports, varying from a low of 2.6 per cent in Honduras to a high of 17.9 per cent in Guatemala.

The decline of CACM in the 1970s was only relative, although this was still of serious concern (see below). In 1980, however, the CACM experienced a huge increase ($215 million) in intra-regional imports; this was almost entirely due to a 171 per cent increase in Nicaraguan imports from CACM as the Nicaraguan economy began the work of reconstruction following the 1979 civil war and the defeat of Somoza.

The Nicaraguan 1980 level of CACM imports could not be sustained and the value of trade fell back in 1981, although still exceeding 1979 levels. The real crisis of the CACM began in 1982, however, with a series of adverse shocks all combining to produce an 18 per cent fall in the value of intra-regional trade.

The most important of these shocks was the decline in the value of extra-regional exports, which began in 1981 as the world economy went into recession; this had a predictable effect on the external terms of trade for Central America (which had in any case been falling since 1977 when the coffee price peaked) and on the volume of demand. Since intra- and extra-regional trade are complementary in Central America (see above), the value of CACM trade was dragged down by the fall in extra-regional exports.

The second shock was the adjustment and stabilisation programmes, which all Central American countries were running in 1982. The initial response to the first shock had been to increase domestic demand through an increase in public expenditure; this had produced unsustainable levels of budget deficits, inflation and public external indebtedness, forcing all republics to adopt adjustment programmes.[20] In 1982, real GDP fell in all five republics – the first such occurrence since 1932. The fall in real GDP was accompanied by an even sharper decline in real consumption per head with a predictable impact on the value of CACM trade.

The third shock has been a series of unilateral and '*ad hoc*' measures designed to aid each country's balance of payments problems by restricting CACM imports; these include exchange rate changes, exchange control, delays in the issue of licences and, above all, non-payment of debt arrears. The last problem has been particularly severe; the 'surplus' countries (Guatemala and Costa Rica) have become exasperated at non-payment by 'debtor' countries (Nicaragua, El Salvador and Honduras) and have on occasions unilaterally restricted CACM *exports* in order to force a reduction in the debtor status of trading partners. The impact of all these measures has been to restrict regional trade, while increasing the importance of counter-trade.[21]

The final shock has been civil war and political unrest; while the first two shocks involve a reduction in the *demand* for regional exports, civil war and political unrest has restricted the *supply* of regional exports. Thus, part of the decline in CACM exports from Nicaragua and El Salvador has been due to war-related supply constraints, although in the former case mention should also be made of the unrealistic exchange rate offered exporters to CACM, which has appreciated sharply in *real* terms since 1979.

It will be noted that not much importance has been attributed to the regional political crisis as such in accounting for a decline in intra-regional trade. Hostility between countries is not a sufficient reason for a decline in intra-regional trade and the value of trade has declined between 'friendly' countries as well as between 'hostile' ones; since

1980, for example, the decline in Costa Rican imports from each Central American republic has been very similar. Thus, the decline in CACM is due fundamentally to economic factors.

The decline in the absolute value of CACM trade since 1980 cannot be dismissed as a short-term phenomenon, because relative decline had set in as early as the late 1960s. The most obvious sign of failure in the 1970s was the departure of Honduras, but by general consensus the market had already lost its dynamism. Intra-regional trade was declining as a proportion of total trade, the rate of growth of GDP in several countries was falling and even the industrial share of GDP was no longer rising.

To the architects of the CACM this last point is perhaps the most serious. Industrialisation was to be achieved by import substitution at the regional level, but this industrialisation appears not to have been carried beyond the 'easy' stage of consumer goods production. The result is that the growth in industry is now tied by and large to the growth of real disposable income in the region with the possibility of above proportional growth determined by the size of the income elasticity for consumer goods.

Consumer goods output – in the absence of regional intermediate and capital goods production – is very import-intensive and this is confirmed by input–output analysis for Central America (Bulmer-Thomas, 1979). The direct and indirect requirement for imported intermediate and capital goods inputs to satisfy a given level of consumer goods output is a *potential* stimulus, in the form of high backward linkages, to further industrialisation through a deepening of the import substitution process. That it has not taken place demands some explanation.

High backward linkages are an inducement to invest in supplying industries; the inducement, however, is only a necessary condition, since it does not take into account the profitability of new production. In the context of the CACM, the two most important determinants of profitability are market size and the effective rate of protection (ERP). Indirect evidence[22] suggests that market size was not the prohibitive factor, so analysis must focus on the ERP.

The ERP for an activity measures the protection received by its net output, i.e. the amount by which value added in the protected situation exceeds the value added that would be achieved under free trade. The higher the ERP, *ceteris paribus*, the more resources will be pulled into an activity and vice versa. In Central America, high tariffs on consumer goods imports combined with low or zero tariffs on other goods suggest

*Table* 4.5 Average effective rates of protection for Costa Rica, (%)

| | *1965–7* | *1968–9* | *1970–1* | *1971–4* |
|---|---|---|---|---|
| All manufacturing | 65.9 | 78.8 | 65.9 | 98.6 |
| Intermediate goods | 32.1 | 39.9 | 32.1 | 49.5 |
| Capital goods | 32.3 | 49.1 | 32.3 | 58.8 |
| Consumer goods | 81.8 | 95.7 | 81.8 | 120.2 |
| Agriculture and exported processed food | – 2.5 | – 3.6 | – 2.5 | n.a. |

n.a. = not available
*Source*: V. G. Bulmer-Thomas, 'The Structure of Protection in Costa Rica – a new Approach to Calculating the Effective Rate of Protection', *Journal of Economic Studies*, Vol. 6 (1976) Table 3.

that the ERP for consumer goods production will be very high, while that for intermediate and capital goods industries will be very modest.

There have been a number of studies of the ERP in Central America and, fortunately, they reach a common conclusion. The only one of these to use an actual input–output table (Bulmer-Thomas, 1976) is restricted to Costa Rica, but – given the use of a CET – the results should not differ too much among the member countries.[23] Table 4.5 shows that the ERP on consumer goods output has been high and rising and is between two and three times higher than that found in other industries.[24]

If industrialisation through a deepening of import substitution is ruled out by the structure of protection, it is tempting to ask why further industrialisation could not be pursued through export promotion of those consumer goods industries in which the CACM has a comparative advantage *vis-à-vis* the rest of the world. The answer is again provided by the structure of protection, although this time in a slightly different form; when an industrialist considers the merits of exporting relative to home (regional) sales, he is concerned with the proportionate difference between net output[25] in the two markets. If home net output is greater, there can be said to be a bias against exports and the bias is an increasing function of the difference between the two output measures.

When considering exports to the rest of the world, the Central American industrialist can expect to lose the protection he enjoys on his output, while at the same time continuing to pay above world prices for his inputs (both domestic and imported). The result is that net output in third markets is likely to be smaller than net output under free trade with the result that anti-export bias will exceed the ERP for any activity. Indeed, this is in general confirmed by empirical studies (Bulmer-Thomas, 1979) with the result that net output on sales to the rest of the world is on average about 50 per cent of that achieved on sales within the CACM.[26]

Further industrialisation, therefore, either through a deepening of import substitution or through exports to the rest of the world appears unlikely without radical changes in the market's structure; the analysis so far, however, does not explain why industrialists did not form a pressure group sufficiently powerful to push successfully for the necessary changes.

Traditionally, industrialists have been marginal in Central American politics with political power (even in Costa Rica) concentrated above all in the hands of those with landed interests. The initial drive towards industrialisation was supported by these groups and indeed many of them invested heavily in new industries, the most spectacular example being that of the Somoza family in Nicaragua. For such investors, however, the correct comparison is not between the profitability of one type of industry over another, but between the marginal rate of return in industry as against the return in agriculture. In this calculus, world prices for primary products are all important and it is no surprise to find that the stagnation of the CACM in the early 1970s coincided with a sharp increase in the price of Central America's traditional exports, reaching its climax with the coffee boom of 1975–7.

The attachment of many industrialists, therefore, to industrial development is skin-deep. The rate of profit on existing industry is generally thought to be high (cf. Cline and Rapoport, 1978a), but the profits will be reinvested outside industry if the rate of return on non-industrial investment justifies it. The result is that the power of industrialists to speak and act as a group is still very limited.

The failure to evolve a framework within which further industrialisation could proceed must be considered as a major cause of failure in the CACM. Apart from the weakness of industrialists as a pressure group, it can also be explained by the lack of supra-national agencies with sufficient authority to galvanise member governments into concerted action. Although SIECA (the regional secretariat) has performed excellently at a *technical* level and has offered its own blueprint for the future success of the CACM (the so-called Rosenthal Report, see SIECA, 1973), it has not exerted much political influence.

The SIECA plan called for institutional changes, including a council of ministers and a permanent committee similar to the European Community Commission; the proposals were agreed in principle by the ministers of finance and economy, as well as the presidents of the Central Bank, and a high-level committee (*Comité de Alto Nivel* – CAN) was set up to review the proposals. The CAN studied the proposals for two years and in 1976 presented the region's governments with a draft treaty which was never adopted, the main reason being the opposition of governments to the implied erosion of national sovereignty.

None of the explanations of the causes of failure so far given justify the departure of Honduras. Following the war with El Salvador, Honduras declared herself willing to remain in the CACM, provided that a new treaty could be signed which gave her preferential treatment in such things as tariff and fiscal policy. The proposals proved unacceptable to El Salvador and Honduras left the CACM at the end of 1970. Significantly, she has remained outside the CACM despite the signing of a peace treaty with El Salvador in October 1980.

Honduras' departure was mainly effected by the strong feeling that she was not benefiting as much as the other countries from membership, a feeling that is confirmed by Table 4.4. Subsequently, she signed a series of bilateral trade treaties with the other CACM countries, which have undoubtedly worked in her favour. It is perhaps not surprising, therefore, that Honduras has shown little inclination to rejoin the CACM.

## THE ROLE OF MULTINATIONAL COMPANIES

Prior to the formation of the CACM, there was virtually no investment by multinational companies (MNCs) in Central American industry, direct foreign investment being restricted mainly to agriculture, transport, communications and public utilities (see Rosenthal, 1973). The CACM changed this picture completely and, since 1960, there has been a marked increase in direct foreign investment (see Table 4.6), most of which has been earmarked for investment in industry (see Willmore, 1976a, Table 13.1). As a consequence of the rise in direct foreign investment, the repatriation of profits has increased in importance and now represents an important debit in the current account of the balance of payments.

The role of MNCs attracted by the CACM invites analysis, because

*Table* 4.6 Direct foreign investment in the CACM. Annual flows (m. US $)

| | *Estimated book value at end 1959** | *Direct foreign investments* | | | | |
|---|---|---|---|---|---|---|
| | | *1960* | *1970* | *1975* | *1978* | *1983* |
| Costa Rica | 73.2 | 2.4 | 26.3 | 69.0 | 47.0 | 55.3 |
| El Salvador | 43.0 | 4.4 | 3.1 | 13.1 | 23.3 | 28.1 |
| Guatemala | 137.6 | 16.8 | 24.6 | 80.0 | 127.2 | 45.0 |
| Honduras | 115.5 | 7.6 | 8.3 | 7.0 | 13.1 | 21.0 |
| Nicaragua | 18.9 | 1.7 | 15.0 | 10.9 | 7.0 | 7.7 |

*Taken from G. Rosenthal, *The Role of Private Foreign Investment in the Development of the Central American Common Market*, mimeo, Guatemala, 1973, p. 86 (in millions of dollars).

*Source*: United Nations, *Yearbook of National Accounts Statistics*; International Monetary Fund, *International Financial Statistics*.

they have been singled out by many economists (cf. Vaitsos, 1978) as a destabilising force leading to *disintegration* of the market. Furthermore, the Sandinista government in Nicaragua has made it clear that its continued participation in the CACM depends on restructuring the market in a way that no longer works principally in the interests of the MNCs (as Nicaragua claims).

That the formation of the CACM was the crucial incentive for investment by MNCs cannot be doubted; out of 155 foreign manufacturing subsidiaries setting up after integration, only ten established plants in more than one country (see Vaitsos, 1978, note 151), suggesting that market size was the all-important determinant of investment flows. Much of this investment, as was noted earlier, simply would not have come at all had it not been for regional integration.

The performance of MNCs in CACM can be summarised as follows: most of them eschew local participation, restricting it at best to a minority stake (Rosenthal, 1973); foreign firms tend to be larger than their domestic counterparts in terms of number of employees and control about 30 per cent of industrial production; direct foreign investment, however, is unevenly distributed across the industrial spectrum, being most heavily concentrated in activities such as tyres, glassware and chemicals.

In a statistical test on 33 pairs of foreign and domestic firms in Costa Rica, each pair being matched for size and product mix. Willmore (1976a) found no statistically significant difference for the two types of firm other than that MNCs employ relatively more administrative personnel, export a greater proportion of their output to the CACM and employ a *lower* capital–output ratio.

This is hardly the sort of evidence with which to build a case against the MNCs, so we must look elsewhere for an explanation of the hostility they have generated. The net welfare gain associated with direct foreign investment will be determined principally (cf. MacDougall, 1960) by the proportion of net output retained in the country through taxation; this proportion has been exceptionally low in Central America and figures are available (Cline and Rapoport, 1978b) to show that in a majority of industries the proportion of profits tax exempted has varied from 70 per cent to 100 per cent.[27]

This, however, only shows that the net gain is likely to have been small. In order to demonstrate a welfare loss, we have to suppose that direct foreign investment has introduced distortions in individual markets sufficient to outweigh the potential net gain; this is not impossible and, indeed, it is most likely to arise when direct foreign investment takes place through acquisition of existing firms, thereby increasing sellers' concentration and reducing competition.

There is some slight evidence in support of this point of view (see Willmore, 1976a), but it cannot generally be sustained. In his monumental study of direct foreign investment, Rosenthal (1973) found that in the case of 299 MNCs' subsidiaries in Central America, only 46 had been established as a result of take-overs of domestic firms and in half these cases domestic capitalists retained a minority interest.

In one respect, however, direct foreign investment has or could lead to serious problems. The attraction of the CACM to the MNCs was the captive home market; such firms have no interest in sales to the rest of the world and, indeed, several cases have been found (Rosenthal, 1973) where sales outside the CACM were specifically forbidden by the terms of the agreement between the subsidiary and head office. Such restrictions do not as yet have much force, but if policy in the CACM should turn more radically in favour of export promotion, it could prove awkward.[28]

We are forced to conclude, therefore, that the hostile attitude to MNCs' investment in the CACM is largely misplaced. Although the net benefits associated with direct foreign investment are probably small, they are likely to have been positive rather than negative. In a restructured market, however, it is legitimate to expect the distribution of benefits to be more favourable to the CACM and we shall return to this point in the next section.

## CONCLUSIONS

By general consent, the CACM is at present in deep crisis. In all member countries, real GDP per head has fallen sharply in recent years, there are civil wars in two countries (El Salvador, Nicaragua), deep hostility between Nicaragua and its immediate neighbours and a public external debt problem which forces all countries to adopt unpopular adjustment programmes. The future of CACM is therefore very much in the balance.

It is clear that a radical restructuring of the CACM, along the lines proposed by the Comité de Alto Nivel (CAN) in the early 1970s, is not currently feasible. Radical changes presuppose a degree of political consensus among the member countries, which is manifestly absent at present. At the same time, the current emphasis should be on making the CACM merely *a* dynamic factor (along with extra-regional manufactured exports) rather than *the* dynamic factor (which was the CAN's proposal); thus, a more modest set of reform proposals is not only more realistic, it is also more desirable.

It should also be clear that a necessary condition for the revival of CACM is a recovery in extra-regional exports and regional growth rates. The essential complementarity between intra- and extra-regional trade will remain for some time, because only the latter can provide the scarce foreign exchange on which the former depends.

The prospects for extra-regional trade are better now than for some time; although this is a necessary condition for the revival of CACM, it is unlikely to be sufficient. The latter requires that CACM countries start to dismantle the barriers they have erected against intra-regional trade since 1980.

The biggest barrier is the accumulation of debt arrears between pairs of CACM countries, because it restricts both CACM imports *and* CACM exports. In the hierarchy of unpaid debts, those owed by one LDC Central Bank to another are given the lowest priority; this has to be changed and international financial institutions and international agencies should give the same priority to intra-CACM debts as is currently given to debts owed to international commercial banks, while at the same time Central American countries need to implement more flexible arrangements for settling inter-country debts than currently exist through the regional clearing house.[29] It is a matter for regret, therefore, that the IMF – which in 1983 had agreements with four of the five republics – did not include as a condition of its lending the settlement of intra-CACM debts.

The second barrier is the uncertainty surrounding exchange rates and the frequent changes in rates applied to CACM trade. Central America's reputation as a region of stable exchange rates and low inflation has now disappeared. The promotion of extra-regional exports (including manufactured goods) requires flexible exchange rates, but this conflicts to some extent with the stability required to promote regional trade. The only solution is to operate a two-tier exchange rate with target zones set for the exchange rates applied to intra-regional trade; the zones should be set in such a way as to minimise the risk of one republic emerging as a persistent deficit or surplus country within the CACM.

The removal of these barriers, together with the revival of extra-regional exports and regional growth, should go some way towards reversing the decline in CACM. Coupled with an export promotion strategy, it would deal with some of the criticisms of the CACM mentioned in the first part of this chapter (e.g. the dependence of the CACM/ISI strategy on the performance of traditional exports). It would not, however, eliminate the problem of:

(a) Ensuring an equitable distribution of net benefits among members.
(b) The bias implied by the structure of protection against intermediate and capital goods.

Both of which remain very difficult to resolve.

Ever since the demise of the Regional Integration Industries' scheme and the failure to adopt a fiscal incentives scheme which favoured the weaker members of CACM, the only major institutional mechanism for countering the impact of market forces on the distribution of net benefits has been the Central American Bank for Economic Integration (CABEI). Since its creation, CABEI's lending has favoured the economically weaker states in Central America (Honduras, Nicaragua) over the stronger, but this has not been sufficient to counteract the impact of market forces in favour of the dominant countries.

One easy, but misguided, way to resolve this dilemma would be to restrict CACM membership to the stronger countries (i.e. Guatemala, El Salvador and Costa Rica), because in that case market forces would probably achieve an equitable distribution of net benefits; it is misguided, however, because CACM (like other regional integration schemes) cannot be judged purely in economic terms. Thus, the continuation of Nicaraguan membership is very important if Nicaragua is not to become even more isolated within Central America, while the re-entry of Honduras into CACM is an important goal for those who wish to see Central America speak with one voice in international trade and finance negotiations. The anomalous position of Honduras has, in any case, become a source of friction as other countries (notably Guatemala) have reacted to the preferential status accorded to Honduras after 1970.

There is therefore a strong case for reviving the Integration Industries' Convention (IIC), under which firms can be granted a regional monopoly subject to various controls on their behaviour. The IIC was always intended as a counter to market forces, since no country would be allowed a second regional monopoly until all other countries had received one. The IIC fell into disuse for various reasons (see above), but it would suit the next stage of import-substituting industrialisation (ISI) admirably. While there is little justification for a regional monopoly in the case of firms producing consumer goods, the same is not true of firms producing intermediate and capital goods; significantly, the regional monopolies set up in the 1960s under the IIC involved intermediate goods.

The IIC would therefore meet two targets with one instrument; it would go some way towards ensuring an equitable distribution of net benefits, while at the same time pushing the CACM towards the next stage of ISI. In addition, the fact that the Convention already exists (and needs only to be revived) means that a long and difficult debate over the introduction of new policy instruments can be avoided.

The final question to be resolved concerns the optimal size and character of the CACM. Although it has always been called a 'common market', this is misleading because free movement of labour and capital is not permitted. At best, it has operated as a 'Customs Union', although in recent years the absence of a CET has meant that 'Free Trade Area' would be a more accurate description.

The CAN in the early 1970s pressed for a genuine common market. This is now unrealistic, because 'free movement of labour and capital' could be used to justify wholesale out-migration on the one hand and capital flight on the other. A 'Customs Union', however, remains a realistic goal, but this means the adoption of a CET by all members; as a first step, therefore, all states must implement the new Arancel de Aduanas and harmonise the exchange rate basis on which trade taxes are collected. A genuine 'Customs Union' also implies the removal of any remaining restrictions on intra-regional trade (e.g. in agricultural products).

The *de facto* membership of CACM at present is three countries: Costa Rica, El Salvador and Guatemala. Nicaragua is a member in name only, while Honduras has not yet rejoined. These two countries should be urged to become full and active members again bringing the total back to the original five.

Should other countries be asked to join? The only possible candidates are Panama and Belize. Membership by the latter presupposes a settlement of the Anglo-Guatemalan dispute[30] (which now looks feasible), but would complicate the problems of CACM enormously. It would be difficult to apply the IIC if Belize were a member and Belize's size (population of 160 000) means that national ISI has not been a serious option: thus, the structure of the Belizean economy is very different from the rest of Central America and the economy is much more export-orientated.

Panama's service-based economy is also very different from the rest of Central America. Panama, however, has pursued national ISI, although it has produced major inefficiencies. Regional ISI coupled with an export promotion strategy, on the other hand, could prove attractive to Panama.

Average real income in Panama is high and the extension of CACM southwards would therefore prove attractive to the rest of Central America. Interestingly, the recent Cooperation Agreement between the European Community (EC) and Central America treated Panama as part of CACM.[31] Panama, therefore, should also be urged to join a revitalised CACM.

## Notes

1. It might also be argued that Panama's exclusion from the CACM owed something to its separate colonial and post-colonial experience, but this is not really so. Many attempts have been made to secure closer economic ties between the CACM and Panama, but the main stumbling-block has always been the service-dominated nature of the Panamanian economy.
2. The list of traditional exports excludes cotton, sugar and beef, although these are now important sources of foreign exchange earnings for several of the CACM members. The reason is that these products were developed for the export market comparatively recently (since 1950) and are therefore regarded as non-traditional.
3. The General Treaty provided for free trade among member countries with a common external tariff, but did not countenance the free movement of labour or capital. It therefore established a customs union, not a common market, but the use of the latter term is so widespread, that it would be pointless to try and change it.
4. Before the CACM, the share of industry in GDP was approximately 10

per cent (see Table 4.1). This corresponds to the 'floor' level found in Chenery's cross-section work (Chenery, 1960) and is made possible by the large number of manufactured goods (e.g. bread, bricks) which receive almost infinite rates of effective protection through high international transport costs.

5. In the 1950s, a great deal of attention was given to the equal distribution of benefits (see Delgado, 1978). The chief instrument conceived was the Regime for Central American Integration Industries, signed in 1958, which was intended to achieve a 'fair' spatial distribution of 'basic industries' among the five republics. Unfortunately, the freeing of trade on a *product* basis within the CACM, made possible by the General Treaty, effectively cut the feet from under the Regime, which relied on the adoption of a (temporary) monopoly by a particular *plant*.
6. This war is often called the 'football war', because it occurred shortly after a soccer match between the two countries (see Cable, 1969). In fact, the origins of the war lie elsewhere (see Durham, 1979) and Central Americans prefer the term '*guerra inutil*'.
7. Agricultural products were in the main excluded from the General Treaty, although several years later an agreement was reached on free trade in basic grains (corn, beans, rice and sorghum).
8. The principal items excluded from the free trade provisions of the Treaty are cotton, coffee, sugar and various goods subject to a government monopoly, such as rum and ethyl alcohol, which remain important sources of tax revenue.
9. The main stumbling-block between member countries over the agreement on uniform fiscal incentives was provided by Honduras' insistence on special treatment. The need for this was not denied by the other members, but the distance between what they were prepared to offer and what Honduras demanded proved too great (see Delgado, 1978, pp. 36–9).
10. In fact, the Régime distinguished whole sectors as 'integration industries', so that in principle the scheme could have applied to several firms in each industry; in practice, however, it was clear that it would only be used where a single plant (firm) was coterminous with the industry.
11. The two are a tyre factory in Guatemala and a caustic soda plant in Nicaragua.
12. Since this hypothesis was first put forward, it has been tested empirically with mixed results. MacBean (1966) found no evidence that export instability was inversely correlated with the rate of growth of GDP, whereas Yotopoulos and Nugent (1976) actually found a positive association. Other studies, however, notably Glezakos (1973), have found a negative correlation and there is an overwhelming feeling on the part of LDC policymakers, enshrined in the proposals for a New International Economic Order, that export instability is harmful to growth.
13. The study in question, however, suggests that the CACM has had a stabilising influence in the case of Costa Rica and Nicaragua. In the case of the former, it is due to the counter-cyclical nature of the change in the value of traditional exports relative to the change in the other republics.

14. At the time the employment study was carried out, no input–output tables for Central America were available, so that calculations were performed on an adapted Colombian coefficients matrix. It should be noted that this is likely to bias upwards the measurement of indirect employment effects, given the greater import-intensity of Central American over Colombian industry.
15. If, for example, the transfer of labour to industry results in the modernisation of agriculture through labour-saving technological change, the net gain in employment will be much more modest than the figures in the text. This line of reasoning is pursued in Reynolds and Leiva (1978).
16. The shadow price of labour ($W^*$) was estimated according to the formula:

$$W^* = W_R(1 - U_R)$$

where $W_R$ is the rural wage rate and $U_R$ is the rural underemployment rate. The latter varies from 58.3 per cent in the case of El Salvador to 14.7 per cent in the case of Costa Rica and is the main source of the difference in shadow prices by country.
17. The shadow price of foreign exchange is derived in three ways: through the tariff-based Harberger (1965) and Bacha and Taylor (1971) methods and through the solution to an econometric model for Central America (Siri, 1978).
18. The final 'static' gain (loss) listed in Table 4.4 is the 'industry intermediate effects'. The net gain in production in each sector gives rise to additional output and import requirements in each sector via input–output relationships; these requirements can then be converted to welfare gains (losses) through the three effects listed above; labour opportunity cost, economies of scale and foreign exchange savings. The reason why this effect appears in Table 4.4 with a minus sign is because the indirect requirements are mostly met by imports, which generate a loss of foreign exchange.
19. The formula used by Cline for the foreign exchange saving net welfare effect (*BFE*) is:

$$BFE = (f^* - 1)(DELTX + TS - TCCE - ETA)$$

where $f^*$ is the shadow price of foreign exchange estimated as the premium over the market rate. *DELTX* is the increase in exports to partners, *TS* is trade suppression, *TCCE* is trade creation and *ETA* is external trade augmentation. According to this formula any saving in foreign exchange (through, for example, trade suppression) is converted to domestic currency via the shadow exchange rate; the domestic resources used in production, however, are not costless and must be evaluated at shadow prices before being deducted from the gross domestic currency equivalent of the foreign exchange saving to give the net welfare gain. This will only give the same result as the above formula in exceptional circumstances. This interpretation of *BFE* implies that the four terms in the brackets should be measured at world prices. If, in fact, domestic prices are used (as happened in Table 4.4), it will impart a bias to *BFE* according to the extent and size of trade taxes. For both these reasons, the estimates of *BFE* in Table 4.4 must be considered *maxima*.

20. For details of these adjustment programmes, see Chapter 7.
21. A shrinking proportion of total intra-regional trade is now handled by the Cámara de Compensación Centroamericana.
22. Many feasibility studies, some by ECLA, have considered the possibility of establishing intermediate and capital goods industries and have in general concluded that the small market size need not be prohibitive.
23. In Rapoport (1978), similar results are found for Costa Rica, but the average ERP and its spread is estimated to be lower in the other republics.
24. On 1 January 1986, a new tariff system (*Arancel de Aduanas*) was adopted by CACM. The new system is based on *ad valorem* tariffs and a change of nomenclature; there are no studies available so far on the impact of the new system on the ERP.
25. In reality, he considers the proportionate difference in profits, but no satisfactory method has been developed for measuring the impact of protection on one primary input, so that the effect of protection is measured in terms of its impact on all primary inputs.
26. Efforts by Central American countries to offset this bias through drawback schemes, Free Trade Zones, tax credit certificates, etc., applied to manufactured exports have so far been very limited except for Costa Rica (see Chapter 10).
27. With the adoption of the new tariff system on 1 January 1986, the CACM also took steps to cancel many of the tax privileges enjoyed by existing firms.
28. The countries of Central America (excluding Nicaragua) are now beneficiaries of the Caribbean Basin Initiative (CBI), which gives duty-free access to the US market for a very broad range of primary and secondary products. The governments of these Central American countries have been encouraging foreign companies to invest in the region to take advantage of the favourable treatment for exports under the CBI. So far, however, these efforts have met with only modest success.
29. Such a scheme (Derechos de Importaciones Centroamericanas – DICA) was adopted at the end of 1986. The DICA is a financial instrument issued by Central Banks to importers for payment of exports; exporters can then use the DICA to purchase CACM imports or exchange it at their Central Bank for *local* currency. The DICA therefore avoids the need for foreign exchange in settling intra-regional debts, although it is still too early to evaluate the success of the scheme.
30. Guatemala's long-standing territorial claim to Belize, a former British colony, has blocked Belize's entry to various regional organisations (including the Organisation of American States). A settlement of this dispute, which Guatemala still considers to involve Great Britain, now

looks more promising following the election of a civilian President in Guatemala at the end of 1985.

31. In November, 1985, the EC signed an agreement with all the Central American countries (together with Panama), which calls for a 'substantial' increase in multilateral EC aid in support of regional integration.

# 5 Regional Integration within a Policy Regime of Openness

## INTRODUCTION

The focus on import-substituting industrialisation (ISI) within the Central American Common Market (CACM) in the 1960s was always seen by policy-makers as a prelude to manufactured exports towards the rest of the world (ROW). During the 1970s, tentative efforts were made in several republics to combine the two industrialisation strategies, although the results were generally disappointing. Now, in the mid-1980s, governments in each republic are under considerable pressure from external and internal sources to abandon the inward-looking strategy and focus exclusively on manufactured exports to ROW as a way of promoting industrialisation.

This chapter addresses the issue and is divided into two parts. The first examines whether strategies of ISI within a regional framework and of increasing extra-regional manufactured exports[1] are mutually exclusive or whether they can coexist within the same policy framework. The second part examines the question of whether economic cooperation at the regional level can be conducted outside the framework of CACM and, if so, in what areas.

It is appropriate to begin, however, with some definitions. The term ISI is straightforward and covers the process of import substitution in industrial goods either at the national or regional level. In the latter case, it is assumed that imports are replaced by regional production behind a tariff or protective barrier which applies equally to all countries of the region. In the former case, imports are replaced at the national level by local production behind a protective barrier which applies only at the national level. In the case of regional ISI, therefore, it is assumed that the movement of industrial goods between countries is not subject to restrictions additional to those which apply at the national level.

There is much greater ambiguity, however, regarding the term 'export diversification'. Where a strategy is contemplated of dismantling a national protective structure in order to increase extra-regional exports, I shall talk of export substitution (ES). Where the strategy contemplates maintenance, by and large, of the national protective structure coupled with encouragement of extra-regional exports, I shall refer to export promotion (EP). Regional ES therefore refers to a situation where a group of countries acting together dismantle their national protective structures and regional EP to a situation where the regional protective structure remains intact and the countries of the region co-ordinate their policies in favour of EP.

## ARE REGIONAL STRATEGIES OF ISI AND ES/EP MUTUALLY EXCLUSIVE?

If it is possible to combine ES/EP with ISI, the combined strategy must overcome at least some of the worst failings commonly associated with ISI. It is appropriate therefore to begin by recognising the problems of ISI in general and, in particular, the difficulties raised by regional ISI in CACM.

A major problem is that ISI, far from reducing balance-of-payments (BOP) problems and foreign exchange bottlenecks, frequently increases them. The reason is threefold: first, ISI is itself very import-intensive and new industrial activities typically generate a high demand directly and indirectly for imports from ROW as intermediate goods, spare parts, capital equipment, etc.; secondly, the policies designed to favour ISI frequently discriminate against exports, so that the *supply* of foreign exchange is lower than it might otherwise have been; thirdly, ISI (which almost always begins with consumer goods) shifts the structure of extra-regional imports in favour of intermediate and capital goods, any reduction in which is much more damaging than in the case of consumer goods.[2] As Table 5.1 shows, this was a serious problem for CACM as early as 1970, with 55 to 74 per cent of all earnings from extra-regional exports swallowed up by industry's need for foreign exchange to buy intermediate and capital goods.

A second problem, related to the first, is that the success of the ISI strategy becomes heavily dependent on the performance of traditional exports. In other words, ISI – far from competing with the traditional export-led growth model based on primary products – is actually complementary to it. This criticism is supported by the experience of CACM, in which the most successful years coincide with a boom in

*Table* 5.1 Import intensity of industry in Central America in 1970 ($ million)

| | *Costa Rica* | *El Salvador* | *Guatemala* | *Honduras* | *Nicaragua* |
|---|---|---|---|---|---|
| (1) Total imports of raw materials for industry | 111.3 | 80.8 | 107.8 | 75.0 | 68.1 |
| (2) Percentage of (1) from outside CACM | 76.9 | 74.3 | 76.1 | 76.2 | 76.2 |
| (3) Total imports of capital goods for industry | 51.5 | 27.1 | 43.9 | 32.3 | 32.6 |
| (4) Percentage of (3) from outside CACM | 98.6 | 95.0 | 97.7 | 96.5 | 96.6 |
| (5) Extra-regional imports for industry as % of | | | | | |
| (a) Extra-regional imports | 55.0 | 56.0 | 57.0 | 53.3 | 56.1 |
| (b) Extra-regional exports | 73.7 | 55.4 | 66.5 | 58.3 | 62.9 |

*Source*: Derived from SIECA, *VII Compendio Estadistico Centroamericano* (Guatemala, 1982).

primary product (traditional) exports[3] and the least successful with the reverse.

The third problem is the bias associated with ISI against production of intermediate and capital goods in favour of production of consumer goods. The structure of protection adopted under ISI involves changes in the nominal rate of protection (i.e. changes in nominal tariffs). The combination of changes in tariffs on firms' inputs and outputs has the effect of altering their value added or net output; economists describe the change in value added relative to the free trade situation as the Effective Rate of Protection (ERP).[4] The higher the ERP, the higher the incentives for industrialists to produce the goods in question.

The ERP varies from sector to sector. Where nominal tariffs are low, however, on intermediate and capital goods and high on consumer goods, the ERP will typically be much higher for consumer goods than for the other branches of industry. This was certainly the case of CACM (see Table 4.5). There is therefore the danger that the ISI process becomes exhausted following import-substitution in consumer goods (the so-called 'easy' stage of ISI) and is unable to advance into more complicated industrial ventures because of the bias built into the structure of protection. Thus, one of the main aims of regional integration is undermined, because the regional grouping was designed to achieve a market large enough to support production of intermediate and capital goods.

The fourth problem concerns the bias against manufactured exports under ISI. The ERP for any given sector ($j$) measures the percentage change in value added per unit of output in the post-tariff situation ($V'_j$) compared with the pre-tariff free trade situation ($V_j$) i.e.

$$\text{ERP}_j = [(V'_j - V_j)/V_j] \times 100 \qquad j = 1, \ldots, n \tag{5.1}$$

If in the post-tariff situation industrialists try to export their output outside the region they lose the protection offered by the nominal tariff on their output, but continue to be subject to tariffs on their inputs. Thus, their value added per unit of output on exports ($V^e_j$) will be less even than value added in the free trade situation (under the latter at least inputs are not subject to tariffs). If we now define the bias against exports ($B_j$) as the percentage by which value added per unit of output in the post-tariff situation exceeds value added per unit of output in extra-regional markets i.e.

$$B_j = [(V'_j - V^e_j)/V^e_j] \times 100 \qquad j = 1, \ldots, n \tag{5.2}$$

then it will always be the case that the bias against exports in any given sector will be at least as great as the ERP in the same sector, i.e.

$$B_j \geqslant \text{ERP}_j \quad j = 1, \ldots, n \tag{5.3}$$

The extent of the bias against manufactured exports clearly depends on the size of the ERP. Table 4.5 suggests, however, that in the CACM (particularly for consumer goods) the ERP has been quite high. Thus, there has been a bias against exporting *outside* the region precisely those commodities which have done well *inside* the region.

The fifth problem associated with regional ISI (very important in the case of CACM) is the difficulty of providing an institutional framework which guarantees that all countries in the region receive an equitable share in the distribution of net benefits. The most careful and thorough study of the CACM (see Cline, 1978) concluded that it had indeed generated net benefits at the regional level, but that the distribution of these net benefits was very unequal. This is frequenly given as a major reason for Honduras's departure from the CACM in December 1970. The problem is a very old and very familiar one: exclusive reliance on market forces will ensure that the most developed countries within the region receive the lion's share of regional net benefits, while interference with market forces to ensure a more equitable share of the benefits may lower the growth rate of the most developed members.

It would be easy to continue this list of difficulties associated with ISI in general and CACM in particular, but the above problems are the major ones. In addition, a successful regional ISI policy presupposes some harmonisation of exchange-rate policy between the countries of the region, which may be inconsistent with the exchange-rate flexibility demanded by an ES or EP strategy.

It is very tempting, when faced with such a formidable list of problems, to conclude that any form of export diversification is preferable to ISI. In the matter of trade policies to be adopted by less developed countries (LDCs), however, there are no easy options and it is salutary to remind ourselves that export diversification strategies also involve major problems. Consideration of ES strategies will illustrate this point.

Under an ES strategy (such as was followed in the Southern Cone of Latin America in the late 1970s), tariffs are systematically lowered or dismantled, producing a depreciation of the nominal (and hopefully real) exchange rates. Whatever the stimulus for non-traditional manufactured exports, it is more likely that a substantial part of the industrial base will be wiped out by imports (this is sometimes called negative ISI). Some of these firms forced to close will be high-cost, inefficient producers, which could never be expected to compete internationally under free trade; others, however, might have made the transition to international competition under different circumstances, but negative ISI will lead to their permanent closure.

The shift in the allocation of resources within an ES strategy encourages industrial specialisation. There is the danger, however, that the country will become as dependent on a few manufactured products as it previously was on a few primary commodities. Exploitation of the opportunities for forward and backward linkages in the industrial sector (potentially very great) will be impossible if the industrial base rests on a handful of manufactured products.[5]

Nowhere is this problem more vividly illustrated than in the free trade zones established by a large number of LDCs (including Central American countries) in the last decade. In return for duty-free imports, cheap labour and tax holidays, companies (often foreign-owned) export their output to earn valuable foreign exchange. As a strategy for earning hard currency, it has some arguments in its favour; as a strategy for industrialisation it is very weak, because it allows little or no opportunities for the exploitation of backward and forward linkages.

The depreciation of the nominal exchange rate associated with the ES strategy sets up inflationary pressures, which require further large nominal depreciations to achieve a small real depreciation of the exchange rate. The latter is bought at a high price, however, in the form of an acceleration of inflation and (usually) a fall in real wages together with a deterioration in the distribution of income in favour of greater inequality. The latter changes aggravate the bias against production for the home market under the ES strategy and may provoke further de-industrialisation.

Finally, no discussion of the ES strategy would be complete without reference to market access. It is precisely in those commodities where LDCs might be expected to have a comparative advantage (e.g. textiles) that protectionist barriers in the developed countries (DCs) are at their greatest. These obstacles consist more of non-tariff barriers (NTBs) than of tariffs and LDCs have lobbied for years for their removal. The results have been mixed; while the LDCs have secured the Generalised System of Preferences (GSP), the Lomé Convention and the Caribbean Basin Initiative (CBI) as partial compensation for the spread of NTBs, protectionist sentiment among the DCs has increased rather then decreased in recent years. The result is that a successful ES strategy (e.g. Taiwan) needs to be supported by a formidable trade lobby in the capitals of DCs in order to guarantee access for an increased flow of manufactured exports.

Given that there are no easy options for LDCs in the matter of trade policy, it is now appropriate to consider whether the ISI strategy can be made consistent with export diversification in such a way that it offers the advantage of both without the disadvantages of either. We must therefore consider the possibility of (a) linking ISI with ES and (b) linking ISI with EP.

The possibility of linking ISI with an ES strategy is remote. Almost by definition, an ES strategy implies negative or reverse ISI and, in practice, it would not be possible to combine the two; most of the instruments favouring one strategy discriminate against the other. Only in the case of real exchange rate depreciation (RERD) does the same instrument favour both sets of strategies, but RERD is unlikely to be sufficient to compensate industrialists producing for the home market for the reduction in ERP consequent upon the lowering of nominal tariffs.

The prospects for linking ISI with EP might seem equally gloomy. After all, this was the combination of strategies favoured by several Central American republics in the 1970s and the results were very disappointing. In the Plan Nacional de Desarrollo published in Costa Rica in 1974 (while Oscar Arias Sánchez was Minister of Planning), projections for manufactured exports implied that the growth of extra-regional exports would be the same as intra-regional exports (see Oficina de Planificación, Plan Nacional de Desarrollo, Sectores Productivos, B. Sector Industrial, Cuadro 6, San José, 1974), but the actual performance of extra-regional manufactured exports fell short of projections.

Despite the disappointment of the 1970s, the combination of ISI and EP strategies is in fact feasible and the failures of the 1970s are due more to an inappropriate combination of policy instruments than to any logical inconsistency beteen the two strategies.

Let us return to equation (5.2). As long as $V_j^r > V_j^e$, there will be anti-export bias and a preference for sales to the home market. Analytically, therefore, a combination of ISI and EP strategies requires a choice of policy instruments pushing $V_j^r$ and $V_j^e$ towards equality – at least in those sectors where extra-regional exports are considered feasible.

What policy instruments do $V_j^r$ and $V_j^e$ depend on? Let us take the former first; it can be defined as

$$V_j^r = P_j e_j(1 + t_j) - \sum_i a_{ij} e_i(1 + t_i) \tag{5.4}$$

where $P_j$ is the world (dollar) price of commodity $j$, $e_j$ is the nominal exchange rate applied to imports of the $j^{th}$ commodity, $a_{ij}$ is the requirement of the $i^{th}$ commodity per unit of output in the $j^{th}$ commodity at world (dollar) prices, $e_i$ is the nominal exchange rate applied to imports of the $i^{th}$ commodity, $t_j$ is the nominal tariff on the $j^{th}$ commodity and $t_i$ is the nominal tariff on the $i^{th}$ commodity.

In equation (5.4), value added per unit of output in the post-tariff situation is seen to depend on five variables, four of which ($e_j$, $e_i$, $t_j$, $t_i$) are instruments controlled by the authorities. The latter can lower $V_j^r$ by lowering $e_j$ and $t_j$ and by raising $e_i$ and $t_i$.

The definition of value added per unit of output if exported ($V_j^e$) is:

$$V_j^e = P_j e_j - \sum_i a_{ij} e_i(1 + t_i) \tag{5.5}$$

which is similar to equation (5.4) except that the output is now sold in world markets and therefore loses the protection offered by the nominal tariff on competing imports ($t_j$). From equation (5.5), we can see that the authorities can raise $V_j^e$ by raising $e_j$ and by lowering $e_i$ and $t_i$.

There appears therefore to be a possible conflict in the use of some instruments. The authorities, it is assumed, wish to lower $V_j^r$ and raise $V_j^e$ in order to make firms in the $j^{th}$ sector indifferent between selling to the (protected) regional market and selling to the (unprotected) world market. A lowering of $e_j$, however, and a raising of $e_i$ and $t_i$ lowers $V_j^r$, but also lowers $V_j^e$. Similarly a raising of $e_j$ and a lowering of $e_i$ and $t_i$ raises $V_j^e$ but also raises $V_j^r$.

This dilemma can only be resolved by distinguishing between exchange rates and tariffs by end-use. Thus, the authorities need to operate one set of exchange rates for goods sold in the regional market ($e_j^r$, $e_i^r$) and one for goods sold overseas ($e_j^o$, $e_i^o$). Similarly, the nominal tariffs on inputs need to vary for the same reason. Thus $t_i^r$ would be the nominal tariff on the $i^{th}$ commodity used in products sold in the regional market, while $t_i^o$ would be the nominal tariff on the $i^{th}$ commodity used in goods sold abroad.

It is therefore possible to rewrite equations (5.4) and (5.5) to take account of these qualifications. Before doing so, however, it is necessary to introduce one further complication. Industrial firms will respond to the value added per unit of output net of direct taxes; by taxing $V_j^r$ and $V_j^e$ at different rates of tax, the authorities have two further instruments for moving $V_j^r$ and $V_j^e$ towards equality.

Equation (5.4) now becomes:

$$V_j^r{}^* = \tau_j^r V_j^r = \tau_j^r[P_j e_j^r(1 + t_j^r) - \sum_i a_{ij} e_i^r(1 + t_i^r)] \tag{5.6}$$

where $\tau_j^r$ is the direct tax rate on value added for the $j^{th}$ commodity when sold in the regional market and $V_j^r{}^*$ is the post-tax value added for the $j^{th}$ commodity when sold in the regional market and equation (5.5) now becomes:

$$V_j^e{}^* = \tau_j^o V_j^e = \tau_j^o[P_j e_j^o - \sum_i a_{ij} e_i^o(1 + t_i^o)] \tag{5.7}$$

when $\tau_j^o$ is the direct tax rate on value added for the $j^{th}$ commodity when sold in the world market and $V_j^e{}^*$ is the post-tax value added for the $j^{th}$ commodity when sold in the world market.

The authorities' task is now to choose some combination of instruments such that $V_j^r{}^* \approx V_j^e{}^*$. Since there is in principle a large number of possible combinations, it is worth setting out the options in Table 5.2 in the form of a box diagram.

Although in principle many combinations of instruments can achieve the desired objectives, the authorities' choice will be guided by other considerations. Thus, for example, any combination which relied exclusively on decreases in ($V_j^r{}^*$) would run counter to the ISI strategy (under the latter, incentives must be available for 'deepening' ISI

*Table* 5.2 Policy instruments for combining import substitution with export promotion

| | *Increases in* $V_j^e{}^*$ | *Decreases in* $V_j^r{}^*$ |
|---|---|---|
| $e_j^r$ | | Down |
| $e_j^o$ | Up | |
| $e_i^r$ | | Up |
| $e_i^o$ | Down | |
| $t_j^r$ | | Down |
| $t_i^r$ | | Up |
| $t_i^o$ | Down | |
| $\tau_j^r$ | | Up |
| $\tau_j^o$ | Down | |

through production of intermediate and capital goods). Similarly, the authorities may well find it unduly complicated to work with '2*n*' exchange rates (two for each commodity) and may prefer to operate with only two exchange rates ($e^r$, $e^o$) which vary by end-use, but not by commodity.

We can now use Table 5.2 to evaluate what has been done in Central America in order to combine ISI with EP strategies. Most republics at various times have worked with differential tax rates ($\tau_j^r > \tau_j^o$); typically, this has been achieved through Certificados de Abono Tributario (CAT) estimated as a fixed percentage of the FOB value of exports.[6] Most republics have also discriminated between tariffs on inputs through drawback schemes favouring firms which export all their production (in the extreme case $t_i^o = 0$). Similarly, some republics have allowed exporters to sell part of their foreign exchange earnings at more favourable rates of exchange than applied to firms selling the same output in the regional market. Finally, efforts have been made to lower nominal tariffs on competing imports.

The impact of all these changes, however, has been very modest and has not been enough to bring ($V_j^r$*) into equality with ($V_j^e$*). The CATs, for example, have been insufficient to compensate for the tax holidays and widespread exemptions enjoyed by many firms selling in the regional market. The advantages conferred by lowering ($t_i^o$) have been small, because ($t_i^r$) has also been very low; the exchange rate privilege has applied, in general, to exporters of non-traditional *agricultural* products rather than manufactured goods.

The most serious problem, however, has been the adoption of the new *Arancel de Aduanas* on 1 January 1986. Although the new Arancel has the great merit of using *ad valorem* rather than specific tariffs and has also been accompanied by a sharp reduction in the tax holiday exemptions offered to existing firms selling to the regional market, it has on balance probably increased ($t_j^r$) rather than lowered it. The situation has been aggravated by the decision of some countries to calculate the tax due on the local currency cost at the parallel exchange rate; this has the effect of raising ($V_j^r$*) and increasing the gap over ($V_j^e$*).

The most effective way for the authorities to achieve the desired equality is through a rise in $e^o$ (or $e_j^o$), a fall in $t_j^r$, an increase in $\tau_j^r$ and a fall in $\tau_j^o$. A change in $e^r$ is not desirable, because the regional ISI strategy works best when members maintain fixed exchange rates within the region; changes in input tariffs are unlikely to be very effective, because the starting rates are so low. Finally, the combination of rising $\tau_j^r$ with falling $\tau_j^o$ will help to prevent a fiscal shortfall as a result of extending tax privileges to extra-regional exports.

The ease with which these instruments can be changed varies enormously. Changes in nominal tariffs (e.g. $t_j^r$) require regional co-operation, since the basis of a Customs Union/Common Market is a common external tariff (CET). Changes in tax rates (e.g. $\tau_j^r$) may require regional co-operation if the member countries are subject to fiscal harmonisation; finally, differential exchange rates (e.g. $e_j^o > e_j^r$) are unpopular with international financial institutions, such as the International Monetary Fund and the World Bank, and external financial support is sometimes made conditional on their removal.

It is worth re-emphasising, however, that there are no easy trade policy options for LDCs in general and Central America in particular. Despite the difficulties outlined in the previous paragraph, it *is* possible to make the necessary changes and combine an ISI with an EP strategy. This is likely to be preferable to an ISI or ES/EP strategy on its own for reasons already given.

An ES strategy minimises state intervention, which is a major source of attraction for many policy-makers. An ISI/EP strategy cannot work in this way, however, because market forces cannot be relied on exclusively; by definition, market forces in the post-tariff situation favour production for the regional market; interference with market prices (using the instruments described above) can reduce or eliminate the bias against extra-regional exports. The bias, however, varies from sector to sector; if the authorities eliminate the bias against exports in the sector with the greatest comparative *disadvantage*, they will offer too much incentive to those sectors with greater prospects for extra-regional exports.

The authorities must therefore use *selective* discrimination. They must identify those sectors with the highest potential dynamic comparative advantage in international trade and adjust their policy instruments so as to eliminate anti-export bias in those sectors.

The record of governments in 'picking winners' is not a good one. The problem is, however, that the authorities have typically been ambiguous about the criteria employed to determine 'potential dynamic comparative advantage'. A brave attempt to resolve these problems can be found in the Brookings Institute Study of the CACM (see Cline, 1978, Ch. 6). In that study, a series of indicators are used to identify out of 75 industrial sectors the 25 with the greatest potential dynamic comparative advantage (see Table 5.3).

The Brookings Institute Study, for lack of suitable data, did not use

*Table* 5.3 Twenty-five industrial sectors ranked highest for overall comparative advantage, Central America

| *Sector* | *Description* | *Combined rank, static and dynamic comparative advantage* |
|---|---|---|
| 3839 | Electrical apparatus not elsewhere specified | 75 |
| 3140 | Tobacco manufacturers | 74 |
| 3131 | Distilling spirits | 73 |
| 3832 | Radio, television, communication equipment | 72 |
| 3111 | Meat: slaughter, preparation | 71 |
| 3512 | Fertilisers, pesticides | 70 |
| 3843 | Motor vehicles | 69 |
| 3312 | Wooden containers | 68 |
| 3114 | Canning, preserving fish | 67 |
| 3559 | Rubber products not elsewhere specified | 66 |
| 3113 | Canning, preserving fruits and vegetables | 65 |
| 3813 | Structural metal products | 64 |
| 3521 | Paints, varnishes | 63 |
| 3311 | Sawmills, planing mills | 62 |
| 3823 | Metal- and wood-working machinery | 61 |
| 3213 | Spinning, weaving, finishing textiles | 60 |
| 3831 | Electrical industrial machinery | 59 |
| 3116 | Grain mill products | 58 |
| 3411 | Pulp, paper, paperboard | 57 |
| 3132 | Wine industries | 56 |
| 3118 | Sugar factories and refineries | 55 |
| 3412 | Paper, paperboard containers and boxes | 54 |
| 3134 | Soft drinks | 53 |
| 3710 | Iron and steel basic industries | 52 |
| 3551 | Rubber tyres and tubes | 51 |

*Source*: W. R. Cline, 'Benefits and Costs of Economic Integration in Central America', in W. R. Cline and E. Delgado (eds), *Economic Integration in Central America* (Washington, DC: Brookings Institution, 1978), p. 282.

what I believe to be the most appropriate methodology for identifying sectors in need of export promotion. This is the Domestic Resource Cost (DRC) criterion and it works as follows: for each industrial sector, an estimate is made (using input–output tables) of the direct and indirect foreign exchange requirements needed to earn one dollar's worth of exports; the difference between the two then gives net earnings of foreign exchange. For each sector, an estimate is then made of the direct and indirect domestic factor requirements (e.g. capital and labour) required to produce one dollar's worth of exports. These factor requirements are then valued at their shadow or accounting prices and added together. By dividing the total for each sector by the net earnings of foreign exchange, one obtains the value of domestic resources in each sector needed per unit of foreign exchange earned (i.e. the DRC criterion). Sectors with a high DRC are inefficient and should not be promoted, because they require 'excessive' domestic resources to earn foreign exchange; sectors with low DRCs should be promoted, because they are very efficient at converting domestic resources into scarce foreign exchange. The equilibrium exchange rate is sometimes used to provide the dividing line between sectors with high and low DRCs.[7] Needless to say, the choice of which sectors to promote should also be influenced by considerations of market access. It is no use promoting textiles, for example, even if the sector enjoys a low DRC, unless there are realistic chances of overcoming protectionist barriers in overseas markets.

## REGIONAL ECONOMIC CO-OPERATION OUTSIDE THE CACM

Although I have argued that the 'first-best' policy for Central America is an ISI/EP strategy with ISI conducted at the regional level through CACM, there are many obstacles which block progress towards this goal; in this section, therefore, we shall examine a 'second-best' policy in which regional economic co-operation is conducted outside the CACM, i.e. co-operation does not presuppose the existence of a Customs Union. This 'second-best' policy is consistent with either an EP or ES strategy, but is more likely to accompany the latter.

What are the obstacles blocking progress towards the 'first-best' policy? The main one is geopolitical: a strengthening of CACM would benefit all members, while the main thrust of current US policy has been to isolate the Sandinista government in Nicaragua. (This contradiction was explicitly recognised – but not resolved – in the Kissinger Report.) Thus, the US administration is not prepared to support the increase in capital flows at the *regional* level which would be needed to revive CACM.

This is a serious problem, although it is not decisive. While the current US administration is unlikely to give active support to CACM, it is now clear that it will not try to block *other* initiatives to revive regional integration. Thus, for example, the recently signed Co-operation Agreement between the EEC and Central America envisages a 'substantial' increase in multilateral aid which will be used to promote *regional* projects and programmes (from which, in principle, Nicaragua will also benefit). Although US Secretary of State Schultz tried in September 1984 to block the possibility of EEC aid benefiting Nicaragua, the diplomatic repercussions led the USA to drop its original objections.

Nevertheless, the revival of CACM without US support would be very difficult; the two regional powers (Mexico and Venezuela) can no longer be expected to provide substantial capital flows to Central America, without which the elimination of debt arrears will be difficult to achieve. US support is also important, because direct foreign investment to take advantage of regional ISI is needed and much of this would almost certainly have to come from North America; although these are private capital flows, the leverage of the US administration remains considerable.

Another major obstacle blocking progress towards the 'first-best' policy is the lack of trust between various Central American countries. The most important example is the tension between Nicaragua on the one hand and Costa Rica, El Salvador and Honduras on the other; there is also a lack of trust between Honduras and El Salvador, whose border dispute has still not been resolved.

Finally, one must mention ideological and political differences among the countries of the region. The basic issue, of course, is the possibility of cohabitation between a Marxist government in Nicaragua and non-Marxist governments elsewhere, although it would foolish to rule out the possibility of a return to military rule in some republics and the tensions this would create.

The problems posed by a Marxist Nicaragua can be exaggerated. Past experience has shown that this has not ruled out collaboration between all Central American countries on a range of issues (e.g. the joint approach to the EEC in September 1983 under the auspices of the Inter-American Development Bank). However, the revival of CACM does presuppose a harmony of interests between the members which might be very difficult to achieve under present circumstances.

Thus, it is realistic to explore the possibility of regional economic co-operation outside CACM. Furthermore, this is a very topical question since the recently opened EEC office in San José is expecting to receive requests for funding regional projects which need not be directly linked to CACM.

There are several areas where regional economic co-operation is desirable and – given the political situation in Central America – feasible. The first is energy projects; the huge hydroelectric and geothermal projects begun in the 1970s, when external funds were cheap and easily available, are now coming on stream. With regional co-operation, the efficiency of these projects could be increased through external trade in energy; the political benefits are also likely to be considerable, because one country will now have a vested interest in political stability in its neighbours (the destruction by the *contras*, for example, of electricity pylons in northern Nicaragua has disrupted Honduran energy exports).

The second is education; the export diversification strategy – whether EP or ES – requires the acquisition of new skills and techniques by the labour force. There are substantial economies of scale in these forms of vocational and technical training, which can only be enjoyed through regional co-operation.

A third area is the elimination of diseases, both those which afflict the human population and the animal/plant kingdom. A programme to eliminate coffee rust, for example, is much more likely to succeed if neighbouring countries participate. The same is true of malaria control and the elimination of other tropical diseases.

A fourth area is transport and communications; this is familiar territory, since Central American countries have been collaborating on these social infrastructure projects since the 1950s (e.g. the Pan-American Highway) and in some cases even earlier (International Railways of Central America linked El Salvador with Guatemala in the 1920s). Much remains to be done, however, as technological progress in these two fields has generated new demands.

Regional economic co-operation could also bring substantial benefits in international negotiation. A joint CACM position, for example, could help Central America in negotiations under the International Coffee Agreement (ICA), the International Sugar Agreement (ISA) and even the Multifibre Agreement (MFA). The experience of the Unión Países de Exportadores de Bananos (UPEB) in the 1970s showed what could be done through co-operation, and – even more – what could be lost through lack of co-operation.

Finally, regional co-operation could help to strengthen the Co-operation Agreement with the EEC. The agreement, scheduled to run until 1990 in the first instance, is subject to annual review at ministerial level; a strong regional negotiating position could do much to extend the scope and impact of this agreement (currently rather limited). The EEC, a regional body itself, finds it easy to negotiate with other regional bodies and the EEC remains a vital potential market for any export diversification strategy.

## Notes

1. During the 1960s and 1970s, the value of both intra-regional and extra-regional exports increased rapidly; the latter, however, was based on primary products. The main concern now is whether it is possible to combine an increase in intra-regional trade with an expansion of extra-regional *manufactured* exports.
2. These arguments are developed more fully in Chapter 4.
3. In the current Central American context, 'traditional' primary product exports includes coffee, bananas, cotton, sugar and beef.
4. For a case study of the ERP in Central America, see Bulmer-Thomas (1976).
5. Backward and forward linkages are of enormous importance for an understanding of the industrialisation process in LDCs. For a fuller treatment, see Bulmer-Thomas (1982, Ch. 12).
6. For a useful summary of these schemes, see Central American Bank for Economic Integration (1984).
7. See Bulmer-Thomas (1982, pp. 259–60).

# 6 Economic Relations Between Central America and Western Europe

## INTRODUCTION

Economic relations between Central America and Western Europe historically have been dominated by trade in commodities. In return for Western European manufactured goods, Central America has supplied coffee, bananas, cotton and other primary commodities. Only recently has Central America seriously considered the possibility of supplying Western Europe with non-traditional (i.e. manufactured) goods, although progress so far has been very limited. Given the difficulties, however, of increasing the volume of primary product exports absorbed by Western Europe, both sides have been examining ways of removing obstacles to an expansion of trade in non-traditional goods.

The second most important feature of economic relations has been capital flows from Western Europe to Central America. Before the First World War Central American bonds were regularly floated on European stock markets, although direct foreign investment never achieved much importance. Following the First World War, European portfolio investment declined as the main source of external finance shifted to the United States; Western European direct foreign investment revived in the 1960s with the formation of the Central American Common Market, while private commercial capital flows accelerated in the 1970s with the growth in syndicated loans. Finally, official capital flows (both bilateral and multilateral) from Western Europe have slowly expanded over the last twenty years to the point where their combined total is now not insubstantial.

Attracted by the prospects for expanding primary product exports from Central America, a trickle of Western Europeans have emigrated to the region over the last century. The most important group was the German coffee growers of Alta Verapaz in Guatemala, but European interests figured prominently in the expansion of exports from Nicaragua, El Salvador and Costa Rica. These groups, however, have either been assimilated (as in El Salvador) or expropriated (as in Guatemala during the Second World War) so that the European colony in each Central American republic is now dominated by those linked to multinational investments or those working under contract with funds provided by official development assistance.

Western Europe, as one of the world's richest regions, plays an important part in international and regional organisations with considerable influence over Central American economic affairs. These institutional economic relations form a third link between Central America and Western Europe, which has grown in importance as the European Economic Community (EEC) has achieved greater unity. The EEC is now dominant within Western Europe and, to the extent that it speaks with one voice, its international influence has grown. This has been reflected in the Co-operation Agreement signed in November 1985 between the EEC and Central America (including Panama), which commits the EEC to a significant increase in multilateral resource transfers to the region.

## TRADE RELATIONS

As far as understanding the dynamics of the Central American economy is concerned, there is no more important question than trade. The region has, for a century at least, had the characteristics of a 'small, open economy' and this openness has increased, not diminished, in recent decades. Indeed, as Table 6.1 shows, while middle-income oil-importing countries in general have experienced an increase in the ratio of exports to GDP (from 14 per cent in 1960 to 18 per cent in 1979), in Central America the ratio rose to nearly 40 per cent in the cases of El Salvador, Honduras and Nicaragua and nearly 30 per cent in the case of Costa Rica. Only in Guatemala, the least trade dependent of the Central American economies, was the share below 25 per cent and even there the ratio rose from 13 per cent in 1960 to 21 per cent in 1979.[1] This high degree of export specialisation has a number of obvious consequences. Economic growth is in general not only export-led, it is also export-determined; this has prompted one economist to observe:

> A striking feature of econometric models of income determination in the region is the evidence of the continuing dominating effects of terms of trade and other export-related fluctuations on the level of domestic income and product. This is so, despite two decades of integration policy designed to diversify these economies to reduce

*Table* 6.1 Ratio of exports to Gross Domestic Product (%)

| | | *1960* | *1979* |
|---|---|---|---|
| (A) | Low-income countries* | 14 | 20 |
| (B) | Middle-income countries† | 14 | 18 |
| (C) | Central America‡ | | |
| 1. | Costa Rica | 21 | 27 |
| 2. | El Salvador | 20 | 36 |
| 3. | Guatemala | 13 | 21 |
| 4. | Honduras | 22 | 38 |
| 5. | Nicaragua | 24 | 37 |

*Notes*: *Excluding China. †Oil-importers only. ‡Considered part of (B) by World Bank.

Although more recent data are available, the year 1979 has been chosen because it is less affected by the regional crisis and world recession.

*Source*: World Bank, *World Development Report 1983* (Washington, 1983), Table 5.

their vulnerability to foreign trade cycles (Reynolds in Cline and Delgado, 1978, p. 288, n. 2).

A further point worth remembering in considering the future of trade to Central America is the region's high degree of commodity and geographic concentration. Coffee and bananas continue to dominate foreign exchange earnings in all republics (see Table 6.2), while the five principal export crops account for between 50 per cent and 70 per cent of total foreign exchange earnings. At the same time, the three principle export markets – the EEC, the United States of America (USA) and the Central American Common Market (CACM) – account for over 75 per cent of the value of commodity trade for all republics, except in Nicaragua where the share has fallen below 50 per cent.

Until the First World War, with the exception of Honduras, the major market for Central American exports was Western Europe. This market was eclipsed by that of the United States following the outbreak of hostilities. In more recent decades, however, there has been a revival in the importance of the EEC market, so that the US market for Central American exports is now dominant only in the case of Honduras. Current trade relations (see Table 6.3) are dominated by

*Table* 6.2 Proportion of total exports accounted for by principal export crops in 1984 (%)

| *Country* | *Bananas* | *Coffee* | *Sugar* | *Cotton* | *Beef* | *Total* |
|---|---|---|---|---|---|---|
| Costa Rica | 25.9 | 27.1 | 2.1 | — | 4.4 | 59.5 |
| El Salvador | — | 61.4 | 3.6 | 1.3 | 0.4 | 66.7 |
| Guatemala | 4.9 | 32.4 | 5.6 | 6.4 | 1.1 | 50.4 |
| Honduras | 34.6 | 23.8 | 3.7 | 1.1 | 2.8 | 66.0 |
| Nicaragua | 4.4 | 24.1 | 1.5 | 36.4 | 5.3 | 71.7 |

*Source*: SIECA, *Series Estadísticas Seleccionadas de Centroamérica, No. 20* (Guatemala, December, 1985), Tables 71 to 75.

Central American exports of three primary products (coffee, bananas, cotton). A study of EEC trade with Latin America[2] shows that these three commodities account for 90 per cent of all exports to the EEC from Costa Rica, El Salvador and Nicaragua, over 80 per cent from Honduras and nearly 70 per cent from Guatemala.

Although Latin America's share of total EEC imports has declined since 1960, the importance of the EEC market for Latin American exports has actually increased. This is true of Central America as well, although the share tends to fluctuate dramatically as coffee prices vary.

As far as Central America is concerned, exports to the EEC are virtually confined to agricultural products. Of these by far the most important is coffee, where the market is segmented into four types: unwashed Arabicas (produced mainly by Brazil), Robustas (produced mainly by African growers), Colombian Milds (produced mainly in Colombia) and Other Milds, where Central American producers are dominant.

While world trade in coffee grew at a comparatively modest rate between 1950 and 1980 (2.5 per cent annum), most Central American producers were able to improve on that and the region's share of world exports in volume terms rose from 8.9 per cent in 1950 to 11.9 per cent in 1980. During the same period, there has been a marked shift in the coffee market away from unwashed Arabicas to Robustas and Other Milds, while at the same time the EEC's share of world imports of 'green' coffee has gone from 18.9 per cent to 36.2 per cent. Thus, Central America's growing trade with the EEC has been based essentially on a decline in Brazil's market share and a change in tastes in favour of the higher quality Other Milds.

*Table* 6.3 Central American trade with Western Europe ($ million) in 1984. Figures in parentheses refer to percentages of each Central American country's total trade

| | *Exports to Western Europe* | | | *Imports from Western Europe* | | |
|---|---|---|---|---|---|---|
| | *EEC** | *EFTA†* | *Total* | *EEC** | *EFTA†* | *Total* |
| Costa Rica | 256.0 (26.0) | 17.1 (1.7) | 273.1 (27.7) | 154.8 (14.2) | 17.2 (1.6) | 172.0 (15.8) |
| El Salvador | 185.2 (25.8) | 1.2 (0.2) | 186.4 (26.0) | 99.8 (10.2) | 10.2 (1.0) | 110.0 (11.2) |
| Guatemala | 163.7 (15.0) | 6.5 (0.6) | 170.2 (15.6) | 174.7 (12.1) | 29.1 (2.0) | 203.8 (14.1) |
| Honduras | 154.8 (22.3) | 16.3 (2.3) | 171.1 (24.6) | 120.6 (14.8) | 18.8 (2.3) | 139.4 (17.1) |
| Nicaragua | 106.2 (29.1) | 2.8 (0.8) | 109.0 (29.9) | 134.8 (19.2) | 28.8 (4.1) | 163.6 (23.3) |

*Defined to include Spain and Portugal (i.e. membership of twelve).
†European Free Trade Area (Austria, Iceland, Norway, Sweden and Switzerland).

*Source*: SIECA, *Series Estadísticas Seleccionadas de Centroamérica, No. 20* (Guatemala, December 1985), Tables 78 to 82 and 85 to 89. For El Salvador, figures are derived from *Revista del Banco Central de Reserva de El Salvador* (Julio–Agosto–Septiembre, 1986, p. 67.

These long-run favourable trends in the coffee market may be difficult to sustain. First, a continued decline in Brazil's market share is something which can no longer be assumed; indeed, there are signs that Brazil may be forced to increase its world market share in order to ease its problems of external imbalance. Secondly, the existence of an International Coffee Agreement, of which both the EEC and Central American countries are members, based on exportable quotas, means that a growing proportion of coffee exports have to be sold in non-traditional markets.

In its trade with the EEC, Central America (like the rest of Latin America) suffers from a number of disadvantages. One of these refers to its exclusion from the group of so-called ACP countries, which enjoy preferential access to the EEC market under the Lomé convention. In 1975, there were 46 ACP countries; by the time of the third agreement in 1985, there were 65. Thus, whatever its shortcomings, Lomé remains popular among LDCs and this suggests that excluded regions are at a serious disadvantage.

The preferential treatment given to ACP countries takes many forms, including duty-free access for many primary products to the EEC on a non-reciprocal basis. Thus, coffee from Latin America must pay a 5 per cent *ad valorem* tariff (7 per cent before the Tokyo round), while coffee from ACP countries pays no tax.

Since coffee from ACP countries (Robustas) is only an imperfect substitute for coffee from Central America (Other Milds), this price advantage has not been too serious and in any case the EEC has agreed to lower the duty on coffee imports from Central America under the Co-operation Agreement. This is not the case for all agricultural commodities, however, and bananas are a case in point. Several EEC countries (Belgium, Netherlands, Luxemburg, Ireland and Denmark) impose a 20 per cent *ad valorem* tariff on banana imports, which is not applicable to ACP countries (Langhammer, 1980). So far, ACP countries have been unable to exploit this advantage, but it must put future Central American exports to those countries at risk.

A further impediment to Central America's trade with the EEC is the Common Agricultural Policy (CAP). In order to defend CAP prices, a variable levy is applied to imports into the EEC which eliminates any price advantage an exporter might have. The main affected products which might be of interest to Central America are sugar, beef and maize.

In all three cases, ACP countries enjoy preferential treatment over Latin America. Maize enjoys a reduced variable levy, while beef from

Botswana and Swaziland (two ACP countries) is allowed in duty-free up to a pre-fixed maximum amount. In the case of sugar, the EEC operates a system of quotas and guaranteed prices for ACP countries, which does not apply to Latin America.

The inclusion of sugar in the CAP and the preferential treatment given to ACP countries has been particularly serious for Central America. High internal prices for beet sugar had converted the EEC from a net sugar importer to a net exporter by 1977; thus, Central America has lost a profitable market and, in addition, EEC exports dumped on the world market have pushed world prices down to levels below or close to cost of production.

The problem of the world sugar market has been compounded by the reluctance of the EEC to support the International Sugar Agreement (ISA). With EEC support, it is generally assumed that an agreement similar to that applied in the case of coffee could be made operational even without reform of the CAP. Without EEC support the ISA is unworkable.

The inclusion of Central America in the associate states benefiting from Lomé III would offer substantial benefits. Coffee and bananas would profit from tariff-free access to the EEC market with a corresponding increase in the price received by exporters and in the case of bananas (not subject, unlike coffee, to quotas), a possible increase as well in the volume of sales. Access to STABEX[3] would prove a useful supplement to the IMF's Compensatory Finance Facility to deal with fluctuations in export earnings; Central America would gain access to the European Investment Bank (EIB), which under Lomé III is permitted to provide finance for industrial rehabilitation; membership of Lomé III would ensure that Central America shared in any future (as well as current) agreement, so that individual countries would benefit even if regional peace efforts should fail. An extension of Lomé to include Central America might receive US support (even if Nicaragua was a beneficiary) and would help to forge much-needed links between Central America and other LDCs (including Belize).

The greatest problem with the Lomé proposal would be ACP resistance to Central American membership. The population of Central America, however, is only 23 million compared with nearly 400 million for ACP countries as a whole and membership has already grown from 46 to 65 states. Another problem is cost, assuming existing resources are not simply spread more thinly; cost, however, has to be seen in the context of expected benefits and the cost-effectiveness of Lomé is likely to be considerably higher than realistic alternatives.

The EEC, however, has so far shown no willingness to increase ACP membership to include Central America. There are therefore serious barriers in the way of expanded trade between the EEC and Central America. There are also various opportunities, which should not be overlooked; the most important of these refers to the Generalised System of Preferences (GSP). The origin of the GSP scheme lies in UNCTAD I, which resulted in 1971 in the establishment of preferential treatment for manufacured goods from most LDCs to most DCs; the scheme was renewed in 1981 with minor modifications.

Unlike the Lomé agreements, the GSP puts Latin America and ACP countries on an equal footing as far as access to the EEC market is concerned. Unfortunately, preferential treatment has not always meant preferential access and the EEC has operated the GSP scheme in such a way that only the most aggressive exporters (mainly from Asia) have been able to extract much benefit. In addition, textile exports are already covered by the highly restrictive Multifibre Agreement (MFA) and the GSP comes complete with such an elaborate system of quotas and ceilings that there is little immediate prospect for exporters of manufactured goods from areas such as Central America.

In the medium term, however, the prospects are better. The present GSP distinguishes between four categories of industrial products: textiles, very sensitive products, less sensitive products and non-sensitive products, and the degree of restriction applied to LDC exports is in descending order. Thus, some 1700 non-sensitive products face unrestricted duty-free entry, although this can still be withdrawn at any time at the request of an EEC state after ten days' notice.

In the medium term, the enlargement of the EEC to include Spain and Portugal could have an important bearing on EEC relations with Latin America in general and Central America in particular for several reasons. First, the enlargement of the EEC must surely lead to the breakdown of the CAP. The entry of Spain alone has added substantially to the arable land of the Community, many of the products from which qualify for CAP status. The breakdown of the CAP, however, would represent important new trading possibilities for Central America not only in maize, beef and sugar, but also in seasonal fruits and vegetables. Second, as the Lomé Conventions have shown, trade agreements and patterns are not unaffected by colonial experience and history and Spain's membership could prove interesting in this respect. In addition, Spain is one of that growing number of countries which wish to see Western Europe exercise a relationship with Latin America independent of US policy towards the region.

## CAPITAL FLOWS

Accurate figures on Western European direct foreign investment in Central America are hard to obtain. The formation of CACM in the 1960s stimulated multinational investment, but interest waned in the 1970s as CACM lost much of its dynamism. In more recent years, Western European countries have again begun to consider investment in Central America, as a possible base for non-traditional exports to the United States. These exports would enjoy duty-free access to the North American market for a twelve-year period (beginning in 1984) under President Reagan's Caribbean Basin Initiative (CBI).

The CBI offers a variety of aid and trade measures to all Central American countries except Nicaragua. The CBI is very similar to Lomé III, except that no provision is made for compensating countries for fluctuations in export earnings (the so-called STABEX and SYSMIN provisions of Lomé III). Although nearly 90 per cent of the Caribbean Basin's exports to the USA already enjoy duty-free access, the CBI is intended to apply for twelve years and this might encourage a shift of resources into activities which previously faced tariff barriers. Non-tariff barriers are likely to be less severe than those facing ACP countries in the EEC market or those facing all LDCs under the GSP scheme. The CBI may therefore offer in the medium term an avenue for the above proportionate expansion of certain manufacturing activities. So far, Western European companies have shown themselves reluctant to commit themselves to new investment in Central America to take advantage of the CBI. Political uncertainty, regional instability and a fear of foreign exchange restrictions have proved more powerful than the prospect of greater profits from duty-free access to the lucrative US market.

Private commercial capital flows to Central America from Western Europe expanded in the 1970s. Only Costa Rica and Nicaragua, however, owed a high proportion of this public external debt to private creditors at the end of the 1970s and in the Nicaraguan case this was owed mainly to US banks. The exposure of Western European banks to Central America has therefore been very minor. They have also shown an extreme reluctance to commit additional credits to the region since 1980; as a result, all five republics have relied heavily on official capital flows to ease their severe balance-of-payments problems in the 1980s.

While the main official creditor for all republics (except Nicaragua) has been the United States (for Nicaragua it has now become the Soviet

Union), Western Europe has been an important source of official development assistance (ODA) for all five republics. Bilateral ODA (see Table 6.4) has provided most of the resource transfer with Nicaragua receiving nearly 50 per cent of the cumulative total between 1982 and 1985. The burden of bilateral ODA has fallen most heavily on West Germany and the Netherlands, who between them have accounted for 47.7 per cent of the cumulative resource transfer from 1982 to 1985. Sweden has also been an important contributor over the same period (nearly 10 per cent of the total) with France and Italy contributing a similar share (see Table 6.4).

Multilateral ODA from the EEC has been much less important than bilateral assistance (see Table 6.5). In 1982, for example, multilateral ODA from the EEC only reached $16.3 million and was absorbed entirely by Honduras and Nicaragua. By 1984, the flow had risen to nearly $30 million and was shared by four republics. The Co-operation Agreement between the EEC and Central America (see below), envisages a 'substantial' increase in multilateral ODA (perhaps to $100 million per year), although this will still be much less than bilateral Western European assistance and only a small fraction of United States bilateral ODA, which reached $700 million in 1985 (see Table 6.5).

## INSTITUTIONAL ECONOMIC RELATIONS

There are three types of international organisations through which the economies of Central America are linked to those of Western Europe: international commodity organisations, international financial institutions and regional (Central American) institutions. Through these organisations the economies of Western Europe influence economic performance in Central America, although the influence is exercised in an indirect fashion.

The main commodity institution is the International Coffee Organisation (ICO) and the related International Coffee Agreement (ICA). As major consumers, Western European countries are in a strong position to determine the success or failure of the ICA which sets a price range for coffee exports and adjusts exportable quotas to maintain prices in this range.[4] Since coffee remains the single most successful export from Central America (see Table 6.2), the successful functioning of the ICA is of vital importance to the region. A second commodity institution is the International Sugar Organisation (ISO). Most Western European countries (including the EEC) now belong to the ISO,

*Table* 6.4 Cumulative gross flows of Official Development Assistance (ODA). $ million. 1982–5

| *Donor* | *Costa Rica* | *El Salvador* | *Guatemala* | *Honduras* | *Nicaragua* | *Central America* | *Donor contribution to total* (%) |
|---|---|---|---|---|---|---|---|
| Belgium | 0.8 | 0.6 | 0.9 | 0.5 | 2.0 | 4.8 | 1.0 |
| Denmark | 0.3 | 1.0 | 0.3 | — | 3.6 | 5.2 | 1.1 |
| France | 3.2 | 0.7 | 1.5 | 9.2 | 32.7 | 47.3 | 9.7 |
| West Germany | 27.4 | 16.1 | 19.3 | 26.0 | 24.9 | 113.7 | 23.3 |
| Italy | 19.9 | 10.5 | 1.7 | 2.7 | 12.8 | 47.6 | 9.8 |
| Netherlands | 15.0 | 6.3 | 5.4 | 13.9 | 78.4 | 119.0 | 24.4 |
| United Kingdom | 2.4 | 0.4 | — | 6.5 | 0.4 | 9.7 | 2.0 |
| Subtotal | 69.0 | 35.6 | 29.1 | 58.8 | 154.8 | 347.3 | 71.3 |
| Austria | — | 0.1 | 5.1 | 0.1 | 21.7 | 27.0 | 5.5 |
| Finland | — | 0.4 | — | 0.4 | 10.3 | 11.1 | 2.3 |
| Norway | 1.5 | 2.3 | 1.6 | 1.3 | 15.1 | 21.8 | 4.5 |
| Sweden | 0.4 | 0.4 | 0.4 | — | 46.2 | 47.4 | 9.7 |
| Switzerland | 2.0 | 1.2 | 0.5 | 21.0 | 8.9 | 33.6 | 6.9 |
| Total | 72.9 | 40.0 | 36.7 | 81.6 | 257.0 | 488.2 | 100 |

*Source*: OECD, *Geographical Distribution of Financial Flows to Developing Countries, 1982–5* (Paris, 1987).

*Table* 6.5 Total gross Official Development Assistance (ODA). $ millions. MU = EEC multilateral; BI = EEC bilateral; US = United States

| | *1982* | | | *1983* | | | *1984* | | | *1985* | | |
|---|---|---|---|---|---|---|---|---|---|---|---|---|
| | *MU* | *BI* | *US* | *MU* | *BI* | *US* | *MU* | *BI* | *US* | *MU* | *BI* | *US* |
| Costa Rica | — | 14.1 | 44 | 0.5 | 8.8 | 201 | 2.7 | 13.2 | 170 | 0.9 | 32.7 | 199 |
| El Salvador | — | 3.6 | 171 | 0.3 | 6.0 | 233 | 0.8 | 5.0 | 223 | 0.3 | 20.9 | 288 |
| Guatemala | — | 7.4 | 22 | — | 7.4 | 38 | — | 6.3 | 31 | 0.3 | 7.4 | 52 |
| Honduras | 9.0 | 13.4 | 70 | 6.4 | 15.1 | 66 | 10.9 | 16.8 | 125 | 2.9 | 13.6 | 161 |
| Nicaragua | 7.3 | 44.3 | 6 | 6.9 | 39.0 | 3 | 14.7 | 38.1 | — | 12.7 | 33.5 | — |
| Total | 16.3 | 82.8 | 313 | 14.1 | 76.3 | 531 | 29.1 | 79.4 | 549 | 17.1 | 108.3 | 700 |

*Note*: Bilateral EEC aid in the above table refers only to those EEC countries which are members of OECD, i.e. Belgium, Denmark, France, West Germany, Italy, Netherlands, United Kingdom.

*Source*: See Table 6.4.

but the sugar policy of the EEC has prevented the EEC from playing a constructive role in the establishment of an effective International Sugar Agreement (ISA). As a result, the ISA exists only on paper; there is no price range for sugar exports and world sugar prices fluctuate violently from one period to the next.[5]

The international financial institutions, to which Western European countries belong and which carry influence in Central America, are the World Bank (WB), the International Monetary Fund (IMF) and the Inter-American Development Bank (IDB). The World Bank, traditionally concerned with project finance, has altered its priorities and is now also engaged in structural adjustment loans (SALs). Both Costa Rica and Panama have received SALs from the World Bank, which involve the recipient country in fairly stringent conditions. The World Bank continues to finance projects in all Central American republics (except Nicaragua) and is expected to play a more influential role (together with the IMF) through its structural adjustment facility.

The IMF has, in recent years, signed standby agreements with all Central American republics except Nicaragua. While Nicaragua accumulated debt arrears with the World Bank, risking expulsion at one point, it has scrupulously serviced its debts inherited from Somoza with the IMF. As a result, relations are formally correct, but the Fund has received no formal request for a standby credit from Nigaragua since the 1979 revolution. Elsewhere, the IMF has had mixed success with its policy of lending subject to conditions. The majority of loans since 1980 have eventually been suspended because of non-compliance, but the Fund has nevertheless helped to push through some of the structural reforms required for a successful external and internal adjustment, especially in Costa Rica and Honduras.[7]

The IDB remains committed fundamentally to project finance and its lending remains least subject to conditionality. This policy came under attack at the March 1986 meeting of the IDB in San José, Costa Rica, but it is expected to survive. At the same meeting, the IDB created the Inter-American Investment Corporation as an instrument for promoting the private sector; Western European countries[8] are entitled to participate in the Corporation and by April 1986 both France and Switzerland had ratified the agreement. Like the World Bank, the IDB ceased lending to Nicaragua despite repeated requests by the latter for loans.

The regional organisations consist of those Central American institutions which receive funding from Western Europe in support of their operations. The most important is the Central American Bank for

Economic Integration (CABEI), which has altered its regulations to permit membership by Western European countries; several Western European countries (notably Spain) have indicated their willingness to join. CABEI continues to lend for project and balance-of-payments purposes to all countries of the region, including Nicaragua, and maintains a high reputation for technical competence and resistance to political pressures. It is one of the few institutions of the CACM which has continued to function efficiently in recent years.

Western Europe's combined voting power in all these organisations (except CABEI) is substantial; with the exception of the IDB (where the combined vote is 11 per cent), the voting power of Western Europe rivals that of the United States. This electoral strength has not been used, however, because neither Western Europe as a whole nor the EEC countries have voted in harmony. On the contrary, voting patterns have conformed to narrowly conceived national interests; the British, for example, have voted against loans for Nicaragua on spurious technical grounds, the Swedes have voted against all lending to Guatemala, the Dutch opposed loans to the Magaña government in El Salvador, the Germans changed their policies as soon as Christian Democrats were elected in Guatemala and El Salvador and so on. As a result, there has been a serious inconsistency between publicly-stated Western European policies and the behaviour of some of the international institutions. In particular, the EEC's efforts to support the Contadora countries in their search for a peaceful solution to the Central American crisis and the EEC's public statements in favour of an even-handed approach to Nicaragua have been undermined by the isolationist policies of the WB, IMF and IDB to which Western European countries belong. There is therefore a sharp contrast between the lending policy of these institutions and the bilateral/multilateral lending policy of Western Europe as a whole, which (see Tables 6.4 and 6.5) has shown a bias towards Nicaragua.

## THE CO-OPERATION AGREEMENT

Central American countries (including Nicaragua) have been keen to see Western Europe play a more active role in the region for several reasons; first, increased access to the wealthy Western European market is seen as important; secondly, Western European involvement is seen as a useful counterweight to US influence and, thirdly, it has been thought desirable to strengthen cultural ties.

The initial efforts to provoke a greater involvement by Western Europe were most unsuccessful. A major regional effort (co-ordinated by the IDB) to increase funding (private and public) from Western Europe was launched in September 1983; despite the fact that all five Central American countries had participated seriously in this venture, it was a resounding failure with no response at all from Western Europe.

A year later, however, all EEC foreign ministers took part in the San José conference together with the Contadora group (Mexico, Venezuela, Colombia and Panama) and the Central American republics. Credit for achieving this high-level commitment by the EEC to Central America has been claimed by various governments (and individuals); whatever the reasons for the EEC's change of heart it did produce a transformation in the priority attached to Central America by the Community and a commitment to increased economic assistance.

Some of the details of this commitment were revealed fourteen months later in November 1985, when the EEC signed a Co-operation Agreement with Central America (including Panama). Emphasis was placed on efforts to promote regional integration and a revival of intra-regional trade; to find ways of increasing trade between the two regions and overcoming trade barriers (including the application of most-favoured-nation treatment to all eligible trade flows);[9] to examine through a Joint Committee ways of improving the Generalised System of Preferences to the advantage of Central America. Finally, the EEC committed itself to a 'substantial' increase in the total volume of aid given to Central America during the five-year duration of the agreement.

Central America, it is fair to say, was somewhat disappointed by the Co-operation Agreement. The preference given to ACP countries by the EEC was not eroded and an increase in multilateral aid even to $100 million per year would still represent a minor contribution compared with bilateral aid from the United States and (in the case of Nicaragua) the Soviet Union. None the less, the Co-operation Agreement must be put into perspective; compared with the negative response given to Central America in September 1983, the Co-operation Agreement represents a positive step forward. The EEC has moved slowly, but the direction of change has each year been in favour of greater commitment. Given the flexible nature of the Agreement and the commitment of the EEC to a meeting at ministerial level with Central America once a year, it is by no means impossible that the Agreement could be strengthened and extended over the next few years.

Success in this area will depend on co-operation among the Central American states (which include Panama for purposes of the agreement). A united front of Central American republics with a clearly-defined agenda for increased economic co-operation could possibly extract additional concessions from the EEC. A divided Central America, on the other hand, is unlikely to persuade the EEC to risk offending the ACP states by increasing co-operation with the region.

## Notes

1. Since 1979, the ratio of nominal exports to nominal GDP has declined in all republics as the terms of trade have turned against Central America. The decline in the ratio has been particularly severe in Nicaragua.
2. See Eurostat, Analysis of EC–Latin American Trade, Brussels, 1984.
3. STABEX is the scheme in Lomé under which exporters of certain primary products receive compensation for shortfalls in earnings.
4. These quotas were suspended early in 1986 following a surge in prices in consequence of a fall in Brazilian production. They were reimposed in October 1987.
5. Most of the world's sugar exports are not in fact sold in world markets. Central America (except Nicaragua) sells most of its exportable production to the United States under quotas, while Nicaragua's former US quota was absorbed by Algeria and Iran.
6. The Baker plan, named after the US Treasury Secretary, calls for an increase in multilateral and private commercial lending to fifteen of the most hard-pressed debtor countries. None of them are in Central America, although debt problems in Costa Rica and Nicaragua are as severe as anywhere.
7. For further details, see Chapter 4.
8. Not all Western European, or even EEC, countries are members of the IDB; only members are entitled to participate in the Corporation.
9. The practical importance of most-favoured-nation treatment is likely to be small. The Co-operation Agreement specifically excludes advantages granted under Customs Unions or advantages granted to certain countries in conformity with the General Agreement on Tarriffs and Trade. Most-favoured-nation treatment does not therefore mean that Central America will enjoy the same advantages as ACP countries.

# Part III

# Central America in Crisis

# 7 The Balance-of-Payments Crisis and Adjustment Programmes in Central America

## INTRODUCTION

Four events of unusual significance for Central America occurred in 1979: oil prices rose sharply, world interest rates started to increase, the Sandinista-led revolution succeeded in overthrowing Somoza's government in Nicaragua, and General Romero was ousted in El Salvador. The first two events had a direct impact on the region's external payments, but the other two (although usually viewed in political or even geopolitical terms) also had a profound influence on the regional balance of payments. In the years after 1979, each republic at one time or another experienced a major problem of external disequilibrium, and it is for this reason that the title of this chapter refers to the balance-of-payments *crisis* in the singular.

The initial response to the crisis was uniform. Each republic tried to surmount the disequilibrium through additional finance, the implicit assumption being that the disequilibrium was temporary;[1] at first, no serious effort at adjustment was made, although El Salvador and Nicaragua could argue with some justification that their economies had already 'adjusted' through the decline in economic activity associated with civil unrest.[2]

The need for adjustment could not be postponed indefinitely, however, and the financing (FN) phase gave way to an adjustment phase beginning in general in 1981. These adjustment programmes varied in content and impact, as each republic adapted the policy mix to its own peculiar socioeconomic and political environment. Thus, we may talk of adjustment *programmes* in the plural.

Unlike many other republics in Latin America, the Central American republics had in general avoided the need for adjustment at the time of the first oil crisis (1973–4). This was due to the sharp improvement in the external terms of trade (TOT) starting in 1975, which by 1976 had pushed TOT above the pre-oil crisis level.[3] Deviations of real GDP from the trend rate of growth during much of the 1970s are therefore more easily explained by natural disasters (hurricanes, earthquakes) than by adjustment programmes.[4]

Consequently, Central America entered its adjustment phase after the second oil crisis with no recent experience of International Monetary Fund (IMF) conditionality. Talks did take place with the Fund and several credits were approved subject to conditionality;[5] all such credits agreed before the second half of 1982 were suspended, however, as a result of the recipients failing to meet IMF-agreed targets.

We may therefore speak of an 'adjustment without conditionality' (AWOC) phase covering in each republic part of the period 1980 to 1982. As we shall see, adjustment certainly occurred, but it did not in general comply with IMF conditions, while two republics (El Salvador and Nicaragua) did not in any case operate under IMF conditionality during this phase.[6]

In 1982, the need for an IMF-agreed programme of adjustment subject to conditionality became more pressing, as the problem of external finance and debt rescheduling became more acute. By 1983, all Central American republics (except Nicaragua) were involved in IMF-inspired adjustment programmes. Thus we may speak of an 'adjustment with conditionality' (AWIC) phase covering part of the period 1982 to 1984, while the performance of the Nicaraguan economy deviates from the general pattern after 1982.

The AWIC phase (excluding Nicaragua) had ended everywhere by early 1984; by the end of the year the beginnings of a very modest recovery were apparent in Central America and it is tempting to speak of a 'post-adjustment recovery' phase. Only Costa Rica reached a new agreement with the Fund,[7] although Guatemala and Honduras may do so.[8] The recovery since the end of 1983 lacks firm foundations, however, and the underlying external disequilibrium has not been resolved; there is also an inconsistency between short-term policy and the region's long-term needs.

## ORIGINS OF THE BALANCE-OF-PAYMENTS CRISIS

The choice of finance over adjustment is appropriate where the balance-of-payments (BOP) disequilibrium is temporary in nature. A disturbance to BOP equilibrium can be external or internal in origin, but this should not affect the choice between finance and adjustment.[9]

The initial decision in Central America to respond to the BOP crisis with finance therefore hinges on whether the disturbances to BOP equilibrium could be construed as temporary.

The outward and visible sign of the crisis was the massive loss of gross international reserves in the years after 1978, although significantly this decline begins earlier in Nicaragua. The problem is therefore one of determining the causes of this reserve loss. The deterioration in the current account BOP deficit is often taken as an indicator of reserve loss, but this is not appropriate where (as in Central America) the current account is traditionally in deficit and financed 'autonomously' through long-term capital flows.

A more appropriate indicator is the basic balance, i.e. the current account deficit adjusted for long-term capital flows. We may therefore ask what proportion of the reserve loss was due to a deterioration in the basic balance and what proportion was due to changes in short-term capital flows (including net errors and omissions).

The answer is provided by Table 7.1, which shows that during the period of heavy reserve loss the major cause of disequilibrium was changes in short-term capital flows in El Salvador, Guatemala and

*Table* 7.1 Balance-of-payments contributions to cumulative reserve losses (inclusive of exceptional financing)

| | *Period* (*end-year*) | (*1*) % | (*2*) % | (*3*) *Total loss* (*million SDR*) |
|---|---|---|---|---|
| Costa Rica | 1978–81 | +72.7 | +27.3 | 774.2 |
| El Salvador | 1978–81 | −8.5 | +108.5 | 399.6 |
| Guatemala | 1978–81 | +21.2 | +78.8 | 492.6 |
| Honduras | 1979–82 | +113.6 | −13.6 | 194.8 |
| Nicaragua | 1977–80 | −67.9 | +167.9 | 288.7 |

*Notes*:
Col. (1) = percentage contribution of current account deficit net of long-term capital flows to cumulative reserve loss.
Col. (2) = percentage contribution of short-term capital flows (inclusive of net errors and omissions, but exclusive of exceptional financing) to cumulative reserve loss.
Col. (3) = reserve loss defined to include exceptional financing, e.g. payments arrears, rescheduling of debt in arrears, loans from Central American Monetary Stabilisation Fund.

*Source*: IMF, *Balance of Payments Yearbook* (1984).

Nicaragua, while in Costa Rica changes in such flows accounted for nearly 30 per cent of the deterioration.

It may be objected that Table 7.1 is distorted by the inclusion of net errors and omissions in short-term capital flows. This is unlikely to be true; the sign of 'net errors and omissions' in Central America's BOP presentations is not random. On the contrary, 75 per cent of all observations in the IMF *Balance of Payments Yearbook* since 1975 (inclusive) have appeared with a negative sign, suggesting that 'net errors and omissions' is a vehicle for capital flight.

The key element in short-term capital flows has been 'other short-term capital of other sectors'. This includes changes in the US bank accounts of Central American residents, the other important entry being trade credits. The drying-up of trade credits after 1978 is clearly related to developments in the international financial system and could therefore be construed optimistically as 'temporary', but the outflow of private capital to US bank accounts requires a more sophisticated explanation.

The two conventional explanations of such outflows are interest-rate differentials and the expectation of exchange-rate depreciation. Neither carries much weight in an understanding of Central America's capital flight problem. It is true that US interest rates rose sharply in 1979, but this was matched to some extent in Central America. Indeed, Costa Rica launched its ill-fated 'financial liberalisation' programme (with a sharp increase in interest rates) in October 1978,[10] but this could not prevent an increase in 1979 of SDR 62.3 million (US $80.5 million) in claims on US banks.

Expectation of exchange-rate depreciation is also unconvincing as an explanation of private capital flows. It is true that Nicaragua devalued in 1979 shortly before the fall of Somoza, but the outflow of private capital began in 1977; similarly, the Costa Rican currency was floated in December 1980, but the outflow began much earlier. Meanwhile, capital outflows were of great importance from Guatemala and El Salvador, two countries with a very long history of exchange-rate stability.[11]

Both interest-rate differentials and exchange-rate expectations no doubt provide part of the explanation for the private capital outflow. More convincing, however, is the concept of political uncertainty as a cause of capital flight; thus, Nicaraguan investors, aware as early as 1977 that the future of the Somoza government was not secure, began to withdraw capital. By the time of Somoza's fall, Nicaraguan capital flight was more or less complete (at least in its first stage), but the

Sandinista victory provoked capital flight elsewhere.[12] This was reinforced by the fall of General Romero in October 1979 in El Salvador and by the sequence of events throughout the region.[13]

Much of this capital flight was clearly not of a temporary nature. In the Nicaraguan case, the capital outflow (much of it belonging to the Somoza family) was lost forever, and the probability of capital repatriation in El Salvador, following the reform programme of early 1980,[14] could only be considered low. Both Guatemala and Costa Rica, on the other hand, could reasonably have expected a reversal of the capital outflow if the regional political environment improved. As the environment steadily deteriorated, however, it became clear that a reversal of capital flight could not be expected in the short term.

Despite the problems created by capital flight, virtually nothing was done to correct it. During 1980, Guatemala and Honduras introduced exchange control, but it was very mild and largely ineffective; El Salvador legalised dollar deposit accounts towards the end of 1980 in an effort to reverse capital outflows, but the result was unimpressive. Nicaragua and El Salvador nationalised their banking systems in 1979 and 1980 respectively, but by then the bulk of the capital outflows had already taken place. In effect, a decision was taken at least tacitly in each republic to finance the outflows by running down reserves accumulated during the years of high coffee prices in the second half of the 1970s.

The other element in the balance-of-payments crisis was the deterioration in some republics of the basic balance (see Table 7.1). In this context, it *is* relevant to ask what happened to the current account deficit, since the cause of the widening basic balance deficit was not a decline in long-term capital outflows, but an increase in the current account deficit not financed by additional long-term flows.

Several factors contributed to the widening of current account deficits in the three republics (Costa Rica, Guatemala, Honduras) where a deterioration of the basic balance was a factor in reserve loss. One was the rise in the price of oil; another was the fall in the price of coffee from its all-time peak in 1977. Between 1978 and 1981, the TOT for the region fell by 29.7 per cent.

The change in the TOT is by no means the whole story, however, as world interest rate rises also added to the cost of servicing external debt. As Table 7.2 shows, this additional interest charge accounts for a substantial part of the deterioration in the current account deficit in the cases of Costa Rica and Honduras.

The table shows that coffee, oil and interest costs are sufficient to

*Table* 7.2 Contributions to deterioration in current account deficit

| | *Period* | *Increase in deficit (million SDR)* | *(1)* % | *(2)* % | *(3)* % | *(4)* % |
|---|---|---|---|---|---|---|
| Costa Rica | 1978–80 | + 219.3 | + 27.3 | + 33.4 | + 39.3 | + 0.1 |
| Guatemala | 1978–81 | + 281.0 | + 38.6 | + 64.9 | + 19.8 | − 23.3 |
| Honduras | 1978–81 | + 131.1 | + 16.7 | + 59.0 | + 48.2 | − 23.9 |

*Notes*:
Col. (1) = fall in value of coffee exports as percentage of increase in deficit.
Col. (2) = increase in value of oil imports as percentage of increase in deficit.
Col. (3) = increase in debt service interest payments as percentage of increase in deficit.
Col. (4) = deterioration in current account other than items (a) to (c) as percentage of increase in deficit (a minus sign denotes an improvement).

*Source*: IMF, *Balance of Payments Yearbook* (1983).

account for most of the change in the current account during the period when the deficit was increasing. In addition, Guatemala suffered badly because of a sharp fall in tourist earnings as a result of the adverse publicity surrounding the country during the Lucas García regime (1978–82). One should also note that the contribution of the 'other' column (4) in Table 7.2 to BOP deterioration was negative or zero. This column is roughly equivalent to movements in the non-oil, non-coffee trade account, and a negative sign means an improvement; much of this was due to favourable movements in the prices of traditional exports (e.g. sugar, bananas, cotton, beef) together with a small decline in the volume of imports.[15]

Following the first oil crisis of 1973–4, adjustment was rendered unnecessary through a sharp increase in coffee prices. This time, however, coffee prices could only be expected to fall, so that the deterioration of TOT from 1979 onwards could not be regarded as temporary; in addition, uncertainties about the world economy and the revival of monetarism suggested that the rise in interest rates might not be temporary either. Thus, prudent policy-making would have counselled at least a modest adjustment programme following the balance of payments deterioration in 1979.

El Salvador and Nicaragua did indeed 'adjust', although policy-making played little part in the programme of adjustment. Both countries ran a trade and current account surplus in 1979, as imports fell even in value terms in response to lower levels of economic activity. In Nicaragua, the value of imports was halved between 1977 and 1979, and the case for financing in response to balance-of-payments pressures after 1979 was very strong; the same could be said for El Salvador, where imports continued to decline in 1980.

Elsewhere, however, the failure to adopt adjustment programmes was a serious error, given that the BOP crisis could not be construed as temporary. The irresponsible resort to finance, particularly in Guatemala and Costa Rica, inevitably increased the burden when adjustment programmes were finally adopted.

## THE FINANCING PHASE

Any division between a financing and an adjustment phase in response to a BOP crisis is to some extent arbitrary, because there will usually be elements of both in any policy mix. Central America is no exception, yet in each republic there is a clear contrast between the first response to the crisis, when financing was dominant, and the second, when adjustment prevailed.

As Table 7.3 shows, the financing (FN) phase came to a halt at the end of 1980 in Costa Rica and El Salvador; in Honduras and Nicaragua it ended by the close of 1981, while in Guatemala the adjustment phase was delayed until 1982. In each case the transition was marked by a package of emergency measures.

Although the initial response to BOP difficulties in each republic was a resort to finance, this was not sufficient to prevent a slowdown in the rate of growth of real GDP. On the contrary, the massive capital outflow documented in the previous section had as its corollary a collapse of private investment; by 1979, private investment had peaked in all republics except Honduras (where it peaked in 1980) and by 1981 it had fallen to nearly half its peak level in Costa Rica and Guatemala, 38 per cent of its peak level in El Salvador and 91 per cent in Honduras.[16]

Two factors helped to offset the rapid decline in aggregate demand implied by the private investment figures. In turn, this made possible positive growth throughout the region, although at a much lower rate than in 1978 and 1979 (except in Nicaragua, where postwar reconstruction lifted the economy by over 10 per cent in 1980).

The first stimulus to aggregate demand was provided by the Central

*Table* 7.3 Responses to balance-of-payments crisis

| | *Costa Rica* | *El Salvador* | *Guatemala* | *Honduras* | *Nicaragua* |
|---|---|---|---|---|---|
| Financing (FN) phase | Up to September 1980 | Up to November 1980 | Up to mid-1982 | Up to April 1981 | Up to September 1981 |
| Adjustment without conditionality (AWOC) phase | Up to December 1982 | Up to July 1982 | Up to September 1983 | Up to November 1982 | Up to end 1982 |
| Adjustment with conditionality (AWIC) phase | Up to January 1984 | Up to August 1983 | Up to July 1984 | Up to January 1984 | Not applicable |
| Post-adjustment phase | In progress | In progress | In progress | In progress | Not applicable |

American Common Market (CACM) with intra-regional trade in 1980 growing by 31 per cent and lifting its value above $1 billion for the first (and only) time in its history. However, nearly 70 per cent of the increase in trade between 1979 and 1980 was accounted for by increased Nicaraguan purchases. This rate of increase could not be sustained, and Nicaragua soon found itself unable to pay its debts arising from the imbalance in intra-regional trade. Between 1980 and 1982, Nicaragua's cumulative deficit with Central America on intra-regional trade reached some $425 million, and the failure of the Sandinista government to service this debt was one of the factors behind the decline of CACM after 1980.

The second stimulus to real aggregate demand came from public investments. While private investment was falling, public capital expenditure rose rapidly between 1978 and 1980 in Costa Rica and Honduras. Expansion continued until 1981 in Guatemala and Nicaragua[17] (where the increase began after 1979) and even in El Salvador a sharp fall in public investment was prevented until 1982.

The increase in public capital expenditure was much faster than the rise in revenue. Indeed, by 1980 (Costa Rica, El Salvador, Nicaragua) or by 1981 (Guatemala, Honduras), government revenue was not even sufficient to cover *current* expenditure and the whole of the capital budget had to be financed by borrowing. The budget deficit as a percentage of GDP rose sharply, reaching over 8 per cent in Costa Rica in 1980 and over 7 per cent elsewhere in 1981.[18]

Between 1978 and 1980 (i.e. during the core of the financing stage), there is a correlation between the size of the budget deficit and the rate of inflation. Only a small part of the variation in the inflation rate, however, can be explained by the budget deficit, as the major factors (as always in Central America)[19] were changes in dollar import prices (including oil) coupled with exchange-rate devaluation (in Nicaragua and Costa Rica). Indeed, as Table 7.4 makes clear, the fall in the inflation rate between 1980 and 1981 in some republics took place against a background of rising budget deficits; the subsequent decline in the budget deficit appears to have had little impact on the inflation rate.

The increase in the size of the budget deficit during the FN phase may not have had much immediate impact on inflation, but it did have an important bearing on domestic credit expansion. Throughout the financing phase the bulk of the deficit was financed internally, with Honduras being the only republic to rely more heavily on external finance (see Table 7.4). As a result, bank credit extended to the public sector rocketed (see Table 7.5) with most of the increase coming from the Central Bank in each republic. This huge increase was not offset by declines in credit outstanding to the private sector (see Table 7.5) and domestic credit expansion (DCE) was substantial during the FN phase, running far ahead of inflation.

During 1978 (i.e. before the BOP crisis), there was very roughly a 1:1 ratio between the stock of bank credit and the flow of imports.[20] After 1978, this ratio (see Table 7.5) rose sharply in all republics, as DCE outpaced the rise in imports even in value terms; this suggests an increase in liquidity, with the public forced to hold unwanted cash balances leading to a rise in inflation. This did not happen, as we have seen; instead, the money stock expanded in line with nominal GDP after 1978, leaving velocity more or less unchanged (see Table 7.5).[21]

What happened is that the public successfully converted its excess money holdings into foreign currency, draining international reserves out of the banking system and forcing the Central Banks in particular to borrow massively in the international capital market. By the end of the FN phase, net foreign assets had turned or were about to turn negative in each republic, and the inflationary pressures usually accompanying excessive DCE were only avoided by converting the excess into

*Table* 7.4 Budget deficits ($ million) and inflation rates (%)

| | 1978 | 1979 | 1980 | 1981 | 1982 | 1983 |
|---|---|---|---|---|---|---|
| *Costa Rica* | | | | | | |
| Budget deficit | 151 | 265 | 428 | 61 | 69 | 134 |
| Internal (net) | 148 | 235 | 342 | 38 | 40 | 110 |
| External (net) | 24 | 49 | 35 | 18 | 23 | 27 |
| Inflation (%) | 5.9 | 9.2 | 18.2 | 37.0 | 90.1 | 32.6 |
| Food (%) | 10.3 | 12.6 | 21.7 | 36.8 | 113.6 | 32.2 |
| Housing (%) | 4.1 | 5.6 | 16.8 | 35.5 | 51.7 | 29.2 |
| *El Salvador* | | | | | | |
| Budget deficit | 63 | 25 | 199 | 283 | 275 | 98 |
| Internal (net) | 26 | 22 | 164 | 226 | 147 | 27 |
| External (net) | 21 | 16 | 50 | 76 | 94 | 105 |
| Inflation (%) | 12.9 | 8.6 | 17.4 | 14.8 | 11.7 | 13.1 |
| Food (%) | 10.6 | 8.7 | 19.6 | 17.9 | 10.6 | 13.4 |
| Housing (%) | 22.9 | 8.6 | 17.1 | 9.3 | 11.7 | 15.1 |
| *Guatemala* | | | | | | |
| Budget deficit | 70 | 179 | 369 | 638 | 410 | 295 |
| Internal (net) | 15 | −50 | 236 | 452 | 441 | 251 |
| External (net) | 94 | 121 | 111 | 96 | 95 | 80 |
| Inflation (%) | 7.9 | 11.4 | 10.7 | 11.5 | 0.2 | 5.8* |
| Food (%) | 4.6 | 10.2 | 11.3 | 11.3 | −2.8 | 7.0* |
| Housing (%) | 12.4 | 16.4 | 15.9 | 12.6 | 0.9 | −1.7* |
| *Honduras* | | | | | | |
| Budget deficit | 124 | 95 | 198 | 203 | 340 | 282 |
| Internal (net) | 37 | 28 | 54 | 92 | 145 | 134 |
| External (net) | 82 | 67 | 127 | 127 | 188 | 125 |
| Inflation (%) | 5.7 | 12.1 | 18.1 | 9.4 | 9.4 | 8.9 |
| Food (%) | 6.2 | 11.4 | 17.1 | 7.3 | 6.7 | 5.3 |
| Housing (%) | 5.3 | 14.7 | 15.5 | 10.3 | 6.6 | 14.0 |
| *Nicaragua* | | | | | | |
| Budget deficit | 166 | 103 | 143 | 262 | 577 | 958 |
| Internal (net) | 85 | 79 | 113 | 91 | 364 | 1000 |
| External (net) | 9 | 15 | 75 | 58 | 99 | 104 |
| Inflation (%) | 4.5 | 48.2 | 35.3 | 23.9 | 24.8 | 31.0 |
| Food (%) | 3.5 | 63.4 | 49.1 | 29.0 | 29.1 | 41.5 |
| Housing (%) | 6.4 | 29.9 | 13.9 | 20.7 | 21.2 | 16.0 |

*Notes*: The difference between (i) internal (net) and external (net) finance and (ii) the budget deficit is accounted for by use of cash balances.

*Obtained by splicing the new index (April 1983 = 100) on to the old series and comparing mid-year figures. See Banco de Guatemala, *Boletín Estadístico*, July–September 1984.

*Sources*: Consejo Monetario Centroamericano, *Boletín Estadístico 1983* (San José, 1984), unless otherwise stated.

*Table* 7.5 Credit, money and quasi-money ($ million), end-year balances

| | *1978* | *1979* | *1980* | *1981* | *1982* | *1983* |
|---|---|---|---|---|---|---|
| *Costa Rica* | | | | | | |
| Credit | 1450 | 2002 | 2525 | 691 | 877 | 1098 |
| Public | 416 | 760 | 1119 | 323 | 420 | 458 |
| Private | 1034 | 1242 | 1406 | 368 | 457 | 641 |
| Credit/imports ratio | 1.24 | 1.43 | 1.66 | 0.57 | 0.98 | 1.11 |
| Money (M1) | 589 | 649 | 741 | 267 | 374 | 443 |
| Money/GDP ratio | 0.17 | 0.16 | 0.17 | 0.096 | 0.15 | 0.15 |
| Quasi-money | 674 | 940 | 1108 | 531 | 701 | 947 |
| *El Salvador* | | | | | | |
| Credit | 1066 | 1299 | 1664 | 1997 | 2228 | 2226 |
| Public | 178 | 304 | 793 | 1018 | 1128 | 1019 |
| Private | 888 | 995 | 871 | 979 | 1100 | 1207 |
| Credit/imports ratio | 1.04 | 1.27 | 1.73 | 2.03 | 2.6 | 2.5 |
| Money (M1) | 451 | 543 | 590 | 582 | 603 | 579 |
| Money/GDP ratio | 0.15 | 0.16 | 0.165 | 0.168 | 0.169 | 0.15 |
| Quasi-money | 494 | 482 | 459 | 583 | 653 | 802 |
| *Guatemala* | | | | | | |
| Credit | 1262 | 1385 | 1831 | 2431 | 3076 | 3469 |
| Public | 382 | 332 | 542 | 983 | 1526 | 1714 |
| Private | 880 | 1053 | 1289 | 1448 | 1550 | 1755 |
| Credit/imports ratio | 0.91 | 0.92 | 1.15 | 1.45 | 2.22 | 3.06 |
| Money (M1) | 624 | 693 | 709 | 738 | 749 | 787 |
| Money/GDP ratio | 0.10 | 0.10 | 0.09 | 0.086 | 0.086 | 0.087 |
| Quasi-money | 865 | 915 | 1074 | 1253 | 1540 | 1473 |
| *Honduras* | | | | | | |
| Credit | 771 | 909 | 1028 | 1182 | 1337 | 1499 |
| Public | 170 | 230 | 296 | 377 | 451 | 516 |
| Private | 601 | 680 | 733 | 805 | 886 | 983 |
| Credit/imports ratio | 1.1 | 1.09 | 1.01 | 1.23 | 1.88 | 1.98 |
| Money (M1) | 267 | 297 | 336 | 353 | 378 | 431 |
| Money/GDP ratio | 0.15 | 0.14 | 0.14 | 0.13 | 0.13 | 0.145 |
| Quasi-money | 305 | 325 | 347 | 387 | 491 | 585 |
| *Nicaragua* | | | | | | |
| Credit | 1146 | 1012 | 1521 | 2020 | 2612 | 3544 |
| Public | 143 | 202 | 498 | 598 | 909 | 1584 |
| Private | 1002 | 810 | 1023 | 1422 | 1703 | 1959 |
| Credit/import ratio | 1.93 | 2.81 | 1.71 | 2.02 | 3.37 | 4.44 |
| Money (M1) | 245 | 302 | 405 | 523 | 641 | 1089 |
| Money/GDP ratio | 0.12 | 0.19 | 0.19 | 0.20 | 0.22 | 0.30 |
| Quasi-money | 347 | 204 | 256 | 307 | 367 | 504 |

*Source*: IMF, *International Finance Statistics, 1984 Yearbook*.

capital flight. This reduced the stock of money of external origin and contributed to a lowering of overall monetary expansion.[22]

The price paid for this largesse on the part of the authorities was a massive rise in external public indebtedness. In the three years after the end of 1978 (see Table 7.6), the disbursed public external debt doubled or more than doubled in all republics; credit from official sources rose most rapidly in the 'war-torn' republics, while elsewhere private credit rose most rapidly. Because of the relatively low starting base for private credit, however, only Costa Rica funded more than 50 per cent of its increase in public external indebtedness from private sources.

The rise in debt during the FN phase was so large that it is not unreasonable to blame much of the current debt problems on the increases incurred in this phase. A considerable share, for example, of the commercial debt (the rescheduling of which has caused such problems for Costa Rica, Honduras and Nicaragua) was contracted during the financing stage. Although adjustment, as we shall see, has its problems, failure to adjust also imposes costs: the increase in the debt burden is one of them.[23]

During the FN phase, several governments paid lip-service to the need for adjustment programmes and some (Costa Rica, Honduras, Guatemala) even reached agreement with the IMF on standby credits (see Table 7.7). In all cases except one these credits were suspended and the exception (Guatemala in November 1981) hardly counts, as the standby was a first credit transfer which is *de facto* free of conditions and is wholly disbursed at the start of the programme; thus it cannot

*Table* 7.6 Disbursed public external debt, increase from end-1978 to end-1981 ($ million)

| | *Total* | % | *Official* | % | *Private* | % | % *Increase due to private sources* |
|---|---|---|---|---|---|---|---|
| Costa Rica | 1302.5 | 137 | 424.2 | 82 | 878.3 | 203 | 67.4 |
| El Salvador | 329.1 | 99 | 339.1 | 108 | − 9.9 | − 47 | Negative |
| Guatemala | 505.5 | 166 | 444.9 | 150 | 60.6 | 904 | 12.0 |
| Honduras | 639.1 | 107 | 381.8 | 79 | 257.0 | 227 | 40.0 |
| Nicaragua | 1126.3 | 116 | 713.0 | 130 | 413.0 | 98 | 37.0 |

*Source*: World Bank, *World Debt Tables* (1983–4).

later be suspended if the borrowing country fails to meet the 'conditions'.

Why did the adjustment programmes in Costa Rica, Guatemala and Honduras fail? In the Guatemalan case, there is no mystery; the Fund's conditions included a rise in interest rates and a reduction in the public sector borrowing requirement (PSBR); interest rates were raised in late 1981, but significantly they were lowered immediately the programme expired,[24] and no action was taken to lower the PSBR other than a cut in capital expenditure.

In the Honduran case, the three-year Extended Fund Facility (EFF) of February 1980 was suspended because the authorities failed to meet PSBR targets. During 1980, Honduras introduced new taxes and raised existing ones (mainly direct) and government revenue rose sharply by 20 per cent. Government expenditure, however, rose even more rapidly on both current and capital account and the PSBR doubled over its 1979 level.

The Honduran failure cannot be attributed to the indexed nature of expenditure. Only half the rise in current expenditure was due to wages and salaries, the remainder being due to the increase in purchases of goods and services. The Honduran public sector is highly decentralised, and the armed forces in particular, in anticipation of the return to civilian rule, appear to have increased their share of the government budget and contributed in no small measure to the failure of the agreement with the IMF.

While the outgoing military administration of General Policarpo Paz García faced few problems in raising public revenue in Honduras, the incoming civilian administration of President Carazo in Costa Rica (1978–82) found itself in the opposite position. Carazo and his economic team were committed to a strategy of financial liberalisation on taking office and looked with favour on a reduced public sector and a shrunken PSBR. Minister of Finance Hernán Saenz recognised early in 1980 that an adjustment programme was needed to solve the BOP crisis, and the Carazo administration welcomed the one-year standby credit agreed with the IMF in March 1980.

The relationship with the Fund, therefore, could not have been more cordial, with both sides taking a similar view on policy. By November, however, the credit had been suspended and a year later Carazo expelled an IMF mission from the country.[25] What went wrong?

The Fund's conditions for the March loan were conventional (see Table 7.7), but the stumbling-block proved to be raising additional tax revenue. While monetary policy (particularly interest rates) was firmly

*Table* 7.7 IMF programmes

| *Country* | *Costa Rica* | *Costa Rica* | *Costa Rica* | *Costa Rica* | *El Salvador* | *Guatemala* | *Guatemala* | *Honduras* | *Honduras* | *Honduras* |
|---|---|---|---|---|---|---|---|---|---|---|
| *Date approved* | March 1980 | June 1981 | December 1982 | March 1985 | July 1982 | November 1981 | September 1983 | February 1980 | August 1981 | November 1982 |
| *Date suspended* | Nov. 1980 (government failed to meet March, June, Sept., quarterly targets) | Oct. 1981 (government introduced new restrictions on imports, defaulted on debt, etc.) | | April 1986, because of budget deficit | | All disbursed in 11/81 because it was a first credit tranche | July 1984 because of refusal to restore VAT to 10% | August 1980 because of budget deficit | Early 1982 because of budget deficit | |
| *Type* | 1-year standby | 3-year extended fund facility | 1-year standby | 13-month standby | 1-year standby | 1-year standby | 16-month standby | 3-year extended fund facility | Extended fund facility (re-established) | 13-month standby |
| *Budget deficit* | Target set for reduction of PSBR in 1980. Government agreed to raise coffee export tax and consumer taxes | Deficit to be limited to 9% in 1981; 7% in 1982 and 5% in 1983. To be achieved through an end of earmarking | Target set at 4.5% of GDP | Target set at 1.5% of GDP. Elimination of subsidies on basic foodstuffs | No target but government spending to be cut by 10% and taxes raised (new sales taxes and revised taxes on selective consumer items introduced mid-1983) | Reduction in PSBR | 3.7% of GDP in 1983; 3% in 1984. Revenue to reach 9.5% of GDP. Reduction in public expenditure (+ wage freeze) | Target stated as cuts in government expenditure programme and reduced number of government agencies | Same as in February 1980 | Curb on government expenditure. Increased customs duties, improved tax administration. Wage and spending cuts |

| | | | | | | | | | | |
|---|---|---|---|---|---|---|---|---|---|---|
| *Net domestic assets of Central Bank* | 3-monthly targets set up to 21.12.80 to limit increases | 3-monthly targets set up to 30.6.82 (falls targeted for 1982) | Ceilings set to increase flow of credit to private sector | | Limited demand management policy | | Limits placed on debt to banking system by government. Overall DCE growth to be consistent with targeted improvement in BOP | No details given | No details given | Reduction in growth of DCE from 20% in 1982 to 9% by end 1983 |
| *Central Bank credit to non-financial public sector* | 3-monthly target set up to 31.12.80 to limit increase in net credit extended | 3-monthly targets set up to 30.6.82 to limit credit to government | Ceilings set to increase flow of credit to private sector | | More balanced distribution of credit between private and public sector | | | No details given | No details given | No details given |
| *Interest rates* | The agreement supported the monetary reform of Oct. 1978, i.e. interest rates to be competitive with those abroad | | | | Rationalisation of interest rate and pricing policies | Rise in interest rates | Flexible interest rate policy to be pursued | | | |

*Table 7.7 cont.*

| *Country* | *Costa Rica* | *Costa Rica* | *Costa Rica* | *Costa Rica* | *El Salvador* | *Guatemala* | *Guatemala* | *Honduras* | *Honduras* | *Honduras* |
|---|---|---|---|---|---|---|---|---|---|---|
| *Public external debt* | Limits set on net increase for each quarter up to 31.12.80 | Increase in 1981 to be a *min* of $350m. ($183m. for non-fin. public sector). Increase in 1982 set at $381m.: 1983 $411m. | Short-term increase (1–5 yr) restricted to $50m. Short and medium-term (1–10 yr) restricted to $100m. Debt rescheduling and resumption of payments | Agreement reached on rescheduling 1985 and 1986 debts. A 10-yr rescheduling with 3-yr grace. $75m. in new money in 1985. None in 1986 | No link to external debt | Increase in foreign borrowing to help finance the public investment programme | Commercial arrears must be reduced by $50m. in 1983 and $100m. in 1984. New public debt ⩽ $300m. | No link to external debt | No link to external debt | Debt rescheduling linked to IMF programme. Finally achieved in 1985 |
| *Exchange rate and trade policies* | No exchange-rate commitment | A commitment to a flexible, but stable unitary exchange rate | Adjustment of exchange rate to narrow spread between interbank rates and free market rates to no more than 2% by end 1983. Achieved Nov. 1983. Revamping of export incentives to promote non-trad products | Devaluation from 45 to 48C. This devaluation, in Oct. 1984, was a precondition | Phased liberalisation of exchange and trade policies. NB: big changes in exchange-rate policy occur *before* and *after* 1-year standby | | Exchange restrictions to be relaxed. No new or stricter controls to be imposed on trade or capital transfers. No devaluation and no multiple exchange rate | No exchange-rate commitment | No exchange-rate commitment | No exchange-rate commitment |

under the control of the authorities, fiscal policy required the support of a national assembly in which the government enjoyed only a paper majority. Time and again, efforts to introduce tax reform packages failed, so that the government could not meet the end-March, -June, -September quarterly targets set by the Fund for fiscal and credit performance.

The lessons of the Costa Rican and Honduran débâcles are clear. Both the Fund and the borrowing government have to take cognisance of political reality. Although revenue increases in Costa Rica were desirable in 1980, it was clear to all neutral observers that they could not be obtained; similarly, the armed forces' desire in Honduras to protect their position after a decade of military rule was wholly predictable. Other programmes could have achieved the same adjustment, perhaps at a higher (economic) cost, but they were not explored;[26] even a higher cost adjustment programme in 1980, however, would have been preferable to a failed programme, because the discounted cost of the future adjustment programmes almost certainly proved greater.

## ADJUSTMENT WITHOUT CONDITIONALITY

The balance-of-payments crisis, with which the FN phase began, did not prove temporary and was reflected in a collapse of net foreign assets. The finance strategy therefore came to a halt when emergency measures were introduced in support of the BOP. This can be dated to September 1980 in Costa Rica, November 1980 in El Salvador, April 1981 in Honduras, September 1981 in Nicaragua and mid-1982 in Guatemala. Each republic then entered an adjustment phase which ended with the approval of a non-suspended IMF credit subject to conditions. This 'adjustment without conditionally' (AWOC) phase therefore runs until July 1982 in El Salvador, November 1982 in Honduras, December 1982 in Costa Rica and September 1983 in Guatemala.[27] In Nicaragua, this stage ended in a different way, as no agreement was reached with the IMF (see the later section on Nicaragua).

As in the FN stage, efforts were made to reach agreement with the IMF; both Costa Rica and Honduras received three-year EFFs in 1981, in June and August respectively, but the Fund suspended both within six months. In the Honduran case the size of the budget deficit proved the stumbling-block, while in Costa Rica the Fund took exception to the introduction of new restrictions on imports and the accumulation of debt arrears.

Adjustment programmes were in force, however, despite the problems with the Fund, and we may therefore observe how the five Central American republics approached the adjustment problem when not subject to IMF conditionality. Unfortunately, this cannot be viewed as a 'controlled experiment', because policy making operated under the shadow of conditionality, but one can still observe a difference of emphasis in policy between adjustment with and without IMF conditions.

The preferred method of adjustment in this phase was without doubt the increased use of import controls. Since such an increase is anathema to the Fund, it is not surprising that relations with the IMF were so strained. The increase in import controls consisted of changes in prior deposits, import licences, quotas, increased taxes and outright prohibition. In effect, the authorities graded imports according to their 'importance' and rationed foreign exchange accordingly.

In most republics this rationing was carried out with the help of multiple exchange rates. In El Salvador, a parallel market was authorised in late 1981,[28] and dealings were brought within the purlieu of the nationalised banking system in August 1982. Nicaragua legalised a parallel market in January 1982, also at a substantial discount, and in both republics a black or free market also operated, without government approval, although in El Salvador the black and parallel markets never drifted too far apart.[29] Guatemala and Honduras, the two republics with the oldest history of exchange-rate stability, did not introduce a parallel market in this phase. A black market existed in both republics, however, with the home currency trading at around 25 per cent below the official rate.

The republic which relied most heavily on the exchange rate as an instrument of policy was Costa Rica. In September 1980, 50 per cent of trade was channelled through a free market, and in December the colón was allowed to float freely. By the end of 1981, there were three exchange rates in force, all of which can be compared with the rate of 8.60 colones per US dollar in August 1980: an official rate of C20, which was used for about 1 per cent of transactions, an interbank rate of C36 (which applied to virtually all trade items) and a parallel rate of C39 for tourism in particular. By the end of 1982, when the adjustment without conditionality phase finished, the interbank rate was C40.50 and the parallel rate C45.

While measures to control imports were adopted vigorously and comprehensively, the same enthusiasm was not displayed in promoting exports. Nicaragua introduced new export incentives for agricultural products in the first quarter of 1982, followed by further incentives in the first quarter of 1983, but neither set of measures came close to compensating exporters for an effective *appreciation* of the real exchange rate. Guatemala also adopted an export incentives law in September 1982, and in December 1981 Costa Rica reduced the exchange taxes on export proceeds (introduced to enable the public sector to benefit from the windfall gains associated with devaluation). Nevertheless, the emphasis on export promotion was very slight during the period of adjustment without conditionality.

The combination of import restrictions, coupled with some export incentives, had a devastating effect on taxes on external trade. The revenue from these taxes fell sharply during the AWOC stage, although the decline began during the FN phase. With taxes on trade accounting for roughly one-third of government revenue in 1978, this sharp decline inevitably provoked a fiscal crisis.

During the AWOC phase, little attention was given to replacing lost income from trade taxes with other revenue sources, so that government revenue declined in real terms (except in Nicaragua) and in three cases (El Salvador, Guatemala, Honduras) was stagnant even in money terms. Nicaragua, on the other hand, succeeded in increasing revenue five-fold between 1979 and 1983, partly through the introduction of new taxes (e.g. a levy on the net worth of private assets), partly through increasing existing taxes (e.g. a 10 per cent surcharge on income tax), but above all through improvements in administration, tax evasion having been such a noticeable feature of the pre-revolutionary period.

Fiscal policy therefore tended to focus on expenditure cuts rather than revenue increases. A key element in several republics was wage restraint, with an outright freeze in El Salvador, strict control in Nicaragua and indexing to a basic wage basket in Costa Rica.[30] Some efforts were made to raise the price of public services, but price control continued to be widespread (making an increase in government transfers inevitable) and food subsidies were common. Even these efforts to lower expenditure, however, tended to be dwarfed by the pressure to raise expenditure in support of increased defence spending.

Under these circumstances, it is scarcely surprising that the size of the budget deficit continued to be a severe problem during the AWOC phase. Only Costa Rica and Guatemala managed to lower the deficit as a percentage of GDP in this phase, while in Nicaragua it reached 12.1 per cent in 1982. Even in Costa Rica and Guatemala, the value of bank credit to the public sector increased sharply, as the opportunities for funding the deficit externally became more and more restricted.

With private credit also increasing, although at a slower rate than public credit, the credit–import ratio continued to rise (see Table 7.5). As in the FN phase, however, this excess credit creation was not monetised; velocity remained stable and the inflation rate declined throughout the AWOC phase (except in Costa Rica where the rise to 90 per cent in 1982 was clearly caused by the collapse of the exchange rate).

There are several reasons why excess credit creation did not result in monetary instability during the AWOC phase. First, all republics except Guatemala raised interest rates, thereby increasing the attraction of non-monetary assets; secondly, the use of advanced import deposit schemes encouraged the growth of quasi-money, which was also promoted by interest-rate changes. Thirdly, capital flight continued during the AWOC phase, so that the decline in net foreign assets (and therefore money of external origin) was not reversed. Finally, exchange rate depreciation (whether *de facto* or *de jure*) soaked up a large proportion of any excess liquidity.

Policy during the AWOC phase relied most heavily on import controls, devaluation (often *de facto*) and exchange restrictions. This was reflected in a sharp fall in imports (see Table 7.8) and an improvement in the current account balance-of-payments deficit. This might be seen as a justification for AWOC phase policy and, indeed, one should not ignore the impact that a direct assault on the balance of payments can have. Nevertheless, several important caveats are in order.

First, the fall in imports was indiscriminate and affected trade within the Central American Common Market (CACM) as much as imports from outside the region.[31] To some extent the fall in the value of CACM trade after 1980 (see Table 7.8) was inevitable, since much of trade consisted of consumer goods, which were the most obvious candidates for import suppression; yet one country's CACM imports are another's exports, so that the effect of import restrictions was to increase the burden of adjustment (see the later section on this) above what was strictly necessary.

Secondly, the improvement in the balance-of-payments position was achieved partly through accumulation of debt service arrears. Costa Rica suspended all service payments in 1981 and resumed interest payments only at a token level in July 1982. By the end of 1982, Guatemalan arrears were estimated at $344 million[32] and Honduras

*Table* 7.8 Imports in nominal and real terms ($ million); real imports at 1982 prices (including service imports)

| | *1978* | *1979* | *1980* | *1981* | *1982* | *1983* |
|---|---|---|---|---|---|---|
| *Costa Rica* | | | | | | |
| Imports (cif.) | 1166 | 1397 | 1524 | 1209 | 893 | 989 |
| Imports (CACM) | 203 | 212 | 220 | 152 | 112 | 120 |
| Imports (ROW) | 963 | 1185 | 1304 | 1057 | 781 | 869 |
| Service imports | 355 | 425 | 522 | 545 | 672 | 665 |
| Real imports | 1708 | 1757 | 1609 | 1185 | 806 | 840 |
| *El Salvador* | | | | | | |
| Imports (cif.) | 1027 | 1022 | 962 | 985 | 857 | 892 |
| Imports (CACM) | 240 | 257 | 320 | 305 | 261 | 223 |
| Imports (ROW) | 787 | 765 | 642 | 680 | 596 | 669 |
| Service imports | 346 | 431 | 392 | 383 | 370 | 386 |
| Real imports | 1514 | 1320 | 1031 | 922 | 768 | 721 |
| *Guatemala* | | | | | | |
| Imports (cif.) | 1391 | 1504 | 1598 | 1674 | 1388 | 1135 |
| Imports (CACM) | 208 | 207 | 155 | 186 | 219 | 225 |
| Imports (ROW) | 1183 | 1297 | 1443 | 1488 | 1169 | 910 |
| Service imports | 451 | 483 | 635 | 650 | 490 | 404 |
| Real imports | 1640 | 1518 | 1387 | 1330 | 1054 | 838 |
| *Honduras* | | | | | | |
| Imports (cif.) | 696 | 832 | 1019 | 960 | 712 | 756 |
| Imports (CACM) | 92 | 98 | 104 | 118 | 87 | 83 |
| Imports (ROW) | 604 | 734 | 915 | 842 | 625 | 673 |
| Service imports | 227 | 288 | 352 | 335 | 361 | 320 |
| Real imports | 928 | 1025 | 1108 | 972 | 671 | 627 |
| *Nicaragua* | | | | | | |
| Imports (cif.) | 594 | 360 | 887 | 999 | 776 | 799 |
| Imports (CACM) | 139 | 111 | 301 | 211 | 117 | 110 |
| Imports (ROW) | 455 | 249 | 586 | 788 | 659 | 689 |
| Service imports | 213 | 206 | 214 | 235 | 254 | 214 |
| Real imports | 581 | 472 | 1058 | 1025 | 764 | 710 |

*Sources*: service imports: IMF, *International Financial Statistics, 1984 Yearbook*; real imports: Inter-American Development Bank, *Economic and Social Progress in Latin America, 1984 Report*; others: Consejo Monetario Centroamericano, *Boletín Estadístico 1983* (San José, 1984).

went into arrears in October 1982. Nicaragua, which had reached agreement with its creditors on debt rescheduling in August 1982,[33] narrowly avoided default in December[34] and was again accumulating arrears in 1983. By the close of the AWOC phase, the external debt problem and the difficulty of obtaining new credits had acquired major significance everywhere except El Salvador and, indeed, was the main reason why Costa Rica, Guatemala and Honduras were prepared to try to honour the IMF agreements which marked the end of the AWOC phase.

Thirdly, the weak fiscal position during the AWOC phase was not very satisfactory. The means by which excessive DCE had not been monetised could only be regarded as temporary, and the rapid growth of quasi-money posed a potential threat to financial stability. In this respect, the IMF proved to be more imaginative (and flexible) than is often realised (see next section).

## ADJUSTMENT WITH CONDITIONALITY

The adjustment with conditionality (AWIC) phase begins with the approval by the IMF of standby credits in support of adjustment programmes which were substantially completed. The dates are July 1982 for El Salvador, November 1982 for Honduras, December 1982 for Costa Rica and September 1983 for Guatemala. No agreement was reached with Nicaragua, which has failed to come to any accommodation with the Fund since the revolution; the exact reasons for this have never been stated publicly, but it is assumed to be due to US leverage over the IMF on the one side and Sandinista reluctance to submit to conditionality on the other (see next section). The AWIC phase therefore excludes Nicaragua.

The central policy element in the AWIC phase has been a reduction in the budget deficit. Although the Fund (as we shall see) has proved flexible in other respects, it has clung to orthodoxy as far as the budget deficit is concerned; targets were set for the deficit as a proportion of GDP (except for El Salvador)[35] and each letter of intent committed the signatories to raising revenue as well as cutting expenditure.

The revenue-raising target took place against a background of falling or stagnant trade taxes; thus, any rise in revenue could only be achieved through disproportionately large increases in non-trade taxes. In each republic the executive was able to secure congressional support, but has faced serious public unrest in consequence; in several cases this led to a reversal or partial reversal of the original tax increases.

The most serious case of reversal occurred in Guatemala, the least democratic of the four republics concerned. The Rios Montt government introduced a value added tax (VAT) at 10 per cent in July 1983 as a precondition for IMF support; the new tax, however, is widely conceded to have been one reason for the fall of Rios Montt in August; the new military government, led by General Mejía Victores, agreed a standby credit with the IMF in September, but promptly lowered VAT to 7 per cent in October. The failure by the Fund to secure a reimposition of VAT at 10 per cent finally provoked suspension in July 1984.

The pressure to raise revenue has also affected the price of public services controlled by decentralised public sector agencies. These increases have in several cases been cancelled, but the Fund has been unyielding in its determination to root out loss-making activities in the public sector. The justification for the Fund's concern has been the fact that a large share of the increase in public external indebtedness is accounted for by the operations of these agencies. The latter include investment corporations, which have become holding companies for a number of private sector lame ducks.[37]

The Fund has not demonstrated the same interest in the expenditure side of the public accounts, although in some respects the two are not independent; thus, central government transfers are lowered if public utility prices rise, and so on. Public sector wage freezes and wage control have continued, but this is a reflection of policy in the AWOC phase. Certainly, large numbers of jobs have been lost in the public sector (an estimated 15 000 in Honduras), but this cannot all be blamed on the Fund; in any case, a government which will not raise new taxes, but wishes to meet IMF targets, is bound to cut jobs.

It was argued in the previous section that the growth of quasi-money in the AWOC phase created a potentially dangerous situation for the preservation of financial stability. In El Salvador and Guatemala, the Fund is credited with pioneering the use of dollar-denominated bonds with a medium-term maturity which served a dual purpose: first, they could be used to soak up the quasi-money overhang and, secondly, they could be used to pay for inports without the need for current dollars.[38] It is possible that this unorthodox measure, which has proved moderately successful, was approved by the Fund in El Salvador and Guatemala because of their relatively low levels of public external indebtedness to private creditors. In any case, such bonds were not issued by Costa Rica and Honduras.

More emphasis has been put on export promotion during the AWIC than the AWOC phase. This is partly due to the opportunities created by the Caribbean Basin Initiative (CBI), which was formally launched in January 1984, but whose probable implementation was known about well in advance.[39] It is also due to the Fund's 'export optimism' and preference for export-increasing over import-decreasing measures. A key element in export promotion has been changes in tax credit certificates (CATs),[40] which have been increased particularly for non-traditional exports outside the region. Other measures include reductions in export taxes and the use of free zones.

The Fund has insisted on orthodox credit policies, with targets set for DCE, but has relied merely on exhortation in the case of interest rates. In fact, interest-rate policy has been extremely inactive during the AWIC phase; nominal interest rates have hardly varied at all despite a big fall in inflation, which has left real interest rates positive for most types of non-monetary assets.

The Fund, perhaps surprisingly, has not given much priority to the exchange rate in establishing preconditions for Fund support. In the case of Costa Rica, the Fund insisted on a narrowing of the spread between the interbank rate and the free market rate to no more than 2 per cent; this was achieved in November 1983, one month before the expiry of the agreement. Elsewhere, the Fund called for the phasing out of exchange restrictions, but nothing substantial was done; the best that could be said is that restrictions were not actually increased.

The Fund gave considerable prominence to questions of external indebtedness. In Costa Rica and Honduras, the agreements were explicitly linked to debt reschedulings; the Fund's approval, however, turned out to be a necessary but not sufficient condition for debt rescheduling. Costa Rica, it is true, came to an arrangement with its official creditors quickly (in January 1983), but agreement with private creditors on debt falling due in 1983–4 was only reached in January 1984 (i.e. after the Fund programme had expired). The Honduran debt problem proved even more stubborn; an agreement in principle was reached in late 1983 covering $230 million of arrears, but was not implemented until 1985.

In the case of Guatemala, the IMF agreement was not explicitly linked to debt rescheduling, but the letter of intent stated that commercial arrears should be reduced by $50 million in 1983 and $100 million in 1984; in the agreement with El Salvador, however, the question of external debt does not appear to have arisen at all.

The Fund's programmes were marked by a large increase in the proportion of the current account deficit financed by the IMF's credits. The sums involved, however, were fairly modest, and the increase in the proportion is also a reflection of the improvement in the BOP position; unlike the AWOC phase, the improvement did not depend wholly on a fall in imports; on the contrary, there was a small increase in export earnings (see Table 7.9), while imports increased even in real terms in Costa Rica. The growth of credit was indeed more moderate during the Fund programmes, and the share of DCE going to the private sector rose sharply.

The inflation rate fell sharply during the AWIC phase in Costa Rica (see Table 7.4), but this cannot be attributed to Fund policies. The massive maxi-devaluations of 1981 and 1982 gave way to mini-devaluations in the AWIC phase which produced an appreciation of the real exchange rate; the deceleration in nominal devaluation, coupled with virtually unchanged dollar import prices and nominal wage restraint, reduced the rise in nominal costs, and inflation began to fall back quickly to its pre-devaluation level. By 1984, Costa Rica had achieved a 30 per cent real depreciation compared with 1980 at the cost of a 466 per cent nominal devaluation, a huge fall in real wages (see next section) and a marked increase in social tensions, but had made no more progress in resolving its external disequilibrium than some other republics which had not devalued and where inflation had been kept to single figures.

Performance gave grounds for cautious optimism during the AWIC phase, and the Fund had shown that it was not as inflexible as its critics have often accused it of being; yet several problems emerged during the AWIC phase, which are also of relevance to other countries.

The first problem is one of timing; it is no accident that the AWIC phase begins after the worst of the BOP crisis was over. Given the lagged response of exports to any efforts to promote them, Central American republics are obliged to deal with a severe BOP crisis through import suppression. To achieve this in the short run requires import restrictions, which are forbidden under AWIC because of the Fund's articles of association.

It follows that Central American republics can only enter into IMF-sponsored adjustment programmes when external conditions have begun to improve; in particular, given the Fund's emphasis on export growth, there has to be some prospect for export recovery. Yet if the worst of the BOP crisis has passed and external conditions are improving, why is there any need for conditionality?

The answer is provided by questions of external debt, and finance, which brings us to the second problem associated with the AWIC phase. The main reason for agreeing to IMF conditionality in the AWIC phase was the need for new credits and debt rescheduling, for which Fund approval of the adjustment programme was a necessary

*Table* 7.9 Exports in nominal and real terms ($ million); real exports at 1982 prices (including service exports)

| | *1978* | *1979* | *1980* | *1981* | *1982* | *1983* |
|---|---|---|---|---|---|---|
| *Costa Rica* | | | | | | |
| Exports (fob) | 864 | 942 | 1001 | 1003 | 869 | 871 |
| Exports (CACM) | 179 | 175 | 370 | 238 | 167 | 187 |
| Exports (ROW) | 685 | 767 | 731 | 765 | 702 | 684 |
| Coffee | 314 | 315 | 248 | 240 | 237 | 230 |
| Non-traditional | 116 | 161 | 162 | 184 | 167 | 166 |
| Real exports | 1349 | 1393 | 1359 | 1510 | 1357 | 1358 |
| *El Salvador* | | | | | | |
| Exports (fob) | 848 | 1129 | 1075 | 798 | 700 | 736 |
| Exports (CACM) | 234 | 264 | 296 | 207 | 174 | 168 |
| Exports (ROW) | 614 | 865 | 779 | 591 | 526 | 568 |
| Coffee | 433 | 675 | 615 | 453 | 403 | 403 |
| Non-traditional | 52 | 66 | 61 | 70 | 59 | 67 |
| Real exports | 971 | 1282 | 983 | 810 | 699 | 770 |
| *Guatemala* | | | | | | |
| Exports (fob) | 1092 | 1221 | 1520 | 1305 | 1170 | 1092 |
| Exports (CACM) | 255 | 307 | 441 | 379 | 337 | 321 |
| Exports (ROW) | 837 | 914 | 1039 | 926 | 833 | 771 |
| Coffee | 475 | 432 | 464 | 325 | 375 | 309 |
| Non-traditional | 141 | 200 | 307 | 260 | 232 | 230 |
| Real exports | 1769 | 1946 | 2047 | 1769 | 1641 | 1429 |
| *Honduras* | | | | | | |
| Exports (fob) | 628 | 757 | 850 | 784 | 677 | 704 |
| Exports (CACM) | 49 | 60 | 84 | 66 | 52 | 61 |
| Exports (ROW) | 579 | 697 | 766 | 718 | 625 | 643 |
| Coffee | 211 | 197 | 204 | 173 | 153 | 151 |
| Non-traditional | 165 | 215 | 231 | 226 | 191 | 220 |
| Real exports | 687 | 766 | 800 | 830 | 749 | 706 |
| *Nicaragua* | | | | | | |
| Exports (fob) | 646 | 616 | 450 | 500 | 406 | 411 |
| Exports (CACM) | 146 | 90 | 75 | 71 | 52 | 34 |
| Exports (ROW) | 500 | 526 | 375 | 429 | 354 | 377 |
| Coffee | 200 | 159 | 166 | 136 | 124 | 149 |
| Non-traditional | 67 | 112 | 92 | 80 | 65 | 37 |
| Real exports | 622 | 714 | 593 | 681 | 614 | 759 |

*Sources*: real exports from IDB (see note to Table 7.8); other data from Consejo Monetario Centroamericano, *Boletín Estadistico 1983*, San José. 1984.

condition. This was made explicit in the case of Costa Rica, while it was implicit in the cases of Guatemala, Honduras and El Salvador.[41]

The Central American experience, however, makes it clear that the IMF seal of approval is neither a necessary nor sufficient condition for a 'successful' debt rescheduling.[42] It is not sufficient, because the private banks are under no obligation to reschedule, yet alone advance new loans. Only Costa Rica was able to complete a rescheduling programme within the AWIC phase, but even that cannot be regarded as successful because it covered two years only (1983–4) and the amount of new credit involved in the package was very small.[43]

The IMF seal of approval is therefore not sufficient for successful debt rescheduling, but the Nicaraguan example shows that it is not necessary either. Nicaragua rescheduled its commercial debt in 1980 and 1982 without reaching an IMF agreement; subsequently, it fell behind in its debt service payments even on rescheduled terms, and it has the unenviable distinction of being one of only five countries in the world for which US bank supervisory authorities have invented a new category of reserve (Allocated Transfer Risks Reserves) for cases of protracted non-service of country debt.[44] It has also been in arrears on payments to the World Bank, an almost unheard-of phenomenon.

It can be argued that Nicaragua has received few additional private credits since the end of 1981[45] and that, therefore, it has paid a high price for not reaching agreement with the Fund. Nicaragua is not alone in this respect, however, and Guatemala in particular received no substantial additional private credits in the two years before July 1983. Consequently, if governments are to be persuaded of the need for painful IMF-sponsored adjustment programmes, there must be a greater degree of reciprocity by the commercial banks, otherwise the Nicaraguan example of *de facto* default will look increasingly attractive.

The third problem relates to the content of the IMF-sponsored adjustment programmes themselves. While the Fund has proved itself to be not inflexible on many issues, it has proved very rigid on the question of budget deficits; this has provided the main source of tension with the host governments, threatening at times to abort the adjustment programmes.

The Fund's position on budget deficits is as follows:

> A rise in the ratio of fiscal deficits to GDP has contributed to the current economic problems requiring adjustment in a good many developing countries. In these countries, excessive deficits have

induced accelerated monetary expansion and inflation. The consequences have included impaired capital investment, loss of competitive position, and generally lower rates of growth. Redressing excessive fiscal deficits has thus become an important element of adjustment policy in developing countries.[46]

While it would be foolish to deny that 'excessive fiscal deficits' can produce serious problems, the Fund's analysis does not appear to have much validity in Central America. 'Excessive deficits' are not in general the cause of accelerated inflation; inflation ratios have risen and fallen, as we have seen, to a large extent independently of the size of the budget deficit. Similarly, the Fund lists as *consequences* of 'excessive deficits' what can more properly be described as *causes* of 'excessive deficits'. Thus, capital investment was certainly impaired by capital flight; private investment collapsed and, with it, imports of capital goods; both lowered government revenue and contributed to 'excessive deficits'.

The rise in the PSBR did, however, contribute to a large and potentially destabilising increase in quasi-money, but this can be (and was) dealt with through other measures than a balanced or nearly balanced budget. Furthermore, the Fund appears not to recognise that the fiscal deficit is linked to the trade cycle, so that the 'full-trade' budget deficit is clearly smaller than the actual deficit during a period of trade recession.

The Nicaraguan PSBR experience makes clear that the Fund's concern with excessive deficits is not wholly misplaced. In Nicaragua, the deficit reached 25 per cent of GDP in 1983, and monetary growth was clearly excessive and potentially dangerous (see next section); there is a difference of quality as well as quantity, however, between a deficit of 25 per cent and one of 5 per cent. Outside of Nicaragua, the budget deficit as a proportion of GDP was falling *before* the AWIC phase, but the Fund has still insisted on targets which cannot be justified in terms of Central American macroeconomics.[47]

Let us suppose, however, that the Fund is correct in its choice of targets for the PSBR. The adjustments needed both to public revenue and public expenditure require time for their completion, particularly the former, so that a medium-term framework is needed for the AWIC phase. This suggests that an Extended Fund Facility (EFF) is appropriate, yet in every case the AWIC phase was marked by standby credits, the longest being for sixteen months. Thus the Fund chose unreasonable targets for the PSBR and then allowed too short a period for adjustment.

The final problem associated with the AWIC phase has been its failure to prevent a further deterioration in CACM. It is true that, with one exception,[48] the Fund's conditions did not countenance *additional* restrictions on intra-regional trade. The IMF, however, exerted no pressure to remove those actually in existence, and its programme of export promotion made no reference to CACM. Given that the Fund has had agreements running contemporaneously with four of the five members (treating Honduras as a *de facto* member), this failure was a serious waste of an opportunity to reduce the costs of adjustment.

The major obstacle to the recovery of CACM, contrary to popular opinion, has not been political differences among the Central American republics, but the accumulation of unpaid debts between various pairs of states. These debts represent arrears just as much as unserviced debts to international banks; it seems strange, therefore, that the Fund has not insisted on repayment of intra-CACM debt as one of the conditions for standby credits. Such a move would have represented a positive step in favour of CACM's revival, despite the fact that the Fund has had no influence over the largest debtor, Nicaragua.

## THE CASE OF NICARAGUA

Although Nicaragua has maintained correct relations with the IMF since the revolution, even settling all its outstanding debts in May 1985 and playing host to a Fund mission the following month, the Sandinista government did not follow the rest of Central America into the AWIC phase; instead, a public-sector boom was engineered from early 1983 (marking the close of the AWOC phase) which lasted until the adjustment programme of February 1985.

Since 1983, therefore, the Nicaraguan case has been *sui generis*; many factors account for this. The most obvious is that it is highly unlikely that the Fund and the Sandinista government could have reached agreement on an adjustment programme, given US influence over the IMF on the one hand and internal Nicaraguan political realities on the other. It was also the case, however, that debt problems (which were forcing other Central American republics into the arms of the Fund) did not have the same significance in Nicaragua; it was clear, for example, by early 1983 that the revolutionary government could not expect any new money from foreign commercial banks or multilateral institutions with strong US participation (above all, the World Bank and the Inter-American Development Bank),[49] while on the other hand its anticipated credits from other sources were not conditional on an agreement with the Fund.

The necessary conditions for avoiding an agreement with the Fund might therefore be said to have existed in 1983, but the external environment deteriorated sharply in that year and the consequent BOP disequilibrium required the continuation and even intensification of adjustment programmes; under these circumstances, the choice of a public-sector boom as the engine of growth of the economy (GDP rose by nearly 5 per cent in 1983) proved to be most unfortunate.[50]

Several factors accounted for the deterioration of the external environment in 1983. Virtually no new loans were forthcoming from multilateral official creditors (although some disbursements continued because of previous commitments) and the increasing intensity of the war against the Contras distorted the allocation of scarce foreign exchange away from the export sector towards the military. The unit value of all major export products (except seafoods) fell in 1983 and gold exports ceased altogether.[51] Finally, Nicaragua lost virtually all its sugar quota to the US market, although this was subsequently picked up by Iran and Algeria at comparable prices.

The public-sector boom in 1983 was the consequence of a 75 per cent rise in central government nominal expenditure unmatched by revenue increases.[52] The central government deficit soared to 24.4 per cent of nominal GDP, with most of it financed internally through the banking system; between the end of 1982 and 1983, the money supply (M1), rose by 67 per cent and the ratio of M1 to nominal GDP rose from about 20 per cent to 30 per cent – a sure sign of short-run, unwanted accumulation of money balances on the part of the public (see Table 7.5).

The huge rise in government expenditure occurred despite a fall in interest payments. Debt repayment problems (see below) led to a virtual 'passive default' and central government interest payments accounted for only 2.5 per cent of expenditure in 1983. By contrast, central government current expenditure on salaries, goods and services rose by around 50 per cent in 1983 compared to 1982, with much of the increase accounted for by additional outlays on defence.

The main reason, however, for the deterioration of the fiscal situation was the 213 per cent rise in 1983 in transfers and subsidies. These reached nearly 20 per cent of total expenditure compared with 7 per cent in 1982; the change is explained by the increasing gap between the producer and consumer prices of controlled goods and services. These included basic foodstuffs (e.g. rice, beans, maize, sugar, milk) as well as the services of public utilities.

The rise in producers' prices for foodstuffs was part of the effort by the state National Foodstuffs Enterprise, ENABAS, to achieve self-sufficiency in food supply.[53] The impact on production of agricultural goods for internal consumption was not unsuccessful,[54] but the state proved incapable of matching supplies through controlled distribution channels to demand (particularly in urban areas). A two-tier market developed for most foodstuffs, with prices in the black market far in execess of official guidelines, although the latter continued to be used in the calculation of the official cost-of-living index.

The Sandinista government denounced speculators and hoarders for the breakdown in the distribution system, but it is clear that the fiscal expansion played a major part in generating an effective demand for foodstuffs which could not be matched by official channels of distribution. Once the two-tier market was in place, moreover, it created a vicious circle: private producers bypassed ENABAS in a search for higher prices, and farmers in the export sector abandoned the production of foodstuffs for their workers since the same commodities could be purchased much more cheaply through official channels. Finally, high prices in the black market attracted migration to urban areas (particularly Managua) and the informal urban sector mushroomed through the expansion of petty commerce.[55]

The scarcity of foreign exchange, coupled with strict import controls, prevented the excess money creation from spilling over into imports, so that financial instability was reflected in domestic inflationary pressures. The rise in inflation (31 per cent in 1983 and 36 per cent in 1984) is not a correct measure of these pressures, because the index relied on official controlled prices. A proxy for inflationary pressures, however is provided by the black market exchange rate; this fell from 70 córdobas to the dollar at the end of 1983 to nearly 500 by the end of 1984.

While the black market exchange rate was rapidly depreciating in 1983 and 1984, the official exchange rate was unchanged at 10 córdobas to the dollar. Since foreign trade had been nationalised by the revolutionary government, the exchange rate that mattered for exporters was the one used by the authorities to convert dollar earnings into actual producer receipts; this varied from product to product, and the authorities adjusted the rates for the main export crops to reflect (at least partially) the rise in domestic prices.

As a result of these efforts, the volume of exports of the main products (coffee, cotton, sugar, bananas) rose in 1983, and there was also an increase in the dollar value of export earnings from these crops (except sugar) despite the falls in world prices. None the less, total export earnings were stagnant in 1983, reaching only 63.6 per cent of the pre-revolution level.

The problem of exports continued to be the decline in non-traditional products (including sales to CACM). Only one-third of the fall in the value of exports from 1978 to 1983 could be explained by the performance of traditional exports,[56] although they accounted for 70 per cent of exports in 1978 and nearly 90 per cent in 1983. The non-traditional products came mainly from the industrial sector, where the unrealistic exchange rate and foreign exchange shortages for the purchase of inputs, spare parts, etc. were the major problems rather than demand factors.

The weakness of exports continued in 1984, aggravated by external aggression,[57] and earnings fell below $400 million for the first time since 1975. This was virtually the same as projected service payments on the public external debt, so that the external disequilibrium became unmanageable; the 'passive default' begun in 1983 was continued into 1984, with no payments even of interest on the commercial debt owed to private, external creditors.

By the middle of 1984, it was quite clear that the Sandinista attempt to circumvent the external disequilibrium through internal demand expansion had failed. Not only had the external environment deteriorated, but real GDP also fell in 1984 by 1.4 per cent; the need for a further round of adjustment was recognised, but electoral considerations postponed a decision until early 1985.

The adjustment programme announced in February 1985 was intended to reduce the fiscal deficit, curb inflationary pressures, and at the same time remove some of the worst distortions in the Nicaraguan economy (the authorities correctly noted that all these were linked). The core of the programme has been the raising of official consumer prices in an effort to end tranfers and subsidies and reduce the fiscal deficit, while operating under a very tight constraint in which security considerations mean that defence will take 40 per cent of the budget. Government investment and other expenditures have been cut and new taxes have been introduced (particularly on petty commerce in the urban informal sector).[58]

Salaries were reorganised into twenty-eight groups and were increased in nominal, but not real, terms. This inevitable element of the adjustment programme was largely nullified in April, when a further round of salary increases was announced to 'compensate' a further round of consumer price increases;[59] the whole package was therefore in danger of simply creating the same set of problems at a higher level of prices; this was confirmed in June when the authorities announced new producer prices for basic foodstuffs[60] and an 'iron fist' offensive against speculation, hoarding, overcharging and contraband.[61]

The adjustment programme legalised the black market exchange rate (which settled at around 650 córdobas to the dollar) and introduced an official multiple exchange rate; the new rates, however, varied from 10 to 50 córdobas to the dollar, so that the devaluation came nowhere near eliminating the gap between the free and official rates and did not compensate exporters (particularly of industrial goods) for the rise in production costs.

While the adjustment programme was being implemented, the external environment was subject to a number of changes, not all of which were unfavourable. In June 1985, an agreement was reached with the creditor banks to postpone all debt service payments for one year,[62] and the Soviet Union agreed to provide 90 per cent of oil requirements, with Mexico supplying the balance,[63] Nicaragua even received a $44 million loan from the Central American Monetary Council to help its industrial exports to CACM.[64] The most spectacular change, however, was the US embargo on trade with Nicaragua in May, which had been anticipated by the authorities for several years and the damage from which is likely to be less severe than at first was believed.[65]

Several lessons can be drawn from the Nicaraguan experience since the end of the AWOC phase. First, external aggression (however unjustified) is not unlike other external shocks in terms of its macroeconomic impact and should not prevent the adoption of adjustment programmes (however painful). Secondly, revolutionary governments ignore the need for internal as well as external balance at their peril, because the eventual costs of adjustment may be so severe as to rob the revolutionary government of its social and political base. Thirdly, the adjustment package of February 1985 is not unlike an IMF-inspired programme, although its impact has been softened by subsequent, inconsistent policies which threaten to cancel the effectiveness of the original package. Finally, the combination of external aggression and internal policy errors have produced a situation where the external debt cannot be serviced; in the Nicaraguan case, passive default is the only 'solution'.

## THE BURDEN OF ADJUSTMENT

Adjustment programmes carry costs, which raises the question of who bears the burden of adjustment. It is a sad comment on the state of economics that the statistics necessary to give a definitive answer to this question are usually unavailable; none the less, with the use of some imagination, one can hazard a guess as to the answers.

The period of adjustment (AWOC and AWIC) corresponds roughly to the period 1981 to 1983.[66] Taking 1980 as the base, one can look at the changes in a number of indicators over the period 1980–3 which are relevant to the question of the burden of adjustment (see Table 7.10).

The first indicator refers to the fall in real GDP per head. As the table makes clear, this has been particularly severe in El Salvador (where the decline actually began in 1978); the inadequacy of this indicator is shown up, however, by the fact that Nicaragua appears to have experienced an increase. If, for example, we take the change in real wages (see column 2), the position of Nicaragua is seen to be very severe; on the other hand, it now appears that Guatemala experienced an increase in real wages, while the unemployment indicator (see column 3) suggests that in this respect Guatemala has been the worst affected.

Data on unemployment and wages (both real and nominal) are notoriously unreliable in Central America; in any case, wage labour only accounts for a part of total labour supply.[67] Consequently, a better indicator of the burden of adjustment (see column 4) is the change in real consumption per head. As Table 7.10 shows, all the republics have been badly affected on this score, with the worst sufferers being El Salvador and Nicaragua.

Real consumption per head is only an average, which implicitly assumes that no group was able to protect its earnings/consumption in real terms. In practice, every country has a 'protected sector', which means that the fall in real consumption per head in the 'unprotected sector' was even greater than implied by Table 7.10. This fall can be simulated on different assumptions about the size of the protected sector (see Table 7.11). The protected sector consists of groups which for one reason or other can manipulate the price of their services to prevent a fall in their real earnings/consumption. They include some (but not all) civil servants, most members of the armed forces, police, etc., some (but not all) employers, members of the professions, politicians, etc. Table 7.11 marks the author's guestimate of the size of the protected sector in each republic, which can be compared with what

*Table* 7.10 Indicators of the burden of adjustment, 1980–3

| | *(1)* | *(2)* | *(3)* | *(4)* |
|---|---|---|---|---|
| Costa Rica | − 18.2 | − 37.7 | + 53 | − 26 |
| El Salvador | − 19.2 | − 35.1 | + 85 | − 39 |
| Guatemala | − 12.5 | + 18.3 | + 264 | − 9 |
| Honduras | − 11.3 | − 4.1 | + 98 | − 19 |
| Nicaragua* | + 3.7 | − 36.9 | − 4 | − 39 |

*Notes*:
*For Nicaragua, the period chosen is 1980–2.
Col. (1) = percentage change in real GDP per head.
Col. (2) = percentage change in real wages.
Col. (3) = percentage increase in unemployment rate (a minus sign indicates a fall). (The unemployment rate in 1980 for the five republics was 5.9%, 16.2%, 2.2%, 10.7% and 18.3% in the order listed above.)
Col. (4) = percentage change in real private consumption per head.

*Sources*: Cols. (1) to (3) from Inforpress, *Centroamericana 1984–6* (Guatemala, 1984); Col. (4) derived from Consejo Monetario Centroamericano, *Boletín Estadístico 1983*, San José 1984.

would have happened if the protected sector were the same as (a) the modern sector and (b) full-time employment.

Table 7.11 suggests that in two republics (El Salvador and Nicaragua) the reduction in real consumption has been massive, in two others (Costa Rica and Honduras) it has been severe, while in one

*Table* 7.11 Fall in real consumption per head in unprotected sector (%)

| Proportion of labour force assumed to be protected (%) | 0 | 10 | 20 | 30 | 40 | 50 |
|---|---|---|---|---|---|---|
| Costa Rica | 26 | 29* | 33 | 37 | 43 | 52‡† |
| El Salvador | 39 | 43 | 52* | 55 | 65† | 77‡ |
| Guatemala | 9 | 10 | 12 | 13* | 16‡ | 19† |
| Honduras | 19 | 21 | 24* | 27† | 32 | 38‡ |
| Nicaragua | 39 | 43 | 49* | 56 | 65† | 78‡ |

*Notes*:
*Author's guestimate of protected share.
†Share of full-time workers in total employment (to nearest decile). For source, see note 67.
‡Share of modern sector in total employment (to nearest decile). For source, see note 67.

(Guatemala) it has been quite modest. This last result is not altogether surprising; Guatemala did not adjust until 1982 and is the least dependent of the Central American republics on external conditions. In addition, the expansion of the oil industry in the period 1980–3 (although far from spectacular) has been a factor contributing towards the relative mildness of adjustment.

The table does not tell us which economic activities have been particularly severely affected by the recent depression. This information is provided by Table 7.12, where it can be seen that the worst affected sectors have been construction, commerce and manufacturing; as these are all predominantly urban activities, it is realistic to assume that it is the urban areas that have carried a disproportionate share of the burden of adjustment.

Agriculture in every case has achieved an above-average performance. This conceals a wide difference, however, between the performance of export agriculture (EXA) and domestic use agriculture (DUA); with the exception of Nicaragua, the performance of EXA has been worse than that of agriculture as a whole, suggesting a relatively strong performance by DUA; this 'defence mechanism' in the Central American context is familiar to students of the 1930s.[68] The Nicaraguan experience, by contrast, has been of EXA constant in real terms, but a

*Table* 7.12 Change (%) in real net output by sector from real GDP peak to trough

| Sector | *Costa Rica 1980–3* | *El Salvador 1978–83* | *Guatemala 1981–3* | *Honduras 1981–3* | *Nicaragua 1978–82* |
|---|---|---|---|---|---|
| Agriculture | + 4.3* | − 10.8* | − 5.1* | + 3.7* | − 12.7* |
| Mining | (a) | 0* | + 5.3* | − 5.0 | − 41.5 |
| Manufacturing | − 16.8 | − 32.5 | − 7.2 | − 2.3* | − 14.9 |
| Public utilities | + 34.7* | + 7.3* | − 3.0* | − 2.8 | − 8.8* |
| Construction | − 50.4 | − 41.6 | − 37.2 | − 7.0 | − 53.8 |
| Commerce | − 26.3 | − 45.0 | − 9.6 | − 3.1 | − 14.3 |
| Public administration | − 0.8* | + 16.3* | + 8.4* | + 3.3* | − 2.9* |
| GDP | − 10.5 | − 22.4 | − 6.2 | − 2.4 | − 13.6 |

*Notes*:
*Above average performance.
(a)Included in manufacturing.

sharp decline in DUA; this has been reversed since 1982, however, as land reform and the removal of price ceilings have begun to take effect.[69]

It would therefore seem that workers and their families in EXA on the one hand and the urban private sector on the other have borne the brunt of the burden of adjustment, while workers and their families in the public sector, together with small-scale agriculture (DUA), have experienced the least hardship. Needless to say, there are exceptions to these generalisations, the most important being EXA in Nicaragua and public employees in Costa Rica and Honduras.

Not all the burden of adjustment can be attributed to the adjustment programmes and even less to the IMF-inspired programmes during the AWIC phase. War-related adjustment has been very important in El Salvador and Nicaragua and is the main reason why those two republics have borne a heavier burden than the others; similarly, once the effects of war are taken into account, it seems safe to assume that most of the burden of adjustment was carried during the AWOC rather than AWIC phase. It would be impossible, however, to quantify the distribution of the burden; in any case it would be inappropriate, as the external environment was much more hostile in the AWOC than AWIC phase.

One final question should be raised, although it cannot be fully answered: what additional costs of adjustment were incurred as a result of delaying adjustment during the FN stage? The answer again cannot be quantitative, but it can be assumed that the additional costs were substantial. Costa Rica in particular would have been able to incur a much smaller burden if adjustment had begun in 1979, while all republics paid a heavy price for their failure to stem capital flight at an earlier stage.

## THE POST-ADJUSTMENT PHASE

At the time of writing (August 1985), the four republics which passed through the AWIC phase (all except Nicaragua) can be said to have entered a post-adjustment phase, the hallmark of which has been a modest recovery in real GDP. This recovery as yet lacks solid foundations, however, and may prove to be temporary in nature; furthermore, the continuation of external financial problems forced Costa Rica to sign a new thirteen-month standby agreement with the IMF in March

1985 (for details, see Table 7.7) and both Guatemala and Honduras are expected to do the same in 1986 following presidential elections.

The recovery of real GDP since the end of 1983[70] in all the republics except Nicaragua has had three principal elements. The first has been export growth, the second a revival in private investment, and the third has been a recovery in imports which has helped to unlock various supply-side bottlenecks.

The dominant factor in export growth in 1984 was better prices for the main traditional exports (particularly coffee and bananas), although there was some growth in volumes exported as well. US imports from the four republics grew rapidly (ranging from 25 per cent in the case of Guatemala to 5.5 per cent in the case of El Salvador), but only a small part of this increase could be attributed to the launching of the Caribbean Basin Initiative (CBI) in January 1984; indeed, in the eighteen months to June 1985, new investments under the CBI in the four republics had only reached $29.7 million (50 per cent of which were in Honduras), compared with $44 million in the Dominican Republic alone.[71]

Import demand since the end of 1983 has been stimulated by the recovery in private investment, but the growth of import supply cannot be explained solely in terms of additional earnings from exports. The four republics have benefited from their strategic geopolitical location and have received increased official capital inflows, mainly from the United States, although on a scale below that envisaged in the Kissinger Report.[72]

The sensitivity of imports to even a modest economic recovery[73] has, however, imposed a very serious strain on the balance of payments and the exchange rate, despite the official capital inflows. The strains forced Guatemala to introduce a parallel exchange market in November 1984, in which the quetzal has rapidly depreciated against the dollar.[74] While some of the explanation is due to the failure of the Guatemalan authorities to reduce the budget deficit,[75] the experience of the other republics shows that the problem runs deeper; Costa Rica has been forced to speed up the rate of mini-devaluations despite its fiscal rectitude, and El Salvador has channelled yet more imports through the parallel market, while the black market exchange rate has fallen dramatically.[76]

The four republics, with the possible exception of Honduras,[77] have therefore effectively broken the exchange link with the US dollar and initiated a period of effective real devaluations. Whatever the impact on non-traditional exports, it is certain that inflation will accelerate (as is confirmed by preliminary estimates). This is likely to aggravate the fiscal situation and increase social tensions in republics which can ill afford it.

Exchange-rate instability, and the consequent acceleration of inflation, is one reason for believing that the modest recovery since the end of 1983 may be short-lived. An additional problem is the dependence of exports on markets where growth is problematical (e.g. CACM, USA) and the reliance on traditional primary products for which world prices have been falling (e.g. coffee, cotton, sugar).

A slowdown in the growth of the US economy, coupled with a fall in nominal dollar interest rates, creates pressures on the balance of payments of Latin American countries whose net effects may be uncertain. In Central America, however, the impact is unambiguous, because so much of the external debt is owed to official creditors at subsidised rates.[78] Thus, the current trends in the US economy can be expected to exert additional strains on the balance of payments of the four republics.

The relatively strong performance of extra-regional exports in 1984 contributed to a slowdown in the decline of intra-regional (CACM) trade. The subsequent exchange-rate instability, however, coupled with the failure to service debts between the member countries, has produced a further deterioration and a shift to bilateral, balanced trade, which the adoption of a new tariff nomenclature is unlikely to reverse.[79]

It is probable that non-traditional exports outside CACM, stimulated by the CBI and real depreciation, will increase in value. Such exports, however, start from a very low base, and it is not to be expected that they can compensate for the weakness of other exports for many years. There are grounds for believing, therefore, that the export performance of the four republics may deteriorate.

Such a deterioration will bring the servicing of the external public debt back to the forefront of discussion. Both Costa Rica and Honduras in the middle of 1985 rescheduled their debts (and arrears) up to the end of 1986, but this postponement of the debt problem is likely to prove short-lived. Both private and official creditors have shown an unwillingness to reschedule the debts of small countries for more than two years at a time, and in the case of private creditors there has been an even greater reluctance to provide new loans. Thus all four republics will continue to be dependent on new official credits, a dependence which will be increased if export earnings deteriorate.

Although the problem of external debt service is most acute in Costa Rica, it has caused increasing strains in the other three republics; a deterioration of the external environment will increase these strains and short-term policy will concentrate on measures to promote export earnings. This raises the question of whether the evolution of the economies in the short run is likely to be consistent with long-term strategies.

Since the start of the AWOC phase, there has been no long-term strategy in the four republics. Analyses of the Central American crisis, however, have achieved a remarkably broad consensus on the need to emphasise food security and a less import-dependent industrialisation in any long-term solution to the region's problems.[80] These are difficult goals, which depend on a diversification of agriculture (in order to supply the urban economy with the raw materials and foodstuffs needed by industrialists and consumers) and a strengthening of CACM (in order to provide a market for the industrial outputs).

Such a strategy saves foreign exchange in the long run and lowers the trade coefficient, making the region less vulnerable to export instability.[81] In the short run, however, it is likely to cost foreign exchange (through the diversification of agriculture away from exports) and therefore runs counter to the short-term strategy imposed of necessity by the hostile external environment in general and the external debt problem in particular. It would seem, therefore, that in Central America the long-term and the short-term strategies are indeed in conflict.

## CONCLUSIONS

The burden of adjustment has been very severe in Central America, but it cannot all be blamed on external factors. One conclusion that emerges clearly from this chapter is that the failure to adjust in 1979, 1980 and (in some cases) 1981 added significantly to the costs of adjustment; in particular, the debt burden was increased enormously as a result of the FN phase.

The failure to adjust could not be excused on the grounds that the balance-of-payments disequilibrium was perceived as temporary; on the contrary, complex though it was, the BOP crisis in 1979 had all the signs of being a medium-term problem. While the position in El Salvador and Nicaragua was complicated by civil war, the failure to adjust elsewhere was inexcusable on economic grounds. Political constraints help to explain the FN phase, but they do not justify it.

Once the decision was taken to adjust, there was a rapid improvement in the BOP position. This was due to the adoption of import-suppressing policies in the AWOC phase, which would not have been permitted as part of an IMF programme; no other policies, however, could have been expected to achieve such a sharp improvement in the BOP in such a short time-period.

The suppression of imports without a corresponding reduction in nominal demand usually produces financial instability and an increase in inflation; with the exception of Costa Rica (where currency depreciation produced an inflation rate close to 100 per cent in 1982), Central America was fortunate to avoid these consequences during the AWOC phase. The credit–import ratio rose dangerously, but excessive DCE was prevented from spilling over into hyperinflation by the rapid growth of quasi-money; this, in turn, was due in particular to increased import deposit requirements.

The transition from the AWOC to the AWIC phase cannot, therefore, be blamed on the failure of the former; on the contrary, judged by the improvement in the BOP, the AWOC stage was successful. It could not, however, resolve the external finance and debt problems, and in three of the four relevant countries[82] these problems were a major reason for sticking to IMF conditionality.

Acceptance of IMF conditions has not solved the debt problem, though. The Fund cannot be blamed for this, but it is a major weakness in the case-by-case approach favoured by the creditor nations. A Fund programme, even if successfully completed, is no guarantee of favourable treatment by creditors; private creditors, in particular, are under no obligation to carry out multiyear reschedulings or lend additional funds.

Net lending by official sources, responding to the internationalisation of the Central American crisis, has continued to flow to the region[83] and the sums involved have even increased; this has gone some way towards easing the debt problem, but official largesse cannot dispose of the problem of the public external debt held privately; projected debt service payments to private creditors are equivalent to 50 per cent of current exports until 1991 in Nicaragua and until 1989 in Costa Rica.[84]

Since 1979, many more IMF programmes have failed than succeeded. The high failure rate cannot be blamed entirely on Fund inflexibility; on the contrary, in its different treatment of El Salvador and Nicaragua, the Fund has shown itself to be politically very flexible, although this sensitivity to the international political environment has not carried over to domestic politics, where the internal obstacles to revenue-raising measures have been ignored.

The Fund has also shown itself flexible in the choice of policy instruments. In the matter of exchange-rate policy, orthodoxy appears to have been abandoned (with the possible exception of Costa Rica) and multiple exchange rates have been tolerated, if not approved.[85] The usual rigid credit ceilings appear to have been progressively relaxed and interest-rate policy has not been very active.

It is only on the question of fiscal policy and the budget deficit that the Fund has proved inflexible. This inflexibility appears to be based on the mistaken idea that the causal link between the PSBR on the one hand and inflation and resource misallocation on the other always runs from the former to the latter.

It would be foolish to deny that fiscal reform is important in Central America. The tax level and revenue structure of several republics, notably Guatemala, is very antiquated and in need of overhaul; fiscal reform, however, cannot be achieved in a short period, and the Fund must either pursue it in a medium-term strategy (e.g. Extended Fund Facilities) or settle for a more flexible fiscal policy in a short-term strategy.

The other major criticism of the Fund to emerge from this chapter is its treatment or lack of treatment of the CACM. The IMF has not tried to reverse the collapse of CACM trade and has focused its export promotion programmes exclusively on exports outside the region. In addition, the Fund has tolerated policies discriminating against CACM imports and has not linked standby credits to the settlement of debt arrears within the CACM.

The IMF's articles of association and its voting structure[86] impose certain limits on the Fund's operations. It follows that Fund programmes will not always be the most suitable way of securing adjustment; the success of the AWOC phase in Central America is an example of this situation. Yet, although a sharp (and rapid) adjustment was achieved, a successful AWOC phase is not usually sufficient to secure favourable treatment by creditors.

There is no real need for this inflexibility on the part of creditors (whether private or public); what matters is the degree of adjustment in relation to the scale of the debt. Creditors (represented by steering committees) do not need the intervention of the IMF in order to judge the results. The Fund's seal of approval does not put the creditors under any greater obligation, but it can impose additional burdens on the debtors.

As the global debt problem moves into its 'mature' phase, a dichotomy is emerging in the treatment of small and large debtors. A successful resolution of the latter's problems is essential if world financial stability is to be assured; as a result, the IMF and the creditors have co-operated with some success to ensure sufficient new finance to prevent collapse.

In the case of small debtors, there is no threat to world financial stability. Creditors therefore feel no obligation to lend additional finance, and assistance is often restricted to rescheduling short-term debts (a highly profitable activity). The burden of adjustment is, therefore, borne entirely by the debtor country, unless it defaults; IMF intervention tends to reinforce this unequal distribution of the burden of adjustment, because it ensures that the debtor has the capacity to service its debts (e.g. through a trade surplus) without increasing the obligations of the creditor. It might, therefore, be more equitable if the debt problems of small debtors such as the Central American republics were resolved bilaterally without IMF conditionality.

## Notes

1. Costa Rica paid lip-service to the need for adjustment. In August 1980, the Minister of Finance, Hernán Sáenz, said: 'we wanted a programme that would adjust through a policy of demand management. We wanted to control the money supply so that the adjustment would be a real adjustment and not just a series of patches' (*Euromoney*, Special Supplement on Costa Rica, August 1980, p. 11). In practice, however, there was no adjustment at all in Costa Rica in 1980.
2. Nicaragua's real Gross Domestic Product (GDP) fell by 7.5 per cent in 1978 and 25.5 per cent in 1979. El Salvador's real GDP fell by 1.5 per cent in 1979 and 8.8 per cent in 1980.
3. See Table 8.1.
4. The fall in Honduran GDP in 1974, for example, can be blamed on Hurricane Fifi.
5. Credits subject to conditionality must be distinguished from the compensatory finance and oil facility drawings which are not so subject and of which all Central American countries have taken advantage.
6. Guatemala completed its one-year standby agreement with the Fund signed in November 1981. This was a first credit tranche, however (disbursed fully at the start of the programme) and there can be no doubt that the performance of the Guatemalan economy did not comply with the Fund's conditions as laid down in the agreement.
7. A new IMF loan to Costa Rica was approved in March 1985, and a standby agreement went into force in May.
8. Nicaragua, as we shall see, has had no agreements with the Fund since

the revolution. El Salvador has had one agreement, but balance-of-payments pressures (and the debt problem) are resolved through exceptionally high levels of official credits on concessionary terms.

9. This point is made very clearly in Bird (1984). In practice, of course, the choice of finance may be ruled out by non-availability.
10. The programme is described in Ministerio de Hacienda, 'La Reforma Financiera en Costa Rica', Banco Central de Costa Rica: Serie Comentarios Sobre Asuntos Económicos', no. 37, 1980. It is discussed more critically in Rivera Urrutia (1982).
11. The Guatemalan quetzal was at par with the US dollar from 1925 to 1986, and the official rate of exchange in El Salvador did not change from 1934 to 1986.
12. In 1979 the Sandinistas were very successful in convincing North Americans and Western Europeans that they were the representatives of a broad-based government which would not interfere with capitalist relations of production. The capitalist class in Central America was suspicious from the start and capital flight was one way of hedging their bets.
13. Table 7.1 suggests that capital flight was not a problem in Honduras. This contradicts a number of contemporary reports (including those provided by the US embassy) and suggests that capital flight from Honduras was concealed. Perhaps it is no accident that the BOP entry 'net errors and omissions' was strongly negative in 1979 and 1980.
14. This included the nationalisation of banks and much of foreign trade, as well as agrarian reform.
15. This small decline is not enough, however, to justify calling this period one of adjustment.
16. Figures are not available on private investment in Nicaragua after the revolution, but it is generally agreed that it also fell to very low levels.
17. It is assumed that virtually all of the increase in investment in Nicaragua can be attributed to the public sector.
18. See Table 8.3.
19. This has been demonstrated using both econometric and input–output techniques. For the former, see Siri and Dominguez (1981); for the latter, see Bulmer-Thomas (1977).
20. In Nicaragua, however, this ratio was nearer 2:1. See Table 7.5.
21. The only sharp changes in velocity are in Costa Rica in 1981 (which can be explained by the conversion of both nominal GDP and the money stock into dollars at the rapidly depreciating exchange rate) and Nicaragua in 1983, when excess money creation was a very serious problem.
22. We should therefore distinguish between the initial capital flight from Central America, which was accommodated by a (passive) financial system, and a later stage of capital flight which was fuelled by the financial system as a result of irresponsible fiscal policies during the FN stage. I am grateful to Jaime Ros for pointing out this distinction.
23. For a similar argument, see Tseng (1984).
24. At the start of the IMF programme, the maximum ceiling for interest rates on commercial bank credits was raised from 11 per cent to 15 per cent; at the end of the programme it was lowered to 12 per cent.

25. See Rivera Urrutia (1982).
26. Import suppression through exchange control and other restrictions is an obvious example.
27. The Guatemalan standby credit of September 1983 was in fact suspended in July 1984 due to the government's failure to meet performance criteria; it is still correct, however, to think of adjustment in Guatemala in two stages: one without and one with conditionality.
28. By December 1981, the parallel market rate was 3.50 colones per US dollar compared with 2.50 in the official market.
29. In Nicaragua, on the other hand, the gap has grown progressively wider. While the parallel market rate remained at 28.50 córdobas per US dollar, the black market rate stood at 70 by the end of 1983.
30. See Rivera Urrutia (1982).
31. Some efforts were made to discriminate in favour of CACM, but they were not sufficient to cancel the forces working in the opposite direction.
32. Between mid-1981 and mid-1983, Guatemala received no major credits from private sources.
33. Agreement had also been reached by Nicaragua with its creditors on part of its debts in the FN phase. See Weinert (1981).
34. Default on payment of $36 million in interest was only avoided when Nicaragua pledged future export earnings against debt service payments.
35. The Salvadorean programme was extremely flexible, so that the risk of suspension was minimal. The charge that the agreement was politically motivated has been made by several observers; see, for example, Arias Peñate (1983).
36. Costa Rican electricity price increases, for example, were suspended in July 1983 as a result of public opposition.
37. The most notorious are the Corporación Costarricense de Desarrollo in Costa Rica and the Corporación Nacional de Inversiones in Honduras; the Corporación Financiera Nacional has also been a heavy loss-maker in Guatemala.
38. There is a good description of the scheme in González (1984).
39. The CBI offers duty-free entry to the US markets for almost all commodities for a twelve-year period. The scheme applies to all countries of the Caribbean Basin except Cuba, Nicaragua and Guyana. See Feinberg and Newfarmer (1984).
40. This has not, however, been important in El Salvador.
41. Although El Salvador cannot be classed as having a major debt problem, it did reschedule its debt with the Dresdner Bank of Germany in June 1983 (i.e. just before the end of the IMF programme).
42. From the point of view of the debtor, 'success' involves multi-year reschedulings together with injections of new credits.
43. In early 1985, Costa Rica rescheduled its debts for 1985–6, but this was outside the AWIC phase (see penultimate section). The partial rescheduling of Honduran debts has already been mentioned.
44. See Crawford, M., 'Third World Debt is Here to Stay', *Lloyds Bank Review*, January 1985.
45. The *World Bank Debt Tables* for 1984–5, however, show that the disbursed debt outstanding to private creditors rose from $832.8 million

at the end of 1981 to $1081.7 million at the end of 1983.

46. See IMF, *World Economic Outlook*, 1984.
47. Throughout most of 1984, for example, the Fund was insisting on a PSBR of 1 per cent in Costa Rica. In the final agreement (implemented in May 1985) a compromise of 1.5 per cent was reached; there can be no macroeconomic justification, however, for such a low figure in Costa Rica or any other Central American country. Furthermore, when the PSBR is adjusted for inflation, it is more than probable that these IMF budget targets would represent a surplus.
48. The exception is Honduras, whose agreement with the Fund in November 1982 allowed for an increase in tariffs on all goods (including those from Central America).
49. Credit from the World Bank was frozen in 1982; the Inter-American Development Bank (IDB) approved its last loan for Nicaragua in 1982, although it was not disbursed until 1984. A $58 million IDB loan was blocked in April 1985, when the USA threatened to reduce its financial commitments to the bank if the loan was approved.
50. In an interview with the *Financial Times* (9 July 1985), the Vice-President of the Central Bank justified the policy as follows: 'At first [1980 and 1981] our expansionist policy brought high levels of growth . . . However, from 1982, external finance began to fall sharply and we were faced with the choice of either stopping growth, or trying to continue with internal finance'.
51. See Banco Interamericano de Desarrollo (1984), Table 1.2.
52. Revenue did rise (by 41.2 per cent) with income tax receipts up by 64.9 per cent, but these efforts were dwarfed by the rise in expenditure. See Banco Interamericano de Desarrollo (1984), Table 7.
53. See Austin *et al.* (1985).
54. By the 1983–4 season, production of rice, beans and sorghum had surpassed pre-revolutionary (1978–9) levels. The growth of maize production was disappointing, however, and the expansion of meat and dairy products was very poor. See Banco Interamericano de Desarrollo (1984), Table 17, and Austin *et al.* (1985), Table 1, p. 25.
55. See Stahler-Sholk (1987).
56. Defined as coffee, cotton, sugar, beef, bananas, shrimps and gold.
57. The crop most seriously affected was coffee. Earnings plunged by 20 per cent despite a rise of 22.8 per cent in its unit value. See IMF, *International Financial Statistics*, July 1985.
58. Further details on the adjustment programme are provided in Stahler-Sholk (1987).
59. See Inforpress, *Centroamericana*, no. 643, 6 June 1985, p. 13.
60. See Inforpress, *Centroamericana*, no. 649, 18 July 1985, p. 8.
61. See *Central American Report*, vol. XII, no. 21, 7 June 1985, p. 165.
62. See Inforpress, *Centroamericana*, no. 650, 25 July 1985, p. 3.
63. See Inforpress, *Centroamericana*, no. 647, 4 July 1985, p. 2.
64. See Inforpress, *Centroamericana*, no. 642, 30 May 1985, p. 6.
65. Exports to the USA (mainly bananas, meat and shellfish) had been reduced to $57 million by 1984, and new markets were found fairly quickly. Imports from the USA (almost double the value of exports in

1984) have proved more difficult to replace, because so much Nicaraguan machinery (particularly within the private sector) is dependent on US spare parts.

66. The main exception is Nicaragua, which pursued a policy of expansion in 1983, so that for Nicaragua the years of adjustment are confined to the period 1981–2.
67. See PREALC (1983), Table 5.
68. See Chapter 3.
69. Land reform began in 1981, but the biggest waves of distribution occurred in 1983 and 1984. Price controls were relaxed a little in May 1984 and loosened substantially in February 1985.
70. In the three-year period 1984–6, real GDP rose by 13.6 per cent in Costa Rica, 9.0 per cent in Honduras and 5.4 per cent in El Salvador. It was virtually unchanged in Guatemala and fell by 5.9 per cent in Nicaragua.
71. See CBI, *Business Bulletin*, June 1985, p. 2.
72. The external financing requirements for Central America and Panama were estimated at $24 billion over the period 1984–90, with $1.5 billion to $1.7 billion in 1984. See *Report of the National Bipartisan Commission on Central America* ('Kissinger Report'), January 1984, pp. 63–7.
73. Guatemalan imports, for example, rose by 13.4 per cent (in value) in 1984, while real GDP rose by 0.5 per cent. This was the most extreme case, but everywhere imports rose much faster than GDP.
74. Guatemala had a three-tier exchange market in 1985. The official rate (at par with the US dollar) was used for essentials (including oil), there were periodic government auctions of foreign exchange for specific goods, and there was also a free market (operated by the banks) where the quetzal had fallen to 3 per US dollar by mid-1985. In 1986, the quetzal was finally devalued.
75. Business pressure groups have consistently and successfully resisted attempts to increase government revenue through tax reform. In April 1985, General Mejía Victores was forced to reverse a number of revenue-raising measures, and the new measures announced in July (including a 3.5 per cent tax on sales in the parallel exchange market) did not have much impact. Although the ratio of tax revenue to GDP is the lowest in Latin America outside Haiti, cuts in public expenditure have prevented an explosion in the PSBR which fell by 47 per cent between 1981 and 1984 (see Inforpress, *Centroamericana*, no. 646, 27 June 1985, p. 2).
76. The parallel market rate was devalued to 4.50 colones per US dollar in July 1985, but the black market rate had fallen by then to C5.80. The official rate was finally devalued to C5.00 in 1986.
77. Honduras has so far resisted the introduction of a parallel exchange market and the official rate remains pegged to the US dollar at two lempiras (L), unchanged since 1918. The black market rate has been stable at around L2.75.
78. Even in Costa Rica, over half of the debt is owed to official creditors with an average interest rate in 1983 of 5.9 per cent. See World Bank, *World Debt Tables 1984/5*.
79. After years of delay, the Central American ministers of economy agreed in June 1985 to adopt the Brussels customs nomenclature, with all tariffs

calculated on an *ad valorem* basis.

80. See, for example, many of the articles in Irvin and Gorostiaga (1985).
81. See Bulmer-Thomas (1985).
82. Nicaragua did not pass through the AWIC phase and El Salvador's debt was not a major reason for seeking an IMF standby credit.
83. Including Nicaragua; a list of socialist country loans/grants to Nicaragua can be found in Acciaris (1984). Mexico has also been a very important creditor.
84. See World Bank, *World Debt Tables 1984/5*.
85. This relaxation of exchange-rate orthodoxy has been noted by Killick (1984), and is explained by the breakdown of the system of fixed exchange rates in the early 1970s.
86. The USA has 19.3 per cent of executive board votes in the IMF; this is three times bigger than the second largest share (the UK with 6.7 per cent), and it is virtually impossible for a country like Nicaragua to secure a favourable vote in the face of US opposition. The Soviet Union is not a member, and the votes of other socialist countries are currently cast by either the Netherlands (Romania, Yugoslavia) or Belgium (Hungary). See *IMF Survey*, September 1984, special supplement on the Fund.

# 8 World Recession and Central American Depression: Lessons from the 1930s for the 1980s[1]

## INTRODUCTION

It is undeniable that the present crisis in Central America has more than an economic dimension. The latter, however, remains an important factor not only in explaining the origins of the crisis, but also in accounting for its continuation. Furthermore, the economic aspects of the crisis have received much less attention than the political and geopolitical.[2] I shall therefore concentrate primarily on economic developments in this chapter.

Although the crisis in Central America is a regional one, not all countries have been equally affected. Special factors, for example, account for the collapse of economic activity in Nicaragua in 1978 and 1979, while the precipitate decline in gross domestic product (GDP) in El Salvador after 1978 is singular to that republic.

If we abstract from the special factors, however, we may observe in Central America the unfolding of an economic depression, whose prime cause is the recession of the world economy. This depression is exacerbated in several republics by features peculiar to that country, but the underlying depression (and the trade-cycle model to which it is related) can be analysed separately.

When the trade-cycle model giving birth to the current depression is analysed, it bears a striking resemblance to the 1929 depression in Central America. Indeed, it is interesting to note that 1982 is the first year since 1932 that economic activity declined in all republics at the same time.[3] This fifty-year lag should not be taken as evidence of a Kondratieff long wave, because the trade cycle is not endogenous to Central America, but it does focus attention on the earlier depression and suggest that a comparison is justified.

Much has changed in the Central American economy[4] since the 1929 depression. Despite the emergence of an industrial sector, however, and the growth of urbanisation, the major source of dynamism remains export agriculture. This is a function both of the openness of the economy[5] and of the high share of total exports taken by agricultural products. Thus, a trade-cycle model with elements common to both periods can be found, as well as a transmission mechanism which feeds through from the export sector to the rest of the economy.

There is an additional and more conventional reason for comparing the present economic crisis with the 1929 depression. My own researches[6] suggest that the recovery from the slump at the start of the 1930s did not have to wait upon a recovery of world commodity prices. This raises the question of whether or not the mechanisms of recovery in the 1930s are applicable to the 1980s.

## THE CENTRAL AMERICAN ECONOMIES IN THE 1970s

The withdrawal of Honduras from the Central American Common Market (CACM) in 1970 symbolised the end of a decade in which import-substituting industrialisation (ISI) had contributed to a rapid rise in real GDP. After 1970, although intra-regional trade continued to expand (at least in value terms), its share of total Central American trade declined.

Despite this, real GDP grew rapidly for most of the 1970s, based on increased earnings from traditional exports[7] as well as the sale of non-traditional exports (agricultural and industrial) outside the region.[8] The ratio of exports to GDP rose throughout the region, increasing the vulnerability of the economy to external shocks.

The rapid growth of the 1970s was affected only slightly by the oil crisis in 1973.[9] The reason for this is that the steep rise in the price of crude oil after October 1973 was matched to some extent by the rise in the price of Central America's traditional exports, particularly sugar, bananas and coffee (see Table 8.1). Thus, the deterioration of the net barter terms of trade after 1973 was much less severe than in many developing countries, where export price movements were not so favourable.[10]

The first oil crisis, therefore, did not seriously undermine the real side of the economy, but it had a profound impact on the financial side. As a small, open economy the rate of inflation in Central America is mainly determined by dollar-import prices adjusted for tariff and exchange-rate changes.[11] With tariff changes limited to once-and-for-all adjustments at the start of CACM and again in 1968 (when the San José

*Table* 8.1 Commodity prices, 1970–84
1980 = 100

| | *70* | *71* | *72* | *73* | *74* | *75* | *76* | *77* | *78* | *79* | *80* | *81* | *82* | *83* | *84** |
|---|---|---|---|---|---|---|---|---|---|---|---|---|---|---|---|
| Sugar† | 12.9 | 15.7 | 25.4 | 33.2 | 103.9 | 71.0 | 40.4 | 28.3 | 23.4 | 33.7 | 100.0 | 58.9 | 29.3 | 29.5 | 14.1 |
| Petroleum‡ | 6.3 | 8.0 | 8.6 | 12.9 | 37.1 | 39.4 | 40.9 | 45.0 | 45.0 | 60.8 | 100.0 | 116.1 | 116.1 | 101.6 | 97.9 |
| Bananas§ | 44.3 | 37.4 | 43.1 | 44.0 | 49.1 | 65.3 | 69.0 | 72.9 | 76.4 | 86.9 | 100.0 | 107.0 | 99.9 | 114.4 | 90.6 |
| Beef¶ | 47.0 | 48.5 | 53.3 | 72.5 | 57.0 | 47.8 | 57.2 | 54.3 | 77.1 | 104.5 | 100.0 | 89.6 | 86.6 | 88.4 | 78.2 |
| Coffee‖ | 33.3 | 28.8 | 32.2 | 39.9 | 42.2 | 41.9 | 91.5 | 150.2 | 104.3 | 112.5 | 100.0 | 83.1 | 90.6 | 85.4 | 94.2 |
| Cotton** | 30.9 | 36.1 | 38.7 | 66.2 | 69.5 | 56.6 | 82.7 | 76.0 | 76.8 | 82.3 | 100.0 | 89.6 | 77.4 | 89.7 | 80.6 |
| Terms of trade†† | 113.1 | 106.1 | 106.0 | 106.2 | 92.3 | 90.7 | 107.7 | 137.1 | 122.4 | 108.5 | 100.0 | 86.1 | 80.2 | — | — |

*August.
†Caribbean (pricing-point New York).
‡Venezuela (pricing-point Tia Juana).
§Latin America (pricing-point US ports).
¶All origins (pricing-point US ports).
‖Other milds (pricing-point New York).
**Liverpool Index.
††Price index terms of trade. Inter-American Development Bank (IDB) estimate based on official figures and ECLA publications. See IDB, *Regional Report for Central America* (September 1983), p. 33.

*Source*: IMF, *Yearbook*, 1983 and IMF, *International Financial Statistics* (October 1984).

protocol was introduced) and exchange-rate stability the rule rather than the exception, the inflation rate in the two decades before 1970 had been kept close to zero in Central America.[12]

At the beginning of the 1970s, import prices in dollar terms began to rise and this tendency was aggravated by the first oil crisis. The result was the acceleration of the rate of inflation in Central America to double figures (see Table 8.2).

With no previous experience of rapid inflation, but with a strong tradition of fiscal and monetary orthodoxy, policy-makers might have been expected to react through the exercise of stringent financial policies and a cut-back in public expenditure. This did not in general happen,[13] largely because the coffee boom after 1975[14] swelled government revenues and reduced the inflation-induced budget deficits.

The reasons why, in the Central American context, inflation tends to provoke a budget deficit are as follows: the main component of expenditure (current and capital) is wages and salaries and there has been a natural tendency to protect the real earnings of public employees; at the same time, in an effort to keep the inflation rate down, subsidies have been paid to firms in both the public and private sector by the central governments. The revenue side of the central government's account, however, has not exhibited the same tendency to increase, because so much income is still obtained from export duties or specific tariffs (neither of which increases in line with inflation), while the lag in collecting other forms of taxation has often been considerable.

For these reasons, the central government's budget deficit as a proportion of GDP has shown a tendency to increase throughout the

*Table* 8.2 Central America: annual inflation rates 1970–83 (%)

| | *70* | *71* | *72* | *73* | *74* | *75* | *76* | *77* | *78* | *79* | *80* | *81* | *82* | *83* |
|---|---|---|---|---|---|---|---|---|---|---|---|---|---|---|
| Costa Rica | 5 | 3 | 5 | 15 | 30 | 17 | 4 | 4 | 6 | 9 | 18 | 37 | 90 | 33 |
| El Salvador | 3 | 0 | 2 | 6 | 17 | 19 | 7 | 12 | 13 | 16 | 17 | 15 | 12 | 13 |
| Guatemala | 2 | 0 | 1 | 14 | 17 | 13 | 11 | 13 | 8 | 12 | 11 | 11 | 0.4 | 0* |
| Honduras | 3 | 2 | 5 | 5 | 13 | 6 | 5 | 8 | 6 | 13 | 16 | 10 | 10 | 9 |
| Nicaragua | NA | NA | NA | 22 | 13 | 8 | 3 | 11 | 5 | 48 | 35 | 24 | 25 | 31 |

*April to April. Taken From Banco de Guatemala, *Boletín Estadístico* (April–June 1983).

NA = not available.

*Source*: IMF, *International Financial Statistics, Yearbook* (1984).

1970s (see Table 8.3). The coffee boom after 1975 had two contradictory influences on this tendency; first, it swelled government revenue in the short term,[15] thereby reducing the deficit below what it would otherwise have been, while secondly it encouraged governments to undertake grandiose investment projects, which in the longer run contributed to a veritable explosion of capital expenditure.[16]

With recycled petrodollars readily available after 1973, there was a preference for funding the expanding budget deficits with foreign sources of finance, and net capital inflows rose extremely rapidly (see Table 8.4). Indeed, the level of these flows was such that net international reserves rose in more years than they fell between 1973 and 1980.

The consequence of these increased borrowings was an explosion in the rate of increase of external indebtedness. Because so much of the borrowing was carried out by governments, however, the most noticeable increases were in public external indebtedness (see Table 8.5); by the end of the decade, the 'debt problem' was already acute in Costa Rica, Honduras and Nicaragua; in El Salvador and Guatemala, the debt also grew rapidly after 1973, but started from a lower base.

At the end of the 1970s, therefore, the real economy in Central America had shown substantial progress,[17] but the financial side was looking dangerously exposed. Exchange-rate stability was no longer assumed in Costa Rica, where official devaluation had been adopted in 1974, nor in Nicaragua, where the Somoza administration had devalued shortly before its collapse; inflation had become a permanent reality, although the mechanisms for avoiding sharp changes in income distribution had not yet been developed; finally, a high level of foreign borrowing had avoided the need for recessionary policies, which in

*Table* 8.3 Central government budget deficit as a percentage of GDP, 1970–83

| | *70* | *71* | *72* | *73* | *74* | *75* | *76* | *77* | *78* | *79* | *80* | *81* | *82* | *83* |
|---|---|---|---|---|---|---|---|---|---|---|---|---|---|---|
| Costa Rica | 0.6 | 4.7 | 4.2 | 4.1 | 1.7 | 2.7 | 4.8 | 3.0 | 4.3 | 6.6 | 8.2 | 3.6 | 3.0 | 2.7 |
| El Salvador | 0.9 | 0.6 | 1.4 | 0.8 | 1.2 | 1.3 | 0.8 | 2.5 | 2.0 | 0.9 | 6.6 | 8.0 | 7.7 | 5.8 |
| Guatemala | 1.3 | 0.8 | 2.4 | 1.8 | 1.3 | 0.3 | 3.7 | 0.7 | 1.2 | 2.6 | 4.7 | 7.3 | 4.0 | 3.9 |
| Honduras | 3.3 | 3.1 | 3.8 | 1.8 | 2.9 | 6.0 | 5.4 | 5.0 | 6.9 | 4.4 | 4.7 | 6.2 | 7.4 | 7.1 |
| Nicaragua | 1.3 | 2.4 | 3.2 | 3.3 | 5.3 | 5.7 | 5.7 | 7.1 | 8.1 | 6.6 | 9.0 | 10.4 | 19.5 | 26.8 |

*Sources*: 1970–9: Consejo Monetario Centroamericano, *Boletín Estadístico*, various years; 1980–3: Inter-American Development Bank, *Annual Report* (1984).

*Table* 8.4 Central America: net balance on capital account, 1974–83 (millions of dollars)

| | *74* | *75* | *76* | *77* | *78* | *79* | *80* | *81* | *82* | *83* |
|---|---|---|---|---|---|---|---|---|---|---|
| Costa Rica | 187.1 | 182.1 | 259.6 | 357.7 | 440.8 | 358.8 | 826.1 | 283.2 | 210.9 | 300.0 |
| El Salvador | 154.2 | 112.9 | 100.3 | 41.7 | 369.9 | – 49.1 | 214.5 | 160.5 | 279.1 | 290.4 |
| Guatemala | 87.9 | 180.4 | 242.6 | 241.8 | 398.9 | 224.4 | – 74.4 | 290.8 | 353.4 | 263.3 |
| Honduras | 91.9 | 166.0 | 129.7 | 201.6 | 154.1 | 230.8 | 278.0 | 237.6 | 91.5 | 204.3 |
| Nicaragua | 240.6 | 223.2 | 40.6 | 194.7 | – 49.0 | – 145.6 | 210.9 | 561.8 | 383.5 | 535.9 |

*Source*: Inter-American Development Bank, *Annual Report* (1984).

*Table* 8.5 Central America: external debt outstanding, end-period, public and publicly guaranteed (including undisbursed), 1973–82 (million dollars)

| | *73* | *75* | *77* | *78* | *79* | *80* | *81* | *82* |
|---|---|---|---|---|---|---|---|---|
| Costa Rica | 344 | 732 | 1292 | 1619 | 1934 | 2523 | 3127 | 3395 |
| El Salvador | 183 | 383 | 451 | 647 | 717 | 926 | 1049 | 1335 |
| Guatemala | 206 | 268 | 625 | 745 | 820 | 1050 | 1384 | 1510 |
| Honduras | 215 | 449 | 810 | 977 | 1269 | 1716 | 1956 | 2044 |
| Nicaragua | 497 | 823 | 1108 | 1199 | 1417 | 2145 | 2639 | 3472 |

*Source*: World Bank, *Debt Tables* (1983).

other circumstances would have had to be adopted to deal with both the deterioration in the net barter terms of trade and the tendency of government expenditure to outstrip revenue in an inflationary environment.

## THE 1979 DEPRESSION

As with its predecessor the 1929 depression, 'the 1979 depression' is a phrase covering a series of events spread over several years. Certain export prices started falling before 1979, others not until the 1980s, and the cumulative effect of these changes did not produce a decline in economic activity throughout the region until 1982, a decline which (except in Costa Rica and Nicaragua) continued throughout 1983.[18] Provided this is clearly understood, no great harm is done by referring to these events as the 1979 depression.

Coffee prices, which had soared as a result of the 1975 frost in Brazil, peaked in 1977 and fell sharply the following year. As coffee is a major source of export earnings for all five Central American republics,[19] this fall reversed the sharp rise in export unit values of the 1976/7 period; import unit values, however, continued to rise after 1977 and the net barter terms of trade throughout the region began to decline in 1978.

The deterioration in the terms of trade in 1978 accelerated in the following years as a result of two factors: the rise in import unit values and the fall in non-coffee export prices. The former reached double figures in 1979 and 1980,[20] while beef prices started to fall after 1979, sugar and cotton prices after 1980 and banana prices after 1981 (see Table 8.1).

The impact of these unfavourable export price movements on export earnings could not be reversed by increases in the quantum of exports as a consequence both of the world recession beginning in 1979 and of supply-side constraints. The latter were most apparent in war-torn Nicaragua, where export earnings peaked in 1978, and in post-Romero El Salvador, where the nationalisation of the export trade and the first stage of the land reform programme had a predictable impact on traditional exports and export earnings after 1979. Elsewhere in the region, however, exports peaked in 1980 (see Table 8.6).[21]

As in the rest of Latin America, one consequence of ISI has been to change the structure of imports away from consumer goods towards intermediate and capital goods. In the case of Central America, this must be qualified by distinguishing between extra- and intra-regional imports, the latter still being dominated by consumer goods. Despite

*Table* 8.6 Central America: imports, exports and balance-of-payments current account (million dollars), 1977–83

| | *77* | *78* | *79* | *80* | *81* | *82* | *83* |
|---|---|---|---|---|---|---|---|
| *Costa Rica* | | | | | | | |
| Exports f.o.b. | 828 | 864 | 942 | 1001 | 1003 | 869 | 853 |
| Imports f.o.b. | 925 | 1049 | 1257 | 1375 | 1090 | 805 | 898 |
| Current account balance | − 226 | − 364 | − 558 | − 663 | − 409 | − 267 | − 284 |
| *El Salvador* | | | | | | | |
| Exports f.o.b. | 974 | 802 | 1132 | 1075 | 798 | 704 | 735 |
| Imports f.o.b. | 861 | 951 | 955 | 897 | 898 | 826 | 831 |
| Current account balance | + 31 | − 286 | + 21 | + 31 | − 250 | − 152 | − 65 |
| *Guatemala* | | | | | | | |
| Exports f.o.b. | 1160 | 1092 | 1222 | 1520 | 1291 | 1170 | 1092 |
| Imports f.o.b. | 1087 | 1284 | 1402 | 1473 | 1540 | 1284 | 1056 |
| Current account balance | − 35 | − 271 | − 206 | − 163 | − 573 | − 399 | − 224 |
| *Honduras* | | | | | | | |
| Exports f.o.b. | 530 | 626 | 757 | 850 | 784 | 677 | 699 |
| Imports f.o.b. | 550 | 654 | 783 | 954 | 899 | 681 | 756 |
| Current account balance | − 129 | − 157 | − 192 | − 317 | − 303 | − 228 | − 219 |
| *Nicaragua* | | | | | | | |
| Exports f.o.b. | 637 | 646 | 616 | 450 | 508 | 406 | 428 |
| Imports f.o.b. | 704 | 553 | 389 | 803 | 922 | 724 | 778 |
| Current account balance | − 182 | − 25 | + 180 | − 379 | − 506 | − 471 | − 444 |

*Source*: *International Financial Statistics, Yearbook*, 1986.

this, the import bill now consists mainly of goods which are complementary to domestic production, so that a decline in imports implies a decline in economic activity.

In order to avoid the fall in imports, with its predictable effect on output, incomes and employment, several republics tolerated a huge rise in their current-account deficits, financed in large part by a fall in net international reserves. In Guatemala, for example, the rise in imports in 1981 provoked a $573 million current-account deficit, while net capital inflows were only $288 million, and total international reserves collapsed from $445 million at the end of 1980 to $150 million at the end of 1981.

In Costa Rica and Honduras, the attempt to increase imports by value was abandoned after 1980, as the current-account deficit in that year widened to unprecedented levels (see Table 8.6). In El Salvador, the decline in imports by value began as early as 1979 as a consequence of capital flight which dried up the supply of foreign exchange for imports of goods. In Nicaragua, imports by value reached their first peak in 1977, falling in 1978 and 1979 as a result of capital flight and the civil war. The recovery after the war was short-lived, however, and imports by value reached their second peak in 1981 when the current account deficit ($506 million) equalled the value of exports f.o.b.

The effort to increase the value of imports despite stagnant or declining export earnings was financed not only through falls in international reserves (see Table 8.7), but also through increases in foreign borrowing, and the public external debt climbed steadily throughout the early 1980s (see Table 8.5). By 1981, Costa Rica had defaulted on its external obligations and in 1983 Nicaragua again ran into difficulties with its creditors.[22] In 1983, Honduras was also unable to meet its commitments to its external creditors in full.

The external-payments strain experienced by Central America in the period 1979–81 financed an increase in the price of imports rather than their value. The real value of imports (see Table 7.8) had peaked by 1978 in Guatemala, El Salvador and Nicaragua and only in Honduras did their level increase significantly in 1979. By 1981, the volume of imports was falling in all republics except Nicaragua and by 1982 a dramatic decline was experienced everywhere.

The recent sharp fall in the real value of imports has been due to the austerity programmes carried out in each republic, in several cases as part of the conditions attached to IMF loans.[23] Exchange-rate stability was abandoned explicitly in Costa Rica after December 1980[24] and there have been *de facto* devaluations in El Salvador, Guatemala and

*Table* 8.7 Net change in official international reserves 1977–83 (million dollars)
A minus sign indicates an increase.

| | *1977* | *1978* | *1979* | *1980* | *1981* | *1982* | *1983* |
|---|---|---|---|---|---|---|---|
| Costa Rica | 119.6 | − 27.3 | 119.8 | − 91.6 | 52.3 | − 118.1 | 59.1 |
| El Salvador | − 41.0 | − 55.5 | 133.9 | 74.6 | 48.9 | − 70.1 | − 179.0 |
| Guatemala | − 179.6 | − 72.7 | 25.5 | 256.7 | 303.6 | 34.9 | − 30.0 |
| Honduras | − 66.3 | − 9.4 | − 19.8 | 77.7 | 71.8 | 88.5 | 8.0 |
| Nicaragua | − 9.1 | 83.6 | − 5.0 | 196.9 | − 57.7 | 99.5 | − 70.5 |

*Source*: Inter-American Development Bank, *Annual Report* (1983), Table 55.

Nicaragua.[25] In Honduras, tariff surcharges have reduced the demand for imports[26] and throughout the region non-price rationing has been applied to reduce the demand for foreign exchange.

The most notable feature of the austerity programmes, however, outside of Nicaragua, has been the restraint on the public sector. The contribution of the government sector to GDP in real terms has shown no increase since 1980[27] and the budget deficit as a proportion of GDP fell sharply in 1982 in Costa Rica and Guatemala (see Table 8.3), while even in El Salvador there was a modest decline.

The continued effect of the decline in export earnings, the restraint on the public sector and the fall in real imports was sufficient to provoke a fall in real GDP throughout the region in 1982. The decline had begun a year earlier in Costa Rica, and as early as 1979 in El Salvador, while Nicaragua had experienced two years of rapid decline in 1978–9 followed by two years of economic recovery (1980–1). By 1982, however, the whole region was in the grip of a severe depression. In the period 1980 to 1983, real GDP per head had fallen by some 25 per cent in El Salvador, some 20 per cent in Costa Rica and nearly 15 per cent in Guatemala and Honduras.

The recent decline in GDP has been disproportionately concentrated in those sectors dependent on imports for their survival, in particular manufacturing, construction and commerce. The latter, which has traditionally earned a high share of its income from the resale of imported consumer goods, has been very severely hit by import restraint; in Costa Rica, for example, its share of GDP fell from 18 per cent in 1980 to 13.5 per cent in 1982.

Manufacturing production has been affected not only by the shortage of complementary imports, but also by the shrinking of the regional market. The value of CACM trade declined sharply after 1980,[28] as regional tensions led to a closing of borders and the scarcity of foreign exchange produced a series of beggar-my-neighbour policies designed to produce an export surplus with CACM partners. Paradoxically, those countries which have realised a surplus on trade within CACM have seen their advantage eroded as payment has often been blocked.

A further problem affecting manufacturing output, as well as several other sectors, has been the shrinking of the domestic market not only through the fall in mean real income, but also through a deterioration in the distribution of income. Real wages (see Table 8.8) have fallen sharply in Costa Rica, El Salvador and even Nicaragua since 1979, while their level in Guatemala is far below that recorded in 1970.

The agricultural sector has been subject to two contradictory forces in the recent period, as so often in the past. While export agriculture (EXA) has tended to shrink in real as well as money terms, agriculture for the home market – domestic-use agriculture (DUA) – has been able to benefit from the restrictions on imports[29] and deliberate government policies. The two effects have tended to cancel each other out in Costa Rica, Guatemala and Honduras, while the decline in EXA has been dominant in El Salvador (producing an overall fall in agricultural net output).

The 1979 depression has therefore not fallen with equal severity on all sectors; while real net output in agriculture has tended to stagnate, increasing the sector's share of real GDP, value added by industry,

*Table* 8.8 Central America: real wages, 1979–82 (index numbers)

| | *Base year* (= 100) | *1979* | *1980* | *1981* | *1982* |
|---|---|---|---|---|---|
| Costa Rica* | 1975 | 140.5 | 136.5 | 121.2 | 92.6 |
| El Salvador† | 1970 | 88.3 | 82.9 | 72.2 | 64.6 |
| Guatemala* | 1970 | 68.6 | 62.0 | 66.7 | 65.2 |
| Honduras | 1976 | 102.0 | 96.0 | 104.0 | 104.0 |
| Nicaragua | 1975 | 95.9 | 81.7 | 79.7 | 69.8 |

*Based on wage data held by social security institute.
†Agricultural labourers only.

*Source*: Inforpress, *Centroamericana* (June 1983), no. 548, p. 10.

commerce and construction has fallen quite sharply.[30] Changes within the agricultural sector, however, have been of importance and the rural economy has not been spared the dramatic fall in real income per person which has afflicted the urban economy.

## THE 1929 DEPRESSION AND THE MECHANISMS OF RECOVERY

As with the 1979 depression, the '1929 depression' is a phrase covering the decline in economic activity over a period of years, which began in Costa Rica as early as 1927, but which did not affect Honduras until the fiscal year 1931/2.[31]

The 1929 depression in Central America was brought on by a collapse of export earnings. With exports dominated by earnings from coffee and bananas,[32] the sharp fall in the price of the former and the volume of the latter[33] provoked a collapse in foreign-exchange receipts to about one-quarter of the pre-depression peak. For a brief period, an attempt was made to sustain the level of imports, but the difficulty of securing a net capital inflow from abroad and the requirements of public external debt-servicing forced each republic to run a trade surplus during the worst years of the depression (1930–2) and the value of imports collapsed even more rapidly than exports.

The decline in the value of external trade provoked a fiscal crisis through its impact on trade taxes and government revenue. Efforts to cut back government expenditure, consisting mainly of wages and salaries, contributed to the political crisis in 1930 and 1931 and were not wholly successful; public-sector deficits then had to be financed through increases in the internal debt.[34]

The public-sector deficits were not the result of Keynesian demand management (although a half-hearted attempt at a public works programme was made in Costa Rica)[35] and government expenditure in money terms declined.[36] With private consumption and investment (both private and public) adversely affected by the fall in imports, all items of expenditure moved pro-cyclically with exports, and the money value of GDP declined dramatically.[37]

Expressed in money terms, there is clearly no comparison between the 1929 and 1979 depressions. The former was much more severe and the collapse of export prices (particularly coffee and sugar) has no parallel with today. In real terms, however, the parallels are much closer: the volume of traditional exports kept up surprisingly well in the worst years of the depression and, although the net barter terms of trade of coffee producers deteriorated,[38] import prices also fell quite sharply.

Thus, the decline in real GDP and real GDP per head (see Tables 2.1 and 2.2) bears comparison with the falls in recent years. Indeed, the collapse of economic activity in El Salvador since 1979 and in Nicaragua between 1978 and 1979 is much more severe than during the 1929 depression.

Furthermore, the dominant role played by external factors in both depressions is readily apparent. In both cases, the depression was triggered off by unfavourable commodity-price movements; in the 1929 depression this leads to a collapse of export earnings, while in the 1979 depression it leads to a stagnation of earnings; since the latter depression, however, is taking place against a background of rising rather than falling world prices, the impact on real imports in both depressions is the same and their volume declines.

The fiscal crisis in the 1929 depression was provoked by the collapse of revenue from taxes on external trade. These have declined in importance in the intervening years, but some two-thirds of government revenue are still obtained from indirect taxes, which tend to move pro-cyclically with the value of external trade.

In both fiscal crises, however, an important role has been played by service payments on the external public debt. In the 1929 depression, fixed nominal payments in a period of falling prices together with currency depreciation (Costa Rica, El Salvador) pushed service payments to between 20 per cent and 30 per cent of government revenue. In the more recent crisis, fixed nominal payments would have been a blessing rather than a burden (because of inflation), but interest rates have been flexible upwards and currency depreciation has added to the problems in Nicaragua and Costa Rica.

In the 1929 depression, there were no international lending agencies to lay down conditions for borrowing. Nevertheless, the governments' hands were frequently tied either by the presence of a foreign controller of customs or by agreements with foreign bond-holders on the disposition of revenues. In both periods, an attempt was made to cut the public-sector deficit back to a level which could be financed without an increase in the internal debt, although in neither case was it very successful.

As Table 2.1 makes clear, the five-year period after 1934 was marked by rapid growth in several republics. This recovery is all the more surprising, given that coffee prices remained close to their floor throughout the 1930s and that banana exports continued to be affected by disease in Honduras and Costa Rica.

The collapse of coffee prices after 1929 put at risk the leading export sector in all Central American republics outside Honduras. Property values fell and growers were threatened with foreclosure by their creditors (mainly commercial banks and exporters). Associations grew up to defend growers, and the authoritarian state, which after 1930 replaced its liberal, oligarchic predecessor,[39] intervened by declaring a debt moratorium and aiding coffee growers in several other ways.

State intervention made possible the continuance of the volume of coffee exports at pre-depression levels and this helped to prevent further falls in real GDP. It was not, however, a mechanism of recovery and the export sector did not play a dynamic role in the 1930s.

The dynamic role was provided essentially by import-substitution; this was not so much import-substitution in industry (ISI) as in agriculture (ISA). The development of export specialisation in Central America in the half-century up to 1930 had led to the neglect of agriculture for domestic use (DUA) and food imports in 1929 represented some 20 per cent of the import bill. The shortage of foreign exchange throughout the 1930s contributed to the development of ISA, a development which was further assisted by an improvement in the distribution of income.[40]

Import-substitution of both types was aided by tariff increases and currency depreciation (in Costa Rica and El Salvador). Nevertheless, ISI played only a minor role because the almost complete absence of an industrial base in the 1920s meant that there was no spare capacity to take advantage of import restrictions. The development of new industrial capacity makes much use of both foreign exchange and credit, and neither were available in the 1930s.[41]

An additional recovery mechanism was provided by debt default. Central American republics, in common with most of Latin America, withdrew from the gold standard after 1931, and after 1932 defaulted on their external debt obligations.[42] This eased the fiscal crisis considerably and freed a substantial part of government revenue for deployment elsewhere.[43]

## LESSONS FOR THE 1980s

In the 1920s, the Central American import bill was dominated by consumer goods. Their suppression in the 1930s led to a fall in the living standards of the urban middle and upper classes, but *ceteris paribus* import restrictions had little impact on production outside of the unimportant non-food-processing industrial sector. That is why EXA was able to maintain its previous level of output and DUA to expand despite a fall in real imports.

In the 1980s, the industrial sector contributes some 20 per cent to GDP and is highly dependent on imports for machinery, raw materials and spare parts. Furthermore, EXA is now more mechanised and more import-intensive (fertilisers, insecticides, etc.) than in the 1930s, while even DUA in certain cases (e.g. rice) has become dependent on complementary imports.

Thus, all tradable activities exhibit import-dependence, and production is likely to be adversely affected by import restrictions. In addition, the scope for ISA is much less in the 1980s than in the 1930s, for three reasons: first, the share of food imports in the total import bill in 1979 was much less than in 1929, and secondly, movements in income distribution have been, if anything, in favour of greater inequality.[44] Thirdly, land is much scarcer and the expansion of DUA no longer has a zero opportunity cost.[45]

Despite this, however, there are signs that DUA might again contribute to recovery, albeit in a more modest way. Although it exhibits a certain import dependence, it is much less than that exhibited by other sectors so that a shortage of foreign exchange is not so critical. Furthermore, land-reform programmes in El Salvador and Nicaragua have led to an increase in the relative importance of DUA, although in both cases this has occurred to some extent at the expense of an absolute decline in EXA.[46]

The problem of preventing a fall in the volume of traditional exports presents similar difficulties in the 1980s to the 1930s. In the 1930s, prices were falling faster than costs, while in the 1980s costs are rising with prices stable or falling; in both cases there has been a profit squeeze and coffee-growers in El Salvador, for example, in an echo of the 1930s, have called on the government to impose a debt moratorium.[47]

Through its control of export taxes, the exchange rate, import tariffs and credit, the state is in a powerful position to manipulate the net price received by growers and there is ample evidence that this process is well under way.[48] As in the 1930s, however, this is unlikely to do more than stabilise the volume of traditional exports, as world market conditions will remain unfavourable for these crops.[49]

The third recovery mechanism from the 1930s (debt default) does not look so promising. In the 1980s Central America cannot afford to run the risk of zero or negative capital inflows, because the cost of running a current-account surplus in terms of lost output would be very high. That is why all republics, even Nicaragua, have been anxious to reschedule their external obligations rather than default unilaterally.

Rescheduling, however, as Nicaragua has found since 1981, does not represent a panacea. Indeed, the burden of debt-servicing remains very high even after a sucessful rescheduling and puts a continuing squeeze both on non-debt government expenditure and on merchandise imports. This reduces the degrees of freedom of Central American governments in the 1980s compared with the 1930s and it must be remembered that for several years to come a large share of any fresh capital inflow will be required simply to refinance the external debt.

The choice of rescheduling rather than debt default makes impossible two other possible recovery mechanisms, neither of which was attempted in the 1930s; the first is Keynesian demand management based on deficit financing, while the second is ISI in intermediate and capital goods. The first mechanism has never made much sense in the context of small, developing countries and is in any case ruled out by the conditions attached to loans contracted with the IMF (a precondition for loans from other sources).[50] The second mechanism is very import-intensive and is therefore ruled out by the squeeze on imports which can be expected to continue for some years to come. Furthermore, ISI in non-consumer goods is possible only at the regional level, which presupposes a degree of regional harmony totally lacking at present.

## CONCLUSIONS

The above study of recovery mechanisms in the 1930s suggests that, if repeated in the 1980s, they would produce only a modest improvement in economic performance. This is true, despite the many parallels which exist between the 1929 and 1979 depressions.

The reasons why the old recovery mechanisms are no longer sufficient are related to changes in the structure of the economy in the intervening period. First, the composition of the import bill has changed in such a way that the level of home output is now much more sensitive to an import squeeze. There are no longer branches of the economy where production does not require complementary imports. Within DUA, there are some crops which are not particularly import-intensive (e.g. maize), but land is no longer costlessly available for their expansion.

Secondly, the 1979 depression is taking place against a background of rising rather than falling prices. With money-wage rigidity apparent in both periods, the consequence was an improvement in income distribution in the 1930s, but probably a deterioration in income distribution in the 1980s. Thus, the market demand for many consumer goods in the 1980s has exhibited a further contraction in addition to that implied by the fall in mean real income.

The prospects for the 1980s therefore look more gloomy than the outcome of the 1930s and it is worth considering whether alternative recovery mechanisms may be available. After peaking in the late 1920s, Central America's net barter terms of trade went through a period of secular decline until the late 1940s. If this decline was reversed more rapidly after the 1979 depression, then clearly the foreign-exchange constraint would be eased. Import-intensive activities could then expand and the recovery would be on its way.

It is difficult to predict the course of commodity prices, but the prospects for Central America's traditional exports do not look particularly bright. Alone of the region's republics, Honduras in the 1930s had to wait on an improvement in the fortunes of export agriculture before a weak recovery could get under way. It seems equally probable that in the 1980s only a modest improvement can be expected from a change in the fortunes of EXA on its own.

Another possibility is that the production of manufactured goods for export outside the region may increase. Certainly, there is spare capacity in the many duty-free export-processing zones throughout the region and market opportunities have increased since the passing by the United States Congress of the Caribbean Basin Initiative. However, these exports are starting from a very low base and would have to grow very rapidly to make much impact on the growth of real GDP, even if they can overcome the formidable obstacles presented by the shortage of investment, skilled labour and management expertise.

It is not inconceivable that the foreign-exchange constraint, the principal barrier to growth at present throughout the region, will be lifted as a result of international initiatives through a mini-Marshall Plan for the region.[51] Over the last few years, several voices have been raised to this effect; without US support, however, such an initiative will not operate and at present neither the US Congress nor the Administration appears well disposed towards a massive injection of economic aid to the region.

We must conclude, therefore, that the prospects for economic recovery in the 1980s and for a resumption of rapid growth are poor. This prognostication could change if regional harmony were restored and economic cooperation resumed at the regional level; this, however, is a political question involving not just the Central American republics and, when the international dimension is introduced, the prospects are indeed more gloomy than they were fifty years ago.

## Notes

1. The title of this chapter was chosen before coming across an article by Carlos Díaz Alejandro comparing Latin America in the 1930s with the 1980s. Díaz Alejandro's article, however, does not in general draw on the Central American experience. See Díaz Alejandro (1983).
2. Two recent exceptions are Feinberg and Pastor (1984) and John Weeks (1985), particularly Chapter 8.
3. In both 1929 to 1931 and 1979 to 1981, Honduras enjoyed positive, if modest, growth of real GDP. From 1979 to 1981, there was positive growth in Guatemala, and real GDP increased in Nicaragua in 1980, 1981 and 1983. These are the exceptions, however, and after both 1929 and 1979 falls in real GDP were common throughout Central America.
4. Some readers may object to the use of the singular 'economy' rather than the plural 'economies'. There are, of course, many important differences between the economies of the Central American republics and, where these are relevant, I shall use the plural form. Nevertheless, the region's economic performance over the long run can be analysed in terms of a model common to all republics and this similarity can be captured by the use of the singular form.
5. One way in which the openness of the economy can be expressed is through the ratio of exports to GDP. In 1979, for example, which comes close to the last 'normal' year, exports were just over 35 per cent of GDP in El Salvador, Honduras and Nicaragua, were 27 per cent in Costa Rica and 21 per cent in Guatemala. For middle-income countries as a whole, the percentage was 18 per cent, a figure which is easily surpassed by all Central American republics except Guatemala even when extra-regional exports alone are considered.
6. See Chapter 3.
7. In the 1920s, 'traditional' exports refer to coffee and bananas only. By the 1970s, the list had been expanded to include cotton, sugar and beef.
8. Examples are provided by cardamom from Guatemala, clothing from El Salvador, timber from Honduras and light manufactures from Costa Rica.
9. In Honduras, hurricane damage in 1974 contributed to a fall in real GDP in 1974 and 1975, but this was independent of the oil crisis.
10. See Chapter 2, Figure 2.1.

11. See Bulmer-Thomas (1977), pp. 319–32.
12. Between 1950 and 1970, the annual average rate of change of prices was below 1 per cent in Guatemala, below 2 per cent in El Salvador and Honduras and 2.1 per cent in Costa Rica. Figures are not available for the whole period for Nicaragua, but there is no reason to believe that the inflation rate was not in the same range.
13. Although at first there was a movement in this direction. See Siri and Dominguez (1981).
14. The coffee boom was sparked off by severe frost in Brazil in 1975.
15. In Costa Rica, for example, the yield from the coffee tax rose from 79.4 million colones in 1975 to 257.4 million colones in 1977.
16. In 1976, capital expenditure by central government rose by 66 per cent in El Salvador, 92 per cent in Costa Rica, and 151 per cent in Guatemala. See Inforpress (1982).
17. Except in Nicaragua, where rapid growth up to 1977 was reversed in 1978 and 1979 as a consequence of the civil war.
18. In the reports prepared by each government in consultation with the Inter-American Development Bank for presentation to the EEC in September 1983, all countries predicted either a fall or zero growth in real GDP for 1983. Nicaragua, however, finally achieved a 4.6 per cent, and Costa Rica a 2.9 per cent increase in real GDP.
19. The share of coffee earnings in total exports in 1978 was as follows: Costa Rica 43.5 per cent, El Salvador 51.9 per cent, Guatemala 43.5 per cent, Honduras 33.0 per cent and Nicaragua 30.8 per cent.
20. Except for 1979 in Honduras, where the rate of increase was 7 per cent. Figures are not given for Nicaragua, but are assumed to be in the same range (see Inforpress (1982)).
21. Export earnings in Costa Rica peaked in 1981, but the level was virtually the same as 1980.
22. The Nicaraguan external debt was renegotiated successfully in December 1980. Despite this, debt-servicing rose to 40 per cent of exports in 1982, forcing the government to seek a further accommodation with its creditors in 1983.
23. In addition to the compensatory financing facility, which comes without conditions when export earnings fall below trend, all Central American countries other than Nicaragua have received IMF loans subject to various conditions on domestic economic policies. The cornerstone of these conditions has been restraint on the public sector.
24. The collapse of the Costa Rican exchange rate has been dramatic since December 1980. While the official rate fell from 8.60 colones to 20 colones to the US dollar, the inter-bank rate has fallen to 44 colones and the free-market rate touched 80 colones to the dollar at one point. Virtually all merchandise trade is conducted at the inter-bank rate.
25. Official devaluation was delayed until 1985 in Nicaragua and 1986 in El Salvador and Guatemala.
26. An additional 'temporary' tax of 20 per cent was imposed on all imported goods in 1982.
27. Except in Nicaragua, where value added by public administration rose by 12.6 per cent in real terms between 1980 and 1982.

28. Intra-regional exports in 1980 were valued at $1,129 million. These fell to $947 million in 1981 and $765 million in 1982.
29. Food imports at the beginning of the 1979 depression accounted for some 5 to 10 per cent of the import bill.
30. See Chapter 7, Table 7.12.
31. Real GDP for these years is given in Bulmer-Thomas (1987), Table A.1.
32. In 1929, coffee and bananas accounted for some 90 per cent of exports from Costa Rica, El Salvador (coffee only) and Guatemala. In Nicaragua and Honduras, the export of precious metals pushed the figure for coffee and bananas down to 73 per cent and 87 per cent respectively.
33. After 1929, the banana trade was dominated by two multinational fruit companies, United Fruit and Standard Fruit. By cutting back on global production, they were able to avoid a sharp fall in banana prices in consuming countries; the impact of the depression in Central America was therefore experienced through reductions in banana volumes rather than prices, the exact opposite of coffee exports.
34. The internal debt rose sharply in all republics, except Nicaragua where government finances were directly controlled by US officials under the Financial Plan of 1917. See Cox, (1927).
35. See Soley Güell (1975), pp. 100–8.
36. See League of Nations (1937).
37. There are official estimates for money GDP (i.e. at current prices) for both Guatemala and Honduras. In the former case, nominal GDP is estimated to have fallen to one-quarter of its peak level (see Banco Central de Guatemala, 1955).
38. See Chapter 3, Figure 3.2.
39. Not all scholars of Central America would explain the political changes in these terms, but there is general agreement that the period marks a change in the dominant political model. See, in particular, Torres Rivas (1973).
40. The question of an improvement in income distribution during a period when governments were avowedly 'anti-labour' is a controversial one, although it is the only one consistent with the statistical evidence; see Chapter 3.
41. Before 1929, expansion of industry had relied either on self-finance or immigrant capital. An examination of bank balance sheets in the inter-war years suggests that credit for industry was virtually zero, in sharp contrast to the case of export agriculture (particularly coffee).
42. Honduras defaulted on her internal debt obligations only, however, honouring her external debt payments.
43. Between 1932 and 1934, external debt service in Costa Rica, for example, fell from 30 per cent to 12 per cent of government revenue.
44. Real wages gave fallen (risen) faster (slower) than real GDP. This suggests a deterioration in the functional distribution of income; figures are not available on movements in the size distribution of income.
45. A surplus of both labour and land is responsible for the argument that DUA had a zero opportunity cost in the 1930s (capital not being used in significant amounts in DUA's production). Elsewhere, however, I have argued that even in the 1930s there were important differences in the

availability of land between 'coffee republics' (El Salvador, Costa Rica and Guatemala) and 'banana republics' (Nicaragua and Honduras). See Chapter 3.

46. See Bulmer-Thomas (1987), Table A.4.
47. See Inforpress, *Centroamericana*, 11 August 1983, no. 554, p. 10.
48. The multinational fruit companies, for example, pressured the Honduran government into reducing the banana export tax in 1983.
49. Trade prospects for traditional exports over the medium term are considered in Bulmer-Thomas (1985).
50. IMF conditionality does not apply to Nicaragua, which has no stand-by arrangement with the Fund. Keynesian demand-management techniques, however, remain as difficult to apply in Nicaragua as in the rest of Central America.
51. The Bipartisan Commission on Central America (the Kissinger Report) called for a massive injection of external finance between 1984 and 1990. Of the total of $20.6 billion (excluding Nicaragua), some $8.5 billion was to be provided by the US Government. Congress, however, has shown little support for voting such sums of money.

# 9 The Kissinger Report

The National Bipartisan Commission was set up by President Reagan in 1983 to explore solutions to the Central American crisis. Chaired by Henry Kissinger, it sought evidence from a number of specialists on the region. Each specialist was sent a set of questions and was asked to reply by 30 September 1983. The evidence was then sifted by the Commission and used to prepare the Kissinger Report published in January 1984. Below is the list of questions sent by the Commission and my response.

## QUESTIONS ON CENTRAL AMERICA

1. What do you conceive US interests to be in Central America? Is the area important to our national security? How? Is it important to our economic interests? How so?

2. How important is it for the United States to help countries in the region eliminate hunger, malnutrition, illiteracy? What concrete measures should we take?

3. How important is it for us to help countries in the region with economic growth and development? How significant is economic development to future peace in the region? What is the appropriate US role? What practical concrete measures can we take? Assistance to land reform? Rural cooperatives? Assistance in developing economic infrastructures? Intermediate credit institutions?

4. How significant is the international financial crisis for Central America? Ought the United States to make proposals for special institutional arrangements to manage the financial difficulties of the Central American countries? Should the IMF and/or the World Bank undertake emergency programs?

5. How important is it that democratic governments be established in the countries of Central America? Is democracy a precondition to peace and security in the region? If so, what can the US do to help further the process?

6. What can the US do to foster the establishment of free and

democratic non-governmental institutions and organisations in the region?

7. Is it important for the US to support more educational and cultural exchange with countries of the region. If so, how?

8. Should the United States consider the establishment in Central America of totalitarian governments tied to the Soviet Union as a security threat? Or doesn't it matter much? Should all Marxist-Leninist governments be considered tied to the Soviet Union? If not, where is the dividing line?

9. What can be done to prevent indigenous revolutionary movements in the region from coming under the control of Marxist-Leninists?

10. Do you believe the national independence and self-determination of countries in Central America are threatened by Soviet/Cuban support for guerrilla wars?

11. What are the Soviet interests and designs in the region? How important do you think it is to the Soviets to prevent the defeat of the Salvadoran insurgents? And what means are appropriate?

12. Is it appropriate for the United States to provide military assistance to governments whose opponents are receiving military assistance from the Soviet bloc?

13. Are there any circumstances under which the US should use military force in Central America? What are these circumstances?

14. Should arms aid to El Salvador be conditioned on progress on human rights? Do you accept the notion that in the event there was no progress on human rights we should terminate military assistance?

15. What role should our European allies play with regard to the region? Japan?

16. What of the Latin Americans? How useful a role can groups such as the Contadora Group play in the search for peace? For development? What about the OAS?

17. What multilateral institutional arrangements can promote economic advance and social and economic progress in Central America?

18. How effective do you find American policymaking machinery as it bears on Central America today? What is the appropriate role of the President? The Congress? The State Department? The National Secur-

ity Council? The Defense Department? The Foreign Service? The Armed Services?

19. What are the possibilities for building a public consensus for policy in Central America?

20. What other practical, concrete efforts can and should the United States undertake to enhance an evolution of Central America compatible with democracy and the security of the hemisphere?

## EVIDENCE TO THE NATIONAL BIPARTISAN COMMISSION ON CENTRAL AMERICA

Although the origin of United States interest in Central America in the nineteenth century is to be found in the possibility of building an inter-oceanic canal through Nicaragua, present interest stems much more from the region's proximity to Panama and Mexico. The latter is of concern because of the possibility that developments in Central America might spill over into the United States' most immediate southern neighbour (a version of the domino theory), while the former is of key interest because the Panama Canal is a vital factor in US strategic planning and because so much oil and other essential resources required by the US economy pass through it.

Despite substantial US investments in both bananas and manufacturing, it cannot be argued that the US has important economic interests in the region and there is very little evidence that the main thrust of US policy has been determined by such consideration. Even the US-inspired coup against the Arbenz government in 1954, often described as carried out in the interest of the United Fruit Co., is better understood if seen in geopolitical terms.

Because of its major strategic interest, it is unrealistic to expect the United States to be unconcerned about developments in the region. Furthermore, because of its size and power, the US is in a strong position to influence the outcome of events in the area, although this ability to influence events can easily be exaggerated. The US, for example, failed despite considerable efforts to prevent the establishment of the Martínez administration in El Salvador in the 1930s and on subsequent occasions was outwitted, for example, by both Ubico in Guatemala and Somoza in Nicaragua.

The United States has therefore not been able to dominate political developments in the region completely and this was made abundantly clear in 1979, when the US tried unsuccessfully to promote Somocismo without Somoza. At the same time, there is a well-founded suspicion that successive administrations have been much more likely to intervene when developments move to the left than when they move to the right. In brief, there has been a tendency to over-react against regimes with left-wing sympathies and to under-react against regimes with repressive tendencies.

The reasons why the United States cannot wholly control political developments is straightforward. The political systen to a large extent is a reflection of the economic system and, in particular, of the model of export-led growth adopted by Central America. The authoritarian regimes to be found in several republics arose from the political crisis after the 1929 Depression, when the survival of the export-led model was called into question. The new political regime ensured the continuation of export-led growth, but the price in terms of repression was high. The political system inherited from the 1930s therefore has its own logic and US powers to reform it are strictly limited. However, although the United States lacks the power to reform politically repressive regimes in the area, it has been in a position to prevent their overthrow through military and other forms of aid. It is this asymmetry in US power, which has contributed substantially to the present crisis.

It will be argued that Costa Rica has pursued the same model of export-led growth as the rest of the region and yet has been able to establish a stable democracy. This is true, but Costa Rica's uniqueness stems from two considerations, which can offer little comfort to US policy-makers in the short run; first, the benefits of export-led growth have been more widely distributed in Costa Rica over the years, because initially (although no longer) it had an egalitarian pattern of land ownership; secondly, Costa Rica in the twentieth century has reaped the benefit of the heavy emphasis on education starting in the 1880s.

One should not, however, exaggerate the uniqueness of Costa Rica. The path to stable democracy has been tortuous at times and the vote was not extended to women until 1949. The last military dictatorship was 1917–19, in the overthrow of which the US played an honourable role, but repressive tendencies have been apparent on several subsequent occasions and the present crisis will test Costa Rica's democratic traditions to the absolute limit.

Outside of Costa Rica, it is difficult to believe that a shift to stable democracies will occur without a change from the model of export-led growth inherited from the past. The establishment of the Central

American Common Market (CACM) in the 1960s offered the prospect of just such an alternative model, but CACM is now in ruins and it is increasingly accepted that one of the major causes of its failures was the attempt to graft an industrialisation strategy onto the model of export-led growth without adequate recognition of the political realities of the region. As long as CACM did not challenge the export-led model, it was allowed to thrive, but when a clash of interests appeared it was CACM which suffered.

The economic system of Central America is still based on export-led growth. With given world prices for her primary exports, Central America's profits and rents from export agriculture are maximised through a policy of low wages for rural labour, although these low wages are an obstacle to industrial development throughout the region. The low wage policy is secured through the repression of rural trade union activity, although there is less such resistance to urban trade unions.

The cheapness and ready availability of rural labour has led to a massive expansion of export agriculture in the last three to five decades, which has provoked a serious crisis in the agricultural economy. I have discussed this crisis in detail elsewhere, but I consider it to be an important element in the current political crisis. Thus, although export-led growth has led to a rapid rise in Gross Domestic Product (GDP) and GDP per head, it has contributed to the marginalisation of the peasantry and to the present problems of Central America.

It is imperative in the longer term that Central America reduce its dependence on export-led growth, where exports consist of its traditional primary products. The extreme openness of these economies makes them too vulnerable to movements in world commodity prices and their small size, given their openness, makes it impossible to carry out an effective counter-cyclical policy, so that employment conditions are at the mercy of external factors beyond the region's control.

The United States has an important role to play in shifting Central America towards an alternative model of economic development. I have argued elsewhere that an important element in this model of economic development must be the strengthening of the Central American Common Market (CACM), so that the region may advance beyond the early stages of industrialisation. In addition, the United States remains potentially the most attractive market for Central America's non-traditional exports and much could be done to encourage their growth.

It may be argued that the Caribbean Basin Initiative (CBI) goes some way to meeting this last point. This is true, although the product restrictions under the CBI (e.g. sugar, textiles) are in some way more important than the list of products given preferential access. It is unfortunate, however, that the CBI has been presented as a political instrument by confining its benefits to 'friendly' countries. It would have been more sensible to mirror the Lomé Convention, which is applied to countries irrespective of their political system and has earned the European Economic Community (EEC) much goodwill in the African, Caribbean, Pacific (ACP) countries.

It is sometimes claimed that the main support the US can give Central America is through capital flows and finance for land reform. I think this is misleading; capital flows will certainly be needed in the short run to help with the present financial crisis, but in the longer term the emphasis should be on financing a much higher proportion of investment through domestic resources. Central America is not a desparately poor region; it is the distribution of income, not income itself, which is at fault.

In the case of land reform, there can be no doubt that the pattern of land ownership is seriously distorted and that this contributes to the present crisis. It is unrealistic, however, to suppose that an effective land reform programme can be implemented without a prior change in both the political system and the model of export-led growth. Land reform in isolation is not a serious option and the US should resist the temptation to belief that it is.

In summary, therefore, I would argue that in the economic sphere the US can contribute most effectively in the longer run by helping to breathe new life into CACM and by encouraging a shift away from excessive dependence on export-led growth. Despite this, it should be pointed out that Central America will continue to export traditional primary products in considerable quantities and the US can contribute at the global level towards a more orderly market, particularly in sugar and cotton.

Once Central America has shifted towards an alternative model of economic development, the opportunities for political progress would be much more favourable. This is because the alternative model would go some way towards eliminating the conditions, such as low wages and under-employment, which militate against the establishment of stable democracies.

All this will take time, however, and meanwhile the US is faced with a political crisis of gigantic proportions in Central America. Although it is important to keep the longer run in view, it is impossible for the US to ignore the short-term; policy should be adopted, however, consistent with the longer-run objectives.

It is this inconsistency between assumed long-run objectives and short-term requirements which has earned the US considerable criticism in the last two years. The effort to destabilise the Sandinista government and to support political reaction in El Salvador and Guatemala is not in the long-run interests of the United States. The same must be said of the militarisation of Honduras and the attempt to reintroduce an army to Costa Rica.

In both El Salvador and Guatemala, and to a lesser extent in Honduras, electoral fraud over the years has forced reformist parties into an uneasy alliance with revolutionary groups. The former tend to be more influential in the political, the latter in the military sphere. Thus, the longer the actual fighting in, for example, El Salvador, the greater the likelihood that the revolutionary element will predominate.

The revolutionary groups usually pay lip-service to Marxism-Leninism. This is undoubtedly disturbing to policy-makers in the United States, although the greatest danger is that of over-reaction. The Marxist wing of the revolutionary movement is not monolithic in Central America and there are important differences between the groups; it is most likely to become monolithic, however, if – as in Nicaragua – it meets with blanket hostility from the US.

Faced with a potentially embarrassing situation for the United States, the Soviet Union finds it difficult to resist the temptation to become involved. This involvement extends to military supplies in the case of friendly governments (Nicaragua), but is much more limited in the case of revolutionary movements. Here, the influence of Cuba is much more important, because Cuba has the moral authority in revolutionary circles to establish the movement's unification and to end factionalism. Throughout Central America, one of the critical moments in the development of a guerilla movement has been an end to the constant bickering among rival groups.

While the revolutionary movements look to Cuba for inspiration, they are also conscious of the problem which isolation has brought the island economy. The economic policy of the Sandinistas, for example, is very different from Cuba's despite the numerous Cuban advisers and the tension with the United States. The relationship with the Soviet Union appears even more pragmatic; it should not be forgotten that many of Central America's guerilla leaders have a Trotskyist background, which does not endear them ideologically to the USSR.

It is clear, therefore, that the revolutionary opposition in Central

America represents a coalition of interests, most of whom are not intrinsically hostile to the United States. It is also the case that the civil wars in El Salvador and Guatemala (as earlier in Nicaragua) are a consequence of internal conditions and not initiated by external aggression. Under these circumstances, there is a strong case for the United States to take a neutral position and confine its role to preventing the internationalisation of the conflicts.

The single, most positive step the US can take in Central America is to stop its harassment of the Sandinista government in Nicaragua. Quite apart from the legality of US operations, there can be no justification for supporting the rump of Somoza's army in an effort to turn back the political clock.

A change in US policy towards Nicaragua should be unconditional; it would be foolish to try and extract various concessions from the Sandinistas in return. The Sandinista government is here to stay and improving relations with it should be a high priority for the US administration.

This change in US policy should go some way to reversing the deterioration of political conditions in Honduras, which has become a virtual US protectorate in the last few years. There is every reason to believe that a continuation of this policy would provoke the same reaction in Honduras as occurred in Nicaragua between 1927 and 1933, when Sandino fought a guerilla war against US marines.

In El Salvador, US emphasis must be on scaling down its commitment to the Magaña administration. It is simply not possible for a regime, dependent on the Salvadorean army, to become the vehicle by which a stable democracy is established. It is not a question of the US switching sides; it is more a question of becoming less committed to the final outcome.

In El Salvador, and possibly Guatemala, negotiations between both sides in the civil war will sooner or later be inevitable. In view of its high profile in support of one side, the US may find it difficult to carry out the task of mediation. For that reason it is important to encourage the continued existence of the Contadora Group; the latter is more likely to prove acceptable as a mediator to both sides in the dispute.

# 10 The New Model of Development in Costa Rica

## INTRODUCTION

Although the Latin American debt crisis is conventionally dated to 1982 (the year of the threatened Mexican default), it struck Costa Rica as early as 1980 when arrears of interests first began to accumulate.[1] In the last seven years there have been a continuous series of adjustment and stabilisation programmes, as Costa Rica has struggled to come to terms with the harsher international and regional climate. These programmes, short-term by nature, have given many the impression that Costa Rica has simply been living in a state of semi-permanent crisis since 1980; in one sense this is true, yet it obscures the fact that Costa Rica has slowly but surely edged towards a new model of economic development in the last few years, which differs both qualitatively and quantitatively from its predecessors.

The new model emphasises non-traditional exports to the rest of the world (ROW) excluding the Central American Common Market (CACM). It is therefore the logical successor to the previous model which emphasised traditional exports to ROW[2] and non-traditional exports to CACM. The emphasis on non-traditional exports to the rest of the world is not necessarily meant to take place at the expense of the previous model – policy-makers would prefer to see it as complementary – but, given the difficulties faced by traditional exports to ROW and non-traditional exports to CACM, the growth of the economy now depends to a large extent on the performance of this third export pillar.

All Costa Rican development models since independence have emphasised exports, and changes in the model have not been frequent. It is worth emphasising that previous changes often took many years to establish themselves before they could be deemed successful. Thus, the introduction of coffee as an export product in the 1830s was revolutionary, but it was twenty years before coffee dominated exports and became the engine of growth. Similarly, it took fifteen years from the start of banana exports in the 1870s (following the construction of the

Atlantic railway) to put the new crop on an equal footing with coffee in terms of foreign exchange earnings. The introduction of new agro-exports after 1945 (principally sugar, beef and cacao) also took fifteen years to become collectively a rival to coffee and bananas, although the expansion of exports to CACM was achieved in a relatively short space of time in the 1960s.[3]

The fact that Costa Rica has embarked on a new stage in its model of development does not mean that it will necessarily succeed. There have been plenty of failures in the past to set against the undoubted successes.[4] Even if the new model does prove to be successful, it does not follow that it is appropriate for other small states in the Caribbean region. The prospects for the model, an evaluation of its performance to date and its relevance for the rest of the region will be the purpose of this chapter.

## EXTERNAL AND INTERNAL PRESSURES FOR MODEL CHANGE

To imagine that Costa Rica has begun to emphasise non-traditional exports to ROW simply as a result of pressure from international agencies committed to the counter-revolution in development economics[5] would be a serious error. Although those pressures, as we shall see, have been enormously important, internal pressures in favour of a change have also been present. Furthermore, the internal pressures are of older vintage and have helped to shape a national consensus, which was a major factor in the country's willingness to respond positively to the international agencies in the 1980s.[6] This response, portrayed misleadingly as capitulation by the harshest critics of the new model,[7] was typically Costa Rican in that it absorbed from the external sources only that part of the recommendations which were consistent with the policy-makers' goals; the rest of the advice was, and still is, ignored – much to the fury of the more ideologically inclined members of the international agencies.

The first reason why Costa Rica was willing to countenance a change in the model was disillusion with CACM, which came to the fore in the early 1970s. It should not be forgotten that Costa Rica was the most reluctant of the five Central American states to become a member of CACM, joining only in 1963 after the common market had been in operation for nearly three years. As early as 1974, the national development plan (drafted by Oscar Arias Sánchez as minister of planning) was forecasting balanced development of non-traditional exports to both CACM and ROW for the rest of the decade. Policy-makers were dismayed by the consequences of the war between El Salvador and Honduras in 1969 and the failure of the lengthy negotiations in the Comité de Alto Nivel (CAN) in the 1970s to restructure the market. Finally, the tension between Costa Rica and the Somoza regime in Nicaragua between 1977 and July 1979, which led to the closing of the frontier and the breaking of diplomatic relations, convinced many Costa Ricans that its economic future lay elsewhere.

A second, related, reason favouring a change in the economic model was the growth of anti-protectionist sentiment. The tariffs associated with the CACM had created an obvious tension between industrialists on the one hand, who stood to gain from the tariff structure, and the agro-exporters and import merchants on the other who favoured lower duties. The bargaining power of the industrialists, never very great, was undermined by the disillusionment with CACM and the growing conviction at the end of the 1970s in the Carazo administration that lower tariffs would act as an anti-inflationary device. As a result Costa Rica has been pressing consistently for changes in the CACM tariff structure for nearly a decade, often taking unilateral action to achieve her aims.

A third reason for a change in the model has been the conversion of many industrialists to an outward-looking strategy. This conversion has a pragmatic origin: the deep recession beginning in Costa Rica in 1980/1 produced massive excess capacity in most manufacturing sectors; at the same time, many industrialists shared the anti-Sandinismo of the Costa Rican leadership and became convinced that there was little mileage left in the CACM. Thus, faced by a recession at home and a common market in crisis, the industrialists' conversion to a more outward-looking strategy was a matter of economic necessity.

Industrialists, agro-exporters and import merchants are pressure groups, but changes in a development model require shifts in policy. To make these shifts consistent and not contradictory, there has to be something of a revolution among a nation's policy-makers. This revolution began under the two *Liberacionista* governments in the 1970s, but was taken much further by the team responsible for economic policy under President Carazo (1978–82). The economic ideas of the Carazo administration were often confused and inconsistent, but they did represent a definitive break with the consensus developed over the previous 25 years. It has been the intense pressure from the international agencies in the last few years, which has forced

Costa Rica's policy-making élite to think through its ideas in a more consistent fashion and bring to fruition an intellectual revolution which is still not wholly complete.

The external pressures in favour of a change in the development model are the same for Costa Rica as for many other developing countries. The most important, of course, has been the international *coyuntura* and in particular Costa Rica's debt crisis. With one of the highest per caput debts in the world and debt service payments never much less than 50 per cent of exports (even after rescheduling), Costa Rican economic policy has been the focus of attention for the private creditors (organised in a steering committee), the government creditors (organised in the Paris Club) and all the multilateral agencies concerned with the region.

Although the international banks and creditor governments have watched developments closely in Costa Rica, they have (with the exception of US institutions) been content to take their lead from the multilateral agencies. Foremost among these has been the International Monetary Fund (IMF), which has had a semi-permanent presence in Costa Rica since 1980. As we shall see, the major contribution of the IMF has been to persuade Costa Rica to institutionalise the system of exchange-rate flexibility which was begun in December 1980; the IMF has had far less success in persuading Costa Rican governments of the virtues of balanced budgets and a reduced public sector, since neither of these goals (unlike exchange-rate flexibility) command overwhelming support in Costa Rica.

The World Bank, with whom Costa Rica has signed Structural Adjustment Loans (SALs), is the second most influential multilateral agency. The preference of the Bank for privatisation, tariff reductions and an end to export taxes has been only partially heeded, however, although Bank strategists were delighted to see Costa Rica recently ask to join the General Agreement on Tariffs and Trade (GATT). World Bank advice for Costa Rica has often been interpreted very loosely and the Bank's major contribution has been to persuade policy-makers to rationalise the tariff and export incentive systems in favour of greater administrative efficiency and a reduction in bureaucratic delays.

The Inter-American Development Bank (IDB), although a major lender to Costa Rica, has not sought to exercise much influence on policy and has continued to confine its activities in the main to project finance. This is in keeping with the IDB's traditional role of avoiding controversial policy questions, although the organisation is now under enormous pressure from the US administration to change its character.

The interest of the US administration, and its numerous agencies, in Costa Rican economic policy has of course been increased by the country's strategic location on the southern border of Nicaragua. US economic and strategic concerns have, however, often had contradictory results with USAID in particular unable to give unconditional support to the IMF and World Bank for a change in policy, because of the possible damaging short-term consequences. Thus, Costa Rica has been able to appeal to the agency for pressure on the IMF in favour of a more lenient fiscal policy. The risk, therefore, to Costa Rica of a united front among donor agencies in favour of a policy change considered inexpedient by the government has often been avoided as a result of a lack of consensus among the agencies themselves.[8]

The impact of the external pressures on the change in Costa Rica's model of development should not be exaggerated. Where the external actors have appeared to achieve success, they have often found themselves pushing on an open door as a result of Costa Rica's prior acceptance of the need for such changes. Where there has been no such consensus (e.g. over privatisation of the clearing banks), the external actors have made little or no progress. The result is a new development model, which embodies many features from the new orthodoxies in development economics, but which remains quintessentially Costa Rican. Its successes or failures should therefore be credited to the Costa Ricans themselves.

## THE INSTRUMENTS OF THE NEW POLICY

The shift to a new model of development has been reflected in four areas of policy: price policy, fiscal policy, monetary policy and institutional reform. Each is important, but the whole is greater than the sum of the parts and the qualitative change in the Costa Rican model is a consequence of the impact of the four policy initiatives taken together.

Price policy refers to changes in instruments which affect directly the profitability of tradeable goods in general and non-traditional exports in particular. It therefore includes the exchange rate, export taxes and tariffs, as well as the various schemes in force for exporters to reclaim tariffs paid on imported inputs.

The most important, and powerful, instrument is the exchange rate. Without a flexible exchange rate, it is doubtful if the other policy instruments open to the authorities would be very efficacious, although – as we shall see – exchange-rate flexibility on its own is not sufficient for non-traditional export growth. As Table 10.1 makes clear, the exchange rate has been subject to massive nominal devaluation since the end of 1980 which in turn has yielded a significant real devaluation. This is a revolutionary change in the Costa Rican (and Central American) context, where nominal exchange rates have been traditionally pegged to the dollar and other policy instruments have been adapted to preserve the fixed exchange rate.

The policy of real exchange-rate depreciation has had two predictable adverse consequences, which the authorities have reluctantly accepted. The first is its impact on inflation, which rose to nearly 100 per cent in 1982 (see Table 10.1) and which remains in double figures even today; although the exchange rate now is expected to reflect the difference between world and domestic inflation rates (leaving the real exchange rate unchanged), it has always been accepted that nominal

*Table* 10.1 Costa Rica: nominal exchange rates, real effective exchange rates and inflation (1978 = 100)

| | *Nominal exchange rate** (1) | *Real effective exchange rate*† (2) | *Inflation*‡ |
|---|---|---|---|
| 1978 | 100 | 100 | 100 |
| 1979 | 100 | 102 | 109 |
| 1980 | 100 | 96 | 129 |
| 1981 | 254 | 186 | 177 |
| 1982 | 436 | 179 | 336 |
| 1983 | 480 | 160 | 446 |
| 1984 | 520 | 166 | 499 |
| 1985 | 589 | 169 | 574 |
| 1986 | 653 | 171 | 642 |
| 1987§ | 735 | 172 | 738 |

*Defined as the colon–US dollar exchange rate (period average). The nominal rate in 1978 was 8.57 colones per US dollar.

†Defined as a weighted sum of nominal exchange rates (based on main partners) adjusted for changes in relative prices (period average). An increase in the real effective exchange rate represents a real depreciation.

‡Consumer Price Index (period average).

§Estimate.

*Sources*: For the nominal exchange rate and consumer price index, see International Monetary Fund, *International Financial Statistics*. For the real effective exchange rate (1978–84), see W. Loehr, 'Current Account Balances in Central America 1974–84: External and Domestic Influences', *Journal of Latin American Studies*, Vol. 19, Part I (May, 1987), Table 8. For the years 1985–87, author's estimates based on US – Costa Rican comparisons only.

devaluation is itself a major cause of domestic inflation. Thus, the policy prevents Costa Rica from returning to the remarkable price stability associated with a fixed exchange rate up to the early 1970s, although there is no longer a risk (as seemed possible in 1982) that exchange-rate devaluation would be associated with hyperinflation.

The second adverse consequence has been the impact of exchange-rate flexibility, via inflation, on real wages. The real wage trend, however, is not uniformly downward; after falling severely until 1982, they staged a partial recovery under the Monge administration. They remain, however, well below their peak in 1979 and a source of frustration and popular discontent.[9] The authorities seem to have accepted, however, that real wage restraint – if not falling real wages – is a necessary ingredient in the promotion of non-traditional exports.

The most important change relating to import duties has been the adoption of a new nomenclature, a shift to *ad valorem* duties and the adoption of a new Common External Tariff (CET) within the context of the CACM. The changes have resulted in a lower average CET, although levels of nominal and effective protection are still quite high.[10] It is fair to say that the tariff changes, pressed for by both the CACM Secretariat (SIECA) and the World Bank, reflect the interests of the former more than the latter, but the World Bank has argued that they represent a move in the right direction and is reasonably satisfied.

As part of the tariff reforms, the myriad exemptions under which firms could qualify for tariff relief on imports have been withdrawn. Instead, Costa Rica has strengthened the drawback schemes in force for some years, under which firms can reclaim duty paid on intermediate imports provided that the finished product is exported to ROW. Thus, the new tariff policy, *cet. par.*, implies a bias against exports to CACM, since only those non-traditional exports destined to the world market qualify for duty exoneration on imported inputs.[11]

Fiscal policy has been revised to favour non-traditional exports to ROW. This reform began in the 1970s with the introduction of Certificados de Abono Tributario (CATs) – a certificate linked to the f.o.b. value of exports which can be used to offset tax liabilities; in more recent years, all export taxes on non-traditional exports to ROW have been scrapped (some remain in force on traditional exports), a new tax certificate (Certificados de Incremento de las Exportaciones – CIEX) has been introduced linked to the growth in value of non-traditional exports to ROW and, finally, under the 1984 export law a 100 per cent income tax exemption on profits generated by non-traditional exports has been introduced. Thus, firms selling non-traditional exports to ROW face almost an over-abundance of incentive schemes, with some of the incentives appearing to overlap.[12]

Monetary policy has been much less active than fiscal policy in promoting non-traditional exports to ROW. The traditional Costa Rican policy of using differential interest rates to promote favoured sectors has largely collapsed; interest rates are now positive in real terms (a change that began under the Carazo administration with the experiment in financial liberalisation) and largely neutral as between different sectors. Credit, at least from the clearing banks and their secondary banking subsidaries, remains under state control, but the old system of 'topes' in favour of particular sectors has also been effectively abolished. In theory, the Central Bank still promises to provide lines of credit for certain (favoured) activities, but it is frequently unable to meet its commitments. Monetary policy is perhaps the weakest element in the package of measures adopted in support of non-traditional exports to ROW.

Institutional reform, after a slow start, has become an important feature of the new policy. Three new ministries/institutions have been created in support of non-traditional exports to ROW. The first is the Centro para la Promoción de las Exportaciones y de las Inversiones (CENPRO), set up in 1968 and the institutional counterpart to the CATs scheme. The second is the Costa Rican Coalitional of Development Initiatives (CINDE), which is not exclusively concerned with non-traditional exports, and the third is the Ministerio de Exportaciones (MINEX) set up in 1983 to oversee the whole process of non-traditional export promotion.

MINEX now plays a key role in the whole process. It has helped to simplify the procedures for exports and under the 1984 export law signs contracts with individual companies which speed up the administrative side of export promotion. Both innovations figured largely in the first SAL signed between Costa Rica and the World Bank in 1985 and the task of simplifying paperwork is taken so seriously that even the President's office has become involved.

Training programmes are also an important feature of the new policy. Programmes for workers are handled by the Instituto Nacional de Aprendizaje (INA), which has expanded its operations significantly since its foundation in the 1950s. Management training programmes are largely the responsibility of the Instituto Centroamericano de Adminstración de Empresas (INCAE), an organisation funded by USAID which moved its headquarters from Managua to San José following the deterioration of relations between the Sandinistas and the US administration.

Perhaps surprisingly, export-processing zones – so common in other parts of the developing world – are not a major feature of export promotion in Costa Rica. Two such zones exist, in Moín on the Atlantic and at Puntarenas on the Pacific, but most of the advantages obtained by firms in the zones can be secured by firms located anywhere in Costa Rica under the numerous incentive schemes available. These zones are really a hangover from the earlier period, when the authorities were inching their way towards a new export promotion policy without being fully committed.

So far, this description of the policy instruments adopted to promote non-traditional exports to ROW refers exclusively to changes introduced by the Costa Rican executive albeit with some prodding from the international agencies. No description would be complete, however, without recognition of the changes introduced by foreign countries which have created new opportunities for non-traditional exports and opened up new markets. Clearly, without the new market opportunities there would have been much less enthusiasm in Costa Rica for the new policy.

The best known change involves the Caribbean Basin Initiative (CBI), in which the USA extended to all beneficiaries (including Costa Rica) tariff exemptions on a wide range of non-traditional products for twelve years from 1 January 1984. The CBI has been widely, and rightly, attacked for its exclusions (products and countries), but at least as far as Costa Rica is concerned some of the exclusions have been covered by the extension of tariff codes 806 and 807, so that such sensitive items as textiles can still be exported by Costa Rica to the USA with low or zero tariffs. The other potentially important market for non-traditional exports is the European Economic Community (EEC), which has signed a Co-operation Agreement with all Central America. The Agreement does not offer anything as radical as the CBI, but it does hold out the prospect of a negotiated entry to the EEC for non-traditional exports through mutually agreed tariff reductions and the elimination of non-tariff barriers.[13]

## EVALUATION OF THE NEW POLICY

The shift of resources towards non-traditional exports to ROW has not been a smooth process. On the contrary, as Table 10.2 makes clear, it is

*Table* 10.2 Costa Rica: traditional and non-traditional exports ($ million)

| | (A) *Traditional** | (B) *Non-traditional* *CACM* | (C) *ROW* | (D) *Total* | (E) *(C)/(D) × 100* |
|---|---|---|---|---|---|
| 1980 | 567 | 270 | 164 | 1002 | 16.4 |
| 1981 | 581 | 238 | 189 | 1008 | 18.8 |
| 1982 | 535 | 167 | 169 | 870 | 19.4 |
| 1983 | 526 | 198 | 148 | 873 | 17.0 |
| 1984 | 570 | 193 | 212 | 976 | 21.7 |
| 1985 | 554 | 128 | 214 | 895 | 23.9 |
| 1986 | 686 | 102 | 305 | 1093 | 27.9 |
| 1987† | 660 | 98 | 407 | 1165 | 34.9 |

*Coffee, bananas, sugar and beef.
†Preliminary.

*Source*: 1980–4, Central Bank of Costa Rica and IMF. 1985–7, USAID compilation of Central Bank data.

only since 1983 that the new policy has really taken effect. Yet there can be no doubting its current importance; non-traditional exports to ROW had reached $407 million by 1987, more than four times greater in value than exports to CACM.[14] With the new exports now accounting for over 30 per cent of exports in a country where exports also account for 30 per cent of the Gross Domestic Product (GDP), the promotion of non-traditional exports to ROW clearly has important macroeconomic implications.

Table 10.2 also shows that the increase in the new exports is similar in value to the fall in exports to CACM. This might prompt the charge that firms have simply shifted non-traditional exports from one market to another without any net increase in resources. Such a conclusion would be false. As we shall see, although both types of exports are labelled 'non-traditional', they do in fact represent different types of commodities. Furthermore, the decline in exports to CACM between 1980 and 1982 was not matched by any increase in non-traditional exports to ROW. It remains posible that the same set of entrepreneurs/firms are responsible both for the decline in exports to CACM and for the increase in exports to ROW, but this is not inconsistent with a change in the commodity mix.

A comparison of Table 10.1 with Table 10.2 shows that the massive real depreciation of the exchange rate engineered between 1980 and 1982 had little impact on the new exports, while the 175 per cent increase in value of the new exports since 1983 has taken place against the background of a virtually unchanged real exchange rate. This is not altogether surprising. The period 1980 to 1982 marked the worst years of Costa Rica's recession with the complementary inputs needed for export expansion (e.g. imported inputs, bank credit) in short supply. On the other hand, the fact that the major increase in non-traditional exports has taken place without further real depreciation is surely important; it suggests that the other elements in the promotion package have been essential for the success of the new policy.

The purpose of the tax and tariff reforms described in the previous section was to reduce the bias against non-traditional exports to ROW and create a climate in which such exports are at least as attractive, if not more so, to entrepreneurs as exports to CACM. Making the small country assumption, we can calculate the profit per unit of output on ROW exports as:

$$\pi_j^{\text{ROW}} = \left[ p_j^* e - \left( \sum_i ad_{ij} + \sum_i m_{ij} \right) \right] \tag{10.1}$$

and the profit per unit of output on CACM exports as

$$\pi_j^{\text{CACM}} = (1 - \tau) \left\{ p_j^* e(1 + t_j) - \left[ \sum_i ad_{ij} + \sum_i m_{ij}(1 + t_i) \right] \right\} \tag{10.2}$$

where $p_j^*$ is the world market price, $e$ is the nominal exchange rate, $\Sigma_i ad_{ij}$ is the sum of all domestic inputs per unit of output (including primary inputs other than profits), $\Sigma_i m_{ij}$ is the sum of all foreign inputs per unit of output, $t_j$ is the nominal rate of protection on output, $t_i$ is the nominal rate of protection on all imported inputs and $\tau$ is the average tax rate on corporate profits.

Since non-traditional exports to ROW now pay no export taxes, no tariffs on imported inputs and no taxes on corporate profits, these parameters do not appear in equation (10.1). On the other hand, exports to CACM enjoy the advantage of the CET still applied to competing goods from outside the region, which is why the parameter $t_j$ appears in equation (10.2).

The question of whether the tax regime is neutral between the two kinds of exports is therefore an empirical one. On the basis of a number of stylised facts about the economy (see Table 10.3), it is possible to

*Table* 10.3 Profit per unit of output for non-traditional exports

| | *CACM* | *ROW* |
|---|---|---|
| $p_j^*$ | 1.0 | 1.0 |
| $e$ | 1.0 | 1.0 |
| $\Sigma_i ad_{ij}$ | 0.5 | 0.5 |
| $\Sigma_i m_{ij}$ | 0.2 | 0.2 |
| $t_i$ | 0.2 | 0 |
| $t_j$ | 0.6 | 0 |
| $\tau$ | 0.5 | 0 |
| $\pi_j$ | 0.43 | 0.3 |

hazard an answer to this question. It would appear from Table 10.3 that the new tariff and tax system has not eliminated anti-export bias and the reason is straightforward: the concessions offered to non-traditional exports to ROW are still not enough to offset the advantage of a relatively high CET. Even major changes in the other parameters in Table 10.3 do not eliminate this advantage.[15]

Yet it is surely significant that, despite the failure to eliminate anti-export bias, the new policy appears to be working. This again suggests that the non-price elements in the promotion package are highly efficacious. It is difficult to single out any one element as being particularly important, but the preferential treatment in the US market, the contracts between firms and MINEX to avoid bureaucratic delays and the training programmes provided by both INA and INCAE have all been very influential in building confidence among industrialists in favour of the new policy.

The macroeconomic implications of the new policy cannot be gauged merely by reference to the total value of the non-traditional exports to ROW. This is because the new exports consist of two rather separate categories of goods, each of which has different macroeconomic implications although both categories are favoured by the new policy. The first category are produced by *maquiladoras* using a high proportion of imported inputs, female labour and with close links to multinational companies; examples of the goods produced by such firms are electronic products, brassières and other items of clothing and the stimulus for their location in Costa Rica has often been provided by articles 806 and 807 of the US tariff code. The second category consists of agro-industrial goods, where Costa Rican raw materials have been subject to a degree of processing before export. Examples of such goods are cut flowers and ornamental plants, fruits, vegetables, spices and essential oils; the stimulus for the expansion of these activities, which are less dependent on foreign capital, has been mainly the CBI.

A survey of both types of firms carried out by the Banco Central de Costa Rica (BCCR) in 1984 (i.e before the CBI was fully in effect) suggested that two-thirds of non-traditional exports came from agro-industrial firms and a third from the *maquiladoras*.[16] These proportions are probably still valid, since there is circumstantial evidence that both types of operation continue to be attracted by the incentives on offer.

Although the new policy does not discriminate between the two categories of exports, the multiplier effects are likely to be very different. Consider the following simple Keynesian model:

$$Y = C + I + G + X_T + X_{NT} - M \qquad (10.3)$$

where $Y$ = GDP
$C$ = Private consumption
$I$ = Investment
$G$ = Public consumption
$X_T$ = Traditional exports and exports to CACM
$X_{NT}$ = Non-traditional exports to ROW
$M$ = Imports

Having distinguished two types of exports, we must now recognise:

$$I = I_1 + I_2 \qquad (10.4)$$

$$M = M_1 + M_2 \qquad (10.5)$$

where $I_1$, $M_1$ refer to investment and imports linked to non-traditional exports ($X_{NT}$) and $I_2$, $M_2$ refer to all other investment and exports.

Making the simplest possible behavioural and technological assumptions:

$$C = cY \qquad (10.6)$$

$$I_1 = iX_{NT} \qquad (10.7)$$

$$M_2 = m_2Y \qquad (10.8)$$

$$M_1 = m_1X_{NT} \qquad (10.9)$$

we then find:

$$Y = cY + I_2 + iX_{NT} + G + X_T + X_{NT} - m_2Y - m_1X_{NT} \quad (10.10)$$

and

$$(1 - c + m_2)Y = I_2 + G + X_T + (1 + i - m_1)X_{NT} \quad (10.11)$$

Assuming $(I_2 + G + X_T)$ all exogenous, we obtain

$$\partial Y/\partial X_{NT} = (1 + i - m_1)/(1 - c + m_2) \quad (10.12)$$

Clearly, the value of the multiplier in equation (10.12) will vary for the two categories of export according to the assumed value of $m_1$. With $c = 0.6$, $i = 0.25$, $m_2 = 0.3$ and $m_1 = 0.45$ (a reasonable assumption for the *maquiladoras*), then the value of the multiplier is a modest 1.14. With $m_1 = 0.1$ (a reasonable assumption for the agro-industries), then the multiplier increases to a more respectable 1.64.[17]

These different multiplier effects have not been given sufficient weight by the authorities. Although the *maquiladoras* bring in much needed foreign investment and employ significant quantities of unskilled (mainly female) labour, these advantages have to be set against the weak interindustrial linkages created by such firms. Furthermore, the footloose character of the *maquiladora* firms makes them much more resistant to real wage increase than the agro-industrial firms; indeed, the attraction of Costa Rica to many *maquiladora* firms has undoubtedly been its low real wages in dollar terms as a result of currency depreciation.

Although the *maquiladoras* are generally labour-intensive, the indirect employment generation is very small. By contrast, many agro-industries are capital-intensive, but generate substantial employment indirectly because of their use of domestic raw materials. Furthermore, this indirect employment generation primarily affects the rural sector, relieving the pressure in favour of rural–urban migration and promoting greater equality between the rural and urban sectors.

For many developing countries, the choice between *maquiladoras* and agro-industries is not a real one. Market restrictions facing agricultural goods (raw or processed) limit the scope for expansion of agro-industries. Costa Rica is relatively privileged in that market opportunities for the expansion of both types of firms do exist. It is regrettable, therefore, that policy has not been adapted to provide special incentives for agro-industrial firms.

## VIABILITY OF THE NEW MODEL

Although the new model appears to have made a good start in Costa Rica, particularly in view of the hostile regional and international environment the country faces, it is subject to a number of problems which deserve further consideration. These can be broadly labelled supply-side and demand-side problems.

Costa Rican industry is small-scale by world, or even Latin American, standards. The increase in non-traditional exports is therefore by and large in the hands of companies which lack detailed knowledge of overseas markets and which cannot afford to devote their own resources to increasing market information. As a result, many firms are obliged to make agreements with foreign companies for the sale of their products. In the case of subsidiaries of multinational companies this may not cause too many problems, but domestically owned firms have been left at the mercy of foreign import houses who have been known to demand expensive changes in a product line and later cancel the order when a cheaper or more reliable source is found.

It may be that these are merely teething problems, but the authorities would do well to consider mounting the sort of public relations exercise through offices abroad for non-traditional exports which they have traditionally done for coffee. The problem is more complicated (coffee is one, virtually homogeneous, product; non-traditional products are extremely varied), but the principles are the same. Costa Rica already mounts a promotional campaign to attract direct foreign investment through offices in the United States and France and the promotion of non-traditional exports could be carried through the same channels.

Much has been done in the last decade to improve port facilities in Costa Rica, which are no longer limited to Limón and Puntarenas. Yet the country is too small to justify the regular shipping services to North America and Western Europe, which many of the new products (particularly those with an agricultural origin) require. There have also been reports of problems with packaging (generally rather expensive in Costa Rica) and with quality control in the case of agricultural goods requiring processing. Nevertheless, the increases in the export figures certainly suggest that these problems are being overcome.

There must also be reservations about the country's ability to maintain the tax and exchange-rate regime, which has contributed to the expansion of non-traditional exports. Although it was argued above that price policy (broadly defined) is not a sufficient condition for the expansion of the new exports, it is certainly necessary and a reversal of the tax and exchange-rate regime would be very damaging.

The exchange-rate regime, basically a crawling peg, now seems to be broadly accepted. Its most undesirable byproduct is the maintenance of double-digit inflation, but Costa Rican society is slowly adapting to the strains imposed by regular price increases. A major real depreciation does not appear to be necessary and the maintenance of a stable real exchange rate looks like a realistic goal.

The maintenance of the tax regime is more problematic. The tariff and export tax reductions, together with generous exemptions for firms producing the new products, put strains on the weak fiscal system; these problems, coupled with the debt service burden, have made the fiscal system an area of special interest for the IMF and the World Bank, both of which have urged on Costa Rica the introduction of new taxes and cuts in expenditure. Successive governments since 1980 have remained largely immune to these pressures, so that fiscal policy has been a running sore between Costa Rica and the international agencies.

With a significant proportion of economic growth coming from the new activities, which are tax exempt, the inelastic nature of the tax system is exacerbated. The danger, therefore, exists that Costa Rica will adopt emergency measures on a 'temporary' basis to strengthen government revenue and that such measures (e.g. a surcharge on imports) will discriminate against non-traditional exports. The continuing reluctance of the Legislative Assembly to vote the tax increases sought by the executive is therefore disturbing.

On the demand-side, the major problem arises from the protectionist threat in the US market. Already manufacturers of brassières and cut flowers have been subject to anti-dumping legislation, which has affected their sales as the result of the imposition of countervailing duties. The US case, based on alleged 'unfair' government subsidies, is flimsy in the extreme, since Costa Rica has simply implemented the kind of 'subsidies' approved by US-dominated international agencies. Nevertheless, the restrictions are very damaging for several reasons.

First, there is an immediate loss of markets as a result of outright restrictions or increases in sale prices from the countervailing duties. Secondly, private investors are reluctant to increase capacity in non-traditional exports until they are sure that their product lines are not subject to a protectionist threat. Thirdly, the reorganisation of Costa Rican agriculture on more specialised lines has been postponed in view of the market uncertainties; thus, the authorities are reluctant to withdraw subsidies to producers of domestic use agriculture, although the same goods can be imported more cheaply, because there is no guarantee that a switch of resources by farmers into non-traditional exports will find a market. The protectionist threat is therefore intertwined with fiscal policy, since the subsidies are an important part of government expenditure.

The twelve-year period offered by the CBI for duty-free access to the USA is long enough for competitive firms to establish a presence in the US market. The beneficiary countries of the Caribbean Basin, however, are potential competitors since many are capable of producing the same agro-industrial products and are all capable of hosting the footloose *maquiladoras*. Costa Rica's success therefore depends in part on its ability to attract demand by undercutting its competitors, although it should always be remembered that even with these new products price is not the sole determinant of the level of demand.

Studies by management consultants suggest that Costa Rican wage rates in dollar terms are by no means the cheapest in the area; similarly, freight rates to and from the United States are among the highest in the region. On the other hand, electricity prices in Costa Rica compare very favourably with other countries in the Caribbean Basin and building rental rates are also cheap. With a very high literacy rate and good training facilities for workers, wages per efficiency unit are probably lower in Costa Rica than implied by monetary rates; price competition in foreign markets is therefore manageable provided that the exchange rate is not subject to real appreciation.

The new model of economic development in Costa Rica can be described, with some reservations, as a success. Inevitably, the Costa Rican example will be held up by international agencies as an example for others to follow. It is worth stressing that several features of the Costa Rican experience distinguish it from other Central American republics and from several countries in the Caribbean. At the very least, these differences will make it much harder (if not impossible) for other countries to follow the Costa Rican example.

First, it is nearly twenty years since Costa Rica first began to think seriously about promoting non-traditional exports to ROW. The intervening years witnessed a public debate within the country's democratic framework, which laid the foundations for the national consensus on this question which is apparent today. That consensus, in turn, was a precondition for the application of consistent policies over a broad range in support of the new model. Without such a consensus, policy would have been fragmented, inconsistent and contradictory with obvious implications for the new exports.

Secondly, the national consensus made possible the adoption of a flexible exchange-rate regime. Other countries in the Caribbean Basin have been forced by the debt crisis to abandon fixed exchange rates, but they have almost all considered parity to the dollar as the preferred long-term goal. As a result, they have lost the advantages of a stable nominal exchange rate (e.g. low inflation) without reaping the benefits of a truly flexible regime.

Thirdly, Costa Rican governments are ideologically well disposed towards foreign capital in general and direct foreign investment (DFI) in particular. In theory, it is possible to promote non-traditional exports to ROW without DFI; in practice, it is difficult because even the domestically-owned export firms must come to some arrangement with foreign import houses and this is often a prelude to joint ventures. Furthermore, foreign firms have been willing to accept Costa Rican assurances on remittance of profits, royalties, dividends, etc., because of the country's long experience in this field and its democratic traditions.

Fourthly, the new model requires policies which put severe strain on the fiscal system and may worsen income distribution. Costa Rica has been able to withstand these strains with some difficulties as a result of an economy which has grown in every year since 1982. Other countries of the Caribbean Basin have not been so fortunate, so that the strains associated with the new model could well prove intolerable.

Finally, Costa Rica has an enviable tradition of education and literacy, which has produced a flexible and adaptable labour force. The new firms in the export sector demand skills from the labour force, which are not found in traditional export enterprises or even in firms exporting to CACM. Yet a well-trained labour force cannot be produced overnight and the leads and lags in educational planning are considerable.

If the new model continues to flourish, as seems on balance likely, the gap in living standards between Costa Rica and its Central American partners will widen still further. At the same time, Costa Rican interest in the moribund CACM will wane. This is a depressing prospect, since exporters of manufactured goods in the other Central American countries continue to depend heavily on the CACM in view of their failure to take advantage of the CBI. I have argued for over ten years that policy ought to be broadly neutral between exports to CACM and ROW in view of the advantages that both can confer, but it is hardly surprising that Costa Rica – faced with a choice between a shrinking regional market and an international market with demand curves that are effectively horizontal – has opted for the latter.

## Notes

1. See Chapter 7.
2. 'Traditional' exports in Costa Rica are defined as coffee, bananas, sugar and beef.
3. For an overview of these changes in the Costa Rican economy, see Bulmer–Thomas (1987), Chapters 1, 8 and 9.
4. The most serious failure in recent years was the creation of a state-holding company (CODESA) to promote industrialisation through joint ventures with the private sector or through publicly owned firms. See Vega (1982).
5. This counter-revolution is competently, and critically, discussed in Toye (1987), especially Chapter 4.
6. See Artavia *et al.* (1987).
7. Urrutia and Sojo (1986), pp. 55–65, come close to this position.
8. This is in marked contrast to the experience of neighbouring Panama, where the IMF and World Bank appear to have collaborated closely in an effort to force through structural reforms (particularly in the labour market).
9. See Fields (forthcoming).
10. Nominal tariffs on competing final goods range from 35 to 70 per cent. Non-competing final goods, imported intermediates, raw materials and capital goods are subject to tariffs in the range 5 to 30 per cent. Thus, the effective rate of protection for most consumer goods is still likely to be high.
11. As we shall see, this is not the full story. The *cet. par.* qualification is very important.
12. See Artavia *et al.* (1987).
13. A mixed EEC–Central American Commission is in place, which meets approximately once a year to review progress and consider new initiatives. At the meeting in Brussels in July 1987, the Central American countries (led, one suspects, by Costa Rica) presented a list of non-traditional exports which they would like to see included in the Generalised System of Preferences (GSP). They also presented a list of products which are in the GSP, but where the Central American countries want to see tariff reductions.
14. Non-traditional exports to ROW even surpassed earnings from coffee in 1987.
15. For example, an increase for exports to CACM in $t_i$ to 0.5 and in $\tau$ to 0.6 would still leave $\pi_j$ at 0.32.
16. See Banco Central de Costa Rica (1984).
17. Interestingly enough, this is close to the value of the multiplier for non-traditional exports obtained for Peru using a much more sophisticated model. See Schydlowsky (1986), Table 5, p. 505.

# Bibliography

ACCIARIS, R. (1984) 'Nicaragua – Pays Socialiste: Vers la consolidation des liens economiques?', *Problèmes d'Amérique Latine*, No. 74.

ADLER, J. H., SCHLESINGER, E. R. and OLSON, E. C. (1952) *Public Finance and Economic Development in Guatemala* (Stanford).

ANDERSON, T. (1971) *Matanza – El Salvador's Communist Revolt of 1932* (Lincoln).

ARIAS PEÑATE, E. (1983) 'El F. M. I. y La Política Contrainsurgente en El Salvador', *Cuadernos de Pensamiento Propio*, I (Managua: INIES/CRIES).

ARTAVIA, R., COLBURN, F. and SABALLOS PATIÑO, I. (1987) 'La Experiencia con Exportaciones en Costa Rica', in F. Colburn (ed.), *Centroamérica: Estrategias de Desarrollo* (San José: EDUCA).

AUSTIN, J., FOX, J. and KRUGER, W. (1985) 'The Role of the Revolutionary State in the Nicaraguan Food System', *World Development*, January, pp. 15–40.

BACHA, E. and TAYLOR, L. (1971) 'Foreign Exchange Shadow Prices: A Critical Review of Current Theories', *Quarterly Journal of Economics*, vol. 85.

BALOYRA, E. (1982) *El Salvador in Transition* (Chapel Hill: University of North Carolina Press).

BANCO CENTRAL DE COSTA RICA (1984) 'Las Exportaciones y la Incidencia del Sector Externo en el Desarrollo Económico' (mimeo).

BANCO CENTRAL DE GUATEMALA (1955) *Memoria* (Guatemala).

BANCO CENTRAL DE HONDURAS (1956) *Cuentas Nacionales 1925–55* (Tegucigalpa).

BANCO INTERAMERICANO DE DESARROLLO (1984) *Informe Económico – Nicaragua* (Washington).

BARRACLOUGH, S. (1982) *A Preliminary Analysis of the Nicaraguan Food System* (UNRISD).

BEACH, C. and MACKINNON, J. (1978) 'A Maximum Likelihood Procedure for Regression with Auto-correlated Errors', *Econometrica*, No. 46.

BELL, J. P. (1971) *Crisis in Costa Rica – The Revolution of 1948* (Austin).

BIRD, G. (1984) 'Balance of Payments Policy', in T. Killick (ed.), *The Quest for Economic Stabilisation* (London: Heinemann).

BLACK, G. (1981) *Triumph of the People – The Sandinista Revolution in Nicaragua* (London).

BULMER-THOMAS, V. (1976) 'The Structure of Protection in Costa Rica – A New Approach to Calculating the Effective Rate of Protection', *Journal of Economic Studies*, vol. 3.

BULMER-THOMAS, V. (1977) 'A Model of Inflation for Central America', *Bulletin of the Oxford Institute of Economics and Statistics*, vol. 39, pp. 319–32.

BULMER-THOMAS, V. (1979) 'Import Substitution v. Export Promotion in the Central American Common Market', *Journal of Economic Studies*, vol. 6.

BULMER-THOMAS, V. (1982) *Input–Output Analysis in Developing Countries* (New York: John Wiley).
BULMER-THOMAS, V. (1985) 'Central American Integration, Trade Diversification and the World Market', in G. Irvin and X. Gorostiaga (eds), *Towards an Alternative for Central America and the Caribbean* (Allen & Unwin).
BULMER-THOMAS, V. (1987) *The Political Economy of Central America since 1920* (Cambridge: Cambridge University Press).
CABLE, V. (1969) 'The Football War and the Central American Common Market', *International Affairs*, October.
CACERES, L. R. (1979) 'Economic Integration and Export Instability in Central America: A Portfolio Model', in S. Smith and J. Toye (eds), *Trade and Poor Economies* (London: Frank Cass).
CANTARERO, LUIS A. (1949) 'The Economic Development of Nicaragua, 1920–1947', Unpublished PhD thesis, University of Iowa.
CENTRAL AMERICAN BANK FOR ECONOMIC INTEGRATION (CABEI) (1984) *Investment in Central America and Panama.*
CEPAL (1978) *Series Históricas del Crecimiento de América Latina* (Santiago).
CHENERY, H. (1960) 'Patterns of Industrial Growth', *American Economic Review*, 50.
CHENERY, H. and SYRQUIN, M. (1975) *Patterns of Industrial Growth* (OUP).
CHENERY, H. and TAYLOR, L. (1968) 'Development patterns: among countries and over time', *Review of Economics & Statistics*, no. 50.
CLINE, W. R. and DELGADO, E. (eds) (1978) *Economic Integration in Central America* (Washington, DC: Brookings Institution).
CLINE, W. R. (1978) 'Benefits and Costs of Economic Integration in Central America', in W. R. Cline and E. Delgado (eds), *Economic Integration in Central America* (Washington, DC: Brookings Institution).
CLINE, W. R. and RAPOPORT, A. (1978a) 'Industrial Comparative Advantage in the Central American Common Market', in W. R. Cline and E. Delgado (eds), *Economic Integration in Central America.*
CLINE, W. R. and RAPOPORT, A. (1978b) 'Industrial Comparative Advantage: Supplementary Tables', Appendix F of W. R. Cline and E. Delgado (eds), *Economic Integration in Central America.*
COHEN ORANTES, I. (1972) *Regional Integration in Central America* (Lexington, Mass.: Lexington Books).
COX, J. J. (1927) 'Nicaragua and the United States', Boston: *World Peace Foundation Pamphlets*, vol. 10, no. 7.
DELGADO, E. (1978) 'Institutional Evolution of the Central American Common Market and the Principle of Balanced Development', in W. R. Cline and E. Delgado (eds), *Economic Integration in Central America* (Washington, DC: Brookings Institution).
DÍAZ ALEJANDRO, C. (1983) 'Stories of the 1930s for the 1980s', in P. Aspe Armella, R. Dornbusch and M. Obstfeld (eds) *Financial Policies and the World Capital Market: The Problem of Latin American Countries* (Chicago: University of Chicago Press).
DORNER, P and QUIROS, R. (1983) 'Institutional dualism in Central America's Agricultural Development', in Stanford Central American Action

Network (ed.), *Revolution in Central America* (Boulder, Colorado: Westview Press).

DURHAM, W. H. (1979) *Scarcity and Survival in Central America* (Stanford: Stanford University Press).

ELLIS, F. (1983) *Las Transnacionales del Banano en Centroamérica* (San José: Costa Rica: EDUCA).

EMMANUEL, A. (1972) *Unequal Exchange: An Essay on the Imperialism of Trade* (Monthly Review Press).

EVANS, D. (1981) 'Unequal Exchange and the Neo-Ricardian Theory of Comparative Advantage', in I. Livingstone (ed.), *Readings in Development Studies* (London: Allen & Unwin).

FEINBERG, R. and NEWFARMER, R. (1984) 'The Caribbean Basin Initiative: Bold Plan or Empty Promise?', in R. Newfarmer (ed.), *From Gunboats to Diplomacy – New U. S. Policies for Latin America* (Baltimore: Johns Hopkins University Press).

FEINBERG, R. and PASTOR, R. (1984) 'Far from Hopeless: An Economic Program for Post-War Central America', in R. Leiken (ed.), *Central America: Anatomy of Conflict* (New York: Praeger).

FERGUSON, E. (1940) *Guatemala* (New York).

FIELDS, G. (forthcoming) *Employment and Economic Growth in Costa Rica* (World Development).

FRANK, C. (1978) 'The Demand for Labour in Manufacturing Industry in Central America', in W. R. Cline and E. Delgado (eds), *Economic Integration in Central America* (Washington, DC: Brookings Institution).

FURTADO, C. (1970) *Economic Development of Latin America* (Cambridge).

GLEZAKOS, C. (1973) 'Export Instability and Economic Growth: A Statistical Verification', *Economic Development and Cultural Change*, vol. 21.

GONZÁLEZ, C. H. (1984) 'Experiencia de Guatemala con el Proceso de Ajuste en 1982–3', *Centro de Estudios Monetarios Latino-americanos (CEMLA), Boletín*, Mayo–Junio, vol. 30, no. 3, pp. 157–65.

GRIEB, K. (1979) *Guatemalan Caudillo – the Regime of Jorge Ubico* (Columbus, Ohio).

HANSEN, R. (1967) Central America: Regional Integration and Economic Development (Washington, DC: National Planning Association).

HARBERGER, A. (1965) 'Survey of Literature on Cost Benefit Analysis for Industrial Project Evaluation', paper presented at the UN Inter-Regional Symposium in Industrial Project Evaluation, Prague.

INFORPRESS (1982) *Centro América 1982: Análisis Económicos y Políticos Sobre La Región, Guatemala.*

IRVIN, G. and GOROSTIAGA, X. (eds) (1985) *Towards an Alternative for Central America and the Caribbean* (London: Allen & Unwin)

JOEL, C. (1971) 'Tax Incentives in Central American Development', *Economic Development and Cultural Change*, vol. 19.

JOHNSON, H. G. (1965) 'An Economic Theory of Protectionism, Tariff Bargaining and the Formation of Customs Unions', *Journal of Political Economy*, vol. 73.

JOHNSTONE, B. F. and KILBY, A. (1975) *Agricultural and Structural Transformation* (Oxford, OUP).

JONES, C. L. (1940) *Guatemala Past and Present* (Minneapolis).

KARNES, T. L. (1961) *The Failure of Union: Central America, 1824–1960* (New Chapel Hill: University of North Carolina Press).
KARNES, T. L. (1978) *Tropical Enterprise: The Standard Fruit and Steamship Co., Baton Rouge* (Louisiana).
KEPNER, C. D., (1936) *Social Aspects of the Banana Industry* (New York).
KEPNER, C. D. and J. H. SOOTHILL (1935) *The Banana Empire: A Case Study in Economic Imperialism* (New York).
KILLICK, T. (ed.) (1984) *The Quest for Economic Stabilisation* (London: Heinemann).
KISSINGER REPORT (1984) *Report of the National Bipartisan Commission on Central America* (Washington, DC).
KOEBEL, W. H. (n.d.) *Central America* (New York).
KRAVIS, I. B., HESTON A. and SUMMERS, R. (1978) 'Real GDP Per Capita for More than One Hundred Countries', *Economic Journal* (June).
KRUGMAN, P. and TAYLOR L. (1978) 'Contractionary Effects of Devaluation', *Journal of lnternational Economics* (November).
LANGHAMMER, R. (1980) 'EEC Trade Policies and Latin American Export Performance', *Intereconomics*, September/October.
LEAGUE OF NATIONS (1937) *Public Finance, 1928–35* (Geneva).
LIPSEY, R. G. (1960) 'The Theory of Customs Unions: a General Survey', *Economic Journal*, vol. 70.
LIZANO, E. and WILLMORE, L. N. (1975) 'Second Thoughts on Central America: the Rosenthal Report', *Journal of Common Studies*, vol. 13.
LOEHR, W. (1987) 'Current Account Balances in Central America 1974–84: External and Domestic Influences', *Journal of Latin American Studies*, vol. 19, Part I, May.
MACBEAN, A. (1966) *Export Instability and Economic Development* (New York: Allen & Unwin).
McCLELLAND, D. H. (1972) *The Central American Common Market: Economic Growth and Choices for the Future* (New York: Praeger).
MACDOUGALL, G. D. A. (1960) 'The Benefits and Costs of Private Investment From Abroad: A Theoretical Approach', *Economic Record*, vol. 36.
MAY, S. and OTHERS (1952) *Costa Rica: A Study in Economic Development* (New York).
MONTEFORTE TOLEDO, M. (1972) *Centro América: Subdesarrollo y Dependencia*, 2 vols (Mexico).
MONTGOMERY, T. S. (1982) *Revolution in El Salvador* (Boulder, Colarado: Westview Press).
MOONEY, J. P. (1968) 'Gross Domestic Product, Gross National Product, and Capital Formation in El Salvador, 1945–65', *Estadística*.
MUNRO, D. G. (1918) *The Five Republics of Central America* (New York).
NUGENT, J. B. (1974) *Economic Integration in Central America* (Baltimore: Johns Hopkins University Press).
PARKER, F. D. (1964) *The Central American Republics* (Oxford: Oxford University Press).
PREALC (1979) *Diagnóstico de las estadísticas y Bibliografía sobre el Empleo en Centroamérica y Panama* (Santiago).

PREALC (1980) *Empleo y Salarios en Nicaragua* (Santiago).

PREALC (1983) *Producción de Alimentos Básicos y Empleo en el Istmo Centroamericano* (Santiago).

RAPOPORT, A. (1978) 'Effective Protection Rates in Central America', Appendix K of W. R. Cline and E. Delgado (eds), *Economic Integration in Central America* (Washington, DC: Brookings Institution).

REYNOLDS, C. and LEIVA, G. (1978a) 'Employment Problems of Export Economies in a Common Market: the Case of Central America', in W. R. Cline and E. Delgado (eds), *Economic Integration in Central America* (Washington, DC: Brookings Institution).

REYNOLDS, C. (1978b) 'Appendix E – A Model of Employment and Labor Shares in an Export Economy with Import Substituting Industrialisation', in W. R. Cline and E. Delgado (eds), *Economic Integration in Central America* (Washington, DC: Brookings Institution).

RIVERA URRUTIA, E. (1982) *El Fondo Monetario Internacional y Costa Rica 1976–82* (San José: Colección Centroamerica).

ROBINSON, S. and KUBO, Y. (1979) 'Sources of Industrial Growth and Structural Changes: a Comparative Analysis of Eight Countries', paper presented to Seventh International Conference on Input–Output Techniques, Innsbruck.

ROSENTHAL, G. (1973) 'The Role of Private Foreign Investment in the Development of the Central American Common Market. Guatemala' (mimeo).

SCHYDLOWSKY, D. (1986) 'The Macroeconomic Effect of Non-traditional Exports in Peru', *Economic Development and Cultural Change*, vol. 34, no. 3, April.

SELIGSON, M. (1980) *Peasants of Costa Rica and the Development of Agrarian Capitalism* (Madison: University of Wisconsin Press).

SIECA (1973) *El Desarrollo Integrado de Centroamérica en la Presente Década: Bases y Propuestas Para el Perfeccionamiento, y la Reestructuración del Mercado Comun Centroamericano*, 13 vols, Institute for Latin American Integration, Inter-American Development Bank (Buenos Aires).

SIECA (1985) *Series Estadísticas Seleccionadas de Centroamérica, No. 20* (Guatemala, December).

SIECA (1987) *El Comercio Intracentroamericano en el período 1980–86* (Guatemala, May).

SIRI, G. (1978) 'Calculation of the Shadow Price of Foreign Exchange Based on the Central American Econometric Model', in W. R. Cline and E. Delgado (eds), *Economic Integration in Central America* (Washington, DC: Brookings Institution).

SIRI, G. and DOMINGUEZ, R. (1981) 'Central American Accommodation to External Disruptions', in W. Cline (ed.), *World Inflation and the Developing Countries* (Washington, DC: Brookings Institution).

SOLEY GÜELL, T. (1949) *Compendio de la Historia Económica y Hacendaria de Costa Rica*, 2 vols, San José (Costa Rica: Editorial Universitaria).

SOLEY GÜELL, T. (1975) *Compendio de la Historia Económica y Hacendaria de Costa Rica, Biblioteca Patria No. 12, San José* (Costa Rica: Editorial Costa Rica).

SOUTAR, G. (1977) 'Export Instability and Economic Growth', *Journal of Development Economics*, vol. 4.

STOKES, W. S. (1950) *Honduras – an Area Study in Government* (Madison, Wisconsin).

STAHLER-SHOLK, R. (1987) 'Foreign Debt and Economic Stabilisation Policies in Revolutionary Nicaragua', in R. Spalding (ed.), *The Political Economy of Nicaragua* (London: Allen & Unwin).

TORRES RIVAS, E. (1973) *Interpretación de Desarrollo Social Centroamericano* (San José: EDUCA).

TOYE, J. (1987) *Dilemmas of Development* (Oxford: Blackwell).

TSENG, W. (1984) 'The Effects of Adjustment', *Finance & Development*, December.

URRUTIA, E. and SOJO, A. (1986) 'El Perfil de la Política Económica en Centroamérica: la Década de los Ochenta', in E. Urrutia, A. Sojo and R. López (eds), *Centroamérica: Política Económica y Crisis* (San José: ICAIS).

VAITSOS, C. V. (1978) 'Crisis in Regional Economic Cooperation (Integration) Among Developing Countries: A Survey', *World Development*, vol. 6, pp. 722–3.

VEGA, M. (1982) *El Estado Costarricense de 1974 a 1978: CODESA y la Fracción Industrial* (San José: Editorial Hoy).

VINER, J. (1950) *The Customs Union Issue* (New York: Carnegie Endowment for International Peace).

WAGLEY, C. (1941) 'Economics of a Guatemalan Village', *Memoirs of the American Anthropological Association, no 58*.

WEEKS, J. (1985) *The Economics of Central America* (New York: Holmes & Meier).

WEINERT, R. (1981) 'Nicaragua's Debt Renegotiation', *Cambridge Journal of Economics*, vol. 5, pp. 187–94.

WHITE, A. (1973) *El Salvador* (London).

WILFORD, W. T. (1970) 'Trade Creation in the Central American Common Market', *Western Economic Journal*, vol. 8.

WILFORD, W. T. (1978) 'On Revenue Performance and Revenue-Income Stability in the Third World', *Economic Development and Cultural Change*, April.

WILKIE, J. W. and REICH, R. (1978, 1980) *Statistical Abstract of Latin America*, vols 19, 20 (Los Angeles: UCLA).

WILLIAMS, R. (1978) 'Economics of Scale Parameters for Central American Manufacturing Industry', in W. R. Cline and E. Delgado (eds), *Economic Integration in Central America* (Washington, DC: Brookings Institution).

WILLMORE, L. N. (1976) 'Trade Creation, Trade Diversion and Effective Protection in the Central American Common Market', *Journal of Development Studies*, vol. 12, no. 4.

WILLMORE, L. N. (1976a) 'Direct Foreign Investment in Central American Manufacturing', *World Development*, vol. 4.

WILSON, E. A. (1970) 'The Crisis of National Integration in El Salvador 1919–35', unpublished PhD thesis, Stanford University.

WILSON, C. M. (1947) *Empire in Green and Gold: The Story of the American Banana Trade* (New York).

WIONCZEK, M. S. (1972) 'The Central American Common Market', in P.

Robson (ed.), *International Economic Integration* (Harmondsworth: Penguin).
WORLD BANK (1983) *World Development Report 1983* (Washington).
YOUNG, J. P. (1925) *Central American Currency and Finance* (Princeton, NJ).
YOTOPOULOS, P. and NUGENT, J. (1976) *The Economics of Development: Empirical Investigations* (New York: Harper & Row).

# Index

CATHOLIC AND REFORMED

# CATHOLIC AND REFORMED

*A Study of the Anglican Church, 1559–1662*

by

FLORENCE HIGHAM

LONDON

S·P·C·K

1962

*First published in 1962*
*by S.P.C.K.*
*Holy Trinity Church*
*Marylebone Road*
*London N.W.1*

*Made and printed in Great Britain by*
*William Clowes and Sons, Limited, London and Beccles*

# CONTENTS

# PREFACE

This study of Anglicanism in its early days grew out of an attempt to understand the position of Church of England men in the turbulent years of the mid-seventeenth century, to see something of the effect of those years on the ordinary life of the parish, and to discover to what extent the course of events had vitiated the ideal of a middle way, Catholic and Reformed. I found, however, that I must go back behind the Civil Wars, not only to Laud but to Andrewes and Hooker and the "settlement" of 1559, although it was not possible to do more than suggest the main lines of development and the character of the men who guided the Church of England in these formative years. Others, I hope, may be tempted to pursue more thoroughly the various paths from which I have had to turn aside.

I would like to acknowledge my debt to the late Dr Norman Sykes, who encouraged me to attempt this study. I hope I have indicated clearly in my notes how much I owe to the work of modern scholars, but I must refer again to my use of Dr R. S. Bosher's book *The Making of the Restoration Settlement*. My thanks are due to Dr G. V. Bennett of New College, Oxford, for advice in regard to my final chapter and to Dr D. M. Barratt for allowing me to read her illuminating thesis on the condition of the parochial clergy between the Reformation and 1660. I am particularly grateful to Dr Tindal Hart not only for his books on the country clergy but for the detailed criticism and constructive advice that he has given me.

A certain use has been made of parochial records and other contemporary sources, and in quoting from these spelling has sometimes been modernized to make for easier reading. I am glad to acknowledge the courtesy and co-operation I have received from the staff of the London County Record Office,

the Kent Archives Office and the Southwark Central Library, as well as from Miss W. D. Coates and her colleagues at the National Register of Archives. I am indebted to Lord Hampton for permission to print excerpts from the Pakington Manuscripts and to Major E. H. Lee Warner for allowing me to examine and quote from the papers of Bishop Warner. Permission to quote from T. S. Eliot's "Little Gidding", in *Four Quartets*, has kindly been given by Faber & Faber Ltd and Harcourt, Brace & World Inc. Finally I would thank Mr Cyprian Blagden and Mrs Guy Rogers, the one for counselling me when the book was half-written, the other for her help in the arduous business of reading proofs.

F. M. G. H.

# CATHOLIC AND REFORMED

# I

# TUDOR BACKGROUND

At a time of challenge and adversity, when the Anglican Church went down in defeat in the civil wars of the seventeenth century, the loyalty and endurance of many ordinary people saved it from extinction. Yet in 1559, a hundred years before, the compromise Church of Elizabeth I seemed to many merely an expedient, set up by Act of Parliament and the will of a Tudor sovereign. The growth that took place in the intervening years, the emergence of Anglicanism as a living way against the background of a world in turmoil, forms the theme of the ensuing pages. The natural starting-point for any such story is Hooker's inspired blueprint of the *Ecclesiastical Polity*, but in order to understand the circumstances and the setting in which that masterpiece was written, something must first be said of the religious settlement which, for more than thirty years before Hooker wrote, had been struggling into existence, even as England herself had been struggling towards stability and internal peace.

When Henry VIII had broken with Rome and dissolved the monastic orders, he endeavoured to halt the course of the Reformation in England by forbidding doctrinal change. It was by no means unreasonable. The denial of the Pope's supremacy, whether justifiable or not, did not run counter to the temper of a rising nation-state; it was a different matter to introduce new dogma which would breed disunity in the Church and might well give rise to faction in the secular sphere.[1] There was, however, already in existence a native Protestant sentiment going back to the days of Wyclif, whose

[1] P. M. Dawley, *John Whitgift and the Reformation* (1955), p. 15.

Lollard disciples continued underground to exercise a good deal of influence in various parts of the country.[2] There was also at a different level a Cambridge group, Hugh Latimer its most distinguished member, whose interest in the new learning was combined with a burning desire for reform, while the ups and downs of Henry's Church policy had already caused a number to withdraw into enforced or voluntary exile and thus to act as a link between their friends in England and Protestant movements on the Continent. It was not a propitious moment to prohibit change![3]

In one respect, the use of the vernacular, Henry continued to encourage the new developments. Before the reaction of his final years set in, he had authorized the publication of Miles Coverdale's translation of the Scriptures, largely based on Tyndale's pioneer work, and Thomas Cromwell had issued injunctions that an English bible should be kept in every parish church. In 1539, after many setbacks, the Great Bible appeared, to be cherished as a precious possession, safely chained, in the churches of the land. Instructions were issued that a chapter of the Scriptures should be read each week in the course of divine service, and thus for the first time a people, in the main illiterate, were made familiar with the words of Holy Writ. It was a vital innovation, for the whole basis of Protestant teaching was the Bible—the Word of God accessible to all men and the supreme authority in life and doctrine.

With Edward VI's accession in 1547 the changes multiplied. Already, under Cranmer's direction, an English form of the Litany had been authorized, and now an English Order of Holy Communion was incorporated in the Latin Mass. It provided for the administration of the sacrament to the laity in both kinds, though in the country at large this important alteration probably made less impact than the discontinuance

[2] Erik Routley, *English Religious Dissent* (1960), p. 20; cf. A. G. Dickens, *Lollards and Protestants in the Diocese of York, 1499–1558* (1959), pp. 242 ff.

[3] E. G. Rupp, *Studies in the making of the English Protestant Tradition* (1947), pp. 1–19, 47.

of old Catholic customs such as the lighting of candles at Candlemas or the blessing of the palms on Palm Sunday. There were many who grumbled, but in the King's Council the power of the Reformers grew; and if some were influenced by greed and ambition, others were stirred by genuine fervour, as clerics of the calibre of Bishop Ridley espoused the new religion and Hugh Latimer in his forthright sermons demanded social justice in the name of Christ.

Archbishop Cranmer, however, was in less of a hurry than many of his lay colleagues in the Privy Council. In 1549 Parliament issued an Act of Uniformity which enjoined the sole use of the Book of Common Prayer. The book had been drawn up by a small committee under Cranmer's guidance, and his genius secured a beauty of language and a spiritual awareness that was to give the English liturgy a sure place in men's affections and enable it to outlast the changes and chances of ecclesiastical politics. But this first Edwardian Prayer Book bore few signs of doctrinal change.[4] Its main purpose, according to the Preface, was to standardize in an English version the various uses employed in worship throughout the country. A few months before Edward's death, however, in 1552, a second Prayer Book was authorized by Parliament and this was firmly Protestant in tone and teaching. The commemorative nature of the Communion Service was stressed and a statement, which came to be known as the Black Rubric, was added to the effect that kneeling to receive the sacrament did not indicate an idolatrous adoration of the elements. Before the new book was in general use the King had died. His sister, the unhappy Mary, reconciled England to Rome but alienated her people's affection by her unpopular marriage with Prince Philip of Spain and by the abortive attempt to eradicate heresy by burnings at the stake. When Mary died after only five years' rule, there was no Roman Catholic heir to complete her work, and the war with France,

[4] *The Booke of Common Prayer . . . 1549–1561*, introd. E. C. Ratcliff (1949), pp. 12–17.

upon which she had embarked as Spain's ally, led only to the loss of Calais, England's last foothold on the Continent.

Elizabeth I thus found herself Queen of a country discredited abroad and insecure at home. Most of her subjects were uncertain in matters of belief, neither Papist nor Protestant in the later sense of the terms but anxious for quiet days and a measure of stability. For herself there could be no question of returning to the Roman allegiance, since her position as Queen and her very legitimacy depended upon the recognition of Catherine of Aragon's divorce. Her advisers, like those of Edward VI, were drawn in the main from the men who had established themselves upon the monastic lands. Nor was it only a case of policy or possessions, as the martyrs of Mary's reign had proved; now the friends who had survived them returned from exile, confident and eager for a further advance. It was inconceivable to them that the good work of purifying God's Church according to the Scriptures should not be carried forward to a glorious conclusion.

At once they were disappointed. The Queen forbade any immediate change. It was essential for England's safety to be prudent, at least until peace was made with France, but it was more than political necessity that made her procrastinate. Her action in regard to the Litany illustrated the way she wished to go. She restored its use in the English form but excluded one clause, never to be restored, which asked for deliverance from "the tyranny of the Bishop of Rome and all his detestable enormities". It was a sign of her genuine desire for a compromise settlement which would be sufficiently palatable to all but a few extremists to enable her and the bishops of her choosing to restore ordered rule and worship after twenty years of turmoil.

As soon as Parliament met it was clear that Elizabeth would not have it all her own way.[5] Protestant feeling was strongly

[5] For details of the settlement see W. H. Frere, *The English Church in the Reigns of Elizabeth and James I* (1904), pp. 14–49; cf. J. B. Black, *The Reign of Elizabeth* (edn of 1949), pp. 1–29.

represented in the Commons, and in the Lords the Marian bishops fought a rearguard action in defence of their faith. After three months of debate and negotiation, the Acts of Supremacy and Uniformity were passed. The Queen, relinquishing the title of Head, became Supreme Governor of the Church in England and, as in the Edwardian Acts, attendance at church was made obligatory and the sole form of service was to be that set forth in a revised Book of Common Prayer.

Within this legal framework a settlement of sorts could be gradually worked out in a series of royal and episcopal injunctions. Its nature was already apparent in the changes in the Prayer Book. The Liturgy, as now revised, went further than the first Prayer Book of Edward's reign but excluded some of the radical changes of his second book. The doctrine of the Holy Communion was left intentionally vague. In the words of administration the sentences from each of Edward's Prayer Books were retained: "The Body of our Lord Jesus Christ . . ." accepted the dogma of a spiritual Presence, while "Take and eat . . . in remembrance . . ." satisfied those who were furthest from the doctrine of the Roman Mass. Elizabeth herself regarded the sacrament as a mystery which it was wiser to accept than to analyse; on one occasion she put her admirable sentiments into rather less admirable verse:

> Twas God the word that spake it,
> He took the Bread and brake it;
> And what the word did make it,
> That I believe and take it.[6]

To her it did not matter that there should be diversity of belief within the Anglican Church. She had no wish to "make for herself a window into men's souls". What she did require was quiet and law-abiding behaviour, not least because a lack of conformity in things of the spirit too often went hand in hand with a disregard of authority in secular affairs. As she declared, a few years later: "We know not, nor have any

[6] S. Clarke, *The Marrow of Ecclesiastical History* (1675), II.94.

meaning to allow, that any of our subjects should be molested . . . in any matter either of faith . . . or for matters of ceremonies . . . as long as they shall in their outward conversation show themselves quiet and comfortable. . . ."[7]

Circumstance and the intractable consciences of men made Elizabeth's proviso less simple than it sounded. At the very start all of Mary's bishops, except one, relinquished office since they could not take the requisite oath to the Queen as Supreme Governor. It was no easy matter to fill so many vacancies, for the obvious leaders of Protestant opinion had, most of them, perished in Mary's reign and those who remained were too radical for Elizabeth's liking. Her choice as Archbishop of Canterbury was Matthew Parker, a former Dean of Lincoln and Master of Corpus Christi College, Cambridge. As a married priest he had lost his preferments in Mary's reign and had lived in precarious retirement in the country. His one wish now was to return to the academic life he loved, but in the summer of 1559 he was summoned to London and, in spite of his repeated *nolo*, the primacy was thrust upon him.

Cardinal Pole's death, within a few days of Queen Mary's, had left the office vacant, and in the election and consecration of his successor every possible care was taken to follow the accustomed practices and traditions of the Church and to leave no loophole for the assertion that the appointment had not been entirely regular. The episcopal bench was in a chaotic condition, and it was December before Parker was consecrated at Lambeth by William Barlow, Bishop-elect of Chichester (formerly of Bath and Wells) and three others, Scory (formerly Bishop of Chichester), Coverdale (formerly Bishop of Exeter), and Hodgkins (Suffragan Bishop of Bedford). It was not till the next century, when polemical debate with Rome was at its height, that the regularity of the

[7] *Burghley State Papers*, ed. Haynes (1740), pp. 591 f, quoted by Dawley (op. cit., p. 61) in a clear and balanced account stressing the comprehensiveness of the settlement.

proceedings was impugned. Parker safeguarded himself by leaving a detailed account of his consecration for inclusion in the archives of Corpus Christi, understanding more clearly than most how much the validity and continuity of the English Church depended on the preservation of the sacramental tie which linked the bishops, old and new, in the Apostolic descent.[8]

It was continuity that Parker and the Queen both wished to stress. He was still a scholar at heart, and the studies in early Church history which had first won him distinction coloured his whole approach to his work as archbishop. He saw the Anglican Church as part of the Church Universal, tracing its proud heritage back to the first centuries after Christ, and the Reformation was not for him a denial of that heritage but a rooting out of the corruptions that had adhered to it during the passage of the years. His most congenial colleague was Bishop Jewel of Salisbury, a man of similar background, whose *Apology* for the Church of England, written in Latin in 1562, first tried to express the principles which lay behind the compromise. It was men such as these, university scholars turned bishops often against their will, who gave to the Anglican Church from the beginning its marked characteristics of sound learning and sober piety.

In Matthew Parker, the Queen had secured an able and conscientious primate who persevered for sixteen years in making her settlement work. He proved himself both patient and realistic, determined when necessary but never tendentious. His wife went with him to Lambeth, gracious and tactful and very uneasy, for married priests were an innovation that few people liked and that the Queen disliked intensely. She could not stay the practice, but in the Injunctions she issued in 1559 she laid down that wives of clergy must first be

[8] See John Strype, *The Life and Acts of Matthew Parker* (1821), I.101–125; and cf. *An Account of the Rites and Ceremonies which took place at the Consecration of Archbishop Parker*, with introduction, preface, and notes, by James Goodwin (1841).

approved by the local magistrates, and not till the next reign were their children accorded legal status. Elizabeth, however, came to give Mrs Parker grudging acceptance, and in his family life and the pleasure of collecting books the Archbishop found some solace and refreshment in a task that grew more difficult with every year.

It had seemed at first as if conformity would be obtained without very much resistance. There were a number who refused the oaths, many of the best men among them, but they were fewer than in recent times of crisis. The chief signs of disorder in the first year came from the zeal of the Londoners in obeying instructions to remove images and other Popish ornaments from St Paul's and the City churches. Rood lofts and altars were torn down and burnt in huge bonfires lit in Cheapside and at St Bartholomew's Fair in Smithfield. In the country as a whole there was less enthusiasm, and sufficient signs of secret activity on the part of "massing priests" for Parliament, in 1563, to draw up penal laws against them. At the same time, Convocation framed a new set of doctrinal articles, thirty-nine in number, based on the forty-two articles of Henry's reign. Elizabeth, however, did not agree to the promulgation of the articles for another eight years, while Parker's judicious leniency prevented any marked persecution under the penal laws. His conciliatory attitude, combined with the Queen's refusal to stress matters of dogma and her restraint in the exercise of her supremacy, secured for the settlement a large measure of acceptance during the first decade of the reign.

Much of the time and energy of Parker and the best of his bishops was devoted to a piecemeal but steady attempt to improve the condition of the Church as a whole, but the calibre of many of the diocesans left much to be desired and ecclesiastical administration and control were largely ineffective, in part through lack of co-operation from parish officials and unsympathetic J.P.s. The removal of the last vestiges of Popery and the desecration that had often attended the process

had left many churches in a ruinous condition, while both the shortage of clergy and their ignorance were deplorable. When Bishop Hooper examined just over three hundred of his clergy in King Edward's reign, little more than half could repeat the Ten Commandments.[9] A large number of cures were vacant or held in plurality, for the poverty and lack of status of the average parish priest kept many young men from entering the Church, and the religious uncertainty of the times and the greater attraction of the study of law had further reduced the number of ordinands. Those who remained were not of necessity worse than their medieval predecessors, but the stress that the Reformers laid upon the Bible and the consequent need to expound its meaning, put a premium upon learning and subjected the parish priest who was a "dumb dog" to a battery of criticism from the Puritan wing of the Church. What the latter did not or would not recognize was the extent to which Parker and his successors laboured to improve the situation.[10]

In her Injunctions the Queen laid down that a sermon should be preached in every parish once a quarter, but it was some time before this regulation could be implemented: for only certain clergy were licensed to preach and in spite of the shortage the bishops kept the standards high. In the absence of a "learned divine", duly licensed, a homily was read from an authorized collection made in Edward VI's reign and reissued with additions by Bishop Jewel—sound Protestant doctrine if rather remote from the needs of the ordinary parishioner. In some vacant livings lay readers were appointed to

[9] D. M. Barratt, "The Condition of the Parish Clergy between the Reformation and 1660 with special reference to the dioceses of Oxford, Worcester and Gloucester", p. 71. (Thesis deposited in the Bodleian Library, Oxford [1949].)

[10] These are the conclusions drawn by Dr Barratt in her invaluable thesis, which gives a detailed account of the clergy throughout the years before 1660 in regard to learning, their financial and social status, and questions connected with tithe and patronage. For the Elizabethan parson see A. Tindal Hart, *The Country Clergy in Elizabethan and Stuart Times, 1558–1660* (1958), pp. 24–51.

read the divine service and the homilies, but not to administer the sacraments.[11] In most churches the service of Holy Communion was at least as rare as a sermon: in a well-ordered parish it was usually held four times a year, at the three great festivals and sometimes after harvest-home.

Moral shortcomings were as serious as intellectual ones. Visitation articles continued to inquire "whether doth your Vicar and curate keep any ale-house . . . or keep any suspected woman in his house or be himself an incontinent liver or given to drunkenness or idleness". Nor were the replies always in the negative.[12] Only by an imperceptible alteration in standards, as the Church was revitalized, would the morals and manners of priests and laymen gradually improve. Undoubtedly a great deal was achieved at the start by the clergy who returned from abroad and the younger men who caught their enthusiasm. Their zeal might make them, in their ecclesiastical views, thorns in the flesh for Elizabeth and her primate, but their moral standards and their pastoral devotion gave them a hold on the people of their parishes which had less to do with theological tenets than with Christian discipleship.

The Precisians, as people began to call them, certainly were thorns in the flesh as they made determined efforts to undermine the balance which the Queen and her Archbishop were precariously maintaining. At first they were in no sense an organized group; they had come back from the Continent at different moments in the early years of the reign—some, for instance, tarried in Geneva to finish a translation of the Bible. Some of those who returned, like Grindal, Sandys, and Richard Cox, accepted bishoprics and drifted away from their friends; others were disappointed by the lack of promotion, and their attitude hardened into opposition as the royal and episcopal Injunctions made it clear that the Church, as now

[11] Tindal Hart, op. cit., p. 27. As the situation improved the authorities discouraged the appointment of readers (Frere, op. cit., p. 167).

[12] J. S. Purvis, *Tudor Parish Documents in the Diocese of York* (1948), p. 3, and cf. Tindal Hart, op. cit., pp. 31–4.

established, was to retain certain ceremonies and vestments which the Precisians could not accept. In the Lower House of Convocation in 1562–3 their numbers predominated and they proposed certain liturgical reforms with every hope of success. But the Crown held the larger number of proxies, and to their intense disappointment they were defeated by one vote. During the next few years many of them adopted a policy of non-co-operation and, particularly in London and the eastern counties, clergy refused to wear the accredited vestments or sometimes even a surplice, while there were strong objections to the square cap enjoined by authority. Parker was reluctant to act against them, but the Queen saw it as a matter of necessary discipline, and eventually after examining the position at law the Archbishop issued his *Advertisements* of 1566. These laid down that certain Catholic practices were to be maintained in worship, but in regard to vestments only insisted on the use of the surplice and a distinctive garb for outdoor wear. Within these generous limits obedience was to be strictly enforced.

The mere question of clothing might seem a small matter upon which to rend a Church, yet behind it lay some serious divergences of principle. The Precisians' dislike of ceremonies, light and colour, copes and candles was not only an instinctive reaction against Popery; whether they were conscious of it or not, it was a sign of their distrust of emotion in worship and their wish for a more intellectual, or at least more rational approach. One of the reforms they put forward in 1563 related to the position of the minister when reading the services and laid down that he should always face the congregation, "that the people may be edified". Dr Routley in writing of English dissent describes this as the key phrase. They had become "suspicious of all the drama and choreography and orchestration of the Mass as being enemies of man's conceptual faculty". What was necessary in illiterate medieval days was no longer desirable for Renaissance man.[13]

[13] Routley, *English Religious Dissent*, p. 38.

Another vital question was involved, more immediate to the practical situation. How far could the diocesan impose obedience in matters of rule and worship which were not specifically enjoined in the Scriptures? How was an ordered Church to be achieved if men's interpretation of the Bible did not tally? These questions, the maintenance of discipline in matters not clearly dealt with in the Scriptures, and the difficulty of reconciling the Protestant stress on the exposition of the Word with the Catholic ideal of corporate worship, were problems over which a running battle continued, fought by the Puritans about matters, apparently non-essential, such as wearing vestments or kneeling to receive communion.

One should note also that these Precisians, who now came to be known as Puritans, did not regard themselves as individualists, in spite of their stress on personal scruples. The separatist strain in Puritanism evolved through the native Protestant element, associated with the Lollard tradition, rather than through the returned exiles. As the latter continued with the task of perfecting the reformation of the national Church to which they belonged, they naturally kept closely in touch with their friends in Europe. Some of them had passed their exile in Geneva; others had remained in Frankfurt; sometimes there had been friction. The advice they now received from their friends overseas did not always agree. Yet they continued to regard themselves as part of a great European movement. Lutherans in Germany and the followers of Zwingli in Zürich and of John Calvin in Geneva might differ in details of doctrine and discipline; but an overall sense of unity prevailed, and the aim of the returned exiles, in the campaign they waged to simplify the ceremonies and modify the government of the Anglican Church, was to bring it into alignment with the Reformed Churches of the Continent, until that fellowship in the faith had grown to be a worthy alternative to the organic unity of Rome.[14]

[14] For a full account of the beginnings of the Puritan movement consult M. M. Knappen, *Tudor Puritanism* (1939).

It was well for the Church of England that during these formative years there was to be found in the Queen herself, in the shrewd and devoted Cecil, and in Archbishop Parker, a triumvirate of wise defenders of the middle way. On the political front under William Cecil's guidance disaster was averted until the country was stabilized, but the flight of Mary of Scotland into England in 1567 and the Northern Rebellion, two years later, began a new period of tension and alarm. The religious situation was entirely changed in 1570 by the issue of a Papal Bull excommunicating the Queen. The threat from Rome naturally strengthened the hands of the Puritans, who began to be openly supported by influential councillors, and, in addition, a leader appeared in their own ranks to give the movement a coherence it had hitherto lacked. Thomas Cartwright, who became Professor of Divinity at Cambridge in the year of the Northern Rising, was still a comparatively young man who made no claim to academic detachment, nor looked back nostalgically to the fellowship of exile. In his first year as professor he gave a course of lectures on the Book of Acts which not only depicted the constitution of the Early Church as Presbyterian in form but indicated that the same pattern was valid for all time. He indicted the whole government of the Anglican Church as at present constituted, claiming that every parish should choose its own minister and that the duties of the bishops should be merely spiritual.[15] Cartwright had many friends and supporters among the younger Cambridge men, not all of whom shared his theological approach; they were all passionately concerned with the Church's obvious shortcomings in such matters as patronage and pluralities and blamed the bishops not only for the peccadilloes of their clergy but for a lack of simplicity in their own lives. So from disputes over details of worship the Puritans advanced to a frontal attack upon the government of the Church.

They would have accomplished more if there had not

[15] Knappen, op. cit., p. 224. For Cartwright see A. F. Scott Pearson, *Thomas Cartwright and Elizabethan Puritanism, 1535–1603* (1925).

emerged at this stage a doughty champion of authority in the person of John Whitgift, the new Vice-Chancellor. There was a good deal of the schoolmaster in Whitgift's make-up and he was shocked by Cartwright's behaviour. He obtained his dismissal from his chair and a year later jockeyed him out of his fellowship. Cartwright went to Geneva, where he studied the Presbyterian system at first hand, but he was back in England to share in the excitement which accompanied the Puritans' first deliberate attempt to gain their ends by parliamentary action. They came near to success but their hopes were unexpectedly foiled by a royal injunction that no motion relating to church affairs should be introduced at Westminster without the bishops' approval. Thus frustrated, the more extreme among them turned their minds to propaganda and published an *Admonition to Parliament*, which attacked episcopacy and various abuses in a vigorous and incisive way. John Field, the most dynamic of Cartwright's associates, was arrested, and with him Thomas Wilcox, as joint authors of the *Admonition*. A *Second Admonition*, less forcible in tone but more constructive in its exposition of Presbyterian principles, is usually though without certainty attributed to Cartwright. He was also involved in a written controversy with Whitgift, who after some hesitation wrote an *Answer* to the *Admonition* to which Cartwright wrote a *Reply*, to be answered in turn by Whitgift's *Defense of the Answer*. The exchange had at least two advantages. It enabled Whitgift to clarify in his own mind the basis of his staunch support of the Elizabethan compromise and it also drew the Queen's attention to his outstanding ability.

Soon after his release Field experimented with an elementary form of presbytery in Wandsworth. During the middle years of the reign, while a growing threat from Rome endangered the Queen's safety, the authorities were reluctant to proceed against the Puritans and there was less propaganda and more experimental work of this kind. To give unity and direction to these experiments, Walter Travers published abroad in 1574 his exposition, *Ecclesiasticae Disciplinae* . . .

*explicatio*, which Cartwright translated into English and was forced to leave the country in consequence. Travers's book gave clear expression to the three characteristics of Calvinist theocracy: a theology resting four-square on the doctrine of Predestination, a strict moral control exercised through exclusion from the sacraments, and a system of ecclesiastical rule vested in ministers and lay elders, meeting periodically in classis, synod and assembly. This was the discipline established in Scotland, and it became eventually the chief objective of the Puritan hopes for the Church in England.[16]

In 1575 Archbishop Parker died, sadly aware of the cleavage in the country that neither his firmness nor his moderation had been able to prevent. Cecil, now Lord Burghley, persuaded the Queen to appoint Edmund Grindal as Parker's successor, in view of the need for a united front against Rome. Grindal was a man of courage and honesty, as well as of deep piety, who thought it more important to make full use of devout and able men in a Church poverty-stricken in regard to personnel, than to enforce ceremonial or refuse a modification of episcopal rule. But he had none of his predecessor's administrative ability, nor indeed of his kindly temper. He never won the Queen's confidence, and he soon found himself in difficulties when a new development in East Anglia attracted her unfavourable attention. The Prophesyings which had been springing up in the eastern counties were at first mainly educational in intent; they were meetings of clergy and leading laymen who came together periodically for mutual exhortation, study, and prayer. Grindal saw clearly the potentialities for good such meetings possessed, and when the Queen ordered their suppression wished rather to control them and only to take action if there were reports of subversive speech. But a certain amount of "voluntary discipline of

[16] Dawley, *John Whitgift and the Reformation*, pp. 135 et seq.; Scott Pearson, op. cit., pp. 58–121. For Field, see Patrick Collinson, "John Field and Elizabethan Puritanism", in S. T. Bindoff, J. Hurstfield, and C. H. Williams (eds.), *Elizabethan Government and Society: Essays presented to Sir John Neale* (1961), pp. 127–62.

evil-doers" had been introduced into some of the meetings which might easily develop into unofficial classes and the Queen regarded them as a dangerous *imperium in imperio*. She insisted on the suppression of the Prophesyings, and when Grindal refused sent instructions over his head direct to the bishops. The Primate was suspended for five years from all but spiritual duties, and died in 1583, a blind and broken man.

In the year that Travers published his *Ecclesiastical Discipline* the first seminary priests had landed in England to win back their country to the Roman Faith. The Counter-Reformation was sweeping across Europe, achieving a triumphant sense of disciplined power, and both Pius V and, still more, his successor Gregory XIII regarded Elizabeth as a Jezebel to be destroyed. In 1570 a Bull of Excommunication had been planned to coincide with the Northern Rising, though it was not smuggled into the country until the rebels had been crushed. Parliament retaliated by a measure declaring it treason to deny the Queen's right to the throne, which made it in effect possible to sentence as traitors any who conceded the Pope's authority to depose a reigning prince. Meanwhile the presence in England of Mary of Scotland placed Elizabeth in a quandary from which she never entirely escaped during the twenty years of her cousin's captivity. Mary, a zealous Catholic, was the rightful Queen if Elizabeth were illegitimate, and her misfortunes and her cause entangled alike able young visionaries and ambitious noblemen. The dangerous years that did not end until her execution were marked by a succession of assassination plots, always effectively foiled by Secretary Walsingham's incredible secret service.

On the spiritual front the Roman Catholics made steady progress. In the late sixties William Allen had founded at Douai a college (later removed to Rheims) where young Englishmen underwent a seven-year training with the vowed intent of returning to England to succour the souls of their countrymen. As the Marian priests who refused to conform

gradually died out, there was dire need of pastoral care among the Roman Catholic recusants, and this the priests from Douai supplied in increasing numbers in the second half of the reign. It was a road that often led to imprisonment or death, for albeit their concern may have been spiritual only, at times of tension the Act of 1571 made it possible to condemn them as traitors. Such a crisis occurred soon after the arrival of the first missionaries. Cuthbert Mayne was executed at Launceston in 1577 and early in 1579 two others were hanged, drawn, and quartered at the gallows at Tyburn.

A daughter house of Douai had been established in Rome and was put under the direction of the Jesuits, who made it a centre of missionary zeal and propaganda famed as the English College in the years to come. In 1580 Gregory gave his blessing to its first mission to England, and although the object of the mission was again said to be spiritual, "the preservation and the augmentation of the faith", a clause in the original instructions permitted political discussions under certain circumstances. The clause was withdrawn but it gave Burghley some excuse in the dangerous summer of 1580 for refusing to distinguish between religion and politics. Some of the missionaries were more disingenuous than others and it was a tragic chance that the Government's first victim was the saintly Edmund Campion who could declare with complete sincerity on the scaffold: "We travelled only for souls, we touched neither state nor policy." But whether or not Burghley and Walsingham were justified in the action they took for the safety of the realm, the faith and courage that brought to the shores of England men of the calibre of Campion and Southwell and a host of humbler priests, obedient unto death, could only serve to underline the tragedy of sundered Christendom.[17]

[17] Frere, *The English Church in the Reigns of Elizabeth and James I*, pp. 206–222; Black, *The Reign of Elizabeth*, pp. 134–51; on Douai cf. Evelyn Waugh, *Edmund Campion* (1935), pp. 53–62, 78 et seq.; cf. also J. H. Pollen, *The English Catholics in the Reign of Elizabeth* (1920), which ends in 1580.

A few years later came open war with Spain within a year of the execution of Mary of Scotland. With the threat of invasion, Catholics and Protestants alike rallied in the defence of England and in allegiance to their Queen. Lord Howard of Effingham, a kinsman of the late Duke of Norfolk and a member of the greatest Roman Catholic family in the land, sailed in command of the fleet that defeated the Armada; Lord Montague, another staunch Romanist, rode out to Tilbury at the head of a contingent of armed men. The Armada was scattered but the war went on and many loyal Roman Catholics were content to stay peaceably away from their parish church, paying the recusancy fines and hearing Mass as best they could in secret. Sometimes they were left in peace if they put in a token appearance occasionally at Mattins, as Montague used to do, slipping in to St Saviour's in Southwark from his house in the adjoining close until a Puritan element in the vestry ordered the door to be blocked up and the customary fine to be collected. The systematic levy of the fines and the amounts extracted varied enormously in different parts of the country, according to the wealth of the recusants and local sympathies, but even when times were comparatively peaceful the tension remained: for the Romanists the constant fear of penury or exile, for the Government the knowledge of a large non-conforming block composed of a cross-section of society. To harbour a priest remained a capital offence, and in the spring of 1588, for this "crime", a woman was pressed to death at York. During the reign as a whole over 120 clergy and about sixty lay men and women were executed, technically as traitors, for loyalty to Rome.[18] Many of them had returned illicitly from banishment, but in the latter years not only the executions but the number of banishments dwindled. In 1593 a new Act of Parliament laid down that recusants must remain within five miles of their homes, and this largely took the place of further punishment. This development was partly due to the lessening of tension but also to the discovery

[18] Frere, op. cit., pp. 220 f.

that the recusancy fines provided a profitable source of wealth to the Exchequer. Periodically troublesome individuals, priests in particular, were imprisoned, mainly in Wisbech Castle where attempts were made by earnest Protestants to convert them. Their effectiveness as a political party was increasingly undermined by the growing difference of opinion between the missionary-minded Jesuits and the secular priests, who like the majority of lay recusants wished only for a *modus vivendi* whereby their love and loyalty to England might be allowed to survive alongside a quiet but persistent practice of their faith.

Before the coming of the quieter years another clash with the Puritans had ended in tragedy. It began with the appointment of Whitgift as Grindal's successor in 1583. This proved a turning-point in the Anglican story, for Whitgift was a born disciplinarian and for good or ill he set the authoritarian tone which characterized the Anglican Church during the next half-century. In an earlier letter to Burghley he had declared that if the dissidents continued unchecked, "nothing else in the end can be looked for, than confusion both of the Church and of the State. But convenient discipline, joined with doctrine, being duly executed will soon remedy all."[19] It was this "convenient discipline" that he now proceeded to exert, yet in enforcing obedience he endeavoured to ensure that the Church itself was made more worthy of the conformity he demanded. He was so far successful in encouraging learning that by the end of his primacy about half the clergy in England were university graduates. The growth of the wonderful network of Tudor grammar schools had a good deal to do with this improvement.[20] Even non-graduate clergy might thus have a smattering of Latin—though fewer knew much of divinity, and it was on this aspect that Whitgift concentrated, developing a scheme initiated during Grindal's term of office. Non-graduate clergy were instructed, with schoolmasterly

[19] Dawley, op. cit., p. 99.
[20] Tindal Hart, *The Country Clergy in Elizabethan and Stuart Times*, p. 26.

thoroughness, each to obtain "a paper book" in which to summarize every day a chapter of the Bible. Once a week they were also to read and note one of the sermons of Heinrich Bullinger, an eminent continental divine. Once a quarter, the note-books were to be shown to a minister in the neighbourhood who was a licensed preacher, these picked clergy being put in charge of some six non-graduates apiece to lessen the burden of supervision that would otherwise fall on the archdeacons.[21]

Thus the work of education went painfully and painstakingly on. Less satisfactory was the imposition of ecclesiastical discipline by methods that were frankly dictatorial. Within two months of his consecration Whitgift had instructed his bishops to demand from their clergy full and complete assent not only to the Royal Supremacy and all the Thirty-nine Articles but to the Prayer Book in its entirety, including "the ordering of Bishops, Priests, and Deacons". Those who refused were suspended, as so many of the best men were to be silenced or ejected in the coming years, as different governments attempted to impose by force the uniformity that as yet appeared the only alternative to the sin of schism. In spite of much hostile criticism Whitgift persisted, with no glimmer of understanding of the depth of religious conviction of those whom he regarded as mere mischief-makers. To enforce discipline he made full use of the prerogative court of High Commission, which he developed into a permanent body out of an *ad hoc* ecclesiastical commission appointed by the Crown. The contrast between its procedure and that of the courts of common law not only offended the sense of justice of ordinary people but alienated the lawyers, who objected in particular to the use of the *ex officio* oath. This oath, tendered not only to the witness but also to the defendant, bound them to answer truly all questions put to them and thus often compelled the accused either to incriminate himself or to commit perjury.

[21] Dawley, op. cit., pp. 200–5; Cardwell, *Synodalia* (1842), pp. 133 et seq.

It smacked too much of the Inquisition, Burghley complained to the Archbishop.[22]

The criticism and hostility of many of the Queen's ministers far exceeded Burghley's, and for a few years Whitgift barely held his own. A new Protestant fervour had been aroused throughout England by the heroic revolt of the Netherlands, and at court there was a strong pro-Puritan faction, led by men of the calibre of Leicester and Walsingham. The Chancellor of the Exchequer, Sir Walter Mildmay, catching the mood of the moment, founded a new college at Cambridge. He named it Emmanuel, appointing Laurence Chaderton, a well-known preacher, to be its Master and stating his aim to be the upbringing of godly divines. His reply is well known to the Queen's challenge that he was setting up a Puritan foundation. With the polished evasiveness of which Tudor statesmen were past-masters, he answered: "I have set an acorn which, when it becomes an oak, God alone knows what will be the fruit thereof."

It was thus with the certainty of a measure of influential support that the Puritans went ahead, encouraged by Cartwright's second return to England and stimulated by men such as Field, who thought in terms of revolution rather than reformation. There was considerable variation among them as to how far they wished to go, but the underground classes were developed in East Anglia and at the same time a detailed survey of the state of the Church was made in various counties. The evidence thus obtained, not only of incompetence but of simony and greed, was made the basis of petitions and Bills presented to the Parliaments of 1584–5 and 1587, a few of the more extreme desiring a completely new start on the Geneva model. In each case firm action by the Queen defeated them

[22] Cf. Dawley, op. cit., p. 170 and pp. 161–94 for a detailed account of these critical years; cf. also Knappen, op. cit., pp. 280 et seq., and R. G. Usher, *The Rise and Fall of the High Commission* (Oxford, 1913), pp. 91–120 (its jurisdiction and procedure), and pp. 121–48 (growth of opposition before 1611).

as it had done before.[23] Her implacable opposition to anything that smacked of insubordination placed her firmly behind her Archbishop, and after 1587 the tide turned in his favour.

The death of Walsingham and Leicester within the next few years changed the balance of power at court, and in the country the Puritans had already been weakened by the first signs of a cleavage in their own ranks which had been slowly becoming manifest since a certain Robert Browne had openly advocated the complete severance of Church and State. For some years Browne's stormy figure had crossed and recrossed the scene. For a time a schoolmaster at Norwich, continually in and out of prison, for a while in Holland, he would have fared worse if he had not been a kinsman of Burghley. Eventually he became an ordained minister of the Church, though never a compliant one. By then he had played his part by his clear proclamation of the revolutionary belief that the Church was not the whole community organized for worship, but a company of "proved Christians", "gathered congregations", taking counsel maybe with neighbouring Churches but independent in their organization and religious life.

Such a theory of the Church was as contrary to the rigid Presbyterian discipline as to the wider view of a fellowship of all believers, and moderate Puritans distrusted it as much as the Anglicans did, not only on theological grounds but as a threat to the whole idea of an ordered society. After Browne's defection a few scattered groups of Brownists continued in being up and down the country and as the more radical of the malcontents began to join them, the more sober of the Puritan clergy, meeting in their unofficial classes in London and East Anglia, waited in vain for a sure sign of God's will as to how to act in the immediate future. As the successful war with Spain swept England into greatness and Puritanism ceased to be fashionable at court, Whitgift found himself no longer alone

[23] J. E. Neale, *Elizabeth I and her Parliaments, 1584–1601* (1957), pp. 20–3, 60–83, 145–65.

either in the Privy Council or in the counsels of the Church. On the High Commission he had now an efficient colleague in Richard Bancroft, a canon of Westminster, a Lancashire man of abrupt speech and tireless energy. At this juncture Bancroft had a chance to show his mettle, for a group of Puritan fanatics, out of patience with the negative result of more conventional methods, embarked upon a campaign of virulent propaganda. By means of a secret and peripatetic press, a series of tracts appeared over the pseudonym of Martin Marprelate. They anathematized the bishops and described Whitgift as the Beelzebub of Lambeth; and although, when a dignified reply had cut no ice, the authorities descended to calumny themselves, they could not match such phrases as Martin's reference to "proud, popish, presumptuous, profane, paltry, pestilent, pernicious prelates, and usurpers".

Under such circumstances, it was not surprising that when Bancroft ran the press to ground in Manchester, those suspected of complicity were treated with scant mercy. Unfortunately the suspect who was first accused was John Udall, a Hebrew scholar of good reputation, who had been concerned with the inception of the tracts but had not been involved in the later compositions. He was, however, tried and condemned to death for sedition on the strength of another publication which he could not deny. Under considerable pressure Whitgift relented and a pardon was issued, but Udall died in prison before he could be released. A year or so later the probable author of the tracts, John Penry, a Welshman of Celtic temperament and fanatic opinion, unwisely returned to London from Scotland, where he had taken refuge. He was arrested with John Greenwood at a conventicle in Islington and was condemned and executed on a flimsy charge of treason. Greenwood, who had been in and out of prison for many years, had during one brief period of freedom helped to found an independent congregation with Francis Johnson as pastor. They had soon been arrested at a haberdasher's house in Ludgate Hill and the little company dispersed, but Johnson,

after four years, was released and joined his friends in Holland where they continued as a Church in Amsterdam. Johnson had been an orthodox Puritan but had been converted to a measure of Independency by one of the writings of Barrow and Greenwood, which he had been instructed by the authorities to burn but which he had first read. Henry Barrow, the most outstanding man in the group, had also been converted in an unexpected way: as a gay young lawyer walking down a London street, he had heard someone preaching and slipped in to listen on a moment's impulse. He had been arrested quite illegally, without warrant, when he was visiting Greenwood in the Clink, and refusing to answer the questions of the Commission had spent the years of captivity in writing tracts against the Establishment, which were smuggled out of gaol by his friends and printed at Dort in Holland. In the spring of 1593 he and Greenwood were condemned for these seditious writings, a crime punishable by death if done "by malicious intent". They were taken once to Tyburn and reprieved upon the scaffold in the hope that the shock would make them conform, but it needed more than the shadow of death to weaken them. A few days later they were again brought to the gallows and hanged. It was more than enough—the sorry end of a deplorable chapter—and an uneasy calm descended upon the religious front.

This was the story that lay behind the *Ecclesiastical Polity*. A copy of the book, either in proof or on publication, appeared on Lord Burghley's desk a month before the Tyburn executions. Written, with Whitgift's encouragement, to provide a reasoned exposition of the official platform, it proved a more magnificent text-book than the Archbishop could ever have conceived, for in the process of dealing with the points at issue—the whole question of authority, the validity of the Scriptures, the present shortcomings and abuses—Hooker gave to the Anglican Church a new sense of direction and a spiritual vitality it had hitherto signally lacked.

Richard Hooker was born in Exeter, like many of his great contemporaries a man of humble parentage, the only son of a widowed mother and something of a child prodigy in her eyes and those of a rich uncle. The latter brought him to the notice of Bishop Jewel, also a Devonshire man, and at the age of thirteen he went up to Oxford as the Bishop's protégé. There he spent sixteen years as scholar and fellow of Corpus Christi College, grounding himself in classical and Hebraic learning and acquiring that tenacious desire for truth, the standards of scholarship, and the sense of proportion which were among the University's best gifts to her children and through them to the Anglican Church.

After Jewel's death Sandys, the Archbishop of York, befriended Hooker and enabled him to stay at the University by sending him as pupils his son, Edwin, and George Cranmer, a kinsman of the Cranmer of the Reformation. These young men became devoted to their tutor, and it was from a member of the Cranmer family that Izaak Walton heard the account of the "judicious" and lovable don which he enshrined for posterity in one of his inimitable *Lives*. Unfortunately the facts, as he heard them, were prejudiced and often inaccurate. In 1581, when he was about 27 years old, Hooker, already ordained, went up to London to preach at Paul's Cross. He stayed with a certain John Churchman in Watling Street and, according to the story Walton heard, he caught a bad chill, was nursed by Joan Churchman, his host's daughter, and precipitately married her. His pupils never quite forgave him and in their eyes Mrs Hooker remained for all time the predatory female. Later research, however, has rehabilitated Joan and her husband's good sense in marrying her.[24] Her father, so far from being a penurious woollen-draper, taking in lodgers to eke out a living, is shown to have been a Merchant Tailor of standing, Master of his Company in the year that his son-in-law published his great book. The marriage, so far from taking place precipitately, did not occur till 1588 when Hooker was

[24] C. J. Sisson, *The Judicious Marriage of Mr Hooker* (1940), pp. 1–44.

living in London as Master of the Temple, and one must jettison rather regretfully his pupils' account of the first country living where Mrs Hooker sent her husband out to mind the sheep and called him from his studies to rock the baby's cradle. In any case Hooker has the last word in the argument, for, as he wrote in the fifth Book of the *Polity*, "that kind of love which is the perfectest ground of wedlock is seldom able to yield any reason of itself".

Whitgift appointed Hooker to be Master of the Temple to offset the influence of Burghley's former chaplain and nominee as Reader, the distinguished Puritan Walter Travers. The two clergymen respected and admired each other's abilities but they differed widely in their views and attacked each other with vigour in their sermons, the points at issue varying from such fundamentals as the nature of the Church to whether one should pray before or after the sermon. It was an impossible situation for they preached alternately to a bewildered congregation. "The Forenoon Sermon spake Canterbury, and the Afternoon, Geneva".[25] The Archbishop broke the deadlock by getting rid of Travers, but Hooker was released soon afterwards to put his arguments into book form. He was given the country living of Boscombe, near Salisbury, which he probably held *in absentia* while he wrote his first four volumes. As soon as they were in the press he and his wife went down to the little village of Bishopsbourne in Kent, the living which he held till his premature death seven years later. He gave to his ministry in Kent the same diligence and devotion that he had given to his studies, and Izaak Walton listened to the reminiscences of an old verger who had loved his rector and drew, in his story of the Bishopsbourne days, one of those portraits of a country priest which adorn like gems the chequered history of the English Church.

In spite of Whitgift's backing, no arrangement seems to have been made for the publication of Hooker's masterpiece

[25] Thomas Fuller, *The Church History of Britain*, ed. J. S. Brewer (1854), V. 183–9. Walton's *Lives*, ed. S. B. Carter (1951), p. 162.

and it all but failed to appear. The first volumes were finished in 1592 and that winter he sent them to William Norton, London's leading publisher, who returned the manuscript with an expression of regret. There was a market for religious writing of a certain sort, witness the Marprelate Tracts, but people were weary of ecclesiastical controversy and neither Norton nor his fellow publishers were prepared to risk their money on a ponderous and judicious examination of contemporary religious problems. Hooker was left with his rejected manuscript and four wasted years.

That at least was the story as Edwin Sandys related it. It was he, always enthusiastic and ready to act, who saved the situation by appealing to David Windet, a kinsman of Hooker and a fellow Devonian, who undertook to print the book at Sandys' expense. For both of them it was a labour of love and Windet turned out a beautiful piece of craftsmanship in a volume worthy of its remarkable contents.[26]

Hooker began his inquiry by a masterly analysis of the whole meaning of law, human and divine. This was no academic digression but an argument strictly germane to contemporary disputes, which all turned upon the question of lawful authority. Whereas in matters of religion the Puritans relied on scriptural revelation alone, Hooker regarded law as being intrinsic to the nature of God, binding upon men not only through the Scriptures, the main source of revelation in matters of faith, but also through the right use of reason and the considered pronouncements of the Church.[27] In his second volume he examined in detail the Puritan claim that the Bible contained explicit directions upon every minor point of worship and rule. Such an argument, he declared, could only bring "the simple a thousand times to their wits' end".

[26] Sisson, op. cit., pp. 49–60.

[27] *The Works of Richard Hooker* (arranged by John Keble; 7th edn revised by R. W. Church and F. Paget, 1888), II.34. For an examination of Hooker's attitude to law and authority see F. J. Shirley, *Richard Hooker and Contemporary Political Ideas* (1949), pp. 71–92.

Hooker, who had a don's tetchiness regarding the foibles of less intelligent people, complained that the Puritan teaching had "already made thousands so headstrong . . . that a man whose capacity will scarce serve him to utter five words in sensible manner blusheth not, in any doubt concerning matter of scripture, to think his own bare yea as good as the nay of all the wise, grave and learned judgements that are in the whole world." He had no illusions about his contemporaries, whom he described as "full of tongue and weak of brain", and he did not scruple to affirm, in the decade in which Shakespeare wrote, that the age "did neither know nor greatly regard true art and learning". There was all the more reason for them to be subject to the authority of the Church, although this did not absolve them from moral responsibility. For the right use of reason, as Hooker conceived it, was a matter of the will as well as the intellect. The distinction between right and wrong was sometimes "more easy for common sense to discern than for any man by skill and learning to determine", and he ended with the solemn reminder of the words: "Behold I have set before you this day good and evil, life and death. Choose life."

In his inquiry into the nature of the visible Church of Christ, Hooker was on more debatable ground. Even Calvin admitted that the Visible Church on earth would include many not of the elect, if only because discipline was not always maintained with sufficient vigour. But there were signs whereby a true Church could be recognized: the Word of God would be purely preached and the sacraments rightly administered.[28] For Hooker, on the other hand, the crucial word was baptism, and the Visible Church was the whole company of baptized Christians, the Body of Christ, "one and indivisible though in this fallen world seldom incorrupt". Even excommunication, the dread punishment for evil-doing, only excluded the sinner from the fellowship of the congregation and "the performance of holy duties", not from membership of

[28] John Calvin, *Institutes of th Christian Religion* (edn of 1935), II.131.

the Church itself. Therefore, despite what he adjudged to be "gross and grievous abominations", Hooker would not deny the Romanists "to be of the family of Jesus Christ" nor allow that Luther or Henry VIII had brought a new Church into being.[29] Thus he stressed the conception of Anglicanism as in no way schismatic, but as the representative in its age and nation of the Church Universal, Catholic and Reformed.

This theory of the Church, which contradicted both that of the gathered congregation and the monopoly of the elect, presupposed the idea of State and Church as one, a community organized with the Crown as the natural Head in an ordered hierarchy both clerical and secular. It was a conception that remained viable only so long as there was one comprehensive and uniform Church acceptable to the community. The existence of dissent, whether within or without its bounds, spelt disorder and disharmony in the national life. This was the sole justification of Whitgift's severity, and this the tragedy of the coming years.

It was the manner of Hooker's writing as much as the matter which made the *Ecclesiastical Polity* a masterpiece, the well-reasoned arguments, moderate yet positive in their conclusions, the juxtaposition of homely phrases and detailed criticism with great sweeps of philosophy expressed in majestic sentences. There was, in addition, his common sense and, less obvious but of the essence of the matter, the true spirituality which underlay it all. "A poor obscure parish priest", so it was reported to the Pope in amazement, had written this remarkable treatise; and though the implication was untrue, for his Oxford career had been distinguished, it should never be forgotten that Hooker was also a parish priest.

Three years before his death in the peace of Bishopsbourne he published the fifth book of the *Polity* and it was the pastor, not the controversialist, who predominated as he wrote of worship and the sacraments and the meaning of the Liturgy.

[29] Hooker, *Works*, I.338–350.

The value of a set place of worship, hallowed by prayer, "where angels mingle as our associates" would, he claimed, if people understood it, draw them eagerly to their parish church without any need of penal statutes to compel. The use of the sign of the Cross in baptism, the cause of so much wrangling, he regarded as an admonition to "glory in the service of Jesus Christ and not to hang down our heads as men ashamed thereof". Of the Holy Communion he was content to wish "that men would more give themselves to meditate with silence what we have by the sacrament and less to dispute of the manner how". And of intercession he wrote: "If we give counsel, they are the simpler only that need it; if alms, the poorer only are relieved; but by prayer we do good to all . . . for this all times are convenient: when we are not able to do any other thing for men's behoof . . . prayer is that which we always have in our power to bestow and they never in theirs to refuse."[30]

Hooker's death in 1600 at the early age of 45 removed one who might have brought to the new century an eirenical spirit of which it would stand much in need. Yet his own views may have hardened in his last years to match a change in the ecclesiastical atmosphere. The three final volumes of his great work were unpublished and probably incomplete when he died. Soon afterwards an open quarrel broke out between his widow, who remarried a man of Puritan affiliations, and Edwin Sandys, and this ended in a chancery suit. In the course of the trial one witness declared that Joan had destroyed the surviving manuscripts. Although no grounds were forthcoming for this accusation, the story of the posthumous books still remains something of a mystery. Two volumes were published in 1648, but not till after the Restoration did Bishop Gauden issue the seventh book which dealt with episcopacy. Its tone approximated more nearly to Laudian views than to those which Hooker once had held, so much so that it is easy to believe that it was Gauden not Joan who tampered with the

[30] Ibid., II.116.

manuscript.[31] On the other hand, in the last years of Queen Elizabeth's reign, an enhanced idea was abroad of the royal prerogative and of the divine origin of bishops which may have affected even the judicious Hooker, at work on his final chapters.

This new stress on the nature of sovereignty was occasioned in part by the great outburst of national feeling which marked the end of the century. Nurtured on the exploits of Drake and Raleigh, given voice by Shakespeare and personified by Essex in the minds of the populace, it gained something of a religious flavour from a group of able churchmen who were coming to the fore under Whitgift's leadership. The whole question of authority, the relation of the prerogative and common law and the divine right of kings and bishops, increasingly exercised their minds—Bancroft's from the practical point of view of his daily work in the Commission and Bilson's (the Bishop of Winchester) from the academic standpoint that came naturally to a prelate of Teutonic stock and monumental learning.

When Whitgift had answered the Puritan's *Admonition* he had regarded episcopacy as the best type of church government but not as sacrosanct. But in February 1589, at the height of the Marprelate troubles, Bancroft preached a sermon at Paul's Cross in which he claimed divine sanction for the bishops in such forthright terms that Lord Knollys, the Queen's Treasurer, a Puritan and an old campaigner, suggested that a charge of treason could lie against him for ascribing such exalted powers to any subject. Elizabeth saw to it that the matter was dropped, but the seeds had been sown and Bancroft's exegesis was contradicted neither by Whitgift nor his successors. Soon afterwards there was a similar foreshadowing of things to come in one of Lancelot Andrewes' sermons. While Hooker had been at Oxford, Andrewes for a similar length of time had been studying languages and

[31] For the posthumous books, VI (Penance), VII (Episcopacy), VIII (The Royal Supremacy), see Keble's introduction to the collected *Works* and Sisson, *The Judicious Marriage of Mr Hooker*, pp. 79–111.

patristic lore at Cambridge. The son of a merchant seaman and a Londoner born and bred, with his full share of the cockney's gift of pithy speech, Andrewes had now emerged from academic calm and as royal chaplain and vicar of St Giles', Cripplegate, was voicing from the pulpit the same ideas of historical continuity and ordered rule that Hooker was enshrining in his balanced prose. The two men were exact contemporaries; but whereas Hooker died in 1600 while still in his forties, Andrewes lived on into the reign of Charles I, bridging the gap between the great Elizabethans and the Laudian régime but still remaining, in his respect for the Crown and his love of decency and order, very much of a Tudor at heart.

It was Sir John Harington, Elizabeth's godson, who noted that Andrewes, quite early in his career as a royal chaplain, preached a sermon which even in those days of intense patriotic feeling left a certain sting behind it. The preacher spoke of authority and described in no uncertain terms the sorry state of the people if they were not adequately led but were left to their own devices. The safety of the community depended upon the King's wise exercise of power in the government of Church and State and upon "a joint reverence for God and the prince" on the part of the people. But Andrewes also stressed the need for self-dedication on the ruler's side, and it is interesting to compare the words he used with those of Shakespeare's Henry V:

> .... What infinite heartsease
> Must kings neglect that private men enjoy!

So Henry meditated as he kept watch before Agincourt and thought of the peasant peacefully asleep. "It is surely supernatural", said Andrewes, "to endure that cark and care which the governors continually do, a matter that we inferiors can little skill of, but to read 'Such a night, the King could not sleep' and again 'Such a night no meat would down with the King and he listed not to hear any music'. To endure this I

say is supernature and it is God which above all nature by his mighty spirit worketh it in them."[32]

Andrewes' sovereign was thus to wear divine right with a difference, just as Hooker's national Church was to include every baptized Englishman. Each for a moment, it would seem, had stepped beyond the bounds of academic certitude into the realms of faith, "the substance of things hoped for, the evidence of things not seen". For there could be no assurance that kings would be always worthy or that the right use of reason would lead men back to unity of faith and worship. As the seventeenth century dawned and the Stuart dynasty came to rule in England these were the unknown factors upon which the future depended. Would James and his successors prove themselves righteous kings to whom in Church and State obedience was justly due, and to what extent could the bishops, as shepherds of their people, lead them to salvation as one undivided flock?

[32] Lancelot Andrewes, *Works*, II.20 f.

# 2

# THE JACOBEAN SCENE

THE Church was established, its personnel had improved, few empty cures were left, and the bishops who worked under Whitgift's direction were a distinguished and devoted group. A generation had grown to man's estate to whom the Liturgy had been known and loved since childhood. The question which faced the Anglican Church was not whether it would or would not survive, but how far it might lose, in the process, the character of a *via media*. It would lose that character if it yielded too much to the demands of extremists on either wing, yet paradoxically it had only been able to maintain control by enforcing uniformity in a manner that belied the very moderation which its nature as a compromise required.

In some ways the new reign exacerbated a cleavage which had been apparent from the moment when the Queen and the Protestant exiles began to reorder the Church from divergent points of view. On the other hand the course of events and the period of comparative calm which succeeded the opening years of the century gave the Church the breathing-space it needed to develop within its own bounds the differing tendencies and emphases in theology and worship implicit in the phrase Catholic and Reformed.

The Queen died at Richmond in the spring of 1603, exchanging in Fuller's grandiloquent phrase "her earthly for a heavenly crown".[1] It had been no easy exchange. For six days and nights Elizabeth's strong will fought a losing battle with her dying body. In the city of London rumours sprang up and

[1] T. Fuller, *The Church History of Britain*, ed. J. S. Brewer (1845), V.258.

multiplied: of men taking up arms for fear of the Catholics, of citizens locking up their jewels, and "every house and everybody . . . in movement and alarm".[2] At the court, in anxious expectation of the end, the Lords of the Council waited. They were not the men of Elizabeth's own age, her councillors and friends of the earlier years, for that generation had gone: these men, in the impatience of their prime, were thinking more of a peaceful entrance for the new dynasty than of a quiet exit for the Queen. At the end she had a few hours' sleep and, wakening with a clear mind, she named as her successor her cousin's son, James VI of Scotland. Then she prepared herself for death, finding comfort in the presence of Whitgift, whom she had come to call her "little black husband" and who now, old and infirm himself, knelt beside her in prayer. In the small hours of 24 March, she died, and her kinsman Robert Carey, already booted and spurred, posted north to Edinburgh to bring the news to James.

Those in authority in the Church took action almost as quickly as Carey and dispatched Dr Nevill, the Dean of Canterbury, to tender to King James the bounden duty of the bishops and clergy in his southern realm. He was also instructed to inquire his Majesty's pleasure "for the ordering and guiding of ecclesiastical causes"; and the dean returned to England with the welcome reply that King James purposed "to uphold and maintain the government of the late Queen, as she left it settled". In this James was moved by conviction as well as policy. He was far better informed than most of his English subjects on the principles underlying the *via media*; it was said that as soon as he reached England he asked to meet Richard Hooker, whose book he had read but of whose death he had not heard. He admired the whole set-up of Anglicanism; his pedagogic mind was attracted by its stress on the historical background and the use of reason and he agreed wholeheartedly with its assumption that Church and State were one, with the King as supreme governor, "the nursing-father

[2] *Cal. S.P. Venetian, 1592–1603*, p. 562 (3 April 1603).

of his people". But he did not like excess and was suspicious of some of the bishops' recent claims. As he rode south through the quiet beauty of an English spring he was convinced that at long last he was to find the law and order and the affection he had missed so sorely in his life as King of Scotland, and he hoped not only to maintain the religious settlement of his predecessor but to achieve what Elizabeth had envisaged in 1559, a national Church to which all but a few extremists would conform.

If the King was optimistic, so were the leaders of the dissidents in England. The Roman Catholics reminded themselves that Mary of Scotland had been King James's mother and reported with satisfaction that his thoughts were returning constantly to her execution. Scarcely a day passed, they said, that he did not refer to the "villainous deed"; various members of the Howard family and others who had befriended her were advanced in office, and the Venetian resident reported that "as long as the Catholics remain quiet and decently hidden" they would neither be "hunted nor persecuted".[3] The Puritans on the other hand remembered that James came from John Knox's country and had been reared a Presbyterian, and they were further encouraged by his response to a petition they presented to him and his promise to hold a conference to settle various outstanding points. Scaramelli, the Venetian, said that the King had ordered it to be proclaimed from every pulpit that he would not alter the state of religion from its "evangelical purity and Christian liberty, phrases most dear to the ears of this people".[4] Thus in affable mood and accepted by all parties James entered his southern capital in June, though the rejoicings and ceremonial were curtailed on account of a virulent outbreak of the plague—a catastrophe that might well be taken as an omen of the ill chances that were to mar the fair intentions of the King.

From the very beginning luck was against him. There were

[3] *Cal. S.P. Venetian, 1603–7*, pp. 21 ff (8 May 1603).
[4] Ibid., p. 33 (22 May 1603).

rumours of rebellion, a "bye-plot" which Fuller dismisses in a few words as the "silly treason" of Watson, a recusant priest, but also a "main plot" engineered by George Brooke and involving, it appeared, Brooke's elder brother, Lord Cobham, and Cobham's brilliant and disgruntled friend, Sir Walter Raleigh. There was no serious threat to James's peaceful succession, but this revelation of treason, real or suspected, came as a sad blow to the King's hope of tranquillity in his southern realm, a shock to which his cruel treatment of Raleigh bore witness. For although James's love of peace was based on logical and moral convictions, it was also a burning emotional need, bred of unhappy and frightening experiences as a youth reared amid scenes of violence and disorder. It was his tragedy that such was his utter lack of charm, his irritability, and the occasional cruelties into which his fear impelled him that he drove away with every word the harmony for which he craved.

At first, however, James was convinced that he would be listened to and obeyed. He set high hopes on the conference requested by the Puritans, and after a postponement due to the plague it was summoned to meet at Hampton Court in January 1604. In the months that intervened his temper was tried by a growth of mushroom petitions from every sort of dissident, including one obscure antinomian sect that called itself the "Family of Love". He was equally annoyed by another group who had the hardihood to thrust their petition upon him when he was out hunting, the greatest pleasure of his life. As for the Puritans proper, who had seemed amenable at first in stressing only minor points of ceremonial, now as they circulated their original petition for further signatures (to justify their use of "millenary" to describe it) they stated that they meant to ask for further changes "agreeable to the example of other reformed churches". Even in regard to non-controversial points it was not easy to initiate reform. The King was genuinely anxious to redress the injury done to the Church at the time of the Reformation through the confiscation

of ecclesiastical endowments, which was the chief cause of the poverty of the clergy. During the Middle Ages many parochial cures had been appropriated by the monasteries and at their dissolution these rectories had passed into the hands of the Universities and the Crown, or been granted by the latter to laymen as part of the monastic property. The lay rector received the revenues of the cure and the right to present to the living, sometimes allowing his vicar the small tithe of mixed products, difficult to collect for anyone not on the spot, or paying him a fixed stipend, usually quite inadequate. In the seventy years since the Reformation prices had trebled: £10 a year was considered an adequate salary for a learned minister in 1535, whereas Whitgift estimated £30 a year as the right amount.[5] Most cures were about half that value and vicars and curates, dependent on stipends, or rectors whose tithes had been commuted for money-payments became increasingly impoverished as prices rose. The value of land had also risen, and those more fortunate incumbents whose tithes had not been expropriated—like the lay rectors—benefited accordingly.

The King, as a first step towards reform, offered to surrender the endowments held by the Crown and suggested that the Universities should do likewise. But nothing came of it. Oxford replied that any such action would impoverish them so much that they would be seriously impeded in their prime task of producing a learned ministry. Even this stress on learning had unfortunate repercussions in that men of academic ability were loath to accept the poorer cures and the rift continued to grow between the well-served parishes and those left destitute of adequate pastoral care. A difference in emphasis had also become more marked during the ten years of comparative quiet after 1593. To the Puritan the need remained paramount to interpret the Scriptures and to stir up the hearts of the people by exhortation and exposition of the Word. The

[5] D. M. Barratt, "The Condition of the Parish Clergy between the Reformation and 1660", thesis in the Bodleian Library, pp. 190–5.

second generation of Anglicans, nurtured on the Book of Common Prayer, which was no longer just a service book imposed by Act of Parliament but the spiritual food upon which they and their children depended, felt the need for more worship and less speech. When at Hampton Court the Puritans demanded a preaching ministry, Bancroft interjected "and a praying ministry, too".

The conference met on Saturday, 14 January 1604. Bancroft's hasty temper and abrupt Lancashire manners did not fit him for the conference table, and the King rebuked him more than once for his interruptions. Whitgift was too ill to make more than a token appearance. At a preliminary meeting on the Saturday, he pleaded with the King to allow no alteration in the Liturgy. The Puritan delegation was called in on the Monday, Bancroft and Bilson being the only bishops present with a selection of deans and members of the Privy Council, and with James himself, half chairman, half schoolmaster, very much the dominant figure.[6] The Puritan representatives were by no means extremists. Their leader, Dr Rainolds of Corpus Christi, Oxford, was a distinguished Greek scholar of an eirenical spirit. Laurence Chaderton, Master of Emmanuel, though convinced in his opinions, was exceptionally gentle in temper; Thomas Sparke kept silence; only Ralph Knewstubs, a man of sixty and one of the Cartwright school, had more than his share of impetuous and fiery speech.

The meeting reached its first and greatest decision early in the session, when a suggestion of Rainolds was accepted that

[6] See Mark H. Curtis, "Hampton Court Conference and its Aftermath", in *History*, Vol. XLVI, No. 156 (Feb. 1961), pp. 1–16. This revision of the standard view of the conference is largely based on the "Anonymous Account" printed by R. G. Usher in *The Reconstruction of the English Church* (1910), II.341–54. Professor Curtis considers that the conference saw a larger measure of agreement between James and the Puritans than is usually supposed and that a genuine chance of a workable compromise was lost through the bishops' lack of co-operation. For the contemporary official account, see "The Summe and Substance of the Conference", printed in E. Cardwell's *A History of Conferences* (3rd edn, 1849), p. 169, and cf. Fuller, *Church History*, V.266–303.

there should be a new translation of the Scriptures. There were two versions in general use: the Bishops' Bible, a rather unsystematic revision of the Great Bible of 1539, and the Geneva Bible made by the scholars in exile—very popular for family worship, vigorous in style, and with copious notes of a strictly Protestant nature. During the forty years since these had been published there had been marked advances in the study of Greek and Hebrew, and James approved the idea of a new translation, free from glosses upon the text and enriched by the best scholarship his new country could produce. There was general assent, although Bancroft was not enthusiastic. If every man's humour were followed, he said, there would be no end of translating.

Their next concern was Prayer Book revision, and here again something of value was achieved, for a further suggestion of Rainolds was adopted that a section dealing with the sacraments should be added to the catechism and Overall, the Dean of St Paul's, a fine scholar of true spiritual perception, undertook the task to the enrichment of the Anglican heritage. It was however over Prayer Book revision that the rift first appeared. Knewstubs threw the measured exchanges out of gear by an incoherent attack on the use of the sign of the Cross in baptism, and James's store of good humour showed signs of running out. It was an apparently innocuous remark of Rainolds that opened the floodgates of the King's displeasure, a reference to the benefits derived from periodic meetings of the clergy. "If you aim at a Scottish presbytery," James interrupted, "it agreeth as well with monarchy as God and the devil", and he launched upon a tirade against the treatment he had received from the ministers in his youth, more in the temper of a neurotic than of the shrewd, well-meaning king he thought himself to be.

Yet in spite of the outburst James was consistent in his attitude. He was ready to be conciliatory up to a point, but there could be no compromise on the matter of sovereignty. Criticisms of Church rule, he saw more clearly than many, impinged

upon the whole question of authority, and No Bishops might well lead to No King. Similarly, in regard to ritual, he believed that he could only interfere justifiably with the accredited Liturgy of the Church if the critics could prove it to be contrary to the Scriptures.[7] At the final meeting on the Wednesday he announced certain changes and promised certain reforms in the ecclesiastical courts and in the matter of non-residence: beyond these limits he would not go and within them he expected his bishops to exercise charity and the Puritans to obey with humility, "the marks of honest and good men".

On this note the conference ended, though Chaderton broke his usual silence to put in a plea for some "godly ministers" in Lancashire, especially the vicar of Rochdale whose zeal he commended. The King had received complaints of the vicar's "irreverent usage of the Eucharist, dealing the bread out of the basket, every man putting in his hand and taking out a piece". However, he gave Chaderton a gracious answer, though he was naturally irritated when Knewstubs at once put in a further plea for some honest ministers in Suffolk. The conference then dispersed, and it is possible that it would not have been regarded as a failure if the various commissions appointed to implement its conclusions had done so in a wholehearted way. But either by lack of interest or design the work was only half done. Some of the agreed changes were not included in the revised Liturgy, the procedure of the church courts went on unchanged, and it was clear that Bancroft, in control after Whitgift's death in February, envisaged his task in terms of discipline rather than conciliation.

During the spring Convocation met and drew up a set of Canons, incorporating the medieval law of the Church and the advertisements and injunctions issued since 1559. Of the 141 Canons, some regulated worship and the administration of the sacraments, others dealt with the procedure of ecclesiastical courts or anathematized dissent of various kinds, while

[7] Curtis, loc. cit., p. 10.

others laid down the rules for appointing schoolmasters or electing parish officials. As many as 46 Canons dealt with the ministry. While they included much that was non-controversial and of spiritual worth, on the matters under dispute there was no compromise. The clergy were to subscribe without qualification to the royal supremacy, the Thirty-nine Articles, and the Book of Common Prayer. Although Parliament refused its assent to the Canons, thus making it doubtful whether they were binding on the laity, the King approved them and they have remained for three and a half centuries the law of the Anglican Church. Bancroft became Archbishop in December and did what he could by way of admonition and persuasion to obtain from the majority of the clergy the subscription required of them. He was now a more mature and charitable person than the young ecclesiastic who had scotched the Marprelate Tracts, and there were many stories of personal kindnesses to his credit, but he could not and did not wish to alter the essential part of the royal edict that those who continued to refuse subscription must be ejected from their cures. It is uncertain how many left their pulpits. The Puritans' estimate of three or four hundred was wide of the mark. Heylyn, after studying the returns at Lambeth, placed the number at 49 and Bancroft certainly gave what latitude he could to those who were hesitant. More significant than the minority who went was the fact that of those who remained many were ill at ease in a Church that became steadily more authoritarian in tone. The minority's views were strongly expressed in an *Abridgement* of their apology published next year by some clergy from Lincolnshire, who affirmed that the Prayer Book as revised contained among other blemishes (which included nineteen "popish errors") "three points that are doubtful, seven that are untrue, seven that are disorderly, five that are ridiculous, besides many evident contradictions". It could not be right, Bancroft argued, for such men to continue to hold livings in a Church of which that Prayer Book was the accredited Liturgy. The answer of the ejected was

that no Church had a right to impose liturgies and modes of worship not specifically ordained in the Bible. It was thus once again a question of authority and an early sign of the conflict that was to become an overriding issue in the troubles of the mid-century—between the liberty of the individual conscience and the duty of rulers to enforce the truth as they saw it.[8]

The King had at least made a genuine attempt to understand the Puritan position. A similar desire to reconcile his Roman Catholic subjects was complicated by fear and marred by a complete lack of consistency. The recusancy fines were waived or imposed with varying severity according to James's own mood or the progress of the negotiations for peace with Spain. An iniquitous system had grown up of farming out the recusancy fines to individuals, whose interest it thus was to spur on the magistrates to prosecute families who might otherwise have been left in peace. In addition to greed, suspicion was a constant incentive to harshness. The great influx of priests in the easier circumstances of the first year of the reign led to so many conversions that in February 1604 they were again ordered to quit the kingdom. So long as the stringent recusancy laws remained on the statute book there could be no easing of the tension; the slightest rumour of plot or change of atmosphere at Whitehall might lead to arrests; and once in prison, whether in the insalubrious Southwark gaols or the comparative comfort of Wisbech, exile or even execution might follow at any moment if fear or policy demanded the rigours of the law.

Any hope of a modification of the statutes vanished with the discovery of the Gunpowder conspiracy. The crazed zeal and twisted courage of Robert Catesby and his friends came perilously near to success. There was the simple logic of madness in their plan to destroy at one stroke the King and his Council

[8] Cf. W. H. Frere, *The English Church in the Reigns of Elizabeth and James I* (1904), pp. 322 f: "... the puritan was contending for the exclusive authority of the Bible against the Churchman's contention for the co-ordinate authority of the Body of Christ, the Church".

by blowing up the House of Lords when James attended to open the new session. The seizure of the Princess Elizabeth, the King's daughter, and the rising on the Welsh borders were planned in equal detail, if less certain in outcome. At Westminster, the cellar was hired, the tunnel made, the gunpowder collected, and a half-confession to Garbett, their spiritual director, salved the souls of the plotters while tormenting the conscience of the priest.

Then fate took a hand, in a repeated adjournment of the meeting of Parliament. The months of delay necessitated more money to meet expenses and to keep the forces in being in the west. Money could only be obtained by sharing the secret with other, less dedicated, persons. As the weeks slipped by, consciences began to stir and nerves to rebel. When the day was fixed at last, a warning letter was sent by a kinsman to Lord Monteagle, one of the Catholic peers. The letter was delivered to Cecil, who was inclined to regard it as a hoax, but the King's fearfulness on this occasion stood him in good stead and he detected the threat of gunpowder in the letter's veiled phrases. The cellars were searched in the small hours of 5 November 1605 and the soldier Johnson, who was known as Guy Fawkes, was found on guard over the hidden store. The others fled to make a last hopeless stand in a Worcestershire farmhouse, and the unfortunate ones, who were not killed, were brought back to share, with Fawkes, torture and execution.

Among those who were to have taken their places in the House of Lords on that tragic fifth of November was Lancelot Andrewes, advanced to the see of Chichester from the deanery of Westminster. In one of his later sermons he described how he had been awakened in the early morning by the sound of uproar without and had been told of the news that was now spreading like wildfire through the City. He never entirely recovered from the shock and horror of that moment, and the merciless words of damnation that he, the most charitable of men, used of the conspirators bear witness to the effect of the

plot upon the people of the time. In James himself it deepened the fear of assassination that had haunted him all his days, until it became an obsession destroying his mental and physical stability. In the country at large it left a neurotic hatred of Rome that undermined for centuries the hope of amity between the mass of Englishmen and the large recusant minority.

The King had thus failed in his hope of reconciliation on every front, yet the first years of his reign were not devoid of glory. The production of Shakespeare's greatest plays, Bacon's *Advancement of Learning*, the hazardous plantation of Virginia, and the Authorized Version of the Bible all combined to give a unique place in the story of England to this first decade of the Jacobean Age. It took seven years to complete the translation.[9] The work was slow in beginning and people grumbled. In November 1604 Andrewes excused himself from a meeting of the newly formed Society of Antiquaries because, he wrote, "this afternoon is our translation time . . . and most of our members are negligent".[10] Six committees had been set up with an average of eight members apiece, centred upon Oxford, Cambridge, and Westminster, and in Westminster in particular the claims of public life were apt to conflict with the work. At Cambridge there was a delay owing to the death of an eminent Hebrew scholar who was to have taken a leading part. At length, however, the project got under way. Each committee was given a section of the Bible to translate: Andrewes' group, for instance, dealt with the Old Testament up to the Second Book of Kings, and the rector of St Clement Danes was co-opted, as he happened to be "skilled in architecture" and "his judgement was much relied on for the fabric of the tabernacle and Temple". At Oxford, Rainolds

[9] An interesting supplement on *The Bible in English* was issued by *The Times*, 27 March 1961, on the publication of the *New English Bible* (*New Testament*).

[10] Lancelot Andrewes, letter to Mr Hartwell, "last of November" 1604, printed in *Two Answers to Cardinal Perron and other Miscellaneous Works* (1854), p. xlii.

did not live to see the completion of his great design but he was hard at work on the Prophets when he died in 1607. Another prominent Oxford scholar was Miles Smith, a Hereford man with Puritan leanings, who had an exceptional knowledge of the languages of the Middle East.

One of the happiest features of the work was the harmony with which churchmen of every shade of opinion worked together, devoting their learning and literary skill, their spiritual insight and their time and energy to the service of God, under the guidance of the Holy Spirit. Thus it was Smith, the Puritan, and Bilson, most rigid of Episcopalians, who were jointly responsible for seeing the book through the press. The deserts of controversy were left behind and the only acrimony engendered concerned the turn of a Greek phrase or the meaning of an Aramaic word. In his *Table Talk*, Selden gave a vivid glimpse of a committee at work. A first draft was made by a member specially qualified to deal with the passage under consideration, "and then they met together and one read the translation, the rest holding in their hands some bible either of the learned tongues or French, Spanish, Italian, etc. If they found any fault they spoke, if not he read on."[11] The agreed version was circulated to the other committees to be approved, and the whole finally edited by Bilson and Smith. The insistence on linguistic accuracy made it likely that some of the phrasing would not be that of common usage, and Selden criticized the translators for retaining too many Hebraisms to the detriment of the English idiom. On the other hand the euphuisms fashionable in contemporary literary circles were rigidly excluded. A large proportion of Tyndale's original wording was retained and wherever possible the English of ordinary speech was used, for, as Miles Smith put it in his Introductory Letter, the translators' aim was "to make God's holy truth . . . more and more known unto the people".

As Andrewes studied the books of the Old Testament,

[11] *Table Talk of John Selden*, ed. Sir F. Pollock (1927), pp. 10 f.

examining and weighing the meaning of every word, the divine sanction that had empowered Moses and Aaron in their dual roles of king and priest impressed itself yet more surely upon him as the proper basis of sovereignty. When he was called upon by James to engage in controversy with the eminent Cardinal Bellarmine upon the subject of the Royal Supremacy, he put forward with conviction his belief that the Kings of England had "the right and power of doing whatever the Kings of Israel did in matters of religion". The controversy arose over the new oath of allegiance, imposed after the Gunpowder conspiracy in an attempt to distinguish between law-abiding recusants and potential traitors. To the regret of many English Catholics the Pope forbade them to take the oath, whereupon James, who prided himself as an author, wrote an *Apology*, which Bellarmine answered using the pseudonym of Matthew Tortus. James found it necessary to call an expert to his aid, and throughout the cold winter of 1608 Andrewes stayed in London writing his *Tortura Torti* and earning the sympathy of his friends, who knew how much he detested argument.[12] Bellarmine replied, working in equal discomfort during a hot Italian summer, and Andrewes countered yet again with his *Responsio*, in this and later writings going beyond the original subject of debate to consider the basis of the whole Anglican compromise. Both Andrewes and Bellarmine indulged in a certain amount of vituperation in racy Latin, but with men of their calibre the exchanges could not be entirely barren. The distinction which Andrewes made between the royal power in ecclesiastical matters and the powers of the priesthood was one that needed to be stressed. Bellarmine taunted the Anglican Church with merely transferring authority from the descendants of St Peter to the descendants of Henry VIII, but Andrewes stated categorically that the King could not order new articles of faith or exercise

[12] John Chamberlain, *Letters*, ed. N. E. McClure, 2 vols. (1935), I.264: "... which task I doubt how he will undertake and perform, being so contrary to his disposition and course to meddle with controversies".

priestly functions. When Elizabeth suspended Grindal, or rebuked Whitgift for issuing a doctrinal statement from Lambeth without her sanction, the distinction had been blurred, and the restatement was timely, though it was not entirely palatable to James. He was more pleased with Andrewes' stress on the divine right of kings, which many of his subjects found less commendable. In the years immediately following the Armada it may have tuned in with the temper of the times, but it ran counter to the dominant forces abroad in the new century. The English people were increasingly familiar with the idea of contract as the basis of their trading ventures, and it already seemed to many a more realistic foundation than divine right for political jurisdiction. Thus Andrewes' political philosophy combined during these formative years with Bancroft's use of the prerogative courts to identify the Anglican Church all too often with the forces of reaction.

Bancroft died in 1610 after a brief but effective primacy, during which he had worked incessantly to better the Church's condition, but the tightening of control, made possible by the completion of the Canons, necessitated a widespread use of the consistory courts and the High Commission, and the quarrels that centred round their procedure placed an unhappy stress on the dictatorial aspect of ecclesiastical discipline. The critics objected at this stage, not to the exercise of spiritual discipline as such, but to the imposition of secular penalties by courts outside the framework of the common law. Thus a running battle developed between the ecclesiastical authorities and the lawyers, paralleled at Westminster, when Parliament was in session, by disputes over privilege and the use of the prerogative. The lawyers were the chief spokesmen in the debates at Wesminster and they allied with the dissidents in the Church in airing their discontents. The deep cleavage which in fact existed between the lawyers' Erastian approach and a Calvinist theocracy did not manifest itself for many years. Meanwhile the alliance, which began with the

refusal to ratify the Canons and did not end until the Civil War was won, strengthened the Puritans as much as their dependence on the prerogative hampered the High Churchmen on the opposing wing.

Notwithstanding this foretaste of future trouble, there was evidence of vitality in the Jacobean Church. In his later controversial writings Andrewes passed on to a new generation of parish priests his clear conception of the grounds on which the Church of England claimed to be, not a schismatic body, but an integral part of Catholic Christendom. The boundaries of the Anglican faith were to be found, he reiterated, as Parker and Jewel had done before him, in the Holy Scriptures and the historic creeds, underlined and clarified by the pronouncements of the Christian Fathers. Yet the Church that Bellarmine defended was very different from the decadent body of the late Middle Ages. Bellarmine spoke with the triumphant assurance of the Counter-Reformation, whose disciplined yet exuberant spirit manifested itself at this very time in the great baroque Churches of Austria and Italy. If Anglicanism, the *via media*, had something of value and particularly its own to merit its survival, it must show itself, not only in controversy but in prayer and worship and Christian living, to be a worthy member of the Holy Catholic Church.

The records of the time are not devoid of signs that some such growth in grace was taking place. Church buildings were looked after with greater care, their inventories were less barren, the number of clergy was increasing—all tangible signs of a real spiritual advance. The decorum and devotion, which is the phrase T. S. Eliot uses to describe the quality of Andrewes' life, became by degrees the pattern for some at least of the parishes; and it was to foster this growth that the last of the great Tudor divines preached and prayed during the years after Bancroft's death. Eschewing theological debate, Andrewes hammered out in his sermons at Christmas, Easter, Whitsuntide the essential truths of the Gospel. He had once said to his students at Pembroke: "What is necessary to be

known, God has made easy and what is not easy is not so necessary." At Whitehall, as at Cambridge, this continued to be his theme, and the courtiers came crowding to hear him, their quick minds delighted by his dissection of words in an age intensely interested in language, their hearts touched by the compassion of one who knew their need to be as great as that of humbler men. He was frequently at court and he admired and liked the King, the link of affection unbroken through the frustrating years ahead. His passionate belief in the Incarnation, which gave to well-doing in ordinary affairs a sacramental grace, impelled him to give meticulous attention to his duties as royal almoner and to the practical affairs of his diocese. Individuals who came to him for help could rely not only on his charity but on a careful and concerned inquiry as to their needs and deserts, and this same quality of intelligent compassion characterized the intercessions that formed so large a part of the private prayers in which much of his time was passed. The standards of beauty and seemliness which he inculcated in his practice of public worship made the chapel in Ely Place, his town house in Holborn, famous for the beauty of its ornaments and the dignity of its ceremonial. This insistence on order and decorum in every department of life was not only consonant with his law-abiding nature (he passed it on to Laud, a man of very different temperament); it stemmed from a belief that order was a thing "highly pleasing to God", the prime virtue without which no Church or State could survive. The ordered beauty of worship, the ordered efficiency of one's practical living, and, sustaining it all in the secular sphere, an ordered hierarchy of rule, in which all from king to commoner had rights and duties to perform—all these were reflections on earth of the ordered harmony of Heaven. Because it led to breach of order he disliked theological dispute; yet in this most important province of belief his gentle temper ensured another emphasis, and one of the most valuable of all his gifts to his Church was his refusal to accept, in matters of faith, the tenets of John Calvin,

ordered and disciplined though they were, as a necessary ingredient of Anglican orthodoxy.[13]

In all the disputes of the past sixty years matters of dogma had seldom been in the forefront, at first because there was not any consciousness of discrepancy among English Protestants and later because Elizabeth had set herself to avoid them. The Thirty-nine Articles duly embodied the central Protestant doctrine of Justification by Faith and bore various signs of the Calvinist beliefs which most of the first Reformers held. But in the latter years of the sixteenth century a reaction had set in both in England, among a group of Cambridge scholars, and at Leyden in Holland, where Arminius, the professor of divinity, waged war on the dogma of Predestination whereby some men were foreordained to absolute perdition. It was to settle a dispute at Cambridge and to establish uniform teaching that Whitgift, himself a moderate Calvinist, issued the Lambeth Articles, but in view of Elizabeth's disapproval they were never enforced in the University, and teachers such as Overall, Regius Professor until 1607, continued to put forward the Arminian belief in salvation freely offered to all men in prayer and sacrament.

James, being a Scot as well as a skilled theologian, was as eager to underline doctrinal issues as Queen Elizabeth had been to avoid them. As a result a divergence was revealed in the belief and attitude of leading English churchmen, which gradually acquired political overtones and made for lack of harmony and effectiveness in the direction of Church affairs. The first sign of this came in James's choice of an archbishop

[13] Andrewes' *Works* (edited by J. P. Wilson and J. Bliss) are published in eleven volumes in *The Library of Anglo-Catholic Theology* (1841–54); *Seventeen Sermons on the Nativity* are published in the *Ancient and Modern Library of Theological Literature* (1887); and of numerous editions of the *Preces Privatae* (first published in 1648) that of F. E. Brightman (1903) has a valuable introduction; see also *The Devotions of Bishop Andrewes*, trans. by Newman and Neale, introd. H. B. Swete (1920). For Andrewes' life see R. L. Ottley, *Lancelot Andrewes* (1894), and P. A. Welsby, *Lancelot Andrewes, 1555–1626* (1958); and cf. T. S. Eliot, *For Lancelot Andrewes: Essays on Style and Order* (1928).

after Bancroft's death. He named not Andrewes, as was generally expected, but George Abbot, a man still in his forties, who had been chaplain to the Earl of Dunbar, a friend of the King. James had promised Dunbar, shortly before his death, to advance his protégé, and Abbot had been made Bishop of London in 1609 and was now "blown over the river to Lambeth".

There were sound reasons for the choice. James had just appointed certain Scottish bishops in the hope of engrafting episcopacy upon his native Church. They would need to be consecrated in England, and Abbot was known to them and his Calvinism acceptable. The new Archbishop lacked both Andrewes' learning and his predecessor's administrative skill but he was honest and in a stubborn sort of way courageous, and his appointment left the door open for policies congenial to the Puritan element in the Church. Had he possessed personal sympathy and spiritual power to match his moderate views, he might have initiated a policy of conciliation and paved the way towards a comprehensive Anglicanism. But a certain worldly-mindedness corrupted his vision and he never made himself popular with the Puritan clergy, in part because he had not had experience as a parish priest and did not appreciate either their difficulties or their achievements as they laboured painstakingly up and down the country. None the less the absence of ecclesiastical turmoil in the earlier years of Abbot's primacy and the fact that Puritan consciences were not stirred by undue harshness or by pronouncements that underlined matters in dispute, gave to the Church a period of quiescence and thus contributed to that steady growth of true religion in the parishes which Bancroft's reforms and Andrewes' influence had encouraged.[14]

On the surface Abbot's primacy was peculiarly unfortunate. The King's militant Calvinism and his Archbishop's compliance were responsible at its start for the burning of two heretics. When Arminius died, his Chair at Leyden had been

14 S. R. Gardiner, *History of England, 1603–47* (1907), III.252 f.

offered to a German, Vorstius, of similar theological views. James had professed himself shocked and had attacked Vorstius so bitterly that the latter had been forced to withdraw. The Dutch were not pleased by the King of England's interference, and James was anxious to give them no chance to accuse him of tolerating in England the unorthodoxy he deplored in Leyden. Unfortunately a victim was ready to hand.[15] Bartholomew Legate had already been condemned as an Arian in the London consistory court and was undergoing a lax imprisonment in the Tower. He chose this moment to sue the authorities for false imprisonment, and when James summoned him to court and attempted to convert him, he declared boldly that he had not prayed to Christ for the past seven years. Faced with this challenge, it was perhaps inevitable that the processes of law should again be set in motion. The Bishop of London's court was enlarged by the presence of other bishops and ecclesiastical lawyers who adjudged Legate to be an "obdurate, contumacious, and incorrigible heretic". Their condemnation was "certified into the Chancery" and here a wiser king and a more charitable primate would have let the matter rest. But a week later on 11 March, by letters under the privy seal, James ordered the Chancery to issue a writ *de heretico comburendo*, according to the law of Henry IV which some declared to be obsolete. Others said conviction by Convocation was necessary in the case of heresy, but James and Abbot disregarded the criticisms and Legate was burnt at Smithfield. Soon afterwards Edward Wightman, "a crazed Antinomian", died at the stake at Lichfield, and here as at London the horrified crowds were revolted by what they saw. In the same year four Roman Catholics—one of them a layman—were executed at Tyburn, technically for treason, so signally had the King failed to impose by force the

[15] Cf. W. K. Jordan, *The Development of Religious Toleration in England* (1936), II.51: "Legate and Whiteman were England's sacrifice to the desperate stand which Calvinism was making against the dissolvents of doctrinal rigidity."

harmony that had eluded him. It was indeed a black year for the Anglican Church, as it proved to be for England as a whole, for in the course of 1612 two deaths had written *finis* to the interlude of comparative prosperity with which the reign began.

Robert Cecil, the Earl of Salisbury, died in the spring of the year. As Lord Treasurer, he had kept the nation solvent and in the secular sphere had endeavoured, as laboriously as Bancroft in the Church, to achieve a measure of order in affairs of State. After his death the national finances knew no such control, and the weakness of the day-to-day administration had much to do with the discontent and disillusion of the succeeding years. In the following November the Prince of Wales also died. Prince Henry had been intelligent and popular, showing in the chaplains he engaged and the friends he made a progressive and moderate attitude towards contemporary problems, and while he lived there was hope for the future and the sense of well-being was maintained. After 1612 there were seven years of ineffectiveness in Church and State alike, although the lack of effective action at the top did not necessarily lead to stagnation in the parishes. It did however lead to a growing amount of stifled criticism—not always stifled when a gifted preacher reached the pulpit—for a series of scandals at Whitehall had repercussions up and down the country, and did much to undermine the confidence of ordinary people in established authority.

After Salisbury's death Abbot soon lost the close confidence of the King, for the Howard family dominated secular politics and the Archbishop not only distrusted their religion but offended them in the matter of the Essex divorce. Frances Howard, married as a child to the young Earl of Essex, had fallen in love with the King's favourite, Lord Rochester. Rochester and Frances, with James's affectionate support, were determined to marry, and a divorce suit was instituted by the Countess on the ground of nullity. Essex fought the case and the commission of judges, composed of bishops and law-

yers, was divided, some giving credence to Frances' statements, others basing their judgement on knowledge of her wanton character. In a private interview the King impressed Andrewes with his own wish and belief that the suit should succeed, and, with reluctance and later regret, Andrewes gave his vote with the narrow majority by which the divorce was granted. Bilson voted with him; Abbot and John King, the Bishop of London, resisted all pressure and refused to agree. Their stock went up in the country in consequence, but at court the marriage took place, Rochester became the Earl of Somerset, and for the next few years he and the Howards were supreme. The weaker side of Abbot's nature revealed itself in his readiness to intrigue with Pembroke, the leader of the rival faction, to introduce George Villiers to the King—a handsome young man who might supplant Somerset in the royal favour. Abbot saw nothing amiss in the design which he himself recounts, recording their appeal to Queen Anne to persuade James to take Villiers into his service, and how he was sworn a Gentleman of the King's Bedchamber in spite of a plea from Somerset that he might only be made a Groom. "George went in with the King", wrote Abbot, "but no sooner he got loose, but he came forth unto me in the privy-gallery and there embraced me . . .".[16] The young man vowed that he owed everything to Abbot, but it was not long before "George" had become the omnipotent Buckingham, forgetful of his earlier obligations. The Somersets fell tragically from power in 1617, when it was discovered that the Countess had been implicated in the murder of Thomas Overbury, and thereafter it was through Buckingham's hands and those of his rapacious family that all patronage passed in Church and State.

These happenings were by no means irrelevant to the fortunes of the Church. It needed no daily press for the gossip of the court to spread through the City, and many country gentry had a regular service of newsletters which recounted the

[16] Arthur Onslow, *The Life of Dr George Abbot* (1707), p. 25, n. K.

events, real or rumoured, that were talked of in the capital. When episcopacy was attacked in 1640 it collapsed the more easily because even those who in theory approved of it had little good to say of bishops, most of whom were believed to have paid cash down for their advancement to one or other member of the Buckingham clique.[17]

This unseemly scramble for places and perquisites was matched by a slow deterioration in the King's own character. Only by degrees did the British Solomon of 1603 become the repulsive old man caricatured in Anthony Welldon's memoirs, and James's acuteness of judgement and sound objectives have seldom received the credit they deserved. Yet as the years went by he neglected the care of his person and indulged increasingly in the pleasures of the table, still eager to debate theological niceties but unable or unwilling to keep a firm grasp of affairs. He was happiest in the country at Theobalds or Royston, for hunting remained his greatest pleasure and in the chase he knew himself as brave as any man. He detested London, for in its crowded streets he went in constant fear of an assassin's knife, and he came and went on his royal journeys by the least frequented ways, while those who still remembered recalled in contrast the happy progresses of Queen Elizabeth. The court was vicious and corrupt and the King had lost control both of it and of himself. Yet this was the King and this the court to which the bishops were tied by the ill-starred theory of divine right, so that even Andrewes lost his way and Abbot, the Primate of England, involved himself, as we have seen, in the intrigues of the royal bed-chamber.[18]

In 1616, the year that Buckingham entered the King's service, the Venetian Ambassador drew up, as was customary, a "relation" of English affairs which throws a flickering light

[17] Cf. H. R. Trevor-Roper, "King James and his Bishops", in *History Today*, vol. V, pp. 571–81.

[18] For James's character see the definitive biography, D. H. Willson, *King James VI and I* (1956), and cf. Charles Williams, *James I* (1934), of particular interest for the analysis of James's religion.

on the state of the Church. The point he stresses is the lack of uniformity. There were, he said, as many as twelve religious parties, "one of Catholics dependent on the Jesuits, two of Catholics who swear fealty to the King and obey his Majesty in temporal matters, three of the indifferent, four of the religion of his Majesty and two Puritan parties."[19] Further analysis is guesswork, for unfortunately Foscarini did not explain his categories nor was he a very reliable observer, but it seemed to him that the number of Puritans were growing while those of "the King's religion" were decreasing.

The tension existing between various recusant groups was an undoubted fact, for the conflict between priests and laymen, those eager to proselytize and those anxious to remain quiet, did not diminish with the years. One distinction made in practice, though unlikely to be that in Foscarini's mind, was between the poorer recusants who filled the prisons to overflowing, and the well-to-do, deliberately left at large and subjected to the spiritual blackmail of repeated fines. The devoted work of pastoral guidance achieved by individual priests is illustrated vividly, at a slightly later date, by the career of Henry Morse in the plague-stricken parish of St Giles; at a different level there continued to be, throughout the reigns of James and his son, a coterie of wealthy and cultured Romanists at court, whose existence continued to keep alive the hysterical fear of Popery among the Protestant middle class.[20] The character and ability of the Spanish Ambassador, Gondomar, was an increasingly important feature of the situation and it was in this year of 1616 that Gondomar began to canvass the idea of a Spanish marriage for the King's surviving son, a diffident and delicate youth who had been brought up in the country and knew little of public affairs.

[19] *Cal. S.P. Venetian, 1617–19*, pp. 386 f (19 Dec. 1618. Foscarini was subjected to trial on various political charges on his return to Venice and did not submit his relation until two years later.)

[20] Cf. Philip Caraman, *Henry Morse, Priest of the Plague* (1957), and see David Mathew, *The Jacobean Age* (1938) for an illuminating picture of the period from the Roman Catholic angle.

The Venetian named three "indifferent parties" in his list. There were the careless and the worldly, as there will be in every generation, and the apathetic humbler folk over whose heads the ecclesiastical changes rolled with little effect so long as the old parochial framework was maintained. Foscarini, using the word in the contemporary sense of impartial, may also have had in mind a small group of men of scientific temper, the precursors of the rationalists, of whom Lord Herbert of Cherbury was an obvious example. This minority of potential free-thinkers (few of them as yet had faced up to the possible development of their thought) approximated to that other enlightened group within the established Church to which, in the succeeding years, Hales and Chillingworth were to belong. These were the men who were to hammer out, from the Anglican viewpoint, the new but essential idea of toleration; and one would like to know more surely whether as early as 1616 this liberal element could be detected among the "four parties of the religion of his Majesty". The two main parties, Arminian and Calvinist, were by now clearly defined, though the term Arminian only came into use, at first in a derogatory sense, in the closing years of the reign. The fourth party may well have been the conforming Puritans, among whom were some of the most conscientious and able parish priests and many whose staunchly Protestant views were accompanied by a critical attitude in politics as well as religion. It boded ill for an harmonious future that among this group there could be found many members of the aristocracy, Herberts, Cecils, Russells, and the stubborn, conscientious Earl of Essex whose dislike of the Howards, and of the King's foreign policy, was equally compounded of patriotism and prejudice. Barely distinguishable were the Presbyterians (though they were not described as such until 1640), the Puritans who took it for granted there would always be a State Church which they hoped to reform to their liking after a continental model. Finally there were the convinced Separatists, who had now once more a foothold in England. A com-

pany of Baptists had returned from Holland, to meet secretly in London, in the year that Legate had been burnt. Thomas Helwys, their leader, had been imprisoned and died soon afterwards, but in 1616, when Foscarini made his report, Henry Jacob had just come over and set up in Southwark a congregation bound together by covenant, which survived the centuries and whose descendants may be found to-day in the Pilgrim Church, rebuilt on the borders of Bermondsey.

Such was the distracted state of the Church of Christ in England. A greater man than Abbot might have fumbled in the direction of so ill-fused a body. Nor had the Archbishop efficient colleagues to assist him. The second generation of Jacobean bishops were not only less eminent in character and learning than their predecessors, but proved on the whole ineffectual as diocesans, the lack of leadership from Lambeth and Buckingham's monopoly of power both having deleterious effects. Under the circumstances the surprising fact is not the mediocrity but the quality of the immediate appointments after the favourite's rise to power. Robert Abbot, who became Bishop of Salisbury in 1615, was more distinguished than the Archbishop in his learning, and able to give his pupils and parishioners that very sense of refreshment and renewal which his brother failed so singularly to give to the Church as a whole. Arthur Lake, one of Buckingham's first nominees as Bishop of Bath and Wells, was rated highly both by Fuller and Izaak Walton, and Thomas Morton, appointed to Chester in the same year, never varied in his goodness and sanity through ninety years of honest living.[21] He belonged in age and outlook to the older generation—a scholar of European reputation and a man of God, who rode through the streets of York in the time of plague, his saddle-bags filled with bread, giving freely and without fear to the crowds who jostled about him.

[21] For Lake, see S. H. Cassan, *Lives of the Bishops of Bath and Wells* (1829), II.27–32, and cf. Izaak Walton's "Life of Sanderson" in *Collected Lives* (ed. S. B. Carter, 1951), pp. 269 f. For Morton, see *The Fight, Victory and Triumph of St Paul*, which is John Barwick's funeral sermon published in 1659.

Of him more will be said, for though he looked back to the Elizabethan Age he lived to suffer the rigours of the Interregnum.

There were a number of less satisfactory prelates: men such as Theophilus Field, who had been Bacon's chaplain and, so it was said, his broker in the matter of bribes, or John Thornborough, Bishop of Worcester, whose sideline was chemistry and whose interests were firmly centred in this world. It was their presumed subservience to Buckingham that undermined the influence of all alike. Rumour said that John Davenant's appointment to Salisbury, in 1621, was the only occasion on which no money passed; and in that case he was the brother-in-law of the previous occupant of the see, who had not held it long enough to provide for his large family. Buckingham asked James to promote Davenant so that he could look after his sister and her children, a reason for an episcopal appointment that nobody seemed to find unseemly.

Davenant was a scholar and a man of strict integrity, with enough of the Puritan in him to fail to attend at court when it meant breaking the sabbath by a journey on horseback. The true reason for advancing him was the service he had rendered at Dort, and no one could quarrel with his promotion. The synod at Dort in 1619 had marked a change in the *tempo* of affairs. Maurice of Nassau's overthrow of Barneveldt in Holland had been linked with the country's religious differences; and the synod was held by the victorious Calvinists, who summoned the Arminian leaders to attend and subjected them to a biased interrogation. King James had encouraged the idea of a synod and sent as observers Joseph Hall, the Dean of Worcester, who returned prematurely because of illness, Dudley Carleton, the diplomat, and Davenant. In spite of their original sympathies they were dismayed and shocked at the lack of all restraint in the treatment of Episcopus, the leading Arminian, and perhaps the most important thing that happened at Dort, from the English point of view, was its effect on an intelligent and sensitive young man who was there in the rôle of secretary. John Hales, who was to become one of

the leaders of liberal thought in the Caroline Church, told his friends in later years that at Dort he said "Good night to Mr Calvin".

The time was passed when disputation of any sort could preserve the peace of Europe. While the theologians met at Dort, to the south, in the mountains of Bohemia, a quarrel over the succession sparked off a religious war which was to last for thirty bitter years. The war became the concern of every Englishman when the crown of Bohemia was offered to the Elector Palatine, the husband of Elizabeth, King James's only daughter. For a brief period it seemed that England was again united, as the courtiers who had idolized the princess as a girl were stirred by old enthusiasms and at one with Puritan zealots, anxious for a Protestant crusade. The King was hesitant, doubting the rebels' right to offer the crown to anyone, but when in August 1620 the Hapsburg forces swept down upon the Palatinate, driving Frederick from his hereditary dominions, James wept angry tears and was as indignant as his subjects, who were clamouring for war. The Bohemian adventure ended a month or so later with the battle of the White Mountain when, according to an English volunteer, a kingdom was lost in less than half an hour,[22] but at Westminster in the new year Parliament heard King James declare in his opening speech that if he could not recover the Palatinate by fair means, he would, "God willing, have it by main force, or it should cost the dearest blood of himself and his son Charles".[23] It was the nearest he ever came to bellicose speech, but neither he nor his Commons proved to be single-minded. The latter were as full of their domestic grievances as of Europe's distress and granted only the most inadequate supplies; James, influenced by Gondomar who had recently

[22] Brit. Mus. Harleian MS. 389, f. 1. "A relation of the manner of the loss of Prague, 21 Nov. (1620); ibid., f. 7d.

[23] A letter to Joseph Meade, 2 Feb. 1621, printed in T. Birch, *The Court and Times of James the First* (1848), II.216. This series of news letters, printed by Birch and contained in Harl. MS. 389, give a lively picture of these critical months.

returned to England, was increasingly attracted by the alternative plan of a marriage alliance with Spain, in the hope of recovering the Palatinate for Frederick through Spanish mediation. Parliament was adjourned in May, its work only half done, and though it was recalled when bad news continued to pour in from the Continent, by the time it reassembled James had either lost interest or changed his mind and had gone to Newmarket. It was not surprising that the session was a brief and stormy one. Many of the members saw in the increasing ferocity of the religious war, and the threat of the advancing Turks on Austria's eastern border, the immediate signs of a coming Armageddon. They drew up an address to the King, informing him in good round terms of their views on foreign policy and the action he ought to take. James was enraged. It was no business of the Commons to discuss foreign affairs. He called for the Journals of the House and tore out with his own hand the page on which the address was recorded. Parliament was adjourned and within a week or two dissolved, thus angrily bringing to an end a year of alarms and excursions in which the last chance of united action passed away.

During this same critical year of 1621, the story of the Church had taken a new turn with the emergence of two dynamic personalities. Buckingham had recently married Catherine Manners, the daughter of a recusant peer. The King insisted that her acceptance of the Anglican faith should precede the marriage and in the formal instruction that was necessary Buckingham had made use of the services of John Williams, a royal chaplain, whose tactful approach to the matter made it easy for the bride-to-be to pronounce herself converted. The grateful Buckingham saw to it that Williams was rewarded by the gift of the deanery of Westminster. The new dean was a brilliant and ambitious Welshman who had been for some years chaplain to Lord Ellesmere, the former Chancellor. From Ellesmere he had imbibed a knowledge of law at least equal to his interest in theology, and his quick, argumentative tongue made him a good sparring-partner for

the King. He was still young, of a good presence and private means, a man of generous impulses but strangely devoid of firm and consistent principles, a lack not yet apparent in the first flush of success. He flourished in the atmosphere of the court and now in 1621, at the age of 39, was nominated Bishop of Lincoln and, to the surprise of all and doubt of many, was appointed to succeed Bacon as Lord Keeper of the Great Seal. His quick abilities were matched with industry, and he saw it as right and fitting that the King should be advised in matters of equity by a clerical Lord Keeper. He also looked forward to being a bishop, though he was anxious not to lose the deanery of Westminster, which provided him with a foothold close to Whitehall and where he delighted to order the music of the Abbey.[24] The probable recipient of the deanery, if Williams gave it up, was William Laud, a man eight years his senior, who had made slow progress up the ladder of preferment though his fortunes were improving with the growing strength of the Arminian party. Laud was not a man who got on well with people: as Dean of Gloucester, he had quarrelled with his diocesan Miles Smith, and during ten years as President of St John's College, Oxford, had shown himself an advanced high churchman and a martinet in matters of discipline. Now, however, Williams, perhaps through genuine friendliness—for he was not a mean-spirited man—and also to secure his deanery, undertook to plead Laud's case as a candidate for the vacant bishopric of St David's. The King was strongly opposed to the appointment. "I find he hath a restless spirit", he commented as to Laud, "and cannot see when matters are well, but loves to toss and change and to bring things to a pitch of reformation, floating in his own brain." "Then take him to you", James agreed in the end, "but on my soul you will repent it."[25]

[24] John Hacket, *Scrinia Reserata: a Memorial of John Williams* (1692), I.46, 62 and *passim* for a contemporary account of the Bishop and his times.

[25] Ibid., I.64. Laud, as Neile's chaplain, had accompanied James on a visit to Scotland in 1616, when the Articles of Perth had been ratified, enjoining certain unpopular points of ritual.

St David's was a poor and distant diocese, to which Laud made only two brief visits, but it was the first step towards future pre-eminence and marked a change in the fortunes of the Arminian divines, partly brought about by a tragic accident which had befallen Abbot. Out hunting with Lord Zouche during the troubled summer of 1621, the Archbishop shot an arrow, which glanced off a tree and struck a keeper in the arm. By ill chance an artery was severed and the man died. James hastened to ensure Abbot of the royal pardon, so far as a civil action was concerned, but not even the King could allay the feeling of dismay and uncertainty that quickly spread. There was an uneasy suspicion that an archbishop could have been better employed than in the chase, and there was doubt whether a priest guilty of manslaughter could rightly administer the holy sacraments. Three bishops, Williams and Laud among them, were awaiting consecration and they refused to accept it from hands stained with a man's blood. Abbot was suspended while the matter was under debate, but, upon Andrewes' more merciful advice, his authority was restored to him. He remained in office until his death twelve years later, but his place in the counsels of the Church was eventually usurped by Laud, as yet working mainly in the background, and more immediately by Williams, the nearest approach on the episcopal bench to a medieval bishop and an unpredictable mixture of worldly ambition, inconstant politics, and occasional spiritual insight. During the final years of the reign, as Laud and Williams strove in secret rivalry for the control of Buckingham's conscience, there lay also in the balance the destiny of England.

It was not long before the scales were tipped in Laud's favour. During the next two years, as the King continued his ineffective parleyings with Spain, Romanism became popular, and a number of conversions took place throughout the country. The most distinguished of the converts was the favourite's mother, the Countess of Buckingham, and the Duke himself was said to be wavering. A full-dress theological debate was

arranged at Whitehall between the Jesuit, Father Fisher, who had won over the Countess, and the Bishop of St David's. Laud distinguished himself, showing to the world for the first time not only his controversial skill and his acute brain but the depth of his devotion and his complete understanding of the Anglican ideal. The Duke's faith was stabilized, and—what was more important for the future—Charles, the young Prince of Wales and Buckingham's inseparable companion, was given a new insight into the meaning of the Church of which he was soon to become the Supreme Governor.

King James, however, continued to prefer Williams, who endeavoured to please both him and the Duke—which was beginning to be less easy than it had been. The marriage negotiations were progressing and in August 1622, as a gesture of goodwill, James ordered the Lord Keeper to issue a proclamation releasing imprisoned recusants, not excepting the priests. The country was profoundly disturbed and the wildest stories circulated: of Jesuits disguised as cooks and falconers, or of bold doings in Lancashire, where the Papists, it was said, had brought a bear into church in the middle of the sermon. From the pulpits less fantastic but no less vigorous opposition caused the authorities to issue instructions to preachers which forbade them to discuss the "power, prerogative and jurisdiction, authority or duty of sovereign princes". At the foreign embassies, where the rites of the Roman Church were permitted, English recusants openly attended the services, but when next year an upper floor collapsed, with considerable loss of life, the Protestant citizens of London had no difficulty in detecting in the tragedy the hand of God.

This obsession in regard to Rome undermined every effort of the Stuarts to grant a measure of toleration in matters of religion. James had expressed his own point of view in his opening speech to the Parliament of 1621: "Faith is wrought by God in the heart, therefore I hold no man's conscience to be compelled. Father Latimer said well that the Devil was a busy bishop and if our Church were as busy to persuade the

right way as the bold Jesuits, Puritans and other sectaries are to supplant and subvert, we should not have so many go astray on both sides."[26] But his subjects must, he hastened to add, obey the laws of the land. It was the attitude which, in the next reign, Laud also adopted: consciences would not be compelled so long as men did not allow their thoughts to bear fruit in illegal action or seditious words. It was, of course, entirely unrealistic, and neither James nor Laud nor Cromwell was able to strike the right balance between freedom and security. The overriding fear of the Papacy added the further complication that any attempt at toleration which James or his successors might make could only rest on the prerogative, for parliamentary assent never came within the bounds of possibility. Thus another barrier arose to prevent success. In 1623 a letter to the King, purporting to come from Abbot but in all probability forged, made both points clear in two sentences, the one hysterical, the other wise. "By your act you labour to set up that most damnable and heretical doctrine of the Church of Rome, the whore of Babylon. . . . This toleration which you endeavour to set up by proclamation cannot be done without a Parliament."[27]

On this occasion the toleration collapsed with the collapse of the marriage alliance. Early that year, Charles and Buckingham had slipped away to Spain to prosecute the suit in person. For a few months Charles thought he was in love with the Infanta, and at Whitehall the marriage articles were signed by James with a bewildered court in attendance. But Madrid had little intention of concluding the match, still less of inter-

[26] Brit. Mus. Harl. MS. 389, f. 5d. The Jesuits claimed to have made 2600 converts in 1623 (Caraman, *Henry Morse*, p. 31).

[27] Cf. *Cal. S.P. Venetian 1623–5*, p. 90. Fuller gives text of the letter, also printed in part and ascribed to Abbot in *The Supplication of all the Papists of England to King James at his first comming to the Crowne for a tolleration of their religion* (1642). Heylyn and Sanderson doubted Abbot's authorship (Fuller, ed. Brewer, V.546 n, 548). Gardiner accepts it as a forgery (*History*, V.71 ff). Further details are in R. A. Christophers' thesis "A Bibliography of George Abbot" (deposited in London University Library) pp. viii f, 94 ff.

vening in the Palatinate, and realizing at last that they were being tricked the Prince and Buckingham returned, full of resentment and wounded vanity. They were now as eager for action as any House of Commons man, and the King was too sick of heart and weary to resist them. Parliament was summoned, the penal laws were reimposed, for a brief while the returned wanderers enjoyed the heady wine of popularity, and in the spring of 1625 the King, who had sought consistently all his life for peace, died in the knowledge that his country was at war with Spain.

# 3

# THE PARISH

STILL to-day in every corner of England, in village and city and sprawling industrial town, there stands the parish church. The tall towers of East Anglia, the shingled roofs of Surrey, the high decorated windows of the Cotswold country alike proclaim man's continuing desire to glorify God by the work of his hands. The fabric often dates back to medieval days, but, in regard to furnishings, many of the most beautiful examples that survive are of Jacobean origin. There are heavy three-tiered pulpits beautifully carved, reading desks of comparable dignity and craftsmanship, innumerable pew-ends decorated with humour and imagination. The lovely rood-screens and altar-rails mark the beginning of the Laudian régime; in the Jacobean age, it is the pulpits and reading-desks that predominate, while the erection of pews and the costly memorial tombs, redolent of family pride and affection, witness to an increasing emphasis on social standing and personal achievement.

These effigies of Jacobean gentry in their stiff ruffs and quilted gowns, attended by a numerous progeny, are the tangible signs of a new age in which the squire and Justice of the Peace had replaced the feudal knight as the dominant figure of the countryside. The great house of the family is often standing in an adjoining park, fortunate if it remains the residence of the descendants of that Jacobean ancestor, who was sometimes a prosperous merchant or lawyer, achieving his ambition of a seat in the country, and sometimes the grandson of a Tudor yeoman, the first of his kin to attain nobility through the success of his sheep-farm, the agility of

his wits, or the payment of a fixed sum to an impecunious king. However the family at the manor house came to be there, both they and their successors served England well in a multitude of ways, as local magistrates, as Members of Parliament, as good landlords, more rarely as patrons of the arts, and when required by the sacrifice of their young men on fields of war in every corner of the world.

The churches bear signs of other less worthy characteristics. There was nothing to commend the exclusiveness of the box-pew, nor the habit of segregating the poor, as at St Saviour's, Southwark, where the merchants of the Borough saw to it that the riff-raff of Bankside remained in the north aisle. One reason for the erection of pews was the increase in income they provided for the overburdened wardens, but a main cause was the Protestant stress on the sermon, which meant that many hours were spent in listening to the preacher, and the necessary provision of seating accommodation, like the exaltation of the pulpit and reading-desk, is a sign of this new emphasis in the services of the Church. In some populous districts where a well-known lecturer might attract strangers to hear him, or the foundation of a free school add a crowd of noisy schoolboys to the congregation at Mattins, it was sometimes necessary to build galleries, with unfortunate results to the aesthetic proportions of the nave, for it was by the work of the craftsmen, rather than the architects, that parish churches were enriched in the years before the Civil War. It is rare to find a church built between the time of the Reformation and the age of Christopher Wren.

This in a sense is surprising in a great age of building, but many churches had fallen into disrepair during the years following the Reformation, and St Paul's was only the chief of many in urgent need of rehabilitation. There was however one interesting exception in an early essay in town planning, the development of Lincoln's Inn Fields, and Inigo Jones's chapel at Lincoln's Inn was built in 1623 to serve the needs of

the new neighbourhood. Elsewhere in England great mansions, such as Knowle and Audley End, were adorned and enlarged or new manor-houses built, while new schools such as Blundell's in Tiverton and Gresham's at Holt and a large number of almshouses witnessed to a growth in wealth and in a sense of individual responsibility. The humbler parishioner, meanwhile, could take his share in the care and upkeep of his church. Moreover in managing its affairs, attending the vestry meeting, and holding office in his turn, burdensome though it might be, he had the chance to exercise to the full those qualities of moderation, common sense and, if need be, obstinacy traditionally associated with the English temperament.

The life of the parish was very much that of a closed community, following in its ordered course the round of the seasons and of the Christian year. In the springtime, at the Easter festival, the new life in field and sheepfold was partnered by new beginnings in the Church, with the annual election of the parish officials and the offer of new life to every soul in the great spiritual experience of the Easter communion. Shortly before the feast of St John the Baptist six days were allotted to the making and repairing of roads, a task in which every householder took a share and contributed a draught of horses if he owned a plough. Thereafter came the harvest, with its assurance of plenty or its warning of dearth, a time of thanksgiving yet of deepened awareness of man's complete dependence upon God; George Herbert was accustomed to hold a service of Holy Communion before the harvesting began as well as at its close. After the festivities of harvest-home, with the coming of winter, the life of the village shut in upon itself, relieved only by the twelve nights of Christmas, when every corner of the church was decked with holly, rosemary, and bays. Thereafter came the turn of the year, the season of ploughing and the stringencies of Lent, until once again it was Easter and the spring.

The regular sequence of country life was interrupted by two

special occasions, regularly noted among the expenses in the churchwardens' annual accounts. The one was a domestic affair, the perambulation of the parish or the beating of the bounds, when the crops were blessed and any doubtful boundaries clearly indicated, an occasion which usually ended with a feast—a formal vestry dinner or a free distribution of cakes and ale. According to Herbert, the "loving walking and neighbourly accompanying one another" was one of the benefits of the perambulation.[1] It gave the parishioners an opportunity to make up some of the little differences of village life. More serious trouble was settled or exposed on the other important occasion, the annual visitation of the archdeacon, or, every third year, of the Bishop's officers. Then, in answer to the articles that had been promulgated, the wardens reported on the material and spiritual state of the parish, presenting those sinners who had committed adultery, sold apples on the sabbath, or proved stubborn on points of ceremonial. The visitation was held in a large church in the neighbourhood, probably in the local market or country town, to which the clergy, officials, and schoolmasters of the neighbouring parishes resorted. Thus it brought the parish into touch with its neighbours, as did the quarter-sessions on the secular front, when the petty constable, an official second only to the wardens in standing, brought rogues and vagabonds and other evildoers before the Justices of the Peace. The latter, leading personalities of the neighbourhood, were familiar with the problems and often with the people with whom they had to deal, and were apt to bend the laws according to their local knowledge and with a sense of rough justice that on the whole worked well. Yet just as in some matters, such as the imposition of the recusancy laws, the hands of the magistrates might be forced by the officiousness of informers, so in the ecclesiastical field, particularly in regard to the regulation of worship, the effectiveness of control might be

[1] George Herbert, *Works*, ed. F. E. Hutchinson (1953), p. 284.

6

vitiated by the reluctance of the churchwardens to present offenders.

Not only were the Justices in close touch with their local world; they also knew something of the world beyond and went up to London periodically, to serve in Parliament or attend to a lawsuit and to bring home in exaggerated form the gossip of Court and City for the scandalized enjoyment of the wardens and their wives. King James, however, did not encourage protracted visits to town and twice in his reign, as Christmas approached, he ordered gentlemen, up from the country, to return to their estates so that, by keeping open house and distributing alms, they might lessen distress among the poor.

Three main types of ecclesiastical document survive to illustrate the life of the parishes. The records of the Church courts are in the nature of things mainly formal, but the deposition books of the bishops' consistory courts contain the statements made by witnesses at trials, of which the outcome can sometimes be traced in the Act Books. There are hints of many personal dramas and small tragedies in the varied testimonies. One can follow, for example, in the deposition book of the London court the story of Elizabeth Castle, of St Leonard's, Shoreditch, accused of being "a common scold". She had found her husband drinking with a friend at a local alehouse, and had turned on Fortune Launcelott, the proprietress, calling her a whore and threatening to have her carted round the town. But Mrs Castle had met her match; Fortune prosecuted her for slanderous words, calling in as witness a neighbour who had looked in at that moment for a pot of beer. That was one type of case; on another page, an inquiry is recorded into the fate of a seaman taken captive by the Turks. A certain John Holt, recently freed, testified that, while he was in slavery in Algiers, the London ship the *Centurion* had been captured and the seaman in question had been brought in, so severely burnt that he was not expected to live

till the morning. No one had heard of him since and the plaintiffs asked for leave to presume death.[2]

Such random examples illustrate the width and thoroughness of the Church's surveillance over people's personal affairs. These unfortunates, however, were exceptions; it is less easy to estimate how far the offender in ceremonial who came before the consistory court was also an exception. If public opinion in the parish backed up a puritan pastor, the chances at first were that he would be left in peace. As the Laudian régime emerged the position altered, until large sections of the local community might decide to sail for the New World to avoid the risk of repeated prosecution and an eventual summons before the High Commission.

The visitation articles, the second source of information, give as it were a picture in the round of the ideal parish, while the replies, when they are still extant, indicate the shortcomings.[3] The articles follow in the main a common form, with a variation in emphasis according to special circumstance or the leanings of those in authority. Questions about the material state of the church and the churchyard and details of church furnishings were more than routine inquiries to men such as Laud and Cosin, earnestly seeking to train the Anglican laity into a new awareness of order and beauty as part of the approach to worship. Davenant, on the other hand, or Hall, at Exeter, might be more concerned to discover the state

[2] Records of London Consistory Court, Deposition Book, Nov. 1637–June 1640 (County Record Office, Westminster Bridge, S.E.1). W. H. Hale, *Precedents in causes of office against church wardens and others* . . (1841) and *A series of precedents and proceedings in criminal causes . . . 1475–1640* (1847), both contain extracts from the Act Books. For a more general account see J. S. Purvis, *An Introduction to ecclesiastical records* (1953). Cf. R. A. Marchant, *The Puritans and the Church Courts in the Diocese of York, 1560–1642* (1960), p. 4: ". . . the legal system of the Church of England was no mere medieval, outworn, outmoded organization, but employed as alert, intelligent and highly-educated men as were to be found in any other profession".

[3] Cosin's articles for his visitation as Archdeacon of the East Riding in 1627 are printed in *The Correspondence of John Cosin* (Surtees Society No. 52, 1869), pp. 106 et seq., and give a good picture of parochial problems.

of the schools in the parish or whether or not the preaching was adequate. Andrewes, always shrewd as well as saintly, inquired in particular as to how the minister had acquired his cure and whether there were any suspicion of simony, and also asked to have particulars of any parishioners who came late to church or "babbled" while the service was in progress. Montagu, in the 1630s, inquired as to whether there was yet a monthly communion.

The parochial records themselves are comparatively scarce for the years before the Restoration. Much was destroyed both by accident and design during the Interregnum, and in the succeeding centuries many have been lost, destroyed by fire or rotted by damp or the ravages of mice in an old church tower or lumber room. A good selection still survive of registers of births, marriages, and deaths, and a smaller number of account-books, while rarer still are the vestry minutes, which generally record only formal business but every now and again bring the past vividly to life.

The impression that emerges clearly and consistently is of the large amount of honest work put in by a succession of parish officials at a task that was rapidly expanding beyond their powers. The parish was both the centre of social and religious life and the unit of local government, responsible through its officials not only for the care of the church but for the welfare of the community, the keeping of the peace, the upkeep of the roads, and the problems of the poor.[4] Chief

[4] See Eleanor Trotter, *Seventeenth Century Life in the Country Parish, with special reference to Local Government* (1919), and W. E. Tate, *The Parish Chest, A Study of the Records of Parochial Administration in England* (edn of 1946). Eleanor Trotter's first three chapters (pp. 1–50) deal with the parochial framework, the churchwardens and the part played by the incumbent; later chapters deal with the duties of the overseers, constables, etc., and draw largely on quarter-session records in Yorkshire. The second section of *The Parish Chest* is also concerned with records, mainly civil; after an introductory account of the parish, Part I deals with parish registers, churchwardens' accounts, charity and tithe records and miscellanea, including visitation records. Cf. Sidney and Beatrice Webb, *English Local Government from the Revolution to the Municipal Corporations Act: The Parish and the County* (1906), pp. 9–60.

among these officials were the churchwardens, surely the supreme example of that untrained yet effective voluntary service so ingrained in the pattern of English life. The office was of ancient origin, owing its authority not to a statutory enactment but to custom recognized in common law, and prior to the time of the Tudors its duties had been confined to the affairs of the Church. It was in Henry VIII's reign, with the general development of local government, that the wardens were invested with a number of secular duties, gradually comprehending every aspect of parochial life from the collection of money for gaols and hospitals to the destruction of foxes and badgers and other vermin. At the beginning of the seventeenth century, the Canons authorized the appointment of sidesmen to help them, which produced the disrespectful jingle, instructing the sidesmen in their duties:

To ken and see and say nowt,
To eat and drink and pay nowt;
And when the wardens drunken roam,
Your duty is to see them home.[5]

The sidesmen were the youngest members, as the wardens were the oldest, of the parish hierarchy.

The election of the wardens in medieval days usually took place after Mattins on a Sunday. The choice, made by the assembled parishioners, was later approved by the archdeacon, but this became by degrees a mere formality. The parson, on the other hand, began to have a say in the election of the wardens during Elizabeth's reign and the Canons of 1604 confirmed that they should be chosen by the joint consent of the minister and the parishioners, but if there were disagreement the minister should choose one warden and the

[5] J. C. Cox, *Church-Wardens' Accounts from the 14th century to the close of the 17th century* (1913), p. 3. This book gives details of and numerous quotations from the early account books and an over-all picture of the wardens' activities and the gradual impingement of secular duties. Cf. Tate, op. cit., pp. 84 ff, and for parochial organization in general cf. C. Drew, *Lambeth Church Wardens' Accounts* (1504–1645) and *Vestry Book* (1610), published by the Surrey Record Society, Vols. XL and XLIII.

parishioners the other. In 1554 new parish officials had been created by law, the surveyors of the highway, to be chosen on the Monday and Tuesday of Easter week. With the growth of sabbatarianism the election of the wardens on Sunday began to appear unseemly, and this also was eventually allocated to the parish meeting early in Easter week. With the Elizabethan Poor Law yet a further pair of officials materialized in the overseers of the poor, and although theoretically these were appointed by the Justices, the post was so burdensome that the outgoing overseers usually nominated their successors and the Justices accepted their choice as willingly as the Archdeacon approved the wardens. All this business was transacted at the parish meeting and the names of the new officials inscribed in the vestry minutes. The constable's name was not usually listed in the minutes, though there are exceptions. He was sworn in by the magistrate with the prime duty of preserving order. In effect he was the wardens' executive arm, but responsible to the magistrates.[6] In fact, men of standing in the parish were expected to fill each office in turn, acting in a voluntary capacity—voluntary in the sense of receiving no pay though by no means necessarily of their free choice, for both in regard to time and money it was an expensive business. It is not to be wondered at that increasingly in the towns the leading citizens preferred to pay large fines to be passed over, a source of revenue which proved a valuable addition to the Church funds. Thus in 1620 the vestry minutes of St Bartholomew Exchange record the receipt of a fine of £20, the more welcome as the great west window was in urgent need of repair. The record adds a note to the name of the donor, John Brown: "being a loving parishioner and much good that he hath done in bountiful manner in the parish . . . to be freed of all offices".[7] In the villages responsibility was usually accepted more readily and in every generation the same names

[6] Trotter, op. cit., pp. 83 et seq.

[7] *The Vestry Minute Books of the Parish of St Bartholomew Exchange*, ed. Edwin Freshfield (1890), Part I, p. 80 (16 July 1620).

recurred, ensuring the continuity of daily living in spite of political changes; at Legh, in Surrey, for example, even Oliver's protectorate did not interrupt the rhythm of the names.[8]

In general it was the right of every parishioner to attend the vestry meetings, but in the early years of the seventeenth century there was a growing tendency for the more "discreet and sober" to monopolize control. By no means all the parishioners were village Hampdens, and unless some vital matter such as the condition of the communal well or gossip about the blacksmith's daughter had aroused them, many stayed away or attended in silence lest onerous duties were thrust upon them. And so in a number of parishes, sometimes by the gradual growth of custom and sometimes by deliberate choice, a select vestry came into being, a small oligarchy of men of substance. Thus in 1605 at St Bartholomew Exchange a small group of energetic members of the congregation constituted themselves a closed vestry by the choice of twenty or twenty-four persons who were to "conclude of all such matters as shall be for the good of this parish, either concerning this church or otherwise".[9] A formal document is copied into one of the parish books of St Mary, Newington, dated 1624 and under the seal of an official of the Croydon deanery, which confirms certain orders the parish has "devised . . . for the establishment and good government of a vestrie". They provided for a select vestry of twenty-five persons, plus the parson and one or both churchwardens, to fill up their numbers as required from the "best, discreetest parishioners". They had power to levy a rate "for the building and repairing of the said church and steeple", and, if any individual complained, could call him before them and either ease him or, if he were an obstinate person, present him to the ordinary. A vestryman could be removed if he behaved himself "unreverently and

[8] Parish register of Legh, Surrey (County Record Office, Kingston-on-Thames).

[9] *Vestry Minute Books of . . . St Bartholomew Exchange*, Part I, p. 53.

unfitting the place by unseemly speeches or usage", and the churchwardens were to present annual accounts and not to spend more than 40*s*. on repairs without consent of the vestry.[10] In the vestry minutes of St Nicholas, Deptford, for 10 May 1629 a similar development is recorded. "It is agreed by us whose names are subscribed", the entry runs, "that the Vicar and Churchwardens for the present tyme shall name six sufficient inhabitantes, to whom we give power to nominate so manie of the parishioners as they shall in discretion think fitt to be a full vestrie, to whom we shall ever committ the care of such businesses as are ordinarily passable by vestrie . . . provided that the number of the vestrie exceed not the number of twentie and that the Vicar, the Churchwardens and constables and overseers of the poore for the tyme being be alwaies admitted to the assistance of that twentie." Two of the six nominations were esquires, two others were described as gentlemen, while the remaining couple were a brewer and a baker. They in their turn nominated fourteen others to make up the vestry, but two years later, on 11 April 1631, three members were replaced by three newcomers as the former, it is recorded, "gave no assistance to the vestrie from which of a long tyme they have absented themselves, so that we were induced to conceive an unwillingness in them to continue longer in the number". The vestry continued its labours even through the critical years of the war and the Interregnum, but little is entered in the minutes beyond the names of the parish officials and occasional lists of pensioners. On the eve of the Restoration the parishioners of Deptford made a new start, reconstructing their select vestry and ordering the wardens and constable to collect the remainder of the rate "that thereby all the parish debts may be discharged".[11]

Until the disruption caused by the civil wars the system

10 St Mary, Newington, Vestry Minutes, 1608–1752, f. 10 et seq. (Southwark Central Library, Walworth Road, S.E.1).

11 St Nicholas, Deptford, Vestry Minutes, 1628–1797, ff. 33–4, 79, 81 (County Record Office, Westminster Bridge, S.E.1. P.78/Nic/44). On select vestries cf. Tate, *The Parish Chest*, pp. 18–21.

worked fairly well. It was still possible to envisage the parish as a community, in which each had his allotted place and men of substance and character, sufficient for the task, took responsibility for the welfare of the whole. The breakdown that was beginning to become apparent by the end of the century was due in part to the problem of the poor but also to the oligarchic nature of the select vestries, for the latter seldom had statutory authority and their validity might well be questioned when they no longer spoke for the parish as a whole. The growing distinction between the families of substance in the township and those of lesser standing, the dissidents of every sort, was bound to lead to trouble, as the sense of community was steadily diminished by greater variations in individual incomes and by the acceptance of Nonconformity as a permanent factor in local and national life.

It was in the all-important task of caring for the poor that the strain imposed by the parochial system first appeared. The Elizabethan Poor Law placed the responsibility of coping with those who could not or would not work firmly upon the parish to which they originally belonged. Those who wandered, either to beg their bread, to live by their wits in places where they were not known, or to prey upon wayfarers on the lonely roads, were to be apprehended and after due punishment to be returned to the parish whence they came. The re-enactment of the law in King James's reign restored the practice of branding rogues and vagabonds, who were then whipped by the constable and dispatched from village to village, sometimes whipped anew at each stopping place until, if they survived, they were returned to their place of birth. If this were not known, they were sent to the "house of correction" which gradually became a usual feature of every township.[12] Often the victim was a pregnant woman, whom

[12] Cf. Trotter, *Seventeenth Century Life in the Country Parish*, p. 166. The House of Correction "occupied an intermediate position between an almshouse and a gaol". Those committed to it came before the quarter-sessions again when their term was completed and "if their report was good were set at liberty".

the authorities endeavoured to deal with speedily lest she fell into labour and the parish found itself with another bastard child to feed and apprentice. There were often strange juxtapositions of cruelty and kindness as in the story, recorded in Tate's *Parish Chest*, of one Magdalen Payne, who took refuge in a barn on the outskirts of Bacton and was discovered by the owner. He "was enforced to runne and to implore for aide and assistance of ye neighbouring wives, by whose good assistance (God so blessing their endeavours) the sayde Magdalen Payne was then and there delivered of a woman childe since christened and named Katherine". None the less two months later Magdalen, having confessed to being a vagrant, was ordered "to be whipped until her body was bloodie" and to be returned with Baby Katherine to Hitcham whence she came.[13] The average Englishman, in an affluent age, found it hard to imagine that a stranger in distress might not necessarily be wandering the roads for choice, and the parish officials had a duty to the community to keep out elements that might disturb its peace. Thus the Cranbrook wardens in 1609 entered a note in their account-book: "No stranger or foreigner" to be received "but such as shall be very well knowen to be persons of honest life and conversation and able to live of themselves."[14] Neither William Perkins, the Puritan scholar, nor George Herbert, at a later date, thought the Poor Law anything but admirable.[15] The duty to work hard at one's vocation was an intrinsic part of Protestant philosophy, while the duty to help one's neighbour in distress was even more fundamental. The distinction, therefore, seemed to them a proper one between the rogues and vagabonds, who must be made to work, and the poor who belonged, the aged and infirm, and orphans needing to be taught a trade.

[13] Tate, op. cit., pp. 211 f.

[14] Cranbrook Church Wardens' Accounts, 1509–1695, f. 131 (Kent Archives Office, Maidstone, P.100/5/1).

[15] See Christopher Hill, "William Perkins and the Poor", in his *Puritanism and Revolution* (1958), pp. 218 et seq.

The regular payment of pensions and apprentice-fees was the pleasanter side of the overseers' responsibilities, and those of the poor who were part of the community received not only relief but genuine compassion and concern. How personal the approach still was, even at a later date, appears from a Cranbrook rate-book of the 1680s: To John Dan, being visited with the small-pox . . . to Thomas Pethurst being lame . . . 3*s*. 6*d*. for mending Cripple Welch's cart . . . 2*s*. 6*d*. to Widow Hope, for looking to old Richeson being sick.[16]

The poor-box was supplied in various ways, including fines for non-attendance and sometimes for contentious talk at vestry meetings. The offerings at the Communion service went by custom to the poor. At St Bartholomew Exchange there was also a weekly distribution of bread, and those in need were instructed to go up into the chancel after the Gospel, "there not only to praise God for his benefits in moving the hearts of godly persons to give relief to their necessities, but also to be ready at the hands of the Church-Wardens . . . to receive the said alms".[17]

After the Reformation, however, the question of poor-relief involved far more than almsgiving either in church or in indiscriminate charity. Within a few years of the suppression of the monasteries it had been seen that the work of the great hospitals must be continued, and the old foundations had been re-established upon a secular basis. During the course of Elizabeth's reign the Justices were empowered to lay a rate on the parishes to aid the hospitals and also for the relief of maimed soldiers and poor prisoners in the county gaol or in the King's Bench and the Marshalsea. The Poor Law of 1601 similarly provided for the levy of a rate for the relief of distress in general, but while the county rate for hospitals, soldiers, and poor prisoners became a regular entry in the wardens' accounts, many parishes hesitated to impose a poor-rate. They

16 Cranbrook Rate Book (Kent Archives Office, Maidstone, P.100/12/1).

17 *Vestry Minute Books of . . . St Bartholomew Exchange*, Part I, pp. 5, 14, 37.

felt it to be, it has been suggested, "an admission of local failure to meet responsibilities", and it was for some while authorized with reluctance.[18]

Many of the wealthier men of the new age felt it incumbent upon them to perform as individual Christians duties that had previously been the immediate concern of the Church. One result of this was the endowment of schools, hospitals, and almshouses, which became so marked a feature of the Tudor and Stuart scene. These private benefactions were made with the utmost care and detail, and the making of a just will was regarded as a Christian duty as well as a social obligation. There is a meticulous document left behind in 1573 by Alexander Dence of Cranbrook, who is chiefly remembered by his provision of an English school for the poor children of the parish. "Being of perfect mynde and whole of remembrance", Dence confessed his sins, left careful instructions for his burial, and bequeathed money and land and clothes to wife and servants and a host of cousins and kinsmen. Then, in addition to a bequest to the school and money for paving the market, he made provision for "the comforte of the poor", in particular for maidens on marriage and "yong folkes to helpe them unto some beginning". And, to crown all, there was to be a dinner every Christmas day "for all the honest householders and farmers", a careful note explaining: "I meane not the poore nor the sick, for they by my will and mynd shall be otherwise provided by my former gifts."[19] Thus confidently Alexander Dence endeavoured to keep an eye on Cranbrook's well-being from the other side of the grave.

While the statutory poor-rate was accepted reluctantly as a necessary evil, the "scot" or "cess" for keeping the church in good repair was a customary levy recognized from medieval times. It was still supplemented on occasion by some of the

[18] W. K. Jordan, *Philanthropy in England*, 1480–1660 (1959), p. 142. Professor Jordan considers that at first only about seven per cent of money expended on the poor came from the statutory rate (ibid., p. 140).

[19] Will of Alexander Dence, 14 Sept. 1573 (Kent Archives Office, Maidstone, P.100/25/1). See below, n. 22.

old customs, such as Church Ales or the collection of Hok-money (a toll levied on a specified day on every passer-by). As the churches began to be furnished with seats a considerable amount was raised by letting out pews, the well-to-do families paying handsomely for good positions in the nave. There were also elaborate scales of burial fees, usually divided between the clerk and the parson, although at St Mary's, Newington, the 13*s*. 4*d*. charged for a burial in the church was kept by the wardens for the use of the parish.[20]

The primary task of the wardens apart from their secular duties was the maintenance of the material fabric of the church. Nails and hinges, tiling and glazing, the upkeep of the clock and bells and the repair of roofs and windows are entries continually repeated in their accounts. In addition, under their guidance, in co-operation and at times in conflict with their minister, the services of the church were conducted, clerk and sexton appointed and kept up to the mark, the pews allotted in due order and bread and wine bought for sacramental use. Moreover on the wardens depended not only the care of the parish property—which might include a herd of cattle as well as a school, an almshouse, or a rickety row of tenements in an overcrowded town—but also the morals of the whole parish. It was they who drew up the answers to the visitation articles and in Southwark on a Sunday morning it was their practice, when divine service had begun, to perambulate Bankside to see which vintners had illegally opened their doors or to track down recusant or sectary who had failed to come to Mattins.

A picture of the wardens at work can be derived more clearly than usual from the collection of Cranbrook records now housed at Maidstone. There is, in particular, one handsome leather volume of accounts that covers the years between the accession of Elizabeth and 1693.[21] It also contains some

[20] St Mary, Newington, Vestry Minutes, 1608–1752, f. 6.

[21] Cranbrook Church Wardens' Accounts, 1509–1694. The book is a solid volume about 2½ in. thick; the entries for the seventeenth century

inventories of the church's possessions, the first dated 1509—before the Reformation. The later inventories make sad reading in comparison. In place of copes of cloth of gold, crosses and chalices of silver and gilt, great brass candlesticks, and fine linen in plenty, they list a table with a cloth and cushion and a silver cup for the Communion, a surplice for the minister, a cushion for the pulpit, two ladders and twelve forms, five great bells and a small one, and a watch bell for the clerk. In addition, in 1604, there were three bibles and four service-books (which was more than most churches possessed) with copies of Foxe's *Acts and Monuments* and of Erasmus's *Paraphrases*, as the injunctions required. At St Mary's, Newington, the account-books contain an annual inventory, and one realizes how much remained the same through all the changes of the mid-century as successive wardens enter such items as "corselet, pike and musket" as well as the green communion cloth "fringed with green silk" which continued in use, come war, come revolution, till in the 1670s it was replaced by purple and gold.

The bells that Cranbrook listed so carefully ranked high in the scale of their possessions, for change-ringing was an art deeply rooted in the habits of the English countryside, and the purchase of a new rope and clappers, regular oiling, and occasional recasting were recurring items in all parochial accounts. Fortunately, neither the Precisians of 1559 nor the Puritans a century later made any attempt to silence the bells, even though Bunyan renounced, for the sake of his soul, the pleasure of ringing them, and every occasion of national rejoicing, from the discovery of Gunpowder treason in 1605 to the marriage of the Protector's daughter in 1657, was celebrated at Cranbrook by a peal of bells, answered triumphantly from every village of the Weald.

---

begin on f. 103d with the record of the election of the parish clerk, and cover the whole of the century. The 1509 inventory is printed in *Archaeologia Cantiana* (Vol. XLI, p. 57), ed. Aymer Vallance. See also W. Tarbutt, *The Annals of Cranbrook Church* (1870–5).

The receipts and expenditure of an average parish approximated to £30 a year and any deficiency (a frequent occurrence) was met by the wardens out of their own pockets and refunded —or not—in the year to come. Regular expenditure included the normal outlay on church repairs, the wages of clerk and sexton and the purchase of the sacramental bread and wine. There were also the expenses of the visitation, the cost of drawing up bills of presentment and the "charges at Canterbury" or other place of meeting. The Cranbrook accounts also contain occasional payments for the "writing up of the registers" and miscellaneous entries such as the purchase of a quire of paper, of lime "for destroying birds in church" and in 1606 for a "Book for the Kinges Ma^ties^ late delivery from the treason". In April 1622 there is a memorandum to the effect that the "teacher of the English free school" shall be allowed 12*d.* a quarter towards the maintenance of every boy he taught, "which was intended by the first donor to the end he may give the better attendance to his scholars".[22] There were no large items such as the salary of a lecturer, which figured frequently in the accounts of city churches; nor was there, in the country, the same amount of parish property to be looked after as there was in London and the crowded suburbs. Yet more than £100 was dispensed annually by Cranbrook's overseers of the poor.

There were, of course, variations in every parish. At Headcorn three assessments were made yearly, one for necessary repairs and furnishings of the church, one for the sacramental bread and wine, and one for the statutory county payments, handed over by the constable at the quarter-sessions. In 1638 over a hundred individuals contributed to the first rate assessed on their holdings of land, paying 1½*d.* an acre and raising over £20. An average of rather more than £2 was required for

[22] Cranbrook Church Wardens' Accounts, 2 April 1622, and cf. W. Tarbutt, *An Historical Account of Dence's School and Schoolmasters* (1866) for the story of the school's troubled beginnings and the loss of its endowments.

hospitals, prisoners, and maimed soldiers; about £2 10*s*. was raised for the bread and wine in payments varying from 1*d*. to 8*d*. a person.[23] The amount expended on bread and wine in many of these churches seems to have been in some such proportion as an eighth, less or more, of the church expenses. According to the rubric, wine not consumed and not yet consecrated went to the incumbent for his private use, so an over-large supply might be a way of adding to the Easter offering. To permit all parishioners to receive the sacrament at Easter three or four services were held, on Palm Sunday and the first Sunday after the festival and on Maundy Thursday and Good Friday as well as on Easter Day itself. The ideal of a monthly Communion was only established by degrees with the wider spread of High Church practices. Cranbrook, although a centre of Nonconformity, had a Laudian rector, one of the dispossessed in 1643, and during the thirties there were nine or ten celebrations in a year (three of them probably at Easter). These Kent clothing towns, during the fourteenth and fifteenth centuries, had enjoyed much prosperity, mirrored in their ancient churches; that at Cranbrook had been enlarged and almost entirely rebuilt by Tudor times, while at Headcorn large sums were expended periodically for buying and laying shingles to keep the lovely roof in good repair. Headcorn had also a particularly fine crop of charities, from the "two Kyne" bequeathed about 1618 for the use of the poor by John Reader, yeoman, to the legacy of £5 in 1701 which provided for two sermons annually, with a gift of 40*s*. on each occasion to the poor who came to hear the sermon. There was £5 also for the Vicars of Headcorn "so long as the world shall endure".[24]

A good all-round picture of the way things were run in a less prosperous area emerges from the records of St Mary, Newington, a busy parish just beyond the bounds of the

23 Headcorn Church Wardens' Accounts, 1637 et seq. (Kent Archives Office, Maidstone, P.181/4/1).

24 Headcorn Records (Kent Archives Office, Maidstone, P.181/25/1–6).

Borough, south-west of London Bridge.[25] Through the heart of the parish ran the Portsmouth road, the Stane Street of Roman times; it was a meeting-place of wayfarers converging on the City, a haunt of malefactors, a breeding-place of overcrowded tenements, and its theatre was the first stop out of London for travelling players from Clerkenwell or Bankside. It had more than its fair share of problems, both of a social and a religious nature, and the vestry minutes note in 1609 that by long experience it had been found "that there is a great inconvenience continually incident to the gentlemen inhabitant in the parish . . . concerning the office of churchwardenship which falleth so oft upon them". It was thereupon agreed that the wardens should be chosen in rotation and abide in office for two years, "this order being made neither in prejudice of the canon nor of the priviledge of the parson". This meant in practice that the minister put forward two nominations and the retiring churchwardens did likewise, and from these a final choice was made. (In 1632 both the wardens eventually elected were nominated by the parson, none of the wardens' nominees being chosen, but usually it was a representative from each group.) No method of choice, however, could make the office palatable, and in 1631, when Richard Cooper was chosen for the second time, he "wilfully" refused to take office, "for the which offence and other ill carriages he was putt ot of the vestry".

In the year after Cooper's disgrace the accounts open with a note of £1 spent on the visitation dinner and of £6 on the perambulation, followed by details of money expended on mending pews. Then comes the item: "Laid out at the Assizes at Kingston for staying an indictment concerning the highways, for our charges: 8*s.* 0*d.*" One entry reads: "Paid Mr Cooke for four several fines entreated against the parish

[25] There are two account books covering the seventeenth century (1632–1657; 1657–1705) and two sets of vestry minutes of St Mary, Newington, housed at the Southwark Central Library, Walworth Road, S.E.1. The first of the minute-books is mainly lists of officials, 1583–1740. The parallel volume contains memoranda and notes of vestry minutes, 1608–1752.

7

concerning the highways £2 16*s*. 8*d*." Another large item of expenditure was £1 13*s*. for "mendinge the well in Newington which the parish stood presented for", while 8*s*. 6*d*. was spent on repairing "the stone bridge by the almshouses", and as much as £5 for "the new fence on the north side of the Churchyard next the Parsonage House". With so many problems to tackle, the chances are that Richard Cooper did not regret that he had been put out of the vestry!

The accounts include each year a list of the outgoings—entries similar to those of other parishes, with such varied items as "Bread and beer which the workman had, 1*s*. 8*d*." or "Box and files for bonds and papers, 3*s*. 7*d*." After a list of church expenses came a detailed list of payments for the use of the poor; pensions and allowances of every sort, which in 1632 filled 6½ pages of the account book and totalled £44 14*s*. 9*d*. The disbursements for the church's general expenses in this year were £46 3*s*. Previous to the lists of expenses came details of the receipts, again divided into the two sections, those for the church in this year totalling £38 16*s*. 10*d*. while £75 11*s*. 11*d*. was received for the use of the poor. The churchwardens, however, did not scruple to regard the combined receipts of £114 8*s*. 9*d*. as their income for all purposes, a procedure, one would have thought, of doubtful legality. They deducted the combined expenditure of £90 17*s*. 9*d*. and noted "Soe there remaineth in stock and is wholy for the use of the poor £23 11*s*. 0*d*." This was an expensive year: in 1633 receipts were £87 odd and expenditure £67, but thereafter the balance dwindled till it was frequently a deficit. The receipts for the use of the church included burial fees and the hiring out of the hearse cloth (£3), money from pews, donations from individual parishioners and special assessments for repairs either of the church or of parish property such as the all-important well. The receipts for the use of the poor included a levy of one penny a week on a rental of £5, paid by the landlords of poor tenements, as well as special items such as the 6*s*. 8*d*. received from the sheriff "being a fine

sett upon a brewer at the sessions" and a similar sum paid by Abraham Bradway "upon his licence for the eating of flesh". The parish also received a regular payment from the county; and in response to a petition in 1612–13 for help for their poor they were allowed £15 yearly from districts including Kingston, Reigate, Godalming, and Farnham.[26]

Though the records are full of illuminating detail, they throw little light on the spiritual state of the parish and fail to show, except on rare occasions, to what extent the man in the pew was conscious of Calvinist theology or Arminian modes of worship or how far his attitude depended on his family background or his personal liking of the parson. Only occasionally does a dispute between the minister and the vestry, a discussion on the choice of lecturers or the character of individual bequests, throw light on the principles or prejudices of the incumbent or of leading members of the congregation.

The trouble was seldom so serious as that which caused the vestry of St Stephen's, Coleman Street, to complain to the Bishop of their vicar, recording "the dislike which they conceive of the conversation and negligence in his ministry, charging of his parishioners with continual calumnies in pulpit and out".[27] Sometimes there was an unexpected stir, as at Bletchingley, toward the end of King James's reign, when the vicar preached a disrespectful sermon on the method of electing M.P.s, and after a scolding at the bar of the House was ordered to confess his fault in the pulpit of the parish church "on Sunday seven night, before the sermon". But such occasions were unusual. When all went well, even the name of the incumbent does not always appear in the vestry minutes, though it can be found in the registers and the imagination has scope to play with the varied clerical signatures, the crabbed scholarly hand of one who wrote always in Latin, the

[26] St Mary, Newington, Vestry Minutes, 1608–1752, ff. 16–19.

[27] E. Freshfield, *History of the Parish of St Stephen, Coleman Street* (1887), p. 6.

flamboyant scrawl of another, the formal rotundity of a third. The centuries have not changed the pattern of English life enough to make one doubt his influence in the parish. On the secular front, the parson's learning, scanty though it might be, would enable him to guide and advise the wardens and overseers in their many administrative duties.[28] Nor is evidence lacking, in the pages of Fuller or in their own writings or the diaries of the time, of the spiritual leadership that the best men of both parties gave to their people in quiet as in stormy days. Fuller records in 1623 the death in his seventies of Henry Copinger, for forty-five years the "painful parson of Lavenham", who had set himself to ease and not to embitter differences of opinion among his nine hundred communicants and had never failed in his purpose. Arthur Hildersham, forty years minister of Ashby-de-la-Zouch, was of less peaceable mould, and his strong views on the subject of separatism earned him the title of "hammer of schismatics". But he won more lasting fame by his treatises and letters, "touching cases of conscience", which showed that he understood his parishioners' need for spiritual guidance and pastoral care such as the Roman Catholic received in confession but which was lacking in the usual Protestant approach. It was the work of such as Hildersham, carried on later by men as diverse in their ecclesiastical politics as Robert Sanderson, Jeremy Taylor, and Richard Baxter, which did something to create a canon of Protestant casuistry, one of the most valuable lines of development in the contemporary Church.

The requirements of an ideal priest are outlined in the thirty-fourth Canon, which declared that every young man before he was made deacon should have reached the age of 23 and have obtained a university degree. He should be "able to yield an account of his faith in Latin" according to the Articles of 1562/3 and to confirm the same "by sufficient testimonies out of the Holy Scriptures". Moreover he must present a testimonial of his "good life and conversation" signed by

[28] Cf. Trotter, *Seventeenth Century Life in the Country Parish*, p. 50.

his college tutors or by "three or four grave ministers". Many of the young men who later obtained good livings in the cathedral cities or in London and the large towns no doubt fulfilled these requirements, but the disparity between the ideal and the actual was painfully apparent—between the scholarly, sometimes too academic occupant of the better cure and the poor vicar who might be saint or might be wastrel. Too many parallels could still be found, in the remoter parts, to Baxter's doleful picture of the Shropshire of his youth. At the village of his birth, he recalled, there were "four readers successively in six years time, ignorant men and two of them immoral in their lives"; at Eaton Constantine an old man of eighty with failing eyesight had charge of two parishes twenty miles apart. One of these he eventually handed over to a kinsman, who thereupon took orders, having hitherto been famed as "the excellentest stage-player in all the country, and a good gamester". Baxter added that there were "three or four constant, competent preachers" in the neighbourhood but any who went to hear them "was made the derision of the vulgar rabble under the odious name of a Puritan".[29] Baxter was born in 1615 and it was still true that, at that time, the better type of clergy usually had Puritan sympathies. With the spread of Arminian ideas in the parishes the balance was rectified; how rich the result, when the best of both schools was combined in one person, the ministry of George Herbert showed in abundance.

The average country priest lived a life in outward form not greatly different from his parishioners, farming his glebe and dependent like them on the work of his hands and the changes of wind and weather. Sometimes there were quarrels about tithes: a greedy or too pernickety parson might complain that the pile of hay left for him had rotted in the fields, or an irascible farmer refuse him the right to drive through the farmyard to collect it. How to assess a tenth if a cottager possessed half-a-dozen lambs, and whether or not one paid for

[29] R. Baxter, *Autobiography* (Everyman edn), pp. 3 f.

garden produce—many such queries abounded, to be answered, not always logically, according to the custom of the parish.[30] John Earle in his character of the Grave Divine described him as being one who would not "wrangle for the odd egg". When there was no altercation, the joint concern of priest and people in the affairs of the countryside had its advantages and avoided the lack of contact in matters of daily living, so tragically common in modern times.

The members of the congregation varied as much as their pastor: the extremists on either wing found their way into the consistory courts; some cared as little as their descendants for churchgoing, others carried inkhorns with them to make précis of the sermons. A few were akin to "Mr Ashton, a conformable citizen" whose epitaph Crashaw wrote, describing him as:

> One whose conscience was a thing
> That troubled neither church nor King . . .
> Sermons he heard though not so many
> As left no time to practise any.

At the beginning of the century there was one outstanding blueprint for the devout layman in Lewis Bayly's *Practice of Piety*, the devotional manual which every good magistrate was said to have on his bedside table alongside Dalton's treatise on the law, and which Bunyan's young wife brought with her when she married—one of the only two books she possessed besides the Bible. Bayly's vigorous account of Judgement Day goes far to explain the terror which obsessed Bunyan in the early days of his conversion, and the conviction and fear of Hell shared so widely by Christians of all sorts is as much a part of the picture of Stuart England as the serenity of Herbert or the deep charity of Andrewes' intercessions.

*The Practice of Piety* grew out of the sermons which Bayly had delivered every Sunday as vicar of Evesham, teaching the

[30] D. M. Barratt, "The Condition of the Parish Clergy between the Reformation and 1660", pp. 228, 322 et al. (thesis in the Bodleian Library).

Christian way of life in one of the twin churches that stand above the Avon in the abbey's ruined grounds. Prince Henry met him at Evesham when he passed through the town as President of the Council of Wales, and later made him one of his chaplains. It was then that Bayly wrote up his sermons, although in his most sanguine mood he could not have foreseen the success that awaited them. The book reached its third edition by 1612, its eleventh by 1619 and so continued through the centuries, until a seventy-fifth was published in 1842. For in every generation there were Christians in need of the guidance Bayly supplied as he counselled his readers to begin the day with prayer, to read their Bible, to meditate at eventide, and to beware in particular of a discontented mind, if they hoped each day to walk with God. He had much of true value to say of public worship and of the Communion service in particular, with many a shrewd aside such as the comment "in the multitude of opinions most men have almost lost the practice of true religion". In the same spirit he wrote: "It is . . . an ignorant pride for a man to think his own private prayers more effectual than the public prayers of the whole Church, . . . therefore . . . (for the avoiding of scandal, the continuance of charity and in testimony of thine obedience) conform thyself to the manner of the Church wherein thou livest."

On one matter, however, Bayly would not compromise, on the keeping of the sabbath, and one sympathizes with the people of Tiverton, whose town was twice burnt down by fire and who found their relief fund suffered from Bayly's strictures, for he regarded their calamities as a direct punishment for the sabbath-day activities that resulted from preparing for the weekly market on a Monday. "God grant them grace when it is next built to change their market-day." Bayly listed "riding abroad for profit or for pleasure, studying any books of science, gross feeding and talking about worldly things" as alien to the sabbath's proper uses, as well as the womenfolk "trimming, painting, and pampering of themselves". Instead

it was to be a day of quiet worship in which the good Christian went reverently to Mattins, listened gratefully to the sermon, gave freely and without grudging if there were a collection for the poor, stayed if there were a baptism to "behold it with all reverent attention" and, if it were Communion day, drew near to the Lord's table "in the wedding garment of a faithful and penitent heart". After dinner, the family was examined on the contents of the sermon; "commend those that do well, yet discourage not them whose memories or capacities are weaker". Later, after Evening Prayer, he permitted "a walk in the fields to meditate upon the works of God", and, "if any neighbour be sick or in any heaviness, go to visit him; if any be fallen at variance, help to reconcile them".[31]

Bayly was made Bishop of Bangor in 1616, but he was soon in disfavour at court, for his sabbatarianism as well as for his zeal for the Bohemian adventure. On one occasion his Celtic temperament got so out of hand that he embarked on an argument with King James, and found himself in the Fleet in consequence. He was reprimanded by his ecclesiastical superiors and allowed to go home, and he was naïvely pleased, when he came up to London for Charles's coronation, that everyone was kind to him and that when he called upon Buckingham he was invited to dine. None the less he was never promoted, for Laud had as little sympathy with his frailties, which were many, as with his moderation, which was a virtue. At the end of his life, in 1630, he was again in trouble for ill-discipline in his diocese, and wrote to the King in justification, listing his activities probably in answer to specific questions.[32] He declared that he had spent £600 on the repair of his cathedral, "planted grave and learned preachers" throughout the diocese and "suffered none to preach but such as were

[31] Lewis Bayly, *The Practice of Piety* (edn of 1842), pp. 91–4, 183, 197, 202 et al. For Bayly, see also John E. Bailey, *Bishop Lewis Bayly and his Practice of Piety: a page in the history of Evesham* (1911).

[32] *Cal. S.P. Dom. 1629–31*, p. 230 (Bayly to the King, 7 April 1630).

conformable". He had preached himself, he said, every Sunday while his health permitted. Catechizing, on which the Anglican authorities laid such stress as a reliable method of instruction, had been duly and regularly observed and he had also, he averred, taken pains in visiting and confirming, and had held synods of his clergy where they gave him an account of "every man's life and doctrine". He and his clergy had provided armour for a hundred men, ready for the King's service, and he was keeping hospitality beyond his means. Such duties, well or ill performed, with all they implied of pastoral care and social responsibility fell to the Bishop's lot, and were as much a part of the picture of the Church in action as was the member of the vestry at the other end of the scale, making his mark or scrawling his illegible signature at the close of the parish meeting.

# 4

# LAUDIAN RÉGIME

In the early years of the reign of Charles I the cleavage both in Church and State was intensified beyond repair against the background of a disastrous war and the coming of a Roman Catholic queen. Charles was married by proxy to Henrietta Maria, the young sister of the King of France, within a month of his accession. The marriage treaty negotiated in the late King's reign contained a secret clause in favour of the recusants, in spite of an undertaking James had given that there should be no such concessions. It did not make it easy for Charles when the Parliament he had eagerly summoned to finance his war with Spain urged that the penal laws should be enforced and granted only an inadequate supply. The debates at Westminster were hurried and anxious, for an outbreak of plague was again sweeping the London streets. Tempers were not improved by the arrival of the young Queen, for she came attended by a bevy of French ladies and a strong complement of Roman priests. The knowledge that English ships loaned to the French king had been used against the Huguenots of La Rochelle further angered the Commons, and when they reassembled at Oxford after a brief adjournment, they found a scapegoat in Buckingham and refused further supplies unless his monopoly of power was ended. Charles in reply dissolved the Parliament, and so within the first six months of his reign the hope of accord had gone.

Religious controversy had played its part in the sorry story. The case of Richard Montagu was outstanding from the previous reign and the Commons had lost no time in giving it their attention. As Archdeacon of Hereford and canon of

Windsor, rector of Stanford Rivers in Essex and afterwards of Petworth, Montagu went some way to justify the gibe which George Morley made in later years. When someone asked Morley what the Arminians held, his reply came pat: "The best livings in England." Montagu's preferments had at least been the reward for much scholarly work; as a young man he had been one of the team collaborating with Sir Henry Savile in his great edition of the writings of St Chrysostom. He possessed in addition to scholarship the gift of lucid and witty exposition and for some time he had been devoting himself to controversy, hoping, as he put it in a private letter, to stand in the gap "against puritanism and popery, the Scylla and Charybdis of ancient piety". Finding that some Jesuits were busy in his parish he challenged them to state their case and replied to their pamphlet, scornfully labelled *A Gag for the New Gospell*, with a tract in like vein, *A New Gag for an Old Goose*.[1]

Montagu's statement of the Anglican position was soundly based on the teaching of Andrewes, but his manner was provocative; "very sharp the nib of his pen", commented Fuller, "and much gall in his ink", and although the tract had been primarily intended for the Romanists, it offended the Puritans equally by its admission that Rome was in essence part of the true Church. In 1624 the Commons committed the book to the attention of Abbot, but meanwhile Montagu took the initiative and in his *Appello Caesarem* he not only amplified his views but appealed to the Crown over the heads of Archbishop and Parliament alike. It was for this contempt of authority that Charles's House of Commons summoned him before them in plague-stricken Westminster and committed him to the custody of the Serjeant at Arms. Charles, vainly hoping to protect him, announced that he was a royal chaplain and that he, the King, was not pleased with the action of his Commons, a statement which did not ease the situation.

[1] See article in *D.N.B.*; Fuller, *Worthies*, ed. J. Freeman (1952), pp. 43 f, *Church History*, VI.15, and cf. *An appeal of the orthodox ministers against R. Montagu* (1641).

The Serjeant, however, allowed Montagu to go down to Petworth on bail, where he fell sick, and although he was summoned to attend at Oxford his plea of illness was accepted and the matter was left in abeyance.

The arid story of religious dispute springs to life in the letters which Montagu wrote to his friend John Cosin, who had been Overall's librarian at Lichfield and was at this stage domestic chaplain to Neile, the Bishop of Durham, whose chaplain Laud had also been in earlier days. At Durham House, in the years before 1627, there were quarters reserved for Laud and Buckeridge, the Bishop of Rochester, whenever they were in town, and the great palace in the Strand became the meeting-place of the Arminian divines, where their viewpoint was developed and adopted as a considered statement of Anglican teaching. Cosin was a familiar figure at their gatherings, and to the older men there was something very attractive in his robust and handsome person, matched to an equally robust and intelligent mind, and they easily forgave his occasional aggressiveness. He belonged to a younger generation than Montagu and Laud; his biographer was able to describe his parents as born and bred in the Anglican faith. They were prominent citizens of Norwich, and Cosin had imbibed from them a knowledge and love of his church and a certain East Anglian stubbornness in defending it. His connection with Bishop Overall had given him a specialized knowledge of liturgical worship, and he had two particular enthusiams of his own, a love of books, both their contents and their format, and a delight in ritual, expressed in music and colour and, above all, in light. Laud turned to him for advice as to the ceremonial to be used at King Charles's coronation and the pattern Cosin set has been followed to this day.[2]

Richard Montagu wrote to Cosin as "dear Jhon" [*sic*], his

[2] See P. H. Osmond, *A Life of John Cosin* (1913), and *The Correspondence of John Cosin*, Part I (Surtees Society, No. 52; 1869). Cosin's *Works* are published in *The Library of Anglo-Catholic Theology* in five volumes, ed. J. Sansome (1843–55).

pages full of phrases in dog-Latin and vivid outlandish words, and every now and again Montagu the man appears behind the figure of the sharp-tongued scholar. When his little girl, Moll, is seriously ill at Petworth he is distracted and asks Cosin's help. "If you can meet with Sir William Paddy [the King's doctor] remember me to him, and desire his advise what to do. We have no phisitions in theise parts worth a beane." Sir William obliged with a prescription, but meanwhile Mrs Montagu had been over to Chichester and secured the help of a local doctor, "Mr Buttler", under whose care the little girl improved. It was during this domestic crisis that Montagu was writing the *Appello Caesarem*, only able to work by snatches in his anxiety. He sent the book to Cosin, to suggest a title and make any alteration he wished, a remarkable tribute to his confidence in the younger man. He himself was intensely anxious about the future. In January 1625 he wrote, only half in jest, of his canonry at Windsor, that he meant to keep it for his old age and he wished "Jhon" could get a reversion, that "we may lay our bones together therein in my grave . . . that if P[uritanism] over-sway they may digg us both up". After Charles's accession, when the new Parliament assembled, Montagu foresaw an attack on the bishops. "I feare I shall live to see their rochetts pull'd over their eares", he wrote and by July, when it is he upon whom the Commons have concentrated their displeasure, he talked of a plot and burnt Cosin's letters, sending word to him to do likewise. He was not as brave a man as he thought a year earlier, and as talk of another Parliament ensued he could see no way to safety except a bishopric, which would remove him to the jurisdiction of the Upper House where at least they knew how to behave.[3]

Cosin was not the sort of man who burnt letters for safety, so Montagu's side of the correspondence survives. Cosin had recently been appointed by Neile to a stall in Durham Cathedral and made Archdeacon of the East Riding of

[3] Cosin, *Correspondence*, I.25 ff, 48 f, 75, 79, 103.

Yorkshire. He was in London in February 1626, the month of the Coronation and of the assembly of Charles's second Parliament, for he took a leading part in a meeting at York House, Buckingham's London home, where the subject under discussion was Montagu and his writings. It was a full-dress theological debate, over which Buckingham presided with considerable ability. The Bishop of Rochester, the Dean of Carlisle, and Cosin defended Montagu's Arminian views, while the Calvinist objections were put by Bishop Morton and John Preston, the Puritan Master of Emmanuel, to whose preaching and personality Buckingham had recently been much attracted. What was behind the Duke's flirtation with Puritanism remains something of a mystery though it had begun naturally enough during the temporary alliance with Parliament at the close of the previous reign. Preston was brilliant and Buckingham had the idea that he would make a good Lord Keeper in place of Williams. But King Charles's growing interest in and liking for the Arminian school damped the Duke's enthusiasm, and the York House debate showed that the interlude was already over. Morton, who bore the brunt of the discussion, was not at his best in theological dispute and the sense of the meeting was clearly against him. The zeal and adequacy, enlivened with occasional flippancy, with which Buckingham and the other lords of the Council listened to and adjudged the niceties of the debate is an interesting comment on the absorption of court and people in religious controversy.[4]

It was a dangerous hobby. The last public pronouncement of old Bishop Andrewes, who died this year, was a statement, which Laud and others also signed, expressing agreement with Montagu's opinions but urging the King to prohibit "any further controverting of these questions by public preaching or writing". In the same month the new Parliament met and Laud, in his opening sermon, took as his text: "Jerusalem is

[4] Cosin, *Works*, II.19–81. For Preston and his influence on Puritan thought, cf. Christopher Hill, *Puritanism and Revolution*, pp. 239–74.

builded as a city that is at unity in itself." That unity could only come through concord between church and state. "For the Church cannot dwell but in the state", he said, " . . . And the Commonwealth cannot flourish without the Church." Laud regarded society as one organic whole; yet to many of his hearers the words seemed mere hypocrisy, for in this very Parliament more seeds of disunity were sown. The Commons were sullen in the knowledge that some of their former leaders had been excluded by the shabby trick of pricking them for sheriffs, while in the House of Lords Bishop Williams among others had been forbidden to attend.

Williams was a rival whom Laud could never learn to treat with Christian charity. He could have afforded to be generous, for it was clear that in the duel between them he had won. Charles had nothing in common with the brilliant, worldly, unreliable Welshman. King James had loved to match his tongue against Williams' dialectical skill, but Charles, not apt in speech himself, distrusted his volubility and the ease with which he moved about the court. In October 1625 he had been relieved of the Great Seal, the advice he had given in the first Parliament not being palatable. He had also been advised to retire to his diocese. Now he was ordered to stay away from Westminster, both for the parliamentary session and for the Coronation. He was allowed to keep his beloved deanery, but only if he entrusted the arrangements for the Coronation to one of the prebends. It added salt to the wound that the senior prebend was Laud, though Williams left the choice to the King rather than name him himself before he reluctantly took leave of Whitehall and retired to his episcopal palace at Buckden in Bedfordshire. It must be said to his credit that, just as he had proved a meticulous Lord Keeper, now that the affairs of his diocese were thrust upon his notice he managed them with ability and expedition.

Charles's second Parliament fared no better than the first, for the Spanish war had gone badly and the Commons now prepared to impeach the Duke. Again, to save his friend, the

King dissolved Parliament and, buoyed up by Buckingham's incurable optimism, proceeded without supplies to embark upon even more disastrous undertakings. Relations with France were steadily deteriorating, primarily on account of Charles's cavalier manner in dealing with his treaty obligations but also through an estrangement between himself and the Queen. Henrietta Maria had a will of her own and had refused on religious grounds to attend the Coronation; Charles had responded by packing her priests and her French attendants back to France. Genuine anxiety about the fate of the Huguenots at La Rochelle added to the tension, and before long the countries were openly at war and Buckingham was planning a glorious come-back in the form of a naval expedition to the island of Rhé. It failed completely; and only Buckingham himself was not dismayed but set about fresh naval and military schemes. In March 1628 the third Parliament assembled. It concentrated at first not on the Duke but on the arbitrary actions of the King. In particular Charles had found it necessary to obtain money by means of a forced loan, and the hostility which the leaders of the Commons felt against the Arminian clergy was embittered by the fact that many of the latter had not hesitated to justify the loan in the pulpit and press.

Archbishop Abbot had refused to license one such sermon and as a result had been relieved of his jurisdiction by the offended King, his powers being entrusted to a commission of five bishops. So closely had belief in the royal power become intertwined with the doctrines of the dominant Anglican group that one preacher, Roger Manwaring, declared that a man who refused the loan was "resisting the ordinance of God and receiving to himself damnation". It should in fairness be noted that Bishop Harsnett, an enthusiastic High Churchman, urged the King in the House of Lords to assent to the Petition of Right. But the overriding influence of such men as Manwaring and the continued danger from Buckingham made the redress of specific grievances, such as the

forced loan and arbitrary imprisonment, only half the battle; in proceeding to the wider issues the Commons were logical, albeit ungrateful. Two days after the bells of London rang out in joy because Charles had given assent to the petition, Manwaring was impeached. He was sentenced to a fine of £1000 (never exacted) and imprisonment during the House's pleasure. On 11 June the Commons completed a remonstrance, in which they attacked Buckingham afresh and inveighed against the opinions of Laud and Neile and the favour which Charles showed to the Arminians.[5]

In August Buckingham was murdered. The problems of Arminianism remained. Strangely, after so many years of domination, the Duke's death made little change in the political and religious situation. The war-fever had burnt itself out and negotiations for peace were on foot. The Puritans no longer thought in terms of a Protestant crusade. To the merchant class, from which so many of them came, trading expansion and prosperity were more desirable than a costly war; and in Europe the religious issue was being submerged by the conflict for power between Spain and the France of Cardinal Richelieu. Charles would have liked to help his sister, Elizabeth of Bohemia, who remained with her family in exile in Holland, but at least peace meant that he could do without further supplies and his turbulent Parliament could be dissolved. For turbulent it had certainly proved when it re-assembled in the new year, deeply disturbed by various episcopal appointments, made by the King during the recess, which showed that Charles had no intention of withdrawing his favour from the Arminian party. Richard Montagu had been given his bishopric, when a vacancy occurred at Chichester, and the rich living of Stanford Rivers passed to Manwaring, the man whom the Commons had impeached. A few months earlier Tobie Matthew's long-expected death had enabled the King to transfer the then Bishop of London to

[5] See H. R. Trevor-Roper, *Archbishop Laud* (1940), pp. 83–96, for summary of the events of 1628–9. For Harsnett, cf. Gardiner, *History*, VI.308.

York, and Laud, who had moved from St David's to Bath and Wells only a year previously, now became Bishop of London. He still looked with exasperation to Lambeth, but at least at Fulham he could control the London clergy and keep his finger upon the pulse of affairs at Whitehall.

So insensitive was Charles to the effect of these promotions on the temper of the Commons that he prepared for the new session in optimistic mood. In a genuine attempt to be conciliatory, he recalled Williams and restored Abbot's jurisdiction. To stress his desire for tranquillity, not debate, the Thirty-nine Articles were reissued with a preface, still to-day embodied in the Book of Common Prayer, which ordained that "all further curious search be laid aside". The Articles should be accepted without comment "in their literal and grammatical sense". Yet such was the masterly ambiguity with which they had originally been framed that the Puritans in the House also upheld them as the true standard of faith, if taken "literally"—free from the glosses of "Jesuits and Arminians". The two parties were in fact so hopelessly at loggerheads that, in the Commons, attempts at reasoned arguments soon gave way to violent attacks upon individuals, attempts to prove Montagu's bishopric invalid and to convict Cosin, of all people, of treasonable words because he had said in conversation that there were limits to the royal power in matters spiritual. Cosin was taking his duties seriously as a prebendary of Durham and, although a junior member of the chapter, he had set about improving the beauty of the cathedral's worship, burning innumerable candles and arousing the anger of a fellow prebendary, Peter Smart, who described him as "our young Apollo [who] repaireth the Quire and sets it out gaily with strange Babylonish ornaments".[6] Cosin had also written at the King's request a *Book of Devotions* for the use of the Protestant ladies of the Queen's

6 *The Vanitie and Downfall of superstitious Popish ceremonies, or a Sermon preached in the Cathedral Church of Durham by one Mr Peter Smart* (1628), p. 24. It is prefaced by a vigorous caricature of Cosin's behaviour.

bedchamber, so that they would not be tempted to use the Roman breviaries of their Catholic colleagues. He had based it, not unnaturally under the circumstances, upon the canonical hours, which was quite sufficient to make it anathema to the pamphleteer, Prynne, who called it *Cosin's Cozening Devotions*. It included Cosin's translation of the *Veni Creator*, "Come Holy Ghost, our souls inspire", which was to hearten so many Christians in succeeding generations, but the Puritans' zeal to break every surviving link with the pre-Reformation Church blinded them to beauty, whether of phrase or thought, if clothed in liturgical form. The attack upon Cosin and the fierce sentence upon Manwaring were signs of a rising tide of feeling, near hysteria, which reached its climax in the final scene of the session when Eliot and Holles made their historic gesture of defiance. With Black Rod waiting at the door and the Speaker restrained in the Chair, the Commons put on record their hatred of "Arminian innovations", declaring that anyone who sought to introduce them was guilty of a capital offence. Thus a tragic impasse had been reached in these first four years of the reign. During the next eleven years of the King's personal rule the initiative would rest with the Arminians to show how far their exposition of faith and worship could be regarded as a valid interpretation of the Anglican middle way.

Laud had few graces in temper or person to help him. He was a stout, rubicund little man, of middle-class birth and an irritable temper. He was always in a hurry, stumbling in awkward haste as he descended from his coach or rupturing himself as he swung a book for exercise with too much energy. He was rather like St Paul as he kicked against the pricks, but like him, too, in striving to obey the heavenly vision. As men came to know him better, they learnt to admire his firm grasp of problems, his genuine piety and his readiness to spend himself, and they discovered an unexpected humour and a depth of affection for those who did not vex him. Wentworth

recognized him as a kindred spirit and men such as Hales and Chillingworth gave him their regard. Yet he remained a difficult person to like, unable to imagine himself mistaken or to attribute to others of opposing views an honesty and consistency equal to his own. The diary that Prynne took from him in his captivity and cruelly revealed to the world betrayed the constant bouts of sickness, the troubled dreams, the lonely heart that lay behind his busy search for perfection. It could not so easily tell of the courage and devotion that were equally a part of his dedicated life.[7]

In his love for order and ceremony and his faith in authority he was a man after the King's own heart. Conscious as a youth of physical handicaps and insecure in his personal relationships, Charles found a framework of order and formality a strength and reassurance, and the Anglican way, as Laud preached it, gave him the sense of balance and certainty he required. To an increasing degree, in his measured devotions and his reliance on the Church's support, he found in it a lasting satisfaction that became the strongest and finest emotion of his life.

Yet he did not give to Laud the intimate affection in which their common purpose might have bound them. After Buckingham's death, he never gave his heart entirely to any man. It was in his wife, whom he now came to love in a way that had been far to seek in the first uneasy years, that he found the vitality and gaiety that Buckingham had possessed in abundance and that his own reserved nature lacked. Henrietta Maria had no sympathy with Laud, and they had nothing in common

[7] Laud, *Collected Works*, ed. Bliss (1852), III.131 et seq.; see *Cyprianus Anglicus*, a life of Laud written by his chaplain Peter Heylyn, published in 1668. Laud's *Works* (ed. W. Scott and J. Bliss) appear in seven volumes in the *Library of Anglo-Catholic Theology* (1847–60). While in captivity Laud wrote an account of his *Troubles and Tryal* which came with the *Diary*, after Prynne's death, into Archbishop Sheldon's hands. They were published by Henry Wharton in 1695 and are printed in vols. III and IV of Laud's *Works*. Professor Trevor-Roper's scholarly work remains the standard modern biography, in spite of his lack of sympathy with Laud's religious aims.

save grit and religious faith. As the "Queen's side" came to count in the court set-up, not only as a centre of frivolous intrigue but as a place where the Roman religion was practised with genuine devotion, Laud was aware of a certain isolation, in spite of the King's unwavering support of all he did.

He experienced a similar sense of frustration in the Privy Council, where he was always conscious of the faction which centred round the Lord Treasurer, the Earl of Portland. Closely linked with Portland was Lord Cottington, affable but unreliable—both of them men of the world, not without ability but with standards not above the average. In the day-to-day administration the King had neither interest nor concern, and Laud fretted and fumed at the lack of integrity and the inefficiency which met him on every hand. The man who shared his annoyance and who, had he been on the spot, might have done something about it was Thomas, Lord Wentworth, whose faith in order and discipline was as great as his own. Wentworth had accepted office under the Crown in 1628 and went first to York as Lord President of the North and later to Ireland; Laud wrote to him impatiently of *Lady Mora*, their code word for the Portland clique, and as they corresponded, in spite of differences of age and temperament, they were drawn closely together by their sincerity of purpose and passion for hard work. There was however one difference between them. Wentworth, a member of the Yorkshire gentry, linked by marriage with the family of the Earl of Clare, was on friendly terms with the better element at court, represented among others by the Earls of Bedford and Northumberland. To them Laud was something of an upstart and, without Wentworth to act as go-between, they disliked him, as much for his lack of social graces as for his disturbing ideas in regard to religion and economics.

Even upon the episcopal bench there was the same ambivalence, although Neile was unswervingly loyal and never grudged Laud his success. Second-rate in many ways, Neile

had a warmth of feeling that made him likeable and a brusque outspokenness attractive after the suavities of the court; among so many donnish colleagues, it was refreshing to find one who avowed that he had been flogged too often at Westminster ever to master Latin. He lacked the character and wisdom to give Laud the support and counsel of an elder statesman; but in 1632 at the age of seventy he became Archbishop of York in succession to Harsnett, whom Prynne described as a furious Hildebrand but who had begun slowly enough with the task of combating the Puritans in the north.[8] Through his officials Neile continued the work of restoring order, prosecuting troublemakers and ending, for good or ill, the passive acceptance of Puritanism which had characterized Matthew's long régime. At the same time Laud's hands were strengthened elsewhere by the appointment of other Arminian bishops, and one in particular, Matthew Wren, who went in turn to Hereford, Norwich, and Ely, proved the strong subordinate he needed. But at least until Wren's emergence the outstanding bishops in piety and scholarship remained the three Calvinists, Davenant, keeping as clear as possible of politics, Joseph Hall at Exeter, amenable but not enthusiastic, and Morton who went from Lichfield to Durham in the same year that Neile went to York. In his rôle of Prince-Bishop of the County Palatine, Morton was as ready to assist the King in the transport of troops or timber as in his ecclesiastical duties. His conception of sovereignty was as high as Laud's, but in his nature as well as his theology he differed profoundly. Whereas Laud scolded victims of the High Commission, Morton reasoned with the offenders, though his words, it must be admitted, usually went well above their heads. From Durham he only sent delinquents south as a last resort, refusing to do so, on one occasion when the prisoner was sick, until a horse-litter could be obtained for the journey. It was a personal kindness that

[8] R. A. Marchant, *The Puritans and the Church Courts* (1960), pp. 50 et seq. Monteigne had only lived for a few months after his translation and Harsnett was Archbishop Nov. 1629–May 1631.

was typical of him. His favourite remedy for insubordinate ministers was to set them to work in remote parts: thus he sent Anthony Lapthorne from Lichfield to Cannock Chase, "the most profane and barbarous parish within that diocese". When Lapthorne turned up in Durham later, Morton repeated the treatment, dispatching him to a Northumberland parish where there had been no preacher of any sort for forty years and one churchwarden did not even know the Lord's Prayer. There Lapthorne's labours were "not unprofitable".[9]

There remained Abbot and John Williams, the former effectively barring Laud's way to full control, Williams still figuring in his uneasy dreams, appearing in chains in one such nocturnal visitation, only to loose himself, leap on a horse and ride away and, recorded Laud, "I could not overtake him". But in reality he had overtaken him. After the collapse of 1629 Williams had again been relegated to his diocese, but not content to leave him there Laud instigated a Star Chamber suit against him on a flimsy charge of revealing counsels of State. The case hung fire, lapsed, and was renewed, at which stage Williams ruined his own chances by suborning witnesses. In the intervening years, in princely retirement at Buckden, he exercised hospitality, encouraged scholarship, and supervised the dignified worship of his chapel. But it did not escape Laud's notice that various noblemen sent their sons to be educated at Buckden, and if the Star Chamber suit hung over Williams' head like a sword of Damocles during these years, so in the background of his rival's anxious mind there was always the consciousness of the large diocese of Lincoln, where insubordinates were unlikely to be harried and Puritan lecturers enunciated the Word of God with more regard to the gospel of Bishop Williams than to that of Bishop Laud.

Laud had two principal objectives. The first and most practical was to silence dispute, whether in press or pulpit or in vestry meeting, and to impose uniformity in external modes of worship; by these means he hoped to inculcate habits of

[9] *Cal. S.P. Dom. 1638–9*, pp. 434 f (*c.* 7 Feb. 1639/40).

unity which would produce, by degrees, unity of the spirit. Secondly, he hoped to restore the Church to the position of pre-eminence which it had held in medieval days. This colossal task had many aspects. It meant among other things that churchmen should take their place among the King's chief advisers in Privy Council and offices of State and, in consequence, Laud was himself increasingly involved in secular politics, although to what extent is a little uncertain. Yet at least there was no denial of responsibility, no belief that a Christian in a sacramental world could rest content with personal piety, unconcerned with the welfare of the State. For to Laud the State, like the Church, was the community, and in the community as he envisaged it each man had his proper place and corresponding duties. Laud had not an analytical mind and probably the nearest he came to expressing the basic pattern of his thought was in his use of the word "thorough" in his letters to Wentworth, but it was the idea of the ordered community which coloured his thinking, with all that it entailed of self-sacrifice and discipline, contrary though it was to the stress on individualism which the Renaissance spirit and Protestant ethic had fostered.[10]

In the economic sphere, Laud's second objective entailed a putting back of the clock that was in fact impossible. As Bancroft had found before him, any attempt to recover the resources of the Church which had been lost in the Reformation, to reassess tithe so that it provided an adequate income for the lower clergy, to buy in or persuade individuals to restore property alienated from the Church, to remedy to even the slightest degree the many abuses that existed, led only to a combined opposition that was invincible. The Crown and the Universities, the bishops and deans themselves were offenders as often as the lay landlords. In the cities, where personal tithe

[10] A most interesting analysis of the philosophy that underlay Laud's policy is contained in E. C. E. Bourne's *The Anglicanism of William Laud* (1947); see in particular pp. 1–24.

had lapsed, incumbents were often dependent on voluntary gifts if there was no levy on rents. Laud did what he could, inevitably in a piecemeal way, but without fear or favour, defending whenever possible the poorer clergy against their superiors. In a list he jotted down on the fly-leaf of his diary, of things he "projected to do", the majority were ticked off before he fell from power. But two that were still outstanding ran: "To find a way to increase the stipends of poor vicars" and "To see tithes of London settled between clergy and city". How much and how little he accomplished has been described by Christopher Hill in his masterly study of the economic problems of the Laudian Church.[11]

The improvement in numbers and in learning which had been marked since the beginning of the century was maintained in Charles's reign, and Laud did his best to secure that the learning should be matched by devotion by the care he gave to his duties as Chancellor of Oxford, an office to which he succeeded in April 1630 on the death of the Earl of Pembroke. He was elected by a majority of nine votes only over Montgomery, Pembroke's brother and heir, who was much discomfited by his defeat. Laud set himself to discipline the University and to put an end to the excesses in behaviour and slackness in morals which were sapping its intellectual life. The statutes were thoroughly revised, his reforms stretching from the introduction of the examination system to the prohibition of wearing boots and spurs with academic dress. He built a fine new quadrangle at John's and endowed a lectureship in Arabic; but above all he stressed the necessity of sound doctrine and spared no pains in obtaining the right men to teach it. This continued concern for Oxford among all the other duties that filled his crowded days would bear good fruit in the years to come, for these young men were the parish priests of the future, trained in their undergraduate days to

[11] Christopher Hill, *Economic Problems of the Church from Archbishop Whitgift to the Long Parliament* (1956), *passim*; see also R. H. Tawney, *Religion and the Rise of Capitalism* (Pelican edn, 1938), pp. 159–62 et al.

appreciate the true meaning and value, not only of the rules and ceremonies so many of their predecessors had resisted, but of Anglicanism as a way of worship and of life.

So far as his aims were constructive, he thus had a measure of success. There is much of value in the Anglican heritage which survived the tumult of the mid-century only because the work of the scholars—Hooker, Andrewes, Overall—was made part and parcel of the life of the parishes through the practical reforms of Bancroft and Laud. In particular Laud's tolerance in matters of belief gave scope to men of diverse character and outlook to enrich and develop the Anglican faith and make it worthy to endure. But he failed in his hope that the uniformity in behaviour, which he enforced, would breed a deeper unity of the spirit: in this sphere equally, and with less justification, he was putting back the clock. To an even greater degree than his predecessors, he dealt with details of behaviour as he dealt with examples of social injustice, by using the conciliar and the Church courts as legitimate means of control, and whether at Fulham or Lambeth, in the Privy Council or as Chancellor at Oxford, he aimed at conformity and correctitude in an age when the trend of fashion, in science, philosophy, and mercantile adventure, was producing on every hand turbulence of thought and independence of action.

The main outline of events during Laud's tenure of the see of London can be traced in the pages of Thomas Fuller's *Church History*, now concerned with the people and events of his own lifetime and displaying in its comments and emphasis the reactions of a man of exceptional moderation and common sense, though not always an accurate historian. It is significant that his record of the year 1630, after a note of the birth of the Prince of Wales, begins with a reference to the Star Chamber sentence on Dr Leighton for his "railing book" and goes on with some misgivings to write of the Puritan feoffees. Leighton's *Sion's Plea* was a piece of hysterical writing, all but

tantamount to treason, that fifty years earlier might well have been punished by death. None the less his branding and mutilation in the pillory occasioned the first of those scenes of anger and dismay that punctuated the succeeding years and did nothing but harm to the Establishment. If only people would refrain from tendentious speech, Laud argued, such tragedies would not occur. He put a large measure of blame upon the lecturers, appointed to preach in many churches and paid by the congregation. They were thus, he said, "the people's creatures", blowing "the bellows of their sedition".[12] It was not feasible nor desirable to suppress all lecturers, but the bishops had already been instructed to tighten their control and a keen eye was to be kept open for any insubordination. The afternoon lecture was to be replaced by the catechism, and it was laid down that divine service should be read on every occasion when a lecturer preached and that, in order to inculcate a measure of responsibility, lecturers were to wear gowns and hoods "according to their degree".[13] It should be added that when the Master of Trinity, Dr Brooke, wanted to write a book that would crush the Puritans, Laud was equally firm in dissuading him from controversy.

It was this danger of subversive preaching that underlay Laud's antipathy to the feoffees, whom Fuller introduces with the words: "My pen may safely salute them with a God-speed, as neither seeing nor suspecting any danger in the design." They were a group of Londoners, four clergy and a similar number of lawyers and of well-to-do citizens, who raised a fund to buy up livings throughout the country and with the proceeds endowed lectureships and supplied vacant cures with "godly and discreet" ministers. They were, in fact,

[12] G. Tatham, *The Puritans in Power* (1913), p. 19.

[13] Cf. *The Vestry Minute Book of the Parish of St Margaret, Lothbury*, ed. E. Freshfield (1887), p. 65, for the vestry's decision, 15 Jan. 1629/30, to buy their minister, Humphrey Tabor, a hood "at the coste and chardge of the parish", on receiving his report of the Bishop of London's instructions that in catechizing, "decencie to be used therein by the minister &c. in wearing of a hoode according to his degree".

quietly getting ahead on a voluntary basis with the tasks which had defeated Laud, buying back lay impropriations and improving clerical stipends, but it was less personal pique than a genuine fear that impelled Laud, after careful inquiry, to lay a suit against them in the Exchequer Court on the technical ground that they had become a property-owning body without the King's consent. They were admirable and, in the main, moderate men and public opinion was shocked by the official attitude, yet there was something wrong in principle in the irresponsible power their financial control gave them. Laud's inquiries had shown that their ideas of sufficiency and conformity in their nominees did indeed vary greatly from his own, and as the lecturers they appointed answered to them rather than to the diocesan authorities, he had some ground for his alarm at this infiltration of a fifth column into his would-be harmonious Church. The feoffees were suppressed and their funds forfeited to the Crown. Later Charles advanced Richard Sibbes, the distinguished preacher of Gray's Inn and a leader of the group, to be vicar of Trinity Church, Cambridge, and Laud spoke with respect of John Davenport, another feoffee who had slipped away from London in disguise, describing him as "a most religious man who fled to New England for the sake of a good conscience". But the lack of personal animosity did not make the action of officialdom appear any less arbitrary, and in Fuller's words "both discreet and devout men were . . . doleful at the ruin of so pious a project".[14]

[14] Fuller, *Church History*, VI.67 f, 86 f, Hill, op. cit., pp. 252–63; and cf. I. M. Calder, "A 17th century attempt to purify the Anglican church" in *American Historical Review*, liii (July 1948), pp. 760–5. Dr Calder points out that the feoffees have "attained perpetuity" through the trustees of the Marshall's Charity who hold the advowson of Christ Church, Southwark. John Marshall left property to the feoffees in 1627 to build a new church in the south-western part of St Saviour's parish and new trustees were appointed after the Restoration and the church built in 1671. Christ Church is now the headquarters of the South London Industrial Mission. For Sibbes and Davenport see *D.N.B.* and Geoffrey Soden, *Godfrey Goodman, Bishop of Gloucester, 1583–1656* (1953), p. 229.

Scenes in the pillory and the downfall of the feoffees were the things that caught the popular imagination. Yet much of the Bishop of London's time was spent in pastoral work in his diocese and in commending, not coercing. In particular he set about with vigour to put his own cathedral in order. Even the time and energy he spent on the repair of St Paul's provoked a grumble, for some said it were better to destroy than to rebuild a monument of superstition and one Derbyshire villager refused to contribute in the belief that the money went to the King for his own nefarious designs. A commission for the repair of the cathedral had been in existence for some time, but little had been done either in the way of rebuilding or imposing order in the notorious Paul's Walk, which the apprentices used as a quick cut across the City and which the citizens frequented with an ear cocked for the latest scandal. In 1631 a new commission was appointed, retaining Inigo Jones as the architect in charge. Laud promised an annual subscription of £100. The King gave generously and eventually undertook the rebuilding of the west end, which included a great portico that must have sat rather awkwardly on the medieval building but which was intended to provide the citizens with an alternative to Paul's Walk. It took many years to complete, Laud's zeal and energy continuing to be the motive force, but when at last it was finished in 1640 Laud was in prison and all that he stood for under attack.

Akin to his interest in St Paul's was his delight in consecrating, with due ceremony, new or restored churches, using for the purposes the special form of service which Lancelot Andrewes had composed. Even this was not a matter above dispute, and when the Bishop appeared in full canonicals at the doorway of the rebuilt church of St Katharine Cree the onlookers made critical or ribald comment, some muttering of popish practices, some gibing at Laud's undistinguished figure which did not match up to the solemnity of the occasion. Yet if some reviled, with many others the habit of seemly worship steadily grew. The week after St Katharine Cree was

consecrated, Laud conducted a similar service at St Giles-in-the-Fields, rebuilt through the generosity of the lady of the manor. He himself gave a chapel to the outlying village of Hammersmith, while a prosperous farmer of the customs made peace with his conscience by endowing a church at Stanmore Magna and Richard Garth, lord of the manor of Morden, built the church of St Lawrence and restored to it the glebe of which his family stood possessed. Laud's young friend, Viscount Scudamore, in temporary retirement at Holme Lacy perfecting his own brand of cider apple, also had time to meditate on the sin of impropriation, and not only rebuilt his parish church but divested himself of some £50,000 in tithe. Not many would obey Laud's teaching to the extent of such self-sacrifice, but men like Scudamore and Garth serve as constant reminders that the repression of nonconformity was only half the picture.[15]

There was an early example of a general growth in piety across the river at St Saviour's, where, in 1623, the vestry decided to rehabilitate the Lady Chapel, which had been let out to a succession of bakers and befouled and desecrated.[16] In the same year a rich lady of the parish presented a new altar table which the vestry agreed to enclose within a "frame of rails", an innovation which commended itself to High Churchmen as a means of securing a permanent position for the table at the east end, protecting it from unseemly use and making it easier to kneel at the administration of the sacrament.

These were the issues upon which Laud waged his battle for uniformity. He quoted St Giles-in-the-Fields as a pattern parish, where Communion was held once a month, the large congregation kneeling before the holy table which was placed

[15] S. C. Carpenter, *The Church in England, 597–1688* (1954), pp. 377 f, and see pp. 374–97 for a sympathetic sketch of the Laudian régime. For Scudamore see Trevor-Roper, *Archbishop Laud*, pp. 95 f and Appendix, pp. 437–56; and for Garth, David W. Pocock, "Morden Parish Church", included in E. M. Jowett, *History of Merton and Morden*, pp. 71 f.

[16] Vestry Minute Book of St Saviour's Church, 1582–1628, ff. 522, 526.

behind a "decent frame of rails". Not all parishes responded with equal enthusiasm: later, at Canterbury, his vicar-general in his reports coined the horrible phrase "non-kneelants" for those who refused to comply. The vestry minute-books of St Bartholomew Exchange give a glimpse of the problem from the parochial standpoint. Here there was a co-operative parson in Mr (later Dr) Grant who, in the difficult years ahead, developed compromise to a fine art. He had permitted the appointment of a lecturer and allowed the vestry to build pews in the chancel, neither of which actions would have commended him to Laud. But he was generally liked and respected, and there are signs that in 1631 the parish was attempting to order its ways according to the Canons and the instructions of the Bishop. On 20 November a vestry minute runs: "there being present Mr Grant our parson, the two churchwardens, with many of the parish there assembled, there was propounded:

1. That there was a great charge laid upon the churchwardens about the great neglect of coming to morning prayer every Wednesday and Friday.
2. That everyone should kneel during time of divine service.
3. That every master should send his youth to be catechized.
4. That everyone when they came to receive Communion should send their names before to the Clerk.

—Unto all which there was promised conformity."

These provisions were amplified two years later when a certain Jeremy Jones was churchwarden, possibly because they had not led to the desired reformation. On 2 June 1633 his record of the vestry meeting details five items which, he writes, "did nearly concern my oath which I took at my admittance". First he reminded the vestry that "one of every house throughout our parish should repair to our parish church on every Wednesday, Friday and holidays to morning prayer", and

secondly that children and apprentices should be sent to be catechized "every Sunday in the afternoon before evening prayer at the tolling of the first peel according to the canons". These were just more detailed reminders of the previous rulings. Nor was there anything original about the third point, that the "battlements of the church" were much decayed, nor about the decision that a subcommittee of twelve should view the damage. It was the fourth item which was controversial, for when Mr Jones dealt with the administration of the Communion, before giving notice that all who wished to receive it should give in their names on the Saturday afternoon or "on the Sunday in the morning before the second peel", he enjoined them to receive it reverently upon their knees, and continued: "It hath been heretofore propounded to make a decent frame about the Communion table as in diverse churches in the city." And here the record adds: "Some thought it good and fit that such a frame should be made and some were against it." A subcommittee were authorized to view the table and give their considered opinion. Mr Jones seems to have gone ahead, probably without waiting for the subcommittee's report. When he presented his accounts on going out of office next spring, the auditors would not pass them and at a special meeting in June explained that they objected in particular to two items, "the locks and keys upon the pews' doors" and the "expense extraordinary . . . in setting up the frame about the Communion table". Eventually the vestry agreed to pass the accounts under protest, "for quietness sake and to avoid suits in law" and in order that Mr Jones could hand over his balance and the vestry have the ready cash to pay the carpenters and plumbers, who had nearly finished work on the church roof.[17]

It was a good, practical reason for accepting a "Laudian innovation", but other parishes were not as amenable as St Bartholomew Exchange. At St Gregory's under St Paul's,

[17] *Vestry Minute Books of St Bartholomew Exchange*, ed. Freshfield, Part I, pp. 108, 114, 118.

certain members of the congregation appealed to the Court of Arches, citing the Elizabethan injunction which allowed the table to stand in the body of the church during the service of Holy Communion, even if its normal position were at the east end. This typical compromise was quite unpalatable to Charles, who decided to make St Gregory's a test case and to judge it himself. The Elizabethan pronouncement was replaced by one of his own, which laid down that the east-end position should be permanent, though this decision of the Supreme Governor of the Church did not prevent Puritan parishes from continuing as before and bishops such as Williams from conniving at their practices. In other cases authority prevailed and the Headcorn accounts in 1639 include 10*s*. 6*d*. "laid out in expenses at Canterbury when we were cited about the church rayles", and 1*s*. 4*d*. "Paid at Canterbury when I tooke a longer time to rayle in the communion table".

High points of doctrine were involved as well as questions of expediency, and it was in an attempt to be true to these that men of both parties made the most sacred service of the Church a matter of passionate dispute. For the Puritans the emphasis was upon the meal of fellowship, and the protesting parishioners of St Gregory's regarded the Holy Communion as primarily a commemoration of the Last Supper, most suitably celebrated if they sat round the table or in their pews in dedicated friendship. The most precious words in the Liturgy were to them, "Take, eat . . . in remembrance of me"; their greatest fear lest the holy table should become an altar whereon the elements, as the Body and Blood of Christ, should be worshipped in an idolatrous way. But for Laud, also, there was essential dogma involved. The real and spiritual presence of Christ, when the bread and wine were consecrated, was reason enough to kneel in reverent humility to receive his gift of himself, and to Laud the sacrament of Holy Communion was a thanks-offering and a showing forth of Christ's sacrifice upon the Cross, not only a bond of fellowship.

Even on less exalted grounds of decency there were arguments on both sides. The irreverent treatment to which the table was exposed, if it were left in the body of the church, and the inconvenience of constantly moving it were practical reasons for placing it permanently at the east end. Some, however, objected that it spoilt the service, because they could neither see the acts of consecration nor hear the celebrant when he stood with his back towards them. This was the attitude of the congregation at St Peter's, Nottingham, quoted by Dr Marchant in his valuable study of the Puritans in the diocese of York. The dissidents at St Peter's said that the crowd of communicants pressing into the chancel made for disorder and irreverence, and one man had not received the sacrament "because of the throng in the chancell and he could not have any meditacion".[18] There was no answer to the impasse except Christian tolerance, either within the bounds of a comprehensive Church or by the recognition of valid dissent. But the ineluctable choice was as yet barely recognized, certainly not by Laud, still convinced that by a mixture of coercion and persuasion men could be induced to live in peaceful conformity.

While Abbot was still at Canterbury Laud's influence, outside his diocese, was exercised mainly through the conciliar courts, and in the imagination of the people the Star Chamber sentences formed a sinister backcloth to all he did. Yet in spite of the vicious sentences in cases of seditious libel, the records on the whole do not give the impression of tyranny so much as of responsible yet puzzled men endeavouring to cope with a varied assortment of misfits, firebrands, scoundrels, sometimes saints, whose crimes or idiosyncrasies were disturbing the peace of the realm.[19]

Laud, himself, was made passionately indignant by the corruption which some of the cases revealed in Church affairs. There was for instance a grave scandal at Exeter, where a

[18] Marchant, *The Puritans and the Church Courts*, pp. 67 f.

[19] G. Davies, *The Early Stuarts, 1603–60* (1937), pp. 76 f; W. H. Hutton, *The English Church, 1625–1714* (1903), pp. 67–72.

clergyman called Travers, disappointed of a canonry, repaid the dean by accusing him of adultery with his maid. It was "a common fame . . .", Travers said, "in the mouthes not of the meaner sort onlie but of baronetts, Knights, Esquires, Batchelors of Divinity and Women without number". He fanned the flame of rumour, involved members of the chapter, and obtained from the wretched girl a confession, later abjured. The Star Chamber judges were unanimous about the girl: she should be whipped from Cullompton to Exeter while Travers, adjudged to have acted from spite, was to be heavily fined. Most of them placed the fine at £500 but Laud said £1000: because Travers was a churchman. "I will fyne him double whatsoever a lay man shall fyne him." Laud's anger burst out in a passionate speech: "There hath been snapping amongst them both on one side and the other. I made it up betweene them once but they breake out before they came home, out of which hath risen this stincking thing . . . I should not have wondered if it had been by a Papist against a Protestant, or by a schismatick against a regular, but . . . one in the bosome of the Church against another of the same Church . . ." He showed a like concern when vicious or incompetent clerics appeared before the courts (one such was said to practise the art of magic and, in particular, to charm pigs), but he often showed a lack of proportion and seemed as much upset by the unseemly bearing of a priest who turned up in his riding clothes with ruffles almost up to his elbows as with those who haunted alehouses and kept bad company.[20] The hardest of all to deal with were the honest men, whose only crime was inconformity of worship or heretical opinion. On one occasion a number of people were rounded up at a conventicle in Blackfriars, at the house of a brewer's clerk. They were brought before the Court of High Commission with their minister, John Lathrop. Many of them were women and it proved singularly difficult to question them. As Sara Jones, Sara Jacob, Pennina Howse, and the

[20] *Cases in the Courts of Star Chamber and High Commission* (Camden Society, 1886), pp. 153–75, 186, 271 f.

rest quoted scripture in turn, and Lathrop stated with dignity that he had done nothing which had caused him "justly to be brought before the judgement seat of man", the Bishop of London's exasperation grew. His uneasiness appeared in his comment that this little company was "not a fourth part of them about the City" and that they had come from every quarter, and over the river from Southwark.[21] With dissidents within the Church he thought he knew how to deal, but he could not cope with those who were separatists on principle.

After a brief imprisonment and a few uncertain years, John Lathrop and many of the others made their way to Massachusetts, the settlement, half refuge, half trading station, founded successfully to the north of the Pilgrims' original colony. It was in 1630 that John Winthrop, an able East Anglian squire, made up his mind to emigrate, and as Governor of Massachusetts he transformed the precarious settlement into a thriving but certainly not a libertarian state. In the same year Thomas Hooker, who had crossed swords with Laud in London, made his way to Holland and some time later to New England, to settle at length in the new state of Connecticut, while in 1631 from the storm-centre of East Anglia a young man called Roger Williams rode across England to sail the Atlantic, looking for liberty and determined to find it.

Roger Williams was Nonconformity personified and could have settled in no State Church, but when John Winthrop and his friends set sail they spoke of themselves as loyal members still of their "dear mother" the Church of England. Their going meant a loss of spiritual power which Laud recognized and endeavoured to check, but imagination was not the King's strong suit and when Wren reported to Laud that William Bridge, an eminent preacher, had left for Holland rather than

[21] Ibid., pp. 278–81, 292–5; cf. Allen French, *Charles I and the Puritan Upheaval* (1955), pp. 313 f. This is a stimulating study of the causes of the great migration and the conditions in England which occasioned it.

conform, Charles on seeing the dispatch wrote in the margin: "Let him go: We are well rid of him."

Bishop Wren had suspended Bridge and his friend, Jeremiah Burroughs, for their refusal to read from the pulpit the new issue of James I's Declaration of Sports. The *Practice of Piety* shows how deeply sabbatarianism had embedded itself in the Protestant viewpoint, and the Declaration of Sports, which James had issued, had never been popular. Its aim had been to establish order rather than to undermine sabbatarian views, and if it laid down that traditional games were permissible after church on Sunday it stressed that divine service must be observed with reverence and by all. Now the matter was raised again, with the emphasis subtly changed, when the Somerset magistrates forbade the holding of wakes and Church Ales upon the Lord's Day. The prohibition was upheld by Chief Justice Richardson on the western circuit in 1632, partly because of the drunkenness and whoring the occasions often produced; none the less he was summoned to attend the Privy Council, to justify his decision, and there he was soundly berated by Laud for interfering in the affairs of the Church; "almost choked with a pair of lawn sleeves", he complained. On the wider aspects of the question the King was more enlightened than most of his subjects, but by reissuing the *Book of Sports* and ordering it to be read in churches he pinpointed a divergence of principle it had been well to keep in the background. As it was, Fuller could report at a later date that "this abuse of the Lord's day" was considered by many moderate men to be "a principal procurer of God's anger, since poured out on this land in a long and bloody civil war".[22]

Both the test case at St Gregory's and the reissue of the *Book of Sports* occurred after Laud had become Primate: they were signs of a new decisiveness in policy. During the summer of 1633 he went with Charles to Scotland. At Edinburgh the King was crowned in the full liturgical splendour that he and Laud loved so well and the average Scot disliked so intensely,

[22] Fuller, *Church History*, VI.102.

suspicious alike of Popish practices and of all things that came from south of the border. None the less, in his brief and crowded visit, Charles made it clear that he hoped to reorder the worship and ceremonial of the Scottish Church, and the Scottish bishops were instructed to draw up a Liturgy, based on the English Prayer Book, to be sent to the King for his approval.

Shortly after their return from Scotland Abbot died at Croydon. There and in Guildford, his native town, they mourned him deeply; at Whitehall the passing of his detached yet critical presence caused more than a breath of relief. There was no doubt as to his successor. Charles greeted Laud at his next appearance with the words: "My Lord of Canterbury, you are very welcome." The indomitable little man was supreme at last, and for the last time he made the uneasy journey through the cobbled streets from Fulham. His coach and horses, ferried to Lambeth, sank on the way, but neither man nor horse was lost and Laud refused to regard it as an evil omen. He had no illusions, however, about an easy road ahead. He had more imagination and a stronger will than the King. He knew a little of the forces opposed to him, and he knew also that there was little time to spare. For he was not at the beginning of his course; an aging body and an anxious spirit marked him as past his prime when at last, in his sixty-first year, he found himself in command, setting out to consolidate in a few brief years the labours of a lifetime.

As soon as he was established at Lambeth the new Archbishop set on foot a series of visitations, employing, not without reluctance, Abbot's vicar-general, Sir Nathaniel Brent. Brent was a man of independent character (he sided eventually with Parliament) and he was never in the same relationship to Laud as was the latter's secretary, William Dell. In most things Dell remained the Archbishop's right-hand man, but the continued employment of Brent absolves Laud of overt partiality, and the vicar-general worked loyally and

adequately. His reports bring vividly to life the state of the Church in the country at large and illustrate both the large measure of surface conformity that was secured and the difficulty of tracking down much suspected inconformity, when local loyalties ran counter to official policy.

The smouldering hostility between Williams and Laud was stirred up when the latter exercised his right as metropolitan to hold a visitation in the Lincoln diocese, which at this period stretched south to include the county of Buckingham. Among those presented was John Hampden, "for holding a muster in the church yard of Beaconsfield and for going sometimes from his own parish church", but the presentment did not go forward because Hampden gave "so much satisfaction for that which is past, and so much assurance of his willing obedience unto the laws of the Church hereafter".[23] Yet within a year or two, in the church of Great Kimble, on a ridge of the Chiltern hills, Hampden and his neighbours at their parish meeting entered their resolution, refusing to pay ship-money. So much was happening of portent to the future in this quiet countryside. At Great Tew, in the neighbouring county of Oxfordshire, Chillingworth was writing one of the first reasoned defences of toleration to issue from within the Anglican Communion. Within a stone's throw of Beaconsfield, in a tangle of meadow and beech-woods, William Russell, a prosperous farmer, was enlarging his well-built residence at Jordans, unconscious of the fame that would soon come upon it when it nurtured a Quaker congregation. The roots of dissidence went deep indeed, and Laud's hope of unity through surface good behaviour rested on a complete misconception of the forces that were abroad.

As a first stage in this metropolitan visitation, the Archbishop inquired into the state of the cathedrals, with particular reference to the devotions and regular attendance of the chapter. The results were not very heartening. In Salisbury, in particular, there was conflict within the close, one party

[23] *Cal. S.P. Dom. 1634–5*, p. 250 (27 Oct. 1634).

headed by Dr Seward, well-entrenched in his comfortable canonry, and the other by the precentor, Humphrey Henchman, who was distressed by the chapter's "great neglect . . . of coming to morning and evening prayer" and in practising hospitality "according to the ancient, laudable customs of our Church". Most of the canons agreed that the choristers were not well ordered in the art of singing, but Dr Seward answered: "I never knew them better." Dr Seward was said to be the chief culprit in the matter of non-attendance, to which he made excuse: "My house is more remote, the way in winter very fowle, my body weake", and the weather often tempestuous. The canons confessed themselves negligent in their parishes, "defective in preaching at those churches whence we receive rentes and profits", and there was also a certain amount of scandal and tittle-tattle, Dr Seward being again involved. It was an unhappy state of affairs, for in the city outside the close, in this and many another cathedral town, there was a growing number of serious-minded men whose remedy would be to abolish deans and chapters in entirety, as a hundred years earlier effete monasteries had been destroyed. The first essential was to raise the standard of cathedral worship, which at Salisbury was poverty-stricken, the quire "utterly destitute and naked of all Cathedral ornaments", while the copes had been "sold away about sixty-six years since" or made into pulpit cloths and cushions. One canon wrote: "Men both of ye better and meaner sort, mechanicks, youths and prentises do ordinarily and most unreverently walk in our church in ye tyme of devine service and within hearing of ye same with their hattes on their heades, I have seene them from my seate (and not seldome) so walkinge or standinge still and lookinge in on us, when we have byn on our knees at ye Letany and ye commandments."

Perhaps the picture at Salisbury was more gloomy than necessary, for the rift in the chapter led to recrimination. At Exeter, where all had certainly not been well of recent years,

the replies to the questionnaire were favourable if not complacent. Morning Prayer was said at six o'clock on Sundays with a sermon provided at the cost of the city, while at ten o'clock the dean and residentiary canons preached in turn. There were also lectures on Tuesdays and Fridays; the muniments were safely kept, the choristers well-ordered and the church sufficiently repaired, and there dwelt within the precincts "no usurer, drunkard, fornicator, incestuous person, Symonist, openly recusants of either sect or of any other cryme". Some of the ordinary canons complained that the residentiaries monopolized both the wealth and the control of the cathedral. There was only one other flaw in the picture: all the traffic of the busy streets poured across the close, the very heart of the city and of Devon.

At Wells the choristers were taught their catechism by the head of the grammar school but were not as well ordered by the choirmaster as they should be, and the chief trouble with the chapter, here as in other places, was their rooted objection to wearing the canonical head-gear. Repeatedly Laud's officials had to note in the margin "let caps be worn", as well as gowns and hoods. So the answers continued to come in, revealing in each cathedral in different degree the dangers of non-residence, of strained relations with the city, and of personal animosities. At Bristol it was the common practice of Mr Mayor to arrive at church in time to hear the sermon, and, if he came too soon, for divine service to break off abruptly on his arrival; if late, for priest and congregation to await his coming before the sermon began. The marginal note here runs, not surprisingly: "I like neither of these two and require that both be remedyed." Permanent seats set up for the use of the mayor and corporation and their wives had so filled the nave that "neither knight nor esquire, lady nor gentlewoman had any proper place where to heare the sermon". This complaint came to the ears of the King, who commanded that the seats should be taken down and movable ones put in their place. As at Exeter there was a traffic problem,

and the chapter reported that their pleasant middle walk had become a "common highway for drays".[24]

In the course of the metropolitan visitation of 1635 Brent surveyed the whole of the province of Canterbury, travelling to Norwich and King's Lynn in April, thence to St Edmundsbury and Peterborough, across the Midlands to Lichfield and Shrewsbury and back to Stafford and Derby. At the end of May he was in Coventry, then west again to Worcester, Stratford, Gloucester, and Moreton-in-the-Marsh, and turning homeward by Winchester and Chichester he reached Kingston in July and completed the tour at Southwark on the 14th.[25] If many things were found to be awry, he could usually report a measure of submission, though it is not apparent how far this led to a real change of heart once the Archbishop's official had passed on to the next place of call. Shortcomings were frequently attributed to lack of money. "There are no copes. They are willing to buy some, but protest they are exceeding poor", so they said at Chichester. On other occasions ignorance rather than poverty was the excuse. At Northampton, Brent noticed, "in time of divine service many put on their hats at morning prayer, but in the afternoon (having marked what I did in the morning) they were all bare, and so continued Monday and Tuesday when I visited". All the same Northampton was not satisfactory. Nobody appeared to bow at the name of Jesus, and he suspected the chief minister, Mr Ball, of administering the sacrament to "non-kneelants". At Lynn, on the other hand, Brent considered that "since the Court of High Commission took in hand some of their schismatics, few of that fiery spirit remain there or in the parts thereabout". The migration across the Atlantic was at its height.

The reception which the cities gave the vicar-general natur-

[24] Historical Manuscripts Commission, *Appendix to Fourth Report*, pp. 125–59.

[25] An abstract of the visitation is printed in the preface to *Cal. S.P. Dom. 1635*, pp. xxx–xlv.

ally varied. At Bury St Edmunds "the town music played and many trumpets sounded"; at Cambridge he was treated with "extraordinary kindness". At Coventry he was met by the clergy five miles outside the town and greeted with a very eloquent oration in Latin. There were difficulties here, however, for the mayor invited Brent to a feast before calling formally upon him, on the ground that the mayor of Coventry visited the King and the King only. Brent stood firm and his will proved the stronger. The mayor called, and Brent then attended the municipal feast. Except for this contretemps and the fact that the ministers of the two churches preached at different times, so that enthusiasts could go from one church to the other and hear both, to the neglect of the catechism, everything was as it should be in Coventry, the city almost "wholly conformable", the two churches "beautiful and well-kept", the ministers learned and discreet and the free school and hospital well governed. How very different the drunkenness rife at Moreton-in-the-Marsh, and the backwardness revealed by the visit to Derby! The little villages of the Dales were fortunate to have parish priests of any sort. The curate at Baslow and the rector of Whittington were notorious drunkards; the minister at Buxton was suspended for "absence and inconformity"; some of the chapels had never been consecrated and the curates at Wirksworth and Chapel-en-le-Frith had frequently conducted clandestine marriages; but, commented Brent, "they are so poor that I doubt no man will prosecute against them in the Court of High Commission".

So the great visitation continued. Only occasionally was Brent entirely satisfied, as at Worcester with the church of All Hallows, "very beautiful, there are organs, singing men, second services at the Communion table etc." He also approved of the state of the two schools in Worcester, which counterbalanced the fact that the brass desk in the cathedral was not as it should be. He paid close attention throughout to the schools, reporting the dangerous position in Winchester, where a recusant was a music master in the city and his son

taught grammar in his father's house and many who came to learn their alphabet learnt Popery by the way. At Oundle, on the other hand, Mr Cobbes the schoolmaster was given a canonical admonition for instructing his scholars from an unofficial catechism and for expounding the Ten Commandments "out of the writings of a silenced minister".

In judging the conformity of individual ministers, the vicar-general was hampered by his lack of confidence in the reports of the diocesans. "The notes of the bishop of the diocese were most of them mistaken", he stated at Shrewsbury. "Dr Bolton of St Mary's is as conformable as any." Sometimes, however, the case was so obvious that it was not necessary to have outside proof. At Bury, one young man lost his licence to preach "in regard of his great ignorance, being not able to tell me what *ecclesia* did signify, and in regard of his great boldness in the pulpit because that with stentorian vociferations and secret glancings at the ceremonies of our Church, he drew many after him from neighbouring parishes." Brent had no patience at all with this habit of "straggling" and he abominated galleries built for the purpose of accommodating strangers. At Kingston he refused to allow a second gallery to be built for which the money had already been collected, stating that the church was spoilt by the one already in existence. At Chichester Mr Speed of St Pancras only escaped prosecution because the dean vouched for his good scholarship, and because he confessed "his error in being too popular in the pulpit" and was "very willing the gallery in his parish church should be pulled down, which was built to receive strangers and at their charges". But Brent also refrained from prosecuting a very different sort of person, Dr Daines, the lecturer at Beccles, "a man of more than 70 years of age, who did never wear the surplice nor use the Cross in baptism" but whom succeeding bishops had left in peace because he was a "very quiet and honest man".

At Stratford-on-Avon, the vicar-general suspended Thomas Wilson for a variety of reasons, "for grossly particularizing in

his sermons, for suffering his poultry to roost and his hogs to lodge in the chancel, and for walking in the church to con his sermons in time of divine service." The following November Wilson's case came up before the Court of High Commission, complicated by a suit in Chancery which he had instituted against the town of Stratford, in the hope of getting a larger salary for himself and the schoolmaster. He obtained from Bishop Thornborough, his diocesan, a letter testifying to his improved behaviour and his conformity, but Laud added the succinct comment that, *pace* Bishop Thornborough, Wilson was "conformable in nothing". So by degrees the regulation of the clergy and of the parish churches continued, not in any harsh or rigid way but with inevitable clashes when a man of independent mind or difficult temper came up against the Establishment.

The year 1636 marked the high-water mark of the Laudian régime. It was in that year that the revision of the statutes was completed at Oxford, and the King paid a gala visit to the University to celebrate the occasion. In that year also the Lord Treasurer Portland died, and Juxon, the then Bishop of London, was appointed his successor. Laud wrote in his diary: "I pray God bless him to carry it so that the Church may have honour and the King and the State service and contentment by it, and now if the Church will not hold up themselves under God I can do no more." To him the promotion of a bishop to this, the highest office of State, was the culmination of his life work, fitting in with his whole conception of the Church as a dominant power in every aspect of national life. To the majority, it merely linked the episcopate more closely with an authoritarian and unpopular régime.

To Juxon as a person there could be no objection, though his one passion in life, outside his religion, was his pack of hounds, to whom he was devoted, perhaps finding them more admirable than the average person he met. He was a man of outstanding goodness, so that even Prynne found that he

could not rail against him, and his integrity was naturally reflected in the improved administration of the Treasury. He was, however, no politician and he was content to obey the King and follow the lead of the Archbishop, giving Laud the friendship and support he badly needed as a new crop of libels and increasing tension at court foreshadowed the crisis that was soon to come.[26]

The tension was partly due to the number of conversions to Roman Catholicism which were taking place. As the Queen's influence grew, some optimists had even hoped for corporate reunion, suggesting that Charles would not be adverse to the idea if Romanists were allowed to take the oath of allegiance. Twice before he became primate, Laud received the offer of a cardinal's hat, only to note in his diary that he could not find it in him to accept. To him, with his intimate knowledge of Anglican theology, it was clear that there were doctrinal divergences which could not be bridged as easily as differences regarding the oath, but others saw less clearly, conscious of the attractions of an infallible Church and impressed by the devoted labours of the Capuchin priests who served the Queen's chapel. Among her chaplains was one who had experienced in his own family how bitterly religion can divide—Franciscus a Sancta Clara, whose English name was Christopher Davenport, brother of John, the feoffee, a later stalwart of Massachusetts. Sancta Clara had written a book endeavouring to reconcile the Thirty-nine Articles with the decrees of the Council of Trent, although Laud declared that he could never do it "so as the Church of England might have cause to thank him for it" and Rome placed his book on the Index. Yet Sancta Clara remained a considerable influence at Whitehall, acting as go-between when Rome sent over an agent, Panzani, and introducing him to men in key positions. Among them was Montagu, who thought Laud over-timid, and Goodman, the disgruntled Bishop of Gloucester, who regarded the

[26] See C. V. Wedgwood, *The King's Peace, 1637–41* (1955), for the years leading up to the Civil War.

Catholicism he shared with the Roman Church as more important than the details that divided them.[27] In 1636 the King agreed to an exchange of Residents between Rome and the Queen's court, and a Scottish Jesuit, George Con, came over to Somerset House. He proved a charming and cultured man who could discuss pictures with the King as well as cases of conscience with his courtiers and, discarding illusory dreams of reunion, he concentrated on individual conversions. Portland had refused Anglican rites upon his death-bed, and it was believed that Cottington was prepared to take the same precautions in a like emergency. Recent converts had included Walter Montagu, the Earl of Manchester's son, and the Dowager Countess of Falkland. Con continued the good work and in the country at large the old fears of Popery revived, as a small but steady stream of conversions at the top served as a constant reminder of the Queen's influence and of her religion.

Con's success was facilitated by a new orientation in foreign affairs. The Dutch had become serious trading rivals and they were not liked the more by Charles for harbouring refugee Puritans. They had recently made a new treaty with France, and the King was considering an approach to Spain and savouring the attraction of an active foreign policy. The immediate result of this was the continuance of ship-money, extended to the inland shires as a determined effort was made to improve the Navy; and the prosecution of Hampden and his associates was one of a series of events that marked the beginning of collapse in the summer of 1637. For this summer also witnessed the notorious Star Chamber sentences upon the lawyer, Prynne, and two other professional men, Dr Bastwick, a physician, and Henry Burton, a schoolmaster. Prynne had been condemned three years earlier for a veiled attack upon the Queen in *Histriomastix*, his tirade against stage plays. Back in the Tower after his ordeal in the pillory, he complained of the lack of writing materials, which Laud at once allowed him. The result was *News from Ipswich*, anathematizing bishops

[27] Soden, *Godfrey Goodman, Bishop of Gloucester*, pp. 224–35, 246–58.

in general and Matthew Wren in particular. Burton, for his part, had published two sermons relentlessly attacking Laudian ceremonies, while Bastwick, who had already been fined and imprisoned for writing in favour of Presbyterian rule, now indulged in bitter satire in *The Litany of John Bastwick*: "from bishops, priests and deacons, Good Lord deliver us". In June the three men were condemned to lose their ears, to a fine of £5000 apiece, and life imprisonment (the fines as usual were not exacted). This time the anger of the crowds was more intense than ever before, compounded of many ingredients—religious fervour, political propaganda, and dismay that men of standing were being treated as if they were rogues and vagabonds. The three victims made the most of their opportunity, and by their fortitude and effective words in the pillory did as much for their cause as their writings had ever done. Their journey to their respective prisons in distant parts of the country was more like a triumphant progress than a road to gaol, and when, next year, young John Lilburne was whipped through the streets and stood in the pillory for distributing subversive literature, the Council tried in vain to prevent a repetition of similar scenes. This new victim was a man of exceptional spirit who might eventually prove more troublesome even than Prynne, for, although equally quarrelsome, he had a less jaundiced view of life and dangerous ideas of freedom and equality.

There was another Star Chamber case *sub judice* in the summer of 1637, that of the unhappy Bishop of Lincoln. He had alienated Laud still further by publishing a book entitled *The Holy Table: name and thing*, in which he supported the action of a Lincolnshire minister who had refused to move the holy table to the east end. Laud was shocked that a bishop should approve insubordination, especially "at such times as these", as he said in his speech at the trial of the three libellers. Williams had thrown caution to the winds, knowing he was already ruined. In July 1637 he was sentenced for perjury in the Star Chamber, suspended from his ecclesiastical

functions in the High Commission, and committed to the Tower. But if Laud welcomed his downfall because this was no time for insubordination, he had also been genuinely and justifiably enraged at the moral slur the suborning of witnesses cast on the episcopate. It was episcopacy itself that was at stake. "Our maine crime is that we are bishops . . ." he said; "were we not so, some of us might be as passable as other men."[28]

In this same critical summer of 1637 the spark was lit that was to lead to the eventual conflagration. On 23 July it was ordered that the new Scottish Liturgy should be read in St Giles' Cathedral. The book had been slowly and devotedly compiled in the years since the Scottish visit of 1633. The Scots were to call it the "Popish-English-Scottish-Mass service book" and hold Laud responsible; in fact it was their own bishops who had drafted it, notably John Maxwell, the Bishop of Ross. The draft had been sent to Charles and had been approved by Laud; and it was based on the English Prayer Book with certain deviations and additions of loveliness and worth. Among the latter were the blessing of the water at Baptism and the invocation of the Holy Spirit when the elements were sanctified at Holy Communion; there was also an additional supplication in the prayer for the whole Church for the "saints who have been the lights of the world in their several generations". Yet these very passages, by which the Liturgy was enriched, were the ones which in Fuller's words were "distasting" to its critics. Most of the people had never been reconciled to the new Jacobean bishops, and the riot at St Giles' and Jenny Geddes' fateful stool were symptoms of a deep disquiet. Yet, quite unconscious that an all but unanimous nation was against him, Charles refused to compromise. In the summer of 1638 the National Covenant was signed and the large majority of the Scottish people, stirred as much by

[28] W. Laud, *A speech delivered in the Star Chamber . . . 1637*. As he had been attacked, Laud did not give judgement against the libellers but made a speech of justification afterwards which the King ordered to be printed.

patriotism as by Presbyterian zeal, vowed themselves to the incompatible tasks of supporting alike the authority of the Crown and "true religion" according to John Knox. Only a minority of loyal Episcopalians remained in pockets of resistance, to suffer in the ensuing years persecution such as their English brethren were never called upon to endure.

Charles had no efficient advisers in Scotland, and Hamilton, who came and went between Edinburgh and Whitehall, was as unreliable as the leaders of the revolt were ruthless and determined. The debacle came quickly. A General Assembly at Glasgow, not authorized by the King, deposed the bishops and revoked the unpopular Articles of Perth, and by the spring it was accepted that armed revolt was imminent. It was Laud who called it the Bishops' War and urged his fellow-clergy to contribute to Charles's exiguous funds.

In May the King marched north to Berwick, the men behind him divided in mind and sore of heart, while the Scotsmen who gathered across the border were not only united in spirit but had as their commander-in-chief Alexander Leslie, a professional soldier at the head of a body of trained veterans, home from the German wars. No blood was shed on this occasion, but the Pacification of Berwick was never more than a screen of words. The situation became increasingly intractable, for neither side had any real intention of giving way and each in turn was driven to illegal or unconstitutional action. Charles had a good case: rebellion against a rightful sovereign could not easily be condoned, and in September Wentworth returned from Ireland and urged strong measures and at long last an unqualified trial of "Thorough". He was made Earl of Strafford, and Laud, who was aging rapidly, thankfully surrendered the leadership to him. In May 1640 Parliament was called, with surprisingly little fuss and excitement after so long a lapse, and Strafford had every hope of obtaining the necessary supplies. But intrigue and divided counsels at Whitehall, and sheer mismanagement, if not worse, at Westminster, brought the Parlia-

ment to an end after a few brief weeks. Charles had lost his last chance of controlling the situation. When Parliament was dissolved, Convocation continued to sit, legally justified perhaps but most inexpediently, as Laud himself protested. It had already granted six subsidies to the King, now given as a benevolence, and was engaged in framing additional Canons to give legal status to the developments of the preceding years. The first was an extreme assertion of the royal authority, "being the ordinance of God himself, founded in the pure laws of human nature and clearly established by express texts both of the Old and New Testaments". The sixth Canon imposed an oath on clergy, doctors, and schoolmasters, approving the doctrine and discipline of the Church of England and vowing not to consent to any alteration. By carelessness in phrasing, reference was made to the government of the Church, "by archbishops, bishops, deans and archdeacons &c." and as the "etcetera oath" it earned both derision and notoriety, so explosively expressed in pamphlet and speech that Laud advised the King not to impose it. The outcry over the unhappy etcetera oath masked a merited disquiet. Not only was it a doctrinal test, but it bound the conscience in regard to future action, a course which ran counter to the instincts of every freedom-loving man—and liberty was to be a word very much on people's lips in the years immediately ahead. But it was a quality of which neither party had the monopoly, as was evident from a development that had taken place in Scotland. In the previous autumn, the signing of the Covenant had been made compulsory for all the Scottish nation. It was the first sign of the tyranny of ideas that during the ensuing twenty years would lessen the sanctity of oaths of every sort and make of "covenant", once a symbol of trust and fellowship, a word of ill repute.

As ideologies began to harden, actions became more violent and early signs of the danger of anarchy were manifold throughout the summer of 1640. In Southwark the hostile crowds broke into the churches of St Saviour's and St Olave's

and tore down the offending altar-rails.[29] The White Lion prison was attacked and the doors thrown open. The crowds surged up to Lambeth Palace; Laud slipped across to Whitehall, and the trained bands were called out. There were violent prejudices and principles at work that the country gentry and the burgesses with their strict respect for property would, in the end, find as alien as did Laud himself.

In August Leslie crossed the border in the same week that Charles arrived in York, where a petition from certain noblemen besought him to summon a Parliament for redress of grievances. The Scottish Army advanced and occupied Newcastle, and the King compromised and summoned a Council of Peers. They succeeded in negotiating a treaty at Ripon but it brought little comfort to Charles, for the Scottish Army was to stay where it was and receive for its upkeep during the next two months the daily sum of £850! If only in order to raise the required money, the King could do no other than accept the peers' advice and summon Parliament.

It assembled upon 3 November and struck without delay at the two men it held responsible for the evils of the time. On 11 November Strafford was impeached; Laud, less dangerous now, was left at large for a few more weeks. On 18 December he, too, was impeached and committed to the custody of the Usher of the Black Rod. He was allowed to collect his papers at Lambeth, and was a little comforted by the crowd of poor people who thronged about him wishing him a safe return. It was not the poor whom he had offended. A few months later he was sent to the Tower, in time to watch Strafford pass his window on the way to the scaffold, to lift up his hands in blessing, and fall in a faint as his friend went from his sight. For four years he remained in the Tower before he, too, was executed with no semblance of necessity to justify the action. During the time of waiting he saw the Church he loved threatened with destruction. One may hope that, at times, his thoughts turned to pleasanter subjects—to the occasion, if

[29] *Lords' Journals*, IV.270 a, 271 b, 277 b et al.

legend is correct, when he persuaded the diffident Herbert to accept a cure of souls, to an interlude on the way to Scotland when he and the King had turned aside to visit Little Gidding, to his lenience to John Hales and friendly talks with his godson, William Chillingworth. For, if his work in any way survived, it would be because of the encouragement he had given to people such as these, and it was because of them and a host of younger men, who would test his teaching in years of adversity, that by the grace of God the Anglican Church would live.

# 5

# QUIET INTERLUDE

In no respect was the Anglican Church more truly a synthesis of Catholic and Reformed than in the patterns of its piety. There was room within its bounds at the beginning of the century for Andrewes' *Preces Privatae*, liturgical in form and derivation, and for the sober Calvinism of Lewis Bayly; as in the years to come there would be room for the mystical poetry of Vaughan and Traherne and the down-to-earth guidance of *The Whole Duty of Man*. There was even room for those who were not particularly pious, for Herrick's songs "of brooks, of blossoms, birds, and bowers", and for those whose piety was more like to a passionate flame, a ruthless search for God as John Donne conceived it:

> Batter my heart, three personed God:
> . . . for I
> Except you enthrall me, never shall be free,
> Nor ever chaste, except you ravish me.

Yet certain patterns there were, varying according to the theological and devotional slant of the time. Donne's personality and genius were such as to fit him into no pattern; yet even he, in spite of or in reaction from the Roman Catholicism in which he had been reared, shared—so a modern scholar suggests—the intellectuality which Anglicanism derived from its concentration upon the writings of the patristic ages.[1] This line of approach, combined with the Protestant stress on the Bible and on personal effort in reading and interpreting the word of God, gave to the piety of the later

[1] John Donne, *The Divine Poems*, ed. with introd. and commentary by Helen Gardner (1952), p. xxvii.

Tudors, whether expressed in the pages of Hooker or William Perkins, an individual and rational character remote from the warmth of medieval worship. It was perhaps to offset this intellectuality that Andrewes furbished his altar at Ely Place and John Cosin lit his candles at Durham; and, in the next reign, Cosin's blunt and healthy churchmanship and Laud's militant faith brought to their wing of the Anglican compromise a sense of commitment as deep as the Puritans' and a new awareness of the corporate life of the Church. It was Donne, preaching at St Paul's in the years between Andrewes' prime and Laud's emergence, who bridged the gap between the two approaches. His own spiritual travail was reflected in the directness and power of his sermons, their close reasoning and emotional depth and the imagination that gave them life and relevance. He stirred his congregations to a response that was a matter of the heart and will, no less than of the brain; perhaps only Milton, under a differing religious discipline, equalled Donne in the combination of intellectual power, poetic genius, and a fervent emotional response.

It had been no easy road that brought him at length to the pulpit at Paul's Cross. Behind him lay the memory of a brother who had died a prisoner for loyalty to the Roman faith, his own excesses in an irresponsible youth, and the secret marriage which ruined his hopes of preferment and led to the frustrated years in the little house at Mitcham. He had been employed by Thomas Morton in the polemical debates with the Jesuits that the Oath of Allegiance had provoked, and Morton with characteristic kindliness had offered to surrender to Donne a benefice he held, if he would be ordained. "Remember, Mr Donne, no man's education or Parts makes him too good for this employment. . . "[2] But if Donne by this stage had accepted the Anglican faith with his mind and was ready to write in its defence, he was not yet sufficiently aware of spiritual reality to act as "Christ's ambassador". It was not until 1612, five years later, that he entered the ministry, and

[2] K. W. Gransden, *John Donne* (1954), p. 22.

it brought him no automatic security. The *Divine Sonnets* that were probably written during these first years as a priest witness to the continuance of struggle and to the deepening of spiritual vision. His wife died in 1617, and thereafter Donne's thoughts were never far from the contemplation of death. Three years later he became Dean of St Paul's and henceforth in the eyes of the world he was a revered and brilliant figure in the ecclesiastical scene. The love-poems of his youth and the religious verse of his maturer years were alike unpublished till after his death; only the passionate appeal of his sermons gave to contemporaries a clue to his burning quest for the divine. For though in his Litany he prayed, "That we may change to evenness this intermitting anguish piety", his religion remained for him a venture across a stormy ocean with faith as the only compass, a humble but determined assault upon the mercy of God.

Donne's friendship with Magdalen Herbert, which linked him with the other great religious poet of the period, is one of the happy accidents of history. Utterly different in career and personality, the two men were alike in working their way uneasily to salvation. A bare three years as rector of a country parish and one slim volume of religious verse sufficed to give George Herbert an abiding place in the story of the seventeenth-century Church, and he needs no epitaph beyond the words of his own poems which were to a large extent spiritual autobiography, depicting his hopeful youth, his ambition, his hesitations, the way so nearly lost, and, at the end, the brief, rich period of fruition.[3] In the next century Samuel Johnson,

[3] Cf. Izaak Walton's *Life of George Herbert*, written in 1670, which is the basis of all later works. Herbert's poems were published in 1633 under the title of *The Temple; sacred Poems and private ejaculations*. There were eleven editions before the end of the century. His collected *Works* have been edited with a commentary and introduction by F. E. Hutchinson (3rd edn. 1953). Among modern biographers see *inter alia* A. G. Hyde, *George Herbert and his times* (1906); Margaret Cropper, *Flame touches Flame* (1949), pp. 1–28; M. Bottrall, *George Herbert* (1954); and Marchette Chute, *Two Gentlemen* (1959).

in disparagement, gave the title of "The Metaphysicals" to Donne and Herbert and other poets, who seized the attention of their readers by extracting unexpected meaning from the conjunction of disparate images and ideas. There are times when the form and sense of their poetry is in danger of being clogged with artificial twists and a surfeit of symbols and metaphors, yet it was this determined effort to find the essence of truth, the meaning behind the symbol, that gave to their verses potency and makes them relevant to-day.[4]

George Herbert was born in 1593, the fifth son of Richard Herbert, who was custodian of Montgomery Castle on the border of Wales and a distant cousin of the Earl of Pembroke, head of the great Marcher family of the Herberts. George was said to inherit his family's hot temper; he certainly possessed his full share of their pride of race. His father died when he was three years old and the dominant person in his earlier years was his mother, Magdalen, one of the exceptional women in which the century was so rich. Not long after her husband's death she moved to Oxford to be with her eldest son, who later as Lord Herbert of Cherbury won unequal fame as the author of a jejune autobiography and of the studies in philosophy that earned him the title of the first English deist.[5]

When he was twelve, young George was entered at Westminster School and his mother moved to a house near Charing Cross. In the next few years he would take his part in those Abbey services that Bishop Williams enjoyed so much and may thus have learnt to love and understand the meaning of the Anglican Liturgy and the significance in worship of order and harmony. Those other requisites of the good life, a careful

[4] Cf. Rosemond T. M. Tuve, *A reading of George Herbert* (1952), and J. H. Summers, *George Herbert, his religion and art* (1954), for two modern studies of his metaphysical thought and his use of language.

[5] See *The Autobiography of Lord Herbert of Cherbury*, introd. C. H. Herford (1928), and Lord Herbert of Cherbury, *De religione laici*, ed. and trans. H. R. Hutcheson (1944); cf. W. K. Jordan, *The Development of Religious Toleration in England in the 17th Century*, II.435–44.

reading of the Scriptures and the pious practices of a Christian home, he had in abundance in his family circle, for Magdalen Herbert's affection and charm bound brothers and sisters closely together in love to her. In 1608 she married for her second husband Sir John Danvers, a large-hearted man of affairs, who was twenty years younger than his new wife and so handsome that people turned to look at him in the street. It was one of those unsuitable matches that turn out extraordinarily well, and Sir John Danvers's home in Chelsea, near to the river and the old parish church, became in the succeeding years a place of call not only for his brood of stepchildren, always sure of a welcome, but also for many eminent visitors. Among them was Donne, who had known Magdalen at Oxford and now, watching her grow in depth and serenity in her middle years, wrote his lovely lines:

> No spring nor summer beauty hath such grace
> As I have seen in one autumnal face.

Yet it may well have been that her love for her children was somewhat too possessive, for the elder ones cut loose as soon as they could. Magdalen's hopes centred, increasingly, on George. He went up to Cambridge as a scholar of Trinity in the autumn of 1609, and when he left Westminster his headmaster predicted a brilliant future, adding as a word of warning that he must not overwork and undermine his health.

It was not entirely wise to caution him. His delicacy and his mother's cosseting were offset by his ambition to do well, but his over-scrupulous care of himself so as not to become a permanent invalid produced the very thing he wished to avoid, hesitation in the face of action. It also tended to mark him out from his fellows; he was not allowed to fast in Lent and he left Cambridge every now and again for a few days at Newmarket, where the dry air did him good—precautions which tended to turn his thoughts in upon himself, and he did not mix easily enough with others to be able to afford any such indulgence.

At first, however, all went well. It was during his first year

that he sent his mother some immature sonnets and told her in a covering letter that he intended henceforward to "consecrate to God's glory his poor abilities in poetry" and to become a writer of religious verse.[6] Meanwhile he was studying the classics, and the remaining verses of his Cambridge years were written in Latin. He did well academically and in due course became a fellow of his college. In 1618, he was appointed to give the Barnaby Lecture in rhetoric. His choice, on that occasion, of one of King James's books for analysis and adulation, in place of the usual classic, half amused, half shocked University opinion, and perhaps as a direct result, when the post of Public Orator fell vacant in the following year, Herbert's name was canvassed as one who could combine classical ability and grace of expression with considerable skill in the needful art of flattery.

He was now 26 years old and it was time that his brilliant future began to materialize. In his post-graduate work he was studying divinity, but this young Herbert of the Cambridge days, a little remote from his fellows, careful about his dress, more enthusiastic at times about his music than about his books, was subjected to a number of conflicting hopes. He was not so sure as he had been as to where the study of divinity would lead him, and he desired the Orator's post not only for the honour, which as he confessed to his stepfather "would please a young man well",[7] but also because he hoped it would prove a stepping-stone to a diplomatic post. He was after all a Herbert, whose kinsman the Earl of Pembroke was not only a doyen of the world of letters but a senior statesman at King James's court. Pembroke's mother had been Philip Sidney's sister, and the legend of Sidney was still potent. As he studied his verses, young Herbert no doubt studied Sidney's life and saw himself in similar guise, serving alike God and his king.

[6] Izaak Walton, *Lives*, ed. S. B. Carter (1951), pp. 206 f.

[7] Letter [Sept. 1619] included in first editions of Walton's *Life* (Hutchinson's *Works of George Herbert*, p. 370).

He became Public Orator in January 1620 and for the next few years was busily and happily employed. He frequently attended the court when it came to Royston and among the persons of importance he met was Lord Chancellor Bacon—a friendship to which Herbert remained loyal after Bacon fell from power in 1621. Two years later he helped to translate the *Advancement of Learning* into Latin, and in acknowledgement Bacon dedicated to him his book of witty sayings and a translation of certain of the Psalms.[8] Francis Bacon's intellectual grasp, his cold, ruthless spirit, and the insatiable curiosity of his scientific mind were in many ways far removed from the pattern of Herbert's thinking, yet Bacon's conception of an ordered universe must have made a strong appeal to him and that conjunction of law and harmony which spelt goodness in the world of science was the very stuff of Herbert's life at Bemerton and exactly what he lacked in the disordered years of the immediate future.

The advancement at court, which had seemed to be merely a matter of time, never materialized. The last extant oration that Herbert made at Cambridge celebrated the safe return of the Prince of Wales from the visit to Madrid. But the Public Orator did not voice the mood of the moment; he devoted a great part of his speech to the praise of James as peacemaker. In recent years two of his brothers had died fighting on the Continent, and it is not difficult to imagine how ruthlessly their deaths cut across Herbert's academic calm. In his oration, neglecting his own interests, he spoke with feeling of the miseries of war, the new evils unloosed by the increasing use of gunpowder, the fact that in war innocent and guilty, victim and aggressor, suffer alike. War, however, was the order of the day and during the next two years Herbert's last chances of preferment vanished, with changes in policy and personnel and the death of James I. Herbert had left Cambridge, for the first signs of tubercular trouble had appeared, and he spent the greater part of 1625 with an unknown friend in Kent. It

[8] Walton, op. cit., p. 212.

proved the turning-point of his life, for it was now that he finally accepted the fact that for him God's will did not lie in the paths of public service. If it might seem that he merely submitted to circumstance, it was characteristic of his day and his religion to see in circumstance the hand of God. The Christian response was a glad acceptance of the divine will, and for Herbert it was not an easy surrender. It was probably at this stage that he was made deacon, for he was so described on 5 July 1626, when he was instituted at Lincoln *in absentia* to the prebend of Leighton Ecclesia. Not till four years later, when he went to Bemerton, was he ordained priest, and they were years of spiritual conflict in which the mood of *The Collar*:

> I struck the board and cry'd "No more.
> I will abroad" . . .

was gradually resolved into the serene acceptance of the final couplet:

> Methoughts I heard one calling "Child!"
> And I reply'd, "My Lord".

During these years of orientation he was much helped by Nicholas Ferrar, to whom he had written for counsel as to the right use of his prebend, receiving the typical advice to get ahead with some practical piece of well-doing until his mind was clearer. With the financial help of a London goldsmith, Arthur Woodnoth, who was Ferrar's cousin, Herbert set about rebuilding the ruined church of Leighton Bromsgrove, mulcting for the purpose his rich kinsman at court and drawing upon a fund of energy that his new activities seemed to have released in him. To his mother's objection, "It is not for your weak body and empty purse to undertake to build churches", he replied that he had vowed to God to do the work and after 33 years of obedience to her will he must ask her permission "to become an undutiful son".[9] In June next year Magdalen Danvers died, and immediately afterwards Herbert relinquished the Orator's post. He then went down to Wiltshire

[9] Ibid., p. 218.

to visit his stepfather's brother, Lord Danby, where before long a little kindly matchmaking began. George Herbert, himself, thought of the ideal parish priest as celibate, but the long passage on virginity in *The Country Parson* shows how hard he found it to reconcile this ideal with the needs and passions of the full-blooded man. It was well for him that Danby or his wife conditioned him successfully to the idea of matrimony, so that when he met Jane Danvers, Danby's cousin, they agreed to marry after the briefest of courtships. For if Herbert's remarks on wives in *The Country Parson* do not sound as if he were ever wildly and romantically in love, it may well be that this happy marriage—for so it proved—was more than any other single factor the cause of the last three gloriously productive years.

In 1630 Herbert was offered the cure of St Andrew, Bemerton, and Fuggleston St Peter, hard by the gates of Wilton Park where the Earl of Pembroke lived. Herbert hesitated, not, as the King had expected, because he did not think the living worth accepting, but because he still doubted his own worthiness to guide and cherish other human souls. Izaak Walton tells the story, probably apocryphal, of a visit to Wilton Park to consult Philip, the new Earl, and of Laud, who was present by chance and who was so persuasive that a tailor was summoned then and there from Salisbury to take measure for the "canonical clothes" Herbert would require. True or not, the incident is symbolic of the new fervour which inspired Herbert in the Bemerton days.

He was inducted by Bishop Davenant in April and ordained priest five months later. Henceforward the plain little church of St Andrew, Bemerton, and the rectory across the way became the centre of a full and happy life. Not only were his duties as a parish priest meticulously carried out; he also did a large amount of reconditioning of the neglected buildings, composed many new poems and carefully revised those of an earlier date, and in addition to some work in Latin wrote the treatise on *A Country Parson*, which mirrors the daily

pattern of his life.[10] Time has not dealt unkindly with this corner of England, and at Bemerton the church still stands very much as it was in Herbert's day. Behind the rectory across the road, the garden that he loved stretches to the river and the water-meadows beyond; and as one follows the meandering stream one sees of a sudden Salisbury spire in all its loveliness, as Herbert saw it when he walked to his music-meetings with his friends in the cathedral close.

In such a case as Herbert's it is superfluous to ask to what "party" in the Church he belonged. One at least of his poems is pure Calvinism, yet a letter he wrote about Predestination pleased Andrewes so much that he was said always to carry it with him. At Leighton the pulpit and prayer-desk, as Herbert planned it, were to be of equal height, signifying the equal value of prayer and preaching, while the basis of the whole of his teaching at Bemerton was the Church Catechism. His ruling on such moot points as bowing at the name of Jesus or kneeling at the receipt of the sacrament was the typical comment that "contentiousness in a feast of charity is more scandal than any posture". In his love of music and order and of all that was sweet-savoured and seemly, he was certainly attuned to the new spirit of worship with which the Arminians had enriched the Anglican compromise. Humphrey Henchman, canon of Salisbury, was one of his most congenial neighbours; and Henchman's knowledge of the primitive Church and his care for ceremonial made him at a later date one of the most distinguished of the Caroline divines. In his sacramental approach, also, Herbert was closely akin to the Laudians. Both in his preaching and in his verses he used the symbol and the hieroglyphic to convey and drive home the spiritual truth that otherwise eluded description. Throughout his ministry he saw the priest as a symbol of Christ himself, one "whose very business and aim was love"; and as he tried in his own life and in the worship of the Church to reveal God to man, so in

10 *A Priest to the Temple or The Country Parson: his character and rule of holy life* (*Works*, ed. Hutchinson, pp. 223 et seq.).

his poems he used the things of everyday life—the collar, the pulley, the tiles in the church floor, and even the very shape and metre of the verses—to depict the pattern of Christian living and the joys and doubts that beset the Christian pilgrim.

*The Country Parson* is full of shrewd comment as well as spiritual insight and discusses with equal conscientiousness and common sense how best to deliver a sermon and how to be sure not to eat too much at dinner. It is easy to see how by careful visiting and genuine interest in his neighbours' welfare, no less than by his teaching and his prayers, Herbert earned the reputation of a near-saint throughout the countryside. Yet he remained a man of his class and age, as appears clearly in the passages that deal with dispensing charity and hospitality, in which one misses the loving abandon of a St Francis or even the easy friendliness of less saintly men. He certainly spoke from experience in his suggestion that those "of better sort" should be invited in due order to the parsonage throughout the year "because country persons are very observant of such things". Equally practical was his advice to the parson to gain a knowledge of tillage and pasturage and to make use of it in his teaching "because people by what they understand are best led to what they understand not". He was in fact to make all the affairs of the parish "his joy and thought", so that he was ready to act if need be as lawyer and doctor as well as a shepherd of souls. His parishioners should be equally occupied, for he regarded idleness as the greatest evil of the times. When they had finished money-making, they should devote themselves to work for the community, as magistrates or Parliament men (not omitting to attend when the House was in committee), or in travels abroad to study problems of trade, or at least by keeping an eye on the village's woods and commons. It is this sense of being involved in life, fully committed as a Christian and a citizen, which redeems the precepts of *The Country Parson* from being merely shrewd; it is the attitude of "The Elixir":

Who sweeps a room as for Thy laws
Makes that and the action fine.

The rhymed maxims in "The Church Porch" have something of the same character.[11] "Do all things like a man, not sneakingly", "Who keeps no guard upon himself is slack", "By all means use sometimes to be alone". So one comes by stages to the act of worship. "Let vain or busie thoughts have there no part. Bring not thy plough, thy plots, thy pleasure thither." For good behaviour by itself only led one to the threshold of religion. Beyond the church porch lay the path to the altar where the priest ministered as Christ's vicegerent, sublime in his office, though his Latin might be shaky and his stipend a bare £10 a year.

The one shadow deepening over the years of Herbert's ministry was his increasing weakness and the growing realization that his time was short. It was hard not to rebel; had he achieved serenity by so hard a path to be left with so brief a time to reap the harvest? These moments of depression survived in an occasional poem, in writing which he lightened his mood and his pain, but the years as a whole, with the daily worship at home and in the church, with their prodigious activity and his deepening love for his parishioners, were happy and serene. A friend, who was also in touch with Little Gidding, came to visit him shortly before his death, and he sent back to Ferrar his manuscript book of verses with a message that in it he would find a picture of the many spiritual conflicts that Herbert had undergone before he could subject himself to the will of Jesus his master, "in which service", he concluded, "I have now found perfect freedom". Soon afterwards he died, in the spring of 1633, and was buried before the altar at Bemerton on Quinquagesima Sunday, the day on which the Church of England in Collect and Epistle extols the gift of love.

What can one say of that other poet-parson who was making

[11] "The Church Porch" is the first section of *The Temple* and the main body of the poems are given the heading "The Church" (*Works*, ed. Hutchinson, pp. 6–24).

music in the England of the day? The average incumbent fitted in, no doubt, between the country rector, as Herbert envisaged him, who could talk with his parishioners of their own skills yet never forgot that he was the deputy of Christ, and the legendary Herrick, who wrote rude squibs about his less attractive neighbours and had been known according to the story to throw his sermon at the heads of his congregation.[12] Yet if Herbert is a precious jewel in the pattern of the Church's piety, it is also the fairer for a shining thread of lyrical beauty which Herrick alone could give. He was a parson almost completely against his will, but his pet pig and delectable ladies and his rough words when he spoke of his Devonshire cure did not prevent his parishioners from being proud of him and telling stories about him that were handed down from generation to generation.

Herrick was a Londoner born and bred, in spite of the country verses that won him immortality. He was apprenticed to his uncle as a goldsmith, but his heart was not in it; he already fancied himself as a poet and, when at length his uncle released him, he went up to Cambridge to study at the late age of 22. He sampled the law, as earlier he had experimented with precious metals, and with as little satisfaction, and when ten years later he was ordained, in 1623, his priestly vocation seemed equally unlikely to be his main concern. He revelled in the life of London and the company of poets, as he had revelled in the poets of Rome in his university days. He made friends with Henry Lawes, whose music fitted his lyrics to perfection, and attached himself to Ben Jonson with a sense of kinship more genuine than that of many of the latter's devotees. But he never belonged to that society of young noblemen, poetasters, and amateur philosophers who were sealed of "the tribe of Ben", and when Jonson died no poem

[12] F. W. Moorman, *Robert Herrick, a biographical and critical study* (1910), p. 107. A certain Barron Field, writing in the *Quarterly Review* of 1810, described a visit to Dean Prior and the continuance of these legends.

of Herrick's was included in the memorial volume, though there lay among his papers the moving lines:

When I a verse shall make
  Know I have prayed thee,
For old religion's sake
  Saint Ben to aid me.[13]

Herrick had been appointed a chaplain in Buckingham's household and sailed with him on the expedition to Rhé. Later, after his friend's death, King Charles attempted to reward those who had shared the ill-fated adventure, and, in the same year that Herbert went to Bemerton, Herrick found himself in theory advanced, but in fact banished, to the living of Dean Prior, a remote village on the edge of Dartmoor. There he remained writing verses, which he reluctantly admitted to be better than those he wrote in town, shaping them with the careful skill of a true craftsman. The care he bestowed upon his parishioners was of a more rough and ready sort. Rose Macaulay has sketched it with a sure touch in *They were Defeated*, and the happiness that, at times, broke through his homesickness for town. Once, in 1640, he did get away, staying some months in Westminster and earning an official reprimand. He had come up to town in the hope of publishing his verses, but for some reason the venture was postponed, perhaps because it was thought the volume would look better with a larger proportion of sacred poems to offset the far from sacred lyrics. Eight years had passed, war and revolution had overwhelmed the country, and he himself had been turned out of his cure before the precious poems at last saw the light of print.[14] A world out-of-tune took little notice of them, and Herrick remained, with fame eluding him, in a London so much less jocund than of old, that even "dull Devonshire" must have come as a pleasant change when he and Charles II returned to their own again.

[13] Marchette Chute, *Two Gentlemen*, pp. 184–7, 217 f.
[14] Moorman, op. cit., pp. 137 ff.

Not a great man and certainly not a saintly one, yet he never entirely lost the innocence of childhood, which was why he could write a child's grace or a verse to a budding flower with a sense of immediacy that the years have not destroyed.

> Love bade me welcome yet my soul drew back,
> Guilty of dust and sinne . . .

wrote Herbert in perhaps his loveliest poem, and the certainty of God's love, that came with a full surrender, gave him power to comfort and sustain. Yet to Herrick, also, one is grateful for his power to enjoy the beauty of the passing moment. Life would indeed have been the poorer if Corinna had not gone a-Maying, or Julia's loveliness had been unsung, and though Herrick, one may be sure, did not put it into theological terms, he was well within the bounds of Anglican orthodoxy in rejoicing with a thankful heart in the good things of life. Perhaps he came nearer to sin in the undercurrent of melancholy, the poignant realization of the fleeting nature of beauty, no less real, if less laboured, than Donne's preoccupation with death. The sure and certain hope of the Christian was clouded with human regret as he turned away from the fading daffodils; and the ugliness of old age made him angry.

Herbert died in his fortieth year, reconciled to death, but Herrick, who disliked so intensely the business of growing old, lived on into the 1670s and found, one hopes, in his quiet corner, with his pig and his pipkin and the faithful Prue to look after him, that the merciful years brought acceptance, and with acceptance peace.

If one travels the Great North Road to-day one can still turn aside at Stamford and come across the fields to Little Gidding. Nothing that is tangible remains, except the little church, rebuilt in the eighteenth century; even the site of the manor house is not known. Yet a spirit lingers in the quiet spot.

If you came this way
Taking any route, starting from anywhere
At any time or any season
It would always be the same. . . .
. . . You are here to kneel
Where prayer has been valid.[15]

The names of Herbert and Ferrar will always be linked, not only because of their personal friendship but because at Bemerton and Little Gidding they revealed, with a slightly different emphasis, the Anglican way as, at its finest, it had grown to be. Herbert had shown it to be a way of sober piety, grounded upon the scriptures and liturgical prayer and adorned by the fruits of good works, and to this Ferrar added a new interpretation of the Catholic tradition of community living, so that it too should be part of the pattern of Anglican devotion. The experiment at Little Gidding differed from its medieval counterparts in that its unit was the family and that no formal vows were taken, but as much as any monastic foundation it recognized that its prime duty was that of prayer, the giving of glory to God. From that prayer there flowed naturally service to one's neighbour according to his need, whether in the form of almsgiving or teaching or the care of the old and sick. But at the heart of it all was prayer.

Nicholas Ferrar was the younger son of a London citizen of standing. For some years he travelled abroad for reasons of health, at first in Germany, later in Italy and Spain, and he had thus been in touch at Padua and Madrid with some of the finest Catholic scholarship of the day. Yet however much he was influenced by the Counter-Reformation, his own personal sense of sin and the firm biblical foundation of his devotional life were essentially Protestant, and behind the Little Gidding experiment lay not only the years in Europe but the background of Ferrar's London home, where equal stress was placed upon personal piety and a concern for public affairs. In Nicholas's case the piety, inculcated by nature and

[15] T. S. Eliot, *Four Quartets* (1943), p. 31.

upbringing and enriched by the years in Europe, was enhanced in a strange way by his delicate health, not only because he had become used on medical advice to habits of abstinence but because the periodic recurrence of serious illness set all his plans in the context of eternity.[16]

In 1618 Nicholas returned to England, for his father's health was rapidly failing and the financial affairs of his elder brother, John, were in a hopeless tangle. Nicholas set himself to straighten things out and took over his father's duties on the board of the Virginia Company, in whose fortunes the family was deeply involved. John Ferrar served as deputy treasurer under Sir Edwin Sandys, an old man now but still capable of impulsive action as in the days when he had helped Hooker to publish his book. King James disliked Sandys almost as much as he disliked tobacco, and as the Spanish interest at the court increased the company was subjected to repeated criticism and attacks from the Crown. In the period that remained before the company's charter was abrogated Nicholas took an increasing part in its affairs, earning a high reputation for his organizing power and his honesty of purpose. When the crisis came he acted with amazing efficiency in arranging for all the company's records to be copied at top speed before the originals were confiscated.[17] His qualities became known to a wider circle in the final Parliament of James I's reign, when he assisted ably in the impeachment of the Lord Treasurer, Middlesex.

It was therefore at the start of a career by no means undistinguished that he decided deliberately to withdraw from public life. In 1624 he bought for his mother the decayed estate of Little Gidding, which included a commodious manor house and a dilapidated church. As much as any Puritan, he looked for the will of God in the coincidence of events, and if the collapse of the Virginia Company impelled him and his

[16] A. L. Maycock, *Nicholas Ferrar of Little Gidding* (1938), pp. 29 f, 51–5.

[17] Ibid., p. 100, and see pp. 65–104, for an account of the connection with the Virginia Company.

brother to a fresh assessment of their future, the outbreak of plague in London, in the summer of King Charles's accession, signalled in dramatic way the right moment to act. Nicholas dispatched his mother and his younger relatives to Hertford and sent John Ferrar to prepare Little Gidding for occupation, and there they were reunited in the autumn. They spent a strenuous winter reconditioning the church, where every day with the Bishop of Lincoln's special permission they said the Litany in a service of intercession for plague-stricken London. But when the plague subsided and the silent streets began to fill again, the Ferrars did not return. Only at Whitsuntide in 1626 did Nicholas and his mother and certain others of the family revisit London to say goodbye to their friends, and on Trinity Sunday Ferrar was made deacon by Laud, then Bishop of St David's. The news that he had taken orders caused some consternation among his friends, and more than one countered with the offer of a rich living. But Ferrar made it clear that he wanted no living and did not intend to become a priest. Deacon's orders gave him authority to conduct his family's devotions and be their spiritual guide, and he read to them a solemn undertaking to fulfil his calling among them in the service of God. Soon afterwards they returned to Little Gidding.[18]

Thus the adventure began. Nicholas's mother, Mary Ferrar, though well over seventy, gave him sensible and zealous support, and his brother and his sister came with their families to Little Gidding so that the community numbered some twenty or thirty persons at its prime. John, less efficient in action than his brother and more involved in personal relationships, was loyalty personified, but his wife, Bathsheba, left London more reluctantly with their one son, a child of six, another Nicholas. Two more children, a girl and a boy, were born later and the girl was called Virginia as a constant

[18] *The Ferrar Papers*, ed. B. Blackstone (1938), pp. 25 ff. "A Life of Nicholas Ferrar", written by his brother John Ferrar, is printed in *The Ferrar Papers*, pp. 9–94, with a note on the texts, pp. xvii–xxi.

reminder of the beloved colony for whose well-being the brothers continued to pray. Up from the country came the Collett family, John and Susannah (née Ferrar) with their two younger sons and eight daughters, of whom the elder two had been brought up by their grandmother and had watched the plans develop. The eldest girl, Susannah, married an Essex clergyman, Josiah Mapletoft, and their home in Margetting was a frequent and refreshing place of call for any member of the family. But Mapletoft died after a few years and the three children of the marriage were sent to Little Gidding to be reared, replenishing the nursery population just as the younger Collett girls and Nicholas Ferrar junior were beginning to grow up. There were other young visitors as the reputation of the place began to spread, and in this way the small community maintained its peculiar character of a family group. There were always children at Little Gidding.

To meet the needs of the young people an old dovecot was transformed into a schoolhouse and three masters were engaged to teach them and, with them, any children of the neighbourhood. Old Mrs Ferrar sat each morning in the Great Chamber and those who were not old enough to go to school played quietly about her, while the grown-ups came and went on their allotted tasks. The practical activities outside the house arose naturally from the needs of the neighbourhood, as the original reconditioning of the church and the setting up of the school had done. Before she died, eight years later, Mrs Ferrar had provided quarters in the house for the use of four poor widows, and under the supervision of Mary and Anna Collett, hesitantly at first but with growing confidence, an infirmary was set up and a "surgeon's chest" of oils and ointments provided, with the aid of which they ministered to their neighbours' ills. Nicholas, who had once thought of becoming a doctor, warned them that "physic was a choice and nice thing" with which they should not meddle, but that good broths and cooling drinks, "kitchen physic" as he termed it, were much to be commended. So a careful in-

quiry was made of the sick in the neighbouring villages and soups and salves were sent out to them, while three times a week at the manor house there was a free distribution of gruel to needy wayfarers.

But it was not the good broth nor the schoolhouse that made Little Gidding famous, it was the framework of prayer and praise in which it was set, which gave meaning to the whole. There was, it is true, a certain formalism in Ferrar's approach, that carried too far might hinder the working of the Spirit. It worried Arthur Woodnoth, who tried rather uneasily to maintain the standards of Little Gidding in the business world of London and who asked Nicholas if he did not perhaps "ascribe too much to the very bodily exercises of devotion and religion . . . setting a high value on the very saying of prayers". But to Ferrar a methodical rendering of the work on hand, whether it was estate management or the worship of God, was not only an integral part of his own nature but a necessary framework without which the household would lose its way in ineptitude or excess. Regularity and discipline, as he saw it, not only saved time and energy but freed mind and body from unnecessary strain, the better to apprehend and fulfil the will of God. Therefore the worship was as ordered as the life. Three times a day a small procession made its way from the house to the church, for Mattins and Evensong and before the midday meal, when the Litany was read as had been the custom since the first months of decision in the time of the plague. Nicholas taught his family to regard themselves as responsible citizens with a duty to understand and ponder upon public affairs, and so it was right and necessary to pray for the needs of the world. These daily services he conducted himself, but the curate of Steeple Gidding came over each Sunday after Mattins, bringing his congregation with him, to conduct the second service of Ante-Communion and to preach. Once a month the sacrament was administered, and on that Sunday the servants dined with the family. Everyone went to church, and household tasks were cut to the minimum

"by causing ovens to be heated and all the dinner to be sett into that, before church-time". Nicholas, a born organizer, spent as much care on such details as on wider issues, sometimes to the chagrin of the less amenable women of the household.

After Mattins on a Sunday, the children of the neighbourhood came into the house and repeated before the sisters one or more Psalms learnt by heart during the week. For every Psalm correctly repeated, each child received a penny and they all stayed for dinner, "which well pleased them and their parents".[19] The Psalms were at the very heart of the worship of Little Gidding. The children of the household also learnt them by heart, without the penny reward, and recited them in the first act of joint worship in the morning. Every hour during the day, a portion of the Psalms and a passage from the Gospels were repeated by the two or three whose turn of duty it was. At the end they sang a brief doxology to the soft playing of the organ and, as surely as the church clock, the sound of the music marked the passing hour. These hourly devotions were gradually extended throughout the night, those who wished taking turns to keep awake till one o'clock, when Nicholas was aroused and kept watch until dawn. By this means the complete Psalter was repeated in the course of the twenty-four hours, and their lives were lived to the echo of "My soul truly waiteth still upon God . . . he verily is my strength and my salvation: he is my defence, so that I shall not greatly fall."

It was not so simple to provide a straightforward reading of the gospel story, from which nothing should be omitted, and in order to make a continuous narrative which could be read through in the course of a month a concordance or "harmony" of the four Gospels was compiled, amounting in all to 150 chapters. A special room was set apart for the work and the daughter of a Cambridge book-binder was hired to

[19] Ibid., p. 35. Dr Maycock gives a detailed account of the members of the household (op. cit., pp. 155–94).

give the girls the necessary instruction; Mary and Anna wielded the scissors and paste and by degrees the Harmonies came into being, beautiful specimens of ingenious craftsmanship. King Charles, on his visit, was delighted with them and asked that a similar Harmony of the Books of Kings and Chronicles should be made for him, as well as a concordance of the Gospels for the Prince of Wales.[20]

Another activity that evolved which gave Nicholas much satisfaction was his "Little Academy", a solemn and rather pedantic study-group in which those who took part assumed allegorical names (the Cheerful, the Patient, the Moderator). Here Nicholas could instruct his nieces how to use their brains, as they discussed, with the aid of classical and renaissance learning, the theory and practice of virtue. Some of them perhaps were more at home in the care of the household, which each undertook in turn for a month at a time. Five of them thus fitted themselves for the rôle that Nicholas intended for them, and in due course became the wives of clergymen. Margaret, who never quite fitted in, succeeded in marrying a layman; Mary and Anna remained unmarried by choice. It was these two who came nearest to Nicholas in spirit, and after his mother's death Mary Collett became the natural leader on the women's side while Nicholas Ferrar junior grew up to be a youth of brilliant promise, his uncle's obvious successor. Among the younger children it was little John Mapletoft who entered most fully into the spirit of the dedicated household, which one either accepted and loved or remained uneasily aloof.

John Ferrar, in his life of Nicholas, said nothing of the friction between his wife and his brother and the inevitable tensions which can be traced in the collection of family letters, which make it clear that, even if the Civil War had not intervened, the reluctance of the female "in-laws" to settle at Little Gidding would have made its permanence unlikely.

[20] See J. E. Acland, *Little Gidding and its inmates . . . with an account of the Harmonies* (1903); Maycock, op. cit., pp. 279 et seq.

Bathsheba Ferrar stood by her husband, but she was homesick for London all the time and she resented Nicholas's assumption of authority in small matters as in great. Nicholas's first great disappointment came when one of the Collett sons brought his wife to Little Gidding, intending to settle there, but after a couple of years they decided not to stay but to make a more ordinary home for themselves in Highgate.[21] The whole idea of combining family and community life had psychological difficulties which even Nicholas could not overcome, yet for twelve years Little Gidding prospered and into the disciplined pattern of its life much satisfying work was fitted as well as a certain amount of tranquil leisure. At the end of the day when the five o'clock supper was over, until at eight o'clock all went to their own rooms, "there was liberty given to retire where each would, in summer time walking abroad; in winter there was a great fire in the roome, so some went to one thing, some to another, to learne against next morning, there being many candles in the Roome in severall places".[22] One can sense the nostalgia in John Ferrar's words as he thinks of the candles and the fire-lit room, writing some fifteen years after his brother's death.

Yet though he has given us this record of the days, neither John's *Life* nor the letters give a clear picture of Nicholas himself. Methodical, meticulous, something of a martinet—so he would seem in the close control he kept over every detail, even such matters as putting young Nicholas into trousers and whether or not it was necessary to buy a new coat for Joyce. But, either because his genuine concern for their welfare warded off criticism or because he had a way with him, he won the affection and co-operation of all but a few. In the travesty of Little Gidding published in 1641 and called *The Arminian Nunnery*, the satirist "improved" on an account given

[21] *The Ferrar Papers*, p. 308. This fascinating selection of private letters (pp. 231–312) gives a very human background to an experiment by no means free of strain. Dr Blackstone also prints, with a note on the Little Academy, one of its discourses, "The Winding Sheet" (pp. 95–201).

[22] Ibid., p. 49.

by a certain Edward Lenton to Sir Thomas Hetley several years earlier. In the tract Nicholas is described as a "jolly, pragmaticall and Priest-like fellow"; Lenton speaks of him as "of a plaine presence, but of able speech and parts". Lenton thought John was the more priest-like in appearance; Mrs Ferrar, one is not surprised to hear, was "tall, straight, clear-complexioned, grave".[23]

Ferrar died towards the end of 1637 and within the next year Anna died also. John tried to continue the old way of life as his brother had bidden him, and the younger Nicholas gave him support and hope. But it was not to be. In the spring of 1640, as the last hopes of reconciliation were vanishing in the State, John and his son came up to town to present some rare specimens of their work to the King and the promised Harmony to the Prince of Wales.[24] There were two wonderful days of recognition and joy, at Whitehall on Maundy Thursday and at Richmond, where they visited the young princes, on Good Friday. On Easter Day Nicholas complained of feeling unwell; and a few weeks later, on his twentieth birthday, he died. Thereafter calamities multiplied. The wars began, and at some period the estate was sequestered and John Ferrar and his family went abroad. Mary Collett was in Brussels in 1643, but did not remain there as is suggested in *John Inglesant*. On her return to England she lived with Thomas and Martha at Highgate, where she died in 1680. John Ferrar came home before the end of the war and was back at Little Gidding in 1646, on the tragic night when the King came thither as a fugitive and John led him across the fields to a place of refuge. Soon afterwards the house and church were burnt and ransacked but only partially destroyed, and the Ferrars lived on there undisturbed till John died in 1657. Then Bathsheba was so much in a hurry to be gone that

[23] A. L. Maycock, *Chronicles of Little Gidding* (1954), pp. 40, 49; see the whole chapter (pp. 39–58), for an account of Lenton's visit and text of *The Arminian Nunnery*.

[24] Ibid., pp. 19–29; and see C. Leslie Craig, *Nicholas Ferrar Junior, a linguist of Little Gidding* (1950).

she could not wait for the coach from Oundle, but hired a seat in a wagon, "and after a tedious journey and well-shaking of bones came safe to London".[25] The Little Gidding that had been was no more, though it lived on in the memory and affection of a second generation of Ferrars and Colletts and Mapletofts and has remained for all time a unique and treasured chapter in the story of the Anglican Church.[26]

There was yet another strand in the Anglican tradition, preserved somewhat precariously through the coming years of hardening ideologies and civil strife, and a third quiet spot as worthy of pilgrimage as Bemerton or Little Gidding. The village of Great Tew still lies unspoilt between Cotswolds and Chilterns, to be found only by those who turn aside from the crowded roads that run from Oxford to the Midlands through Banbury or Shipston-on-Stour. In the years before 1640 Lord Falkland's home at Tew stood for the intellectual freedom and for the tolerance in matters of doctrine which remained, in spite of so much that was authoritarian in tone, implicit in the Anglican stress on the use of reason.

As Herbert's poems preserved the spirit of Bemerton and John Ferrar's self-effacing *Life* of his brother painted in loving detail the picture of Little Gidding, so a man's desire to leave a memorial of his friends kept alive the story of Great Tew. During an enforced breathing-space in a life of incessant activity, Edward Hyde, in Jersey, at the close of the first Civil War, began to write his *History of the Great Rebellion*; twenty years later, again in exile, he completed the record of his *Life and Times*. During the intervening years he had known many great men, had become Earl of Clarendon, Lord Chancellor

[25] *Ferrar Papers*, pp. 309 f (John Ferrar, Junior, to his wife, 3 Nov. 1657).

[26] The *Chronicles of Little Gidding* cover the years after Nicholas Ferrar's death, giving some account of the life at Little Gidding during the civil wars and the Interregnum. There is an interesting sketch of Virginia Ferrar, showing the continued interest of her father and herself in the colony after which she was named (pp. 75–86, 102–5), and of her cousin, John Mapletoft (pp. 110–16).

of England, and had shaped the destinies of his land. But as he looked back the most vivid of his memories was of a small group who met together, at Burford in the earlier days and later at Great Tew, guests of Lucius Cary, the second Lord Falkland, best of hosts and most lovable of men. "There were Dr Sheldon, Dr Morley, Dr Hammond, Dr Earles, Mr Chillingworth", and as Clarendon wrote he recalled the faces behind the names, "and indeed all men of eminent parts and faculties in Oxford, besides those who resorted thither from London."[27] To a later list he added Sidney Godolphin and "Mr John Hales of Eton". They met as friends, differing widely in character and attainments but united by their Oxford background and a certain liberal temper of mind. Falkland in his self-imposed seclusion welcomed them without formality; there was an open invitation and they came and went unheralded, but when they were there he put aside his Greek Grammar or the tract he was writing on *Infallibility*, content to talk and to listen and to make them feel at home. The *convivium* and its members live for posterity in Clarendon's balanced prose while the harsh record of history completes the story of their varying fates, against the backcloth of a world in turmoil. Some like Falkland himself, Godolphin, and Chillingworth died of wounds or on the field of battle in the course of the Civil War; some like Hyde and Sheldon lived to achieve high office in the England of the Restoration; all who survived the wars experienced in the Interregnum hardship or exile and in many cases penury. Yet they remained a company of friends, destined to become the chief champions

[27] *The Life of Edward, Earl of Clarendon*, written by himself (edn of 1827), I.48; cf. Clarendon's *History of the Rebellion*, ed. Macray (1888), III.180. For the Great Tew group see also Kurt Weber, *Lucius Cary, 2nd Viscount Falkland* (1940), which gives a detailed account of the days at Burford and Tew and a sketch of the members of the "Convivium": full bibliography is attached (pp. 327–49). J. A. R. Marriott, *Life and Times of Viscount Falkland* (1907), is a readable biography covering Falkland's whole life. For the thought and influence of the group see J. Tulloch, *Rational Theology and Christian Philosophy in England in the 17th century* (1874), I.76–343, and Jordan, *The Development of Religious Toleration*, II.349–421.

of the Anglican way in the years of adversity, and accomplishing what they did, at least in part, because they *were* friends and because of their knowledge of each other's minds, gained in the discussions at Great Tew in the days of peace.

Although John Hales may not have visited Tew, for he seldom left Eton except to lecture in Oxford, he was in many ways most truly representative of the attitude of mind which gave the group its value.[28] His love of moderation was bred not of indifference but of charity, and imbued with a hatred of all that divided man from man. He was considerably older than Falkland's other friends. He was born at Bath in 1584, the son of the agent of a neighbouring estate, and to the end of his life he remained a countryman, who had no desire to settle in London or to share in great affairs. He went up to Oxford as a scholar of Corpus Christi, when Rainolds was President, and thus gained first-hand knowledge of the best type of scholarly Puritan. It was the period when Henry Savile, at Merton, was recruiting his team of scholars to assist him in his mammoth task of translating and editing the works of St Chrysostom. His talent scouts, who had picked out Richard Montagu, discovered Hales also, and in 1605 he was offered a fellowship at Merton. For the next eight years he immersed himself in Chrysostom, one of the few Christian fathers whose eirenical philosophy matched his own. The teaching of the Antioch school may well have helped to mould his thought, though admittedly it had no such effect on Montagu. Hales's choice of friends, however, showed that already he was averse to the factious spirit which even in the universities was beginning to be rampant. Among his associates were moderates such as Dudley Carleton, Henry Wotton, and Sir Thomas Bodley, who was busy setting up his new library.

[28] See J. H. Elson, *John Hales of Eton* (1948). *The Golden Remaines of the ever-memorable Mr J. H.* were collected and edited by Peter Gunning in 1659 with a preface by John Pearson. Some of Hales's writings and sermons are included in Vol. V of Jared Sparks, *A Collection of Essays and Tracts in Theology* (1823–6).

Hales assisted him for three or four years, recording the accessions in the library catalogue in his exceptionally neat hand.

When Chrysostom was finished and published, Hales resigned the fellowship at Merton in favour of one at Eton where Savile was Provost. He visited Oxford regularly for a while, as the public lecturer in Greek, but an unexpected break came when he accepted the appointment of chaplain to his friend Dudley Carleton, who had been made ambassador to the Hague. In this capacity Hales accompanied Carleton to Dort in 1619 and saw at first hand the bitter dissension that arose from theological dispute. He returned thankfully to Eton, his task, as he saw it, not to decry Calvinism nor to advocate Arminianism but to preach peace, the peace and mutual forbearance of reasonable men.

Reason played as large a part as peace in John Hales's thinking. He was not only a man of gentle temper, he was a man of complete integrity and a scholar. It was therefore inconceivable to him that men should not follow out their inquiry into truth, wherever it might lead them. He believed reason to be a divine gift which it was a sin to neglect. "And how can it stand with reason", he queried, "that a man should be possessor of so goodly a piece of the Lord's pasture as is the light of understanding . . . if he suffer it to be untilled, or sow not in the Lord's seed?"[29]

Yet honest inquiry might lead a man into strange pastures, and the sceptical turn of mind which made him eschew all dogma beyond the fundamentals of the Christian faith, and hesitate to specify those fundamentals, made Hales a suspect when two Socinian tracts were published anonymously and by many were attributed to him. His own faith was securely anchored in "the plain places of the Scriptures" but the danger of rational inquiry leading to heresy was one that had to be faced, and probably he was never entirely happy about it. He could only stress the need for honesty and charity,

[29] Jordan, op. cit., II.403 ff.

agree reluctantly to the use of force by the civil arm if—and only if—heretical beliefs led to action endangering the security of the State, and hope for a national Church based on so broad a foundation that all who professed and called themselves Christians could worship together in unity.

He had a further reason for his ardent desire for a comprehensive Church. As inherent to his nature as his love of peace and his intellectual integrity was his dislike of schism. He had no love of innovation for its own sake; he possessed the innate conservatism of the countryman and the academic's abhorrence of disorder. Thus he saw no reason to alter the existing framework of church government, albeit episcopacy was to him a matter of expediency rather than of divine right. But a rigid imposition of specific modes of worship was as uncongenial to him as detailed confessions of faith. Any such attempt to achieve uniformity might cause the very schism it aimed at preventing, and he did not hesitate to add that in this case "not he that separates but he that causes the separation is the schismatic".

In spite of his friends' persuasions Hales never published a *magnum opus* but was content with a few tracts, one of which grew out of a private letter he had written to William Chillingworth summarizing his ideas on toleration and schism. It was enough in itself to make him "ever-memorable", for embodying as it did not merely the fruits of study but a man's whole way of looking at life, it gave in a few clear pages the first considered exposition of the Anglican case for liberty of thought. Laud summoned him to Lambeth soon after the publication of the tract, and may have warned him he was on dangerous ground. But no record of their talk remains, and instead of a reprimand Hales was offered in 1639 a canonry at Windsor, a promotion he accepted with reluctance and one that has puzzled his biographers. Yet in that year of crisis Laud must have felt the need of honest and pacific men with an urgency sufficient to explain his action.

Of Hales himself and his twenty years at Eton an attractive

picture remains in one of John Aubrey's vivid lives.[30] It depicts the quiet pleasures of a scholar and describes Hales's "noble librarie of bookes and those judicially chosen", his occasional glass of Canary, and the joy he derived from his numerous godchildren, who knelt for his blessing when he passed them on his walks and received a coin in addition to the blessing, so that "by the time he came to Windsor bridge he would have never a groate left". He was a small, neat man, careful of his clothing, courteous and kindly but with the gift of silence, entirely devoid of personal ambition and indulging in no vice beyond the accumulation of books; he has had many successors at Eton and in the senior common-rooms at the University, all ever-memorable in the affection of their friends.

John Hales was certainly rich in friends. There is a delightful verse of Sir John Suckling inviting him to come to town for a session of the poets. "Sir", Suckling wrote:

Whether these lines do find you out,
Putting or clearing of a doubt
(Whether predestination,
Or reconciling three in one,
Or the unriddling how men die,
And live at once eternally,
Now take you up) know 'tis decreed
You straight bestride the college steed,
Leave Socinus and the schoolmen . . .
And come to town . . .
The sweat of learned Jonson's brain,
And gentle Shakespear's eas'r strain
A hackney coach conveys you to,
In spite of all that rain can do;
And for your eighteenpence you sit
The lord and judge of all fresh wit.
News in one day as much we have here
As serves all Windsor for a year.

Occasionally Hales complied and joined the band of poets and playwrights who met under Jonson's leadership at

30 Aubrey's *Brief Lives*, ed. Oliver Lawson Dick (1949), p. 117.

various favourite inns. The scholar from Eton generally said little.

> Hales, set by himself, most gravely did smile
> To see them about nothing keep such a coil,
> Apollo had spied him, but knowing his mind
> Passed by, and called Falkland . . .[31]

On one occasion however, when Jonson and Suckling were disputing hotly about Shakespeare's claims to greatness, Hales could keep silence no longer and put up such a good case for Shakespeare that it was agreed to continue the argument in a set debate in his own rooms at Eton. "A great many books were sent down" by those who preferred the ancient writers, "all the persons of Quality that had wit and learning and interested themselves in the quarrel" came down for the occasion, and after numerous quotations from the classical poets and a "thorough disquisition" a unanimous decision gave the preference to Shakespeare.[32]

The seclusion at Eton was not quite the self-imposed exile it might appear to Hales's London friends, for the court was often at Windsor and Aubrey noted that "the learned courtiers much delighted in his company". In addition, during the greater number of the twenty years, Hales had a friend close at hand in Sir Henry Wotton, the former diplomat who became Provost of Eton in 1622. Wotton borrowed books from him and regaled him in return with good conversation, enriched by his experience as ambassador to Venice and elsewhere. Until Wotton's death just before the troubles in the State began they lived out together his philosophy of life:

> How happy is he born and taught
> That serveth not another's will,
> Whose armour is his honest thought
> And simple truth his highest skill.

[31] Quoted by Elson, op. cit., pp. 16 f. See David Masson, *Life of Milton* (1859), I.387–514 for a survey of British literature during this period.

[32] Charles Gildon, ed., *Miscellaneous Letters and Essays on several subjects* (1694), pp. 85 f, Elson, op. cit., p. 17.

Who God doth late and early pray
More of his grace than goods to lend;
And entertains the harmless day
With a well-chosen book or friend.

Wotton was Hales's senior by some years, but the latter was fortunate in finding among his juniors another rare spirit whom the world had not corrupted, the young man who had sat next to him at the session of the poets. This was Lucius Cary, eldest son of the first Lord Falkland, Lord Deputy of Ireland. At first sight the two men had little in common, except their lack of inches, their love of books, and their amiability. Hales was essentially a recluse, a friendly onlooker, young Cary was impetuous and eager to be involved. In the first four years of King Charles's reign, he was a familiar figure in London, usually in the company of Henry Morison, his close friend, whom he talked of joining in a military career. But the death of Cary's maternal grandfather, Sir Lawrence Tanfield, thrust other responsibilities upon him. His mother, Lady Falkland, Tanfield's daughter, was a strong-minded and rather eccentric lady just about to join the Roman Church, and in his will Sir Lawrence completely passed her over, leaving his estates at Burford and Great Tew, after his widow's death, to his grandson Lucius. The consequent family estrangement was the young man's first disillusionment, followed almost at once by the early death of Henry Morison, the golden youth for whom Ben Jonson wrote his famous elegy. A year later Cary married Lettice Morison, his friend's sister, a young woman of a rather neurotic piety. She had watched with great interest the inception of Little Gidding, and probably by her persuasion Cary made a deliberate choice, similar to Ferrar's, and withdrew from London to the seclusion of his Cotswold inheritance.[33] He did so, at first, with great reluctance and did not immediately achieve a tranquil life. His

[33] John Duncon, *The Holy Life and Death of the Lady Letice, Viscountess Falkland* (3rd edn 1653), pp. 6 ff et al. Duncon, who was Lady Falklands' chaplain after Falkland's death, was the mutual friend of Ferrar and Herbert and was with the latter shortly before his death.

father died in 1634 and Cary, now Lord Falkland, spent the following winter in the capital, trying to disentangle his parents' chaotic finances and provide for his widowed mother. To do this adequately he eventually sold Burford, and the latter years were spent entirely at Great Tew. The Dowager Lady Falkland became increasingly difficult to satisfy or control, and his feelings and his pride were deeply wounded by her successful attempts to win over her younger sons to Rome. To achieve this, she used shock methods, for while the youths were staying at Tew under Chillingworth's tutelage, they were abducted. Two of their sisters, who were also at Tew, were going on a visit to town and, on the pretence of rousing them at three in the morning in time for the early start, the two boys were able to get up and out of the house without rousing their tutor's suspicions. The rest was easy. They slipped down the gardens, somewhat noisily, to a rendezvous a mile away, where two hired men awaited them with horses and bore them to Abingdon and thence by boat to London. Thence they were smuggled abroad to the Jesuits and salvation.[34]

Falkland never saw his brothers again, and it was against this background of a bitter personal experience that he wrote his tract on *Infallibility*, which was circulated in manuscript among his friends, together with an earlier letter he had written attempting to dissuade his kinsman, Walter Montagu, from being reconciled to Rome. In both writings he examined the question of schism from the opposite angle to Hales, not that of the Church endeavouring to forestall dissent but that of the unwilling dissident. For Rome's chief weapon against the Anglican Church was this very charge of schism. If Rome were indeed infallible, what right had Anglicans to withstand her claim? Hence Falkland's attempt to assess infallibility in a discourse in which emotion as well as reason played a part. From both viewpoints he could not but conclude against "this supposed necessity of an infallible guide"

34 Weber, *Lucius Cary*, pp. 177–80.

and "the supposed damnation for want of it". To all "who follow their reason in the interpretation of the Scriptures, God will either give his grace for assistance to find the truth or his pardon if they miss it."[35] It is the same argument as that of Hales, a blending of rational thought and a charitable temper, and the writings had an immediate value in that they gave to this growing idea of toleration the *cachet* of Falkland's high repute. But the classic work on the subject, written in the library of Great Tew during 1636, was the book which William Chillingworth completed after his pupils' abduction, *The Religion of Protestants: a safe way to Salvation.*

Chillingworth was a man of a restless mind, with an insatiable thirst for truth, who worried himself into doubts at every stage of his spiritual journey. Clarendon described him in a few cogent words as one who had "an indefatigable desire to do good: his only unhappiness proceeded from his sleeping too little and thinking too much". He had been one of those who could not resist the able persuasions of the Jesuit, Fisher, and after many heart-searchings in 1630 he had given up his fellowship at Oxford and entered the Jesuit seminary at Douai. He found that certainty was as far to seek in the infallible Church of Rome as in the Anglican *via media* and after a year he returned to England and a fresh period of hesitation, under the anxious eye of Laud, his godfather. He was much helped by the wise counsel of William Juxon, the President of St John's, and by Gilbert Sheldon's firm direction and in 1634 he returned to the Anglican allegiance, still unhappy about the Athanasian creed, which did not seem to him, in its damnatory clauses, to be "agreeable to the word of God".[36]

A sharp controversy had arisen, when Chillingworth first went over to Rome, between the Jesuit Edward Knott and

[35] *A discourse of Infallibility . . . by Sir Lucius Cary, late Lord Viscount of Falkland. Also Mr Walter Mountague . . . His Letter against Protestantism; and his lordship's answer thereunto* . . . [1660]. The Discourse was first published in 1645, and with the letter attached in 1651.

[36] Tulloch, *Rational Theology and Christian Philosophy*, I.283, n 4; cf. Weber, op. cit., pp. 169–212.

Dr Potter, the Provost of Queen's, and the *Religion of Protestants* was a section-by-section examination and denial of Knott's assertions, combined with a defence of Dr Potter. Under these circumstances it could not be expected to have literary form, but the clarity and sincerity of its thought rises above the straitjacket of the enforced line of argument. The point at issue was once again that of infallibility. It was the great question of the seventeenth century both in Church and State. "By what authority . . . ?" Where was the final word to be found upon which mankind could rest? Chillingworth gave a clear answer: for Protestants it was the Bible—not Luther, nor Calvin, nor Melancthon, but the Bible. "I for my part after a long and (as I verily believe and hope) impartial search of the true way to eternal happiness, do profess plainly that I cannot find any rest for the sole of my foot but upon this rock only." It was a statement to which all Protestants would say "Amen". Whether or not it led to a tolerant approach depended on the way in which the argument was developed. Chillingworth, in denying that any Church was infallible and in asserting that salvation was to be found in the Bible alone, went on to declare that "nothing is necessary to be believed but what is plainly revealed", thus making that distinction between the fundamentals and the accessories of faith which was at the basis of the moderates' case for freedom of thought. "For to say", he continued, "that where a place [of Scripture] by reason of ambiguous terms lies indifferent between divers senses, whereof one is true and the other is false, that God obliges man, under pain of damnation, not to mistake through error and human frailty, is to make God a tyrant." To impel people to believe was foolish and indeed impossible, for belief was a thing that could not be forced. Believe what one could, and live in the spirit of one's faith, this was basically his counsel. "If all men would believe the Scriptures and freeing themselves from prejudice and passion would sincerely endeavour to find the true sense of it and live according to it and require no more of others than to do so . . . those wretched contentions

which now rend and tear in pieces not the coat but the members and bowels of Christ . . . should speedily receive a most blessed catastrophe."[37]

It was here that Chillingworth, like Hales, trod less surely in the assumption that the "fundamentals" would always be acceptable to rational men. It was possible to argue, as Hammond put it later, that these truths were so plainly revealed in the Word of God that it would be unreasonable not to believe them. None the less their validity must rest on religious experience, rather than on rational proof, and the strength of the Great Tew group as compared with men such as Lord Herbert of Cherbury lay in the fact that they possessed in abundance a deep personal piety. They none of them believed that correct thinking was in itself enough; if the Scriptures were a safe way to salvation then one must live according to the Word. And while Chillingworth's able and incisive pen claimed for all men the right to find out the truth for themselves, the link between truth and goodness was shown forth by other members of the group, particularly by Earle and Hammond, in the whole tenor of their lives.

Falkland's first target, when he retired to the Cotswolds, had been to learn Greek, and in Earle he had a friend ready to help him with the classics and also to criticize his not very admirable verse. John Earle was a fellow of Merton—the only scholar, it was said, whom Sir Henry Savile had been willing to accept despite the reputation of a wit. Humour was not the strong suit at Great Tew, and Earle must have been a particularly welcome guest. He was reputed to be the author of

[37] See Tulloch, op. cit., I.326–37, summarizing the scattered argument of *The Religion of Protestants:* "Scripture on the one hand, therefore, and the free, honest, open mind on the other hand—these are, with Chillingworth, the factors, and the only factors, of religious truth—the essential elements of religious certitude" (p. 330). Cf. Paul Elmer More, "The Spirit of Anglicanism", pp. xxiv f, an essay prefaced to *Anglicanism: the thought and practice of the Church of England, illustrated from the Religious Literature of the 17th century*, compiled and edited by P. E. More and F. L. Cross (1935).

the *Microcosmography*, a collection of character-sketches published anonymously in 1628—an assumption he never denied. The sketches are full of a salty humour and when he castigated the pompous and the insincere he could be scathing. He wrote of the Formalist, whose religion was "a good quiet subject", and the Female Hypocrite who "so overflows with the Bible that she spills it on every occasion and will not cudgel her maids without Scripture". But when he described "The Grave Divine", it was with a sympathy as characteristic of him as his wit. His Divine is "a Protestant, out of judgement not faction; not because his country but his reason is on this side. . . . Inciting of Popish errors, he cuts them with arguments, not cudgels them with barren invectives, and labours more to shew the truth of his cause than the spleen. . . . In matters of ceremony he is not ceremonious but thinks how he owes that reverence to the Church to bow his judgement to it, and make more conscience of schism than a surplice. . . . He is no base grater of his tithes and will not wrangle for the odd egg. . . . He is the main pillar of our Church though not yet Dean or Canon and his life our religion's best apology."[38]

Earle might well have been writing of his friend Henry Hammond, who may have ridden over to Burford as frequently as the others, but cannot often have been at Great Tew, for in 1633 he moved to Kent. Hammond was a scholar of outstanding repute, but he had little of Chillingworth's thirst for philosophical inquiry. Chillingworth's second love was engineering, and it would have needed only a twist of destiny to make him a scientist, rather than a theologian; whereas Hammond's learning was deeply rooted in the writings of antiquity, and his value to his friends and to his Church

[38] John Earle, *Microcosmography, or a piece of the world discovered*, ed. H. Osborne (1933): 1st edn 1628; 7th edn 1638. For a well-argued suggestion that the true author of the sketches was Charles Herle, the Puritan, see J. D. Ogilvie, "Earle and Herle and the Microcosmography" in *Journal of the Presbyterian Historical Society*, XXV.246; but it seems unlikely that a man of Earle's character would have allowed the assumption of his authorship to go uncontradicted if it were false.

came as much from his personality as his learning. His genius was a practical one; he was energetic and precise, vigorous in thought and action and exceptionally sweet-tempered, not a very usual combination. As a child at Eton his precocity was already balanced by this tranquillity of spirit, rather to the confusion of his master who thought that it denoted indolence but had to think again when young Hammond was ready for Oxford at the age of thirteen. He was made a fellow of Magdalen when he was twenty, and was ordained in 1629 upon reaching the canonical age. Four years later, the President of Magdalen, unable to fulfil an engagement at court or wanting to give his young colleague his opportunity, sent him to preach at Whitehall in his stead. Among those present was the Earl of Leicester, who was profoundly moved by the sermon and offered Hammond the vacant family living at Penshurst. His acceptance changed the course of Hammond's life, and for more than ten years he remained a parish priest, giving himself wholeheartedly to the work.

The life which Dr Fell wrote of him a year or so after his death is one of conventional eulogy, but the picture of the days at Penshurst rings true; diligent and constant preaching, the daily service and the monthly Communion, regular teaching of the catechism in which Hammond excelled, and the steady practice of the Christian virtues of "relieving the poor, keeping hospitality, reconciling of differences among neighbours, visiting the sick". He was as practical as Herbert in his good deeds, and it was never forgotten how in times of scarcity he would buy in corn at the enhanced rate and resell it to his parishioners at normal prices.[39] Hammond's father had been one of the royal physicians, and he had considerable private means which he regarded as a trust to be used punctiliously in the service of his fellows and his Church. One of the few early sermons of his that remain pleads for systematic

39 Henry Hammond, *Miscellaneous Theological Works* (1847–50), I.xxiii. John Fell's *Life* written in 1661, is prefaced to Vol. I of the *Works,* edited by N. Pocock in 3 vols. in the *Library of Anglo-Catholic Theology.*

almsgiving. It was preached at Paul's Cross and so may have had reference to the repair of the cathedral, but he dealt with wider issues and impressed upon the distinguished gathering that salvation did not depend merely upon "the diligence of a bended knee"; the teaching of Micah and St James was also relevant and Christ's own words, "For I was an hungered and ye gave me meat."[40]

It is not entirely chance, nor entirely due to their biographers' rose-coloured spectacles, that at least three of Falkland's friends, Hales, Earle, Hammond, were men of outstanding goodness and kindliness of heart. The ethos of Burford and Tew, the belief that the tangled problems of politics could only be solved by the fearless application of intelligence and charity combined, appealed strongly to men who abhorred the lack of single-mindedness in public life. Yet the men, whose names Clarendon listed, were not by any means all of a similar type. There was, for instance, a doctrinaire streak in Gilbert Sheldon; as Warden of All Souls he had not hesitated to cross swords with Laud when the latter attempted to jockey young Jeremy Taylor into a fellowship, contrary to the regulations. Sheldon's friends at Great Tew used to say from the start that he was meant to be Archbishop of Canterbury. Sheldon's close friend, George Morley, differed from the rest in still professing Calvinist doctrine which he managed to combine with liveliness of mind and a generous if hot temper. Edward Hyde himself came to Tew from an active life in the Inns of Court, very different from the common-rooms of Merton and All Souls.

When Falkland first became intimate with Hyde, during that winter in London in 1634, the latter was at the parting of the ways. He had been called to the bar in the previous year and was an ambitious and able young man, the centre of a brilliant circle of friends including the erratic Kenelm Digby and the clever but detached politician, Selden. He was at once

[40] Hammond, *Miscellaneous Theological Works*, III.239–69, "The Poor Man's Tithing" (12 April 1640): see pp. 256 f in particular.

eager for action and uncertain where he belonged, when the meeting with Falkland and an invitation to Great Tew introduced him to a fresh group of men, with whom he found himself in surprising accord. He remained a man of affairs, but the serious cast of mind which was natural to him was accepted as right and proper by his new friends and, while his zeal for the public service was stimulated rather than abated, his religion was deepened by their influence and his ambition was tempered by contact with men whose scale of values was based, not on worldly success, but on sound learning and an honest life.[41]

It was with his host that the ties were closest. Falkland was no recluse; the surprising thing is that he had kept so long to his resolution to stay out of London. For Lettice, his wife, the quiet and ordered days were years of content, which came to an abrupt end in the summer of 1639. For Falkland himself there may have been an element of relief in his decision to volunteer to march in the King's forces against the Scottish rebels. It was an impetuous, generous action though it did not prove a happy experience. He enjoyed neither the deepening conviction that matters were seriously awry nor such minor discomforts as the shortage of butter in County Durham.[42] But afterwards it was quite impossible to return to a life of seclusion in the southern Midlands. It was the hour for action, not for meditation, if the rising tide of discontent were to be directed aright. Those in university posts had still their jobs to do, but he and Edward Hyde had now the opportunity to stand in public for the way of life—reasonable, just, charitable —that they had envisaged at Great Tew.

So the *Convivium* was adjourned *sine die* and the two friends stood for Parliament. At Westminster, in the spring of 1640, they made their first acquaintance with the House of Commons. Falkland, an inveterate romantic, was tremendously impressed

[41] Sir Henry Craik, *The Life of Edward, Earl of Clarendon* (1911), I.28–32.

[42] *Cal. S.P. Dom. 1639–40*, p. 578 ([Thomas] Triplet to Laud, 4 March 1640).

by the quality of the knights and burgesses who came together in sober mood to set their country right. He was the more shocked and angered by the court's mismanagement that led to the breakdown of the abortive Parliament. Six months later the new House assembled and Hyde and Falkland, sitting side by side, were soon known to be inseparable, as they joined without hesitation in an all but unanimous attack on the King's evil counsellors and his arbitrary rule. They did not doubt that the pulling down would be followed in due course by a building up, and by the restoration of an ordered realm and a Church in which the Spirit burnt more brightly for the dead wood that had been cut away.

# 6

# DOWNFALL

IN November 1640 the burgesses and gentry of the shires came up to Westminster in an angry and determined mood. Arbitrary rule must go in Church and State, the Popish menace must be uncovered and destroyed, evil counsellors removed, and the victims of the prerogative courts indemnified. In the face of a responsible section of the nation, all but a few hostile to the régime if not to him, the King was helpless and his servants hopelessly at odds. Effective measures by the advocates of *Thorough* were forestalled by the prompt action of the Commons, led by John Pym, the member for Tavistock, a man whose sober zeal for the laws and liberties of England was combined with a subtle and ruthless gift for organizing and directing parliamentary strategy. A week after the session opened Strafford reached London from the north and within twenty-four hours, after a secret session of the Commons, he was impeached at the bar of the Upper House, arrested, and sent to the Tower. By that swift attack all that followed was made possible.

The new House of Commons was not in any way a revolutionary body. The great majority of the members were men of property, well known in the local community which had chosen them and which they had served as magistrates, lords of the manor, churchwardens, and the like. They were a wealthy group: out of a total of more than five hundred it is estimated that close to half "were in the category of rich men".[1] In his great opening speech Pym referred to the

[1] M. F. Keeler, *The Long Parliament 1640–1*, a biographical study of its members (1954), pp. 21–6.

"liberty and property which was their birthright by the laws of the land", and it was the restoration of security and the preservation of the law which most concerned them. Hence their unanimity in attacking the arbitrary acts of the King and their distrust of innovations which were likely to upset the economic framework—the more so in the case of members who chanced to hold the tithes and patronage of the parish church. How they felt about religion depended mainly on local affiliations and personal experience. The events of the next two years had still to mould them into opposing parties; as yet they were less conscious of the differences that would eventually divide them than of the family relationships and neighbourhood loyalties that even in those later days were never entirely forgotten.[2]

Pym was a loyal adherent of the middle way, a Church of England man with a tincture of Puritan zeal the strength of which it was hard to estimate. He certainly considered the Arminian trimmings of recent years to be a dangerous approach to Popery, and thus a threat to the safety of the kingdom; but he was not concerned immediately with fundamental issues of doctrine and church government, partly because it was more consonant with his nature to deal with the facts that revealed abuses than with the theories that may have caused them, and also because many matters of law and politics clamoured for attention and too detailed a consideration of religion would, he knew, be likely to sunder the House's unity. He directed attention to specific points: the employment of Roman Catholics in positions of trust at Whitehall and in the Army, the attempt to crush Puritan opinion in the parishes by prosecutions upon "things indifferent", and the bishops' insufferable claims in regard to their temporal powers.[3] A Grand Committee of Religion was appointed to

[2] J. H. Hexter, *The Reign of King Pym* (Harvard Historical Studies, No. 48; 1941), pp. 73 et seq.

[3] John Rushworth, *Historical Collections* (1721), IV.22. The main authority for the ecclesiastical history of the period is W. A. Shaw, *The*

deal with these questions, while the House proceeded on the political front with the urgent business of framing the charges against Strafford and introducing a Bill for annual Parliaments, later modified as the Triennial Bill. The Lord Keeper, Finch, was impeached as the defender of ship-money, Falkland attracting attention by the ability with which he conducted the case, but Finch evaded arrest and slipped away to France. Before long his example was followed by Secretary Windebank, who had been the official responsible for the issue of the writs that had waived proceedings against the recusants. A timid man, longing to be justified, he enjoyed exile no more than authority—one of the first of the company of the uprooted who in the succeeding years were to haunt the capitals of Europe.

In the first weeks of its existence the Grand Committee was inundated with petitions for redress from victims of the Star Chamber and High Commission Court, so much so that the chairman, Sir Edward Dering, reported in vigorous if somewhat muddled metaphors that the axe should be laid to the "long and deep fangs of superstition and Popery".[4] Until Strafford was destroyed, however, and the passage of the Triennial Bill ensured, Pym preferred to continue the piecemeal treatment of religious grievances, and deflected enthusiasts from more controversial measures by encouraging attacks upon individual churchmen and by directing attention towards the unpopular Canons of 1640. In mid-December these were declared illegal, Lord Digby, the brilliant but erratic son of the Earl of Bristol, declaring that Convocation, by continuing to sit after the dissolution in the spring, "had usurped to itself the grand pre-eminence of Parliament". This focused attention on Laud and two days later he was impeached, the Peers committing him to the custody of Black Rod until the

---

*History of the English Church, 1640–60* (2 vols., 1900): the first half of Vol. I deals with the ecclesiastical debates of 1640–3 (pp. 1–144). Cf. D. Neal, *History of the Puritans* (1822), I.318–44.

[4] Shaw, op. cit., I.14.

Lower House sent up the Articles of impeachment. Wren was ordered to appear when required and in the Commons John Cosin was attacked. Cosin had been for the past five years Master of Peterhouse, where he had adorned the college chapel with all the beauty of worship that meant so much to him.[5] Recently he had been appointed Dean of Peterborough, but now the old charges were revived against him and he was ejected from his deanery and condemned by a vote of the whole House. He was allowed bail and remained for a while in Cambridge, increasingly isolated in that Puritan stronghold whose Member of Parliament was Oliver Cromwell. His old friend, Montagu, escaped retribution, for both he and Archbishop Neile had died earlier in the year.

One of the first petitions with which the Grand Committee had to deal came from the wives of Henry Burton and Dr Bastwick, and within a few weeks they and Prynne had been released. Burton and Prynne met at Southampton and rode up to London together. Some distance from the city they were met by "multitudes of people of several conditions, some on horseback, others on foot", and were brought with tumultuous rejoicing into London by way of Charing Cross. They themselves and those who followed carried sprigs of rosemary, "for remembrance", and others waved the branches of bay that symbolized victory, as they hurled their anathemas against the bishops who were held responsible for all that the returned heroes had suffered. In Southwark, a few days later, Dr Bastwick was greeted in the same way. To Hyde it was evident that behind the tumult there was a good deal of careful organization, "to publish the temper of the people",[6] and this shrewd use of public opinion to influence the debates at Westminster and the decisions of the King was to be a marked feature of the succeeding months. Hyde believed that a good deal of "uningenuity and mountebankry" went into the work

[5] Rose Macaulay gives a sympathetic description of Cambridge in 1640–1 in her historical novel *They were Defeated.*

[6] Clarendon, *History of the Great Rebellion,* ed. Macray (1888), I.269.

of circulating and presenting petitions to the House, which was the chief way, except for exploiting mob emotions at times of crisis, in which the temper of the people was brought to bear on events. But neither Hyde nor the majority of his fellow members had any conception of the strength of feeling that had been growing in the capital during recent years, directed not merely against the excesses of individuals but against the system itself. Sir Richard Gurney, the Lord Mayor elected this November, was a loyal servant to the King and the civic authorities were still closely linked with the Crown, but radical views and a closely knit body of Puritan devotees might be found, not only among the craftsmen and journeymen and the noisy apprentices, but in the sober ranks of middle-class merchants, who had sat under John Davenport at St Stephen's, Coleman Street, or worshipped at Henry Burton's church, St Matthew's, Friday Street. Their leaders had worked together in the colonizing and trading ventures of the thirties, or shared in the activities of the feoffees, and they scored their first all-important success in Common Hall in the autumn of 1640, when they secured the election of four members of Parliament, led by Isaac Penington, who represented their point of view not that of the loyal Lord Mayor and aldermen.[7] Left-wing Puritan opinion was thus effectively expressed at Westminster by the London members, whose position was strengthened not only by petitions presented at crucial moments but by the need to raise money in the City to pay the Scottish Army—loans which Penington and his colleagues became adept at promising or holding up according to their liking for the mood of the House.[8]

The continued presence of this army in the north of England was a factor not to be disregarded and strengthened the hands of the parliamentary leaders. At the end of November Scottish

[7] Valerie Pearl, *London and the Outbreak of the Puritan Revolution* (1961), pp. 193 et seq., et al.

[8] Ibid., pp. 201 ff.

commissioners arrived in London to treat for peace, and in attendance upon them was Robert Baillie, who wrote home to his wife or his presbytery a full account of all that occurred. "All here are weary of Bishops", he reported on arrival, and as soon as "his little Grace", Archbishop Laud, was impeached Baillie expected "to get Bishops, ceremonies and all away".[9] It was not, however, as simple as he thought, and the zeal with which the Scots proffered advice in the matter of religious reform remained an embarrassment to Pym, even if it encouraged those of his colleagues who thought the time had come for fundamental change.

To a certain extent they forced Pym's hand, by the presentation of a petition from the City of London. On 11 December, four days before the debate on the illegal Canons, a crowd of some hundreds with two aldermen at their head bore down upon Westminster. This was no mob of firebrands and apprentices; they were led by gentlemen of quality and worth, and Baillie described them as "a world of honest citizens in their best apparel". None the less the number of signatures to the petition was alarming (some estimated it at 15,000). The petition itself was revolutionary, for it asked for the complete abolition of episcopal government, "with all its dependencies, roots and branches". It thus raised the very issue Pym had hoped to avoid, the basic question of church government and the nature of episcopacy, and the cleavage in the House that was immediately revealed showed that his reluctance had been more than justified. He succeeded in shelving the matter until February, by which time there had been other expressions of opinion, one petition, signed by a more moderate section of the Puritan clergy, asking for reform rather than basic change. On 8 February the House debated whether this and the London Petition should be committed for further consideration, and the subsequent discussion—which began in the morning, went on all day, and continued on the

[9] *The Letters and Journals of Robert Baillie* (edn of 1841) I.274, 278. (Baillie to his wife, 18 Nov., 12 Dec. [1640].)

morrow—proved to be a landmark in the history of the Parliament.[10]

It was the first occasion of conflicting opinions and emotions that the House had witnessed. Baillie asserted that those in favour of the petition had only expected a formal debate on its committal, and found that they had to rebut without preparation a determined defence of episcopacy in general. It was Digby who most impressed the House. His approach was empirical; he claimed that any other form of church government might have as great or greater inconveniences than limited episcopacy, and he stressed the way in which the petition had been presented and the dangers of "irregular and tumultuous assemblies". This matched the temper of many of the members, who were conservative by instinct and were already beginning to feel that they were yoked with dangerous colleagues in the business of setting the country to rights. Falkland followed in a rather different vein. "He is a great stranger in our Israel," he began, "who knows not that this kingdom has long laboured under many and great oppressions both in religion and liberty, and that a principal cause of both has been some bishops and their adherents. . . ." He charged the bishops with the destruction of unity, "who under pretence of uniformity have brought in superstition, and scandal under the title of decency", and criticized their efforts to increase their temporal power. But then, with a sudden switch, Falkland declared that the blame did not lie with episcopacy itself but with individual bishops who had abused their function. "There are some that have been neither proud nor ambitious." He thereupon urged that they should not root up the "ancient tree" of the episcopacy until they had tried lopping its branches. With logical if fallacious optimism, he concluded: "Let us but give good men

[10] Pearl, op. cit., pp. 213 et seq.; see *The Journal of Sir Simonds D'Ewes from the beginning of the Long Parliament to the opening of the Trial of the Earl of Strafford*, ed. Wallace Notestein (1923), pp. 335 et seq. For the text of the petition see Rushworth, op. cit., IV.93 ff.

good rules and we shall have good government and good times."[11]

In the interchanges on 9 February, it was not Falkland's argument but Digby's that was taken up, the more vigorously in that a number of citizen-politicians had marched down that morning to the entrance of the House to "countenance their petition". Penington answered Digby's criticisms with vigour. The petition had been warranted by "men of worth and knowen integritie". If pressure had been used, not 15,000 but four times as many would have signed it, "and if ther weere anie meane men's hands to it yet if they weere honest men ther was noe reason but ther hands should bee received". That, to most, was dangerous doctrine; the "meaner sort" should not have views of their own. Later Sir John Strangeways of Dorset hinted at the fear that was at the back of many minds: "if we made a paritie in the Church we must at last come to a paritie in the Commonwealth". At that stage the M.P. for Cambridge rose to contradict him, and there were calls to the bar and a few minutes' uproar before Cromwell repeated more quietly that he saw no reason to make the comparison.[12]

The petition was eventually committed for consideration, and two weeks later the committee made recommendations on the lines suggested by Falkland. The bishops' claims to jurisdiction, their intermeddling with secular affairs, and their "too great rents" were listed as true grievances, and two Bills were introduced, the one to abolish the High Commission and Star Chamber courts and the other to exclude the bishops from their seats in the House of Lords. Upon the latter Bill, for probably the only occasion in their parliamentary career, Falkland and Hyde differed, and Falkland voted for the

[11] Neal, *History of the Puritans*, II.365 ff; Rushworth, *Historical Collections*, IV.184 ff. Cf. Baillie, I.302: ". . . they contested on together from eight acloak till six at night. All that night our party solisted as hard as they could. Tomorrow some thousands of citizens bot in a verie peaceable way went down to Westminster Hall to countenance their petition."

[12] D'Ewes, *Journal* (ed. Notestein), p. 339.

bishops' exclusion, which Hyde opposed. Falkland, deeply concerned with the welfare of the Church, was persuaded that only by such a concession could further attacks upon it be prevented. To Hyde, the bishops were part of the hierarchical framework, not only of the Church but of the Constitution, a landmark not to be overturned if order were to be maintained.[13]

In March the Earl of Strafford's trial began, and until the bitter end, in the early days of May, the eyes of all were focused upon the tragedy of a great man fighting a losing battle for his life. The impeachment failed, and Strafford was condemned by an Act of Attainder, to which the King miserably gave his consent, unnerved by the threatening mob and his Queen's terror, conscious of guilt even in the doing of the act, a hundredfold remorseful afterwards. He had asked advice of the bishops at hand and each had replied as might be expected. Williams, whom the whirligig of fortune had restored to a measure of favour, distinguished between a king's public and private conscience and tried to justify compliance; Ussher of Armagh had been more recondite than helpful and Bishop Juxon had urged him to do what was right, whatever the cost. Charles gave way, but his surrender helped neither the nation nor himself; for the problems that had now to be faced—the control of the armed forces and the restriction of episcopal power—were fundamental to the authority of Church and Crown and Strafford's death had not answered either question. The King's policy veered between conciliation and the encouragement of army plots, evolved by the hotheads on the "Queen's Side". In May, the Lords rejected the Bill for the exclusion of the bishops, but the committee of divines which they had set up under Williams' chairmanship to advise them on the matter of Church reform had ceased to

[13] Clarendon, *History of the Great Rebellion*, I.311; Christopher Hill, *Puritanism and Revolution* (1958), p. 202. Cf. B. H. G. Wormald, *Clarendon: Politics, History and Religion* (1951), pp. 5–12, 286 et seq. for an interesting examination of the difference in attitude of Hyde and Falkland.

sit after only six meetings. Three days after the Peers' rejection of the Bishops' Bill, in the House of Commons, one morning, Sir Edward Dering rose unexpectedly from his seat in the gallery and introduced a measure for the total abolition of bishops, deans, and cathedral chapters. Dering, a somewhat mercurial student of antiquities, was to change his tune more than once in his parliamentary career; he was said on this occasion to be the mouthpiece of two men—Cromwell, whose reputation was steadily growing, and the younger Henry Vane, who had already tasted authority as a youthful governor of Massachusetts. Had the Upper House agreed to exclude the bishops these two might have bided their time, but the refusal of the Lords to "lop and prune" gave to the extremists their chance to push forward with their policy of extirpation, "root and branch".

Throughout the summer the Root and Branch Bill was debated in the Commons, but in part through Pym's continuing effort to soft-pedal the religious issues and also through Hyde's clever management as chairman of the relevant committee, the Bill was still under discussion when the House adjourned in September. A change was taking place in the political atmosphere. In July the King had given his assent to the abolition of the conciliar courts and, in August, ship-money was declared illegal. These measures completed, it seemed to many that the Revolution had gone far enough. The unanimity of the previous autumn was already far to seek, and on the question of basic changes in the Church the House was all but equally divided. A motion for the revision of the Liturgy was defeated just before the adjournment, Sir John Culpepper declaring in debate that if steps were not taken against "such as did vilify and contemn the Common Prayer-book, . . . it might be the occasion of many tumults in Church and State".[14] The fear of tumults began to loom large in the minds of many. Peace had been made with the Scots in the late spring and the armies were in process of being dis-

[14] Gardiner, *History of England, 1603–1642* (1904), X.14 f.

banded, so that the countryside was infested with discharged soldiers rapidly deteriorating into rogues and vagabonds. Matters were not mended by the instructions, issued by the Commons with doubtful legality, dealing with the removal of offending images and communion rails. The growing number of local disturbances made men see that there were drawbacks even to the abolition of Star Chamber and High Commission, for now there was no effective and expeditious way for dealing with mob violence or eccentric speech. On more counts than one, this was the time when a consistent attempt at conciliation might well have succeeded; but the King was not even in England. In August, to the annoyance of his Parliament, he had journeyed north to Scotland, thinking in terms of a counter-offensive and hoping to rally support.

Charles did not return till November. Parliament had reassembled a month earlier with Pym on the defensive. No attempt was made to enforce the instructions as to images and the Root and Branch Bill was not revived. But Pym continued with a plan, conceived earlier in the autumn, of framing a Remonstrance which would, he hoped, stir up his party's flagging spirits by recapitulating all they had achieved. At the same time a second Bill excluding the bishops from the Upper House was passed through the Commons in the space of two days. Tactically it had become an essential measure, for the bishops represented a solid block of votes for the King, and, with tension increasing between the two Houses and the parties more evenly balanced, this factor was more important than any religious scruple. The King, however, continued to play his cards badly and chose this moment, while still in Edinburgh, to fill up five vacant bishoprics. No action could have exasperated the Commons more at this particular juncture, although the choice of men like Ralph Brownrigg and Humphrey Prideaux was excellent in itself as well as acceptable to the moderates. Bishop Hall was advanced to Norwich and Skinner, a High Churchman, went to Oxford, though both were lying under the Commons' impeachment for

imposing the illegal Canons. Williams, too late to glory in it, found himself at York.

At this stage a new urgency was injected into the situation by the news of the Irish Rebellion. The native population had turned upon the Protestant settlers, burning and killing in a mood of fear and revenge; nor had the Anglo-Normans of the Pale given adequate help to Strafford's ineffective successors. The truth was tragic enough, but it was bolstered up by atrocity-stories of every kind and London was soon in the throes of hysteria, spying a Popish plot at every corner of the street. What was far more serious was the growing belief that the rebels had acted with the King's connivance and the more justifiable anxiety that he might attempt to make capital out of the rebellion rather than crush it speedily. One thing was certain: neither he nor anyone else could crush it effectively without raising an army, which posed the question of whether it was safe to leave the control of the militia in the hands of an impenitent King. In the next few months this became the crucial issue.[15]

It was thus in a fighting mood that the Grand Remonstrance was hurriedly completed in November. Every grievance of the reign was meticulously listed and the blame placed firmly on bishops and evil councillors. The King was urged to agree to the curtailment of the bishops' temporal power and to choose only such councillors as Parliament approved. Conscious that the cleavage as to religion lessened their chance of success, Pym and his associates had restrained their more violent colleagues. A clause was dropped which attacked the liturgy, and an attempt was made to reassure those who feared disorder. "It is far from our purpose", the Remonstrance stated, "to let loose the golden reins of discipline and government in the Church, to leave private persons or

[15] C. V. Wedgwood, *The King's War, 1641–1647* (1958), pp. 23–107, where the story of the drift into war and the prime importance of the control of the armed forces is told with admirable clarity. The interaction of Irish and Scottish affairs with the course of events in England is stressed throughout the volume.

particular congregations to take up what form of divine service they please, for we hold it requisite that there should be throughout the whole realm a conformity to that order which the laws enjoin, according to the word of God." To this end, a general synod was suggested "of the most grave, pious, learned and judicious divines of this island; assisted with some from foreign parts. . . ." It was in such clauses that the original intention of the Remonstrance appeared most plainly, to serve as propaganda in the country as a whole. "I imagined", grumbled Dering, "that . . . we should hold up a glass to his Majesty . . . I did not dream that we should remonstrate downward and tell stories to the people."[16] But Pym all but overreached himself, for his action compelled those within the House as well as those without to think clearly where they stood. When the measure was debated on 27 November, it proved that there was little to choose numerically between the parties. Throughout the day the discussion went on, candles were called for, and the debate continued. In the small hours the motion was put and carried by a bare eleven votes. The minority asked leave to enter a protest, and swords were drawn, as overwrought tempers snapped, until Hampden's voice brought members to their senses. As Falkland and Cromwell went out together, Cromwell declared that if it had gone otherwise, he would have sold all he had and left for New England. It was the unconsidered comment of a tired and excited man but it showed how near the moderates had come to success.

Charles replied to the Remonstrance in a dignified manner, using a draft of Hyde's which asserted the King's right to choose his own councillors and refused to deprive the bishops. His return to London had been something of a triumph, and although it had been carefully encouraged by a loyal Lord Mayor and aldermen, out of tune with the prevalent tone of the City, there was sufficient reality in the people's welcome for him to feel that he might still be master of the situation.

[16] C. V. Wedgwood, *The King's Peace, 1637–1641* (1955), p. 483.

For Charles it was a dangerous mood, and during December the situation deteriorated on every hand. There was no consistency in the King's policy and any ground he had gained in London was lost by the end of the month. Another mammoth petition from the citizens, judiciously presented by a few, gave full support to the extremists in the House, and at the election to the Common Council, which took place just before Christmas, many changes occurred, putting the Puritans securely in control.[17]

To Pym and Cromwell, a Militia Bill which advanced through the two Houses alongside that for the curtailment of the bishops' temporal power was the more urgent and important of the two measures. But as the sense of crisis increased, the excited Londoners centred their attention on the bishops. Petitions poured in which made the wretched prelates responsible for every ill, including the "general decay of trade".[18] Violence was in the air; when the Houses met on St Stephen's Day after only two days' break the apprentices, at the start of their twelfth-night holiday, were completely out of hand. The mob joined in, and as the author of *Hudibras* wrote:

> The oyster women locked their fish up
> And trudged away to cry "No Bishop",
> Some cried the Covenant instead
> Of puddings, pies and gingerbread.

As some of the bishops came by water to Westminster, they found an angry crowd awaiting them at the landing-stage and "were so pelted with stones and frighted" that some withdrew and others, who reached the security of the Upper House, were warned not to venture forth again. Williams, who had given as good as he got, arrived with a torn tippet and an angry temper, and next day he persuaded eleven of his colleagues to join him in a Protestation, declaring that they were debarred by force from attending at Westminster and that in

[17] Pearl, *London and the Outbreak of the Puritan Revolution*, p. 132.

[18] See Neal, *History of the Puritans*, II.447 ff, for the numerous petitions received from the counties both by King and Parliament.

consequence further measures taken in their absence were invalid. The Lords took umbrage at the implication that they were not a free Parliament, and the Protestation was remitted to the notice of the Commons who retaliated by impeaching the twelve signatories for treason. Morton and Wright of Lichfield, whose age and reputation secured them some favour, were sent to the custody of Black Rod; the others found themselves within the Tower.

This was the beginning of the end. Each side believed that the other was planning a *coup d'état*. Pym professed himself in danger of attack and on one occasion the House removed itself ostentatiously for safety to the Guildhall. Rumours reached Charles of the Commons' intention to impeach the Queen, and there was suddenly a flurry of action at Whitehall. The King took a surprising step and offered Pym the vacant post of Chancellor of the Exchequer. It was either a farce or an insult—or a last attempt at a desperate remedy. Pym refused: and Charles bestowed the post on Sir John Culpepper and at the same time made Falkland a secretary of state.[19] They were sworn in on 2 January, and on the 3rd, in complete contravention of any advice his new councillors might have given him, the King impeached six leaders of the opposition, Lord Mandeville in the Upper House and the famous five members, Pym, Hampden, Denzil Holles, Valentine, and Strode. Digby was probably behind both moves. He had been made a peer and was in the King's close confidence, but though he was a man fertile in bright ideas he was singularly inept in translating them into effective action. The advancement of the moderates was valueless so long as they were given no real say in policy, and the attack on the five members proved disastrous. On the morning of 5 January Charles bore down on Westminster to arrest them in person, but "the birds had flown" and all that greeted the King was the bleak hostility of a House angered and amazed at his

[19] Clarendon, *History of the Great Rebellion*, I.256 ff; cf. J. A. R. Marriott, *Life and Times of Viscount Falkland*, pp. 223–8.

ill-judged invasion of their privileges. In the City, the five members took refuge in Coleman Street, and Charles going in pursuit of his quarry found no friendly welcome. The citizens were terrified, fearful of an attack from the Tower by the Royalist officer in command. Chains were drawn across the streets, while the housewives prepared buckets of boiling water. All the King achieved was a broadsheet thrust into his coach, "To your tents, O Israel". By his precipitate departure next day from Whitehall, with the Queen and his elder children, to the palace at Hampton Court, he acknowledged the severance of his realm into opposing parties. The members returned triumphantly to Westminster; the two Bills completed their passage through the House of Lords and in February were submitted to Charles for the Royal Assent. In the case of the bishops he gave way, thus avoiding a complete breach till the Queen had left England to see what help she could muster in France and Holland. On the question of the militia he remained adamant and the Bill was issued by the Houses as a parliamentary ordinance. Charles went to York and, throughout a miserable summer, there slipped away from Westminster—from the Lords and Commons alike—those who knew that when it came to the push they could not desert their King.

The question of episcopacy in its political aspects, which had loomed so large in the debates of the Long Parliament, ceased to be a primary concern when the duel at Westminster gave place to the battlefields of the Civil War. Nor did the bishops recover in 1660 anything like their earlier political influence, even though they regained their seats in the House of Lords: clerical ministers of state were no more and diocesan duties, pastoral and administrative, became increasingly their main concern. Yet it is as well to bear in mind the earlier conception of a bishop's duties, as voiced for instance by the Earl of Kingston in the Lords' debate on the second Exclusion Bill. He was a wealthy Midland landowner, not involved in

the political issues, and he declared that it did no harm for the prelates to be absent from their diocese if they had good subordinates to act on their behalf, concluding that they were better employed, as they had been since the days of the Norman Conquest, in making "wholesome and good laws for the happy and well-regulating of Church and Commonwealth".[20] Even Lord Brooke, in his *Discourse upon Episcopacy* published in the summer of 1641, took it for granted that a main part of a bishop's task was to advise his king. His complaint was that neither by birth nor education were they fitted to do so. They were, he said, "of the lowest of the people", with nothing to commend them but a dry-as-dust education at grammar school and university. Skimming through Aquinas and Scotus, "with some other school trifles", was no fit preparation for the King's Council-Chamber or the House of Peers, nor did their lack of roots in the country fit them to make wise decisions for the good of posterity. The lay lords, whose estates would pass in due course to their sons or grandsons, had a care for the future, they would live on "in their names, honours, posterity". But the bishops, who had no family tradition behind them, were like "meteors that must quickly blaze out", at the beck and call of the patrons who had advanced them, and they would be concerned only to "humour the present times".[21]

It was certainly true that the characteristics of academic learning and a middle-class origin were distinguishing marks of the Tudor and Stuart prelates, though it was not necessarily a matter of reproach. Most of those who had moulded the Anglican Church into its present form were men of an academic turn of mind, who had come to the episcopal bench after distinguished careers at the university. Many of them were also products of the Tudor grammar schools, who had

[20] Fuller, *Church History*, VI.222–6.

[21] Robert, Lord Brooke, *Discourse upon Episcopacy* (2nd edn, 1642), pp. 3, 34 f. (A facsimile is printed in Vol. II of W. Haller's *Tracts on Liberty in the Puritan Revolution* [1934].)

become what they were not only through the intellectual ability that had won them scholarships to Oxford and Cambridge and fellowships thereafter, but because of the training in thrift and diligence in humble homes in the city of London and the provincial towns. They could not have been more different—the flamboyant Williams only excepted—from the prelate-statesmen of the pre-Reformation Church, but in many cases their shrewd practical wisdom brought the affairs of their diocese into a far better shape than had ever seemed possible in the first uneasy years after 1559. Their training as scholars helped them not only to understand the subtleties of the *via media* but to express it in controversy, and thus to provide Anglicans with terms of reference *vis-à-vis* their Romanist and Puritan opponents. Yet Brooke had certain grounds for his criticism, and there were weaknesses even in the fine group who were Whitgift's colleagues and immediate successors, still more in those who had been Buckingham's nominees and in the congenial colleagues whom Laud gradually acquired. Among the less dedicated churchmen there was a concern for their families' welfare, a hoarding of possessions, and a readiness to advance relations that bordered on nepotism and was in part traceable to the humble origins Brooke so much deplored. In the best of them there was a certain donnish remoteness from ordinary men that generally disabled them from grasping the wider issues involved in the political disputes of the day. In their lack of contact with the hopes and frustrations of seekers after truth, less intellectually able than themselves, they were often too ready to equate awkward gestures and stupid words with a stubborn temper rather than with confused thinking, and thus they alienated when they should have helped. Laud and his team had more drive but little more understanding; what they did have, in contrast with some of their predecessors, was an enhanced sense of their duties in the secular sphere and of the status and authority of the Church. Thus Juxon became Lord Treasurer, and Laud, often unfairly, was regarded as the king-pin of an arbitrary

régime. But in addition, as the attacks of the excited mob bore witness on St Stephen's Day, there was in existence a more fundamental hostility than any Brooke expressed, concerned not only with temporal power but with the bishops' whole way of life. "He hath scattered the proud in the imagination of their hearts . . . the rich he hath sent empty away." Sunday by Sunday, men repeated the words that the years had not yet staled, and the solvent of the New Testament scriptures was at work in the land. Among a large section of the community a sturdy conviction grew that the great palaces, the train of servants, the large rent-rolls were not fitting attributes of true shepherds of souls. Few spoke, at this stage, of the "divine right of bishops"; many hoped like Baillie "to get Bishops, ceremonies and all away".

When Baillie used that phrase he already saw the sign of a split in the Puritan camp through the inclination of many of the lay lords to the party of the Separatists. Brooke's aim in the *Discourse on Episcopacy* was not to advocate a closed Presbyterian system as a valid alternative, but to suggest the free association of mutually tolerant but independent congregations. Lord Brooke was no ordinary man. He had succeeded in combining a left-wing position in religion and politics with a considerable reputation as a student and philosopher. His marriage with a daughter of the Earl of Bedford had linked him closely with the opposition peers, and his trading ventures in the New World had brought him in close contact with Puritans of varying shades of opinion and made his town-house in Holborn a centre of activity, as it continued to be when Parliament met in 1640. The shape of his philosophic thought had been outlined in an earlier disquisition on *The Nature of Truth*. His beliefs were not dissimilar to those of the Platonists, who were beginning to make themselves felt, particularly at Cambridge. He identified reason with the divine light which men enjoyed in their inmost being. This divine indwelling Spirit he described as "the All in us . . . besides which we are wholly nothing" and, foreshadowing the holism

of Smuts and the shared unconscious of Jung's philosophy, he stressed repeatedly this conception of the "All". "Unity is God's essence, unity is all what we are. . . . Harmony, proportion, . . . so many severall names of the same Unity."[22] Thus by these two lines of thought, the divine light of reason and the wholeness, the harmony that was characteristic of the divine, he came to attack the separation of learning into different compartments. Hence came his criticism of the bishops' erudition, which he considered to be too specialized and academic to equip them fully either to counsel kings or to shepherd their flocks.

Separation in religion should have been, and in one sense was, antipathetic to him, but the wholeness he desired was a spiritual quality; unlike Laud, he saw no necessity for uniformity as its necessary precursor and declared that if he deported himself "without faction, turbulent commotion, or uncharitable censure . . . no power on earth ought to force my practice more than my judgement". So he placed himself wholeheartedly alongside his friend, Lord Saye and Sele, as spokesman of the Independent party in the Lords. Thus the force of circumstance in his troubled generation led him into a strangely contradictory rôle: for he whose philosophy of life was based on unity, on the oneness of truth, advocated the necessity of the toleration of the sects and became known to his enemies as the most obstinate of schismatics. At the same time the cause which he fostered—he an aristocrat *par excellence* —became increasingly identified with the demagogues he abhorred. There would have been little peace of mind and small hope of consistency in action for the second Lord Brooke, had not a stray bullet within a year of the war's beginning put an end at Lichfield to his unfulfilled but not ignoble career.

Others there were in 1641, this year of angry debate, whose names are linked with the attack on episcopacy. Bishop Hall had written rather reluctantly at Laud's request a defence of

22 Robert, Lord Brooke, *The Nature of Truth; its union and unity with the soule* ("at the Bible in Duck Lane", 1640), pp. 21–44.

the order in 1640, when a detached attitude could still be maintained. He was an able and moderate thinker, whose stress on fundamentals and on the importance of spirit rather than form were in fact not very different from Brooke's own. There was not much that was tendentious in his tract except what was implicit in the title, *Episcopacy by Divine Right Asserted*, which in itself was like a red rag to a bull so far as the majority of the House of Commons was concerned. Next year he wrote two tracts, *An Humble Remonstrance to the High Court of Parliament* and *A Defence of the Humble Remonstrance*, neither outstandingly humble.[23] In the latter, however, he was fighting a rearguard action and professed himself ready to cede many of the bishops' powers if thereby the order might be preserved. The *Humble Remonstrance* had been answered by five Puritan ministers who slung their initials together to produce the atrocious pseudonym "Smectymnuus". The arid learning and confused syllogisms of their treatise were as much out of tune with the passionate intensity of the times as Bishop Hall's mild worldliness and academic snobbery. But after a further exchange a contribution came from a very different sort of person, and the bishop was aghast and bitterly offended when he read the *Animadversions upon the Remonstrants Defence against Smectymnuus* which was written by John Milton. Milton began with some vigorous and well-rounded sentences which referred to the "pseud-episcopacy of prelates with all their ceremonies, liturgies and tyrannies which God and man are now ready to explode and hisse out of the land" and described Hall as a "notorious enemie to truth and his country's peace",

[23] Hall argued in *Episcopacy Asserted* that episcopacy had been ordered and settled by apostolic direction and was therefore of divine institution; that it was the universal practice of the Church, was approved by the Christian Fathers, and that scriptural evidences against it were few and doubtful, so that to depart from the apostolic practice "cannot but be extremely scandalous and savour too much of schism". The change of temper appears in the contrast between this balanced judgement and the tone of the *Humble Remonstrance*: "I am confounded in myself to heare with what unjust clamour it is cried down abroad by either weak or factious persons."

asserting that it would be "nothing disagreeing from Christian meeknesse to handle such a one in a rougher accent and to send home his haughtiness well bespurted with his own holy water". The paragraph rose to a fine crescendo, with a reference to a "slye shuffle of counterfeet principles", and the tract continued in like vein. Unfortunately Bishop Hall lost his temper, and either he or his son replied with *A modest Confutation* in the preface to which the author of the *Animadversions* was described as a "grim, lowring, bitter fool": "it is like he spent his youth in loytering, bezelling and harlotting".

Milton was as shocked by *A modest Confutation* as Hall had been by the *Animadversions*. He was over-sensitive about his own reputation for he regarded himself as a dedicated person, already planning, reading, meditating on the mighty poem he meant to write, which could only be written by a man whose own life was free of all that was paltry and mean. He wrote immediately *An Apology* against *A modest Confutation*, speaking of his "own wearisome labours and studious watchings wherein I have spent and tir'd out almost a whole youth".[24] He had written his tract, one among others he wrote against episcopacy, moved in part by affection and loyalty to Thomas Young his former tutor, the T.Y. of Smectymnuus. He had also been irritated by Hall's style. The latter's use of monosyllables and of curt gibes annoyed him as much as his religion and politics, and he described him as "one who makes sentences by the statute as if all above three inches long were confiscate". "Can nothing then but Episcopacy teach men to speak good English, to pick and order a set of words judiciously?" By the time this second essay had been published the war was at hand, and it is doubtful if the tracts counted for much in the scales in which the bishops were weighed and found wanting. But they came

[24] The *Animadversions* was printed by Thomas Underhill and "sold at the sign of the Bible in Wood Street." *A modest confutation of a slanderous and scurrilous libell entitled Animadversions &c.*, was answered by *An Apology against a Pamphlet call'd a modest confutation* . . . (1642) "to be sold at the signe of the Sunne". On the whole the tone of the *Apology* is much quieter than that of the *Animadversions* (cf. pp. 2, 5).

as a further reminder of the new force of propaganda which had been growing steadily throughout the reign, and in the pamphlet warfare of the forthcoming years John Milton would be a giant among pygmies, giving his very eyesight for his cause and laying aside his great work till England needed him no longer.

The outbreak of war, in August 1642, was as complete and unredeemed a tragedy for England as that other August tragedy of 1914. The old order was ended and in the ensuing twenty years there were few who had not to revalue their way of life and their conceptions of truth and freedom before the stark challenge of death and penury or the disillusion that came with apparent victory or defeat. In 1642 there was the added bitterness of internecine strife; there were many to whom the way was clear from the start, but there were others who were as men beating the air in a fog of uncertainty, conscious only of great issues confronting them and of conflicting loyalties of family and friendship. Perhaps the majority wished only to be left in peace; it was impossible to conceive that this horror of Civil War was one that all must face.

Among those who knew exactly where they stood was Isaac Penington, who was chosen Lord Mayor in August when Sir Richard Gurney was impeached, dying an unsung hero in the Tower. The majority in the City and in most of the large towns were of Puritan sympathies and knew something of the issues involved; to the scattered population of the countryside, the opposing causes were often personified in the squire or parson, and when the great lord of the neighbourhood raised a force for King or Parliament, those who marched out at his behest were more conscious of loyalty to him who rode at their head than to any distant symbol of authority. The great lords, themselves, were often uncertain. Northumberland, chief of the Puritan aristocrats, continued to take his place at Westminster in the much depleted House of Peers, and was given custody at Sion House of the King's younger children; Leicester, his sister's husband, was an uneasy Royalist, and he and

Northumberland did not meet again as friends until, in 1660, Leicester left the seclusion of Penshurst and the two old men rode out together to welcome the return of Charles II. Leicester's daughter, Waller's "Sacharissa", had married Henry Spencer, the first Earl of Sunderland, one of the finest of the younger Cavaliers. He wrote to his wife, not long before his death by Falkland's side at Newbury, that he would rather be hanged than fight for Parliament, yet in the next letter he was talking of exile if the King won and extreme counsels prevailed.[25] It was the claims of honour, the knowledge that for years he had served the court, that impelled Edmund Verney of Claydon to join the King at York, and to die at Edgehill with the royal standard clasped in his hand, while Ralph Verney, his son, continued to sit in the House of Commons and contributed horses to the Parliamentary cause.[26]

In recent years modern historians have been at pains to stress how many forces other than religion had driven England into war.[27] The rivalry between landowners and merchants, changes in class-structure owing to inflation, the need to preserve the common law, and not least the King's own inconsistencies had all been in part responsible. In so far as religious issues were concerned, they centred on church government and the power and pomp of bishops and were thus in part economic and political in intent. Clarendon saw this clearly, and even Hammond wrote: "No man can believe that these armies were raised or continued to subdue the Common Prayer book." Yet, the point having been made, it can perhaps be over-stressed; people thought and lived in the seventeenth

[25] A. Collins, *Letters and Memorials of State* (Sydney Papers) (1746), II.667.

[26] *Memoirs of the Verney Family* (3rd edn 1925), II.16, 33; Ralph Verney's Notes of Proceedings in the Long Parliament are published by the Camden Society as *The Verney Papers* (1844–5).

[27] Hill, *Puritanism and Revolution*, pp. 6–31; H. R. Trevor-Roper, "The Gentry" in *The Economic Historical Review*, Supplement (1953), and W. H. Coates, "An analysis of major conflicts in seventeenth century England", included in *Conflict in Stuart England* (1960).

century in the framework of religion and expressed themselves through theological terms, not so exclusively as fifty years earlier but sufficiently so for it to be the impact of religion which clearly divided the parties. And when war came and men and women were brought face to face with death, it was religion that increasingly dominated the minds of those who suffered of either party, whether it were the King himself or the young widow left with a family to rear and the need for a strength beyond her own.

For the ordinary congregation at the outbreak of war, there does not seem in most cases to have been an immediate change. Familiar faces vanished as the squire and his humbler associates went off to the war, and those who were left became increasingly preoccupied. At Charing, the Kentish village on the road to Canterbury, the accounts in 1643 were presented as usual, checked by Sir Robert Honeywood, the great man of the neighbourhood. But when they are next presented two years later Honeywood has scribbled beside them: "I have exactly cast over receipt and payments and find them just but you must look over payments and check that which is not fitt, for I have no time to look it over."[28] One catches an echo of the disturbed days. But elsewhere the interruptions were more violent than an intermission in good book-keeping. At Westminster, in April 1643, a committee was appointed "for demolishing monuments of superstition or idolatry" and instructions were issued to the churchwardens to destroy crosses and images and any stained glass that depicted the Virgin or the persons of the Trinity. Some parishes obeyed in an ordered manner. In Chatham the changes were carefully noted in the records. The scriptural sentences regarding the sacrament

[28] Charing Church Wardens' Accounts, 1617 et seq. (Kent Archives Office, Maidstone, P.78/5/1). The accounts for 1643–5 included "our charges being warned to bee at Ashford to take ye Covenant 4/-". This large volume was the original Register of Tudor times, but after 1598 a new Register was begun and the wardens began to use the old book again, as a book of accounts, in 1617. A new account-book begins in 1672 (P.78/5/2).

which were painted on the pillars of the chancel were washed out, "partly in regard ye communion table was removed from that place and partly for new plastering of the walls". The images in the church porch, tending to superstition, were broken down and some further "painted works" washed out, "with the consent of some knowing men of the parish". The churchwarden then received a letter pointing out the "onely popish relique remaining, . . . ye seates in the chancell, formerly used by ye fryars", so these also went and eight new pews were made in their place, "to ease those that were crowded and to accommodate others". In addition, "two long pewes were made in ye gallery to containe ye yongmen who formerly sate in the chancell", and one Nicholas Pinder, the local shoemaker, agreed to attend on Sundays and fast days to keep the boys in order, and any others that should breed disturbance in the congregation.[29]

This combination of zeal and good order was by no means always to be found, and in the theatres of war the approach of Parliamentary forces, with sanction from Westminster to smash and destroy, might bring desolation and despair to many parishes. Sometimes, as at Lichfield, the nave of the church might be used as a stable for cavalry or a bastion of defence, or it might be a band of ill-disciplined Royalists who swept into the village, plundering as they went. Yet for all these disturbances, to a surprising degree ordinary life went on; the parochial framework of government was maintained, wardens and overseers and surveyors were duly elected, days set aside for the mending of the roads, and the constables kept busy with vagrants and evil-doers.

In regard to the incumbents, there was not immediately any large-scale ejection. When the Long Parliament first met, a committee was set up "to discover the sufferings of ministers by ecclesiastical proceedings" and another subcommittee, which later became a full committee of the House, was known

[29] Chatham Vestry Book. "Records of manie things done in the parish of Chatham anno [1643]" (Kent Archives Office, Maidstone, P 85/8/1).

indiscriminately as the Committee for Preaching or the Committee for Scandalous Ministers, according to whether one had in mind its attacks on unsatisfactory incumbents or its honest attempts to find suitable substitutes. To the Puritan, "unsatisfactory" might mean anything from "popish practices" to gross ignorance or immoral lives. A measure against pluralities was passed and stringently enforced, so that Cranbrook's Robert Abbott had eventually to go. On the whole the committee acted fairly, concentrating on individual cases, and in spite of the ejection of some good men, such as Benjamin Spencer of the hospital church of St Thomas, Southwark, the desperate shortage of suitable clergy to replace those who went acted as a brake on the committee's zeal.[30]

With the outbreak of war the *tempo* naturally quickened and the supply in the London area was also increased by refugee clergy, whose parishes had been overrun by Royalist troops. The existing bodies in Parliament were supplemented and eventually superseded by yet another committee to assist these "plundered ministers", and it was soon found that the simplest way to provide for them was to sequester the cures of any of the City incumbents suspect either in character or churchmanship. A large number of ejections took place during 1643. In February, Humphrey Tabor left St Margaret's, Lothbury, and at St Mary's, Newington, in June, James Meggs gave place to Henry Langley. At St Bartholomew's, Exchange, the transition was managed more smoothly than in many parishes. The vestry had donated Dr Grant £5 in April for giving them leave "to chuse Mr Lightfoot for the lecturer", and when the latter left in January 1644 the accommodating rector leased his rectory for £50 to a body of trustees who appointed Thomas Cawton.[31] Dr Grant lived on peaceably in the parish,

[30] Spencer was imprisoned for a short while but released on bail. The Lords laid down that £30—about half the value of the rectory—should be allowed annually for the support of his wife and children (*Lords' Journals*, VI.7b, 39a).

[31] *Vestry Minutes of St Bartholomew Exchange*, ed. Freshfield, Part 2, pp. 1, 5, 10 ff.

in spite of editing, at an earlier date, a defence of the Liturgy of the Church of England, and when he died in 1654 he was buried at the parish's expense and gifts were made to his widow when in need. The personal element often intruded in this way. Among the higher clergy, Juxon at Fulham and Morton at Durham House were unmolested until the end of 1643, the latter making use of every opportunity which the leniency of Parliament afforded to give food and shelter to ejected clergy or scholars in distress. The other bishops, when they were released from the Tower, were allowed to return to their dioceses, but their properties were in many cases lost, when it was laid down that the estates of certain named persons and of any absent in the King's forces should be sequestered and the revenues used as Parliament should direct.

In the country parishes, circumstances naturally varied according to the exigencies of war. Some of the Puritan clergy left their cures voluntarily to act as army chaplains, among them Richard Baxter, but Baxter was a near-saint with a worrying temperament and found little of profit in his adventure. The chaplains in the Royalist army tended at first to be of inferior quality, for most devoted men, like Henry Hammond at Penshurst, felt it their duty to remain in charge of their flock as long as they could escape the attention of Parliament. In the country the work of the Committee of Plundered Ministers was supplemented by local committees, who came into being to deal with ecclesiastical problems as similar county associations were attempting to deal with the military ones.[32] Composed of leading figures of the locality, knowing each other's circumstances and character, they continued to wield a considerable influence in a variety of ways. When they turned out their vicar, they did not usually want him to starve and would allow to him or his family a proportion of his revenue, which varied enormously in different cases. Eventually

[32] *The Committee at Stafford, 1643–45: the Order Book of the Staffordshire County Committee*, ed. D. H. Pennington and J. A. Roots (1957), pp. xv ff; Paul H. Hardacre, *The Royalists during the Revolution* (1956), pp. 27 f, 40 f.

the central committee standardized this allowance to a fifth, to be paid to the dependants of the ejected minister by his successor. At the same time they sought means to "settle" a preaching ministry by raising "the poor vicarage and cures" of the kingdom to a competent maintenance. Money, however, was desperately short, and often the legal "fifth" was never paid, let alone the maintenance increased. All these matters concerned the Committee of Plundered Ministers, which continued in being long after its title had ceased to be apposite. It dealt systematically with all questions of ejection and replacement and became as the years passed a compact and experienced body of men, competent to deal with the involved questions of patronage and ecclesiastical finance, which every turn of the wheel of fortune rendered more complex.[33]

The abolition of episcopacy was a foregone conclusion, but it was by no means clear what exactly should take its place. A few days before the King raised his standard at Nottingham, the General Assembly in Scotland had forwarded a declaration to Westminster expressing its concern at the delay in establishing "a uniformity in Kirk government". "For what hope can there be of unity in religion, of one confession of faith, one form of worship and one catechism, till there be one form of ecclesiastical government?" Parliament resolved unanimously that the government of the Church of England by "archbishops, bishops, their chancellors and commissaries, deans and chapters, archdeacons and other ecclesiastical officers" was "very prejudicial" and should be taken away, but none the less they did not in their reply to their Scottish brethren commit themselves to anything beyond pious hopes of future harmony and further references to an assembly of divines. At this stage they hoped for a speedy victory, so that they could settle the matter to their own liking without too close interference from their friends north of the border.

[33] Shaw, *History of the English Church*, II.194–9, 221–4, 457 et seq.

It did not happen that way. After Edgehill, the King marched to the very outskirts of London. The trained bands of the City lined up on Turnham Green, encouraged by a throng of excited citizens, stirred by reports, suitably embroidered, of Prince Rupert's sack of Brentford. There was, however, to be no sack of London; Charles withdrew his troops and made Oxford his headquarters. Both parties saw that there was to be no quick conclusion, and a declaration was issued from Westminster inviting Scottish aid. But no further action was taken until the alternative of a negotiated peace had been essayed; and in February Northumberland headed a delegation that visited the King at Oxford, asking his consent, among much else, to a Bill abolishing episcopacy which had passed both Houses in the previous month. It was given no serious consideration and the negotiations foundered on the more urgent question of the armed forces. Soon afterwards the peace party at Westminster was shocked almost out of existence by the discovery of a plot engineered by Edmund Waller during the negotiations. A covenant was drawn up, to be taken by all men over the age of fifteen, in which they undertook, after expressing their abhorrence of "the wicked and treacherous design lately discovered", to assist the forces raised by Parliament for their just defence and for the defence of the true Protestant religion and liberties of the subject. The Chatham vestry-book recorded not only the text of the covenant but the steps taken to ensure that none avoided it. Due notice was to be given, and those concerned were to attend before the minister on a given date. After solemnly taking the oath, they were to sign or make their mark opposite their names in a register of the adult males in the parish, compiled by the wardens from a list supplied by the constable. The wardens called personally on those who failed to turn up on the appointed date and they were given a second chance; if again they did not attend, their names were sent in to the authorities.[34]

[34] Chatham Vestry Book (Kent Archives Office, Maidstone, P 85/8/1).

It was this July covenant which disturbed the as yet quiet existence of those two moderate men, Thomas Fuller and John Evelyn. Fuller, who had given up his country benefices and was living in London and preaching at the Savoy, offered to take the covenant with reservations; but these were unacceptable to the authorities, so he left London and joined the court at Oxford. In that hotbed of royalism, however, he felt very much odd man out and attached himself as chaplain to Sir Ralph Hopton's Army, and as he travelled up and down war-time England he collected data for his *Worthies* in the towns and villages through which he passed. John Evelyn tried to avoid the oath by alternating between his houses in Deptford and Surrey, in perpetual motion between London and his country home, as he described it in the diary he so carefully kept. But, "finding it impossible to evade doing of very unhandsome things", he, too, applied for a licence to travel and withdrew to the Continent.[35]

A succession of Royalist victories during the summer months of 1643 underlined the urgency of the Scottish alliance. Pym was a dying man, but, for the last time, he rallied Parliament behind him and in August a commission led by Vane arrived in Edinburgh. Within a few weeks the Solemn League and Covenant was drafted and, with some modifications, accepted at Westminster. In return for military aid the English Church was to be reformed on a strict Presbyterian model, and on 5 September the two Houses solemnly assembled in St Margaret's and vowed to extirpate Popery and prelacy, to preserve the liberties of the country and to bring the Churches of England and Scotland into close uniformity, "according to the word of God and the example of the best Reformed Churches". Vane had secured the saving reference to "the word of God", which gave him and many others a loophole

[35] Dean B. Lyman, *The Great Tom Fuller* (1935), pp. 63–78, and cf. John Freeman's introd. (p. xi) to Fuller's *Worthies* (edn of 1952); *The Diary of John Evelyn*, ed. E. S. de Beer (1955), II.81 f (23 July 1643).

for conscience as they raised their right hands and swore. Some, like Ralph Verney, had less adaptable consciences and, refusing the covenant, slipped away to the Continent to join the growing number of English refugees of every political colour and creed.

How systematically the National Covenant was administered throughout the country remains something of an enigma. How soon did it become merely a shibboleth to be taken in the course of compounding with the victors and as a mere matter of form? The military crisis of the summer was already past, and it is probable that there was not the careful imposition of the oath in the parishes that there had been in the case of the July covenant. None the less, the majority of the three thousand clergymen ejected between the outbreak of war and the first months of the Commonwealth régime left their living in 1643–4, and it is perhaps significant that in the parochial records themselves the dates that mark the periods of greatest derangement are not 1642 and 1649, when war began and the King was executed, but 1643 and 1653, the dates of the Scottish alliance and Cromwell's Protectorate. Even so, a good number of loyal Parliamentarians were mistrustful of Scottish control from the beginning, and so long as the county committees had a say in the matter there was room for a certain amount of leeway. In 1645–6, as sequestrations increased and as the system of compounding was developed, the central committees took over most of the work and the position hardened, until with Cromwell's emergence as the strong man of the hour the Presbyterian domination itself was threatened and the covenant lost its potency. In 1644 it could still inspire a zealous and predominantly religious response, and the minutes of St Margaret, Lothbury, contain not merely a note of the two covenants of 1643 and of those who swore to them, but also the names of a large number of parishioners who renewed their covenant a year later and, before the administration of the sacrament, took a further oath, "To walk in all the ways of God" and "to be willing to be lovingly admonished

and reproved", when they had gone astray.[36] It was against this background of intense religious zeal in some quarters, and growing doubt and cynicism elsewhere, that the promised reform of the Church was being carried on at Westminster, as the Scottish forces advanced into the country and the balance of the war turned against the King.

The Assembly of Divines which met on 1 July 1643 after a long and complicated period of gestation consisted on paper of 121 members, assisted by ten members of the House of Lords and twenty members of the Commons and attended by three secretaries and eight Scottish commissioners (lay and clerical). The latter arrived in September, and fortunately for the records the voluble Baillie was among them. Only 69 of the 121 clergy attended the first session, and this number or rather less remained the average; invitations had been sent to some moderate Episcopalians, including Ussher and Brownrigg and Earle, who naturally did not appear, but a small critical minority was provided by a compact group of Independents, led by five ministers who had recently returned from exile in Holland. The statesmanlike Thomas Goodwin and the other "dissenting brethren", Philip Nye, Sidrach Simpson, William Bridge, and Jeremiah Burroughs, formed the spearhead of a small but voluble opposition. Prominent among the Puritan ministers were Stephen Marshall, a lecturer at St Margaret's, whose influence had been strongly felt in the political arena since the first petitions against episcopacy, and Edmund Calamy, the popular preacher of St Mary Aldermanbury.

The assembly was at work on a revision of the Thirty-nine Articles and was discussing the nature of Grace when urgent instructions reached them from Parliament in October 1643 to take in hand "the Discipline and Liturgy of the Church", and during the next three years, as the fate of the country was hammered out on the battlefields of England, the Assembly

[36] *St Margaret's Lothbury Vestry Minute books*, ed. Freshfield, pp. 77 et seq., 85 f.

concentrated on a task that proved far more arduous and intricate than had been imagined. There were various complications: the most fundamental, which only gradually emerged, was the determination of Parliament to keep the threads in its own hands and to modify or reject any conclusions that were not pleasing to it. In the Assembly itself, there was the dissidence of the five dissenting brethren to be reckoned with. Independency was rather a habit of mind than a sect, and had social and political connotations not always identical with its religious significance.[37] There were as yet no clear-cut lines of division among the anti-Prelatists, and many of the more conservative Independents were ready to take office as Elders in their Church, within the Presbyterian framework. Socially there was obviously a wide gap between the outlook of Lords Saye and Brooke and that of the dissenting brethren, and between the latter and the camp-fire theorists of Cromwell's Army. Yet during these years there was steadily developing a force loosely described as Independency, which was opposed to the whole idea of a closely-organized state Church. It was characterized by the conception of the gathered Church, a group of people of a like mind managing their own affairs under the hand of God, and by a belief in toleration, expressed less as a philosophic concept on the lines of the Anglican thinkers but as the necessary concomitant of Independent views. The clarification of these ideas in the Westminster Assembly, through the speeches of Thomas Goodwin and his friends, was paralleled by the growing domination of Cromwell, their greatest exponent, on the field of battle.

As Cromwell and his Ironsides went from strength to strength, the handful of Independents held up proceedings at Westminster, jumping up to speak whenever the Holy Spirit

[37] Cf. George Yule, *The Independents in the English Civil War* (1958), "an attempt to discover the connexion between the Parliamentary Independent party and Religious Independence". See pp. 20 et seq. and, for the social background of the group, pp. 47–53.

prompted them, so that Baillie declared: "Nothing in any Assemblie that ever was in the world, except Trent, [was] like to them in prolixitie."[38] Their Presbyterian brethren took a like pleasure in debating theological minutiae instead of getting ahead with the vital business of working out details of organization and drawing up a new catechism and a Directory of Worship. For the space of some eighteen months, the Assembly debated and debated yet again such topics as the nature of the ministry, the shortcomings of liturgical prayer, methods of ordination, and a fitting catalogue of sins. In August 1645, Parliament issued the ordinance that provided for the election of elders and the setting up of classes, synods, and assembly. In the same month the Directory of Worship was published for a second time, after another attempt to treat for peace had failed at Uxbridge, and penalties were now imposed on the use in public of the Book of Common Prayer. It was not until eleven months later, in October 1646, that the ordinance for the abolition of episcopacy was eventually issued and the lands and revenues of the bishops, many already sequestered, were confiscated in entirety.

The delay was caused by the lengthy disputes which took place between the House and the Assembly over the matter of discipline. This was an integral part of the Presbyterian system, which could not be set up until its details were settled. Nobody doubted that persons of scandalous lives or "without competent knowledge of the faith" should be excluded from participation in the sacrament, but there was considerable argument as to how it should be done. The Commons refused to give the elders general powers of excommunication for unspecified offences and, in order to avoid doing this, spent an incredible amount of time in trying to define "competent knowledge", and in compiling a list of additional sins so that

[38] Baillie, *Letters and Journals*, II.164 (12 April 1644). His account of the Assembly had begun in the previous December (II.107 et seq.) with considerable enthusiasm, which slowly waned as the greatness of the prolixity and the slowness of the progress wearied him.

no scandal should be overlooked. To those suggested by the Assembly for excommunication, they added "makers of images . . . senders or carriers of challenges, any using dancing, gaming, masking on the Lord's Day . . . any repairing to witches, wizards or fortune tellers", as well as keepers of stews and persons married to Papists.[39] At the same time, jealous of any usurpation of power by the Church, they laid down that offenders had the right to appeal to Parliament. For, as Baillie complained, the House remained "either half or whole Erastian", regarding the Church as "a human institution depending on the will of the magistrate", and in their anticlericalism the Erastians had the support of the Parliamentary Independents. In January they gave up the attempt to enunciate every possible sin but resolved that County Commissioners should be appointed to judge of "any scandalous unenumerated offence" and if necessary to issue certificates to the elders to suspend the offender. It seemed an eminently sensible arrangement to those accustomed to regard the J.P.s and the county committees as the pivot of local affairs, but it drove Baillie and his clerical friends to the brink of despair. A few months later, however, Charles surrendered to the Scots, and the Commons were brought up sharply against the fact that they must not quarrel with their allies. In June 1646 the Ordinance for Scandal was finally passed, and the idea of local Commissioners was dropped in favour of a standing committee of Parliament whom the elders were to certify in the case of offences not on the specified list.

Thus slowly and painfully (in our sense of the word as well as that of the seventeenth century) Parliament and Assembly worked out a system of rule and worship, consonant with the reformed churches of Scotland and Geneva. But this was neither Scotland nor Geneva, and the system, duly established, failed entirely to take root. There were many ways of

[39] Shaw, *History of the English Church*, I.275 ff. The second half of Vol. I (pp. 145 et seq.) gives a detailed account of the proceedings of the Assembly and of its constructive work.

sabotaging it, beyond the obvious one of procrastination. On one occasion, when lay elders were duly chosen, an ejected Anglican priest was included among them; another parish, disliking the Directory, refused to pay tithe, taking as their slogan, "No paternoster, no penny".[40] London was an exception, and here elders were elected and steps were immediately taken to group the parishes of the City and Southwark into thirteen classes, which continued to meet sporadically over the next twelve years. In Lancashire, also, something definite was accomplished. Elsewhere there was considerable hesitation: local committees reported that they were waiting for further instructions from Parliament before ordering the election of elders, or that they had decided to take no immediate action; and before this reluctance had been overcome the change in the climate of opinion, mirrored in the quarrel between the Army and the Parliament, made it impossible to enforce any rigid ecclesiastical system upon those who did not willingly co-operate.

In spite of such reservations, the system established by parliamentary ordinance in 1645–6 remained the law of the land, and though elders might or might not be appointed and the difficulties of discipline could be avoided by law-abiding parishioners, no one could escape the impact of the new dispensation in the regular use in the churches of the Directory of Worship. As Presbyterians and Independents had an equal dislike of liturgical prayer, the cleavage between them was less marked on the subject of the Directory than of Church discipline and it was drawn up in 1644, when tempers were less strained. None the less the inclusion of Goodwin in the subcommittee of five, which laboured at the business over a period of six months, meant a certain measure of dispute, especially when he brought Philip Nye uninvited to a meeting.[41] The service of Holy Communion was still the source of difference. The Presbyterians were as strict in their manner of administration

[40] Paul H. Hardacre, *The Royalists during the Puritan Revolution* (1956), p. 49.

[41] Baillie, op. cit., II.123 (1 Jan. 1644).

as Laud himself and thought that the Independents "mangled" the sacrament by celebrating it each Sunday, without preparation beforehand or thanksgiving afterwards, and by receiving it in their pews in silence instead of in the Scottish manner, sitting round the holy table after an exhortation and the words of institution. Eventually there was a compromise: the Directory laid down that the table should be "decently covered and so conveniently placed that the communicants might orderly sit about it or at it", but a cynic overhearing the disputes of the subcommittees and recalling the test case at St Gregory's, might well have meditated that the more things change the more they remain the same.

A small sum for the purchase of the Directory appears in many of the wardens' accounts, and if the parliamentary ordinance were obeyed, the superseded books were carried by the wardens and the constable to the county committees for them to destroy. Hence the shortage of prayer books in 1660. The Directory was supplemented in many congregations by a metrical version of the Psalms and it was suggested that "all not disabled by age or otherwise should be exhorted to learn to read", so as to sing the Psalms with understanding.[42]

As the Directory was more concerned with ordaining the shape of the service than in providing specific prayers, the character of the resulting worship depended largely on the ability and beliefs of the incumbent. Where there had been no change or where the new vicar was, like Thomas Malory at Deptford, a moderate and peaceable man, the parishioner who regretted the Liturgy might yet attend without undue dismay. If the minister had been episcopally ordained, the Anglican authorities did not frown upon their adherents receiving communion at their parish church, as Evelyn did on at least one occasion at Deptford. It is true that the Direc-

[42] Ibid., II.120 f, and Shaw, I.377 et seq. The translation approved by the Commons was by Francis Rouse but the Lords preferred a more "poetical paraphrase" by William Barton, and never gave Rouse's version their official blessing.

tory criticized "the many unprofitable and burdensome ceremonies", enjoined in the Book of Common Prayer, which had kept "divers able and faithfull ministers" from seeking ordination. But it denied any particular liking for novelty and there was much in it to which moderates of all schools could say "Amen". The congregation were told to enter "not irreverently but in a grave and seemly manner" and to abstain from "all private whisperings, conferences, salutations or doing reverence to any persons present or coming in, as also from all gazing, sleeping or any other undecent behaviour". The minister was instructed how to read the Scriptures, one chapter at a time to be followed by a short exposition, and he was advised in his sermons to avoid strange phrases or the "unprofitable use of unknowne Tongues" and to be sparing of quotations, "be they never so elegant". The central point in Presbyterian worship was the prayer before the sermon, and this was to begin with the confession of sins and include a number of intercessions, not only for the King but "for the conversion of the Queen, the religious education of the Prince . . . for the comforting of the afflicted Queen of Bohemia and . . . for the restitution of the Palatinate". A blessing was asked on all reformed Churches, especially those of the three kingdoms, "now more strictly and religiously united in the Solemn National League and Covenant".[43]

It was not so much in what it enjoined as in what it excluded that the Directory offended those who loved the Anglican way. When the King was attempting to rally Royalist opinion in 1648 before the Second Civil War, he instructed Henry Hammond to write a defence of the Liturgy and Hammond examined the changes entailed in the use of the Directory in 88 rather tedious pages. Among much else, he attempted to explain the value of those outward signs and

[43] "A Directory for publique Prayer . . ." was annexed to an ordinance "for taking away the Book of Common Prayer . . ." dated 4 January 1644–5. It is printed in *Acts and Ordinances of the Interregnum, 1642–60*, comp. and ed. C. H. Firth and R. S. Rait (1911), I.582 et seq.

ceremonies, which the Puritans so firmly excluded but which were to Anglicans part of the worship of the whole man, an act of obedience to the precept that God should be glorified "in our bodies as well as souls". In addition he stressed the conception of the Church as the company of all faithful people, militant on earth, triumphant in Heaven. Thus the absolution gave "the pardon and peace of the Church to all her penitent children", the commemoration of festivals served as a reminder of "one of the noblest priviledges of which this earth is capable, to be a fellow-citizen with the saints", and the loss of the Sanctus and the Gloria, in which the congregation "bear the angels company here", was deplored as "little better than fury . . . to think it necessary to throw this bit of heaven out of the Church".[44]

The average parishioner might not be conscious of the full richness of the Holy Catholic Church, as Hammond conceived it, but he soon became aware of the shortcomings of the new dispensation in regard to Holy Communion. The Directory laid down that the sacrament should be frequently celebrated after morning prayer and made provision for a seemly and decorous service. One of the few references to matters of worship in contemporary church accounts is to the washing of the cloth upon the communion-table. On the other hand the accounts, in almost every case, showed a marked drop in the purchase of bread and wine, which in some cases lapsed entirely. At St Mary's, Newington, where a special rate which raised about £5 a year was levied for the bread and wine, the entries were normal for the first three-quarters of 1643 but dropped in 1644–5 to an income of 7*s*. 6*d*. and an outlay of 4*s*. 2*d*. and thereafter completely disappeared. At Cranbrook after Abbott's departure in 1643, the item drops immediately out of the accounts. At Headcorn the notes of small payments for bread and wine continue until 1653, and appear again in 1657, no accounts being entered for the intervening years, but

[44] [Hammond,] *A view of the new Directory and a Vindication of the ancient Liturgy of the Church of England* (1645), pp. 32, 39 f.

there is no separate assessment for bread and wine after 1641. At Charing the Easter Communion is recorded until 1653, but disappears from later entries except in the year of 1655–6. When Oliver Heywood, a staunch Presbyterian from Lancashire, crossed the Pennines to a Halifax parish in 1655, one of his first acts was to restore a monthly celebration of the Communion which had not been administered for many years, and similarly Henry Newcome reintroduced it at Gawsworth. It is clear that for a while the sacrament was neglected and one of the reasons for this was the old trouble of discipline. The close moral surveillance exercised by the elders, before a person could be admitted to communion, offended the average man's sense of decency as well as his pride. Isaac Allen of Prestwich put his finger on the trouble when he pointed out that people of competent knowledge and blameless life had to apply to the elders for admission alongside the scandalous and ignorant. Respectable folk objected to having their private lives scrutinized by their neighbours, and the simplest way out of the difficulty was not to apply for admission and quietly to stay at home.[45]

A London example shows that even here there were similar difficulties. At St Bartholomew's, Exchange, Thomas Cawton was a person of some importance in the new ecclesiastical hierarchy. He was an orthodox Presbyterian and one of the Triers for Ordinands attached to the seventh London classis. But before long his vestry proffered a request that at St Bartholomew's the sacrament should be administered "without coming before the elders". "When Cawton came into the vestry," runs the record, "Lamotte told him the sense of the parish and desired him to deliver the sacrament to all his parish to beget love one with another; his answer was that he would take it into consideration and satisfy the

[45] S. Hibbert [Ware]. *The History of the College and Collegiate Church, Manchester* (Vol. I of *The History of the Foundations in Manchester of Christ's College, Chetham's Hospital and the Free Grammar School*, [1834]), I.313.

parish in a short time [that] what did lie in him to do should not be wanting."[46]

"To beget love one with another"—those were the operative words; for as the cleavage grew between the strict Presbyterians and the Independents with their gathered churches, the position in some London parishes could only be described as confusion worse confounded. At St Stephen's, Coleman Street, Davenport's successor was John Goodwin, a brilliant, restless individual who was a republican in politics and a High Churchman in his theology. Bishop Juxon had turned a blind eye to his vagaries, but in 1645 he was involved in a dispute with his vestry and was eventually evicted by the Committee of Plundered Ministers for refusing to baptize or administer the sacraments indiscriminately. His successor, William Taylor, was hedged round with disciplinary restrictions; a committee of four was appointed to judge the fitness of those who wished to receive communion; these were to attend on the previous Tuesday or Thursday, write their names in a book and receive a token which they gave up at the subsequent service. In Goodwin's case, it was less a question of discipline than of his Independent views as to the nature of a church. For four years Goodwin ministered elsewhere in Coleman Street to a "gathered" or separated congregation, but he returned to St Stephen's in 1649, bringing his congregation with him and making an amicable agreement with the parishioners whereby they allowed the newcomers any spare room in their pews. The gathered church still used their previous meeting-place, "to receive the Lord's Supper so oft as they see cause after the sermon ended and to make collections among themselves at such time for their own poor", but sat under Mr Goodwin at St Stephen's for his sermons, in which in due course he attacked the Cromwellian system as he had thundered in the past against Presbyterian and Laudian alike.[47]

[46] *Vestry Minutes of St Bartholomew Exchange*, ed. Freshfield, Part II, p. 26 (27 Aug. 1649).

[47] E. Freshfield, *The Book of Records of St Stephen's, Coleman Street*, pp. 8–11.

During 1647 the Assembly drew up a larger and shorter Catechism and a Confession of Faith which in the words of the latest historian of the Scottish Church "set forth in the clearest terms, a Calvinism more rigid than Calvin's". They were adopted with some reluctance by the Scottish General Assembly in the hope of uniformity, but by 1648, when the Assembly at Westminster ceased to sit, Parliament had only authorized the Shorter Catechism. Its opening question and answer, "What is the chief end of man? . . . To glorify God and to enjoy him for ever", ring down the centuries in jubilant contradiction of the more negative aspects of the Puritan way of life.[48]

A more pleasing picture of the Presbyterian divine than that of the rigorists of the Westminster Assembly emerges from the diaries and journals of a group of clergy in Lancashire, where the system was established more consistently than elsewhere outside London. The first classis, established in October 1646, centred upon Manchester, and at the centre of Manchester was the collegiate church, founded in the first years of the fifteenth century and since that date three times suppressed and re-established. The Warden, Richard Heyrick, was a Londoner whose father had obtained the post in reversion, in return for large sums of money loaned to the Crown; Heyrick thus regarded it as payment for services rendered and stuck to it through thick and thin, against Laud's reforming zeal in the 1630s and the parliamentary sequestration of the college lands as Church property in 1646. He was a man who fitted into no category but was content to be "anti" most things; in 1640 he had admonished his flock to "pray that there be no heresy, no Trent determinations, no Socinian blasphemies, no Arminian quiddities, no Antinomian wickednesses", and he added, "no schism, no separation, no walls of partition, no heathenish customs, no Samaritan rites, no idolatrous superstitions, no Popish ceremonies, no Canons to

[48] J. H. S. Burleigh, *A Church History of Scotland* (1960), p. 226. Cf. Shaw, *History of the English Church*, I.357 et seq.

batter and terrify the consciences of God's people".[49] The answer, as Heyrick saw it, was Presbyterianism and as a member of the Assembly he welcomed the establishment of the system, though with more enthusiasm for the discipline than the Directory as he happened to have a particular liking for liturgical prayer. What he required was an established framework of rule and worship to prevent schism and the excess he detested, and within that framework as much latitude as possible. Heyrick's colleague, Martindale, described him as "so perfect a Latitudinarian" as to affirm in a fast-day sermon "that the episcopal, presbyterian and independents might all practise according to their own judgements yet each by divine right". Martindale obviously thought it was nonsense, yet Baxter, phrasing the idea more succinctly in the term "mere Christian", was working along the same lines in his church at Kidderminster.

It was, after all, the only possible answer for the moderates, who could accept neither the authoritarian Anglicanism of Laud's making nor yet a toleration that resulted in a wild proliferation of sects, such as occurred in the years between Naseby and the execution of the King. The trouble with Heyrick was that no policy appeared moderate when he was voicing it. In a sermon before the House of Commons he rated them for the toleration that was being shown on every hand, even towards Royalist malignants, if they were prepared to pay a fine and settle down. "Little know we what Gunpowder plots are now hatching", he declared. Those who had loyally supported the Parliamentary cause were the ones who should not be forgotten. He reminded them of Manchester's brave resistance at the beginning of the war. "There are seven thousand at least that have not bowed their knees to Baal", he cried, and proceeded to draw a vivid picture of the Almighty asking in a divine assembly, "Shall I destroy England?", to which Heyrick appeared to suggest that, for Manchester's sake, God would give the recalcitrant country

49 Hibbert, op. cit., I.180.

another chance. The practical aim of this outburst of local patriotism was the removal of the sequestration order upon the college lands and this Heyrick obtained, with the restoration of those members of the college who were prepared to take the Covenant. Prebendary Johnson, who refused, was arrested so precipitately that he had not even time to put on his boots, but was led through the streets "on a ragged colt" with straw wrapped round his legs for protection.[50] The jeers and the stones cast by an angry crowd come as a sudden reminder of the age's peculiar mixture of brutality and piety.

This brutality was a growing feature of political occasions as the Army dominated the scene. The soldiers who hustled Johnson on his nag and who roughly evicted Morton from Durham House in 1648 were no worse than the apprentice mobs who terrified the bishops in 1640, but now they had authority on their side and their gestures of defiance or effrontery had the chance to erupt in action, which increasingly disturbed those to whom the restoration of order was a prime concern. The eight hundred signatories to the *Harmonious Consent*, which Heyrick published as a protest from the Lancashire ministers against the toleration of sectaries, included not only men such as himself but even John Angier, most friendly and kindly of clergymen, who yet believed that schism must be combated, even at the cost of freedom, by every means in one's power. Otherwise there would be chaos, the antithesis of good.

John Angier was the doyen of the Lancashire Presbyterians. He had first come north in 1630 from East Anglia where he was a friend and disciple of the famous John Cotton of Boston, Lincolnshire. He had married Mrs Cotton's niece, Ellen Winstanley, who came from Wigan, and he intended to emigrate with the rest of the family to Massachusetts after paying a visit with his young wife to her relatives in Lancashire. But

[50] Ibid., I.238–42. Chapter XVIII (pp. 247–67) gives a detailed account of the Presbyterian discipline as it was practised in the Manchester classis.

there he remained, for during the visit he preached at Bolton and at Ringley, so moved by the Spirit on the latter occasion that he fainted in the pulpit! The congregation, deeply impressed, at once invited him to come and be their minister. He accepted the call and was ordained by Lewis Bayly, who did not insist on the customary oaths. Bishop Bridgeman likewise turned a blind eye to Angier's unorthodoxy, knowing saintliness when he saw it. After eighteen months Laud's rebukes caused the Bishop to suspend Angier though he only moved as far as Denton where the congregation had for some time been putting out feelers to secure the services of "the little man at Ringley". At Denton he remained for more than forty years, becoming indeed with the passing years "the idol of Lancashire", praying without ceasing, healing whenever healing was possible, firm when necessary (he was imprisoned for a while for refusing to sign the Engagement), ever ready with counsel in the cases of conscience submitted to him, unweary in good works in disregard of delicate health that would have made a lesser man an invalid. He even managed to remain human. His first wife died on the eve of the Civil War, and—it was said on her suggestion—he married Margaret Mosely of Ancoats, whose kinsman was Lord of the Manor of Manchester. Some of his colleagues were a little uneasy about this alliance with wealth and influence, and were not quite sure whether to disapprove or be impressed when the marriage took place (as Oliver Heywood, Angier's biographer, records) "very publicly in Manchester church in the heat of the wars, which was much taken notice of as a great act of faith in them both". Twelve years later, when civil marriages were the law of the land, Heywood married Angier's daughter and notes that on that occasion his father-in-law entertained a hundred guests at Denton, for "he loved to have a marriage like a marriage".[51]

It is not surprising to read that the minister at Denton lived peaceably with his neighbours. He was not at first very happy

[51] Oliver Heywood, *Life of John Angier*, with introd. and notes by Ernest Oxon (Chetham Society: *Remains* . . . new series No. 97; 1937), p. 63.

about the Presbyterian system, because of the exclusiveness of its discipline, but he returned from a visit to London, where he had gone to see a book through the press, prepared to co-operate but making the mental reservation that he "hoped never to trouble the classis with any controversies concerning his own congregation". Thus sympathizing with the Independent point of view, he had no difficulty in remaining on good terms with them as their strength and influence increased in the county. Adam Martindale, another Lancashire Presbyterian, did not find it nearly so easy to live in friendly communion either with his own brethren or with "the good and learned men" who stood for the congregational way, and his diary contains a detailed account of the clash of interest and the contest for pulpits between the two Puritan parties in a county whose inhabitants had more than their fair share of stubborn individuality.[52]

Martindale was twenty years younger than Angier, and the diary gives not only a vivid account of the contemporary scene but a picture of his own spiritual pilgrimage from the days of his early schooling with "a humdrum curate that had almost no scholars nor deserved any, for he was both a simpleton and a tippler". After many vicissitudes, Martindale emerged as something of a scholar, and when the Civil War began he took to schoolmastering and began to write a text-book on arithmetic. But no man of conscience could escape the inexorable pressure of the war, and Martindale went as chaplain to the Parliamentary troops, based on Liverpool, where his religious education was intensified by the "sweet communion" he enjoyed with the officers of the foot regiment. Imprisoned for a while upon the surrender of Liverpool, he found himself in the last year of the war back at his schoolmaster's desk, and set himself at the age of 21 to a disciplined course of reading in Hebrew, logic, ethics, and European culture.

[52] *The Life of Adam Martindale, written by himself*, ed. R. Parkinson (Chetham Society: *Remains* . . . No. IV; 1845), pp. 61 et seq., and on ordination, pp. 80–7.

The shortage of clergy, when the war was over, led to the offer of a lectureship at Middleton, which he declined as the vicar's assistant was one of his old, less satisfactory teachers whom he did not wish to turn out. He accepted instead a call to lecture at Gorton provided the consent of the chapelry was obtained, testified under the hands of the inhabitants. He remained there for a year or two, but the congregation was divided and there were continuous bickerings through the oo great zeal of one thorough-going Presbyterian and the unwillingness of others to submit to the discipline of "such as they accounted over-rigid, though otherwise worthy men". "To be familiar with them of one partie was to render me suspected to the other", Martindale wrote, and uncertain of his own liking for the classis system he argued in turn with those of both persuasions, and failed to reconcile them. He was glad to move in 1649 to Rosthorne in Cheshire, where he received the living rather against the will of a section of the parish, who would have preferred the nominee of the former patron. Martindale's supporters applied to the Committee of Plundered Ministers and Martindale dashed up to London to be ordained, which entailed the approval of specified Triers among the elders appointed for that purpose. The diary contains a vivid if not very edifying account of the way in which Martindale gatecrashed the classis of St Andrew Undershaft just before it adjourned for a month—a delay which would have given his opponents a chance to outwit him, a sorry comment on the disadvantages of the new way of doing things. At Rosthorne he remained for thirteen years, not without a number of the disturbances which always seemed to dog him.[53]

Such things did not happen to Henry Newcome, the last of these Puritan worthies of the North Midlands whose habits of introspection led them to keep the journals that give body to the tangled story of Church politics at the close of the Civil War. Newcome was a sensitive, gentle Puritan, the great-grandson of that Thomas Sparke who had attended the

[53] Ibid., pp. 124 ff.

Hampton Court Conference with Rainolds and Knewstubs. His father was a Huntingdon man but his mother came from Salford, and he was a schoolmaster at Congleton when he decided to be ordained in 1648, to help fill the depleted ranks of the clergy after the war. He became minister in the small village of Goostrey, and two years later, when only 22 years old, he was made rector of Gawsworth, one of the loveliest of the Cheshire churches. There he ministered for six years, as truly as Herbert had done at Bemerton and Hammond at Penshurst, encouraged till her death by his friend and patron Lady Fitton, the lady of the manor. He was an over-anxious young man, who could not, like Angier, take goodness in his stride, and after Lady Fitton died in 1655 he was hampered by poor health and a number of debts. The heart-searchings as to whether to move ended when he accepted the invitation of the congregation at Manchester to become their minister. A long life lay ahead of him, in which, for all his sensitivity, he responded with courage to the challenge of the times. But the happiest years were the early ones at Gawsworth, and they serve as a reminder that the true pastor is not circumscribed by law and can preach Christ's gospel whether he abide by the Directory or the Book of Common Prayer.[54]

The anxiety that Heyrick expressed in his sermon before the House and that the Lancashire clergy voiced in the *Harmonious Consent* was shared by many in all parts of the country, as enthusiasts endeavoured to transform their camp-fire politics into a programme of immediate action. The bickerings in the Assembly's subcommittees appeared as judicious and academic argument when compared with the rantings of fifth-monarchy men and the dangerous claims of "democraticall" dreamers, and Thomas Edwards gave to his list of heresies, flourishing unchecked, the significant title of *Gangraena*. Yet it

[54] *The autobiography of Henry Newcome*, ed. R. Parkinson (Chetham Society: *Remains* . . . Nos. 26, 27; 1852), I.16–70 covers the years at Gawsworth.

was impossible to silence them, and these seminal years between 1644 and 1647 contained, in addition to the *Gangraena* and the Assembly debates, three great tracts on liberty of conscience as well as those other debates in Putney church in which the men of the new model proclaimed their democratic faith. Yet landmarks as they are in the story of freedom, neither tracts nor debates were merely statements of theoretical belief; they were strictly relevant to practical issues and occurred it would seem almost by chance, as if Freedom were a germ in the air to be caught in passing.

Milton's *Areopagitica* was less a statement of a considered philosophy than an impassioned plea for liberty, immediately occasioned by circumstances. He had written a tract on divorce, after making a disastrous marriage with a slip of a girl who had been overwhelmed alike by his love-making and his arrogance. He had not submitted his tract to the censor and it was suppressed. That the authorities were technically within their rights did not save them from the full force of Milton's scathing pen, as always turning his personal feelings into potent phrase. "I cannot praise a fugitive and cloistered virtue . . .", he declared, "that never sallies out and sees her adversary; . . . who ever knew Truth put to the worse in a free and open encounter?" It is true that, in the next decade, as the advocate of the republican government, he begged the question by his assertion that "none can love freedom heartily but good men; the rest love not freedom but license". Even Roger Williams, the author of the second great tract, used the analogy of the ship of state, admitting that, as in a storm at sea the passengers must not hinder the crew, so in times of crisis individual interests must be sacrificed for the safety of the whole. Yet with these moral and political reservations, which must always provide an element of tension in the practice of liberty, Milton's and Roger Williams' dynamic faith in freedom of thought gave an impetus to the idea of toleration as it was germinating in the minds of more ordinary men.

Williams wrote *The Bloody Tenet of Persecution* to beguile the

tedium of an Atlantic crossing, as he came over to England to obtain a charter for his plantation at Providence and Rhode Island. Throughout the winter of 1643/4, he was a familiar figure in the streets of London, encouraging the citizens, who were short of the coal held up in Newcastle, by sawing down trees and scavenging for wood as he had learnt to do in his frontier home. He saw his tract through the press and framed his charter, which endeavoured to secure liberty of conscience by the complete separation of Church and State. In Rhode Island in the succeeding years he succeeded in living out his faith in man's right to find out his own way to salvation, but in London in 1644 his tempestuous advocacy of freedom appeared as revolutionary as the aberrations of the wilder sects, and Parliament ordered both the *Areopagitica* and the *Bloody Tenet* to be called in and burnt by the common hangman.[55]

Throughout the months before and after the battle of Naseby the influence of the sectaries grew, matching the military successes of the Army. "This was that bustling year", wrote Martindale in 1646, "wherein the Presbyteriall and congregational governments were like Jacob and Esau struggling in the womb." For a while after the surrender of the King to the Scots the Presbyterians were again uppermost, but the coup at Holmby, whereby the Army obtained control of the King's person, once more altered the balance in their favour.

It was at this juncture that Jeremy Taylor wrote the third great plea for liberty of thought that these years produced. Taylor had been turned out of his living at Uppingham and after an uneasy period in Oxford had found refuge with Lord Carbery, a moderate Parliament man, at whose home in South Wales Taylor and some friends set up a school. But like Milton, Jeremy Taylor found schoolmastering a second best to practising the magic of words and, deprived of books of reference as he was at Golden Grove, he discovered in the topical question of toleration a suitable subject to tackle in

[55] For Williams, cf. W. K. Jordan, *Development of Religious Toleration* (1936), III.472–506.

retirement. In spite of innumerable quotations from memory from the Christian fathers the *Liberty of Prophesying* was eminently practical, a plea for peace in a distracted world. Taylor had been one of Laud's protégés, jockeyed into All Souls to preserve him from the subversive influence of Cambridge, but he was more of a poet than an academic and more than once on the verge of unorthodoxy. The colour of his mind is illustrated by his conviction that it was more important for people to live well than to believe in this or the other disputed doctrine. "I am certain", he wrote, "that a drunkard is as contrary to God and lives as contrary to the laws of Christianity as a heretic, and I am also sure that I know what drunkenness is, but I am not sure that such [and such] an opinion is heresy."[56] So in the name of charity and common sense he pleaded for toleration, following the classic lines of Anglican thought as laid down by Hales and Chillingworth. Taylor's sensitive prose was better reading than Chillingworth's dialectic, and though he broke no new ground he reasserted at a critical moment the belief of an Anglican in freedom as part of the Christian heritage. For that reason it is hard to over-emphasize its importance, for in the harsh antithesis of war two facets of Anglicanism—the Catholicity of its faith and worship and the Protestant reliance upon scriptural revelation—stood out clearly and men were ready to defend them both, but the third all-important strand, the zeal for truth, "the quest for intellectual freedom", the ethos of Tew and Golden Grove, might all too easily have perished in a totalitarian world.[57]

In the summer of 1647 the war seemed to be over, but first men must tread the hard path of peacemaking. Before the King there lay the bitter choice of abandoning his realm or the episcopal Church, before Cromwell the conflicting claims

[56] C. J. Stranks, *Life and Writings of Jeremy Taylor* (1952), pp. 70–87.

[57] Cf. the sermon preached by the present Archbishop of Canterbury at his enthronement on 27 June 1961: "We are a Church reformed and scriptural. . . . We rejoice too in our Catholic continuity. . . . No less must we cherish that quest for intellectual freedom, that passion for truth, which has marked our great thinkers and teachers. . . ."

of statecraft and his men's Utopian dreams. During July and August the Army marched towards London, while at Hampton Court the King had his last glimpse of joy, as his captors allowed him to visit his children at Sion House and to hunt in Richmond Park. Cromwell, advised by his able son-in-law Henry Ireton, offered terms that a wiser man might have accepted, but Charles could not conceive of treating with the Army, whose leaders were much less congenial to him than either his fellow Scotsmen or the lords of the Parliament. He professed himself in danger of assassination and meditated flight, while the last chance of a treaty slipped away.

During October the Army was billeted at Putney, and it was there, in the old parish church on the banks of the Thames, that the men's agents or "agitators" met the "grandees" led by Cromwell and Ireton. In a series of debates, begun and interspersed with meetings for prayer, the agitators expressed the soldiers' discontent with the terms that the grandees had offered to the King. It was not so much the specific terms but the fact of negotiation itself that had angered them, and they urged that any agreement should be disregarded, which led to a heated argument with Ireton on the sanctity of the given word. Ireton was a sober, conservative-minded lawyer, who did not speak the same language as the demagogues among the troops. The magna carta of the men was the *Agreement of the People*, drawn up by John Lilburne, which demanded annual Parliaments and universal suffrage, advocated toleration, and declared roundly that power in the last resort lay neither with the King nor with the Parliament, but with the people. It stopped short only at demanding economic communism, which some of the more advanced thinkers would have liked to add. To Independents of means and respectability such ideas were as antipathetic as they were to the right-wing Puritans and the Cavaliers themselves. At Putney, when the discussion passed to universal suffrage, Ireton urged with unusual warmth of feeling that only men of property, who had a stake in the country's welfare, should have a say

in its control and management. But his opponent, Colonel Rainsborough, spoke bluntly and to the point: "For really I think that the poorest he that is in England hath a life to live as the greatest he."[58]

With religious problems, as such, the soldiers' spokesmen at Putney were not immediately concerned; though their antipathy to all that betokened the Establishment was implicit in every word. Social aspiration and fundamental political reform, with a dislike of legal abuses and of feudal survivals that were linked together as "the Norman yoke"—these were the matters that the agitators voiced; but it was in religious terms that the ideologies of the day were framed, and it was the teaching of the inner light, of the rule of saints and the company of the elect that provided the dynamic from which their social and political aspirations sprang. Charles was perhaps realistic in feeling that in spite of the grandees' proffered terms he had no basis of agreement with the Army. It is doubtful, however, whether his flight from Hampton Court was planned with any preconceived idea of what he hoped to accomplish or avoid. It was in the mood of a gambler that he made his final throw, still unable to conceive that he had lost the war beyond repair to a body of men untrained in politics or warfare, who had no qualifications for victory except their belief that they were better men than he.

The King's flight, mismanaged as his more precipitate actions usually were, landed him at the Isle of Wight, whose governor, Colonel Hammond, albeit he was Henry Hammond's kinsman, remembered he was the Parliament's servant and confined his unwelcome visitor in Carisbrooke Castle. Parliamentary commissioners came down to negotiate, but the King would not give way on the question of the militia. Already he had other plans on foot: he had made through the agency of Hamilton, a repentant rebel and now a courtier once more, a secret treaty with the Scots and he did not hesitate

[58] *Puritanism and Liberty, being the Army debates from the Clarke manuscripts* . . ., ed. A. S. P. Woodhouse (1938), p. 53.

to plunge his country again into war. A Royalist rising in the Home Counties was timed to coincide with an invasion of the Scottish Army. Laying aside for a while the Agreement of the People, Cromwell and his men, in a mood of grim and justifiable anger, marched out to meet the Scots in Lancashire and routed them at Preston, while Fairfax stormed Colchester, and even he showed merciless severity in the bitterness of heart the renewal of war had caused. The Army returned victorious but with every shred of confidence gone in Charles Stuart, to them a "man of blood". They found the Parliamentary commissioners again at Newport, attempting to treat with him; this time, the stumbling-block was the refusal of an amnesty to certain of his followers. As his cause became hopeless, Charles gained unwonted courage and staunchness of behaviour, refusing to sacrifice Church or friends. Parliament could find no way out of the dilemma, and the Army cut short the treaty and demanded the King's trial. Cromwell, convinced that peace and stability would return only when Charles had been removed, lost no time in completing an unpleasant job. Colonel Pride, his subordinate, was placed at the doors of Westminster one December morning, and refused to admit to the Commons any members upon whose votes the Army could not rely. Thus purged, the Rump that was left set up a court of justice to try the King in that same Westminster Hall where eight years before Strafford had faced his accusers. The sense that he was redeeming his earlier sin of compliance nerved the King to play his part with dignity. Refusing to plead before an illegal court, he placed upon those who signed his death-warrant the burden of a great wrong, which lay like a blight across the dreams of the Levellers and the visions of the Saints, and across all the honest attempts which Cromwell made to "heal and settle" and to give to his country sound administration and enlightened rule.

# 7

# YEARS OF ADVERSITY

THE King was dead, but the millennium tarried. The Rump, as men had come to call it in derision, organized itself at Westminster so that the machine of State should run effectively, and in the next year or two it won for the Commonwealth the recognition of the states of Europe. An efficient secretariat was developed under the Walter Frosts, father and son, with John Milton acting as Secretary for Foreign Tongues. Yet to many the rule by parliamentary committees seemed but a poor exchange for the reforming zeal of the *Agreement of the People* or Winstanley's visions of Utopia, which nerved the Diggers in their abortive attempt to establish communism in the heart of respectable Surrey.

Such excesses could not be permitted with Ireland still to be subjugated and a king in exile, a continuing threat, in the person of the young Charles II. "The Levellers must be levelled", and a mutiny was firmly crushed before Cromwell set out on his tragic Irish campaign. For two more years the security of the country was in jeopardy; for, to the chagrin of his Anglican councillors, Charles came to terms with the Scottish covenanters and attempted to regain his southern realm by way of invasion from the north. Not till Dunbar and Worcester had been fought, and he had returned in chastened mood to Paris, did peace come at last to an exhausted country, and with it the need for defeated Royalists to come to terms with the facts.

The convinced Anglicans of the Laudian school could not consider compromise with the new régime. It was not only

that the neglect of the sacrament and the proscription of the Liturgy struck at the very means of grace whereby Anglican piety was nourished, nor that the abolition of episcopacy challenged their claim to be heirs to the apostolic Church and part of the Church Universal; the execution of the King and the usurpation of power by the Rump of the Long Parliament struck at the whole idea of divine authority mediated in human affairs through an ordered hierarchy in Church and State. This conception of the God-given nature of sovereignty had already linked Anglicanism too closely for its health with the arbitrary acts of Charles I, and it would lead it into an insoluble dilemma before the century was out; it was significant in the Interregnum, because it meant that allegiance due to the rightful king was not something that could be given or taken away according to variations in character or circumstance. Charles II's activities in exile, whether personal or political, were not always easy to approve—witness a prayer that Lady Pakington composed, asking the Almighty to keep the young King true to the Church of Israel, and praying that he should learn to control his passions, which was "more valuable than a thousand kingdoms", an assumption with which Charles might not necessarily agree.[1] None the less, however anxious they might be and however weary they might grow of the shifts and insecurity that hedged about their life in England, their obedience to the King was not a matter of debate; Hyde's unfortunate brother, who died on the scaffold in 1651, put it into words: "My allegiance hath been incorporated into my religion and I have thought it a great part of the service due from me to Almighty God, to serve the King."[2]

At some point, therefore, the defeated, whether squire or

[1] MS. belonging to Lord Hampton, with whose kind permission it is quoted (registered at the National Register of Archives, Quality Court, London, W.C. 2).

[2] James Heath, *A new book of Loyal English Martyrs and Confessors* (? 1665), p. 308.

parson, had to make a decision: after Worcester, if he had been able to postpone it for so long, more probably when the war was lost in 1646, or three years later when the King's execution had shut the door on hope. He must, if he remained true to the High Church conception of sovereignty, go into exile or, if he stayed in England, remain intransigent, a potential rebel and a fifth columnist in the Commonwealth régime. Alternatively, if he belonged to the moderate school or if he were a cleric and felt that his first duty was the welfare of his flock, he could opt for peaceable acquiescence in things as they were, waiting upon the event in matters political and hoping that it might be possible to preserve something of the spirit of Anglican worship in the inchoate Church of the Interregnum.

Many went into exile, some driven by fear or necessity like the first refugees from parliamentary attack, some unable to take the Covenant, but like Verney and Evelyn ready to return when the obnoxious oaths were waived, the majority still regarding themselves as men under orders ready to fight with sword or pen whenever and however they could. To Edward Hyde, it was unthinkable that anyone should stay in England. It was in May 1650 that he wrote to his wife: "Can it be possible that the Warden [Sheldon] can find it safe to stay in that cursed country . . . it is madness to stay upon the confidence that they can get away when they will."[3] Young William Sancroft, a fellow of Emmanuel, wrote to his father, when he heard of the sentence passed upon Charles I: "For my part if once I see the fatal blow struck I shall think of nothing but trussing up all and packing away, and nothing but your command shall stay me long in a nation which I am persuaded will sink to the centre, if it suffer so horrid a wickedness without chastisement."[4] Sancroft's father died within a few weeks, his heart broken by the news of the King's death, and his son, like many others, felt himself bound by family

[3] Hist. MSS. Com. *Bath MSS.* (1907), II.90 (Bosher, p. 51 n).

[4] H. Cary, *Memorials of the Great Civil War in England*, II.103.

duties to remain in England. But now and in the next few years there was a fresh crop of exiles to swell the ranks of the British refugees in the Normandy towns of Caen and Rouen, in the friendly cities of the Spanish Netherlands, and in Paris and Cologne.

They were helped by many, not least by Mary of Orange, Charles I's elder daughter, whose marriage as a child had interrupted so strangely the stark gloom of the week before Strafford's execution. Other ruling princes became less forthcoming as the Commonwealth established itself more securely, and as one year gave way to another there was much hardship and mental distress and, even for those who prospered, the incurable malaise of being uprooted. The wilder spirits indulged in plots which always proved abortive, while those of a different mould were often tempted to join the Roman Church and thus to secure themselves a spiritual home. In Paris, in particular, the presence of the Queen Mother increased the temptation, and it was an uphill fight for the little group of Anglican divines who were centred upon the chapel which Sir Richard Browne, the Resident, had built on to his private house. The chaplain was John Cosin, very different now from the "young Apollo" of Prebendary Smart's strictures, but still, in spite of intense poverty and failing health and a cataract developing on his only "reading eye", a man who knew where he stood. He had been one of the first to send his plate to be melted down when the wars began, as he was to be the first to order the use of the Prayer Book in cathedral worship after 1660. Meanwhile, as he put it to a friend: "The time hath been wherein good orthodox Christians have suffered more than we do and continued firm and constant in their ways, nor do I see any better way to recover our station again than this."[5]

Cosin worked without ceasing to maintain the morale of the refugees in Paris, though he lost the support of the King's

[5] Cosin, *Works* (1851) IV.387; *Correspondence* (1869), I.288; P. H. Osmond, *A Life of John Cosin* (1913), p. 144.

presence after a treaty between Cromwell and France necessitated the removal of Charles's court. Another stalwart was John Bramhall, the Bishop of Derry, who with the exception of one brief visit to Ireland was sixteen years in exile. He spent the years writing in defence of the Anglican Church against adversaries on every side—militant Rome, the Presbyterian discipline, and the forces of materialism soon to be strikingly deployed in Hobbes's *Leviathan*. It was no easy life, as Bramhall wrote in reference to his literary work: "Those who have composed minds, free from distracting cares, and means to maintain them, and their books and notes by them, do little imagine with what difficulties poor exiles struggle whose minds are more intent on what they should eat tomorrow than on what they should write."[6] But he persevered, and in 1654 there was published in London his *Just Vindication of the Church of England* in which he expounded the orthodox Anglican defence against the Roman accusation of being a Church in schism.

Others there were in abundance, among them the old friends, John Earle and George Morley. Earle, appointed tutor to the Prince of Wales in 1640, had followed his charge into exile, and now that the years of tutelage had passed, Charles had no mind to lose sight of a man upon whose goodness he could always rely. It was Earle who married John Evelyn to Sir Richard Browne's daughter on one of the rare occasions when happiness broke through. Morley came out in 1649 when he lost his Oxford fellowship, and during the uncertain winter that Charles spent in Scotland, Morley and Earle were together in Antwerp. Hyde's family were also there, while Hyde himself was away on an embassy to Madrid, and when Earle returned to Paris to attend the Duke of York at Charles's command, Morley remained and "for friendship's sake" looked after Lady Hyde and taught her boys, until he declared that he could no longer at his age bear "the vexatious

[6] Robert S. Bosher, *Making of the Restoration Settlement* (1951), pp. 66 et seq., and see Chapter II, pp. 49–87 for the clergy in exile.

employment of teaching little children".[7] An invitation from Elizabeth of Bohemia to go with her as chaplain to Heidelberg solved his immediate difficulties. Of all these plans he wrote to Sheldon in England, sending messages to Hammond arising from their joint guardianship of Falkland's unsatisfactory sons, and wherever the group of friends might be, a close correspondence was maintained between Hyde and Sheldon, Hammond and Morley, telling of their personal fortunes but discussing also the problems of the Church.

After Charles's disillusionment in Scotland and his defeat at Worcester, Hyde became his chief adviser, and there was thus a small but compact group who by their writings and their worship and their political skill succeeded in keeping intact the Anglican faith and ensuring at length the full restoration of an episcopal and sacramental Church. The moderates of Great Tew became, in this way, the die-hards of the Interregnum. Sheldon was something of a rigorist by nature and Hyde had been hammered by experience into a very different person from the young lawyer who urged moderation in 1640. He still retained his capacity to balance and compromise, particularly in political matters, and he was consistent in his main contention that continuity, not revolution, was desirable in Church and State alike. Ten years later he was to bring back the King by means of a clever use of the disillusioned Presbyterians, but he avoided any commitment on the religious front such as Charles had given by taking the Covenant in 1650, and certainly his clerical friends had never any intention of compromising on the religious issue.[8] There can be little doubt that the liberal element of the Great Tew group,

[7] Letter to Sheldon, 8 June 1653, printed in *The Ecclesiastic and Theologian*, XIII.242 f; Anthony Wood, *Athenae Oxonienses*, ed. Philip Bliss (1813–20), IV.151.

[8] Dr Bosher's able study in conjunction with A. G. Matthews' *Walker Revised* (1948) makes possible a new understanding of the position of Anglicans during the Interregnum. Dr Hardacre in *The Royalists during the Puritan Revolution* writes from the social and economic point of view. I would wish to acknowledge fully the use I have made of these accounts.

for which Falkland and Chillingworth had been mainly responsible, had been overlaid, if not eradicated, by the experiences of the war years, and this was not only because the evils of disorder had become manifest but because they had become convinced of the value of dogma and of the power to say: "This is the truth, for which I am prepared to die!" One legacy, however, remained of the Great Tew days: they were all old friends, and this maybe was one reason why this small group did so much to preserve the Anglican way during its years of eclipse. They knew from the discussions and the comradeship of the *convivium* how each other's minds worked, and thus were able to trust each other and to work together, though some remained in the English Midlands and others journeyed uneasily to Paris or Antwerp or Cologne.

The decision of Sheldon and Hammond to remain at home when Morley went abroad in 1649 proved, in spite of Hyde's original doubts, to be of the greatest value to the Church. The exiles on the Continent, often penurious, always uprooted, knew only that they had chosen the harder part and forgot at times how important it was to have spiritual guides still viable among the dispossessed at home. When Oxford was purged and after a brief period of restraint Sheldon and Hammond had to decide upon their future course, the latter wrote to his friend: "Whether the judgements that hang over us should at all incline us to leave this nation which yet is our lot, I am as unresolved as you."[9] But he felt increasingly that there was work for him to do in England. Sheldon made his headquarters in the Derbyshire village of Snelston; Hammond went eventually to Westwood in Worcestershire, the home of Sir John Pakington, a wealthy ex-Royalist with a charming and intelligent wife, the daughter of the former Lord Keeper Coventry. At Westwood, Hammond remained until his death a few weeks before the King's return, using his private means to help poor students and writing treatises at every hour of the day and night, to confirm the waverers and to explain to those

[9] Brit. Mus. Harl. MS. 6942, No. 14.

who stood firm the meaning and significance of their faith. As the years passed and the prospect of change receded, the dangers of spiritual *accidie* increased, and the bracing effect of Hammond's personality, kindly yet robust, balanced yet disciplined, made itself felt far beyond the bounds of Worcestershire. Meanwhile at Golden Grove, rather apart from the other Anglican leaders, Jeremy Taylor followed up his *Liberty of Prophesying* by a *Life of Christ* and his two great masterpieces, *Holy Living* and *Holy Dying*, which gave to loyal churchmen in these disastrous years the spiritual food and devotional guidance they needed as surely as the sound doctrine that came from Hammond's pen.

The leadership that was gradually assumed by Hyde and Sheldon and their friends was to a certain extent thrust upon them by the lack of effective guidance from the bishops, either to individual Christians or in the politics of the Church. There were not, by the 1650s, very many of them still alive. When the war began, Williams betook himself to Wales and garrisoned Conway Castle for the King. But he proved himself as inconsistent in war as in peace and switched his allegiance to Parliament when a professional soldier supplanted him in his command. He died in retirement on one of his Welsh estates, a painful example of a near-miss to greatness. Of his colleagues on the episcopal bench, Wright of Lichfield died in his house at Eccleshall while it was under bombardment by the Parliamentary forces, and Walter Curll, that dignified prelate, hid ignominiously in a dung-cart to escape from Waltham to Winchester, his cathedral city. Bishop Hall wrote of his experiences in his *Hard Measure*, which described the desecration of the Norwich churches and his forcible eviction from his episcopal palace in 1647—sad memories redeemed by the kindness of friends, who bought in some of his books when his goods were confiscated and a sufficient amount of furniture and household utensils for him to live in comparative comfort in his sister's cottage at Higham. One April day,

two years before Hall's death, there was an interruption of the cottage's quiet routine. Four young men appeared at the door; their leader introduced himself as Simon Patrick, a fellow of Queens' College, Cambridge. Later he recorded the event. He had wished some time earlier to be ordained. "I knew no better," he wrote, "than to go to a classis of presbyters, who then sat, and was examined by them and afterwards received the imposition of their hands. This afterwards troubled me very much when not long after I met with Dr Hammond upon *Ignatius' Epistles* and Mr Thorndike's *Primitive Government of the Church*, whereby I was fully convinced of the necessity of episcopal ordination. This made me inquire after a Bishop to whom I might resort; and hearing that Bishop Hall lived not far from Norwich, of which he was bishop, thither I went with two other Fellows of our College and a gentleman (Mr Gore, with whom I had contracted a great friendship) as a companion and witness of what we did. There we were received with great kindness by that rev[erend] old Bishop, who examined us and gave us many good exhortations, and then ordained us in his parlour at Higham about one mile from Norwich, April 5th, 1654."[10]

This problem of securing a continuance of the ministry was one of increasing urgency and there were many such secret ordinations particularly by Robert Skinner, the Bishop of Oxford, who in a peripatetic life in the West Country was regularly resorted to by young men anxious to receive the episcopal laying-on of hands. It was less easy to secure the consecration of new bishops, and eventually this became an urgent matter if the apostolic succession were to be preserved. Their number steadily dwindled, though Bishop Morton, the senior in age, went near to outliving them all. More fortunate than many, he had been given £1000 by Parliament upon the loss of his estates and, with the Earl of Rutland's help, bought himself a small annuity. But he would not accept the Earl's offer of a home, and went into the country with no fixed plan

10 *The Autobiography of Simon Patrick* (1839), pp. 23 f.

in mind. A year or so later, he decided to return to London and as he was riding towards the capital he was overtaken by Sir Christopher Yelverton whom he recognized as the son of an old friend of his. To Yelverton's inquiry as to who he might be, Morton replied with a flash of the old spirit: "I am that old man, the Bishop of Durham, in spite of all your votes." But when Yelverton asked him whither he journeyed he answered sadly: "To London, to live there a little while and then to die." They rode on together, so the story goes, but when they came to the parting of the ways Yelverton persuaded the bishop to turn aside with him on the road to Easton Maudit, and there he stayed, outliving his benefactor but remaining a beloved and respected member of the family till his death at the age of 95 on the eve of the Restoration.[11]

Matthew Wren, Laud's loyal henchman in earlier days, lived out the Interregnum a prisoner in the Tower. Cromwell, when he became Protector, would have liked to have released him, but Wren refused to accept a pardon because it would have implied a recognition of the usurper's authority. His days were not idle; young men came to him for ordination and through John Barwick, an indefatigable intermediary who had met Wren while temporarily in prison himself, he kept in touch with Hyde and Sheldon and with the other leaders of Anglican opinion. Bishop Juxon remained undisturbed at Fulham until after the King's death and then retired to the Oxfordshire village of Little Compton, to cherish his master's memory and the royal bible and, scarcely less precious, his pack of hounds. He must have kept his books too, or some of them, for in 1657 he gave to the Bodleian certain Oriental manuscripts in his possession. He ministered to the family at Chastleton nearby and went out hunting—for his health's sake, his friends rather apologetically asserted. So he remained

[11] Walker, *Sufferings of the Clergy* (1714), II.18; cf. John Barwick, *The Fight, Victory and Triumph of St Paul . . . a Sermon preached at the funeral of . . . Thomas, late Bishop of Durham, together with the Life of the said Bishop* (1660), pp. 122 f.

as serene in his country village as he had been in the bustle of the Treasury, a good man but never given to heroics.

In much the same mood of quiet acceptance, although in closer touch with the more dynamic group, Brian Duppa, Bishop of Salisbury, lived out the years in a cottage on Richmond Hill. He was secured possession of the little house through the generous help of Justinian Isham, a Northamptonshire gentleman whom he had met by chance at the home of mutual friends at Petersham nearby. When Isham returned to Northampton after his visit he kept up a regular correspondence with the Bishop, and the letters, published by Sir Gyles Isham in 1950, give an attractive picture of a deepening friendship. More fortunate than most of his colleagues, Duppa had a devoted wife to look after him, "a bosom friend", he described her on a wedding anniversary, "who hath so faithfully and affectionately gone along with me through all the variations of my life and fortunes".[12] There was the underlying sadness of the uncertain days and some material hardship—above all no money to buy books—but there were kind neighbours and occasional gifts of tasty venison, the pleasure of a walk up the hill to look out over one of England's loveliest views, all the small change of life in addition to the more solid comfort of reading, and the occasional flurry of business when the available Anglican leaders converged upon the Richmond house.

Of these private meetings, as of political events in general, Duppa said nothing in his letters to Isham, for security depended upon prudence. At least one such meeting seems to have been held not long before Cromwell became Protector, when the matter under debate was the provision of an alternative liturgy along Anglican lines. A few years later, in 1655, and again after Cromwell's death, there was much correspondence and anxious discussion—but no subsequent action—in

[12] *The Correspondence of Bishop Brian Duppa and Sir Justinian Isham, 1650–1660*, ed. Sir Gyles Isham (Publications of Northamptonshire Record Society, XVII [1950/1]), p. 146.

regard to the consecration of new bishops, but no joint statement was made on any of these occasions, and by the time the Restoration occurred Duppa, though he served loyally to the end, was more concerned with the approach of death than with ecclesiastical politics.

More energetic than Duppa, though less in the confidence of those upon whom the direction of Anglican affairs devolved, were Skinner of Oxford, who at least tried to keep in touch with his diocese, and Warner of Rochester, a robust and wealthy prelate, old-fashioned in his theology but a vigorous supporter of the Crown. None the less he had the uneasy distinction of being the only bishop who had compounded. His troubles had begun in 1643, when he had stubbornly refused to pay the parliamentary levy and was one of twelve named bishops whose property was sequestered. For three years he was up and down the West Country, more or less a fugitive, but, as he put it, "preaching the Truth boldly and plainly in all places against our enemies". In April 1646 he had come up to London to compound but his reluctance to admit that his presence in the King's quarters amounted to delinquency and his stubborn refusal to take the Covenant helped to delay a settlement which took more than a year to reach. During the year he fought a rearguard action for his rights as he saw them, quibbled about the details of his estate, and got increasingly annoyed with his lawyer. The Bishop had some rough treatment from the committee at Haberdashers' Hall; he was "reprehended" for calling himself a bishop and subjected to the jeers of the soldiers. "See how like a Rogue the Bishop stands now bareheaded", cried one; "I warrant he would heretofore have stood with his hatt on, but the times are well amended."[13] Warner protested in vain, and not all his vigour of mind and keen business sense could prevent the

[13] An account by Bishop Warner, included in the MSS. belonging to Major E. H. Lee Warner of Denton Hall, Harleston, Norfolk, which are deposited at the Bodleian. The papers regarding the composition are at the P.R.O. (*S.P. Dom. Interregnum*, 19/92).

twelve months' wrangling from ending with the imposition of an extra fine of £850 in addition to the original confiscation of a third of his estate. It was not till 1649 that the sequestration was removed, by which time Warner had been forced to relinquish his episcopal palace at Bromley to a Mr Augustine Skinner who had leased it from Parliament. He had not given in easily: according to his own account written in 1660, "I, after threatts and proclamations to leave my house at Bromley, yet I alone of all the Bishops kept my possession against the sheriff, armed with two several ordinances. I kept it till Christmas Eve, 1648, I was forced out by Skinner, who with new Engl. men, Smyths, Carpenters &c. broke open five doors [which] were lock'd and bolted." He remained in lodgings in the neighbourhood of Bromley and was thereafter undisturbed, using the remnant of the fortune he had rescued to help many fellow-Anglicans in distress. In 1648 he was engaged in writing, at Charles I's request, a lengthy dissertation against the sale of church lands, and had the courage in 1649 to preach a sermon within a week or two of the King's execution in which the crime of killing an anointed ruler was compared in no uncertain terms with "the devilish conspiracy . . . and damnable murder of Christ by the Jews".[14]

Warner, one would have thought, was a man after Sheldon's own heart. He was certainly treated with respect and took a leading share in any discussions on policy or practice that took place. Jeremy Taylor dedicated to him, unfortunately without his consent, his tract on repentance, *Unum Necessarium*, and had his knuckles rapped for impertinence and unorthodoxy. But Warner was a strict Calvinist, which may have kept him to a certain degree outside the Hyde-Sheldon group; although it must be remembered that George Morley also remained a Calvinist to the end, and probably more personal reasons, lack of intimacy and maybe a clash of temperament, had as much to do with it as any question of theology.

[14] Brit. Mus. Add. MS. 32096, f. 182d; cf. Edward Lee Warner, *The Life of John Warner* (1901), pp. 31–46.

Bishop Warner's composition and the shelter given to Morton at Easton Maudit are a reminder of what happened to those defeated Royalists who remained in England. It was not an easy decision, either for layman or cleric, whether to go or to stay. There were many laymen, less committed than priests or politicians, who desired only to recover a semblance of ordinary living. There were dependants to be thought of, fields to be harvested, the ravages of war to be repaired: to many it seemed right as well as sensible to compound.

This practice of composition, which reached its two peaks in 1646–7 and after the execution of the King, had grown up in a somewhat haphazard way, as Parliament's urgent need for money caused them to permit those whose estates had been sequestered to recover them on the payment of a fixed fine. In the case of certain named persons and of the clergy, this was a third part of the estate; in other cases it might be as low as a tenth. The value of the estate was supplied by the county committee and the fines were fixed by a body that met at Goldsmiths' Hall in the City and was composed of leading citizens and members of the House. In addition to the fine, those who compounded had to take the Covenant and the negative oath, which bound them not to take up arms again; that done they could go in peace, to make the best of what was left of a tattered fortune and a conscience ill at ease.[15]

Compositions did not always work out as planned. A portion of the fine was paid on the nail and the remainder over an agreed period, and all too often, when this proved impossible, instead of recovering his place in society the ex-Royalist found himself a prisoner for debt. Among some letters and accounts of the Pakington family, there is a paper drawn up by Lady Pakington recording her husband's "sufferings and expenses"

[15] On compositions cf. *Calendar of the Committee for Compounding, 1643–60*, Part 1, Preface, pp. v et seq.; and see Paul H. Hardacre, *The Royalists during the Puritan Revolution* (1956), Chapters 2 and 3, pp. 17–64.

for adhering to the King. The family had large estates in Buckinghamshire, including a remunerative toll in Aylesbury, all of which had been sequestered in addition to the land at Westwood for which Sir John had compounded. His wife estimated his losses at £20,358, and adds: "The best house in Buckinghamshire pulled down with vast destruction of wood not reckoned." Nearly half the total was money lost through the Buckinghamshire sequestrations, and Lady Pakington also included her husband's army expenses and his charges while he was a prisoner in the Tower. Westwood had been compounded for in 1646 for the sum of £5000, paid over four years, and then in 1651, just as Sir John thought he was getting straight, the battle of Worcester took place. Sir John was in Worcester at the time and he was said to be wearing a sword; as a result Westwood was sequestered again. This time he had to compound for £1000 and, to add insult to injury, it cost him £200 to repair his house, which had been used as a billet by the Scottish invaders.[16] On a smaller scale Sir John's experiences were those of many others, and one of the main causes of the decay in morale among the defeated Royalists must have been the constant struggle with poverty, the financial straits and contrivances which were not merely the background but the immediate pressing concern of every malignant's life.

The other demoralizing factor was the oaths. The large majority of the cases recorded in the State Papers include a certificate to the effect that the two oaths have been taken; yet this must have been a sore stumbling-block to many of tender conscience, albeit every Anglican did not regard episcopacy as sacrosanct, as did the Laudians. Loyal Church of England men like Pakington himself took the oath, though doubtless with mental reservations. All too many took it as a matter of form in the cynical mood of the topical song, quoted by Dr Hardacre:

[16] Pakington MS., belonging to Lord Hampton. Lady Pakington adds up the items incorrectly, making the total £20,858.

Since Goldsmiths' Committee
Affords us no pity,
Our sorrows in wine we will steep 'em.
They force us to take
Two oaths, but we'll make
A third, that we ne'er meant to keep 'em.[17]

All the same, the oaths were sometimes refused or avoided. The aim of the composition was not ideological but strictly practical—to raise money—and if a malignant like Bishop Warner proved stubborn, the committee would be more likely to raise his fine than to refuse his composition. This was certainly the case when the matter rested with the county committee, and in this respect as in many others it is probably safe to say that the treatment given to a malignant depended, at least to some degree, on the colour of the local community and also upon himself—whether over the years, politics apart, he had proved himself a good neighbour and a peaceable man.[18]

In 1649–50 there was yet another oath imposed by Parliament, an Engagement to be "faithful and true" to the Commonwealth, as then established, without a King or a House of Lords. This occasioned much heart-searching, particularly among Presbyterians, who had no republican leanings and whose Scottish friends were now in alliance with Charles II. Newcome took the Engagement, but could never persuade himself that he had not sinned in doing so; Martindale had fewer qualms at first but was equally regretful later and reflected, in reference to the Independent politicians now in charge, "how hardly those tender people that pretended so much to liberty of conscience had dealt with their brethren in

[17] Hardacre, op. cit., p. 22; cf. C. V. Wedgwood, *Poetry and Politics under the Stuarts* (1960), pp. 108 ff.

[18] See D. H. Pennington and J. A. Roots, *The Committee at Stafford, 1643–5* (1957), introd., p. li: "Questions about readiness to subscribe to the Parliamentary Covenants do arise but they are not common. So long as there was no active support of the enemy," the Committee's main concern with the compounders was to extract money from them.

imposing burdens upon them". Among conscientious Anglicans there was much anxious consultation, some arguing that one could take the oath if one intended to live peaceably under Commonwealth rule for the time being, without betraying one's basic allegiance to the Crown, should circumstances change. Young Sancroft at Emmanuel was one of those who could not square it with his conscience, and giving up his fellowship he retired to the country and later went abroad to study.

Sensible men on both sides saw that an impossible situation was arising. Algernon Sydney said bluntly that the vague wording of the Engagement made it an oath that would prove a snare to every honest man but every knave would slip through it. Even Hyde urged Charles Cavendish to return to England to compound, for the desperate purpose of selling his recovered estates to raise money for the refugees; when Cavendish declared that he would rather "submit to nakedness or starving in the street" than subscribe to the Covenant or Engagement, Hyde argued that the two oaths were so contrary and had "so much justled and reviled each other" that they were seldom pressed upon a person unless the Government had some particular reason for doing so. Eventually Cromwell put an end to them with the fitting epitaph, "many . . . oaths and engagements have proved burthens and snares to tender consciences". He was even prepared to compensate those whose inability to swear had prevented them from bringing suits at law.[19]

Whatever compromises and economies compounding might entail, it did mean that in the England of the Interregnum there were a number of ex-Royalists, anxious to live normal lives again but unchanged at heart in their faith and their opinions. For one group of malignants, the ejected clergy, it was well that this was so, for many moderate men, setting about the work of rehabilitation, saw it as part of their duty

[19] Clarendon, *Life* (edn of 1857), I.251–4; Firth and Rait, *Acts and Ordinances of the Interregnum* (1911), II.830 f.

to give them shelter, as Pakington at Westwood had welcomed Henry Hammond. Royalists who had never been happy about compounding could persuade themselves that they had acted rightly, when the money that remained enabled them to help a priest or scholar in distress. Members of the gentry who had supported the Parliamentary cause, and found it hard to forgive themselves when the King was killed, slept more easily at night if an old and grateful clergyman was in the room next door. There were humbler folk also who now had a chance to help, as John Hales discovered when he lost his fellowship at Eton. He found lodging with a former maidservant, whom he had treated kindly upon her marriage many years before. Mrs Powney was devoted to him, looking after him until his death with warm proprietary affection, and it was at her house that Aubrey visited him and found him "very gentile and courteous", reading Thomas à Kempis, still neatly dressed and still able to enjoy a glass of "canarie".

A very great deal depended on the women. There were so many of them, their husbands in exile or dead on the battlefields of Naseby or Marston Moor. They carried on, cherishing their memories, looking after their depleted estates, and above all, with the aid of the Anglican priest to whom they had given shelter, bringing up their sons in the old faith and the old loyalties. In the privacy of countless country homes the one-time vicar in the role of chaplain and tutor gathered about him a new sort of congregation; he taught the children, christened the babies, churched the mother, prayed for the dying and administered Communion to the whole household and to the neighbours who slipped in unobtrusively at the appointed hour. In telling the story of Morton's stay at Easton Maudit, John Walker refers to young Henry Yelverton, the son and heir, "whom the good old bishop made a true son of the Church of England".[20] Multiply this a hundred times and one begins to understand the zeal and the certainty of the

[20] Walker, *Sufferings*, II.18; cf. Bosher, *The Making of the Restoration Settlement*, pp. 39 f.

young squires who came up from the country to take their seats in the House of Commons when the King came into his own again.

There were many others among the clergy who remained in their cures throughout the Interregnum, and the extremists in exile and the dispossessed given shelter by the faithful must be balanced by those who by conviction and a measure of good luck continued to minister in the parish churches of England. As events since 1559 had repeatedly testified, there were the two traditions in the Anglican heritage: the one developed by the High Churchmen, the other held by those who were always mindful of the need for Protestant unity and sought to avoid sectarianism through a broadly based comprehensive Church. In the crisis of these years the staunch defence of episcopacy and the preservation of the apostolic succession became a matter of urgency to a forceful minority, who regarded them as essential to the historic continuity and the sacramental doctrine at the very centre of the Church's life. But it was no less important that the other tradition should also be preserved: the distinction in framing dogma between accessories and fundamentals, the elbow-room for freedom of thought, the continued trust in the unity of the Holy Spirit. John Owen, the religious spokesman of the Commonwealth Government, like Cromwell when he became Protector, hoped to build a harmonious Church on some such basis. They failed, and their work died with them, and after 1660 the immediate future lay with the rigorists. Yet the idea of comprehension did not perish at the Restoration, for there remained within the established Church the moderates with their own insights, no less sincere if less clearly etched than those of the men who would not compromise. That this tradition survived was largely due to the Anglican priests and scholars who stayed in their posts during the Interregnum.

Dr Matthews' revision of Walker's *Sufferings of the Clergy* gives the number of sequestered cures as 2425 out of a total of

8600 parishes. In addition there were certain of the university fellows and members of cathedral chapters, not holding a living, which brought the number of ejected up to about 3600.[21] According to this computation more than half of the parishes were not disturbed. A comparatively small, if vocal, section of the incumbents who remained were convinced advocates of a Presbyterian system, but the large majority were middle-of-the-road men. Many had been left in peace because their livings were so poor that it was worth no one's while to turn them out. They were often simple men, like Parson Higham at Evelyn's home at Wotton, or the old chaplain of the Cecil household, whom John Lambert left undisturbed at Wimbledon until the board of Triers stirred him up to make a change.[22] Occasionally they were men whose age or reputation secured them special treatment, like Abraham Colfe at Lewisham who had been vicar since 1610 and might well be regarded as an institution. Evelyn heard him preach an "honest sermon" in February 1652, but it was sufficiently an occasion for him to add, "it being now a very rare thing to find a Priest of the Church of England in a parish pulpit". Colfe trod carefully (he did not for example hold a service on Christmas Day, though he spoke his mind about the Incarnation on the Sunday following) and he was left undisturbed by the authorities until his death in 1657—a forbearance from which posterity has benefited, for it was during these years of the Interregnum that he founded the Lewisham Grammar School that bears his name.

It was not however just a question of inadvertence or of local partiality. The majority of the men in authority who had the well-being of the Church at heart were as anxious as ever Bancroft had been to increase the supply of learned and devout clergy, and once the sense of emergency had diminished,

[21] A. G. Matthews, *Walker Revised*, introd., pp. xiii ff; Bosher, op. cit., p. 5. In addition one should note that many vacancies occurred through death during the decade after 1642, which would normally be filled by men of a Puritan allegiance (e.g. at St Nicholas, Deptford).

[22] W. Bartlett, *History of Wimbledon* (1865), p. 110.

they were not anxious to exclude. Similarly among the Anglicans, in cures that had not been sequestered, the decision to stay was often deliberate. Among the bishops there were at least two who saw a measure of compromise as a Christian duty: Brownrigg of Exeter, who lived and preached in London and was eventually made Chaplain of the Inner and the Middle Temple, and the learned and moderate Ussher, who was appointed preacher at Lincoln's Inn and was given a state funeral by the Protector when he died. Another man of this mould was, of course, the genial Tom Fuller, who often lectured in London. Comfortably settled as curate of Waltham Abbey, he married again, and set about finishing his *Church History*. Someone who did not like him described him as "running round London with his big book under one arm and his little wife under the other, and recommending himself as a dinner guest by his facetious talk".[23] But his friendliness and moderation were of the dyed-in-the-wool variety and he even maintained his good humour in replying to Heylyn, when Laud's former chaplain pulled his *History* to pieces.

For many who stayed in their livings it was less a question of logical adherence to one school of thought or the other, but a desire to continue to minister to their congregations. In the middle years of the Interregnum, Evelyn records with pleasure a sermon he heard in a village near Uppingham, by a man who had been vicar since 1637 and who preached "touching the love of God very excellently well". Many such as he felt it better to serve within the bounds of the Commonwealth Church than to leave their flocks without a shepherd. Certainly this was the view of the most influential and one of the best beloved of those who remained, Robert Sanderson, the rector of Boothby Pagnell. In the year the war began he had been appointed Regius Professor of Divinity at Oxford. He could not take up his post till the fighting was over, and meanwhile Boothby Pagnell was sequestered and he himself was

[23] Fuller's *Worthies*, ed. John Freeman (1952), introd., p. xiii; cf. Dean B. Lyman, *The Great Tom Fuller* (1935), p. 128.

taken prisoner. He had been exchanged for a neighbouring minister of a different political colour on the understanding, according to the story, that neither should be disturbed thereafter. Sanderson's own character had probably as much to do with his subsequent immunity as any tacit agreement, for he was a shy, sensitive man, without a touch of arrogance in his make-up but with exceptional powers as a spiritual director. When, in 1647, he was able to take up his post at Oxford he gave a course of lectures on cases of conscience which proved him to be a master of casuistry, that neglected art of guidance in matters of ethics and behaviour, which was as urgent a need in these uncertain days as Hammond's teaching tracts or Taylor's devotional works. Sanderson's lectures were in Latin and were not translated (except, it was said, by the King in his captivity) nor published till after the Restoration, but when Sanderson returned to Boothby Pagnell in 1648 he thought it his clear duty to stay, using his expertise in casuistry not only for the comfort of his parishioners but for the many who wrote to him for advice as to the right course of action at a time when the old standards had gone and values were all awry.

One of the matters upon which he was often consulted by other Anglican clergy still in harness was the use of the Liturgy. This was forbidden by the ordinance of 1645, and although the Directory allowed scope for a good deal of extempore prayer in which many of the Prayer Book phrases could be used, this was as far as it was expedient to go. Sanderson's own practice was to use a modified form of the Liturgy, with sufficient omissions and adjustments to satisfy the law, so that the new generation would grow up with at least some knowledge of the spirit and shape, if not the exact wording, of the Book of Common Prayer.[24] In November 1652

[24] Sanderson, *Works* (1854), V.37–59; Jeremy Taylor, *Works* (1847–54), VIII.571 f. In the Lee Warner MSS. there is an all but indecipherable copy among the innumerable loose sheets of sermon notes, memoranda, accounts, which Warner hoarded. The arguments against compromise are as always fear of scandal and schism: the arguments in favour include the plea of necessity and the duty of not deserting one's flock.

Sanderson circulated an answer he had given to a clergyman who had consulted him upon this point, for the High Church extremists argued that even this amount of adaptation was not permissible, that it would cause scandal and appear to condone schism. Sanderson in reply urged the argument of necessity, in times of danger and confusion, and suggested that there could be no scandal when the only alternative was to leave the sheep without a shepherd. By the repetition of the creed and decalogue and by one's sermons it was possible to safeguard "the old theology". Hammond watched with anxious solicitude his old friend's progress, as he trod the razor's edge between charity and compliance. Every clergyman had sworn at his ordination, according to the terms of the Act of Uniformity, to use the Prayer Book and the Prayer Book only in his public worship; so to Hammond it appeared as a simple question of obedience, and obedience had become a key-word to him in the tangle of opposing duties. One way out of the dilemma would be the joint issue by the surviving bishops of an episcopal dispensation, which would give a measure of legality to a regrettable irregularity in practice. The rigorists felt that either this step should be taken, or the practice condemned, and after much anxious correspondence in the spring of 1653 a meeting was arranged at Richmond. Hammond urged Sheldon to attend, to interpose his "judgement and authority". Jeremy Taylor, the only man with the requisite literary skill, had drawn up an alternative form of the liturgy, but it is not known whether this was discussed in detail or what the outcome of the meeting was. Certainly no dispensation was issued and the decision seems to have been left to the individual conscience, at the cost of consistency but not without valuable results.

Official action may well have been postponed, because a change in the political situation gave rise to hopes of a legal toleration which would permit the Prayer Book to be used. In April 1653 Cromwell dispersed the Rump, and took upon himself the ordering of England. Though one of his generals,

"honest John" Lambert, urged the need of a strong executive, Cromwell followed the counsel of Major-General Harrison, the leader of the Fifth Monarchists, who dreamt of a rule of Saints. Representatives of the gathered churches were summoned to Westminster, where the nominated Parliament soon came to be known as "Barebones", from the name of one of the members. To them, in a great opening speech, Cromwell entrusted the charge of setting the country to rights, adding significantly: "If the poorest Christian, the most mistaken Christian shall desire to live peaceably and quietly under you . . . let him be protected." Francis Rouse, who had written the paraphrase of the Psalms and was now appointed Speaker, had expressed the same principle, which was an essential part of Independent doctrine, in the words: "When Christ speaks to thee to follow him one way, thou mayest not with Peter make quarrels and questions concerning John's other way." Yet when it came to practical details a deep cleavage of opinion was revealed. The idealists among the Saints urged the abolition of tithes and the complete separation of Church and State so that every man could in truth follow Christ in his own way. But Cromwell's stress was on the "living peaceably" and his answer to the danger of fanatics on both wings was an established Church, comprehensive and tolerant in tone but under strict state control.[25] His first glimpse of disillusion came with the realization of the disparity between him and the Saints both in church affairs and secular matters. Before the end of the year the members had returned to their homes, Harrison was in disgrace, and John Lambert was back at Whitehall, his scheme for a strong executive ready to hand. The Instrument of Government invested authority in a single person, assisted by a Council of State and an elected assembly which was to meet for not less than five months in every three years. Cromwell accepted the office of Protector, and on

[25] For Cromwell's religious settlement, based upon John Owen's, see Gardiner, *History of the Commonwealth and Protectorate* (edn of 1903), III.19–25.

16 December 1653, in a ceremony of some magnificence, he was installed at Whitehall and the first step was taken on the road back to the monarchy.

Lambert, a generous and brilliant soldier, was also an ambitious Yorkshireman, without any of Harrison's religious fervour. What spiritual sustenance he needed he derived from growing flowers in his Wimbledon garden. He gave lip-service to the idea of toleration, which was indeed congenial to him, but neither he nor the new secretary of state, John Thurloe, regarded it as entirely practicable. Thurloe was an honest and devoted civil servant, and as great a genius as Queen Elizabeth's Walsingham in managing his intelligence system. No Royalist plot escaped his detection, whether it emanated from an irresponsible few or from the band of distinguished plotters known as the "Sealed Knot". He knew that in many cases an Anglican clergyman was involved as intermediary, and it needs only a glance at his massive collection of State Papers to understand how immediate and ubiquitous was the danger of assassination or revolt. The *Instrument of Government* therefore laid down the principle of toleration but stated categorically that "Papists and Prelatists" should be excluded. It was a bitter blow to those who had been counting on a measure of liberty in meeting together for worship. Yet the assembly of potential rebels in one place, where plots could be concerted and secret instructions passed from hand to hand, was the very thing the Government could not allow, not at least by legal right. In practice Cromwell did for a while permit it, either in private houses or in certain London churches, still hoping that by tolerant administration he would win over the greater part of the nation.

It was an illogical arrangement but for a while it worked, and the sense of more settled times at hand persisted. Ralph Verney was back at Claydon, planting his orchard and planning to build. He had come home in the previous year, prefacing his return by a letter inquiring as to the state of his house, the quantity of table linen, the present price of beef and

butter and "green morning milke cheeze", and innumerable other details. "Tell me what scollop dishes there are at Claydon, for frute?"[26] A still greater act of faith in a future of sorts was that of Sir Robert Shirley who built a new church at Staunton Harold. An inscription over the west door reads:

In the yeare 1653
When all things sacred were throughout ye nation
Either demolisht or profaned
Sir Robert Shirley, Barronet
Founded this church
Whose singular praise it is
to have done ye best thinges in ye worst times
And
hoped them in ye most callamitous.
Ye righteous shall be had in everlasting remembrance

Despite the inscription no one attempted to demolish or profane Shirley's handiwork and, for a few more years, his home was a shelter for the dispossessed, in particular for two Cambridge scholars, Peter Gunning and Robert Mapletoft.[27] But "living peaceably" was still the crux of the matter, and Shirley was not content with such service to the cause of Church and King as the building of churches provided. He was involved in more than one Royalist conspiracy and died in captivity in 1656.

Where men were content to be quiet, they were usually undisturbed. For instance at Little Gidding, which Robert Mapletoft, for one, knew so well, there was no interference with the subdued tenor of the days. John Ferrar once contrasted them with the bitter years when Little Gidding had been sequestered and the family went beyond the seas but, he added, "God almighty brought us home againe to the admiration of all men [and] had Giddinge restored to us without our

[26] *Memoirs of the Verney Family* (edn of 1925), I.523 f.

[27] A. L. Maycock, *Chronicles of Little Gidding* (1954), pp. 65 f. Robert Mapletoft (1609–77) was the brother of Josiah Mapletoft, Susannah's husband. He preached Nicholas Ferrar's funeral sermon, and frequently visited Little Gidding.

Composition or Covenanting". In a memo connected with his son's marriage, which took place in 1657, he refers to the worship at Little Gidding as still including "on Sundays, divine service fully and Communion each first Sunday month, and go daily all the week".[28]

In the summer of 1654, John Evelyn thought things sufficiently settled to take a journey across England to visit old friends, among them the affable Dr Wilkins, the Warden of Wadham, who entertained him to a magnificent feast in Oxford. (Later, to Evelyn's way of thinking, he carried his affability too far by marrying the Protector's sister.) The acceptance of things as they were by men such as Wilkins and Verney added to the Protector's sense of security: he could permit the news-sheets to record that "conventicles of common prayer are frequent and much desired in London". Even the cautious Dr Duppa wrote to Isham, who had hitherto addressed his letters to Mrs Duppa: "The times being now more open and our intercourse so innocent, you may safely change the style and direct what you write to the Bishop of Salisbury and possibly the empty title may bring it the sooner to me."[29]

John Evelyn was among those who returned from Europe, intending "to endeavour a settled life in England". His first bout of travel had lasted for four years, and ended in Paris with his marriage to the twelve year old daughter of Sir Richard Browne. He left her in the care of her parents during a two years' visit to England, but returned to France in the summer after the King's death and only came home for good in the early months of 1652. His young wife and her mother followed him and they made their home at Sayes Court, which the Brownes had leased from the Crown at Deptford and which the Commonwealth had confiscated and sold. Evelyn succeeded in buying out the present owners and it remained his headquarters during the succeeding years, with

[28] Ibid., pp. 87 f; *Ferrar Papers*, p. 302.

[29] *Duppa-Isham Correspondence*, p. 94.

periodic visits to his own family estates at Wotton which he would eventually inherit.[30]

His diary remains the surest guide to the life of the ordinary peaceable Anglican during the days of the usurpation. It is perhaps rather too urbane to give a true picture of the uncertain times, but it indicates clearly how the Anglican attitude hardened by degrees into opposition, and the more optimistic atmosphere of 1653–4 foundered on the intransigence of a few and the growing doubts of Cromwell's own supporters.

St Nicholas, Deptford, was now Evelyn's parish church and at the beginning of the period, whether he was at home or at Wotton, he used to go fairly regularly to his local church on Sundays, though in Surrey he found the "very plain sermons" of Parson Higham rather hard to bear. He was more fortunate at St Nicholas in Thomas Malory, who was not only "peaceable" but a man of learning. In the October after their return to England Lady Browne died, and Malory permitted her to be buried in the Browne tomb at St Nicholas according to Anglican rites. "We carried her in a hearse to Deptford", the diary records, "and interr'd her in the church near Sir Richard's relations ... accompanied with many coaches of friends and other persons of qualitie with all decent ceremonie, and according to the Church Office, which I obtained might be permitted after it had not been used in that church for seven yeares before, to the greate satisfaction of that innumerable multitude who were there."[31] It was a tribute to the moderation and courtesy of all concerned, and a reminder of the continued importance of personal relationships.

When Evelyn's son was born, however, no such co-operation could be practised, for Malory was a sound Puritan, at one with the law in forbidding at St Nicholas the use of the sign

[30] *The Diary of John Evelyn*, ed. E. S. de Beer (1955), II.535, 537 n. 6; III.59 n. 1.

[31] Ibid., III.76.

of the Cross, so integral a part of the Anglican baptismal service. Evelyn, like many others, had his children christened in private by a dispossessed priest, in his case Richard Owen, the previous incumbent of Eltham, to whom he referred as early as 1649 as a "sequestered and learned minister [who] preach'd in our parlor and gave us the Blessed Sacrament which was now wholy out of use in the Parish Churches. . . ." Three years later Owen baptized Evelyn's son "about four in the afternoone in the little drawing-roome next the Parlor in Says Court, many of my relations and neighbours present".[32] So usual did these private christening parties become, such bright spots in the sequence of dull, uncertain days, that when things were normal again after 1660 the clergy found it hard to persuade the mothers to bring their babies to church for the ceremony.

On one occasion in 1654, a few days after Mr Owen had celebrated the Communion privately in the library at Deptford, Evelyn went to church and heard Malory preach "preparatory to the sacrament", which "was a very rare thing in these daies". It was not till three weeks later, on 23 April, that the Holy Communion was administered at St Nicholas, an indication of the solemnity with which it was regarded in the time allowed for due preparation. Evelyn attended the service and recorded that "considering the vastness of the Parish" there were very few communicants.[33]

There are no further entries in the diary of communions at Deptford until 1659, though this is not proof that none occurred for, after 1654, Evelyn like many other devout Anglicans made it a habit to come up to London where, as he

[32] Ibid., II.552; III.75. Cf. the Diary of R. Fog, of Danes Court, Tilmanston [*Archaeologia Cantiana*, (1862–3), V.112f], which records the baptism of three infants in the course of eight years: the first in 1645 "after the new fashion of the Directory"; the second in 1647 "christened by Mr Thomas Russel, a great Cavalier with the Book of Common Prayer and signed with the Cross in the chamber over the kitchen"; and a third in 1654 in "the old way cum signo Crucis", by the schoolmaster.

[33] Evelyn, *Diary*, III.94 f.

records, "privately some of the orthodox sequestered Divines did use the Common Prayer and administer the sacraments". Only once, at Whitsuntide 1655, was he not able to find the service he required, and at a rough computation he received communion, either in his private house or in the City, on an average of once in three months in addition to the great Christian festivals. One of the things the ordinary churchgoer resented most during the Interregnum was the ban that was placed on the celebration of Christmas, both on account of the excesses in eating and drinking to which it often led, and for fear of idolatry, which the Puritans associated with the cult of the Virgin Mary. Many churchmen on the other hand had been given a new appreciation by patristic scholars of the doctrine of the Incarnation, and thus theological as well as moral questions were involved. At Christmas therefore, as on other special occasions, Evelyn made his way to London, although he still continued to attend St Nicholas periodically, justifying himself by the fact that Malory was duly ordained and preached "sound doctrine"[34] albeit he was "Presbyterianly affected".

When he first went up to London, Evelyn usually attended the church of St Gregory's under St Paul's, where George Wild and later John Hewit ministered with the open connivance of the Protector. They were men in their early forties, who were beginning their ministry when Laud was the dominant influence in the Church, and added to a deep sense of pastoral duty an unwavering adherence to High Church doctrine in religion and politics. Hewit's pleasant voice and excellent diction gave to his reading of the Liturgy a poignant sweetness, though one description suggests the danger of excess, "doctor mellifluus, doctor altivolans, et doctor inexhaustibilis".[35] There are references, elsewhere, to Anglican services in Garlick Hill and a church in Westminster, where

[34] Ibid., III.185 (30 Nov. 1656).

[35] Article on John Hewit in *D.N.B.*, quoting a note in the Ashmole MS. at the Bodleian.

Timothy Thurcross preached, while at Anthony Farindon's church, St Mary Magdalene, Milk Street, it was said that one could find a choir and a priest in full canonicals. But by degrees the meeting-place which overshadowed the rest was the chapel at Exeter House, the home of the Earl and Countess of Rutland. The Earl, Bishop Morton's friend, was himself a moderate Parliamentarian, with no liking for the illegalities that had paved the way for Cromwell's assumption of power. His wife was a Montagu, the daughter of a Royalist peer, a "prayer-book puritan" as they used to call him. With her at Exeter House was her sister, Lady Hatton, an able and devout woman whose unsatisfactory husband was in exile and who had taken in Peter Gunning as tutor for her son after Shirley's death. Gunning ministered regularly at Exeter Chapel in the later years and the attraction of his lucid brain and passionate churchmanship, combined with the *cachet* of his aristocratic patrons, drew so many to the great house in the Strand that it came to be known as the "Grand Assembly".[36]

By the time Gunning was established as the leading Anglican divine in London the tension had increased again and those who came to hear him needed the example of his integrity and conviction. In the spring of 1655 there was an abortive Royalist rising in Dorset and the West and rumours of more serious plots, all sooner or later uncloaked by Thurloe and his agents. Suspects of every sort were rounded up, and for some weeks both Verney and Isham were confined in St James's Palace, with other country gentlemen whose sense of decency was outraged by this brusque treatment. They were released after signing various guarantees of good behaviour, which Verney found it very hard to stomach. He returned to Claydon to find his estate threatened by a decimation tax of ten per cent to be imposed upon all delinquents; to find himself classed as a delinquent hurt almost as much as the fine, and his old steward was particularly angry and wrote an indignant, breathless letter protesting at such harshness after

[36] *Athehae Oxonienses*, IV.141; Bosher, op. cit., p. 12.

all that Claydon had suffered from the Royalists in the war.[37]

The magistrates treated Verney with courtesy and as much consideration as they dared, for, as the Protector alienated the sympathies of the local gentry, he found himself faced with a new difficulty in the reluctance of the magistrates to discriminate against a neighbour. It was in order to circumvent this policy of stonewalling, as well as to impose order on the more unruly elements in the countryside, that he appointed Major-Generals, officers empowered to act in an executive capacity and each given a group of counties to control. To these counties they came as outsiders and were inevitably very much resented, the more so as the decimation tax had been levied to pay for their upkeep. They were not all petty tyrants. Major-General Berry, for example, in Wales and the West Midlands was a man of good humour and honesty who coped without viciousness or brutality with dissidents of all sorts, whether Papists or Quakers, Levellers or malignants, vagrants or offenders against the Puritan moral code.[38] Others were only too ready to exercise their powers of interference to the full, and there were few who had a good word for them. So signally had Cromwell failed to "heal and settle". The feeling steadily grew that if indeed there were to be rule by a single person it were better to be by a King, bound by the laws of the constitution and the tradition of the centuries.

As Thurloe revealed to his chief the irrefutable evidence of Royalist conspiracies, and as the "Grand Assembly" and St Gregory's gave visual proof of the determination of Anglicans to keep aloof, Cromwell's hopes of harmony were replaced by anger at Anglican recalcitrance. In October 1655, a declaration was issued forbidding the employment of sequestered

[37] For Verney's difficulties in 1655 see Chapter 36 of *Memoirs of the Verney Family* (edn of 1925), II.26–45.

[38] Cf. Sir James Berry and S. G. Lee, *A Cromwellian Major-General* (1938), illustrated by extracts from Berry's correspondence.

clergy as chaplains or schoolmasters and prohibiting the use of the Prayer Book services under pain of exile or imprisonment. The declaration came in force at the end of the year and the general feeling of anxiety is mirrored in Duppa's letter to Isham a fortnight before the ban came into effect. "We are yet suffered to offer up the public prayers and Sacrifice of the Church though it be under private roofs, nor do I hear of any for the present either disturb'd or troubled for doing it. When the persecution goes higher we must be content to go lower and to serve our God as the ancient Christians did in dens and caves and deserts."[39] On 30 December Evelyn went up to St Gregory's to hear "the funeral service of preaching", and described it as "the mournfullest day that in my life I had seen or the Church of England herself. . . ."[40]

Yet nothing drastic occurred immediately. A month later, Duppa reported: "I am in the same condition as a low shrub is in a tempest, for the winds blow over me but shake me not. For as yet I am undisturb'd but not secure, for I see as low shrubs as myself rooted up, which is worse than shaking." Anthony Farindon of Milk Street was turned out at last and, "being barred from the pulpit", was "fain to betake himself to the press" that he might "get bread for himself and his children".[41] Dr Wild of St Gregory's continued resolutely to administer the sacrament in a private house in Fleet Street. Evelyn attended a service in August and commented bitterly, "The first time the Church of England was reduced to a chamber and conventicle"; yet he was forced to add that it was a "great meeting of zealous Christians who were generally much more devout and religious than in our greatest prosperity". Indeed at Christmas the crowd was so considerable that Evelyn, arriving late, could not get near enough to hear the sermon, which must have disappointed him, for only

[39] *Duppa-Isham Correspondence*, p. 113.

[40] *Diary of John Evelyn*, III.164. "God make me thankful", Evelyn added, "who hath hitherto provided for us the food of our souls as well as our bodies."

[41] *Duppa-Isham Correspondence*, p. 155.

a month earlier he had noted the dearth of practical counsel from the pulpits of the parish churches.[42]

During 1656 Cromwell's difficulties had been increased by his war with Spain, in which he saw himself as the champion of Protestant Christendom. In the minds of Thurloe and the Protector there was the ever-present fear of an invasion from the Spanish Netherlands, where so many of the exiles had found a home. During the spring the Royalists were planning an unlikely alliance with the Levellers in support of some such project, and one of the main reasons for the Major-Generals was to maintain order in case of disturbances at home, if any invasion occurred. When the Protector's second Parliament met in September, however, no arguments of necessity could persuade it to legalize either the Major-Generals or the decimation tax. Soon after Christmas the discovery of a plot concerted by both Levellers and Royalists to assassinate Cromwell, followed next month by a new invasion scare, hammered home the necessity of securing the succession and of regulating the Protector's powers. Those who disliked the arbitrary nature of his rule presented Cromwell with a *Humble Petition and Advice* which offered him the Crown, declaring that if he would be pleased to take upon him the Government according to the ancient constitution, "their liberties and peace . . . would be founded upon an old and sure foundation". Cromwell shared the general desire for security, but he refused the title of king because of the implacable hostility of Lambert and other of his old comrades in arms. He accepted the substance of the Petition, however, and in June 1657 was installed a second time Protector, with the right to name his successor and an Upper House of nominated members. Except for Lambert, who refused the new oaths of allegiance, the Army accepted the situation. For a few months there was a lessening of the tension but there was no fundamental change, although

[42] *Diary of John Evelyn,* III.184 (2 Nov. 1656). "Now nothing practical preached, or that pressed reformation of life, but high speculative points and straines."

the position of the Anglicans seemed to have eased during the summer. Gunning was preaching regularly at Exeter Chapel, assisted by Jeremy Taylor, whose presence in London brought refreshment to many, not least to Evelyn himself. Dr Hewit was reinstated at St Gregory's, and the fact that the services were sometimes attended by the ladies from Whitehall may indicate the reason for the Protector's continued forbearance. When Mary Cromwell married Lord Fauconberg in November, Dr Hewit officiated at Hampton Court at a religious service, following the civil ceremony. Rumour even had it that he used the Prayer Book forms.

Yet the political danger was still there and Thurloe knew that designs were on foot, considerably more serious than those of 1655. It was essential for the Protector to show that he had still a complete control of the situation. Hence the alarming experience which befell Evelyn when he came up to Exeter Chapel on Christmas Day.

Gunning was preaching and the congregation was particularly large, as no service was being held at St Gregory's. "Sermon ended", as the Communion was being administered, a troop of soldiers surrounded and entered the chapel. Gunning did not falter but continued the service, and the soldiers, it would seem, were a little at a loss. "These wretched miscreants", wrote Evelyn, "held their muskets against us as we came up to receive the Sacred Elements as if they would have shot us at the Altar, but yet suffering us to finish the office of Communion, as perhaps not in their Instructions what they should do in case they found us in that Action." When the service was concluded, some of those present were hustled away to prison. Evelyn himself was confined to Exeter House, and cheered up a little when the Earl of Rutland asked him to dine with the family. In the afternoon he was interrogated by the Major-Generals Whalley and Goffe. He was reminded that it was illegal to observe Christmas, told that the Prayer Book was only the Mass in English and asked why he had prayed for Charles Stuart. He replied that he had prayed for "all Christian

Kings, Princes and governors". "They replied in so doing we praied for the K. of Spaine, too, who was their Enemie and a Papist. . . ." At length, with much pity for his ignorance, he was dismissed. The raids on Exeter Chapel and other Anglican centres were reported fully in the *Mercurius Politicus* and, as the type of questions indicated, their purpose was political; a piece of propaganda to remind loyalists and dissidents alike that malignants were only left at large so long as the Protector willed.[43] In the following March Evelyn records that he received communion in a private house where Jeremy Taylor preached, and on the same day in the afternoon he heard Dr Gunning preach at Exeter House, so that the Christmas raid does not seem radically to have changed the situation.

Tragedy erupted, with the uncloaking of the plots which had been simmering all the winter. An invasion from Flanders had been planned for February; ships and men were being collected and Charles had been ready to embark. But the dilatory preparations of the Spaniards had been matched in England by friction and mistrust between the elder, somewhat disillusioned members of the Sealed Knot and the younger Royalists, among whom Dr Hewit and the Earl of Peterborough's son, Lord Mordaunt, took the lead. Hewit was issuing commissions to young gentlemen in Sussex to rise at a given signal and was also involved in a plot centred upon the City. Ormonde, coming over secretly and for once hoodwinking Thurloe, decided it was all too risky and in spite of rumours to the contrary did not even see Hewit. Soon afterwards the invasion was postponed as impracticable. But meanwhile Thurloe struck. Mordaunt and Hewit were arrested and a special court set up to try them. Mordaunt, against whom the evidence was incomplete, was acquitted by a single vote; Hewit lost the sympathy of the court by a speech which an onlooker described as "starched on purpose for the lady spectators, towards whom he often turned on each side". He refused to plead and was condemned to death, "without law,

[43] Ibid., III.203 f, 204 n. 6.

jury or justice", Evelyn commented, though it is hard to see where the injustice came in. Hewit had played for high stakes and lost; but in his own eyes and those of his friends he was a martyr. "That excellent preacher and holy man Dr Hewit was martyred", is Evelyn's entry on 8 June, the day of the execution. Hewit spoke of himself on the scaffold as a martyr to the people, while his friends, with a courage that verged on effrontery, made his execution an occasion for an open act of worship of the Anglican kind. Hewit in his lengthy prayers brought in innumerable phrases from the Book of Common Prayer. Dr Wild, who attended him, added his own petitions in liturgical form, and as the *Mercurius Politicus* was careful to report next day, his friends added Amen "after the old Cathedral manner".[44]

For John Evelyn the year was steeped in sadness, for at the end of January his son Richard had died, and another infant son only a few weeks later. "Here ends the joy of my life", records the diary. Jeremy Taylor wrote to condole with him on the loss of "that pretty person, your strangely hopeful boy", and followed up his letter with a visit. He had become Evelyn's spiritual director in recent years and for a year or two, before going to Ireland as Lord Conway's chaplain, he was living in the capital, preaching frequently at Exeter Chapel and working hard at a gargantuan ethical guide-book, *Ductor Dubitantium*, of which he read passages to Evelyn. He hoped it would be his greatest work, but by the time it was published after 1660 the mood of the nation had changed, and it was no longer fashionable to be concerned about one's conscience.

It was amazing how many good books were being written and published during these years of adversity. The Isham-Duppa correspondence is full of them, and though occasion-

[44] Cf. Heath, *Loyal English Martyrs*, p. 429, for Hewit's speech on the scaffold and *Thurloe State Papers*, ed. Birch (1742), VII.65–9 for the information given against him. Cf. also Mary Coate, *Cornwall in the Great Civil War and Interregnum* (1933), p. 298.

ally the bishop felt that at his age he should not indulge in each new book that came his way, he had the honesty to add: "I confess I have not yet so far conquered myself (where either the arguement or the style is pleasing) that I can refrain from reading it." "It is a writing age", he commented, on another occasion, "and the swordsmen having assumed the liberty of acting what they please, the pen-men are as venturesome." All the publications were not polemical but quite a number of them were, and it is a fine tribute to Cromwell's censorship that so much Anglican literature was allowed to go through the press. London was full of former University dons who had to write to save their souls and their reason, and often to earn their bread and butter. Half or more of the works upon which the reputation of the Caroline divines depended were written or planned during the Interregnum. John Pearson's *Exposition of the Creed* was based on lectures he delivered regularly at St Clement's, Eastcheap; Anthony Sparrow's *Rationale upon the Book of Common Prayer* was written by him when his insistence on reading the Liturgy drove him out of his country living after a bare five weeks.[45]

It was largely with a view to helping the out-of-work scholars that Brian Walton, the previous incumbent of St Martin's Orgar, Cannon Street, launched his project for a Polyglot Bible. Herbert Thorndike, an ex-fellow of Trinity College, Cambridge, was one of his main coadjutors and every available scholar not otherwise engaged was brought in to help. In six huge tomes of beautiful craftsmanship, with lengthy prefaces that dealt in turn with chronology, weights and measures, and the science of languages, the Scriptures were set forth in parallel columns in various eastern tongues, and the Hebrew and Greek originals collated with passages in Syriac and Ethiopic, Persian and Chaldean. Walton sent out a circular letter appealing for funds in 1652 and raised the

[45] For excerpts from the writings of the Caroline divines, see More and Cross, *Anglicanism*, and the commentary prefacing them, "Anglicanism in the seventeenth century", by Felix R. Arnott (pp. lvi–lxiv).

surprising amount of £8000. The Elector Palatine headed the list of patrons; the bishops gave the project their blessing; Cromwell allowed them the paper, duty-free—and very fine paper it was—and the scholars got down to their task. The bible was published in 1657. "The work . . . has not yet been superseded" is the comment of the *Oxford Dictionary of the Christian Church*, exactly three hundred years later.

Bramhall, in exile, and Hammond, at Westwood, were the chief protagonists of the more controversial type of writing. They belonged to the older generation, whose whole life had been changed and moulded by the wars. Hammond's first important book, his *Practical Catechism*, was based on the instruction he had given at Penshurst, and he had permitted it to be published anonymously at Oxford to help the bewildered and often ignorant mixture of courtiers, soldiers, and hangers-on that thronged the streets of the university city when it was also the headquarters of the King. Similarly he gave guidance to the household at Westwood and all who came that way.[46] His essay in biblical criticism, *A Paraphrase of the New Testament*, was one of the most valuable of his later works, published in 1653, but he decried those who escaped from the times by embarking upon lengthy academic treatises; "the present importunity of affairs" necessitated writing that was strictly relevant. In the latter years of the Interregnum the Pakingtons' Worcester home became to a growing degree the centre of what, for want of a better term, one may call the neo-Laudian school, and after Hammond's death his friend John Fell, who had frequently visited him, wrote a life of his beloved master and described the sequence of the Westwood days. Beneath the gloss of hagiography, one catches a glimpse

[46] *The Whole Duty of Man*, the popular devotional treatise published anonymously, had a foreword by Hammond and probably owed much to Westwood. It was divided into seventeen chapters to be read over three times a year, on consecutive Sundays, and dealt with man's duty to God in worship, to himself (including temperance and contentedness), and to his neighbour. See J. H. Overton, *Life in the English Church, 1660–1714* (1885), pp. 261 et seq.

of Hammond at work, his writing and proof-correcting and research, interspersed with "his reception of visits, whether of civility or for resolution of conscience . . . his agency for men of quality, providing them schoolmasters for their children and chaplains in their houses, . . . his general correspondencies by letter, whereof some cost him ten, others twenty, forty nay sixty sheets of paper and ever took up two days of the week entirely to themselves."[47] Hammond wrote as he lived, clearly and without hesitation, beginning a tract at 11 p.m. and finishing it before he went to bed, writing a defence of episcopacy all through the night and sending it off to the printers first thing in the morning, a thing it was only possible to do because he was drawing on a fund of knowledge and conviction, garnered from a lifetime of study and from hours spent upon his knees in prayer. The flavour of his personality still lingers in one of his letters to Sheldon, outlining his plan for helping less fortunate scholars. "Let me mention to you an hasty undigested fancy of mine suggested to me by reading the conclusion of Bishop Bramhall's excellent book on Schism. It is this. What if you and Dr Henchman and I should endeavour to raise £600 per an: (each of us gaining subscriptions for 200 l.) for seven years to maintain a society of twenty exiled schollars. When we discern the thing feasible, communicate it to Bishop Bramhall and require of him a catalogue of twenty such whose wants and desires of such a recess in some convenient place . . . might make it a fit charity to recommend to pious persons. . . . Tell me . . . what else you can think of to perfect and forme this sudden rude conceit, which when I have also communicated to Dr Henchman I shall be content to be laughed at by either of you." After some initial hesitation on the part of his friends, the scheme would appear to have gone ahead.[48]

To Hammond, his polemical writing was part of his duty as a loyal churchman. Yet the times were slowly changing and

[47] Fell, "Life of Hammond" (Hammond's *Works*, I.lxii f).

[48] Harl. MS. 6942, Nos. 18, 21, 24, 35.

the Puritan challenge, which still exercised those who had been in their prime before the wars, was already giving ground to the new challenge of rationalist and materialistic thought. Three years before the publication of Bramhall's *Just Vindication of the Church of England* against the charge of schism, Hobbes's *Leviathan* appeared, which Duppa read with some concern as a strange mixture of some things well said and others "wildly and unchristianly". Bramhall replied to the book with *Vindication of True Liberty*, in which he inveighed against Hobbes's neglect of all spiritual values. After the *Leviathan* was published, Hobbes found himself unpopular with his fellow exiles and returned to make his peace in England. He was an intellectual giant, but always odd man out among the philosophers, and as timid in person as he was courageous in thought. As a young man he had walked and talked with Bacon, travelled much abroad, and suffered one day a sudden mental awakening upon sight of a page of Euclid and the unerrant certainty of Q.E.D. His terms of reference were entirely different from the theologians' and he knew nothing of the mystique of "divine right". But he strove to apply to his evaluation of the thoughts and emotions of men the new methods of deduction and experiment, and what he observed in ordinary men was a deep desire for peace and security, which they themselves frustrated by the fear and self-interest that in the main motivated their actions. So he evolved his belief that the natural state was "nasty, brutish, and short", and that man had entrusted to the Sovereign the absolute power which alone could ensure the peace of ordered days. The Church was placed fairly and squarely subordinate to the secular ruler, for Hobbes's logical mind could not approve a clash in authority; and thus he was led to a glorification of the State which was contrary to the whole spirit of Christianity.[49]

49 Basil Willey, *Seventeenth Century Background* (1934), p. 116. Hobbes was treated kindly by Charles II in spite of his submission to Cromwell and lived on to the age of ninety (Aubrey, *Brief Lives*, ed. O. L. Dick [1949], pp. 147–59).

Another odd man out was Harrington, whose *Oceana* appeared five years after the *Leviathan* and also caused Duppa some uneasiness in addition to a measure of boredom. Harrington's ideal commonwealth, which grew out of his admiration of the Venetian oligarchy, was based on the sound idea that power should not remain in the hands of one section of the community but should be exercised in rotation, and suitable citizens be chosen by ballot to act in turn as magistrates and lawgivers. The book was seized on the way through the press but later Cromwell relented, it was said through Elizabeth Claypole's intervention; Royalists liked it little better than he. It was the balloting box that was the novelty, and Aubrey gives a vivid description of the Rota Club which Harrington initiated in 1659, in which the business to be discussed was decided by ballot.[50]

Harrington was a little unbalanced. He had been appointed by Parliament to wait on Charles I during part of his captivity, and he had learnt to love him and never quite recovered from the shock of his execution. There were many like him, slightly disorientated and their brains teeming with new ideas —scholars, scientists, antiquarians. Seldom can so varied a selection of books have appeared, for the decade that began in 1648 with Drake's brave publication of Lancelot Andrewes' *Private Prayers*, and ended with that equally Anglican but very different devotional work *The Whole Duty of Man*, also saw the publication of England's first book of singing games and the performance of her earliest opera. And in these years which produced Bramhall's *Just Vindication* and Hobbes's *Leviathan*, there were two editions of Izaak Walton's *Compleat Angler*, which must have come as a relief to many weary of theological wrangling. Walton, working in his ironmonger's shop and worshipping regularly at St Dunstan's in Fleet Street, writing with love and reverence his lives of the Anglican saints, belonged to an age that would soon be past. One day as he browsed over the second-hand bookstalls he met a fellow biographer

[50] Aubrey, op. cit., pp. 125.

of a very different mould. This was John Aubrey, who had once been a law student and still kept the legal terms, so that he should be in touch with all that happened in the capital. He was at the moment engaged on a *Perambulation of Wiltshire* and thrilled by his discovery of Avebury. He was conscious of a world intellectually alight and himself declared that 1649 had been the turning-point. A number of his friends were on the edge of various Royalist plots, but Aubrey was more interested in men and ideas than in practical politics.[51]

The ambivalence of the age is well illustrated by Sir Thomas Browne's *Religio Medici*, that other classic of the period, published without the author's consent in 1642 but reissued next year with his permission. Thereafter, through all the changing fortunes of his country, Browne continued to practise as a doctor in Norwich, writing with exuberance, investigating and yet giving credence to various forms of witchcraft, devoted to his Church, at one and the same time a modernist and a traditionalist, an attitude of facing-both-ways characteristic of the time.[52] The most eminent of the churchmen interested in science was of course the Protector's brother-in-law, the Warden of Wadham. About him at Oxford and at Gresham College in the City there congregated a group of scientists who were to be the founder-members of the Royal Society. Among them was John Wallis, the mathematician who had held a London living and been secretary to the Westminster Assembly. In 1655 he published his *Arithmetica Infinitorum* and for more than fifty years (from 1649–1703) he was the Savilian Professor of Geometry at Oxford. Equally outstanding in a different way was the lovable though slightly eccentric Anglican layman, Robert Boyle, the Earl of Cork's son, who had been converted to science by the experience of a thunderstorm in the Alps as Hobbes had been converted by a page of Euclid. He established himself with his sister at Oxford when the wars were over, built himself a laboratory, and set to work on

51 Anthony Powell, *John Aubrey and his Friends* (1948), pp. 11, 63, 91.
52 Willey, op. cit., p. 42.

various experiments in regard to pressure and the expansion of air, eventually enunciating the law so well known to schoolboys of successive generations. In between he studied divinity and the biblical languages, but, feeling no sense of vocation, refused to be ordained, although Aubrey felt that there was something pontifical about him ("I had almost sayd Lay Bishop").[53]

While so much exciting experiment was going on at Oxford, at Cambridge another group of thinkers was equating learning and religion in a rather different sphere. The influence of the Cambridge Platonists had made itself felt as early as 1637 when Benjamin Whichcote, a fellow of Emmanuel, was appointed afternoon preacher at Trinity Church and proclaimed from the pulpit the philosophy he summed up in his famous aphorisms: "The spirit in man is the candle of the Lord"; "There is nothing proper and peculiar to man but the use of reason and the exercise of virtue". Whichcote resigned his fellowship on his marriage in 1643, but returned to Cambridge next year as Provost of King's, accepting the post with hesitation as he replaced an ejected divine and refusing to subscribe the Covenant. He was a born teacher, inspiring and guiding a host of eager students and closely associated with three younger men—Ralph Cudworth, the professor of Hebrew and Master in turn of Clare Hall and of Christ's, Henry More, a fellow of Christ's, and John Smith of Emmanuel who died at the age of 34 in 1652. Their approach and emphasis varied according to their differing natures and aptitude, but they shared a devotion to the Platonic ideal and held to the same essentials, which gave the group its distinctive character—a belief in the divine nature of reason and the inseparable union of truth and goodness. Only by purity and self-discipline could one come to know God: it was this that More in particular stressed, himself a mystic rather than a scholar, while Cudworth, a man of ponderous learning, challenged Hobbes's exaltation of absolute power which left no

[53] Aubrey, op. cit., p. 36.

room for the individual man to choose between right and wrong. Smith urged that the only sure basis for believing in God was the recognition of the divine in man, and he himself was a living example of reason, vitalized by love. He was a fine spirit, brilliant of brain and warm of heart, stirred to passion by injustice and cruelty but in all else, not least in his own illness, patient and serene. To-day one would speak of an integrated personality; then they quoted a phrase of Seneca's and said that his life was "all of one colour, everywhere like itself". He did not need to be hammered into shape on the anvil of experience and he died young.[54]

Cambridge Platonism was more vivid in its living, and in Whichcote's preaching at Trinity Church, than in its expression in literary form, which was often overweighted by abstruse classical learning. Though the Platonists accepted the Cromwellian régime and Cudworth was a personal friend of John Thurloe, whom he sometimes advised on academic appointments, their whole line of thought ran counter to religious and political discrimination. At the height of the Presbyterian domination, Cudworth preached before the House of Commons a sermon full of the spirit of reconciliation. This was not merely because they were peaceable men but because they were active protagonists for harmony in a distracted world, and it was as much a matter of principle for them to accept the *status quo* as it was for the High Churchmen to refuse to co-operate with an usurper.

There were some who had little freedom of choice one way or another, and when the picture is drawn of the exiles and the scholars, the uneasy gentry and the parish priests, there still remain the ordinary folk, the shopkeepers and the tillers of the soil and all who went to church, Sunday by Sunday, throughout the eleven years of the Interregnum. Such parochial records as survive throw less light than one could wish

[54] Willey, op. cit., pp. 133 et seq. The second volume of Tulloch's *Rational Theology* deals entirely with the Platonists.

upon the bewildering scene. Perhaps it is the lack of them that is significant, and the increasing disorder of those that remain. Even in cases where a modicum of order had hitherto been kept, after 1653 the records usually dwindle to little more than a list of parochial officers. The recurrence in those lists, however, of the same family names that have persisted through the centuries argues a measure of continuing tradition, and the annual appointment of churchwardens and overseers and of surveyors of the highway remained an essential part of the life of the countryside.

The extent to which the material fabric of the churches were maintained varied enormously, and the new dispensation by no means necessarily entailed neglect. Indeed, a number of new churches were built. Yet much that was beautiful had gone for ever, to the satisfaction of many parishioners and the distress of others; stained glass in abundance had been deliberately destroyed and the great stone altar-screens at St Albans and St Saviour's, Southwark, stood bare of the saints and angels that had adorned them. "Paid John Payne for taking down ye Crosse 1*s.* 6*d.*" runs an entry in the accounts of Holy Trinity, Clapham. In the war years fences had fallen down; the gates of church properties sagged on broken hinges; and in the accounts of the Kentish churches payments are frequently recorded of 1*s.* for foxes' heads, rather less for "grays" (badgers) and a few pence for the inoffensive hedgehog. At Cranbrook, however, well looked after under a succession of Puritan vicars, they got down to work as early as 1645 to tiling and mending the gates and putting in new palings, and the accounts presented in April 1649 record the insertion of 778 panes of new glass "put in here and there about the church which could not be measured" and supplemented next year by 264 additional panes. At Headcorn, in 1649–50, a rate was levied and a large portion of it spent on repairs of every kind. Charing, never able to forget its position astride the Dover road, recorded many payments to travellers, Irishmen, and poor seamen, but its accounts continue through

the Interregnum and the very mixed lists of outgoings include the regular payment of gaol-money to the magistrates, the purchase of spades and mattocks, repairs to the church gate and the pulpit door and the wages of clerk and sexton. In all the parishes, whatever else was done or not done, the bells and the clock were kept in good order, as essential items in regulating the daily round.

In some parishes, where there had been no violent disruption of personnel, there began to be signs of a new prosperity. In June 1650, Holy Trinity, Clapham, made an assessment of £50 at a general meeting of parishioners to enlarge their church "for the benefit of the said church and poor of this parish", improvements extended next year by the building of a belfry and watch-tower near the schoolhouse. Clapham was on the verge of becoming a fashionable suburb. (Forty years later Samuel Pepys chose it as an accessible yet secluded spot for his retirement.) Among the congregation in 1650 was Walter Frost, the secretary to the Council, and upon Frost's death the vestry gave his son leave to erect a chapel over his father's grave in the church. A sign that things were going well was the large sum of £86 sent to Mr Floyd, at the Mermaid in Cheapside, for propagating the Gospel among the Indians of New England, a duty of which the Churches at home had newly become aware through the settlers from Massachusetts who returned to England to fight for the Puritan cause.[55]

Another parish whose surviving records betoken calm was that of St Mary, Newington. The poor and needy were as great a problem as ever, though some help was given from the excise on sea-coal. At least in the spiritual sphere the parish enjoyed a prosperous interlude, for in 1653 "at a full meeting of the parishioners . . . it was agreed with a general consent that Mr Thomas Wadsworth be desired to accept the care of their soules and to be their minister". Wadsworth was

[55] Holy Trinity, Clapham, Vestry Minute Books, 1637–76 (two books bound in one), I.49–57. (County Record Office, Westminster, P.95/Tri.1/1).

one of the finest of the Independent clergy, whose ministrations could not fail to bring balm and healing to the busy highway and narrow alleys of Newington. The records show signs of leadership in practical matters also: fines were imposed for non-attendance at vestry meetings, and some minor abuses were checked. Two letters survive that Wadsworth wrote to Richard Baxter in which he records his success in "gathering a people by public profession". "Some 140 come freely", he wrote, ". . . several of them having been most gross drunkards . . . the whole town is pretty quiet, standing in amaze."[56]

Cromwell's protectorate had an immediate effect on the daily life of the Church in two directions, in the increase of State control and the method of choosing personnel; and the encroachment of the State upon matters hitherto the Church's sole concern was shown in nothing so much as in Cromwell's regulation of marriages. His ordinance of 1654 forbade marriages in church, authorizing a civil ceremony and laying down that after the banns had been published either in the church or the market-place the couple were to appear before the mayor or local justices, who thereupon pronounced them man and wife. Few couples were satisfied with this unromantic procedure or were content to go without God's blessing on their union, and after the first year or two, in an increasing number of cases, the legal ceremony before the local authority was

[56] St Mary, Newington, Vestry Minute Book, 1608–1739, f. 27d; Though many records lapse or show signs of neglect after 1653, there are a number of exceptions, one example being the account books of St Mary, Newington, as one would expect during Wadsworth's ministry. The Newington records are full of interest and deserve further study. For Wadsworth see the *D.N.B.* article; the letters to Baxter are quoted by J. Waddington in *Surrey Congregational History* (1866), pp. 41 ff. All Saints', Wandsworth, is another parish whose accounts remain in good order throughout the period. At Stepney, after a good deal of quarrelling, they formed themselves into a select vestry in 1655, to avoid tumults and supply the want of meetings "for the settling and carrying on of the weighty matters of the parish" (*Memorials of Stepney Parish*, ed. W. H. Frere and G. W. Hill [1890/1], pp. 202 f.)

supplemented by a religious service, either in church or surreptitiously in the parlour. Thus Richard Drake, the sequestered parson of Radwinter, was married before the Lord Mayor at Guildhall but afterwards "Matthew Smallwood, Presbyter more firmly and happily joined" him and his wife in the church of St Martin Outwich.[57] Eventually, under pressure from his own family, the Protector altered the law so as to make such services permissible. But during the years that the ban persisted it perhaps did more than any other single measure to make ordinary folk regret the Church of former days.

In order to record adequately births, marriages, and deaths a registrar was to be appointed in every parish. Occasionally, owing to the dearth of suitable laymen, the incumbent exercised the office. The vicar of Great Easton in Essex was thus appointed civil registrar in 1653. He duly entered a note of the appointment in his parochial records, but thought fit some time after 1660 to insert the word "wicked" before "Parliament"! In a register of a small Shropshire church the pages are blank between 1644 and 1650, and a note added: "Registering neglected, a happy time" as if even war-time conditions were preferable to the close surveillance of the Cromwellian régime.[58]

In regard to patronage and the appointment of the clergy the changes were less abrupt than they might have been. As part of a larger scheme of reform, Cromwell set up a board of Triers entitled "Commissioners for the approbation of public preachers". Local committees were established to deal with undesirables already in possession of a pulpit, but the board of Triers was a central body of forty-three members, twelve of whom were laymen, and who numbered among them men both of Presbyterian and Independent

[57] Harold Smith, *The Ecclesiastical History of Essex* (1933), p. 342; cf. Hardacre, *The Royalists during the Revolution*, pp. 110–11.

[58] E. J. Erith, *Essex Parish Records, 1240–1894* (1950), p. 106; *Shropshire Archaeological Transactions* (1895), p. 144. For the registrars cf. H. Smith, op. cit., pp. 339–45.

views. They did not ordain, nor present to vacant livings, but every new appointment had to be approved by them. The system did not always work smoothly; and there is a vivid picture in the Verney papers of its complications from the point of view of an applicant.[59] Sir Ralph wished to present Edward Butterfield, the parson of a neighbouring parish, to the vacant living of Claydon, and Butterfield went up to London to go before the board. But he was dissatisfied with the only testimonial he had obtained, as possibly out of date, and continued to pull strings, calling first on one person, then on another, and asking Verney to obtain a recommendation from someone in Preston and send it up post-haste. Yet in spite of the creaking of the machinery and the dangers of bureaucratic control, it is hard to over-stress the importance of the fact that Cromwell did not disrupt the parochial system by the abolition of tithe or by taking over in its entirety the task of filling up vacant cures. He himself, or the Commissioners of the Great Seal, presented new incumbents in the case of livings which had been in the hands of sequestered persons. (These cures, with the tithes attached to them, could not be regained by composition, part of their revenues being used to improve the stipends of clergy in poorer parishes.) But moderate men who had escaped sequestration, or Parliamentarians long out of step with the times, retained the right to present to livings and often appointed men of moderate episcopal views who with good fortune might satisfy the Triers. Thus both George Bull and Edward Stillingfleet, two of the most famous of the Caroline churchmen, were presented to country livings in 1657.

Bull had been a pupil at Blundell's School in Tiverton and at the age of fourteen (in 1648) had gone on to Oxford where he signalized his "enjoyment of manly liberty" by easing up on his studies. But nobody who thought and had a conscience could take life easily for long in 1648–9. Faced with the injunction to take the Engagement, Bull refused and left the University. Those responsible for him suggested that he

[59] *Memoirs of the Verney Family* (edn of 1925), II.112 et seq.

should be put under the direction of an eminent divine, and after a careful consideration of the claims of Henry Hammond and a certain William Thomas of Somerset (who later became one of Cromwell's Triers) the latter was selected. Things worked out in a curious way. Young Bull learnt something from Mr Thomas, but a great deal more from his son, Samuel, who had become a devotee of the writings of Richard Hooker, Hammond, and other Anglican teachers. When he was 21, Bull slipped away to be ordained near Bicester by Skinner, and settled near Bristol in a small living worth £30 a year, deciding that he was unlikely to be disturbed in a cure of such small value. In his services he used the Prayer Book phrases which he knew by heart and convinced most of his congregation that they were excellent prayers, though few knew whence they came. Two years before the Restoration he exchanged his small living for Suddington St Mary, nearer to Cirencester, his wife's home, and his labours nearly came to a sudden end next year, when his house was a meeting-place for Royalists involved in the abortive plots of 1659. But he escaped Dr Hewit's fate and went on to complete his two great books in Latin, the *Apostolical Harmony*, published in 1670, and his famous *Defence of the Nicene Creed*, which came out in 1685. He lived until 1710, thus linking up the stormy age of the Interregnum with the more sober chapters of the Age of Reason.[60]

The men, therefore, who ministered in the parish churches during the Interregnum might be Presbyterians—of greater or less rigidity—Independents, Baptists, or moderate Anglicans. They might be presented to their livings by the ordinary methods of patronage, or invited by the congregation to accept the cure or have been intruded in the place of an ejected

[60] See Robert Nelson, *The Life of Dr George Bull* (1714). Pp. 3–52 cover the early years. On pp. 54 f Nelson describes Bull's use of the Prayer Book service at a wedding before 1660, "not concealing from [his parishioners] how much it was in their power to expose him to a malicious prosecution and shewing at the same time the confidence he placed in their kindness and affection". He was given "unanimous approbation".

minister. They must have varied enormously, not only in their tempers and ability but in the extent to which they regarded the whole parish as their care or thought of themselves as the chosen minister of the few. For a real difficulty arose when the Triers approved as the occupant of the parish pulpit a divine who was already the minister of a "gathered church", that is to say of a congregation whose conception of the Church was not the company of all baptized Christians but a gathering of the elect, "saints by calling", as they themselves termed it. In such cases the parish church became merely a place of assembly from which many of the parishioners felt themselves excluded. In some cases a meeting-house existed side by side with the parish church, secure in the toleration granted by the Instrument of Government. It is possible that such a conventicle existed in Clapham Old Town under the shadow of Holy Trinity.[61] Often two congregations shared the parish church, as they did harmoniously at St Stephen's, Coleman Street, and less amicably elsewhere. But when the Independent or Baptist was also the parish priest there was an obvious anomaly, for it was clearly illogical for such to adhere to a State Church of any sort. Their leaders showed that they were conscious of the problem in a declaration on Faith and Order issued from the Savoy at a conference, planned with Cromwell's approval but held shortly after his death. "They who are ingaged in the work of Publique Preaching", the statement ran, "and enjoy the Publique Maintenance upon that account are not thereby obliged to dispense the Seals [i.e. sacraments] to any other than such as (being Saints by Calling and gathered according to the Order of the Gospel) they stand related to, as Pastors or Teachers; yet ought they not to neglect others living within their Parochial Bounds, but besides their constant publique Preaching to them, they ought to enquire after their profiting by the Word, instructing them in, and pressing upon them (whether young or old) the great

[61] F. Reynolds Lovett, *A History of the Clapham Congregational Church* (1912), p. 22.

Doctrines of the Gospel, even personally and particularly, so far as their strength and time will admit."[62]

With the best will in the world, pastoral care, without joint participation in the sacrament, was not likely to satisfy, and sometimes there was a sorry dearth of goodwill. There was an unsavoury quarrel at St Bartholomew, Exchange, when Dr Grant died. St Bartholomew's was a crown living and Cromwell nominated the distinguished Independent Philip Nye, who made a certain John Loder his deputy. Loder and his congregation seem to have moved in a body to take possession of the parish church. The vestry thereupon complained that Loder "would not minister the sacrament or christen those not joined in communion with his church", and declared, not without some justification, that they had no reason to pay tithes when their church was taken up and their pews filled with strange congregations. "Mr Nye's congregation", a rougher type no doubt than the parish worthies, had done considerable damage to the pews and offered to repair them, but they were dealing with businessmen who refused the offer, lest the invaders "should claim thereby an interest in the church and pews".

The dispute was still unsettled when General Monck marched on London in the month before King Charles's happy return. That April the Commissioners of the Great Seal examined Loder and, though the position was not clear, they gave Nye permission to try a suit at law with anyone appointed. At that critical moment a letter arrived from General Monck which was handed round the table and which countermanded a previous letter of his recommending Loder as a fit man. If the parish representatives were still in the room, one can imagine the exchange of glances, for in the wardens' accounts there is an entry of "10*s.*, To Lord Generals secretary for a letter to reverse a letter Mr Loder had obtained from General Monke". Loder and Nye were dis-

[62] A. G. Matthews, *The Savoy Declaration of Faith and Order 1658* (1959), pp. 27 et seq., 123 f.

missed and a new nomination made, though even so it was necessary in July 1660 for the vestry to order that Loder should not preach any more, the clerk adding the note: "Voted that I with the assistance of some gentlemen of the Parish keep him out"[63]

These unhappy clashes between different brands of Christians distressed no one so much as Richard Baxter who was the outstanding advocate of a comprehensive Church. It was in an attempt to counteract the insularity of the sects that he had evolved his plan of an association of clergy, meeting parochially for mutual counsel and a measure of united action. The scheme had developed naturally out of the meetings which he had held in his own house as vicar of Kidderminster; in 1652 he endeavoured to extend it throughout the country, and all ministers of piety and "competent ability" were invited to join. At their monthly meetings there was to be a public lecture, differences of judgement were to be debated, and complaints as to discipline considered—a course that would not only strengthen fellowship but enable them to act wisely over debatable points such as exclusion from the sacraments, on which young and inexperienced ministers were asked not to take action without consulting their colleagues. The fact that similar associations grew up in Cumberland and in the southern counties showed that there was some response, but Baxter ruefully admitted that in spite of the broad terms of membership no convinced Presbyterian joined them in Worcestershire nor any Independent, "though two or three honest ones said nothing against us". Nor were there any of "the new Prelatical way (Dr Hammond's)" but "three or four moderate conformists that were for the old episcopacy, and all the rest were mere Catholics, men of no faction, nor siding with any party".[64] One regrets that when so many of the experiments of the Protectorate reappeared with a new look after the

[63] *Vestry Minute Book of . . . St Bartholomew Exchange*, Part 2, pp. 61, 70, 73 f, 77. Account Books, p. 168.

[64] Richard Baxter's *Autobiography* (Everyman edn), p. 84.

Restoration, Baxter's fine venture in Christian fellowship should prove so transitory. Yet the practical difficulties for men of decided allegiances were very real. The association at Grantham put the issue to the test by inviting Sanderson to join them. He was very anxious to do so, but Hammond heard of it and wrote with unaccustomed heat, pleading with him not to consent. The combination was not legal nor by the authority of the bishop, and as in the case of modifying the Liturgy that was Hammond's criterion. The Commonwealth Church was in schism, and to comply with its ministers in their schismatical acts was, said Hammond, "to put a stumbling-block in their way to reformation". Sanderson agreed to abstain, only hoping that by doing so he was not hindering a meeting "which to some men's apprehensions seemeth to tend so much to Christian peace and edification".[65]

As year followed year without hope of a break in the régime, so the fear grew that the perpetuation of Anglicanism as a separate unit might become impossible in England. In September 1658 Cromwell's death caused an upsurge of hope but the confusion of the distracted months that followed brought spirits near to breaking point. Even Hammond was disheartened and wrote: "The truth is unless some care be otherwise taken to maintain the Church it is to little purpose what any write in defense of it. For it will soon be destroyed." The old problem of the dwindling number of bishops was becoming urgent. Twice already, in 1655 and just before Cromwell's death, the matter had been raised by those in exile. The usual procedure was impossible, for there were no deans and chapters in existence to nominate new bishops when a see fell vacant. It had been suggested that the precedent of 1559 be followed and a royal mandate issued, instructing the bishops in England to meet and consecrate certain specified persons. Hitherto the bishops, not eager to assemble even in secret, had taken no action, but in May 1659 Richard Allestree, an Anglican clergyman and a Royalist agent, brought over to Duppa

[65] Brit. Mus. Harl. MS. 6942, No. 23; Sanderson, *Works*, VI.379 f.

a message in cipher requiring him, "all pretences whatsoever laid aside, without delay", to bring the bishops together to consecrate certain named persons "to secure the continuation of the order in the Church of England". Duppa, who was worried by his wife's illness and described himself as in an "eddy of confusion, whirl'd about as in a great fall of waters", delayed once more, and early in 1660 Allestree was arrested. The matter was then allowed to lapse, as Morley had followed him to England and was in treaty with the Presbyterians, whom it was undesirable to alarm.[66]

Hammond had been among those named in the King's letter and was designated to the see of Worcester, and as the spring of 1660 approached he prepared to leave for London "to assist in the great work of the composure of breaches in the Church". But on the eve of the journey he was taken seriously ill, and three weeks later he died.[67] To the sorrowing household who gathered about his bed, as to his friends on both sides of the Channel, it seemed an irreparable loss. "The beloved man of God" they called him, and Morley wrote to Lady Pakington, grieving that he had not seen him at the end. "Perhaps some of his spirit by God's mercy might have rested on me, if I had been by him and seen him and spoken with him as Elisha did with Elijah when he was taken away from him."[68] But Morley was held up in London with public affairs, and on the day that Hammond died, the Convention Parliament met that invited the King to return.

It was a tragedy for his country as well as for his friends that Hammond would not be there, to take a convinced yet charitable part in the reconstruction of the English Church. Yet perhaps he was more blessed than those who lived to see the hopes of that glorious spring clouded over by the old shadows of greed and suspicion. At the time, it seemed an Easter of

[66] See Bosher, *The Making of the Restoration Settlement*, pp. 107–14 for Morley's negotiations, although Dr Bosher perhaps overstresses the case for a concerted "neo-Laudian" plan.

[67] Fell's "Life" (Hammond, *Works*, I.cix).

[68] Pakington MS. belonging to Lord Hampton.

miracle. John Evelyn went to Greenwich openly to Communion with all his family, a simple enough statement to enter in his diary but how much it meant in fact! Duppa wrote in March, "I think myself to be in such a dream as David mentions when God turn'd away the captivity of Sion"; and a month later: "It is yet standing water with us, we neither flow nor ebb." But Isham replied: "Methinks I see your Lordship welcoming your King with tears of joy and even ready with old Simeon to say 'nunc dimittis'." Already a consciousness of the bishop's status has brought in an element of restraint: "My Lord, I know the multitude of business and care will now be upon you. If I may have the favour by letter but some times...." And indeed there was much coming and going, the counties emptying themselves into London and London into Holland, many visitors and a multitude of business which all but overwhelmed the bishop, so that he wrote rather ruefully: "Our letters only are the things that make no noise." It was August before he wrote again, by which time the King was safely home and he himself was to be translated to the see of Winchester and could thus look forward to living once more in his "beloved Richmond". The last letter is dated December 1660, and after an item of business it ends with the words: "And when I have done all I can, I shall still be an everlasting debtor to you for all your acts of friendship." It is perhaps a fitting epitaph upon the years of adversity, for, in the midst of so much that was tragic and insecure, there were many who had learnt anew the meaning of friendship and the value of all that was done in friendship's name.

# 8

# RESTORATION

In the years after 1660, the Anglican Church was restored as the established Church of the country. The bishops came back, though they never recovered the political influence of the former years; the Church courts came back, but not the High Commission and the notorious "ex officio" oath; their archaic methods of punishment and the protracted delays in procedure made them as unpopular as before and increasingly irrelevant. The parochial system was maintained, as it had been throughout the Interregnum, but no attempt was made to develop the Cromwellian efforts to augment stipends and adjust parish boundaries, and the shortcomings of the vestries as units of local administration became the more obvious as the industrial and financial pattern of life grew in complexity. Above all the Liturgy came back, and with it an enforcement of uniformity that rendered null and void the moderates' hope of a comprehensive Church, while the reappearance of the Roman Catholic bogey and the persistent fear of political unrest made toleration still anathema to many.

In the restored Church the process of rehabilitation showed itself on the material level in building and rebuilding, in reordering worship and reforming the select vestries. Whether for good or ill, the settlement of 1662 was a settlement and the Church was free at last from disputes about ceremonies and the origins of episcopacy. The scholastic eminence and pastoral zeal of the leading clergy were in many cases outstanding and, in contrast to the licentiousness of the court, there was a fruitful growth of personal piety among ordinary laymen.

The events that led up to the settlement which eventually emerged have been frequently recounted and variously interpreted, with considerable difference in making up the balance-sheet. Dr Bosher has argued convincingly that the course of events in 1660–1 was due not so much to the exigencies of the situation as to a deliberate policy followed consistently by the small but compact group of High Churchmen of whom Sheldon and Morley were the acknowledged leaders. Their religious principles were fixed and they had no intention of compromising their faith, but there were so many unknown elements in the situation of 1660—the King's own personality, the extent to which the Presbyterians would conform, the possibility of rioting and revolt—that one doubts if their policy were so clear-cut as this thesis would suggest.[1] Baxter himself gives his opponents the benefit of the doubt. "I think that those men are reprovable", he wrote, "who say that nothing but deceit and juggling was from the beginning intended. ... While the diocesan doctors were at Breda they little dreamt that their way to their highest grandeur was so fair and ... when they came in it was necessary that they should proceed safely and feel whether the ground were solid under them before they proceeded to their structure."[2] In fact that structure was being completed at the local level, with what degree of deliberation remains uncertain, while the settlement was being worked out with so many delays at headquarters. Hyde's own ambivalence adds to the difficulty of assessing the position. He still retained something of the Tew approach to religion, but his close intimacy with Morley influenced him in the High Church direction as his earlier friendship with Falkland had once inclined him to a more tolerant approach. But the main characteristic of his attitude was his clear conception of the Church as a bulwark of society

[1] Cf. Norman Sykes, *From Sheldon to Secker* (1959), p. 3; and see R. S. Bosher, *Making of the Restoration Settlement* (1951), pp. 88, 143–218 for a detailed account of events.

[2] R. Baxter, *Autobiography* (Everyman edn), pp. 158 f.

and the prerogative as a necessary part of the constitution. His main antipathy was to disorder, his main guide the law and customs of the country, and his main desire a return to tranquillity, expressed in his hope that England would soon recover "its old good manners, its old good humour and its old good nature".[3]

At Breda, awaiting the summons to return, Charles had given certain undertakings. "And because the passion and uncharitableness of the times have produced several opinions in religion", he promised to all a liberty to tender consciences. "No man", he declared, "should be disquieted or called into question in matters of religion . . . which did not disturb the peace of the kingdom." Personally he would have been glad to have it so and, throughout his reign, he was the one person who tried consistently (though without undue effort) to implement the promises. Nor did Hyde disagree, but he stressed in his own mind the concluding phrase, "which did not disturb the peace of the kingdom", and made a clear distinction between the law-abiding moderates and the "seditious preachers", who had caused so much trouble in 1641 and whom he was distressed to find still preaching seditiously in the London of twenty years later.

None the less in the first few months after the King's return the omens for peace were good, and Baxter, hurrying up to town from Kidderminster, had every hope of a settlement with room in it for all "mere Christians". He was not immediately concerned with fanatics, for he disliked them almost as much as Sheldon did. He was received with courtesy and, with other leading Puritans, was appointed a royal chaplain, with the proviso that they need only preach if it offended them to read the Prayer Book services. The restoration of some form of liturgy and episcopacy was a foregone conclusion, and the Presbyterian divines spent the summer discussing the modifications necessary before they could conform.

[3] *Lords' Journals*, XI.173 ff (speech on adjournment, 13 Sept. 1660).

The Convention Parliament was still sitting at Westminster and in the Lower House the ex-Puritans held a narrow majority. The best hope for the Presbyterians would have been to press ahead with the ecclesiastical settlement while the convention was in session, making the most of the King's assurance of liberty to tender consciences and uniting whole-heartedly with the Independent members to see that the promises of Breda were implemented. But there seemed many other matters of equal or greater urgency, such as questions of land tenure and the Bill of Indemnity, so that it was all too easy to postpone the intricate problem of the Church. Early in July a Bill for the "maintenance of the true reformed Protestant religion" was twice stormily debated but eventually set aside. During the next month, however, as many of the country members went down to see to their harvests the precarious balance swung in favour of the Presbyterians, and Prynne, that old campaigner, seized his opportunity. On 4 September he succeeded in carrying his "Bill for Settling Ministers", which laid down that with certain exceptions present incumbents should be maintained in their cures. Presentations made under the Great Seal or by peers of the realm since May 1660 were recognized as valid, and where sequestered incumbents were still alive or there were claimants who had been legally presented but refused by the Triers, they were to be allowed to recover their livings. Although the exceptions robbed the Bill of its full efficacy, its passing marked the growing ascendancy of the ex-Puritans in the House and thoroughly alarmed those who were determined to achieve as nearly as possible a full restoration of the Laudian Church. The adjournment of Parliament, however, ended the immediate danger and gave them a chance to stabilize their position.[4]

During these first critical months, while the moderates who had engineered the King's return allowed the initiative to slip out of their hands, the authorities were going ahead with the

[4] Bosher, op. cit., pp. 176–81.

reordering of the battered Church.[5] In the first twelve months, in spite of the Bill for settling ministers, nearly seven hundred livings changed hands as surviving clergy returned to claim their sequestered cures, or extremists were refused a licence to preach, or vacancies occurred through natural causes. This was a good example of the way in which administrative action forestalled the decisions at Westminster, for the majority of the new incumbents were men of High Church leanings, an end attained in the case of crown livings by submitting recommendations to a small commission consisting of Sheldon, Morley, and Earle, who naturally approved men of their own way of thinking.[6] It was not at first easy to find good men, and the new bishops made commendable efforts to encourage suitable ordinands; indeed their efforts combined with other causes after 1662—a genuine revival in piety, fashion, the more settled times—to produce more clergy than were needed to fill the available cures. Those who came forward in the first months of the Restoration had a more varied experience than the young graduates who were the candidates in more normal times. Some of them had spent years in exile or had served as soldiers in the wars or earned their living as doctors or schoolmasters in Cromwell's England, and possibly in consequence were more dogmatic in their Anglicanism than those who had suffered less for their faith.[7]

It was easier to return to the old ways in that neither episcopacy nor the Liturgy had been legally abolished. The exclusion of the bishops from the House of Lords had been the last Act of the Long Parliament to which Charles I had given the Royal Assent, and thus the old forms of worship and discipline could be introduced again without fresh legislation. Immediately he reached Whitehall, Charles stipulated that

[5] Cf. Anne Whiteman, "The Re-establishment of the Church of England, 1660–3" in *Transactions* of the Royal Historical Society, 5th series, V.111–31, and her article in the *Victoria County History* for Wiltshire.

[6] Bosher, *Making of the Restoration Settlement*, pp. 159 f.

[7] J. H. Overton, *Life in the English Church 1660–1714* (1885), pp. 309 f; Whiteman, loc. cit., pp. 115 f.

the full Anglican ritual should be practised in the Chapel Royal. But Pepys found the ceremonies uncongenial: "they do so overdo them", he commented, and it was by no means feasible to make the resumption of liturgical worship as speedy as the law permitted. It took some time to accustom a new generation to forms of worship and theology of which they knew little except that they had been brought up to consider them the devices of "malignants". To many, accustomed to the Directory with its scope for extempore prayer, the formal phrasing and the brevity of the Anglican collects were unconvincing, and some took exception to the repetitions and responses of the clerk and people and the alternate reading of the psalms and hymns which caused "a confused murmur in the congregation". The people's part in public prayer, said the Puritans, was to attend to it in silence and reverence and to declare their assent at the close by saying Amen.[8]

Simon Patrick, the young vicar of Battersea, used the Prayer Book for the first time in July, after thinking it over carefully as he walked through the streets of the parish, and he prepared his people "by preaching about forms of prayer, the lawfulness and usefulness of them".[9] All parish priests were not so wise, and although in this same month of July Evelyn recorded "from henceforward was the Liturgy publiquely used in our churches, whence it had been for so many years banished", the statement was only true in a very limited sense. Four months later, Pepys noted in regard to the worship at St Olave's, "Mr Mills did begin to nibble at the Common Prayer, but the people had been so little used to it that they could not tell what to answer", and as late as March 1661 a Londoner computed that there were "more churches that have not the Common Prayer than that have it".[10] In the country there might be less conscious opposition than in London

[8] F. Procter, *A New History of the Book of Common Prayer*, revised and rewritten by W. H. Frere (1902), p. 172.

[9] *The Autobiography of Simon Patrick* (1839), p. 38.

[10] Evelyn's *Diary*, ed. E. S. de Beer (1955), III.251 (8 July 1660); Pepys's *Diary*, ed. Wheatley (1904), I.255 (4 Nov. 1660); *Cal. S.P. Dom.*

but the process was more likely to be delayed by practical difficulties, for a large number of prayer books had been destroyed and the wardens were sometimes hard put to it to obtain new copies. As late as 1662, during Sanderson's first visitation, the churchwardens in the little village of Fingest replied to the inquiry as to their possessions: "Noe cover to the Chalice. A bible of the last translacon wanting. Wee want a new common Prayer Booke. Noe table of degrees prohibited. Noe surplice. Noe book to register strange preachers. Noe byer [bier], noe herse cloth." They only cheered up when they were able to report that their parsonage house was in fair condition. They planned to improve it further, but not until "after harvest".

Many of the remoter villages were in a similar state to Fingest. Over and over again, the lack of surplice and prayer book was reported—surplices proving particularly difficult to trace, for often they had passed into the possession of a parishioner and been put to other use. There was much to be done even when there were no complications as at West Wycombe, where the wardens reported: "The Church windowes newly broken by a distracted woman. Parte of the leade of the tower lately imbezelled or stollen, but by whome they know not; but now repaired. Book of homielies, canons ecclesiasticall, table of degrees, &c, surplice wantinge."[11]

The state of affairs in the small Buckinghamshire villages could be contrasted with that of such parishes as Headcorn and Charing where the churches had been kept throughout in good condition and seemly worship maintained. In London many parishes prospered, while others had been hard hit by the economic difficulties and the growth of vagrancy. Deptford tried to put its affairs in order as early as 1659, after the departure of Malory to a City living. It brought its select vestry

---

*1600–1*, p. 543, 19 March 1661. The letter continued: "but the bishops have sent readers to some, and will do so to all".

[11] *Episcopal Visitation Book for the Archdeaconry of Buckingham, 1662*, ed. E. R. C. Brinkworth (1947), pp. 13, 24.

up to 36 in number (including Evelyn), instituted suits at law against those who were behind with their rates, levied a cess to discharge the parish debts, and tightened up the regulations in regard to baptism. During the succeeding years parish records, often reduced to a mere list of officials, began to fill out again, although there is seldom any direct reference to the great events which had brought the change about. One exception to this is in a small book, originally a register, belonging to St John's, Hackney, which contains the interpolation: "God be thanked, the King preserved and our times amended. Thankes be to God, obedience to his word, and love and charity unto all men"—a pious hope immediately followed by a note in regard to burial dues that "every stranger that dyeth in the parish shall pay double fees". The accounts of All Saints', Wandsworth, presented in the spring of 1661, include seventeen shillings paid "for the ring of bells on the King going through the town". Next year there is a note of seven shillings for a new Liturgy and a book of the Articles and, later, of £2 10*s*. paid for a surplice, entries paralleled in other parish account-books, on dates that varied according to chance or circumstance.[12]

The bishops' return to office and the filling up of their depleted ranks proceeded alongside the restoration of old ways of worship and was the necessary precursor of rehabilitation. During the summer of 1660 Juxon and Duppa came up from their quiet places of retirement to join the bustling crowds that waited upon the King. Juxon's appointment as Archbishop was a foregone conclusion and Duppa in September was translated to the vacant see of Winchester, but they were old men, too tired and sick to be again involved. Matthew Wren returned to Ely and Skinner, who had ordained so many good men during the Interregnum, moved to Worcester in 1663 but Warner, who had helped many financially and suffered

[12] St John-at-Hackney, Register (County Record Office, Westminster, P.79/Jn 1, No. 22); All Saints', Wandsworth, Church Wardens' Accounts, 1623–1728. (Ibid., P.96/All 1, No. 45).

much himself, was left—in spite of voluble protestations—unpromoted at Rochester.[13]

The first stage in filling up the many vacancies was the reconstruction of the cathedral chapters so that episcopal elections could proceed in the accustomed way. At Exeter four of the residentiary canons had survived, and during August and September the number was brought up to the statutory nine. At Lincoln a new archdeacon was installed by a prebendary, no higher functionary being present to take action.[14] In each cathedral city up and down the country there were like reunions in which joy and mourning bore an equal part. It was some months before numbers were brought up to strength, new leases issued for cathedral property, services re-established, and where necessary an episcopal nomination made. It was the end of October before Brian Duppa consecrated five new bishops in a great service from which no point of ceremonial was omitted and which was followed by a sumptuous feast at Haberdashers' Hall.

Four of the newly appointed bishops belonged to the group which had played so prominent a part during the years of adversity. Sheldon became Bishop of London and, in view of Juxon's infirmity, the real leader of the Church; he moved to Lambeth when Juxon died in 1663. Morley, now made Bishop of Worcester, succeeded Duppa at Winchester within a couple of years. Henchman went, as was fitting, to Salisbury, where thirty years before he had helped to bear George Herbert's coffin to its resting place at Bemerton. Another to be consecrated was Sanderson, the only possible choice for Lincoln. He was well on in his seventies now, and a little crochety, but he had still two duties to perform for his Church, the reordering of his ravaged diocese and his share in the revision of the Book of Common Prayer.

[13] For Warner's protest see Brit. Mus. Add MS. 32096, ff. 182–3. He lists his services in the Upper House in the debates of 1640–1 and two gifts, of £1000 to the repair of St Paul's and £1500 to the King in 1640, in addition to his sufferings during the wars; cf. Sykes, *From Sheldon to Secker*, pp. 6 ff.

[14] Whiteman, *Trans.* Royal Hist. Soc., 5th Series, V.113 f.

By degrees the remaining vacant sees were filled. Cosin became Bishop of Durham in December and John Hacket, the author of the life of Williams, went to Lichfield, where he found the beautiful and comely church so battered by the wars that his sorrow and pity outweighed his comfort in his new promotion. The very next morning "he set his own coach-horses on work together with other teams to carry away the rubbish".[15] Within eight years, through his own bounty and the generosity of the neighbouring gentry, the cathedral was rebuilt at the cost of £20,000.

These large outgoings in rebuilding and repairs formed one of the bishops' most effective answers to a charge soon levied against them. In almost every case the leases on their property had run out and the fines paid by tenants for the leases' renewal reached a total out of all proportion to customary receipts. It began to be felt that a great opportunity had been lost, and that some at least of the money should have been set aside for buying in impropriations and improving the value of poor livings, thus completing the task that both Laud and Cromwell had essayed. Not only ecclesiastical politicians such as Burnet but men of Evelyn's non-aggressive temper felt it was wrong for these exceptional amounts to go into the bishops' private purses. But a great deal of it left those purses again in public works of all sorts, such as the library Cosin built at Durham with so much personal care and anxious inquiry that his secretary was hard put to it to keep his temper. The generosity of Morley and Sheldon was beyond reproach. None the less the criticism had become vocal by the end of 1662, when Sheldon told Cosin that in the coming session of Parliament "we shall be reproached for the great store of money we have received".[16]

If opportunities of reform were lost, both in this respect and

[15] T. Plume, *Life and Death of John Hacket* (edn of 1865), pp. 79 f. See Cosin, *Correspondence*, II.21, for his account of the welcome he was given at Durham.

[16] Cosin, *Correspondence*, II.90–4, 101; cf. Christopher Hill, *The Age of Revolution* (1961), p. 201.

in regard to the Church courts, to which coercive powers were restored in 1661, the cause was partly to be found in the piecemeal way in which the system was restored, officials appointed, and the machine set going again without any considered debate. Yet there was also a lack of dynamic leadership, perhaps inevitable under the circumstances. The bishops were old men in the main and had been through too much to relish innovations. Juxon was eighty in 1662, even Sheldon in his sixties had hardened into a mould; their minds were no longer flexible, nor were the economic and administrative issues clear in the months immediately succeeding that first incredible May. It was sufficient to them to repair the breaches, and, thankfully, they saw the old ways coming back without too much fuss up and down the countryside.[17]

A few days before the consecration of the bishops a meeting had been held at Worcester House (the lodgings of the Chancellor, Hyde) when the King presented to the leaders of both parties in the Church the concessions he was prepared to embody in a forthcoming declaration. The meeting broke up prematurely upon the news that the Chancellor's daughter, the Duchess of York, was in labour; it was not clear that anything had been settled but there had been one significant interchange. Hyde had read out a petition from the Independents and Anabaptists asking for toleration; and very tentatively he had asked the views of those present as to whether other groups might also "be permitted to meet for religious worship so be it they do it not to the disturbance of the peace".

Everyone kept silent; the generous gesture for which the King had hoped was not forthcoming; someone whispered to Baxter to say nothing. But he could not refrain from an attempt to underline the difference between the sort of toleration he could tolerate and any indulgence of Papists and Socinians. The subject was dropped and Baxter went

[17] Whiteman, loc. cit., pp. 129 ff.

dejectedly home, feeling that again he had said too much and that the royal Declaration would be shelved. A few days later, as he was walking through the streets, he heard the newsboys shouting; the King had kept his word, and, eagerly obtaining a copy of the Declaration, Baxter found that it promised a revision of the Liturgy and embodied most of the concessions for which his party had asked.

"I wondered at it how it came to pass", he recorded in his autobiography, "but was exceeding glad of it, as perceiving that now the terms were (though not such as we desired yet) such as any sober honest ministers might submit to." He was not, however, prepared to accept the bishopric which had been offered to him informally shortly before, and which the Chancellor now asked him point-blank whether he would accept. The see of Hereford was intended for him, while Edward Reynolds, the Warden of Merton, was offered Norwich, which he accepted, and Calamy reluctantly said no to Coventry and Lichfield. Baxter would have liked to delay his reply till he knew whether the King's concessions would be given the force of law, but, directly challenged by Hyde, he refused the bishopric on the ground that he could better serve the Church without it, recording in his autobiography a multiplicity of reasons which show how hard he had found it to make up his mind.[18] As he wrote in later years it was all too easy to feel that in these crucial months he had failed his party, through faults of personality or mistaken policy, and an unconscious attempt at self-justification increasingly colours his account.

Baxter could not be blamed for his doubt as to whether or not the Declaration was more than a "sop for present use". The concessions were considerable: ceremonies were not to be enforced for the time being and panels of advisers were to assist the bishops and archdeacons in ordinations and matters of discipline. But it was only intended as a temporary expedient, was perhaps only a means to prevent a precipitate settle-

[18] *The Autobiography of Richard Baxter* (Everyman edn), pp. 155 ff.

ment; and when Parliament reassembled in November, the Government was placed in something of a quandary by a motion that it be at once embodied in a Bill. The King's interest in it had lapsed since he saw no chance of a toleration clause. Sheldon disliked the whole business, and Hyde wanted all drastic action to be postponed till a new Parliament, constitutionally elected, had replaced the Convention. When the suggested Bill was debated before a packed House, who had duly thanked the King for his Declaration, a speech by Sir William Morrice, the Secretary of State, made it clear how those in authority wished the vote to go. It was in vain that Prynne poured scorn on the idea of throwing out the Bill after expressing thanks for the Declaration. Morrice advised that the Bill be "laid aside", and in a vote of 183 to 157 the Bill was negatived by the narrow majority of 26 on a motion to proceed with the previous question. By this small margin of less than thirty votes, the Church was set firmly on the path that led to the perpetuation of dissent.[19] For in December the Convention Parliament was dissolved, and when its successor assembled in the spring not only was the Anglican system firmly established throughout the country, but the new Parliament, overwhelmingly Cavalier in tone, was eager to legislate more rigorously than even the bishops desired.

Certain alarming events occurred in the interim. In January 1661 an open revolt had broken out in London and a group of fanatics, old Fifth-monarchists led by a wine-cooper called Venner, plunged the City into terror till they were routed out and captured by Government troops. Echoes of like disturbances came from other parts of the country, a clear reminder to the King and his ministers of the possibility of rebellion. Giavarina, the Venetian resident, complained again of the slowness and inconsistency of English administration; the latter fault he had attributed, two years earlier, to the effect of the British climate; at this stage hesitation was more probably due to uncertainty as to how far the Presbyterians should be

[19] Bosher, *Making of the Restoration Settlement*, pp. 197 ff.

placated in the interests of peace.[20] In March, at the London parliamentary elections, stormy scenes took place at the Guildhall and, amid cries of "No Bishops" that recalled the scenes of 1640, four opposition candidates were chosen, two of them Presbyterian. Compromise was still an evident necessity, and within a week a royal warrant was issued for a conference to consider the reform of the Liturgy. But by the time the twelve bishops and their assessors, with an equal number of eminent Puritan divines, had assembled at the Savoy, the atmosphere had again completely changed. The new Parliament, which met on 8 May, was overwhelmingly Royalist in sympathy—mostly young men up from the shires and determined to get things done. One of the first acts of the new House of Commons was to order the public burning of the Covenant; on 26 May they attended St Margaret's and received Holy Communion; four days later a Bill was introduced for the restoration of the bishops to the House of Lords. Later in the year, after an adjournment in which there were rumours of fresh unrest, they countered not with concessions but with the passing of the Corporation Act, which imposed upon all local officials an oath of non-resistance and the obligation to take communion annually according to Anglican rites, a prostitution of the sacrament for political ends bound to lead to cynicism and disbelief.

In this atmosphere of mistrust, in the course of 1661–2, the ecclesiastical settlement evolved. The Savoy Conference took the wrong direction from the start, when Sheldon insisted that the Presbyterians should draw up a list of their exceptions to the present Liturgy, thus stressing differences, not the hope of accord. The exceptions were 99 in number, and only seventeen were eventually conceded by the bishops. They dealt with all sorts of minor matters, the observance of saints' days, the choice of lessons, clerical nomenclature, and disputed points of ceremonial, but they also revealed fundamental differences both in theology and in regard to the nature of the

[20] *Cal. S.P. Venetian, 1659–61*, pp. 23, 274 f.

priesthood as well as an utter lack of mutual understanding. Had all the other difficulties been overcome, that of baptism remained. The Presbyterians objected to the inclusion of the phrase, "that it hath pleased thee to regenerate this infant by thy Holy Spirit". "We cannot", they averred, "by faith say that every child that is baptized is regenerated by God's Holy Spirit." On this the bishops could not compromise, and in the eventual revision of the Prayer Book a declaration was incorporated in the baptismal service that "It is certain by God's Word, that Children which are baptized, dying before they commit actual sin, are undoubtedly saved". At a later date Baxter made the comment: ". . . of the forty sinful terms for a communion with the Church party, if thirty-nine were taken away and only that rubric, concerning the salvation of infants dying shortly after their baptism, were continued, yet they could not conform."[21] It was not only the bishops' "duplicity" that made it hard to build a comprehensive Church!

Baxter enlivened his account of the conference with his impressions of his chief opponents. He credited Gunning with being "an able disputant, a man of greater study and industry than any of them, well read . . . a very temperate life . . . but so vehement for his high imposing principles and so over-zealous for Arminianism and formality and church-pomp and so very eager and fervent in his discourse, that I conceive his prejudice and passion much perverted his judgement". Cosin had "a great deal of talk" and little logic to which no one paid much attention, but they respected his patristic knowledge and found him easier to talk to than the others, "of a rustic wit and carriage" and "more affable and familiar than the rest". It was Pearson whom Baxter admired most, as a true scholar who debated "accurately, soberly and calmly"; Morley's hot spirit and ready tongue continued to rile him, and it is tempting to imagine how things might have fallen out if the

[21] Procter and Frere, *A New History of the Book of Common Prayer*, pp. 170 et seq., 200 n; F. E. Brightman, *The English Rite* (2nd edn, 1921), I.cxciv ff; Baxter, *Autobiography*, pp. 162–7.

protagonists at Worcester House and the Savoy had been Hammond and John Angier rather than Morley and Baxter, who were still, twenty years later, brooding with irritation upon each other's opinions.[22]

While the divines had been debating at the Savoy the King had been crowned, Hyde had been created Earl of Clarendon, the new Royalist Parliament had met, and Convocation had been summoned. In the course of the first parliamentary session a Bill for Uniformity had passed the Lower House, but the Lords took no action upon it before the adjournment at the end of July. During the vacation a group of bishops continued to meet unofficially and to work upon the revision of the Prayer Book, with the result that when the Houses reassembled in November Convocation was able to act with remarkable speed. An official committee was now set up under Bishop Wren's chairmanship. It met each evening at Ely House, after the daily session of Convocation, and within a month a draft was submitted for detailed criticism, the amendments considered, a fair copy made, and on 20 December the new book was approved by both Houses of Convocation. It was submitted to Parliament and annexed to the Bill for Uniformity, which was awaiting the Lords' attention. They accepted it without a detailed examination, though the debates on the Bill itself continued throughout February and March. In April, by a margin of six votes, the Commons also agreed to accept the revised book without debate, although by a further vote they declared their right to debate it had they wished. On 19 May 1662 Charles gave his assent to the Act of Uniformity. It decreed that before 24 August, St Bartholomew's Day, all incumbents must be episcopally ordained, must undertake to use the Prayer Book in their churches, and must give their unfeigned assent and consent to all that it contained. Moreover all teachers must be licensed by their bishops and must take the oath of non-resistance and of assent

22 Baxter, op. cit., pp. 168 f; *The Bishop of Winchester's Vindication . . . against R. Baxter* (1683).

to the Book of Common Prayer. In this sweeping manner the triumphant Cavaliers determined to purge the national Church of the Puritan element and to ensure that true learning, as they understood it, should flourish and abound.[23]

The spirit and the promises of the spring of 1660 had thus been entirely reversed, though in the revision of the Book itself the bishops had not been unmindful of their duty of restraint. Both Cosin and his chaplain, William Sancroft, who probably acted as secretary, entered suggested emendations into prayer books of their own, one of which survives at Durham and includes the alterations agreed upon during the informal vacation meetings; Sancroft's fair copy is in the Bodleian. The Durham book makes it clear that the informal group suggested various alterations of a High Church character, largely based on the Scottish Prayer Book of 1637. But a note is added in Sancroft's handwriting: "My Lords, the Bishops, at Ely House ordered all in the old method", and the eventual Book that issued from Convocation contained no "Laudian" innovations beyond the inclusion in the Prayer for the Church Militant of the thanksgiving "for all thy servants departed this life in thy faith and fear". In restoring the Black Rubric of Edward VI's second Prayer Book a change of wording marked an advance in sacramental doctrine. In 1552 the statement ran that the act of kneeling did not imply idolatry "either unto the sacramental bread or wine . . . or unto any real and essential presence of Christ's Flesh and Blood". The restoration of the rubric was a concession to Presbyterian opinion, but by changing the words "real and essential presence" to "corporal presence", a subtle change of emphasis was obtained; transubstantiation was eschewed but the belief in a real if spiritual presence was implied.

Among other verbal changes, the Absolution was to be pronounced by the "Priest", instead of "minister" and in the Litany one prayed for "Bishops, Priests and Deacons", not, as heretofore, for "Bishops, Pastours and Ministers". The

[23] Procter and Frere, op. cit., pp. 194 f.

rubrics were clarified and the collects admirably revised with some additional ones from Cosin's pen. His translation of the "Veni Creator" was also included in the Ordinal. A few extra services, some more successful than others, were added to meet new needs, such as that for Adult Baptism, in view of the conversion of many Anabaptists, and the Forms to be used at Sea, in the years of the Navy's growing prestige. The book was enriched by the addition of some new prayers: Sanderson and Gunning between them were probably responsible for the prayer for "all sorts and conditions of men"; Bishop Reynolds, in Convocation, produced the General Thanksgiving (sufficient cause for posterity to be grateful that he had accepted a see). Finally Sanderson wrote the Preface, catching the spirit of his own ministry in its first phrases: "It hath been the wisdom of the Church of England, ever since the first compiling of her Publick Liturgy, to keep the mean between the two extremes, of too much stiffness in refusing and of too much easiness in admitting any variation from it." Yet even Sanderson had not escaped the temper of the times, and there was a jarring note in his assumption that one could not expect that "men of factious, peevish, and perverse spirits should be satisfied with anything that can be done in this kind by any other than themselves".[24]

As the summer advanced, it became clear that many not noticeably peevish or perverse were preparing to go rather than conform. The Act had been passed without any loopholes, and two amendments approved by the House of Lords, which would have eased the situation, had not been accepted in the Commons. The first would have allowed a fifth of their

[24] Ibid., pp. 196 et seq. for a summary of the changes, and Brightman, op. cit., pp. cxciii et seq. for the work of revision. The official committee of eight consisted of Wren, Cosin, Sanderson, Morley, Henchman, Warner, Skinner, and Bishop Nicholson of Gloucester. James Parker in a detailed analysis, *An Introduction to the History of the successive Revisions of the Book of Common Prayer* (1877), lays particular stress on the part played by Cosin in the revision, but Brightman queries this and attributes a larger share to Wren (p. cxcvii).

stipends to the displaced ministers, the second, proposed by Clarendon, would have given the King leave to suspend the law in the case of individuals of a "pious and peaceable disposition". Clarendon believed that the King possessed a dispensing power in ecclesiastical affairs and, although in his later writings he minimized his own share in events, he was certainly uneasy at the loss of so many eminent men and probably approved the attempts which Charles made to lessen the impact of the law by the use of his prerogative. It was with the Chancellor's connivance that on 27 August some of the leading London ministers petitioned the King for an Indulgence. They were given to understand that there was a likelihood of relief in individual cases but the co-operation of the bishops would be necessary, and on 28 August such as were in London were summoned to a meeting of the Privy Council. Sheldon alone attended, and on behalf of his colleagues he refused to condone any action which ran contrary to the express wishes of Parliament and the law of the land. The suggested Indulgence fell through and the London ministers went with the rest.

Clarendon was not inconsistent in his unease, nor Sheldon in his obduracy. Clarendon's whole view of life was based on Hooker's conception of the Visible Church as the community of all faithful people, the concomitant of the ordered State in the sphere of religion. There could be no harmony except on the basis of law and order, and obedience in the secular sphere meant obedience in religion also; the fact that hundreds of sober and peaceable men were prepared to separate themselves from the established Church, rather than accept a settlement laid down by law, meant in effect the breakdown of his whole conception of community. But his stress was on the political and social aspects of their action, rather than the religious one; and if a measure of toleration would give back to the dissidents a sense of belonging, he was prepared to give it to those whom he felt he could trust.

Sheldon's approach was far less devious. The course

suggested by the King was a hole-and-corner method of procedure, quite uncongenial to him. Rules were made to be obeyed. He had told Laud as much twenty years before, in the case of Jeremy Taylor's fellowship; he had said the same ten years later in regard to a modified Liturgy; he said it again in 1662. "Uniform obedience" had been Hammond's reply, when Lady Pakington asked him on his death-bed which virtue it were best to emulate. It was the basis on which he and his friends had built their lives. It was one of the reasons Sheldon disliked the whole idea of toleration as compared with comprehension, which he could accept in principle even if it were unattainable in practice. But toleration—the acceptance of dissent as a permanent factor in the nation's life—was not only a denial of the whole conception of the Visible Church which he shared with Clarendon, it was also a sop to disobedience.[25]

As for the other protagonists, the attitude of the House of Commons men, who were responsible for the stringency of the Act, is best expressed by some words of Henry Coventry, in no sense an extremist. "I will never receive the blood of my Saviour from that hand that stinks with the blood of my great master."[26] These young men could scarcely be expected to differentiate between different species of Puritan, and the shadow of the late King's death and the memory of a dozen battlefields still lay across the scene. The King himself was preoccupied that summer with his own marriage, and the difficulty of reconciling his Portuguese bride with the continued presence at court of Lady Castlemaine. He could be forgiven for being thoroughly weary of the ecclesiastical settle-

[25] For Clarendon's attitude in general see B. H. G. Wormald, *Clarendon: Politics, History and Religion, 1640–1660* (1951), p. 308, and cf. Keith Feiling, *A History of the Tory Party* (1924), pp. 68–71. See in particular in regard to the Indulgences, G. R. Abernathy, Junior, "Clarendon and the Declaration of Indulgence" in *Journal of Eccles. History*, XI.1 (April 1960), pp. 55 et seq., which stresses Clarendon's wish for indulgences in special cases and a moderate execution of the Act.

[26] Feiling, op. cit., p. 125.

ment, though his dislike of persecution was genuine and his intention unchanged to counteract it, when occasion served, by a judicious use of his prerogative. It is possible he had a glimmering of the one hopeful factor of the situation. After the exodus in 1662, nonconformity no longer consisted of Papists and sectaries alone but included a large proportion of educated and respectable citizens who could not indefinitely be shut out from the affairs of their country and their neighbourhood. Sooner or later toleration must come.

No amount of argument could—or can—make it other than a "Black Bartholomew", for it is estimated that as many as 1760 ministers left their pulpits and 149 teachers were ejected from the Universities and schools.[27] On 17 August Pepys heard Dr Bates preach his final sermons at St Dunstan's; he asked his hearers to believe that it was not "opinion, fashion or humour" that kept him from compliance, "but something, which after much prayer, discourse and study remains unsatisfied". Next Sunday, guards were posted in the City, but there were few disturbances except for the mishandling of one or two orthodox preachers and the misbehaviour of some hooligans in Pudding Lane who tore all the prayer books they could find to pieces, with derisory cries of "Porridge!" Up in Lancashire rumours of the Indulgence arrived by the Saturday post, so on the 24th many of the ministers preached again; but Adam Martindale was ejected in the course of the following week. He protested at unfair treatment, as he had not received a copy of the revised book till 22 August and he had needed "the stomach of an ostrich to have digested that great book, without chewing". Afterwards he taught mathematics at Warrington, which was perhaps his true vocation. Angier, like one or two more of the Lancashire ministers, was undisturbed at Denton. He allowed a visiting cleric to read the Prayer Book occasionally, to satisfy the archdeacon, but he made no subscription himself; and in part because of his connection with the Moselys, and more because of his own goodness, the

27 A. G. Matthews, *Calamy Revised* (1934), pp. xii ff.

magistrates let him alone. Occasionally it was rumoured that a warrant was out, but "the worst men had no heart to meddle with him. Sometimes they searched, but profess'd they would not see him for £100."[28]

The King would have liked more of that spirit to be abroad, and in December 1662 he made another attempt to exercise his dispensing power and issued an Indulgence which extended to Roman Catholics as well as Protestant dissenters. Charles's efforts failed, as they were bound to do, for the same reason that his grandfather failed in 1622–3. The obsessive fear of Popery was beginning to stir again, and suspicion of the prerogative had not grown less in forty years.[29] The politicians behind the Indulgence were the Earl of Bristol, the spokesman of the Roman Catholics, and Arlington, an able politician, who between them were undermining Clarendon's power. The latter was laid up with gout that winter, and he did not associate himself with the measure, though he may have been less opposed to its general principle than he later made out. When Parliament reassembled in February, he spoke against a Bill which had been introduced into the Lords to legalize the Declaration. In consequence it was dropped in committee. The Commons had already expressed themselves strongly through the Speaker, and the Indulgence was withdrawn. Throughout the rest of the reign the pattern was repeated, the attempts at toleration alternating with schemes to win back the moderates by a measure of compromise—both provoking retaliatory measures from a Parliament determined to keep things as they were.

[28] Heywood, *Life of Angier* (Manchester, 1937), pp. 127, 132; Martindale's *Autobiography*, p. 163; A. G. Matthews, *Calamy Revised*, pp. 12, 343. See Baxter, pp. 171 f for his unsuccessful attempts to say goodbye to his Kidderminster congregation.

[29] Osmund Airy attributed to Sheldon, in an article in Vol. 77 of the *British Quarterly Review*, a letter which in so far as he quotes it is identical with that written in 1623, purporting to come from Abbot. The 1623 letter was reprinted, with omissions, in 1663 as anti-Romanist propaganda, but it did not emanate from Sheldon, who was always restrained if decisive in his language. (See p. 66 above.)

The first positive result of the settlement was a new energy in going ahead with the process of rehabilitation. That summer most of the bishops went down to their dioceses, and visitations were set on foot in every part of the country. Much had still to be done in the way of restoring order, but, now matters were settled for good or ill, this part of the task was reasonably straightforward. There was a good store of enthusiasm, and when a neighbourhood had news of a bishop's visitation crowds would pour in to be confirmed. The regular celebration of Holy Communion was re-established, but again only by degrees. In July 1661, more than a year after the Restoration, the new vicar of Deptford felt it necessary to precede a celebration by a sermon "reproving the great neglect of the Holy Sacrament", and at Cranbrook it is not till 1663 that the purchase of bread and wine begins to appear again in the accounts. At first the expenditure was about 10*s.* in the year whereas it had exceeded £6 before the war; a discrepancy in part due to the growth of more seemly manners in regard to the amount of wine consumed. After 1668 a new vicar came to Cranbrook, who stayed out the century and restored a sense of stability after the many changes in personnel since 1642; it is noticeable that in the accounts the 10*s.* now grows to 25*s.* or thereabouts and for some years varies very little. In London a weekly Communion was introduced in certain churches, as in the cathedrals, but the monthly celebration was the usual practice; and in the country there were still many churches that remained content with the crowded services for the whole parish at the great Christian festivals, including Michaelmas, which tallied with the changing seasons of the year.

As emotions and practices steadied down, wise parish priests tended to concentrate upon teaching the Catechism, to remedy the many gaps in knowledge left by the unsettled years. In this connection the village schools became a more regular feature of the scene. Sanderson's articles indicate clearly the two different types of school with which the parish might be concerned. There was the grammar school, possibly founded

by a private benefactor, probably in Elizabethan days, as to which the bishop inquired: "Who was the Founder and is now the Patron thereof? And what is the yearly revenue or stipend belonging to the Governors or Masters of the same? Is the same ordered or governed in every respect as it ought to be?" There was also the village school, which might be a private venture or an "English" school directly under the control of the vestry, and as to which the questions ran: "Doth any man keep a publick or private school in your parish who is not allowed thereunto by the Bishop or his Chancellor? Doth your schoolmaster teach his scholars the Catechism of Religion set forth by authority? Doth he cause them upon Sundayes and Holy dayes orderly to repair to your Church or Chappel? and see they behave themselves there quietly and reverently during the time of Divine Service and Sermon?" One answer revealed that Burnham possessed a private school whose master, Barnard Bartram, was also parish clerk, and the wardens reported that "very manie will not pay him . . . his wages but detaine it from him" and the recorder has added in brackets "*pauperrimus*". This sort of thing had happened too often in the past, but as the reign progressed the parishes began to accept their responsibility for teaching not only the bright boy who went to the grammar school, but the poor children in their care, at least a knowledge of the alphabet, so that they could read their bibles. It was not till the end of the century that individual efforts were co-ordinated in the Charity School movement, but in the years after 1662 there is increasing reference in the parochial records both to parish and private schools, and the tidy pinafores and well-scrubbed faces that began to adorn the galleries of numerous churches on a Sunday morning provide one of the pleasanter aspects of this chequered chapter in the Anglican story.[30]

[30] Brinkworth, *Episcopal Visitations*, pp. 1, 4, 19, 92; cf. M. C. Jones, *The Charity School Movement, a study of eighteenth century Puritanism in action* (1938), pp. 5, 22. For parochial references cf. St John-at-Hackney, Vestry Minutes, 1657–1698 (County Hall, Westminster, P.79/Jn. 1 No. 138), 9 and 26 Jan.

One of the new schools was that founded by Robert Breton, one of Malory's successors at Deptford. He left £200 "for the teaching of twelve poor children, grammar and writing", for, as he put it in his will, he could best express his "unfeigned love for the said parish" by providing "for the educating of their youth in the principalls of religion and learning". Of Breton one knows rather more than of the average parson, for the records of the parish can be pin-pointed from Pepys's diary as well as from Evelyn's. Pepys visited St Nicholas each year on Trinity Monday, when Trinity House held its annual service in the church before the election of its Master and Wardens. Deptford, with its great dockyard, was a headquarters of the Navy, and until its removal to Tower Hill in 1795 Trinity House, whose main function was the training of apprentice seamen, was adjacent to the church. Breton was appointed vicar of St Nicholas early in 1662, Evelyn commending his probation sermon in the previous November as "an excellent discourse on God's free grace to penitents". Pepys's first impression of him was of "a fine man and good company", but when he preached on Trinity Monday the diarist listened to the sermon with impatience adjudging, with his usual common sense and good temper, that a sermon "full of words against the nonconformists" was "not proper to the day at all". Three years later, the vicar has become in Pepys's eyes "that conceited fellow, Dr Bretton", though to Evelyn he remained "our Doctor", the godfather to one of his sons and a valued friend. After Breton's death, when another of the periodic attempts was made to reconstitute the select vestry, Evelyn was again one of the 36 vestrymen, and thereafter his distinctive signature occurs repeatedly in the minute-book.[31]

---

1665–6; 1 Oct. 1671. The earlier entries deal with a dispute between the vestry and the schoolmaster, who refused to be turned out; the later entry gives leave to a Mr Salmon to enlarge the gallery "that his schollers sit in", and to Mrs Freeman to add three pews to the one her scholars used.

[31] Breton's will is inscribed on f. 9, one of the opening pages of St Nicholas' minute-book. Evelyn's signature, clear and florid, and usually

The Deptford minute-book vividly illustrates another aspect of the years after 1662. When the vestry was reconstituted, the regulation was also re-enacted that no children should be baptized "without lawful notice given two days beforehand . . . this article being intended for the prevention of baptizing strangers not belonging to this place". The rules of settlement had been made still more rigid, and a new Act empowered the parishes to send back to their place of origin not only rogues and vagabonds but any strangers liable to be unemployed. In 1672 two pages of the vestry minutes deal with methods of extracting securities from newcomers or removing them elsewhere, and one entry illustrates the particular hazards of the time. It records a bond for £200 given "to discharge the parish by Gilbert Luke". "He and his wife bigg with child going to London from Gravesend, his wife being shott by one, out of a Press boat, fell in labour against our towne and so was brought ashore heere." The naval wars against Holland added to Deptford's anxieties, and one macabre difficulty that occurred was the disposal of the bodies of dead seamen put ashore from passing ships. "There is a great trouble, before there cann be procured persons to carry such corpse to the grave": in consequence four bearers were appointed specially for this purpose.[32]

Despite wars and vagrants Deptford prospered, but the cleavage which the Act of Settlement made between parish and parish was another sign of the breakdown of community which men such as Clarendon deplored. When people's imagination was stirred they could sympathize with their neighbours and be generous, and it was now that the practice of issuing briefs for charitable purposes was developed almost to excess. The most likely calamity was that of fire, and the Cranbrook account-book records various lists of parishes that have been helped; one page dated 1659–61 includes eleven

without an initial attached, occurs *inter alia* on f. 94 et seq. and ff. 157, 159. For further details of the church see John Summerson, "The Monuments in the Church of St Nicholas Deptford" in *Transactions of the Ecclesiological Society*, Vol. I (new series), part 4, p. 226.

[32] St Nicholas, Deptford, Vestry Minutes, ff. 103–7.

names and collections varying from 10*s.* 4*d.* for Chertsey to £1 8*s.* 4½*d.* for Fakenham. But there were many other good causes to be assisted. At Holy Trinity, Clapham, they collected the large sum of £6 3*s.* for "the distressed churches in Lithuania", 24*s.* towards the encouragement of the fishing trade, and 16*s.* 6*d.* for "Philip Dandulo who was converted from the Mahometan profession by Doctors Wilde and Gunning". On another occasion 32*s.* was contributed for the church in Strasbourg "being in great wante".[33]

So the life of the parishes went on, the problems, in most cases, differing in size and complexity rather than in nature from those of earlier years. Yet over-riding them all was one as insoluble as vagrancy, less rewarding than the schools, and bristling with as many difficulties as allotting the best pews—that of living side by side with Nonconformists. The village of Penn, most peaceful of spots to-day, must have seemed a storm-centre in 1662 when there were presented—in addition to the vicar, unsuccessfully charged with "frequentinge of alehouses and keeping of disorderly companie"—twelve reputed Anabaptists and Quakers, two women who were not living with their husbands, and two gentlemen who refused to pay the church rate. The position grew worse after the passing of the Conventicle Act, which forbade more than four persons to meet together, other than the household. The excuse was the imminent war with the Dutch and the interests of security; as an attempt to prevent the Nonconformists from worshipping in private it signally failed. It was increasingly difficult to know what to do with those who were arrested, for it was administratively impossible to send them all to prison. Fines were more usual, and the Cranbrook accounts record in 1665–6 the sum of £3 13*s.* "for being taken at a conventicle", which was handed over by the Justices to the churchwardens and distributed by them to the poor.

The assumption that the dissenters were of necessity

[33] Holy Trinity, Clapham, Vestry Minutes, 8 Dec. 1661 (Part 2, pp. 35, 43).

contumacious foundered in the next few years. Their stock went up considerably in 1665 in the year of the plague. It struck the city in June, when the signs of panic appeared and Pepys noted: "I find all the town almost going out of town." In July the King left Whitehall for Hampton Court, setting a bad example which not only the President of the College of Surgeons but a good many clergymen followed. Henchman, now Bishop of London, threatened to remove those who did not return to their cures, and Sheldon remained at Lambeth. It would never have entered his head to do otherwise. Breton was among those who remained at his post, while the vicar of St Giles-in-the-Fields was as staunch in his stricken parish as Morse the Roman priest had been in the 1630s. Simon Patrick, now rector of St Paul's, Covent Garden, deliberately returned from a holiday to his parish, doing what he could to help and finding he had a good deal of extra time for study. "I . . . read many good authors, for I had seldom any company."[34] But more than sufficient went for the critics' tongues to get busy—chaplains going with their noble patrons or pluralists visiting their country cures, leaving their curates in charge in the City. The ejected ministers, in contrast, perhaps because they had already come to terms with sacrifice, rose magnificently to the occasion. One of the best known among them was Thomas Vincent, who had been vicar of the church in Milk Street where once Anthony Farindon had ministered. He now returned to London and went from empty pulpit to empty pulpit, preaching until he died. For most of them did die. The burial registers of St Giles, Cripplegate, include one page that runs, under the date 1665:

[34] S. Patrick, *Autobiography*, pp. 52–7. In the records of St James's, Clerkenwell, there are some extracts from Vestry Minutes (County Record Office, Westminster, P.76, J.S.1/80), including the entry; "At a vestry held the 11th Feb. 1665[6]. Ordered that Mr Ayloffe, Mr Cole, Mr Dawes, Mr Gibbs, Mr Knight, Mr Jenny or four of them at the least doe attend the Lord Bishop of London, forthwith to acquaint his Lordship . . . of Mr Kingston's greate paines and hazard in the service in the said parish in the late sad visitation." Richard Kingston was vicar 1665–6.

| | | |
|---|---|---|
| August 21 | Samuel Austin, Minister | Plague. |
| Sep. 6 | John Askew, Minister | Plague. |
| Sep. 15 | Samuel Skelton, Minister | Plague. |
| Sep. 16 | Abraham Jennaway, Minister | Plague. |
| Sep. 23 | Henry Marley, Minister | Plague. |
| Sep. 30 | John Wall, Minister | Plague.[35] |

The reward which Parliament meted out to those who survived was the passing of the Five Mile Act, which forbade dissenting ministers to come within five miles of a city or corporate town unless they took a special oath "not to endeavour at any time any alteration in Church or State". The absurdity no less than the savagery of the measure defeated itself and the tide began to turn.

Within a year of the plague the Great Fire swept through the City, destroying in forty-eight hours of nightmare the restored St Paul's and eighty-seven parish churches whose spires had diversified the skyline of medieval London. An indication of what this meant can be gleaned from the minute-books of St Bartholomew, Exchange, whose vestry had recently raised £300 for a thorough repair of the church, completing the work in 1664. Within two years the fire destroyed the building and only three houses were left in the parish. At these in turn the vestry continued to meet, and plans to rebuild the church were immediately put in hand. It was the same throughout the City. Materials, bricks, lead, timber were salvaged from the ruins, rates were levied and subscriptions raised to furnish and adorn the churches, a proportion of which the Government undertook to rebuild. The cost was to come from a tax on coal, used increasingly for domestic purposes. Among those in charge of the work was Sir Christopher Wren, who had deserted the academic life to become an architect and a civil servant.[36]

From his house on the South Bank Wren watched the progress of the new St Paul's, and craftsmen and artists came from

[35] Walter G. Bell, *The Great Plague in London in 1665* (1924), p. 150.

[36] T. F. Reddaway, *The Rebuilding of London after the Great Fire* (1940), pp. 49, 56 ff, et al.

all over Europe to take their part in the work. But the residents, it was noticed, were slower in coming back; life in the suburbs had proved to have its advantages and the City never recovered its old density of teeming life and political influence. After a second Building Act in 1670 the work on the parish churches went ahead. By degrees Wren's great masterpieces arose, St Mary-le-Bow, St Bride's, St Peter's, Cornhill, classical rather than baroque, full of light and space, a new and exhilarating skyline for those who looked across from Southwark where the lovely thirteenth-century arches of St Saviour's, like the stalwart Norman pillars of St Bartholomew's on the City's outskirts, were among the few reminders of a medieval past upon which a new age had resolutely turned its back.

For the architecture of the new churches, the great central dome, the lofty pulpits with their sounding boards, and the flowers and fruit of Grinling Gibbons' altar-pieces were symbolic of a like change of ways of thought and worship, which marked the beginning of a new chapter in the Anglican story. At St Lawrence Jewry, one of the most influential of the City churches, there ministered in turn Dr Wilkins, the incarnation of reason and amiability, and Benjamin Whichcote, who continued in the pulpit and in the quality of his own life to show that the pursuit of reason must be harnessed to moral force. As the decade drew to a close, after beginning so hopefully with the promise of "liberty to tender consciences" and foundering so pitifully not only on men's suspicions but on their conscientiousness, fresh attempts were made to come to terms with dissent in a spirit of charity.

In the year after the fire the Dutch sailed up the Medway, completing the tally of the disastrous years. Clarendon was the inevitable scapegoat, held responsible not only for the punitive laws but for the unsuccessful war and the fact that the Portuguese match, which he had favoured, had failed to produce an heir. He was impeached and banished. His successor as Keeper of the Great Seal was Orlando Bridgeman, a

lawyer rather than statesman, whose father, Bishop Bridgeman, had managed to administer the diocese of Chester in an eirenical spirit even in the days of Laud. Under the aegis of the new Lord Keeper a plan for the reformation of outstanding clerical abuses and for a measure of comprehension was set forward by Dr Wilkins, after consultation with Baxter and his friends. A Bill was drafted by Sir Matthew Hale, an admirable person, who based it on a compromise in regard to ordination and a milder form of subscription. In opening the next session the King asked his Parliament to "think of some course to beget a better union and composure in the mind of my Protestant subjects in matters of religion". But Parliament had not changed its spots; it negatived the proposals for a consultation by 176 votes to 70 and proceeded to pass a second Conventicle Act to replace the one that had expired. Within a year the King had changed his policy, Bridgeman was out of office at his home in Teddington, and Charles countered the Commons' obduracy with a second Declaration of Indulgence.[37]

The Indulgence was issued in March 1672 and was in operation for eleven months. It allowed Roman Catholics freedom of worship in private houses, while Protestant dissenters might hold services in public on receipt of a licence from the Secretary of State.

The Indulgence was linked with the intrigues with France, associated with the politicians who had ousted Clarendon and whose initials conveniently spelt the word "Cabal". Their administration, if it deserves such a description, soon collapsed, for there were no shared principles of statecraft or religion to bind together Clifford, a zealous Roman Catholic, Ashley, the ex-Parliamentarian, and Arlington, an able pragmatist. When Parliament reassembled in February of next year the King made no effort to continue whatever arbitrary designs he had cherished. The Indulgence was recalled, Ashley went into opposition, Clifford resigned the Treasury and committed suicide; Arlington rode out the storm.

[37] Cf. Sykes, *From Sheldon to Secker*, pp. 72–5.

The King was forced to accept a Test Act, which imposed upon all office-holders a denial of the doctrine of transubstantiation in addition to the usual obligation in regard to communion. The Roman Catholics against whom the measure was primarily directed had to wait for one and a half centuries before the full rights of citizenship were conceded to them. But after 1673 the position of the Protestant dissenters subtly changed. While the Indulgence was in force over fifteen hundred licences had been issued, and the congregations which had come into the open in most cases remained in being, suffering intermittent persecution but sufficiently undisturbed to preserve their identity.[38] The ding-dong continued of alternate schemes for comprehending or tolerating a body of citizens whose sober integrity in business and private life was increasingly recognized. In 1677 Sheldon died and William Sancroft, then Dean of St Paul's, succeeded him at Canterbury. He was a milder, less able man than his predecessor, not happy in politics nor easy in personal relationships. But he knew better than Sheldon the danger inherent in too close an alliance between Church and State and he was eager to bridge the gulf between Christians. To the end of his primacy he fostered the idea of a comprehensive Church, but in the years immediately after his appointment the cross-currents of anti-Romanist fears and political corruption swamped the new spirit that was abroad. Such monstrous events as Titus Oates's pretended plot and the futile tragedy of the Rye House conspiracy embittered the closing years of the reign and caused, inevitably, a Royalist reaction. The High Churchmen now spoke of non-resistance, divine right by a modern name, only to find themselves in an insoluble dilemma when the accession of James II put a Papist on the throne. James's attempt to establish toleration by the use of the prerogative failed as surely as his brother's had done, and the Protestant dissenters, by reversing their action of 1672 and refusing to accept a

[38] See Frank Bate, *The Declaration of Indulgence, 1672* (1908), for a definitive study of the subject.

religious freedom that was not sanctioned by Parliament, made possible the concerted action that led to the coming of the Prince of Orange and James's abdication. Their legal toleration was naturally part of the Revolution settlement of 1689. The High Churchmen, Sancroft at their head, remembering non-resistance and the allegiance they had sworn to James, could not take the oaths to his successor; in their turn, as Non-jurors, they separated themselves from the established Church, and thus to the end the story of the generation that grew old between the Restoration and 1688 was confused and darkened by the intermingling of politics and religion.

There remains the balance-sheet, which was not all loss. The courage and faithfulness of the non-conforming clergy, the close fellowship of the conventicles, the educational ventures, and the works of piety and pastoral care that the ministers wrote for their congregations when debarred from the pulpit, all are part of the story of the Free Churches, without which the chronicle of England would be immeasurably poorer. Excluded from the professions, the ablest among them prospered in trade and commerce and in the coming centuries of England's industrial expansion set their own mark upon the character of the English middle class. The Anglican Church suffered in proportion, for the uniformity for which Sheldon had laboured had been bought at a price. The restored Church of England rested fair and square on the authority of Parliament. Henceforward it was Parliament, the organ of the people in their secular capacity, which would regulate both the form of worship and the treatment of dissent. This might have mattered less if Convocation had remained an active body. But in 1664, by a strange error of judgement, Sheldon had agreed that Convocation should waive its right to make a separate money grant to the Crown. The Church's contribution was henceforward included in the Parliamentary supply. Thus deprived of its primary *raison d'être*, Convocation did not meet again during the reign and, after a brief period of

activity, met only for formal business during most of the eighteenth century. There was thus no active body to initiate reform, which was an ever-present need if the cumbersome machinery of the church courts were to be brought up to date or the anomalies of the unwieldy Canon Law to be redressed.[39] Nor was there any comparable body through which the Church could speak with a united voice in matters of social justice or political corruption.

The social and political cleavage which the fact of dissent had introduced into the parish vitiated its corporate life, just as the vain attempt to keep out strangers emphasized the fact that it was no longer viable as an independent economic unit. The old sense of unity—if it were ever other than a myth—was far to seek, and certainly the heyday of the vestry was over. Among the vestrymen themselves, as the offices of churchwarden and overseer were pressed in turn upon them, there was an increasing tendency for the well-to-do to contract out by the payment of a fine. This enriched the poor-box but imperilled the whole system, based as it was on intelligent and conscientious voluntary service. Even where select vestries maintained a modicum of efficiency, the faults inherent in an oligarchic system led to criticism and opposition, which culminated in a parliamentary attack after the Revolution. Although this was defeated in its final stages, the size and complexity of the problems involved in local government led inevitably to the gradual intervention of the State.

There were, none the less, signs of vitality in the spiritual life of the Church in the years immediately after 1662. The Act of Uniformity meant that Anglicans knew where they were; there was a new precision both in teaching and worship, and just as the settlement had at once increased the pace and efficiency of rehabilitation in the material state of the

[39] "There can be little doubt that the failure of the Restoration settlement to reform the ecclesiastical courts and the canon law was one of its gravest defects from which the Church was to suffer increasing disadvantage" (Sykes, op. cit., p. 22). See also ibid., pp. 36 et seq., "The Eclipse of Convocation".

Churches, and in their practices and personnel, so in the realms of scholarship and devotion there was a similar sense of fresh energy and direction.[40]

The lead came naturally from the clergy and here, as the story of the plague year shows, there were as many contrasts as in any other walk of life. In 1670 some stir was caused by a tract entitled "The Grounds and Occasions for the contempt of clergy . . ." written by John Eachard, a university don, whose opinions on the quality of the average sermon and the futility of teaching Latin to small boys have a familiar ring about them. He satirized, among much else, the attitude of superiority adopted by many gentlemen towards their chaplains, who were treated as little better than servants and expected to leave the table before the sweetmeats were served. But the main target of his attack was the poverty and ignorance of the country clergy and he drew a vivid picture of the harassed parson, escaping to the "little hole over the oven with a lock to it call'd his study" to ponder, less upon his text and the authors he should be consulting, than upon his uncertain tithe. "Whence will come the next rejoycing Goose, or the next cheerful Basket of Apples?" Eachard was probably on surer ground in regard to poverty than ignorance; neither of the two writers who answered him—the first in more kindly manner than the second, who added "Facit Indignatio" to his imprint—attempted to deny the poverty and the time wasted in collecting tithe. The trouble lay of course in the discrepancy between the richer livings and those that were totally inadequate; a difficulty which had been enhanced by the increase in prices and land values and was the more apparent as the supply of clergy exceeded the demand. Nor had the unfortunate custom ceased of men of distinction being rewarded by benefices of value, held in

[40] W. H. Hutton, *The English Church from the accession of Charles I to the death of Anne* (1903), p. 192: "Comprehension could only have been achieved by the sacrifice of convictions on both sides . . . When the Act of Uniformity was enforced the Church was in a position to carry out her system consistently. . . "

plurality: even Simon Patrick, with his sensitive conscience, saw nothing amiss in accepting the deanery of Peterborough in 1679 while remaining rector of his London parish.

Ignorance was another matter. Barnabas Oley, the probable author of the first reply, pointed out that it was not the education of the country parson that was at fault, but the lack of books and of time to read them and "the want of converse with learned men". He might as well call his hogs in Latin, he commented, "as make any great use of learning among his neighbours", though there was a satisfaction in seeking their souls' salvation, as solid as any Dr Eachard knew. Here again there were no doubt considerable contrasts, but the majority of the ordinands after 1660 were university men and the *Vindication* published in answer to Eachard claimed that the Church was "more plentifully furnisht with men of singular worth, universal knowledge and great clerks than ever it [had] been since the Reformation".[41] The learning and spiritual power of the finest of the Caroline divines earned them the title of "the wonder of the world". The work that Elizabeth I and Parker had begun, whereby the Anglican Church should grow into a living part of the Church Universal, was completed during the years of adversity and exile by the writings of such scholars as Bramhall and Herbert Thorndike, defending the historical basis of their faith against Romanists and Puritans alike. After 1662, no longer forced by circumstance to concern themselves primarily with controversial matters, they and their successors could concentrate in their studies upon the content of their religion, linking it with the new science of biblical criticism, which paralleled in theology the scientific awareness in other branches of learning. In giving life and shape to the Elizabethan *via media*, Hooker and Andrewes had found in the history of the early Church a

[41] John Eachard, *The Grounds and occasions of the contempt of the Clergy and Religion* . . . (1670), pp. 84 et seq.; *An Answer to a letter of Enquiry* . . . (1671), pp. 44 ff; *A vindication of the Clergy from the contempt imposed upon them* . . . (1672), p. 23.

valuable touchstone in matters to which neither the Scriptures nor human reason gave a clear reply. The need to verify their references and to assess the validity of the writings of the early Fathers, which had led Ussher to investigate the much-debated epistles of St Ignatius, now inspired scholars of the calibre of Pearson and Bull to similar studies. Bull's Latin *Defence of the Nicene Creed* won him the admiration of the Gallican Church in France and it was consonant with the more pacific ethos of the age that European scholars were seeking for a basis of accord on which to build a friendly relationship, in contrast with the acerbities that had characterized earlier interchanges.[42]

Pearson and Bull stood firmly in the High Church tradition and their main concern was to build a bulwark of orthodox theology against the forces of rationalism which were so marked a feature of the times. The clergy of the other tradition, the Latitudinarians as they came to be called, were less conscious of the threat to orthodoxy which was inherent in the stress on reason as opposed to revelation, on morality in contradistinction to sacramental grace. At their best there was a fine charitableness in their desire to do good and a readiness to accept new truth which had been fostered by the teaching of the Platonists, with whom they were closely linked. The Cambridge group were not eclipsed by the changes of the Restoration, although Whichcote had been forced to surrender the provostship of King's. Cudworth remained undisturbed as Master of Christ's, never completing the masterpieces that teemed in his brain but producing in 1676 one massive work, *The true intellectual system of the Universe*, while More in his writings and still more in his personal influence continued to stress the mystical side of the Platonists' approach, a consciousness of the illumination of the Holy Spirit that rooted their goodness firmly in the realms of faith.

It was when they lost this immediate sense of the grace of

[42] Sykes, op. cit., pp. 105 et seq.; cf. J. R. H. Moorman, *A History of the Church in England* (1953), p. 256, for the Latitudinarians.

God, the only sure foundation for good works, that the Latitudinarians were in danger of the mediocrity their name suggests. They were saved from sterility in the earlier years, not only by the mystic awareness of such writers as More, but by the admiration and awe aroused by the scientific discoveries of the day, which bred in them not agnosticism but a deeper sense of order and purpose at the very centre of the universe. The conception of order as a divine attribute, which had imbued the thought and worship of Andrewes, was now given a fresh orientation, and Christian teachers sought to establish it in human affairs, not by the ecclesiastical regimentation, the imposed uniformity which Laud and Sheldon had advocated, but by fostering a personal morality based on intelligence as well as on devotion. Thus Isaac Barrow, scientist and theologian, in one of his famous and over-lengthy sermons, expounded the rules of Christian living and argued that a pious man, governed by such rules, "doth both understand himself and is intelligible to others". "We shall perceive him to have a cheerful mind and composed passions," Barrow said, "to live in comely order, in . . . firm concord with his neighbours. . . . But if you mind a person who neglecteth them, you will find his mind . . . racked with anxious fears and doubts . . . living in disorder and disgrace, jarring with others and no less dissatisfied with himself."[43]

This stress on morality, as opposed to fanaticism, received ready acceptance among reasonable men, disgusted by the brutal treatment of the conventiclers or the viciousness of Titus Oates. Its appeal to moderates such as John Evelyn or the good-hearted Pepys is obvious, possibly with certain reservations in the case of Pepys! It was lived out by the saintly yet very human Thomas Ken (a nephew of Izaak Walton and

[43] Barrow was Professor of Mathematics at Cambridge until he recognized in his pupil Isaac Newton a genius greater than his own and retired in his favour in 1669. Thereafter he was Master of Trinity, but died in 1677 at the age of 47. See P. H. Osmond, *Isaac Barrow, his life and times* (1944), pp. 146 et seq. and cf. Felix Arnott in More and Cross, *Anglicanism*, p. lxiv and ibid., pp. 744 et seq.

chaplain to Bishop Morley), who in his later years as Dean of Winchester and Bishop of Bath and Wells stood for all that was finest in the High Church tradition, tempered by the stress on personal goodness that was the sheet anchor of the Caroline Churchman. It was to be found in the teaching of some outstanding parish priests, but again closely linked with the worship of the Church. For men such as Simon Patrick and William Beveridge who represented the differing traditions of Anglicanism—Patrick a leading Latitudinarian, Beveridge a staunch High Churchman—both trained their people in a "practice of piety" that was the other feature of the personal religion of the reign.

Simon Patrick, who had been tutored at Queens' by the Platonist Smith and tremendously affected by him, ministered at Covent Garden for twenty-seven years. He approached his task with the same meticulous care that he had shown in his Battersea days, of which he records: "One afternoon in every week, I set apart to visit as many families as I could in my parish till I had gone through it, and given them private monitions and catechized their children." There was a good deal of the Puritan in his make-up, but the familiarity with the early Fathers, which had first led him to seek episcopal ordination, had given him a clear and firm churchmanship, which he inculcated into his congregation at Covent Garden. A weekly service of Holy Communion was held, and daily prayers were said at 10 a.m. and 3 p.m., "maintained and attended by the gentry and better sort of people". In 1680 Patrick arranged for two more daily services to be endowed. As much as £400 had accumulated over the years—the surplus of the Communion offertory, after the poor and sick had been sought out and relieved. The wardens thought it should, obviously, be used to lessen the poor-rate, but Patrick pointed out that this would only assist the well-to-do who paid the rate, and it was agreed that a curate should be appointed to say prayers daily, at six in the morning and seven in the evening in summer, "before trading began and

when it was done, that servants might resort unto them". The wardens needed some persuading, but the rector had his way.[44]

Beveridge was a younger man than Patrick, ordained priest and deacon in one day, among the many who came forward in the urgent need for ordinands in 1661. He went first to Ealing and eleven years later to St Peter's, Cornhill, where the daily prayers and weekly Communion featured as at Covent Garden. He was a man of considerable erudition, and a good deal more: Robert Boyle used to say that his ideal Christian leader was Hammond among the dead and Beveridge among the living. Another parish priest, equally devoted, was Anthony Horneck, preacher at the Savoy, a German who had come over to England because he liked the sound of it, distinguished himself at Oxford, and won the respect of his adopted country by a moral uprightness that had something Teutonic about its uncompromising thoroughness. At the Savoy his challenging sermons soon made him popular with a generation that had outgrown both the euphuism of the Jacobean preachers and the verbosity of the Puritans. He stressed worship rather less than Beveridge and Patrick: Communion was held only once a month, but it was a great and solemn occasion with a preparatory sermon on the previous Friday and a great crowd of communicants. For Horneck did not only preach good sermons—had that been the case the distinguished congregations might soon have drifted elsewhere—but, as Patrick and Beveridge were doing, he welded his people into a community of the faithful, winning them by the personal approach, teaching the young, visiting the sick, giving spiritual counsel when required and holding himself in readiness for any who needed him.[45]

[44] S. Patrick, *Autobiography*, pp. 32, 88. Patrick was a voluminous writer of devotional and biblical works, published in nine volumes, ed. A. Taylor, Oxford, 1858. He had been elected President of Queens' College, Cambridge, in 1661, but the election was overruled when the King nominated Anthony Sparrow.

[45] Richard Kidder, *The Life of the Reverend Anthony Horneck, D.D., late*

It was Horneck and Beveridge who were mainly responsible for encouraging the religious societies, which sprang up on all sides in the later years of the reign, as young men and women reacted against the political violence and the licentious habits of the age and banded together to seek salvation by means of good works and a disciplined rule of life. The regulations that governed one such group, dealing with such matters as subscriptions, fines, and an annual "moderate dinner", included an omnibus resolution which ran: "The following rules are more especially to be commended—To love one another—When reviled not to revile again. . . . To pray if possible seven times a day. To keep close to the Church of England. . . . To be helpful to each other. . . . To examine themselves every Night. To give every one their due. To obey superiors, both spiritual and Temporal."[46] Members were not allowed in their weekly meeting "to discourse of any controverted point of divinity" nor of the government of Church or State. It was an inevitable reaction to the excesses of the century now drawing to a close. In the name of Christ, Legate had been burnt, Puritans had been banished, priests had been hanged at Tyburn, the aged Laud had perished on Tower Hill. For conscience' sake, Englishmen had killed each other on the battlefield, wasted their years in exile, rent their Church asunder. It was small wonder that the men and women of the younger generation spoke no word against authority, but concentrated on a training in piety and personal relationships. The danger of too much inward-looking was obvious. Those societies were not particularly successful that attempted later to fight such social evils as prostitution and vice, and in their earlier stage, as schools of discipleship, it is uncertain how much they accomplished. Yet perhaps it is significant that

---

*preacher at the Savoy* (1698), pp. 9 ff; cf. Overton, *Life in the English Church, 1660–1714*, pp. 207 et seq.

[46] Kidder, op. cit., pp. 13–16. *An account of the Rise and Progress of the Religious Societies in the City of London and of their endeavours for Reformation of Manners* was written by Josiah Woodward in 1697 and ran into seven editions in the next century.

the two great societies founded at the turn of the century, for Promoting Christian Knowledge and for the Propagation of the Gospel, came into being and survived the years in part because of the consistent help of devoted and disciplined laymen.[47]

It is the poet who must have the last word, for it is in the writings of Thomas Traherne that the visions of the saints and the scientists caught fire, and morality was seen to be more than obeying the rules. His poems throb with a sense of the joy and wonder in creation, and interpret the scientific excitement of the Caroline age, even as Donne and Herbert had interpreted the sacramental teaching of half a century before.[48]

Traherne was the son of a Hereford shoemaker and was born in the late 1630s, dying before he was forty in 1674. Much of his life was spent in the country about Hereford, where at blossom-time it is easy to feel nearer to heaven than earth. His vivid awareness of beauty was so immediate and compelling that he identified his very self with the natural world through which God manifested his love and his omnipotence. "You never enjoy the world aright till the sea itself floweth in your veins, till you are clothed with the heavens and crowned with the stars . . . till you delight in God for being good to all, you never enjoy the world." This joy—or felicity, as he termed it —seemed to him the sole reason for existence, and after some unsettled years and a period of study at Oxford, he made a deliberate choice, to live upon ten pounds a year and to go in leather clothes, "so that he could have all his time clearly to himself and never be so burdened with care and labour as to be impeded in his search for happiness". After some earnest prayer, to be led to the "fairest and divinest", he chose the life of a country parson.

47 Overton, op. cit., pp. 216–22.

48 *The Poetical Works of Thomas Traherne*, ed. with preface by Gladys I. Wade (1932), including Bertram Dobell's introduction to the first edition (1903, revised 1906); see pp. lxxxvi et seq. for the discovery of the Traherne MSS. A critical biography, *Thomas Traherne*, by G. I. Wade, was published in 1944. Traherne's *Roman Forgeries* was published in 1673.

It was the middle fifties and Traherne went before the Triers in London, his credentials signed by various Puritan clergy of Hereford and Upton-on-Severn; but his studies at Oxford had attracted him to the Anglican interpretation of religion and according to Anthony Wood, who knew him in his Oxford days, he "became much in love with the beautiful order and primitive devotion of this, our excellent church". For ten years he ministered in the parish of Credenhill, but it was a different sort of ministry from that of Herbert, whose own physical suffering was a constant reminder of the Cross. Traherne's message was of the well-being that comes from fellowship with God, the Creator:

The skies in their magnificence,
The lively lovely air,
Oh how divine, how soft, how sweet, how fair.

A native health and innocence
Within my bones did grow,
And while my God did all his glories show
I felt a vigour in my sense
That was all spirit. I within did flow
With seas of life like wine,
I nothing in the world did know
But 'twas divine.

When he was just past his thirtieth year he left his country parsonage, accompanying the Lord Keeper, Bridgeman, as chaplain to his home in Teddington. He acted as curate in the riverside village, wrote one indifferent work of learning, and died soon afterwards, leaving to his brother all he possessed of value, his books and "his best hat". Perhaps it was the latter years that brought another note into his writing, as he experienced the redemptive power of Christian teaching:

Mankind is sick, the world distemper'd lies,

The wise and good like kind physicians are
That strive to heal them by their care

—and find that the only way to heal is to share that felicity which is so abundant

> that we can
> Spare all, even all, to any man.

He no longer sought to avoid "care and labour". "To love one person with a private love is poor and miserable, to love all is glorious. To love all cities and all kingdoms, all kings and all peasants . . . this makes a man a glorious friend to all persons, a concerned person in all transactions."[49]

It was thus that the poet transmuted those qualities of wonder and concern, expressed in a more pedestrian way by the scientists and the pioneers in missionary and educational endeavour. And so the chapter ends, with Traherne on one hand and the religious societies on the other. The experiments of the Royal Society, with eminent divines among its members, the spacious new churches going up in London and the volumes of theological learning, still standing for our edification upon the library shelves, all witness to the vitality and breadth of the Anglican Church in the years that followed the Restoration. They witness also to the complete change that had come over the English scene, after the struggles of the earlier years, by which Anglicanism had been hammered into shape. The hope of a national Church in which the people were at one, united in their worship of God as in their loyalty to their earthly King, had foundered on the stubborn rock of conscience, and often charity had foundered with it. The search for a deeper unity, underlying the divergencies, was a further stage on the Church's spiritual journey, and only a few rare spirits like the "ever-memorable" Hales felt impelled to begin that search in the years before 1662. Yet it was implicit in the whole ethos of Anglicanism at its best, a Church of the middle way, its Catholic heritage preserved by the devotion and "uniform obedience" of a succession of stalwarts from Hooker to Ken, its sure reliance upon the Scriptures and upon the use of

[49] *Centuries of Meditation by Thomas Traherne* (first published 1908; 1950 edition, with introd. by John Hayward), 4th Century, No. 69.

reason placing it firmly in the Protestant tradition, while a certain aversion to doctrinal rigidity, shared by Elizabeth I and Laud alike, left room for the belief that men could not restrict God's mercy to a few predestined souls and for a humble reliance on sacramental grace to enable men to grow into the knowledge and the love of God.

Thus throughout the century the Anglican Church grew to maturity, buttressed by the scholarship of the universities, nurtured by the prayers of the faithful, tested by the sufferings of the years of adversity and in quieter days adorned by lives as fragrant as the English countryside, of saints in the Anglican manner, sober men, not given to excess. The loyal, if at times the grumbling service of innumerable vestrymen kept in seemly order the fabric and furnishings of their parish church, and the work of the craftsmen often still survives, to give joy to a generation less aware of the beauty of holiness. The poetry of Donne and Herbert and Traherne, the rich prose of Sir Thomas Browne and Izaak Walton, the devotions of Andrewes and Jeremy Taylor, and the measured counsel of the *Practice of Piety* or the *Whole Duty of Man* gave to seventeenth-century Anglicanism a character and an appeal that has seldom if ever been surpassed. How often the Church fell short of her calling in the turmoil of politics and through failure of Christian compassion these chapters of her story indubitably show: yet something had emerged worthy of man's devotion, a faith and worship and a practice in well-doing that have given to the Anglican branch of Christendom its own spiritual insights and the validity of a living Church.

# NOTE ON SOURCES

I have included in my notes bibliographical details of the original authorities I have consulted, as well as of the standard biographies and historical works covering the period. As a guide for further reading a selection is added here of a few of the modern books of a more specialized character to which I have been indebted.

P. E. More and F. L. Cross (with an additional essay by Felix Arnott), *Anglicanism: The Thought and Practice of the Church of England Illustrated from the Religious Literature of the Seventeenth Century* (1935).

THE PARISH

J. S. Purvis, *An Introduction to Ecclesiastical Records* (1953).

W. E. Tate, *The Parish Chest: A Study of the Records of Parochial Administration in England* (Cambridge, 1946; 2nd edn, revised and enlarged, 1951).

A. Tindal Hart, *The Country Clergy in Elizabethan and Stuart Times, 1558–1660* (1958).

Eleanor Trotter, *Seventeenth Century Life in the Country Parish, with special reference to local government* (Cambridge, 1919).

1558–1603

M. M. Knappen, *Tudor Puritanism: A Chapter in the History of Idealism* (Chicago, 1939).

P. M. Dawley, *John Whitgift and the Reformation* (1955).

A. F. Scott Pearson, *Thomas Cartwright and Elizabethan Puritanism, 1535–1603* (Cambridge, 1925).

C. J. Sisson, *The Judicious Marriage of Mr Hooker and the Birth of the Laws of Ecclesiastical Polity* (Cambridge, 1940).

1603–40

D. H. Willson, *King James VI and I* (1956).

Christopher Hill, *Economic Problems of the Church from Archbishop Whitgift to the Long Parliament* (Oxford, 1956).

H. R. Trevor-Roper, *Archbishop Laud* (1940) [revised and reissued, 1962].

E. C. E. Bourne, *The Anglicanism of William Laud* (1947).

R. A. Marchant, *The Puritans and the Church Courts in the Diocese of York, 1560–1642* (1960).

# INDEX

# INDEX